The Complete
Ninja Foodi
Digital Air Fryer Oven Cookbook

1500 Affordable & Tasty Air Fry, Air Roast, Air Broil, Bake, Bagel, Toast, and Dehydrate Recipes for Beginners and Advanced Users

Julie Pereira

CONTENT

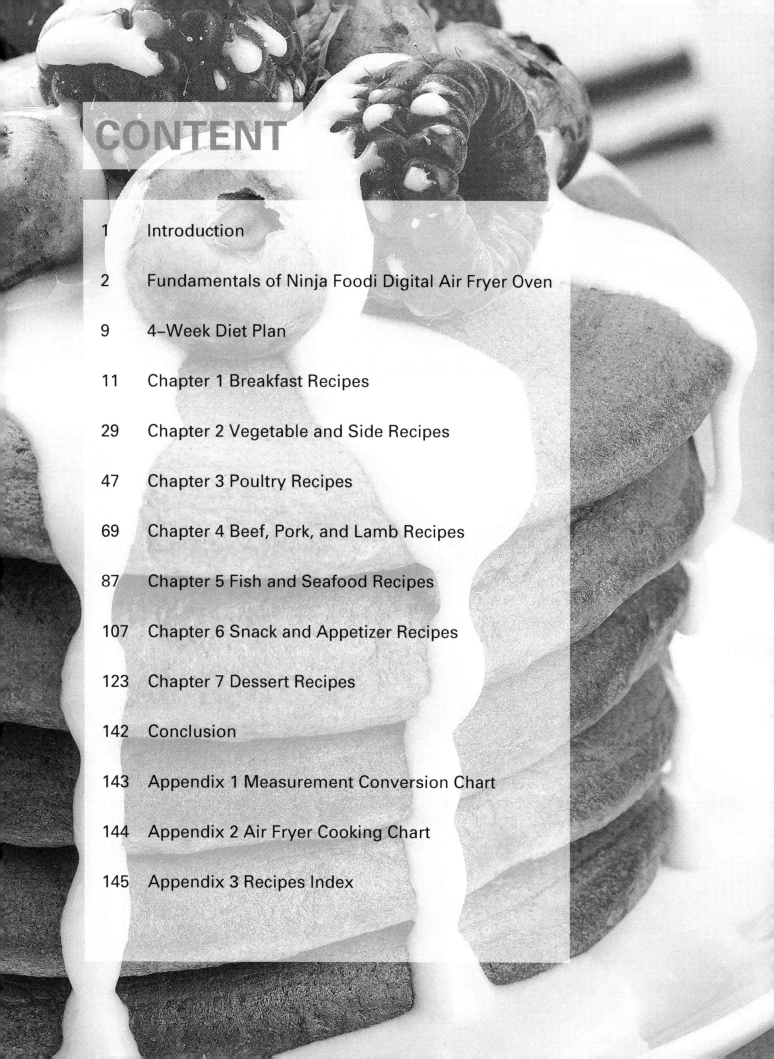

Introduction

Ninja Foodi Digital Air Fryer Oven is a multifunctional cooking oven. With 8 customizable cooking capabilities in one Ninja Foodi, you can create a host of meals. Now family-sized dinners may be quickly and simply made in just about 30 minutes. A super-fast 90-second preheat will put an end to prolonged wait times. This workstation oven is ideal for family-sized dinners and provides rapid and uniform 2-level cooking. There is no need to utilize several appliances to prepare a full dinner because you can accommodate a main course and sides at the same time. With a true surround convection, get quick, sharp, and consistent results. There is no need to flip or rotate cooking trays with a high-velocity fan, back heat source, and surround airflow work together to circulate superheated air throughout the whole oven for uniform cooking on two racks. A temperature range of 40°C/105°F to 230°C/450°F is provided by the top and bottom infrared heating components, and superheated convection air is produced by a third rear heat source that is hidden behind the high-velocity fan in it. With touch screen controls, a digital display, and settings for time, temperature, and shade all conveniently placed on the stylish oven door handle.

Fundamentals of Ninja Foodi Digital Air Fryer Oven

What is Ninja Foodi Digital Air Fryer Oven?

The Ninja Foodi Digital Air Fry Oven combines an air fryer, convection oven, and toaster oven into one appliance. Ninja Foodi Digital Air Fry Oven packs a lot of features and cooking capacity into a small countertop footprint. With its distinctive design, which enables you to fold it up against your backsplash when not in use, you may get extra-large capacity without giving up counter space. The Ninja Foodi is more than simply an air fryer. The original Ninja Foodi is a powerful well-made product. The Ninja Food includes a highly attractive display that provides information on the control panel, like remaining cook time, reminder to flip food and show the unit is hot. Ninja Foodi's instruction handbook is informative and simple to understand. The food crisps up beautifully in the air fryer. Great for desserts (such as crème brulee) or for making individual portions (such as egg muffins). You don't need to remain in the room to turn off the air fryer since it counts down and turns off

when the time is up. There are settings specifically for dehydrating or reheating leftover French fries. You can also roast chicken without using an oven to heat your house (perfect for summer days). Additionally, you can set the timer for up to an hour at a time, and the temperature may reach 450 degrees Fahrenheit. With just one appliance, you can air fry, air roast, air broil, bake, bagel, toast, dehydrate, and keep warm. When you have finished cooking, all you have to do is to flip the oven up and away to clean and store it. Overall, the Ninja Foodi is a great all-in-one product. It does an excellent job of air frying, roasting, broiling, toasting, and dehydrating.

Accessories

Removable Crumb Tray –It is used to collect the crumbs that fall off while baking or grilling. It can be easily cleaned. Always place below the bottom heating elements in your Ninja Foodi.

Wire Rack –A wire rack is used to allow air to circulate freely from the bottom to the top of the food, and to prevent them getting soggy from condensation. Keep wire rack in the bottom rail position in your Ninja Foodi.

Sheet Pan –A sheet pan, also referred to as baking tray, baking sheet, or baking pan, is a flat, rectangular metal pan placed in an oven and used for baking pastries such as bread rolls, cookies, sheet cakes, Swiss rolls, and pizzas. A sheet pan is a wide, shallow baking pan made from aluminum or stainless steel whose low sides encourage airflow and browning. It is the go-to pan for roasting vegetables, meats and often entire meals. Always layer it on top of the wire rack.

Air Fry Basket –It is perfect for frying foods, cooking meats, and baking snacks, the air fry basket also can use for dehydrating fruits, meats. such as frying crispy chicken, French fries, pizza, onions, chicken wings, steak and fried vegetables multiple foods. Use in the top rail position.

A healthier way to cook your favorite meals and snacks, by using little to no oil. More than an air fryer, it quickly and easily air-fry, roast, reheat, and dehydrate, from chunky chips and crispy chicken to roasted vegetables and beef jerky.

Enjoy the same great taste with up to 75% less fat than traditional frying methods. Cooking with little to no oil, Ninja Foodi Digital Air Fryer Oven offers a healthier way to enjoy all your favorite fried foods, from crispy fries to crispy chicken wings.

With so many cooking functions, you can also roast golden vegetables and sides, reheat leftovers to restore that fresh-out-of-the-oven texture, and gently dehydrate ingredients to enjoy homemade dried fruit, vegetable crisps, and beef jerky. Dinner can be on the table in just minutes. Cook from frozen for deliciously crispy results. Fast airflow and precision temperature control ensure your food is cooked exactly as you like it.

Less Fat: When utilizing the Air Fry feature as opposed to conventional deep frying, you may indulge in all of your favorite air-fried foods guilt-free with up to 75% less fat compared deep-fried French fries in a test.

Quicker Cooking: Cook dishes completely with Air Roast function in as little as 20 minutes and up to 60% quicker than a conventional oven.

Large Capacity: Compared to the flat surface area of the Cuisinart toa-60 and toa-65 pan, the useful pan cooking area is 45% greater and fits up to 9 pieces of toast, a 13" pizza, or 6 chicken breasts (6–8 oz. each).

Renew Your Counter Area: When you flip it up and away to store it against your kitchen backsplash, it takes up 50% less counter space.

Doneness of Toast to Choose: With a bread darkness picker to get it just right, toast and bagels are prepared to your preferences.

Easy Cleaning: A retractable crumb tray and an easily accessible rear panel are included for simple cleaning.

Step-by-step Using Tips

Air Fry

Enjoy fast, extra-crispy results using little to no oil. Perfect for frying your favorite fried dishes, like oven chips, crispy French fries, sizzling sausages, breaded chicken goujons, and sizzling sausages.

❶ Turn the dial to select the Air Fry function.

❷ Press the TIME/SLICE button and adjust the cook time with the dial up to 1 hour. Press the TIME/SLICE button to set the time.

❸ Press the TEMP/DARKNESS button for temperature and use the dial to set a temperature between 250°F and 450°F. Press the TEMP/DARKNESS button to set.

❹ To start preheating, press START/PAUSE.

❺ Fill the air fryer basket with the ingredients. Put the basket on the sheet pan if the ingredients are fatty, greasy, or marinated. Don't overcrowd the basket. To get foods crispy and promote even cooking, food should always be in a single layer in the air fryer basket. Do not stack or layer. You can cook in batches as needed.

❻ It's ok to pull the basket out to check on the progress of your food during the cooking cycle.

❼ Shake or flip part way through to cook evenly. When cooking food in small pieces, such as Brussels sprouts or French fries, give the basket a good shake about half way through cooking to promote even cooking and browning. When cooking meat such as pork chops or chicken, flip the pieces over about half way through.

❽ Dry foods well to get them crispy. Moisture is the enemy of crispiness. Before adding oil, seasonings or placing food in the air fryer basket, pat food dry with a clean kitchen towel or paper towels.

❾ Slide the basket into the upper rails of the oven as soon as the device beeps to indicate that it has reached preheating. If using a sheet pan as well, slip both into the oven at the same time, the pan on the wire rack below the basket and the basket on the top rails. Close the oven door.

❿ When cook time is complete, the unit will beep. Your food will be ready.

Air Roast

Achieve a crispy outside and perfectly cooked inside for full-sized sheet pan meals, thicker proteins, and roasted veggies. Perfect with an oven tray to bake meals such as lemon and herb chicken breasts with asparagus and salmon fillets with broccoli and sweet potatoes.

1. Turn the dial to select Air Roast function.
2. Select your time up to two hours by pressing the TIME/SLICE button and turning the dial.
3. Press the TIME/SLICE button again to set the time.
4. Select a temperature between 250°F and 450°F by pressing the TEMP/DARKNESS button and turning the dial. Press the TEMP/DARKNESS button again to set the temperature.
5. To start heating, press START/PAUSE. Place the roast into the basket of the Ninja Foodi. Once the cooking time is up, prepare a sheet of foil to place the roast on.
6. Place the air fry basket on the wire rack as soon as the appliance beeps to indicate that it has reached preheating with crumble tray down. Shut the oven door.
7. When cook time is complete, the unit will beep. Your food will be ready.
8. Carefully remove the roast from the Ninja Foodi and place it on the foil.

Air Broil

Air Broil function can be used to broil meat and fish and evenly brown the tops of casseroles.

1. Turn the dial to select Air Broil function.
2. Select your time up to 30 minutes by pressing the TIME/SLICE button and turning the dial. Press the TIME/SLICE button again to set the time.
3. Select either HI or LO by turning the dial after pressing the TEMP/DARKNESS button.
4. Press the TEMP/DARKNESS button again to set the temperature.
5. Put the ingredients on the sheet pan. Place the pan in the center of the wire rack. Close the oven door after setting the sheet pan on the wire rack and click START/STOP to begin cooking.
6. You may check on or flip items while they are cooking by opening the oven door.
7. When cook time is complete, the unit will beep. Your food will be ready.

Bake

Evenly bake everything from your favorite cookies to homemade pizzas. Create savory foods like spaghetti bakes, handmade quiches, jacket potatoes, fish pies, and more, or bake your favorite cookies, cakes, and pastries with ease.

1. Rotate the dial to select Bake function.
2. Select your time up to two hours by pressing the TIME/SLICE button and turning the dial. Press the TIME/SLICE button again to set the time.
3. Select a temperature between 250°F and 450°F by pressing the TEMP/DARKNESS button and turning the dial. Press the TEMP/DARKNESS button one more to set the temperature.
4. To start preheating, press START/PAUSE.
5. Pour the batter (all ingredients) into the pan and use a spatula to smooth the surface. Put the pan on the wire rack as soon as the appliance beeps to indicate that it has reached preheating. Close the oven door.
6. When cook time is complete, the unit will beep. Your food will be ready.

Toast

Evenly toasts up to 9 slices of bread to your perfect level of darkness.

1. Turn the dial to Toast function.

② Choose the number of slices of bread by pressing the TIME/SLICE button and turning the dial. 9 slices can be toasted at once. Press the TIME/SLICE button once again to set the number of slices.

③ Butter your toast and add any additional toppings (optional) that you are wanting to cook with the bread.

④ Select a degree of darkness by pressing the TEMP/DARKNESS button and turning the dial.

⑤ Press the TEMP/DARKNESS button again to set the darkness level.

⑥ Place your toast on the wire rack and place wire rack into Ninja Foodi Digital Air Fryer Oven with the bread pieces on it. To start cooking, close the oven door and press START/PAUSE.

⑦ You do not need to flip the slices during cooking. When cook time is complete, the unit will beep.

Bagel

Perfectly toast up to 9 slices of bagel when they're placed cut-side up on the wire rack. Restore leftovers to that fresh-out-of-the-oven finish without overcooking, from pizza to spring rolls.

① Rotate the dial to select Bagel function.

② Select the number of slices by turning the dial after pressing the TIME/SLICE button.

③ Up to 9 bagel pieces can be toasted at once. Press the TIME/SLICE button once again to set the number of slices.

④ Select a degree of darkness by pressing the TEMP/DARKNESS button and turning the dial.

⑤ Press the TEMP/DARKNESS button again to set the darkness level.

⑥ Put the cut-side-up bagel slices on the wire rack. To start cooking, close the oven door and select START/PAUSE.

⑦ You do not need to flip the slices during cooking. When cook time is complete, the unit will beep.

⑧ When cook time is complete, the unit will beep. Your food will be ready.

Dehydrate

Dehydrates meats, fruits, and vegetables for healthy snacks. You can create healthy snacks, from beef jerky to dried fruit.

① Turn the dial to select Dehydrate function. The time and temperature will be shown by default.

② To choose a time up to 12 hours, press the TIME/SLICE button and turn the dial. Press the TIME/SLICE button again to set the time.

③ Choose a temperature between 105°F and 195°F by pressing the TEMP/DARKNESS button and turning the dial. Press the TEMP/DARKNESS button once again to set the temperature.

④ Add your ingredients into the air fryer basket.

⑤ Put the air fryer basket in the oven with the items inside over the wire rack with crumble tray at the bottom. To start cooking, close the oven door and select START/PAUSE.

⑥ You may check on or flip items while they are cooking by opening the oven door.

⑦ When cook time is complete, the unit will beep. Your food will be ready.

Keep Warm

Keep food warm for up to 2 hours.

① Turn the dial to select KEEP WARM function.

② Select a time up to two hours by pressing the TIME/SLICE button and turning the dial. Press the TIME/SLICE button once again to set the time.

③ Put the meal on the sheet pan or in an oven-safe dish, then set the dish or pan on the wire rack. To start warming, close the oven door and hit START/PAUSE.

④ The appliance will beep when the warming process is finished.

Cleaning and Caring Tips

Daily Cleaning

The appliance has to be completely cleaned following each usage.

❶ Plug the device out of the outlet and cool down the unit before cleaning.

❷ Slide out the crumbs tray to empty it.

❸ To remove any food stain, wipe the internal walls of the space with a delicate, moist sponge.

❹ To clean the exterior of the main unit and the control panel, wipe them clean using a wet cloth.

❺ Apply the cleanser or a gentle spray solution to the sponge, not on the surface of the oven, before cleaning.

You can quickly clean up spills and crumbs thanks to a retractable crumb tray that pulls out.

Deep Cleaning

❶ Before cleaning, unplug the appliance from the outlet and give it time to cool.

❷ Remove all of the unit's attachments, including the crumb tray, and wash each individually. To wash the air fry basket more completely, use a non-abrasive cleaning brush.

❸ Flip up the oven into the storage position.

❹ To get access to the oven's inside; press the push button to open the back door.

❺ To clean the inside of the oven, use a soft cloth and warm, soapy water. Abrasive cleansers, scrubbing brushes, and chemical cleaners SHOULD NOT BE USED as they will harm the oven.

Frequently Asked Questions

Why is the oven not turning on?

• To turn on the oven, it must be turned down.
• Double-check that the power cord is firmly inserted into the socket.
• Place the power cord in an alternative outlet.
• If required, reset the circuit breaker.
• Click the power switch.

What is an air fryer?

Air fryers are large countertop appliances that offer a bold promise: perfectly fried food using very little oil

Is air frying healthier than deep frying?

Yes, air fryer's intended purpose holds true: Instead of quarts of oil, a cook can use just a small amount and achieve beautifully crisp results in French fries, chicken, fish, and more.

Do I need to preheat the Ninja Foodi Digital Air Fryer Oven?

No. One of the advantages to using the Ninja Foodi Digital Air Fryer Oven as opposed to an oven—it's much faster because you don't have to preheat it.

How do I prevent food from sticking to my air fryer?

For foods that are prone to sticking, such as breaded chicken or delicate fish, we recommend spraying the basket lightly with vegetable oil spray. Using a foil sling can also make cleanup and the removal of certain foods easier, especially fish.

Is a sheet pan an acceptable substitute for an air fry basket with an air fry function?

• The results for crispiness may vary, though.

Is the basket nonstick?

Yes. The basket is nonstick and has a ceramic coating.

How often should I clean the basket?

We suggest cleaning the basket after each use.

What is the capacity of the basket?

The basket holds up to 4 quarts. It can comfortably cook a 2-pound bag of French fries.

Do the cook times and temperatures for conventional oven recipes need to be changed?

Reduce the cooking time when using the Air Roast feature to prepare classic oven dishes by 30% and temperature by 25°F.

Can I reset the device to its factory defaults?

Even if you disconnect the oven, it will remember the last setting you used for each function.

Pressing the TIME/SLICE and TEMP/DARKNESS buttons at the same time for five seconds will reset each function of the oven to its default settings.

Why do the heating components seem to be on and off repeatedly?

This is typical. The power levels of the heating components may be changed to precisely manage the temperature for each function in the oven.

Why does the oven door have steam pouring out of it?

This is normal. The door has vents to let out steam produced by foods with a lot of moisture.

- The cook time and temperature may be adjusted at any time during the cooking cycle.
- Press and hold the START/PAUSE button for 3 seconds to return to the function selection.
- To switch from Fahrenheit to Celsius, press and hold the TEMP/DARKNESS button for 3 seconds while the unit is not in cook mode.
- Time and temperature will always return to the cook time and temperature that was set the last time the oven was in use.
- The light will automatically turn on when there are 30 seconds of cook time remaining.
- The unit preheats quickly, so we recommend prepping all ingredients before turning on the oven.
- The timer will start counting down as soon as the unit has preheated. If ingredients are not ready to go into the oven, simply turn the dial to add more time.
- DO NOT use an extension cord. A short power-supply cord is used to reduce the risk of children grabbing the cord or becoming entangled and to reduce the risk of people tripping over a longer cord.
- NEVER use the outlet below the counter.
- Keep the appliance and its cord out of reach of children. Do not allow the appliance to be used by children. Close supervision is necessary when used near children.
- DO NOT let cord hang over edges of tables or counters or touch hot surfaces, including stoves and other heating ovens.
- NEVER leave the oven unattended while in use.
- DO NOT cover the crumb tray or any part of the oven with metal foil. This will cause the oven to overheat or cause a fire.
- NEVER place aluminum foil on top of the sheet pan or broil pan. This traps grease and can cause a fire.

- To protect against electrical shock. DO NOT immerse the cord, plugs, or main unit housing in water or other liquid.
- DO NOT use the oven with damage to the power cord or plug. Regularly inspect the oven and power cord. If the oven malfunctions or has been damaged in any way, immediately stop use and call Customer Service.
- DO NOT cover the air intake vents or air outlet vents while the unit is operating. Doing so will prevent even cooking and may damage the unit or cause it to overheat.
- DO NOT insert anything in the ventilation slots and do not obstruct them.
- DO NOT place items on top of the surface while the unit is operating except for authorized recommended Ninja accessories.
- Before placing any accessories into the oven ensure they are clean and dry. 19 Intended for countertop use only. DO NOT place the oven near the edge of a countertop. Ensure the surface is level, clean, and dry.
- This oven is for household use only. DO NOT use this oven for anything other than its intended use. Misuse may cause injury.
- DO NOT store any materials, other than supplied accessories, in this oven when not in use.
- DO NOT use outdoors. DO NOT use it in moving vehicles or boats.
- DO NOT use accessories and attachments not recommended or sold by SharkNinja.
- When using this oven, provide adequate space above and on all sides for air circulation.
- A fire may occur if the oven is covered or touching flammable material, including curtains, draperies, walls, or the like when in operation. DO NOT place anything on the oven during operation.
- This oven has a tempered glass door and is more resistant to breakage. Avoid scratching the door surface or nicking the edges.
- DO NOT use the oven without the wire rack installed.
- DO NOT spray any type of aerosol spray or flavoring inside the oven while cooking.
- Use caution when inserting and removing anything from the oven, especially when hot.
- Outlet voltages can vary, affecting the performance of your product. To prevent possible illness, use a thermometer to check that your food is cooked to the temperatures recommended.
- Prevent food contact with heating elements. Excessive food loads may cause personal injury or property damage or affect the safe use of the oven.
- DO NOT place any of the following materials in the oven: paper, cardboard, plastic, roasting bags, and the like.
- Extreme caution should be exercised when using containers constructed of any materials other than metal or glass.
- Spilled food can cause serious burns. Extreme caution must be used when the oven contains hot food. Improper use may result in personal injury.
- Please refer to the Cleaning & Maintenance section for regular maintenance of the oven.
- Cleaning and user maintenance shall not be made by children.
- Press the power button to turn the oven off and allow it to cool completely before cleaning, moving, and flipping for storage.
- Unplug from the outlet when not in use. To unplug, grasp the plug by the body and pull it from the outlet. Never unplug by grasping and pulling the flexible cord.
- DO NOT clean with metal scouring pads. Pieces can break off the pad and touch electrical parts, causing a risk of electrical shock.
- DO NOT use the oven as a source of heat or for drying.
- While the unit is running, DO NOT cover the air intake or air output vents. This will prevent cooking from occurring evenly and might harm the appliance or cause it to overheat.
- Only the officially approved and suggested Ninja attachments are allowed to put on the surface while the unit is running.
- While cooking, AVOID using any kind of aerosol spray or flavoring.
- STAY AWAY from hot surfaces. Oven surfaces get warm both during and after use. Always use protective hot pads or insulated oven mitts, and use accessible handles and knobs to avoid burns or personal damage.
- NEVER put the main unit in the dishwasher or immerse it in water or any other liquid.

4-Week Diet Plan

Week 1

Day 1:
Breakfast: Air Fried Scotch Eggs
Lunch: Jicama Fries with Eggs
Snack: Cheesy Jalapeno Poppers
Dinner: Traditional Orange Duck
Dessert: Sweet Cream Cheese Wontons

Day 2:
Breakfast: Delicious Apple Fritters
Lunch: Cheesy Green Beans
Snack: Mediterranean Herb Potato Chips
Dinner: Air Fried Classic Garlic Shrimp
Dessert: Delicious Mini Strawberry Pies

Day 3:
Breakfast: Sweet Pumpkin Oatmeal
Lunch: Buttery Garlicky Potatoes
Snack: Parmesan Eggplant Fries
Dinner: Beef and Mushroom Meatloaf
Dessert: Buttery Sugar Fritters

Day 4:
Breakfast: Classic Fries
Lunch: Roasted Fennel
Snack: No-Corn Cheesy Dogs
Dinner: Delicious Chicken Goulash
Dessert: Banana & Walnuts Cake

Day 5:
Breakfast: Sweet Apple Compote
Lunch: Smashed Baby Potatoes
Snack: Delicious Hot Dog Buns
Dinner: Butter Lemon Mahi-Mahi Fillets
Dessert: Lemon Tarts

Day 6:
Breakfast: Healthy French Toast
Lunch: Vegetable Stromboli
Snack: Crispy Carrot Chips
Dinner: Roasted Spicy London Broil
Dessert: Mixed Berry Puffed Pastry

Day 7:
Breakfast: Baked Eggs with Bacon
Lunch: Charred Sweet Potatoes
Snack: Crispy Parmesan Dill Pickles
Dinner: Spicy Chicken
Dessert: Delicious Glazed Donuts

Week 2

Day 1:
Breakfast: Delicious Shakshuka
Lunch: Sweet Roasted Tomatoes
Snack: Simple Cashew Bowls
Dinner: Beef-Stuffed Tortillas
Dessert: Peanut Butter Doughnut Holes

Day 2:
Breakfast: Cheesy Egg Pockets
Lunch: Hot Fried Cabbage Patties
Snack: Crispy Pickles Chips
Dinner: Chili and Sweet Paprika Squid
Dessert: Chouquettes

Day 3:
Breakfast: Tasty Spinach Balls
Lunch: Green Tofu Quiche
Snack: Herbed Meat Skewers
Dinner: Turkey Sliders with Avocado
Dessert: Blueberry Tartlets

Day 4:
Breakfast: Pumpkin Pie Toast
Lunch: Healthy Parsnip Fries
Snack: Lemony Shrimp Bowls
Dinner: Fried Beef Taco Egg Rolls
Dessert: Baked Beignets

Day 5:
Breakfast: Vegetable Patties
Lunch: Charred Peppers
Snack: Tangy Tofu Cubes
Dinner: Tuna Stuffed Potatoes
Dessert: Chocolaty Nutella Banana Sandwich

Day 6:
Breakfast: Eggs & Cheese Toast
Lunch: Spicy Black-Eyed Peas
Snack: Herbed Eggplant Sticks
Dinner: Greek Meatballs
Dessert: Chocolate Molten Cakes

Day 7:
Breakfast: Bacon Egg Muffins
Lunch: Zucchini Carrot Muffins
Snack: Herbed Tomato Chips
Dinner: Regular Beef Empanadas
Dessert: Crispy Apple Wedges

Week 3

Day 1:
Breakfast: Salmon & Carrot Breakfast
Lunch: Refreshing Romaine Slaw
Snack: Roasted Baby Carrots
Dinner: Delicious Fish Taco
Dessert: Cinnamon Sugar Roasted Chickpeas

Day 2:
Breakfast: Creamy Biscuits
Lunch: Vegetable Lasagna
Snack: Sweet Glazed Beets
Dinner: Crispy Fried Chicken Skin
Dessert: Super Easy Jelly Doughnuts

Day 3:
Breakfast: Green Feta Frittatas
Lunch: Spicy Gujarati Green Beans
Snack: Yogurt Marinated Endive
Dinner: Spicy Herbed Roast Beef
Dessert: Pineapple Sticks

Day 4:
Breakfast: Sweet Raspberry Yogurt Cake
Lunch: Baked Buffalo Cauliflower
Snack: Tasty Eggplant Cubes
Dinner: Italian Garlicky Chicken Thighs
Dessert: Roasted Cinnamon Pumpkin Seeds

Day 5:
Breakfast: Easy Pecan Rolled Granola
Lunch: Buttery Sweet Potatoes
Snack: Crispy Avocado Wedges
Dinner: Tangy Cranberry Cod
Dessert: Banana & Vanilla Puffs

Day 6:
Breakfast: Beef Cheeseburger Sliders
Lunch: Goluptious Air Fried Kale Chips
Snack: Easy Fried Beetroot Chips
Dinner: Tasty Steak and Broccoli
Dessert: Baked Cheesy Cinnamon Rolls

Day 7:
Breakfast: Spiced Omelet
Lunch: Asian Balsamic Fennel
Snack: Easy Radish Chips
Dinner: Roasted Whole Chicken
Dessert: Easy Air Fryer Busicuits Donuts

Week 4

Day 1:
Breakfast: Crispy Avocado Fries
Lunch: Buckwheat Bean Patties
Snack: Scallions and Spinach Pie
Dinner: Healthy Scallops
Dessert: Air Fried Chocolate Vanilla Cake

Day 2:
Breakfast: Egg Casserole with Ham
Lunch: Healthy Potato Latkes
Snack: Cheddar Tomato Platter
Dinner: Spicy Beef Burgers
Dessert: Chocolate Cake

Day 3:
Breakfast: Air Fried Peppers Hash
Lunch: Cheesy Eggplant
Snack: Bacon Butter
Dinner: Tasty Chicken Piccata
Dessert: Crispy Sweet Bananas

Day 4:
Breakfast: Spicy Sweet Potato Hash
Lunch: Caesar Cauliflower
Snack: Healthy Tuna Bowls
Dinner: Herbed Salmon
Dessert: Tropical Pineapple Cake

Day 5:
Breakfast: Cherry & Almond Bars
Lunch: Zucchini with Kimchi Sauce
Snack: Easy Potato Chips
Dinner: Mustardy Steak Sliders
Dessert: Lemony-Lavender Doughnuts

Day 6:
Breakfast: Italian Sausage Sandwich
Lunch: Veggie and Feta Frittata
Snack: Sweet and Salty Snack
Dinner: Delicious Popcorn Shrimp
Dessert: Healthy Hasselback Apple Crisp

Day 7:
Breakfast: Crispy Fish Sticks
Lunch: Vegetable Spring Rolls
Snack: Spiced Crispy Cauliflower Florets
Dinner: Turkey Meatloaves
Dessert: Strawberry Hand Tarts

Chapter 1 Breakfast Recipes

Baked Green Baby Spinach Scramble

Prep time: 5 minutes | Cook time: 20 minutes | Serves: 4

1 tablespoon olive oil	3 cups baby spinach
½ teaspoon smoked paprika	Salt and black pepper to the taste
12 eggs, whisked	

1. In a bowl, mix all the except the oil and whisk them well. 2. Select the "BAKE" function of Ninja Foodi digital air fry oven, set the temperature to 360 degrees F/ 180 degrees C and set the time to 20 minutes. Press the Start/Pause button and begin preheating. 3. Add the eggs and spinach mix in Ninja sheet pan. When the Ninja Foodi is preheated, place the sheet pan in the wire rack and close the door to begin to cook for 20 minutes, divide between plates and serve.
Per Serving: Calories 429; Fat 32.4g; Sodium 325mg; Carbs 5g; Fiber 1g; Sugar 3g; Protein 28g

Veggie Omelet with Cream and Cheese

Prep time: 10 minutes | Cook time: 14 minutes | Serves: 4

4 eggs, beaten	¼ teaspoon salt
1 tablespoon cream cheese	¼ cup heavy cream
½ teaspoon chili flakes	¼ teaspoon white pepper
½ cup broccoli florets, chopped	Cooking spray

1. Put the beaten eggs in the big bowl. Add chili flakes, salt, and white pepper. With the whisker stir the liquid until the salt is dissolved. Then add cream cheese and heavy cream. Stir the ingredients until you get the homogenous liquid. 2. After this, add broccoli florets. 3. Select the "AIR FRY" function of Ninja Foodi digital air fry oven, set the temperature to 375 degrees F/ 190 degrees C and set the time to 15 minutes. Press the Start/Pause button and begin preheating. Spray the sheet pan with cooking spray. Pour the egg liquid in the pan. Cook the omelet for 14 minutes.
Per Serving: Calories 173; Fat 13.6g; Sodium 281mg; Carbs 3g; Fiber 1g; Sugar 1g; Protein 10g

Air fried Cheddar Turkey Casserole

Prep time: 5 minutes | Cook time: 25 minutes | Serves: 4

1 turkey breast, skinless, boneless, cut into strips and browned	2 cups cheddar cheese, shredded
2 teaspoons olive oil	2 eggs, whisked
2 cups almond milk	Salt and black pepper to the taste
	1 tablespoon chives, chopped

1. In a bowl, mix the eggs with milk, cheese, salt, pepper and the chives and whisk well. Select the "AIR FRY" function of Ninja Foodi digital air fry oven, set the temperature to 330 degrees F/ 165 degrees C and set the time to 30 minutes. Press the Start/Pause button and begin preheating. Add the oil in air fryer sheet pan, heat it up, add the turkey pieces and spread them well. 2. Add the eggs mixture, toss a bit and cook for 25 minutes. Serve right away for breakfast.
Per Serving: Calories 1052; Fat 50g; Sodium 438mg; Carbs 7g; Fiber 0g; Sugar 7g; Protein 132g

Granola-Stuffed Apples

Prep time: 15 minutes | Cook time: 20 minutes | Serves: 4

4 Granny Smith or other firm apples	¾ teaspoon cinnamon
1 cup (100g) granola	2 tablespoons (28g) unsalted butter, melted
2 tablespoons (19g) light brown sugar	1 cup (240ml) water or apple juice

1. Select the "BAKE" function of Ninja Foodi digital air fry oven, set the temperature to 350 degrees F/ 175 degrees C and set the time to 20 minutes. Press the Start/Pause button and begin preheating. Working one apple at a time, cut a circle around the apple stem and scoop out the core, taking care not to cut all the way through to the bottom. Repeat with the remaining apples. 2. In a small bowl, combine the granola, brown sugar, and cinnamon. Pour the melted butter over the ingredients and stir with a fork. Divide the granola mixture among the apples, packing it tightly into the empty cavity. 3. Place the apples in the sheet pan for the air fryer. Pour the water or juice around the apples. Bake for 20 minutes until the apples are soft all the way through. 4. Serve warm with a dollop of crème fraîche or yogurt, if desired.
Per Serving: Calories 200; Fat 15.6g; Sodium 165mg; Carbs 5g; Fiber 1g; Sugar 2g; Protein 10g

Spiced Baked Eggs with Mascarpone

Prep time: 10 minutes | Cook time: 3 minutes | Serves: 2

2 eggs	¼ teaspoon dried cilantro
1 teaspoon mascarpone	¼ teaspoon ground turmeric
¼ teaspoon ground nutmeg	¼ teaspoon onion powder
¼ teaspoon dried basil	¼ teaspoon salt
¼ teaspoon dried oregano	

1. Crack the eggs in the mixing bowl and whisk them well. After this, add mascarpone and stir until you get a homogenous mixture. Then add all spices and mix up the liquid gently. 2. Pour it in the silicone egg molds and place in the Ninja air fryer basket. Select the "BAKE" function of Ninja Foodi digital air fry oven, set the temperature to 400 degrees F/ 200 degrees C and set the time to 5 minutes. Press the Start/ Pause button and begin preheating. Place the cups in wire rack and cook the egg cups for 3 minutes until done.
Per Serving: Calories 134; Fat 9.8g; Sodium 394mg; Carbs 2g; Fiber 0g; Sugar 1g; Protein 9g

Air Fried Peppers Hash

Prep time: 5 minutes | Cook time: 20 minutes | Serves: 4

1 red bell pepper, cut into strips	Salt and black pepper to the taste
1 green bell pepper, cut into strips	2 tablespoons mozzarella, shredded
1 o bell pepper, cut into strips	
4 eggs, whisked	Cooking spray

1. In a bowl, mix the eggs with all the bell peppers, salt and pepper and toss. 2. Select the "AIR FRY" function of Ninja Foodi digital air fry oven, set the temperature to 350 degrees F/ 175 degrees C and set the time to 20 minutes. Press the Start/Pause button and begin preheating. Grease the sheet pan with cooking spray, pour the eggs mixture, spread well, sprinkle the mozzarella on top and cook for 20 minutes. Divide between plates and serve for breakfast.
Per Serving: Calories 227; Fat 9.8g; Sodium 525mg; Carbs 7g; Fiber 2g; Sugar 4g; Protein 28g

Baked Eggs with Bacon

Prep time: 10 minutes | Cook time: 10 minutes | Serves: 3

3 eggs	3 bacon slices
½ teaspoon ground turmeric	1 teaspoon butter, melted
¼ teaspoon salt	

1. Brush the muffin silicone molds with ½ teaspoon of melted butter. Then ar the bacon in the silicone molds in the shape of circles. Select the "BAKE" function of Ninja Foodi digital air fry oven, set the temperature to 400 degrees F/ 200 degrees C and set the time to 8 minutes. Press the Start/Pause button and begin preheating.. 2. Place the bacon on sheet pan and Cook the bacon for 7 minutes. After this, brush the center of every bacon circle with remaining butter. 3. Then crack the eggs in every bacon circles, sprinkle with salt and ground turmeri. Cook the bacon cups for 3 minutes more.
Per Serving: Calories 248; Fat 21.1g; Sodium 429mg; Carbs 2g; Fiber 0g; Sugar 1g; Protein 12g

Eggs in a Basket

Prep time: 10 minutes | Cook time: 10 minutes | Serves: 1

1 thick slice country, sourdough, or Italian bread	butter, melted
2 tablespoons (28g) unsalted	1 egg
	Kosher salt and pepper to taste

1 Select the "BAKE" function of Ninja Foodi digital air fry oven, set the temperature to 300 degrees F/ 150 degrees C and set the time to 6 minutes. Press the Start/Pause button and begin preheating. Brush the bottom of the air fryer sheet pan with melted butter. Using a biscuit cutter, cut a hole out of the middle of the bread and set it aside. 2. Place bread in the air fryer cake pan . Crack the egg in the bread hole, taking care not to break the yolk. Season with salt and pepper. Place the cut-out bread hole next to the slice of bread. Place the sheet pan into the air fryer. 3. Bake at 300 degrees F/ 150 degrees C for 6 to 8 minutes until the white of egg sets and the yolk is still runny. Using a silicone spatula, remove the bread slice to a plate. Serve with the cut-out bread circle on the side or place it on top of the egg.
Per Serving: Calories 134; Fat 9.8g; Sodium 394mg; Carbs 2g; Fiber 0g; Sugar 1g; Protein 9g

Baked Paprika Cauliflower

Prep time: 5 minutes | Cook time: 20 minutes | Serves: 4

2 cups cauliflower florets,
separated
4 eggs, whisked

1 teaspoon sweet paprika
2 tablespoons butter, melted
A pinch of salt and black pepper

1. Select the "BAKE" function of Ninja Foodi digital air fry oven, set the temperature to 320 degrees F/ 160 degrees C and set the time to 25 minutes. Press the Start/Pause button and begin preheating. Grease the Ninja sheet pan with the butter, add cauliflower florets on the bottom, then add eggs whisked with paprika, salt and pepper, toss and cook for 20 minutes. 2. Divide between plates and serve for breakfast.
Per Serving: Calories 200; Fat 15.6g; Sodium 165mg; Carbs 5g; Fiber 1g; Sugar 2g; Protein 10g

Baked Cinnamon French Toast

Prep time: 12 minutes | Cook time: 9 minutes | Serves: 2

⅓ cup almond flour
1 egg, beaten
¼ teaspoon baking powder
2 teaspoons Erythritol

¼ teaspoon vanilla extract
1 teaspoon cream cheese
¼ teaspoon ground cinnamon
1 teaspoon ghee, melted

1. In the mixing bowl mix up almond flour, baking powder, and ground cinnamon. Then add egg, vanilla extract, ghee, and cream cheese. Stir the mixture with the help of the fork until homogenous. 2. Line the mugs bottom with baking paper. After this, transfer the almond flour mixture in the mugs and flatten well. 3. Select the "BAKE" function of Ninja Foodi digital air fry oven, set the temperature to 355 degrees F/ 180 degrees C and set the time to 10 minutes. Press the Start/Pause button and begin preheating. Place the mugs with toasts on the sheet pan and cook them for 9 minutes. 4. When the time is finished and the toasts are cooked, cool them little. Then sprinkle the toasts with Erythritol.
Per Serving: Calories 76; Fat 5.7g; Sodium 63mg; Carbs 1g; Fiber 0g; Sugar 1g; Protein 5g

Cheddar Eggs and Tomatoes Hash

Prep time: 5 minutes | Cook time: 25 minutes | Serves: 4

2 tablespoons olive oil
1 pound tomatoes, chopped
½ pound cheddar, shredded

2 tablespoons chives, chopped
Salt and black pepper to the taste
6 eggs, whisked

1. Grease the Ninja air fryer basket, Select the "AIR FRY" function of Ninja Foodi digital air fry oven, set the temperature to 350 degrees F/ 175 degrees C and set the time to 30 minutes. Press the Start/Pause button and begin preheating., Add the tomatoes, eggs, salt and pepper and whisk. Place mix to sheet pan and add the cheese on top and sprinkle the chives on top. 2. Cook for 25 minutes, divide between plates and serve for breakfast.
Per Serving: Calories 509; Fat 40.6g; Sodium 525mg; Carbs 8g; Fiber 2g; Sugar 5g; Protein 28g

Air Fried Scotch Eggs

Prep time: 15 minutes | Cook time: 13 minutes | Serves: 4

4 medium eggs, hard-boiled,
peeled
9 oz ground beef
1 teaspoon garlic powder
¼ teaspoon cayenne pepper

1 oz coconut flakes
¼ teaspoon curry powder
1 egg, beaten
1 tablespoon almond flour
Cooking spray

1. In the mixing bowl combine together ground beef and garlic powder. Add cayenne pepper, almond flour, and curry powder. Stir the meat mixture until homogenous. After this, wrap the peeled eggs in the ground beef mixture. In the end, you should get meat balls. 2. Coat every ball in the beaten egg and then sprinkle with coconut flakes. Select the "AIR FRY" function of Ninja Foodi digital air fry oven, set the temperature to 400 degrees F/ 200 degrees C and set the time to 15 minutes. Press the Start/Pause button and begin preheating. 3. Then spray the air fryer sheet pan with cooking spray and place the meat eggs in it. Cook the eggs for 13 minutes. Carefully flip the scotch eggs on another side after 7 minutes of cooking.
Per Serving: Calories 314; Fat 25g; Sodium 138mg; Carbs 2g; Fiber 0g; Sugar 1g; Protein 17g

Yummy Egg Cheesy Frittata

Prep time: 10 minutes | Cook time: 20 minutes | Serves: 6

1 cup almond milk
Cooking spray
9 ounces cream cheese, soft
1 cup cheddar cheese, shredded

6 spring onions, chopped
Salt and black pepper to the taste
6 eggs, whisked

1. Select the "BAKE" function of Ninja Foodi digital air fry oven, set the temperature to 350 degrees F/ 175 degrees C and set the time to 25 minutes. Press the Start/Pause button and begin preheating. Grease sheet pan with cooking spray. 2. In a bowl, mix the eggs with the rest of the ingredients, whisk well, pour and spread into the sheet pan and cook everything for 20 minutes. Divide everything between plates and serve.
Per Serving: Calories 288; Fat 23.3g; Sodium 308mg; Carbs 6g; Fiber 1g; Sugar 5g; Protein 14g

Delicious Shakshuka

Prep time: 10 minutes | Cook time: 30 minutes | Serves: 2

Tomato Sauce
3 tablespoons (45ml) extra-virgin
olive oil
1 small yellow onion, diced
1 jalapeño pepper, seeded and
minced
1 red bell pepper, diced
2 cloves garlic, minced
Shakshuka
4 eggs
1 tablespoon (15ml) heavy cream
1 tablespoon (1g) chopped

1 teaspoon cumin
1 teaspoon sweet paprika
Pinch cayenne pepper
1 tablespoon (16g) tomato paste
1 can (28 ounces, or 800g) whole
plum tomatoes with juice
2 teaspoons granulated sugar

cilantro
Kosher salt and pepper to taste

1. Select the "AIR FRY" function of Ninja Foodi digital air fry oven, set the temperature to 350 degrees F/ 175 degrees C and set the time to 10 minutes. Press the Start/Pause button and begin preheating. In a large deep skillet, sauté the onion and peppers in hot oil over medium heat, spice with salt, and sauté until softened, about 10 minutes. Add the garlic and spices and sauté a few additional minutes until fragrant. Add the tomato paste and stir to combine. Add the plum tomatoes along with their juice—breaking up the tomatoes with a spoon—and the sugar. Boil the mix to high heat. Lower down and manage to simmer until the tomatoes are thickened, about 10 minutes. Turn off the heat. 2. Crack the eggs into a 7-inch (18cm) round cake pan insert for the air fryer. Remove a cup of tomato sauce from the skillet and spoon it over the egg whites only, leaving the yolks exposed. Drizzle the cream over the yolks. 3. Place pan in the preheated air fryer. Close the door to begin cooking. Cook for 12 minutes until the whites of eggs are cooked and the yolks are still runny. Remove the pan from the air fryer and garnish with chopped cilantro. Season with salt and pepper. 4. Serve immediately with crusty bread to mop up the sauce.
Per Serving: Calories 429; Fat 32.4g; Sodium 325mg; Carbs 5g; Fiber 1g; Sugar 3g; Protein 28g

Baked Strawberries and Cream Oatmeal

Prep time: 10 minutes | Cook time: 15 minutes | Serves: 4

1 cup (170g) sliced strawberries
1 egg
¾ cup (180ml) milk
¼ cup (60ml) heavy cream
1 cup (80g) rolled oats
2 tablespoons (19g) brown sugar

½ teaspoon baking powder
½ teaspoon cinnamon
½ teaspoon ginger
Pinch salt
1 tablespoon (14g) unsalted butter

1. Place the sliced strawberries in the bottom of the cake pan for the air fryer, reserving a few for garnish. In a bowl, whisk the egg along with milk, and cream and pour it over the strawberries in the pan. 2. In a small bowl, combine the rolled oats, brown sugar, baking powder, spices, and salt. Combine well the dry and wet ingredients in the cake pan and stir to combine. Allow to rest for 10 minutes. Place the reserved strawberries on top of the oatmeal. 3. Select the "BAKE" function of Ninja Foodi digital air fry oven, set the temperature to 320 degrees F/ 160 degrees C and set the time to 15 minutes. Press the Start/Pause button and begin preheating. Place the sheet pan in the air fryer and cook until the oatmeal is warmed through and puffed. Spoon the oatmeal into bowls.
Per Serving: Calories 509; Fat 40.6g; Sodium 525mg; Carbs 8g; Fiber 2g; Sugar 5g; Protein 28g

Toasted Granola with Nuts

Prep time: 5 minutes | Cook time: 8-10 minutes | Serves: 5

⅔ cup rolled oats
⅓ cup shredded sweetened coconut
⅓ cup sliced almonds
1 teaspoon canola oil
2 teaspoons honey
¼ teaspoon kosher salt

1. Select the "AIR FRY" function of Ninja Foodi digital air fry oven, set the temperature to 360 degrees F/ 180 degrees C and set the time to 5 minutes. Press the Start/Pause button and begin preheating. 2. In a medium bowl, combine the rolled oats, sliced almonds, shredded sweetened coconut, honey, kosher salt, and canola oil. 3. Place a small piece of parchment paper on the bottom of the air fryer sheet pan, pour the mixture into the pan and distribute it evenly. Place the sheet pan into the air fryer, cook for 5 minutes, pause the fryer to gently stir the granola and cook for 3 more minutes. 4. Remove the granola from the fryer and place on a wire rack to cool for 5 minutes, then transfer the granola to a serving plate to cool completely. Serve.
Per Serving: Calories 163; Fat 9g; Sodium 94mg; Carbs 18g; Fiber 3g; Sugar 7g; Protein 4g

Cheesy Asparagus Frittata

Prep time: 15 minutes | Cook time: 15 minutes | Serves: 2-4

1 cup (134g) asparagus spears, cut into 1-inch (2.5 cm) pieces
1 teaspoon vegetable oil
6 eggs
1 tablespoon (15ml) milk
2 ounces (55g) goat cheese
1 tablespoon (3g) minced chives
Kosher salt and pepper

1. Select the "AIR FRY" function of Ninja Foodi digital air fry oven, set the temperature to 400 degrees F/ 200 degrees C and set the time to 5 minutes. Press the Start/Pause button and begin preheating. Toss the asparagus pieces with the vegetable oil in a small bowl. Place the asparagus in a 7-inch (18cm) air fryer sheet pan. Close the door to begin cooking. Cook it for 5 minutes until the asparagus is softened and slightly wrinkled. Remove the pan. 2. Whisk the eggs with milk and pour the mixture over the asparagus in the sheet pan. Crumble cheese over the eggs and add the chives, if using. Spice with a pinch of salt and pepper. Air fry at 320 degrees F/ 160 degrees C for 20 minutes, until the eggs are cooked through. Serve immediately.
Per Serving: Calories 173; Fat 13.6g; Sodium 281mg; Carbs 3g; Fiber 1g; Sugar 1g; Protein 10g

Sweet Potato and Black Bean Burritos

Prep time: 10 minutes | Cook time: 30 minutes | Serves: 6

2 sweet potatoes, cut into a small dice
1 tablespoon (15ml) vegetable oil
Kosher salt and pepper to taste
6 large flour tortillas
1 can (16 ounces, or 455g) refried black beans, divided
1½ cups (45g) baby spinach,
lightly packed, divided
6 eggs, scrambled
¾ cup (90g) grated Cheddar or Monterey Jack cheese, divided
Vegetable oil for heating
Salsa, Roasted Garlic Guacamole, and sour cream

1. Select the "AIR FRY" function of Ninja Foodi digital air fry oven, set the temperature to 400 degrees F/ 200 degrees C and set the time to 10 minutes. Press the Start/Pause button and begin preheating. Toss the sweet potatoes with vegetable oil, season with salt and pepper, and place in air fryer basket. Place the basket in air fryer 2. Close the door to begin cooking. Cook the potatoes for 10 minutes Remove and set aside. 3. Take a flour tortilla and spread ¼ cup (59.5g) of the refried beans down the center, leaving a border at each end. Top with ¼ cup (8g) of the spinach leaves. Sprinkle ¼ cup (27.5g) plus 2 tablespoons (14g) of sweet potato cubes on top of the spinach. Top with one-sixth of the scrambled eggs and 2 tablespoons grated cheese. To wrap the burrito, fold the long side over the ingredients, then fold in the short sides and roll. Repeat with the remaining ingredients and tortillas. 4. Wrap each burrito tightly in foil and combine in a large, gallon-size freezer bag. Freeze for up to 3 months.5. To heat, place the burrito, still wrapped in foil, in the air fryer and cook at 350 degrees F/ 175 degrees C for 20 minutes, flipping once halfway through. Remove the burrito from the foil, brush the outside of the tortilla with 1 teaspoon oil, and heat for an additional 3 to 5 minutes, turning once. Serve with salsa, Roasted Garlic Guacamole, or sour cream as desired.
Per Serving: Calories 1052; Fat 50g; Sodium 438mg; Carbs 7g; Fiber 0g; Sugar 7g; Protein 132g

Streusel French Toast with Aromatic Cinnamon

Prep time: 10 minutes | Cook time: 15 minutes | Serves: 4

Streusel
½ cup (63g) all-purpose flour
¼ cup (50g) granulated sugar
¼ cup (38g) light brown sugar
½ teaspoon cinnamon
Pinch kosher salt
4 tablespoons (55g) unsalted butter, melted
French Toast
2 eggs
¼ cup (60ml) milk
1 teaspoon vanilla extract
½ teaspoon cinnamon
Pinch nutmeg
4 slices brioche, challah, or white bread, preferably slightly stale
Maple syrup for serving

1. To make the streusel, combine the flour, sugars, cinnamon, and salt in a medium bowl. Pour the melted butter over the dry ingredients and stir with a fork to combine. Transfer the mixture to a plastic bag and place it in the freezer while you prepare the French toast. 2. To make the French toast, whisk together the eggs, milk, vanilla, cinnamon, and nutmeg in a medium bowl. Select the "AIR FRY" function of Ninja Foodi digital air fry oven, set the temperature to 375 degrees F/ 190 degrees C and set the time to 5 minutes. Press the Start/Pause button and begin preheating. Line the air fryer basket with parchment paper to prevent sticking. Dunk each slice of bread in the egg mixture, ensuring both sides are coated. Hold the bread over the bowl for a moment to allow any excess liquid to slide off. 3. Place the bread in the air fryer basket. Cook for 5 minutes. Open the air fryer and turn the bread over. Top each slice of bread with 2 tablespoons (40g) of streusel. Cook for an additional 4 minutes until the bread is crispy and browned and the streusel is puffy and golden. Serve warm with maple syrup.
Per Serving: Calories 227; Fat 9.8g; Sodium 525mg; Carbs 7g; Fiber 2g; Sugar 4g; Protein 28g

Delicious Apple Fritters

Prep time: 10 minutes | Cook time: 10 minutes | Serves: 5

Fritters
2 firm apples, such as Granny Smith, peeled, cored, and diced
Juice from 1 lemon
½ teaspoon cinnamon
1 cup (125g) all-purpose flour
1½ teaspoons baking powder
½ teaspoon kosher salt
2 tablespoons (26g) granulated sugar
2 eggs
¼ cup (6 ml) milk
2 tablespoons (28g) unsalted butter, melted
Vegetable oil for spraying
Glaze
1¼ cups (125g) powdered sugar, sifted
½ teaspoon vanilla extract
¼ cup (60ml) water

1. Select the "AIR FRY" function of Ninja Foodi digital air fry oven, set the temperature to 360 degrees F/ 180 degrees C and set the time to 7 minutes. Press the Start/Pause button and begin preheating. To make the fritters, toss the diced apples with the lemon juice and cinnamon in a small bowl and set aside. In a bowl, mix the flour with baking powder, and salt. In a bowl, whisk the sugar and eggs until the mixture is pale yellow. mix in the milk with melted butter. Mix the wet and dry ingredients in the large bowl and stir to combine. Fold in the diced apples. 2. Brush the basket of the air fryer with oil or line with parchment paper to prevent sticking. Working in 3 batches and using a spring-loaded cookie scoop, ice cream scoop, or ¼-cup measure, scoop 5 balls of dough directly onto the air fryer basket. Spray the fritters with oil. Place the sheet pan into the air fryer. Cook for 7 to 8 minutes until the outside is browned and the inside is fully cooked. 3. Whisk together the powdered sugar, vanilla, and water in a small bowl. Drizzle the glaze over the fritters or dip the tops of the fritters directly in the glaze, letting any excess drip off.
Per Serving: Calories 248; Fat 21.1g; Sodium 429mg; Carbs 2g; Fiber 0g; Sugar 1g; Protein 12g

Cheesy Eggs with Leeks

Prep time: 5 minutes | Cook time: 7 minutes | Serves: 2

2 leeks, chopped
4 eggs, whisked
¼ cup Cheddar cheese, shredded
½ cup Mozzarella cheese, shredded
1 teaspoon avocado oil

1. Select the "AIR FRY" function of Ninja Foodi digital air fry oven, set the temperature to 400 degrees F/ 200 degrees C and set the time to 7 minutes. Press the Start/Pause button and begin preheating. Then brush the air fryer basket with avocado oil and combine the eggs with the rest of the inside. Cook for 7 minutes and serve.
Per Serving: Calories 160; Fat 8.2g; Sodium 266mg; Carbs 12.6g; Fiber 7.1g; Sugar 4g; Protein 8.6g

Creamy Biscuits

1 cup (125g) self-rising flour
½ cup (120ml) plus 1 tablespoon (15ml) heavy cream

Vegetable oil for spraying
2 tablespoons (28g) unsalted butter

1. Select the "AIR FRY" function of Ninja Foodi digital air fry oven, set the temperature to 325 degrees F/ 160 degrees C and set the time to 15 minutes. Press the Start/Pause button and begin preheating. Place the flour in a medium bowl and whisk to remove any lumps. Make a well in the center of the flour. Slowly pour in the cream in a steady stream. Continue to stir until the dough has mostly come together. With your hands, gather the dough, incorporating any dry flour, and form it into a ball. 2. Place it on a floured surface and pat into a rectangle that is ½ to ¾ inch (1.3 to 2 cm) thick. Fold in half. Turn and repeat. One more time, pat the dough into a ¾-inch-thick (2cm) rectangle. Using a 2-inch (5cm) biscuit cutter, cut out biscuits—close together to minimize waste—taking care not to twist the cutter when pulling it up. You should be able to cut out 5 biscuits. Gather up any scraps and cut out 1 or 2 more biscuits. (These may be misshapen and slightly tougher than the first 5 biscuits, but still delicious.) 3. Spray the air fryer basket with oil to prevent sticking. Place it in the air fryer basket so that they are barely touching. Cook for 15 to 18 minutes until the tops are browned and the insides fully cooked. Remove the biscuits to a plate, brush the tops with melted butter, if using, and serve.
Per Serving: Calories 76; Fat 5.7g; Sodium 63mg; Carbs 1g; Fiber 0g; Sugar 1g; Protein 5g

Smoky Potatoes with Adobo Ketchup

2 cups (220g) diced (½ inch [1.3cm]) waxy red potatoes
2 teaspoons vegetable oil, divided
Kosher salt to taste
½ cup (80g) chopped yellow onion

1 cup (150g) chopped red bell pepper
1¾ cups (420g) ketchup
2 chipotle peppers in adobo
1 tablespoon (15ml) adobo sauce
½ teaspoon smoked paprika

1. In a bowl, toss the potatoes with 1 teaspoon of oil and season with a pinch of salt. Select the "AIR FRY" function of Ninja Foodi digital air fry oven, set the temperature to 400 degrees F/ 200 degrees C and set the time to 10 minutes. Press the Start/Pause button and begin preheating. Place them in the air fryer basket. Cook for 10 minutes. In a bowl toss the onion and pepper with the remaining teaspoon of oil and season with salt. 2. After 10 minutes, add the onion and pepper to the air fryer basket and toss to combine. Cook for further 10 -12 minutes until the peppers are softened and charred at the edges and the potatoes are crispy outside and cooked through. 3. While the vegetables are cooking, prepare the chipotle ketchup. Combine the ketchup, 2 chipotle peppers, and 1 tablespoon (15ml) of the adobo sauce in a blender and purée until smooth. Pour the chipotle ketchup into a serving bowl. 4. Toss cooked vegetables with the smoked paprika. Serve immediately with chipotle ketchup on the side.
Per Serving: Calories 314; Fat 25g; Sodium 138mg; Carbs 2g; Fiber 0g; Sugar 1g; Protein 17g

Sweet Pumpkin Oatmeal

1 cup rolled oats
2 tablespoons raisins
¼ teaspoon ground cinnamon
Pinch of kosher salt

¼ cup canned pumpkin puree
2 tablespoons maple syrup
1 cup low-fat milk

1. Select the "AIR FRY" function of Ninja Foodi digital air fry oven, set the temperature to 300 degrees F/ 150 degrees C and set the time to 10 minutes. Press the Start/Pause button and begin preheating. 2. Combine the rolled oats, raisins, ground cinnamon, and kosher salt in a medium bowl, then stir in the pumpkin puree, maple syrup, and low-fat milk. 3. Spray the air fryer sheet pan with nonstick cooking spray, then pour the oatmeal mixture into the pan. Place the sheet pan into the air fryer and cook for 10 minutes. 4. Remove the oatmeal from the fryer and place the pan on a wire rack to cool for 5 minutes before serving.
Per Serving: Calories 301; Fat 4g; Sodium 140mg; Carbs 57g; Fiber 6g; Sugar 26g; Protein 10g

Fried Apples with Steel-Cut Oats

1 cup dry steel-cut oats
4 cups water
Pinch of kosher salt
1 large gala apple, cored and cut

into 10 slices
⅛ teaspoon ground cinnamon
1 tablespoon granulated sugar

1. In a medium saucepan, combine the steel-cut oats, water, and kosher salt. Bring the mixture to a boil, reduce the heat to a simmer, and cook uncovered for 30 minutes or until the oats are tender. Set aside. 2. Select the "AIR FRY" function of Ninja Foodi digital air fry oven, set the temperature to 390 degrees F/ 200 degrees C. Set the time to 10 minutes. Press the Start/Pause button and begin preheating. 3. Spray the air fryer basket with nonstick cooking spray, then place the apple slices in the basket and place it into the air fryer, cook for 10 minutes. 4. While the apples cook, combine the ground cinnamon and granulated sugar in a small bowl and set aside. 5. Remove the apple slices from the fryer and place on a serving plate. Sprinkle 1 teaspoon of the cinnamon sugar mix on the apples. 6. Allow the apples to cool for 5 minutes, then serve on top of the cooked oats.
Per Serving: Calories 183; Fat 3g; Sodium 36mg; Carbs 36g; Fiber 5g; Sugar 8g; Protein 5g

Blueberry Oat Squares Bites

1 cup all-purpose flour
1 cup quick-cook oats
¼ teaspoon baking powder
Pinch of kosher salt
¼ teaspoon ground cinnamon
1 large egg, beaten

¼ cup light brown sugar, packed
¼ cup unsweetened applesauce
¼ cup canola oil
¼ cup low-fat milk
1 cup fresh blueberries
1 teaspoon confectioners' sugar

1. Select the "AIR FRY" function of Ninja Foodi digital air fry oven, set the temperature to 390 degrees F/ 200 degrees C. Set the time to 14 minutes. Press the Start/Pause button and begin preheating. 2. In a large bowl, whisk together the all-purpose flour, quick-cook oats, baking powder, kosher salt, and ground cinnamon. Set aside. 3. In a separate large bowl, combine the egg, light brown sugar, unsweetened applesauce, canola oil, and low-fat milk. 4. Add the egg mixture to the flour mixture, stirring until just combined, then gently fold in the blueberries. 5. Spray the air fryer sheet pan with nonstick cooking spray, then pour the batter into the pan. Place the sheet pan into the air fryer .Cook for 12–14 minutes or until golden brown and a toothpick comes out clean when inserted in the middle. 6. Remove the pan from the fryer and allow to cool on a wire rack for 10 minutes. Dust the confectioners' sugar on top before cutting and serving.
Per Serving: Calories 236; Fat 11g; Sodium 61mg; Carbs 32g; Fiber 2g; Sugar 12g; Protein 4g

Egg, Bean and Mushroom Burrito

2 tablespoons canned black beans, rinsed and drained
¼ cup baby portobello mushrooms, sliced
1 teaspoon olive oil
Pinch of kosher salt

1 large egg
1 slice low-fat cheddar cheese
1 eight-inch whole grain flour tortilla
Hot sauce

1. Select the "AIR FRY" function of Ninja Foodi digital air fry oven, set the temperature to 360 degrees F/ 180 degrees C and set the time to 5 minutes. Press the Start/Pause button and begin preheating. 2. Spray the air fryer sheet pan with nonstick cooking spray, then place the black beans and baby portobello mushrooms in the sheet pan, drizzle with the olive oil, and season with the kosher salt. 3. Place the sheet pan into the air fryer, cook for 5 minutes, then pause the fryer to crack the egg on top of the beans and mushrooms. Cook for 8 more minutes or until the egg is cooked as desired. 4. Pause the fryer again, top the egg with cheese, and cook for 1 more minute. 5. Remove the pan from the fryer, then use a spatula to place the bean mixture on the whole grain flour tortilla. Fold in the sides and roll from front to back. Serve warm with the hot sauce on the side.
Per Serving: Calories 277; Fat 12g; Sodium 306mg; Carbs 26g; Fiber 6g; Sugar 2g; Protein 16g

Green Feta Frittatas

Prep time: 5 minutes | Cook time: 11 minutes | Serves: 2

1 cup kale, chopped
1 teaspoon olive oil
4 large eggs, beaten

2 tablespoons water
Pinch of kosher salt
3 tablespoons crumbled feta

1. Select the "BAKE" function of Ninja Foodi digital air fry oven, set the temperature to 360 degrees F/ 180 degrees C and set the time to 3 minutes. Press the Start/Pause button and begin preheating. 2. Spray the air fryer sheet pan with nonstick cooking spray, then place the kale in the pan, drizzle with the olive oil, and Place the basket into the air fryer; cook for 3 minutes. 3. While the kale cooks, whisk together the eggs, water, and kosher salt in a large bowl. 4. Pause the fryer to pour the eggs into the pan and sprinkle the feta on top. Reduce the heat to 300 degrees F/ 150 degrees C and cook for 8 more minutes. 5. Remove the frittata from the fryer and place it on a wire rack to cool for 5 minutes before cutting and serving.
Per Serving: Calories 216; Fat 15g; Sodium 354mg; Carbs 5g; Fiber 1g; Sugar 2g; Protein 16g

Cheese Bacon & Egg Sandwiches

Prep time: 3 minutes | Cook time: 8 minutes | Serves: 2

2 large eggs
¼ teaspoon kosher salt, divided
¼ teaspoon freshly ground black pepper, divided (plus extra for serving)

2 slices Canadian bacon
2 slices American cheese
2 whole grain English muffins, sliced in half

1. Select the "AIR FRY" function of Ninja Foodi digital air fry oven, set the temperature to 360 degrees F/ 180 degrees C and set the time to 5 minutes. Press the Start/Pause button and begin preheating. 2. Spray two 3-inch ramekins with nonstick cooking spray, then crack one egg into each ramekin and add half the kosher salt and half the black pepper to each egg. 3. Place the ramekins in the fryer basket and cook for 5 minutes. 4. Pause the fryer and top each partially cooked egg with a slice of Canadian bacon and a slice of American cheese. 5. Cook for 3 more minutes or until the cheese has melted and the egg yolk has just cooked through. 6. Remove the ramekins from the fryer and allow to cool on a wire rack for 2–3 minutes, then flip the eggs, bacon, and cheese out onto English muffins and sprinkle some black pepper on top before serving.
Per Serving: Calories 305; Fat 5g; Sodium 618mg; Carbs 26g; Fiber 3g; Sugar 3g; Protein 22g

Caramelized Banana with Yogurt

Prep time: 5 minutes | Cook time: 5 minutes | Serves: 1

1 banana, cut into ¾-inch slices
6 oz. nonfat plain Greek yogurt

3 tablespoons toasted granola with almonds

1. Select the "AIR FRY" function of Ninja Foodi digital air fry oven, set the temperature to 360 degrees F/ 180 degrees C and set the time to 5 minutes. Press the Start/Pause button and begin preheating. 2. Spray the air fry basket with nonstick cooking spray, then place the banana slices in the basket and place the basket into the air fryer; cook for 5 minutes. 3. Allow to cool in the fryer for 5 minutes, then remove the banana slices from the fryer. 4. Spread the plain Greek yogurt on a serving plate, then place the banana slices on the yogurt and top with the toasted granola before serving.
Per Serving: Calories 249; Fat 1g; Sodium 96mg; Carbs 40g; Fiber 4g; Sugar 23g; Protein 18g

Salmon & Carrot Breakfast

Prep time: 5 minutes | Cook time: 15 minutes | Serves: 2

1 lb. salmon, chopped
2 cups feta, crumbled
4 bread slices

3 tablespoons pickled red onion
2 cucumbers, sliced
1 carrot, shredded

Select the "AIR FRY" function of Ninja Foodi digital air fry oven, set the temperature to 300 degrees F/ 150 degrees C and set the time to 15 minutes. Press the Start/Pause button and begin preheating. Add salmon and feta to a bowl. Add carrot, red onion and cucumber and mix well. In a sheet pan, make a layer of bread and then pour the salmon mix over it. Air fry it for 15-minutes.
Per Serving: Calories 56; Fat 2.2g; Sodium 177mg; Carbs 5g; Fiber 1g; Sugar 1g; Protein 5g

Healthy French Toast

Prep time: 8 minutes | Cook time: 8 minutes | Serves: 2

2 slices whole grain bread
1 large egg
½ cup low-fat milk
⅛ teaspoon ground cinnamon

½ teaspoon vanilla extract
2 teaspoons maple syrup
1 teaspoon confectioners' sugar

1. Select the "AIR FRY" function of Ninja Foodi digital air fry oven, set the temperature to 360 degrees F/ 180 degrees C and set the time to 8 minutes. Press the Start/Pause button and begin preheating. 2. Spray the air fryer sheet pan with nonstick cooking spray, then cut the whole grain bread into small pieces or strips and place in the pan. Set aside. 3. In a medium bowl, whisk together the egg, low-fat milk, ground cinnamon, vanilla extract, and 2 teaspoons of maple syrup. 4. Pour the egg mixture over the bread, then press it down with a spatula to make sure all the bread is coated. Place the soaked toast on sheet pan and cook for 8 minutes. 5. Remove the French toast from the fryer and place on a wire rack to cool for 5 minutes, then dust with the confectioners' sugar and drizzle 2 tablespoons of maple syrup on top before serving.
Per Serving: Calories 221; Fat 4g; Sodium 239mg; Carbs 37g; Fiber 2g; Sugar 21g; Protein 9g

Chicken Almond Casserole

Prep time: 5 minutes | Cook time: 25 minutes | Serves: 4

¼ cup almonds, chopped
½ cup almond milk
4 eggs, whisked
1 cup chicken meat, cooked and

shredded
½ teaspoon oregano, dried
Cooking spray
Salt and black pepper to the taste

1. Select the "AIR FRY" function of Ninja Foodi digital air fry oven, set the temperature to 350 degrees F/ 175 degrees C and set the time to 25 minutes. Press the Start/Pause button and begin preheating. 2. In a bowl, add eggs with the rest of the except the cooking spray and whisk well. Grease a sheet pan with the cooking spray, pour the chicken mix into the pan, put the pan in the machine and cook the omelet for 25 minutes. Divide between plates and serve for breakfast.
Per Serving: Calories 216; Fat 11g; Sodium 230mg; Carbs 5g; Fiber 3g; Sugar 1g; Protein 9g

Cinnamon Buns with Pecan Nuts

Prep time: 10 minutes | Cook time: 30 minutes | Serves: 9

¾ cup unsweetened almond milk
4 tablespoons sugar-free maple syrup
½ cup pecan nuts, toasted
3 teaspoons cinnamon powder
1 ½ cups almond flour, sifted
1 cup whole grain flour, sifted

1 tablespoon coconut oil, melted
3 tablespoons water
1 tablespoon ground flaxseed
1 ½ tablespoons active yeast
2 ripe bananas, sliced
4 dates, pitted
¼ cup icing sugar

1. Heat the almond milk to lukewarm and add the syrup and yeast. Allow the yeast to activate for about 10-minutes. Mix flaxseed and water separately to make egg replacement. Allow flaxseed to soak for 2-minutes. 2. Add coconut oil. Pour the flaxseed mixture into yeast mixture. In another bowl, add both types of flour, and 2 teaspoons cinnamon powder. 3. Pour into the yeast-flaxseed mixture and combine until dough is formed. Knead the dough on a floured surface for about 10-minutes. Place the kneaded dough into a greased bowl and cover it with a tea towel. Leave in a warm and dark area to rise for 1 hour. Make the filling by mixing the pecans, dates and banana slices and remaining teaspoon of cinnamon powder. 4. Select the "AIR FRY" function of Ninja Foodi digital air fry oven, set the temperature to 390 degrees F/ 200 degrees C and set the time to 30 minutes. Press the Start/Pause button and begin preheating. Roll the risen dough on a floured surface until it is thin. Spread the pecan mixture over the dough. Roll dough and cut it into nine slices. Place inside of dish that will fit into your air fryer and cook for 30-minutes. Once cook time is completed, sprinkle with icing sugar.
Per Serving: Calories 69; Fat 7.2g; Sodium 486mg; Carbs 2g; Fiber 1g; Sugar 0g; Protein 0g

Sweet Raspberry Yogurt Cake

Prep time: 10 minutes | Cook time: 8 minutes | Serves: 4

½ cup whole wheat pastry flour	2 tablespoons canola oil
⅛ teaspoon kosher salt	2 tablespoons maple syrup
¼ teaspoon baking powder	¾ cup fresh raspberries
½ cup whole milk vanilla yogurt	1 teaspoon confectioners' sugar

1. Select the "AIR FRY" function of Ninja Foodi digital air fry oven, set the temperature to 300 degrees F/ 150 degrees C and set the time to 8 minutes. Press the Start/Pause button and begin preheating. 2. In a large bowl, combine the whole wheat pastry flour, kosher salt, and baking powder, then stir in the whole milk vanilla yogurt, canola oil, and maple syrup and gently fold in the raspberries. 3. Spray the air fryer sheet pan with nonstick cooking spray, then pour the cake batter into the pan and Place the sheet pan into the air fryer ;cook for 8 minutes. 4. Remove the cake from the fryer and allow to cool in the pan on a wire rack for 10 minutes, then sift the confectioners' sugar on top before cutting and serving.

Per Serving: Calories 222; Fat 8g; Sodium 82mg; Carbs 25g; Fiber 3g; Sugar 12g; Protein 3g

Egg White Cups with Spinach and Tomato

Prep time: 5 minutes | Cook time: 10 minutes | Serves: 1

2 egg whites, beaten	Pinch of kosher salt
2 tablespoons tomato, chopped	Red pepper flakes
2 tablespoons spinach, chopped	

1. Select the "AIR FRY" function of Ninja Foodi digital air fry oven, set the temperature to 300 degrees F/ 150 degrees C and set the time to 10 minutes. Press the Start/Pause button and begin preheating. 2. Spray a 3-inch ramekin with nonstick cooking spray, then combine the egg whites, tomato, spinach, kosher salt, and red pepper flakes (if using) in the ramekin. 3. Place the ramekin in the air fryer basket. Cook for 10 minutes or until the eggs have set. 4. Remove the ramekin from the fryer and allow to cool on a wire rack for 5 minutes before serving.

Per Serving: Calories 40; Fat 0g; Sodium 184mg; Carbs 1g; Fiber 1g; Sugar 1g; Protein 7g

Red Onion Omelet Cups with Bell Pepper

Prep time: 5 minutes | Cook time: 10 minutes | Serves: 2

4 large eggs	¼ teaspoon freshly ground black pepper
½ bell pepper, finely chopped	
1 tablespoon red onion, finely chopped	2 tablespoons shredded cheddar cheese
¼ teaspoon kosher salt	

1. Select the "AIR FRY" function of Ninja Foodi digital air fry oven, set the temperature to 390 degrees F/ 200 degrees C. Set the time to 10 minutes. Press the Start/Pause button and begin preheating. 2. In a large bowl, whisk together the eggs, then stir in the bell pepper, red onion, kosher salt, and black pepper. 3. Spray two 3-inch ramekins with nonstick cooking spray, then pour half the egg mixture into each ramekin and place the ramekins in the fryer basket. Place the basket into the air fryer, Cook for 8 minutes. 4. Pause the fryer, sprinkle 1 tablespoon of shredded cheddar cheese on top of each cup, and cook for 2 more minutes. 5. Remove the ramekins from the fryer and allow to cool on a wire rack for 5 minutes, then turn the omelet cups out on plates and sprinkle some black pepper on top before serving.

Per Serving: Calories 176; Fat 12g; Sodium 333mg; Carbs 2g; Fiber 0g; Sugar 1g; Protein 14g

Delicious Grilled Cheese Sandwiches

Prep time: 5 minutes | Cook time: 7 minutes | Serves: 2

4 slices of brown bread	shredded
½ cup sharp cheddar cheese,	¼ cup butter, melted

1.Select the "AIR FRY" function of Ninja Foodi digital air fry oven, set the temperature to 360 degrees F/ 180 degrees C and set the time to 5 minutes. Press the Start/Pause button and begin preheating. 2. Place cheese and butter into separate bowls. Melt butter and brush it onto the 4 slices of bread. Place cheese on 2 sides of bread slices. Put sandwiches together and place them into the air fryer basket. Cook in air fryer for 5-minutes and serve warm.

Per Serving: Calories 409; Fat 18.9g; Sodium 214mg; Carbs 10g; Fiber 1g; Sugar 9g; Protein 48g

Cheesy Egg Pockets

Prep time: 10 minutes | Cook time: 35 minutes | Serves: 4

1 large egg, beaten	1 slice cheddar cheese, divided into 4 pieces
Pinch of kosher salt	
½ sheet puff pastry	

1. Select the "AIR FRY" function of Ninja Foodi digital air fry oven, set the temperature to 330 degrees F/ 165 degrees C and set the time to 5 minutes. Press the Start/Pause button and begin preheating. 2. Pour the egg into the air fryer sheet pan, season with the kosher salt, and cook for 3 minutes. Pause the fryer, gently scramble the egg, and cook for 2 more minutes. Remove the egg from the fryer, keeping the fryer on, and set the egg aside to slightly cool. 3. Roll the puff pastry out flat and divide into 4 pieces. 4. Place a piece of cheddar cheese and ¼ of the egg on one side of a piece of pastry, fold the pastry over the egg and cheese, and use a fork to press the edges closed. Repeat this process with the remaining pieces. 5. Place 2 pockets in the fryer and cook for 15 minutes or until golden brown. Repeat this process with the other 2 pockets. 6. Remove the pockets from the fryer and allow to cool on a wire rack for 5 minutes before serving.

Per Serving: Calories 218; Fat 15g; Sodium 143mg; Carbs 14g; Fiber 0g; Sugar 0g; Protein 6g

Delicious Huevos Rancheros

Prep time: 20 minutes | Cook time: 25 minutes | Serves: 4

4 large eggs	¼ cup warm water
¼ teaspoon kosher salt	½ cup salsa
¼ cup masa harina (corn flour)	¼ cup crumbled queso fresco or feta cheese
1 teaspoon olive oil	

1. Select the "AIR FRY" function of Ninja Foodi digital air fry oven, set the temperature to 330 degrees F/ 165 degrees C and set the time to 5 minutes. Press the Start/Pause button and begin preheating. 2. Crack the eggs into the air fryer sheet pan, season with the kosher salt, and cook for 3 minutes. Pause the fryer, gently scramble the eggs, and cook for 2 more minutes. Remove the eggs from the fryer, keeping the fryer on, and set the eggs aside to slightly cool. 3. Preheat the air fryer to 390 degrees F/ 200 degrees C. 4. In a medium bowl, combine the masa harina, olive oil, and ¼ teaspoon of kosher salt by hand, then slowly pour in the water, stirring until a soft dough forms. 5. Divide the dough into 4 equal balls, then place each ball between 2 pieces of parchment paper and use a pie plate or a rolling pin to flatten the dough. 6. Spray the air fryer sheet pan with nonstick cooking spray, then place one flattened tortilla in the pan and cook for 5 minutes. Repeat this process with the remaining tortillas. 7. Remove the tortillas from the fryer and place on a serving plate, then top each tortilla with the scrambled eggs, salsa, and cheese before serving.

Per Serving: Calories 142; Fat 8g; Sodium 333mg; Carbs 8g; Fiber 1g; Sugar 2g; Protein 8g

Spicy Sweet Potato Hash

Prep time: 10 minutes | Cook time: 20 minutes | Serves: 4

2 large sweet potatoes	sliced
½ small red onion, cut into large chunks	½ teaspoon kosher salt
1 green bell pepper, cut into large chunks	¼ teaspoon freshly ground black pepper (plus extra for serving)
1 jalapeño pepper, seeded and	1 teaspoon olive oil
	1 large egg, poached

1. Select the "AIR FRY" function of Ninja Foodi digital air fry oven, set the temperature to 360 degrees F/ 180 degrees C and set the time to 4 minutes. Press the Start/Pause button and begin preheating. 2. Cook the sweet potatoes on high in the microwave until softened but not completely cooked (3–4 minutes), then set aside to cool for 10 minutes. 3. Remove the skins from the sweet potatoes, then cut the sweet potatoes into large chunks. 4. In a large bowl, combine the sweet potatoes, red onion, green bell pepper, jalapeño pepper, kosher salt, black pepper, and olive oil, tossing gently. 5. Spray the fryer basket with nonstick cooking spray, then pour the mixture into the basket and cook for 8 minutes. 6. Pause the fryer to shake the basket, then cook for 8 more minutes at 360 degrees F/ 180 degrees C or until golden brown. 7. Remove the hash from the air fryer, place on a plate lined with a paper towel, and allow to cool for 5 minutes, then add the poached egg, sprinkle black pepper on top, and serve.

Per Serving: Calories 121; Fat 3g; Sodium 174mg; Carbs 22g; Fiber 4g; Sugar 7g; Protein 4g

Egg-in-a-Hole

Prep time: 5 minutes | Cook time: 10 minutes | Serves: 1

1 slice whole grain bread
1 large egg
⅛ teaspoon kosher salt
¼ cup avocado, diced
¼ cup tomato, diced
Pinch of freshly ground black pepper

1. Select the "AIR FRY" function of Ninja Foodi digital air fry oven, set the temperature to 360 degrees F/ 180 degrees C and set the time to 5 minutes. Press the Start/Pause button and begin preheating. 2. Spray the air fryer sheet pan with nonstick cooking spray, then use a ring mold or a sharp knife to cut a 3-inch hole in the center of the whole grain bread. Place the bread slice and the circle in the pan.3. Crack the egg into the hole, then season with the kosher salt. Place the pan into the air fryer, cook for 5–7 minutes or until the egg is cooked as desired. 4. Remove the pan from the fryer and place on a wire rack to cool for 5 minutes before transferring the toast to a plate, then sprinkle the avocado, tomato, and black pepper on top before serving.
Per Serving: Calories 220; Fat 12g; Sodium 406mg; Carbs 18g; Fiber 5g; Sugar 4g; Protein 10g

Creamy Mascarpone Eggs

Prep time: 8 minutes | Cook time: 5 minutes | Serves: 6

7 eggs, beaten
¼ cup mascarpone
1 teaspoon ground paprika
½ teaspoon salt
1 teaspoon avocado oil

1. Put eggs in the bowl and add mascarpone, salt, and ground paprika. With the help of the fork whisk the until homogenous. 2. Then Select the "AIR FRY" function of Ninja Foodi digital air fry oven, set the temperature to 395 degrees F/ 200 degrees C and set the time to 5 minutes. Press the Start/Pause button and begin preheating. 3. Spray the basket with avocado oil. Pour the egg mixture in the air fryer basket. Cook the omelet for 5 minutes.
Per Serving: Calories 93; Fat 6.6g; Sodium 277mg; Carbs 1g; Fiber 0.2g; Sugar 0g; Protein 7.7g

Classic Fries

Prep time: 10 minutes | Cook time: 20 minutes | Serves: 2

1 lb. small red potatoes, diced
2 teaspoons olive oil
¼ cup yellow onion, finely chopped
¼ teaspoon kosher salt
¼ teaspoon freshly ground black pepper

1. Select the "AIR FRY" function of Ninja Foodi digital air fry oven, set the temperature to 360 degrees F/ 180 degrees C and set the time to 20 minutes. Press the Start/Pause button and begin preheating. 2. In a medium bowl, toss the red potatoes and olive oil, then add the onion, kosher salt, and black pepper, tossing again to coat. 3. Spray the fryer basket with nonstick cooking spray, then place the mixture in the basket and Place the basket into the air fryer; cook for 20 minutes or until golden brown, pausing the fryer every 5 minutes to shake the basket. 4. Remove the fries from the fryer and place on a plate lined with a paper towel to cool for 5 minutes before serving.
Per Serving: Calories 102; Fat 2g; Sodium 161mg; Carbs 19g; Fiber 2g; Sugar 2g; Protein 2g

Sweet Apple Compote

Prep time: 5 minutes | Cook time: 15 minutes | Serves: 4

2 medium apples, peeled and diced
⅛ teaspoon ground cinnamon
2 teaspoons honey
Juice of ½ lemon
2 tablespoon raisins
⅔ cup water

1. Select the "AIR FRY" function of Ninja Foodi digital air fry oven, set the temperature to 360 degrees F/ 180 degrees C and set the time to 15 minutes. Press the Start/Pause button and begin preheating. 2. Spray the air fryer sheet pan with nonstick cooking spray, then combine the apples, ground cinnamon, honey, lemon juice, raisins, and water in the pan. Cook for 12–15 minutes or until the apples are tender. 3. Remove the compote from the fryer and place on a wire rack to cool for 5 minutes before serving.
Per Serving: Calories 65; Fat 0g; Sodium 3mg; Carbs 17g; Fiber 1g; Sugar 14g; Protein 0g

Creamy Tomato & Egg Scramble

Prep time: 5 minutes | Cook time: 10 minutes | Serves: 2

2 eggs
1 tomato, chopped
Dash of salt
1 teaspoon butter
¼ cup cream

1.In a bowl, whisk the eggs, salt, and cream until fluffy. Select the "AIR FRY" function of Ninja Foodi digital air fry oven, set the temperature to 300 degrees F/ 150 degrees C and set the time to 10 minutes. Press the Start/Pause button and begin preheating. 2. Add butter to the sheet pan and place into the air fryer. Once the butter is melted, add the egg mixture and tomato to sheet pan, then cook for 10-minutes. Whisk the eggs until fluffy then serve warm.
Per Serving: Calories 104; Fat 2.5g; Sodium 29mg; Carbs 18g; Fiber 4g; Sugar 2g; Protein 3g

Cheesy Bacon and Egg Quesadilla

Prep time: 5 minutes | Cook time: 5 minutes | Serves: 1

1 large egg
⅛ teaspoon kosher salt
1 eight-inch whole wheat tortilla
¼ cup shredded cheddar cheese
1 slice cooked bacon, chopped

1. Select the "AIR FRY" function of Ninja Foodi digital air fry oven, set the temperature to 360 degrees F/ 180 degrees C and set the time to 5 minutes. Press the Start/Pause button and begin preheating. 2. Pour the egg into the air fryer sheet pan and season with the kosher salt. Cook for 3 minutes, then pause the fryer, gently scramble the egg, and cook for 2 more minutes. 3. Remove the egg from the fryer, keeping the fryer on, and set the egg aside to slightly cool. 4. Spray the fryer basket with nonstick cooking spray, then layer the cooked egg, shredded cheddar cheese, and bacon on the tortilla. Fold in half, place in the basket, and cook for 5 minutes. 5. Remove the quesadilla from the fryer and allow to cool on a wire rack for 2–3 minutes before serving.
Per Serving: Calories 335; Fat 19g; Sodium 480mg; Carbs 25g; Fiber 2g; Sugar 1g; Protein 19g

Egg Casserole with Ham

Prep time: 5 minutes | Cook time: 12 minutes | Serves: 2

1 cup day-old whole grain bread, cubed
3 large eggs, beaten
2 tablespoons water
⅛ teaspoon kosher salt
1 oz. prosciutto, roughly chopped
1 oz. slice pepper jack cheese, roughly chopped
1 tablespoon fresh chives, chopped

1. Select the "AIR FRY" function of Ninja Foodi digital air fry oven, set the temperature to 360 degrees F/ 180 degrees C and set the time to 12 minutes. Press the Start/Pause button and begin preheating. 2. Spray the air fryer sheet pan with nonstick cooking spray, then place the bread cubes in the pan. 3. In a medium bowl, whisk together the eggs and water, then stir in the kosher salt, prosciutto, pepper jack cheese, and chives. 4. Pour the egg mixture over the bread cubes and cook for 10–12 minutes or until the eggs have set and the top is golden brown. 5. Remove the casserole from the fryer and place on a wire rack to cool for 5 minutes before cutting and serving.
Per Serving: Calories 248; Fat 6g; Sodium 557mg; Carbs 11g; Fiber 3g; Sugar 2g; Protein 19g

Banana Cookies

Prep time: 5 minutes | Cook time: 20 minutes | Serves: 6

3 ripe bananas
1 teaspoon vanilla extract
⅓ cup olive oil
1 cup dates, pitted and chopped
2 cups rolled oats

1.Select the "AIR FRY" function of Ninja Foodi digital air fry oven, set the temperature to 350 degrees F/ 175 degrees C and set the time to 20 minutes. Press the Start/Pause button and begin preheating. 2. In a bowl, mash bananas and add the rest of the ingredients and mix well. Allow ingredients to rest in the fridge for 10-minutes. 3. Cut some parchment paper to fit inside of your air fryer basket. Drop a teaspoonful of mixture on parchment paper, making sure not to overlap the cookies. Cook the cookies for 20-minutes and you can serve with some almond milk.
Per Serving: Calories 288; Fat 23.3g; Sodium 308mg; Carbs 6g; Fiber 1g; Sugar 5g; Protein 14g

Tasty Spinach Balls

Prep time: 10 minutes | Cook time: 10 minutes | Serves: 4

1 carrot, peeled and grated
2 slices of bread, toasted and make into breadcrumbs
1 tablespoon corn flour
1 tablespoon nutritional yeast
½ teaspoon garlic, minced

1 egg, beaten
½ teaspoon garlic powder
½ onion, chopped
1 package fresh spinach, blanched and chopped

1.Select the "AIR FRY" function of Ninja Foodi digital air fry oven, set the temperature to 390 degrees F/ 200 degrees C. Set the time to 10 minutes. Press the Start/Pause button and begin preheating. 2. Blend ingredients in a bowl, except the breadcrumbs. Make small balls with the mixture and roll them over the bread crumbs. 3. Place the spinach balls in a sheet pan and cook for 10-minutes. Serve warm.
Per Serving: Calories 138; Fat 10.6g; Sodium 102mg; Carbs 1g; Fiber 0g; Sugar 1g; Protein 9g

Cheesy Pea Protein Muffins

Prep time: 5 minutes | Cook time: 15 minutes | Serves: 4

1 cup almond flour
1 teaspoon baking powder
3 eggs
1 cup mozzarella cheese, shredded

½ cup chicken or turkey strips
3 tablespoons pea protein
1 cup cream cheese
1 cup almond milk

1.Select the "BAKE" function of Ninja Foodi digital air fry oven, set the temperature to 390 degrees F/ 200 degrees C and set the time to 15 minutes. Press the Start/Pause button and begin preheating. 2. Mix all the ingredients in a mixing bowl and stir with a wooden spoon. Fill muffin cups with mixture ¾ full. 3. Place the muffins in the sheet pan and place in the air fryer. Bake for 15-minutes and enjoy!
Per Serving: Calories 293; Fat 13.8g; Sodium 855mg; Carbs 28g; Fiber 8g; Sugar 11g; Protein 19g

Cherry & Almond Bars

Prep time: 10 minutes | Cook time: 17 minutes | Serves: 8

2 cups old-fashioned oats
½ cup quinoa, cooked
½ cup chia seeds
½ cup prunes, pureed
¼ teaspoon salt

2 teaspoons liquid Stevia
¾ cup almond butter
½ cup dried cherries, chopped
½ cup almonds, sliced

1. Select the "AIR FRY" function of Ninja Foodi digital air fry oven, set the temperature to 370 degrees F/ 185 degrees C and set the time to 15 minutes. Press the Start/Pause button and begin preheating. In a large mixing bowl, add quinoa, chia seeds, oats, cherries, and almonds. In a saucepan over medium heat melt almond butter, liquid Stevia and coconut oil for 2-minutes and stir to combine. 2. Add salt and prunes and mix well. Pour into sheet pan that will fit in air fryer and cook for 15-minutes. 3. Allow to cool for an hour once cook time is completed, then slice the bars and serve.
Per Serving: Calories 151; Fat 7.5g; Sodium 621mg; Carbs 20g; Fiber 5g; Sugar 2g; Protein 5g

Cheese Bread Cups

Prep time: 5 minutes | Cook time: 15 minutes | Serves: 2

2 eggs
2 tablespoons cheddar cheese, grated
Salt and pepper to taste

1 ham slice, cut into 2 pieces
4 bread slices, flatten with rolling pin

1.Select the "AIR FRY" function of Ninja Foodi digital air fry oven, set the temperature to 350 degrees F/ 175 degrees C and set the time to 15 minutes. Press the Start/Pause button and begin preheating. Spray the inside of 2 ramekins with cooking spray. 2. Place 2 flat pieces of bread into each ramekin. Add the ham slice pieces into each ramekin. Crack an egg in each ramekin then sprinkle with cheese. Season with salt and pepper. Place the ramekins into the air fry basket and place it in the air fryer for cooking. Cook for 15-minutes. Serve warm.
Per Serving: Calories 354; Fat 7.9g; Sodium 704mg; Carbs 6g; Fiber 3.6g; Sugar 6g; Protein 18g

Cheesy Bacon Scrambled Eggs

Prep time: 5 minutes | Cook time: 10 minutes | Serves: 4

¼ teaspoon onion powder
4 eggs, beaten
3-ounces bacon, cooked, chopped
½ cup cheddar cheese, grated

3 tablespoons Greek yogurt
¼ teaspoon garlic powder
Salt and pepper to taste

1. Select the "AIR FRY" function of Ninja Foodi digital air fry oven, set the temperature to 330 degrees F/ 165 degrees C and set the time to 10 minutes. Press the Start/Pause button and begin preheating. Whisk eggs in a bowl, add salt and pepper to taste along with yogurt, garlic powder, onion powder, cheese, and bacon, stir. 2. Add the egg mixture into an oven-proof sheet pan. Place it into air fryer and cook for 10-minutes. Scramble eggs and serve warm.
Per Serving: Calories 25; Fat 0.1g; Sodium 546mg; Carbs 3g; Fiber 1g; Sugar 0g; Protein 3g

Cheesy Bacon, Ham and Eggs

Prep time: 5 minutes | Cook time: 10 minutes | Serves: 4

4 eggs
⅓ cup ham, cooked and chopped into small pieces

⅓ cup bacon, cooked, chopped into small pieces
⅓ cup cheddar cheese, shredded

1. In a medium-sized mixing bowl, whisk the eggs, add the ham, bacon, and cheese and stir until well combined. Add to sheet pan that is sprayed with cooking spray. Select the "AIR FRY" function of Ninja Foodi digital air fry oven, set the temperature to 300 degrees F/ 150 degrees C and set the time to 10 minutes. Press the Start/Pause button and begin preheating. 2. Place pan into air fryer and cook for 10 minutes then remove when cooking time is completed and serve warm.
Per Serving: Calories 217; Fat 21.8g; Sodium 207mg; Carbs 7g; Fiber 4g; Sugar 3g; Protein 2g

Easy Pecan Rolled Granola

Prep time: 5 minutes | Cook time: 5 minutes | Serves: 6

1½ cups rolled oats
½ cup pecans, roughly chopped
Dash of salt
½ cup raisins

½ cup sunflower seeds
2 tablespoons butter, melted
2 teaspoons liquid Stevia

1.Select the "AIR FRY" function of Ninja Foodi digital air fry oven, set the temperature to 350 degrees F/ 175 degrees C and set the time to 5 minutes. Press the Start/Pause button and begin preheating. 2. In a mixing bowl, combine oats, pecans and a dash of salt and stir well. 3. In a small bowl mix butter with Stevia then add to the oat mixture. Spray the sheet pan with cooking spray and add in the oat mixture. Place in the air fryer and bake for 5 minutes. Stir halfway through. 4. Remove from air fryer and pour into bowl to cool. 5. Add the sunflower seeds and raisins and stir. Eat immediately or store in an airtight container.
Per Serving: Calories 34; Fat 2.3g; Sodium 122mg; Carbs 1g; Fiber 0g; Sugar 0g; Protein 2g

Cheesy Asparagus Omelet

Prep time: 5 minutes | Cook time: 8 minutes | Serves: 2

3 eggs
5 steamed asparagus tips
2 tablespoons of warm milk
1 tablespoon parmesan cheese,

grated
Salt and pepper to taste
Non-stick cooking spray

1.Select the "AIR FRY" function of Ninja Foodi digital air fry oven, set the temperature to 350 degrees F/ 175 degrees C and set the time to 8 minutes. Press the Start/Pause button and begin preheating. 2. In a large bowl, mix eggs, cheese, milk, salt and pepper then blend them. Spray a sheet pan with non-stick cooking spray. Pour the egg mixture into the pan and add the asparagus, then place the pan into the air fryer and cook it for 8-minutes. Serve warm.
Per Serving: Calories 74; Fat 1.9g; Sodium 685mg; Carbs 9g; Fiber 7g; Sugar 2g; Protein 9g

Baked Eggs with Spinach

Prep time: 5 minutes | Cook time: 8 minutes | Serves: 4

1 lb. of spinach, chopped	1 tablespoon olive oil
7 ounces sliced ham	4 tablespoons milk
4 eggs	Salt and pepper to taste

1. Select the "AIR FRY" function of Ninja Foodi digital air fry oven, set the temperature to 350 degrees F/ 175 degrees C and set the time to 8 minutes. Press the Start/Pause button and begin preheating. 2. Butter the inside of 4 ramekins. In each ramekin, place spinach on bottom, one egg, 1 tablespoon of milk, ham, salt, and pepper. 3. Place ramekins in air fryer basket. Place the basket in the air fryer and cook for 8-minutes.
Per Serving: Calories 23; Fat 1.3g; Sodium 40mg; Carbs 2g; Fiber 1g; Sugar 1g; Protein 1g

Pumpkin Pie Toast

Prep time: 5 minutes | Cook time: 20 minutes | Serves: 4

2 large, beaten eggs	¼ cup pumpkin purée
4 slices of cinnamon swirl bread	¼ teaspoon pumpkin spices
¼ cup milk	¼ cup butter

1. Select the "AIR FRY" function of Ninja Foodi digital air fry oven, set the temperature to 340 degrees F/ 170 degrees C and set the time to 10 minutes. Press the Start/Pause button and begin preheating. In a large mixing bowl, mix milk, eggs, pumpkin purée and pie spice. Whisk until mixture is smooth. In the egg mixture dip the bread on both sides. Place 2 slices of bread onto the air fryer basket and cook for 10-minutes. Serve pumpkin pie toast with butter.
Per Serving: Calories 80; Fat 6g; Sodium 444mg; Carbs 6g; Fiber 1g; Sugar 4g; Protein 1g

Breaded Cod Nuggets

Prep time: 5 minutes | Cook time: 10 minutes | Serves: 4

1 lb. of cod
For breading:

2 eggs, beaten	1 teaspoon dried parsley
2 tablespoons olive oil	Pinch of sea salt
1 cup almond flour	½ teaspoon black pepper
¾ cup breadcrumbs	

1. Select the "Air Fry" function of Ninja Foodi digital air fry oven, set the temperature to 390 degrees F/ 200 degrees C and set the time to 10 minutes. Press the Start/Pause button and begin preheating. 2. Cut the cod into strips about 1-inch by 2-inches in length. 3. Blend breadcrumbs, olive oil, salt, parsley and pepper in a food processor. 3. In three separate bowls, add breadcrumbs, eggs, and flour. Place each piece of fish into flour, then the eggs and lastly the breadcrumbs. Add pieces of cod to air fryer basket and cook for 10-minutes. Serve warm.
Per Serving: Calories 42; Fat 2.8g; Sodium 126mg; Carbs 4g; Fiber 1g; Sugar 1g; Protein 1g

Vegetable Patties

Prep time: 5 minutes | Cook time: 15 minutes | Serves: 2

1 cup almond flour	1 carrot, grated
½ cup milk	1 zucchini, grated
1 tablespoon parmesan cheese, grated	1 tablespoon olive oil
3 eggs	¼ teaspoon nutmeg
1 potato, grated	1 teaspoon onion powder
1 beet, peeled and grated	1 teaspoon garlic powder
	½ teaspoon black pepper

1. Select the "AIR FRY" function of Ninja Foodi digital air fry oven, set the temperature to 390 degrees F/ 200 degrees C and set the time to 15 minutes. Press the Start/Pause button and begin preheating. 2. Mix the zucchini, potato, beet, carrot, eggs, milk, almond flour and parmesan in a bowl, then add the remaining ingredients. 3. Place olive oil into oven-safe dish. Form patties with vegetable mix and flatten to form patties. 4. Place patties into sheet pan and cook in air fryer for 15-minutes. Serve with sliced tomatoes, sour cream, and toast.
Per Serving: Calories 134; Fat 2.8g; Sodium 64mg; Carbs 26g; Fiber 4g; Sugar 8g; Protein 3g

Delicious Oriental Omelet

Prep time: 5 minutes | Cook time: 24 minutes | Serves: 1

½ cup fresh Shimeji mushrooms, sliced	A handful of sliced tofu
2 eggs, whisked	2 tablespoons onion, finely chopped
Salt and pepper to taste	Cooking spray
1 clove of garlic, minced	

1. Select the "AIR FRY" function of Ninja Foodi digital air fry oven, set the temperature to 355 degrees F/ 180 degrees C and set the time to 24 minutes. Press the Start/Pause button and begin preheating. Spray the sheet pan with cooking spray. 2. Add onions and garlic in pan and place in the air fryer. Air fry them for 4-minutes pause. 3. Place the tofu and mushrooms over the onions and add salt and pepper to taste. Whisk the eggs and pour them over tofu and mushrooms. Air fry again for 20-minutes. Serve warm.
Per Serving: Calories 153; Fat 2.8g; Sodium 28mg; Carbs 26g; Fiber 1g; Sugar 1g; Protein 6g

Crispy Avocado Fries

Prep time: 5 minutes | Cook time: 8 minutes | Serves: 2

2 eggs, beaten	Salt to taste
2 large avocados, peeled, pitted, cut into 8 slices each	Juice of ½ a lemon
¼ teaspoon pepper	½ cup of whole wheat flour
½ teaspoon cayenne pepper	1 cup whole wheat breadcrumbs
	Greek yogurt to serve

1. Add flour, salt, pepper and cayenne pepper to bowl and mix. Add bread crumbs into another bowl. Beat eggs in a third bowl. 2. First, dredge the avocado slices in the flour mixture. Next, dip them into the egg mixture and finally dredge them in the breadcrumbs. 3. Place avocado fries into the air fryer basket. Select the "AIR FRY" function of Ninja Foodi digital air fry oven, set the temperature to 390 degrees F/ 200 degrees C and set the time to 6 minutes. Press the Start/Pause button and begin preheating. Place the air fryer basket into the air fryer and cook for 6-minutes. When cook time is completed, transfer the avocado fries onto a serving platter. Sprinkle with lemon juice and serve with Greek yogurt.
Per Serving: Calories 33; Fat 3.5g; Sodium 1mg; Carbs 1g; Fiber 0g; Sugar 0g; Protein 0g

Cheese & Egg Sandwich

Prep time: 5 minutes | Cook time: 6 minutes | Serves: 1

1-2 eggs	A bit of butter
1-2 slices of cheddar or Swiss cheese	1 roll sliced in half, Kaiser bun, English muffin, etc.

1. Butter your sliced roll on both sides. Place the eggs in an oven-safe dish and whisk. 2. Add seasoning if you wish, such as dill, chives, oregano, and salt. Place the egg dish, roll and cheese into the air fryer. Make sure the buttered sides of the roll are facing upwards. 3. Select the "AIR FRY" function of Ninja Foodi digital air fry oven, set the temperature to 350 degrees F/ 175 degrees C and set the time to 6 minutes. Press the Start/Pause button and begin preheating. Cook them for 6 minutes. Place the egg and cheese between the pieces of roll and serve warm. You might like to try adding slices of avocado and tomatoes to this breakfast sandwich!
Per Serving: Calories 292; Fat 24.3g; Sodium 660mg; Carbs 5g; Fiber 0g; Sugar 3g; Protein 14g

Beef Cheeseburger Sliders

Prep time: 5 minutes | Cook time: 10 minutes | Serves: 6

1 lb. ground beef	6 dinner rolls
6 slices of cheddar cheese	Salt and black pepper to taste

1. Select the "AIR FRY" function of Ninja Foodi digital air fry oven, set the temperature to 390 degrees F/ 200 degrees C and set the time to 10 minutes. Press the Start/Pause button and begin preheating. 2. Form 6 beef patties each about 2.5 ounces and season with salt and black pepper. Add the burger patties to the air fryer basket and cook them for 10-minutes. Remove the burger patties from the air fryer; place the cheese on top of burgers and return to air fryer and cook for another minute. Remove and put burgers on dinner rolls and serve warm.
Per Serving: Calories 4; Fat 0.1g; Sodium 0mg; Carbs 1g; Fiber 1g; Sugar 0g; Protein 0g

Zucchini & Cream Muffins

Prep time: 5 minutes | Cook time: 15 minutes | Serves: 5

1 tablespoon cream cheese	oil
Half a cup zucchini, shredded	Pinch of sea salt
1 tablespoon plain yogurt	2 teaspoons baking powder
1 egg	1 teaspoon cinnamon
1 cup of milk	1 tablespoon liquid Stevia
2 tablespoons of warmed coconut	4 cups whole wheat flour

1.Select the "AIR FRY" function of Ninja Foodi digital air fry oven, set the temperature to 350 degrees F/ 175 degrees C and set the time to 12 minutes. Press the Start/Pause button and begin preheating. 2. Mix all your dry ingredients in a mixing bowl. Stir to combine. 3. In another mixing bowl combine all of the wet ingredients (coconut oil, milk, yogurt, liquid Stevia, and egg. Whisk these until evenly combined. 4. In a large bowl, combine both the wet and dry ingredients and use a hand mixer to whisk them. Stir in the shredded zucchini and fold in the cream cheese. 5. Place five muffin cups into your preheated air fryer. Fill each cup ¾ full of mixture. Cook muffins for 12-minutes. Serve warm or cold.
Per Serving: Calories 193; Fat 8.9g; Sodium 93mg; Carbs 2g; Fiber 1g; Sugar 0g; Protein 25g

Peanut Butter & Banana Toast

Prep time: 5 minutes | Cook time: 6 minutes | Serves: 1

2 slices of whole wheat bread	1 sliced banana
1 teaspoon of sugar-free maple syrup	2 tablespoons of peanut butter

1.Select the "AIR FRY" function of Ninja Foodi digital air fry oven, set the temperature to 330 degrees F/ 165 degrees C and set the time to 6 minutes. Press the Start/Pause button and begin preheating. 2. Evenly coat both sides of the slices of bread with peanut butter. Add the sliced banana and drizzle with some sugar-free maple syrup. 3. Place toast on air fryer basket and place it in the fryer; cook for 6 minutes. Serve warm.
Per Serving: Calories 101; Fat 5.4g; Sodium 106mg; Carbs 8g; Fiber 3g; Sugar 3g; Protein 7g

Cherry Tomatoes and Sausage Frittata

Prep time: 5 minutes | Cook time: 15 minutes | Serves: 3

6 eggs	shredded
8 cherry tomatoes, halved	1 Italian sausage, diced
2 tablespoons parmesan cheese,	Salt and pepper to taste

1. Select the "AIR FRY" function of Ninja Foodi digital air fry oven, set the temperature to 355 degrees F/ 180 degrees C and set the time to 5 minutes. Press the Start/Pause button and begin preheating. 2. Add the tomatoes and sausage to sheet pan. Place the sheet pan into air fryer and cook for 5-minutes. Meanwhile, add eggs, salt, pepper, cheese, and oil into mixing bowl and whisk well. Remove the sheet pan from the air fryer and pour the egg mixture on top, spreading evenly. Placing the dish back into the air fryer and bake for an additional 5-minutes. Remove from air fryer and slice into wedges and serve.
Per Serving: Calories 162; Fat 9.4g; Sodium 68mg; Carbs 21g; Fiber 4g; Sugar 16g; Protein 1g

Bacon Egg Muffins

Prep time: 5 minutes | Cook time: 6 minutes | Serves: 2

2 whole wheat English muffins	Pepper to taste
4 slices of bacon	2 eggs

1. Crack an egg each into ramekins. Season with pepper. Select the "AIR FRY" function of Ninja Foodi digital air fry oven, set the temperature to 390 degrees F/ 200 degrees C and set the time to 6 minutes. Press the Start/Pause button and begin preheating. 2. Place the ramekins with the bacon and muffins alongside in air fryer basket and cook for 6 minutes. Remove the muffins from the air fryer after a few minutes and split them. 3. When the bacon and eggs are done cooking, add two pieces of bacon and one egg to each egg muffin and serve immediately.
Per Serving: Calories 716; Fat 62.6g; Sodium 302mg; Carbs 18g; Fiber 8g; Sugar 2g; Protein 34g

Eggs & Cheese Toast

Prep time: 5 minutes | Cook time: 15 minutes | Serves: 2

⅛ teaspoon of black pepper	2 eggs
¼ teaspoon salt	2 slices of whole wheat toast
½ teaspoon Italian seasoning	3 tablespoons cheddar cheese, shredded
¼ teaspoon balsamic vinegar	6-slices tomatoes
¼ teaspoon sugar-free maple syrup	Cooking spray
1 cup sausages, chopped into small pieces	A little mayonnaise to serve

1. Select the "AIR FRY" function of Ninja Foodi digital air fry oven, set the temperature to 350 degrees F/ 175 degrees C and set the time to 10 minutes. Press the Start/Pause button and begin preheating. Spray sheet pan with cooking spray. 2. Place the bread slices at the bottom of the pan. Sprinkle the sausages over bread. Lay the tomatoes over it. Sprinkle top with cheese. Beat the eggs and then pour over top of bread slices. Drizzle vinegar and maple syrup over eggs. Season with Italian seasoning, salt, and pepper, then sprinkle some more cheese on top. 3. Place the sheet pan in the air fryer basket and cook for 10-minutes. 4. Remove from air fryer and add spot of mayonnaise and serve.
Per Serving: Calories 147; Fat 7.3g; Sodium 56mg; Carbs 20g; Fiber 5g; Sugar 11g; Protein 4g

Italian Sausage Sandwich

Prep time: 5 minutes | Cook time: 20 minutes | Serves: 3

1 pound sweet Italian sausage	2 teaspoons mustard
6 white bread slices	

1. Select the "AIR FRY" function of Ninja Foodi digital air fry oven, set the temperature to 370 degrees F/ 185 degrees C and set the time to 15 minutes. Press the Start/Pause button and begin preheating. 2. Place the sausage in a lightly greased Air fryer basket. Air fry the sausage for 15 minutes, tossing the basket halfway through the cooking time. Assemble the sandwiches with the bread, mustard, and sausage, and serve immediately.
Per Serving: Calories 407; Fat 14.5g; Sodium 336mg; Carbs 31.8g; Fiber 6.6g; Sugar 7.6g; Protein 28.8g

Traditional Eggplant Spread

Prep time: 5 minutes | Cook time: 20 minutes | Serves: 4

3 eggplants	2 tablespoons olive oil
Salt and black pepper to the taste	2 teaspoons sweet paprika
2 tablespoons chives, chopped	

1. Select the "AIR FRY" function of Ninja Foodi digital air fry oven, set the temperature to 380 degrees F/ 195 degrees C and set the time to 20 minutes. Press the Start/Pause button and begin preheating. Put the eggplants in your air fryer's basket and cook them for 20 minutes. 2. Peel the eggplants, put them in a blender, add the rest of the ingredients, pulse well, divide into bowls and serve for breakfast.
Per Serving: Calories 190; Fat 7g; Sodium 423mg; Carbs 5g; Fiber 3g; Sugar 2g; Protein 3g

Country Chicken Tenders

Prep time: 5 minutes | Cook time: 15 minutes | Serves: 4

¾ lb. of chicken tenders
For breading:

2 tablespoons olive oil	½ cup seasoned breadcrumbs
1 teaspoon black pepper	½ cup all-purpose flour
½ teaspoon salt	2 eggs, beaten

1.Select the "AIR FRY" function of Ninja Foodi digital air fry oven, set the temperature to 330 degrees F/ 165 degrees C and set the time to 10 minutes. Press the Start/Pause button and begin preheating. 2. In three separate bowls, set aside breadcrumbs, eggs, and flour. Season the breadcrumbs with salt and pepper. Add olive oil to the breadcrumbs and mix well. 3. Place chicken tenders into flour, then dip into eggs and finally dip into breadcrumbs. Press to ensure that the breadcrumbs are evenly coating the chicken. Shake off excess breading and place in the air fryer basket. Cook the chicken tenders for 10-minutes in the air fryer. Serve warm.
Per Serving: Calories 271; Fat 9.3g; Sodium 15mg; Carbs 43g; Fiber 6g; Sugar 2g; Protein 5g

Bacon Salad with Crispy Croutons

Prep time: 5 minutes | Cook time: 20 minutes | Serves: 5

1-pound bacon, cut into thick slices
1 head lettuce, torn into leaves
1 tablespoon fresh chive, chopped
1 tablespoon fresh tarragon, chopped
1 tablespoon fresh parsley, chopped

2 tablespoons freshly squeezed lemon juice
2 garlic cloves, minced
Coarse sea salt and ground black pepper, to taste
1 teaspoon red pepper flakes, crushed
2 cups bread cubes

1. Select the "AIR FRY" function of Ninja Foodi digital air fry oven, set the temperature to 400 degrees F/ 200 degrees C and set the time to 10 minutes. Press the Start/Pause button and begin preheating. 2. Place the bacon in the Air Fryer basket. Then, cook the bacon for 10 minutes, tossing the basket halfway through the cooking time; reserve. 3. Air fry the bread cubes at 390 degrees F/ 200 degrees C for approximately 6 minutes or until the bread is toasted. Toss the remaining ingredients in a salad bowl; top your salad with the bacon and croutons. Bon appétit!
Per Serving: Calories 419; Fat 36.3g; Sodium 455mg; Carbs 13.4g; Fiber 1g; Sugar 2.5g; Protein 13.4g

Sweet Avocado & Blueberry Muffins

Prep time: 5 minutes | Cook time: 15 minutes | Serves: 12

2 eggs
1 cup blueberries
2 cups almond flour
1 teaspoon baking soda
⅛ teaspoon salt
For streusel topping:
2 tablespoons Truvia sweetener
4 tablespoons butter, softened

2 ripe avocados, peeled, pitted, mashed
2 tablespoons liquid Stevia
1 cup plain Greek yogurt
1 teaspoon vanilla extract

4 tablespoons almond flour

1.Make the streusel topping by mixing Truvia, flour, and butter until you form a crumbly mixture. Place this mixture in the freezer for a while. 2. Meanwhile, make the muffins by sifting together flour, baking powder, baking soda and salt and set aside. 3. Add avocados and liquid Stevia to a bowl and mix well. Adding in one egg at a time, continue to beat. Add the vanilla extract and yogurt and beat again. Add in flour mixture a bit at a time and mix well. Add the blueberries into the mixture and gently fold them in. 4. Pour the batter into greased muffin cups, then add mixture until they are half-full. 5. Sprinkle the streusel topping mixture on top of muffin mixture and place muffin cups in the sheet pan. Select the "BAKE" function of Ninja Foodi digital air fry oven, set the temperature to 355 degrees F/ 180 degrees C and set the time to 10 minutes. Press the Start/Pause button and begin preheating. Place the pan in air fryer and cook for 10-minutes. Remove the muffin cups from the air fryer and allow them to cool. Cool completely then serve.
Per Serving: Calories 139; Fat 3.2g; Sodium 45mg; Carbs 26g; Fiber 4g; Sugar 8g; Protein 3g

Cheesy Cheddar Bacon Pancakes

Prep time: 10 minutes | Cook time: 7 minutes | Serves: 2

2 tablespoons almond flour
¼ teaspoon baking powder
1 teaspoon Erythritol
1 teaspoon cream cheese
1 teaspoon butter, melted

2 eggs, beaten
1 bacon slice, cooked, cut into halves
1 Cheddar cheese slice
1 teaspoon sesame oil

1. In the bowl mix up baking powder, almond flour, Erythritol, cream cheese, and 1 beaten egg. Select the "AIR FRY" function of Ninja Foodi digital air fry oven, set the temperature to 390 degrees F/ 200 degrees C and set the time to 15 minutes. Press the Start/Pause button and begin preheating. Then line the air fryer with baking paper. 2. Pour ¼ of the pancake batter in the air fryer in the shape of pancake and cook for 1 minute. Then flip the pancake on another side and cook for 1 minute more. Repeat the same steps with the remaining pancake batter. You should get 4 pancakes. 3. After this, brush the air fryer basket with sesame oil. Pour the remaining beaten egg in the air fryer and cook for 3 minutes. Cut the cooked egg into 2 parts. Place the 1 half of cooked egg on the one pancake. Top it with 1 half of the bacon and second pancake.
Per Serving: Calories 374; Fat 31.7g; Sodium 287mg; Carbs 7g; Fiber 3g; Sugar 1g; Protein 18.7g

Egg Rolls

Prep time: 10 minutes | Cook time: 4 minutes | Serves: 4

2 eggs, hard-boiled, peeled
1 tablespoon cream cheese
1 tablespoon fresh dill, chopped
1 teaspoon ground black pepper

4 wontons wrap
1 egg white, whisked
1 teaspoon sesame oil

1. Chop the eggs and mix them up with cream cheese, dill, and ground black pepper. Then place the egg mixture on the wonton wraps and roll them into the rolls. 2. Brush every roll with whisked egg white. After this, Select the "AIR FRY" function of Ninja Foodi digital air fry oven, set the temperature to 395 degrees F/ 200 degrees C and set the time to 5 minutes. Press the Start/Pause button and begin preheating. Brush the air fryer basket with sesame oil. Arrange the egg rolls in the hot air fryer and cook them for 2 minutes from each side or until the rolls are golden brown.
Per Serving: Calories 81; Fat 4.4g; Sodium 269mg; Carbs 5.7g; Fiber 0.4g; Sugar 0.3g; Protein 4.9g

Cheese Omelet with Onion

Prep time: 15 minutes | Cook time: 13 minutes | Serves: 2

3 eggs
1 large yellow onion, diced
2 tablespoons cheddar cheese, shredded

½ teaspoon soy sauce
Salt and pepper to taste
Olive oil cooking spray

1 Select the "AIR FRY" function of Ninja Foodi digital air fry oven, set the temperature to 350 degrees F/ 175 degrees C and set the time to 7 minutes. Press the Start/Pause button and begin preheating. 2. In a bowl whisk together eggs, soy sauce, pepper, and salt. In a small pan that will fit inside of your air fryer, spray with olive oil cooking spray. 3. Add onions to the pan and spread them around. Air fry onions for 7-minutes. 4. Pour the beaten egg mixture over the cooked onions and sprinkle the top with shredded cheese. Place back into the air fryer and cook for 6-minutes more. Remove from the air fryer and serve omelet with toasted multi-grain bread.
Per Serving: Calories 427; Fat 18.3g; Sodium 603mg; Carbs 44g; Fiber 6g; Sugar 3g; Protein 23g

BLT Sandwich

Prep time: 5 minutes | Cook time: 15 minutes | Serves: 3

6 ounces bacon, thick-cut
2 tablespoons brown sugar
2 teaspoons chipotle chile powder
1 teaspoon cayenne pepper

1 tablespoon Dijon mustard
1 heads lettuce, torn into leaves
2 medium tomatoes, sliced
6 (½-inch) slices white bread

1. Select the "AIR FRY" function of Ninja Foodi digital air fry oven, set the temperature to 400 degrees F/ 200 degrees C and set the time to 10 minutes. Press the Start/Pause button and begin preheating. 2. Toss the bacon with the sugar, chipotle chile powder, cayenne pepper, and mustard. Place the bacon in the Air Fryer basket. Then, cook the bacon for 10 minutes, tossing the basket halfway through the cooking time. Assemble your sandwiches with the bacon, lettuce, and tomato. Bon appétit!
Per Serving: Calories 401; Fat 23.3g; Sodium 411mg; Carbs 32.3g; Fiber 6.4g; Sugar 9.5g; Protein 14.2g

Spiced Omelet

Prep time: 5 minutes | Cook time: 20 minutes | Serves: 4

10 eggs, whisked
½ cup cheddar, shredded
2 tablespoons parsley, chopped
2 tablespoons chives, chopped

2 tablespoons basil, chopped
Cooking spray
Salt and black pepper to the taste

1. In a bowl, Add eggs with all the except the cheese and the cooking spray and whisk well. Select the "AIR FRY" function of Ninja Foodi digital air fry oven, set the temperature to 350 degrees F/ 175 degrees C and set the time to 20 minutes. Press the Start/Pause button and begin preheating. Grease sheet pan with the cooking spray, and pour the eggs mixture inside. 2.Sprinkle the cheese on top and cook for 20 minutes. Divide everything between plates and serve.
Per Serving: Calories 232; Fat 12g; Sodium 578mg; Carbs 5g; Fiber 1g; Sugar 1g; Protein 7g

Delicious Chicken Muffins

Prep time: 10 minutes | Cook time: 10 minutes | Serves: 6

1 cup ground chicken
1 cup ground pork
½ cup Mozzarella, shredded
1 teaspoon dried oregano
½ teaspoon salt
1 teaspoon ground paprika
½ teaspoon white pepper
1 tablespoon ghee, melted
1 teaspoon dried dill
2 tablespoons almond flour
1 egg, beaten

1. In the bowl mix up ground chicken, ground pork, dried oregano, salt, ground paprika, white pepper, dried dill, almond flour, and egg. When you get the homogenous texture of the mass, add ½ of all Mozzarella and mix up the mixture gently with the help of the spoon. 2. Then brush the silicone muffin molds with melted ghee. Put the meat mixture in the muffin molds. Flatten the surface of every muffin with the help of the spoon and top with remaining Mozzarella. Select the "AIR FRY" function of Ninja Foodi digital air fry oven, set the temperature to 375 degrees F/ 190 degrees C and set the time to 10 minutes. Press the Start/Pause button and begin preheating. 3. Then arrange the muffins in the air fryer basket and cook them for 10 minutes. Cool the cooked muffins to the room temperature and remove from the muffin molds.
Per Serving: Calories 291; Fat 20.6g; Sodium 369mg; Carbs 2.7g; Fiber 1.3g; Sugar 1.5g; Protein 23.9g

Delicious Spinach Quiche

Prep time: 5 minutes | Cook time: 15 minutes | Serves: 2

2 eggs
1 large yellow onion, diced
1¾ cups whole wheat flour
1½ cups spinach, chopped
¾ cup cottage cheese
Salt and black pepper to taste
2 tablespoons olive oil
¾ cup butter
¼ cup milk

1. Select the "AIR FRY" function of Ninja Foodi digital air fry oven, set the temperature to 355 degrees F/ 180 degrees C and set the time to 15 minutes. Press the Start/Pause button and begin preheating. 2. Add the flour, butter, salt, and milk to the bowl and knead dough until smooth and refrigerate for 15-minutes. 3. Place a frying pan over medium heat and add the oil to it. When the oil is heated, add the onions into the pan and sauté them. Add spinach to pan and cook until it wilts. Drain excess moisture from spinach. Whisk the eggs together and add cheese to bowl and mix. 4. Take the dough out of the fridge and divide into 8 equal parts. Roll the dough into a round that will fit into the bottom of quiche mold. Place the rolled dough into molds. Place the spinach filling over dough. 5. Place molds into air fryer basket and cook for 15-minutes. Remove quiche from molds and serve warm or cold.
Per Serving: Calories 88; Fat 7.1g; Sodium 143mg; Carbs 4g; Fiber 3g; Sugar 1g; Protein 4g

Crispy Fish Sticks

Prep time: 15 minutes | Cook time: 10 minutes | Serves: 4

8 oz cod fillet
1 egg, beaten
¼ cup coconut flour
¼ teaspoon ground coriander
¼ teaspoon ground paprika
¼ teaspoon ground cumin
¼ teaspoon Pink salt
⅓ cup coconut flakes
1 tablespoon mascarpone
1 teaspoon heavy cream
Cooking spray

1. Chop the cod fillet roughly and put it in the blender. Add egg, coconut flour ground coriander, paprika, cumin, salt, and blend the mixture until smooth. After this, transfer it in the bowl. 2. Line the chopping board with parchment. Place the fish mixture over the parchment and flatten it in the shape of the flat square. Then cut the fish square into sticks. In the separated bowl whisk together heavy cream and mascarpone. 3. Sprinkle every fish stick with mascarpone mixture and after this, coat in the coconut flakes. Select the "AIR FRY" function of Ninja Foodi digital air fry oven, set the temperature to 400 degrees F/ 200 degrees C and set the time to 10 minutes. Press the Start/Pause button and begin preheating. Grease the basket with cooking spray and place the fish sticks inside. Cook the fish sticks for 10 minutes. 4. Flip them on another side in halfway of cooking.
Per Serving: Calories 101; Fat 5g; Sodium 236mg; Carbs 1.9g; Fiber 1g; Sugar g; Protein 12.4g

Eggs with Olives

Prep time: 5 minutes | Cook time: 20 minutes | Serves: 4

2 cups black olives, pitted and chopped
4 eggs, whisked
¼ teaspoon sweet paprika
1 tablespoon cilantro, chopped
½ cup cheddar, shredded
A pinch of salt and black pepper
Cooking spray

1. In a bowl, add eggs with the olives and all the except the cooking spray and stir well. 2. Select the "AIR FRY" function of Ninja Foodi digital air fry oven, set the temperature to 375 degrees F/ 190 degrees C and set the time to 20 minutes. Press the Start/Pause button and begin preheating, Grease the sheet pan with cooking spray, pour the olives and eggs mixture, spread and cook for 20 minutes. Divide between plates and serve for breakfast.
Per Serving: Calories 240; Fat 14g; Sodium 256mg; Carbs 5g; Fiber 3g; Sugar 2g; Protein 8g

Cheesy Cheddar Biscuits

Prep time: 15 minutes | Cook time: 8 minutes | Serves: 4

½ cup almond flour
¼ cup Cheddar cheese, shredded
¾ teaspoon salt
1 egg, beaten
1 tablespoon mascarpone
1 tablespoon coconut oil, melted
¾ teaspoon baking powder
½ teaspoon apple cider vinegar
¼ teaspoon ground nutmeg

1. In the big bowl mix up ground nutmeg, almond flour, salt, and baking powder. After this, add egg, apple cider vinegar, coconut oil, and mascarpone. Add cheese and knead the soft dough. 2. Then with the help of the fingertips make the small balls (biscuits). Select the "AIR FRY" function of Ninja Foodi digital air fry oven, set the temperature to 400 degrees F/ 200 degrees C and set the time to 8 minutes. Press the Start/Pause button and begin preheating. Line the basket with parchment. Place the cheese biscuits on the parchment and cook them for 8 minutes. 3. Shake the biscuits during the cooking to avoid burning. The cooked cheese biscuits will have a golden brown color.
Per Serving: Calories 102; Fat 7.9g; Sodium 456mg; Carbs 1.6g; Fiber 0.4g; Sugar 0.6g; Protein 4.3g

Healthy Sprouts Hash

Prep time: 5 minutes | Cook time: 20 minutes | Serves: 4

1 tablespoon olive oil
1 pound Brussels sprouts, shredded
4 eggs, whisked
½ cup coconut cream
Salt and black pepper to the taste
1 tablespoon chives, chopped
¼ cup cheddar cheese, shredded

1. Select the "AIR FRY" function of Ninja Foodi digital air fry oven, set the temperature to 360 degrees F/ 180 degrees C and set the time to 20 minutes. Press the Start/Pause button and begin preheating. Grease sheet pan with the oil. Spread the Brussels sprouts on the bottom of the fryer, then add the eggs mixed with the rest of the ingredients, toss a bit and cook for 20 minutes. Divide between plates and serve.
Per Serving: Calories 242; Fat 12g; Sodium 366mg; Carbs 5g; Fiber 3g; Sugar 2g; Protein 9g

Crispy Fried Bacon

Prep time: 10 minutes | Cook time: 12 minutes | Serves: 4

10 oz bacon
3 oz pork rinds
2 eggs, beaten
½ teaspoon salt
½ teaspoon ground black pepper
Cooking spray

1. Cut the bacon into 4 cubes and sprinkle with salt and ground black pepper. After this dip the bacon cubes in the beaten eggs and coat in the pork rinds. Select the "AIR FRY" function of Ninja Foodi digital air fry oven, set the temperature to 395 degrees F/ 200 degrees C and set the time to 12 minutes. Press the Start/Pause button and begin preheating. 2. Grease basket with cooking spray and put the bacon cubes inside. Cook them for 6 minutes. Then flip the bacon on another side and cook for 6 minutes more or until it is light brown.
Per Serving: Calories 537; Fat 39.4g; Sodium 745mg; Carbs 1.4g; Fiber 0.1g; Sugar 0g; Protein 42.7g

Cheesy Broccoli Casserole

Prep time: 5 minutes | Cook time: 25 minutes | Serves: 4

1 broccoli head, florets separated and roughly chopped	1 cup almond milk
2 ounces cheddar cheese, grated	2 teaspoons cilantro, chopped
4 eggs, whisked	Salt and black pepper to the taste

1. Select the "AIR FRY" function of Ninja Foodi digital air fry oven, set the temperature to 350 degrees F/ 175 degrees C and set the time to 25 minutes. Press the Start/Pause button and begin preheating. In a bowl, add eggs with the milk, cilantro, salt and pepper and whisk. Put the broccoli in your air fryer, add the eggs mix over it, spread, sprinkle the cheese on top, cook for 25 minutes, divide between plates and serve for breakfast.
Per Serving: Calories 214; Fat 14g; Sodium 332mg; Carbs 4g; Fiber 2g; Sugar 4g; Protein 9g

Creamy Eggs

Prep time: 10 minutes | Cook time: 8 minutes | Serves: 4

4 eggs	1 teaspoon dried parsley
1 tablespoon heavy cream	3 oz kielbasa, chopped
1 oz Parmesan, grated	1 teaspoon coconut oil

1. Select the "AIR FRY" function of Ninja Foodi digital air fry oven, set the temperature to 385 degrees F/ 195 degrees C and set the time to 8 minutes. Press the Start/Pause button and begin preheating. Toss the coconut oil in the air fryer basket and melt. It will take about 2-3 minutes. Meanwhile, crack the eggs in the mixing bowl. Add heavy cream and dried parsley. 2. Whisk the mixture. Put the chopped kielbasa in the melted coconut oil and cook it for 4 minutes. After this, add the whisked egg mixture, Parmesan, and stir with the help of the fork. 3. Cook the eggs for 2 minutes. Then scramble them well and cook for 2 minutes more or until they get the desired texture.
Per Serving: Calories 157; Fat 12.2g; Sodium 695mg; Carbs 1.5g; Fiber 0g; Sugar 0g; Protein 10.7g

Spiced Buttery Eggs

Prep time: 5 minutes | Cook time: 20 minutes | Serves: 4

2 tablespoons butter, melted	6 eggs, whisked
6 teaspoons basil pesto	2 tablespoons basil, chopped
1 cup mozzarella cheese, grated	A pinch of salt and black pepper

1. In a bowl, mix all the ingredients except the butter and whisk them well. Select the "AIR FRY" function of Ninja Foodi digital air fry oven, set the temperature to 360 degrees F/ 180 degrees C and set the time to 20 minutes. Press the Start/Pause button and begin preheating. Drizzle the butter on the bottom, spread the eggs mix, cook for 20 minutes and serve for breakfast.
Per Serving: Calories 207; Fat 14g; Sodium 411mg; Carbs 4g; Fiber 3g; Sugar 1g; Protein 8g

Breakfast Sausage Bake

Prep time: 15 minutes | Cook time: 23 minutes | Serves: 6

2 jalapeno peppers, sliced	1 tablespoon cream cheese
7 oz ground sausages	½ teaspoon salt
1 teaspoon dill seeds	1 teaspoon butter, softened
3 oz Colby Jack Cheese, shredded	1 teaspoon olive oil
4 eggs, beaten	

1. Preheat the skillet well and pour the olive oil inside. Then add ground sausages, salt, and cook the mixture for 5-8 minutes over the medium heat Stir it from time to time. 2. Meanwhile, Select the "AIR FRY" function of Ninja Foodi digital air fry oven, set the temperature to 400 degrees F/ 200 degrees C and set the time to 16 minutes. Press the Start/Pause button and begin preheating. Grease the air fryer basket with softened butter and place the cooked ground sausages inside. Flatten the mixture and top with the sliced jalapeno peppers. 3. Then add shredded cheese. In the bowl mix up eggs along with cream cheese. Pour the liquid over the cheese. Sprinkle the casserole with dill seeds. The cooking time of the casserole is 16 minutes. You can increase the cooking time if you prefer the crunchy crust.
Per Serving: Calories 230; Fat 18.9g; Sodium 354mg; Carbs 1.3g; Fiber 0.3g; Sugar 0.2g; Protein 13.4g

Tropical Coconut Muffins

Prep time: 10 minutes | Cook time: 10 minutes | Serves: 2

⅓ cup almond flour	1 tablespoon coconut milk
2 tablespoons Erythritol	1 tablespoon coconut oil, softened
¼ teaspoon baking powder	1 teaspoon ground cinnamon
1 teaspoon apple cider vinegar	Cooking spray

1. In the mixing bowl, mix up almond flour. Erythritol, baking powder, and ground cinnamon. Add apple cider vinegar, coconut milk, and coconut oil. Stir the mixture until smooth. 2. Spray the muffin molds with cooking spray. Scoop the muffin batter in the muffin molds. Spray the surface of every muffin with the help of the spatula. 3. Select the "AIR FRY" function of Ninja Foodi digital air fry oven, set the temperature to 365 degrees F/ 185 degrees C and set the time to 10 minutes. Press the Start/Pause button and begin preheating. Insert the rack in the air fryer. Place the muffins on the rack and cook them for 10 minutes. Then cool the cooked muffins well and remove them from the molds.
Per Serving: Calories 107; Fat 10.9g; Sodium 471mg; Carbs 2.7g; Fiber 1.3g; Sugar 1g; Protein 1.2g

Fresh Avocado Salad

Prep time: 10 minutes | Cook time: 3 minutes | Serves: 4

1 avocado, peeled, pitted and roughly sliced	¼ teaspoon salt
½ teaspoon minced garlic	1 teaspoon cilantro, chopped
¼ teaspoon chili flakes	1 cup baby spinach
½ teaspoon olive oil	1 cup cherry tomatoes halved
1 tablespoon lime juice	Cooking spray

1. Select the "AIR FRY" function of Ninja Foodi digital air fry oven, set the temperature to 400 degrees F/ 200 degrees C and set the time to 3 minutes. Press the Start/Pause button and begin preheating. 2. Grease the air fryer basket with cooking spray from inside. Combine all the inside, cook for 3 minutes, divide into bowls and serve.
Per Serving: Calories 142; Fat 10.2g; Sodium 269mg; Carbs 4.9g; Fiber 2.7g; Sugar 2g; Protein 8.8g

Cheddar Kale

Prep time: 5 minutes | Cook time: 20 minutes | Serves: 4

½ cup black olives, pitted and sliced	4 eggs, whisked
1 cup kale, chopped	Cooking spray
2 tablespoons cheddar, grated	A pinch of salt and black pepper

1. Select the "AIR FRY" function of Ninja Foodi digital air fry oven, set the temperature to 360 degrees F/ 180 degrees C and set the time to 20 minutes. Press the Start/Pause button and begin preheating. 2. In a bowl, add eggs with the rest of the except the cooking spray and whisk well. Grease a pan that fits the air fryer with the cooking spray, pour the olives mixture inside, spread, put the pan into the machine, and cook for 20 minutes. Serve for breakfast hot.
Per Serving: Calories 220; Fat 13g; Sodium 321mg; Carbs 6g; Fiber 4g; Sugar 2g; Protein 12g

Pepperoni Mozzarella Rolls

Prep time: 15 minutes | Cook time: 6 minutes | Serves: 6

6 wonton wrappers	1 oz pepperoni, chopped
1 tablespoon keto tomato sauce	1 egg, beaten
½ cup Mozzarella, shredded	Cooking spray

1. In the big bowl mix up together shredded Mozzarella, pepperoni, and tomato sauce. When the mixture is homogenous transfer it on the wonton wraps. Wrap the wonton wraps in the shape of sticks. 2. Then brush them with beaten eggs. Select the "AIR FRY" function of Ninja Foodi digital air fry oven, set the temperature to 400 degrees F/ 200 degrees C and set the time to 6 minutes. Press the Start/Pause button and begin preheating. Grease the basket with cooking spray. Put the pizza sticks in the air fryer and cook them for 3 minutes from each side.
Per Serving: Calories 65; Fat 3.5g; Sodium 247mg; Carbs 4.9g; Fiber 0.3g; Sugar 0g; Protein 3.5g

Spiced Paprika Zucchini Spread

Prep time: 5 minutes | Cook time: 15 minutes | Serves: 4

4 zucchinis, roughly chopped
1 tablespoon sweet paprika

Salt and black pepper to the taste
1 tablespoon butter, melted

1. Select the "AIR FRY" function of Ninja Foodi digital air fry oven, set the temperature to 360 degrees F/ 180 degrees C and set the time to 15 minutes. Press the Start/Pause button and begin preheating. 2. Grease a sheet pan that fits the air fryer with the butter, add all the ingredients, toss, and cook for 15 minutes. 3. Transfer to a blender, pulse well, divide into bowls and serve for breakfast.
Per Serving: Calories 240; Fat 14g; Sodium 288mg; Carbs 5g; Fiber 2g; Sugar 1g; Protein 11g

Cheesy Chives Omelet

Prep time: 5 minutes | Cook time: 20 minutes | Serves: 4

6 eggs, whisked
1 cup chives, chopped
Cooking spray

1 cup mozzarella, shredded
Salt and black pepper to the taste

1. Select the "AIR FRY" function of Ninja Foodi digital air fry oven, set the temperature to 350 degrees F/ 175 degrees C and set the time to 20 minutes. Press the Start/Pause button and begin preheating. 2. In a bowl, mix all the except the cooking spray and whisk well. Grease a pan that fits your air fryer with the cooking spray, pour the eggs mix, spread, put the pan into the machine and cook for 20 minutes. Divide the omelet between plates and serve for breakfast.
Per Serving: Calories 270; Fat 15g; Sodium 411mg; Carbs 5g; Fiber 3g; Sugar 2g; Protein 9g

Healthy Boiled Eggs

Prep time: 8 minutes | Cook time: 16 minutes | Serves: 2

4 eggs

¼ teaspoon salt

1. Select the "AIR FRY" function of Ninja Foodi digital air fry oven, set the temperature to 250 degrees F/ 120 degrees C and set the time to 16 minutes. Press the Start/Pause button and begin preheating. 2. Place the eggs in the air fryer and cook them for 16 minutes. When the eggs are cooked, cool them in the ice water. After this, peel the eggs and cut into halves. Sprinkle the eggs with salt.
Per Serving: Calories 126; Fat 8.g; Sodium 477g; Carbs 0.7g; Fiber 0g; Sugar 0g; Protein 11.1g

Greeny Spinach Spread with Bacon

Prep time: 5 minutes | Cook time: 10 minutes | Serves: 4

2 tablespoons coconut cream
3 cups spinach leaves
2 tablespoons cilantro

2 tablespoons bacon, cooked and crumbled
Salt and black pepper to the taste

1. Select the "AIR FRY" function of Ninja Foodi digital air fry oven, set the temperature to 360 degrees F/ 180 degrees C and set the time to 15 minutes. Press the Start/Pause button and begin preheating. 2. In a pan, combine all the ingredients except the bacon, put the pan in the machine and cook for 10 minutes. 3. Transfer to a blender, pulse well, divide into bowls and serve with bacon sprinkled on top.
Per Serving: Calories 200; Fat 4g; Sodium 411mg; Carbs 4g; Fiber 2g; Sugar 1g; Protein 4g

Healthy Egg Peppers Cups

Prep time: 10 minutes | Cook time: 12 minutes | Serves: 12

6 green bell peppers
12 eggs

½ teaspoon ground black pepper
½ teaspoon chili flakes

1. Cut the green bell peppers into halves and remove the seeds. Then crack the eggs in every bell pepper half and sprinkle with ground black pepper and chili flakes. 2. After this, Select the "AIR FRY" function of Ninja Foodi digital air fry oven, set the temperature to 395 degrees F/ 200 degrees C and set the time to 15 minutes. Press the Start/Pause button and begin preheating. Put the green bell pepper halves in the air fryer. 3.Cook the egg peppers for 4 minutes. Repeat the same steps with remaining egg peppers.
Per Serving: Calories 82; Fat 4.5g; Sodium 231mg; Carbs 4.9g; Fiber 0.8g; Sugar 0.6g; Protein 6.2g

Green Omelet

Prep time: 5 minutes | Cook time: 15 minutes | Serves: 4

4 eggs, whisked
1 tablespoon parsley, chopped
½ teaspoons cheddar cheese, shredded

1 avocado, peeled, pitted and cubed
Cooking spray

1. Select the "AIR FRY" function of Ninja Foodi digital air fry oven, set the temperature to 370 degrees F/ 185 degrees C and set the time to 15 minutes. Press the Start/Pause button and begin preheating. 2. In a bowl, mix all the ingredients except the cooking spray and whisk well. Grease a sheet pan that fits the air fryer with the cooking spray, pour the omelet mix, spread, introduce the pan in the machine and cook for 15 minutes. Serve for breakfast.
Per Serving: Calories 240; Fat 13g; Sodium 147mg; Carbs 6g; Fiber 4g; Sugar 2g; Protein 9g

Spinach Frittata with Chives

Prep time: 5 minutes | Cook time: 20 minutes | Serves: 4

1 tablespoon chives, chopped
1 eggplant, cubed
8 ounces spinach, torn

Cooking spray
6 eggs, whisked
Salt and black pepper to the taste

1. Select the "AIR FRY" function of Ninja Foodi digital air fry oven, set the temperature to 380 degrees F/ 195 degrees C and set the time to 20 minutes. Press the Start/Pause button and begin preheating. In a bowl, add eggs with the rest of the ingredients except the cooking spray and whisk well. Grease a pan that fits your air fryer with the cooking spray, pour the frittata mix, spread and put the pan in the machine. 2. Cook for 20 minutes, divide between plates and serve for breakfast.
Per Serving: Calories 240; Fat 8g; Sodium 235mg; Carbs 6g; Fiber 3g; Sugar 1g; Protein 12g

Baked Coconut Veggie and Eggs

Prep time: 5 minutes | Cook time: 30 minutes | Serves: 6

Cooking spray
2 cups green and red bell pepper, chopped
2 spring onions, chopped
1 teaspoon thyme, chopped

Salt and black pepper to the taste
1 cup coconut cream
4 eggs, whisked
1 cup cheddar cheese, grated

1. Select the "AIR FRY" function of Ninja Foodi digital air fry oven, set the temperature to 350 degrees F/ 175 degrees C and set the time to 30 minutes. Press the Start/Pause button and begin preheating. In a bowl, mix all the except the cooking spray and the cheese and whisk well. 2. Grease a pan that fits the air fryer with the cooking spray, pour the bell peppers and eggs mixture, spread, sprinkle the cheese on top, put the pan in the machine and cook for 30 minutes. 3.Divide between plates and serve for breakfast.
Per Serving: Calories 251; Fat 16g; Sodium 235mg; Carbs 6g; Fiber 3g; Sugar 2g; Protein 11g

Healthy Zucchini Cakes

Prep time: 10 minutes | Cook time: 8 minutes | Serves: 4

2 zucchinis, grated
3 tablespoons almond flour
1 medium egg, beaten
¼ teaspoon salt
¼ teaspoon ground black pepper

¼ teaspoon minced garlic
1 tablespoon spring onions, chopped
¼ teaspoon chili flakes

1. Put the grated zucchini in the bowl and add the almond flour. Then add egg, salt, ground black pepper, minced garlic, onion, and chili flakes. Add green peas and stir the with the help of the fork until homogenous. 2. Select the "AIR FRY" function of Ninja Foodi digital air fry oven, set the temperature to 365 degrees F/ 185 degrees C and set the time to 8 minutes. Press the Start/Pause button and begin preheating. Make the fritters and put them on the baking paper. 3.Place the baking paper with fritters in the air fryer and cook them for 4 minutes. Then flip the fritters on another side and cook them for 4 minutes more.
Per Serving: Calories 160; Fat 11.8g; Sodium 255mg; Carbs 9.6g; Fiber 3.9g; Sugar 2g; Protein 7.6g

Traditional French Frittata

Prep time: 10 minutes | Cook time: 18 minutes | Serves: 3

3 eggs
1 tablespoon heavy cream
1 teaspoon Herbs de Provence

1 teaspoon almond butter, softened
2 oz Provolone cheese, grated

1. Crack the eggs in the bowl and add heavy cream. Whisk the liquid with the help of the hand whisker. Then add herbs de Provence and grated cheese. Stir the egg liquid gently. 2. Select the "AIR FRY" function of Ninja Foodi digital air fry oven, set the temperature to 365 degrees F/ 185 degrees C and set the time to 18 minutes. Press the Start/Pause button and begin preheating. Then grease the air fryer basket with almond butter. 3. Pour the egg liquid in the air fryer basket and cook it for 18 minutes. When the frittata is cooked, cool it to the room temperature and then cut into servings.
Per Serving: Calories 179; Fat 14.3g; Sodium 311mg; Carbs 1.9g; Fiber 0.5g; Sugar 0.3g; Protein 11.6g

Tangy Tomatoes Frittata

Prep time: 5 minutes | Cook time: 20 minutes | Serves: 4

4 eggs, whisked
1 pound cherry tomatoes, halved
1 tablespoon parsley, chopped

Cooking spray
1 tablespoon cheddar, grated
Salt and black pepper to the taste

1. Select the "AIR FRY" function of Ninja Foodi digital air fry oven, set the temperature to 360 degrees F/ 180 degrees C and set the time to 20 minutes. Press the Start/Pause button and begin preheating. Put the tomatoes in the air fryer's basket, cook for 5 minutes and transfer them to the sheet pan that fits the machine, greased with cooking spray. 2. In a bowl, add eggs with the remaining ingredients, whisk, pour over the tomatoes and cook for 15 minutes. Serve right away for breakfast.
Per Serving: Calories 230; Fat 14g; Sodium 125mg; Carbs 5g; Fiber 3g; Sugar 1g; Protein 11g

Beef and veggies Wrap

Prep time: 10 minutes | Cook time: 15 minutes | Serves: 2

½ cup ground beef
½ jalapeno pepper, chopped
¼ teaspoon ground black pepper
½ teaspoon salt
1 teaspoon keto tomato sauce
1 teaspoon olive oil
¼ teaspoon minced garlic

¼ teaspoon onion powder
1 teaspoon dried cilantro
½ teaspoon ground cumin
2 oz avocado, chopped
2 big cabbage leaves, steamed
2 tablespoons water

1. Select the "AIR FRY" function of Ninja Foodi digital air fry oven, set the temperature to 360 degrees F/ 180 degrees C and set the time to 15 minutes. Press the Start/Pause button and begin preheating. In the mixing bowl mix up ground beef, salt, ground black pepper, tomato sauce, olive oil, minced garlic, onion powder, dried cilantro, water, and ground cumin. 2. Then add jalapeno and stir gently. Transfer the ground beef mixture in the preheated air fryer basket. Cook the meat mixture for 15 minutes. Stir it with the help of the spatula after 8 minutes of cooking. 3. Then place the mixture over the cabbage leaves. Top the ground beef with chopped avocado and roll into the burritos.
Per Serving: Calories 230; Fat 15.9g; Sodium 300mg; Carbs 15.9g; Fiber 9.3g; Sugar 3g; Protein 10g

Delicious Peppers Bowls

Prep time: 5 minutes | Cook time: 20 minutes | Serves: 4

½ cup cheddar cheese, shredded
2 tablespoons chives, chopped
A pinch of salt and black pepper

¼ cup coconut cream
1 cup red bell peppers, chopped
Cooking spray

1. Select the "AIR FRY" function of Ninja Foodi digital air fry oven, set the temperature to 360 degrees F/ 180 degrees C and set the time to 20 minutes. Press the Start/Pause button and begin preheating. In a bowl, mix all the ingredients except the cooking spray and whisk well. Pour the mix in a sheet pan that fits the air fryer, greased with cooking spray and place the pan in the machine. 2. Cook for 20 minutes, divide between plates and serve for breakfast.
Per Serving: Calories 220; Fat 14g; Sodium 211mg; Carbs 5g; Fiber 2g; Sugar 1g; Protein 11g

Eggplant and Kale Omelet

Prep time: 10 minutes | Cook time: 20 minutes | Serves: 4

1 eggplant, cubed
4 eggs, whisked
2 teaspoons cilantro, chopped
Salt and black pepper to the taste
½ teaspoon Italian seasoning

Cooking spray
½ cup kale, chopped
2 tablespoons cheddar, grated
2 tablespoons fresh basil, chopped

1. Select the "AIR FRY" function of Ninja Foodi digital air fry oven, set the temperature to 370 degrees F/ 185 degrees C and set the time to 20 minutes. Press the Start/Pause button and begin preheating. In a bowl, mix all the ingredients except the cooking spray and whisk well. Grease a pan that fits your air fryer with the cooking spray, pour the eggs mix, spread, put the pan in the machine and cook for 20 minutes. Divide the mix between plates and serve for breakfast.
Per Serving: Calories 241; Fat 11g; Sodium 266mg; Carbs 5g; Fiber 4g; Sugar 2g; Protein 12g

Fresh Green Beans Salad

Prep time: 5 minutes | Cook time: 20 minutes | Serves: 4

2 cups green beans, cut into medium pieces
2 cups tomatoes, cubed
Salt and black pepper to the taste

1 teaspoon hot paprika
1 tablespoons cilantro, chopped
Cooking spray

1. Select the "AIR FRY" function of Ninja Foodi digital air fry oven, set the temperature to 360 degrees F/ 180 degrees C and set the time to 20 minutes. Press the Start/Pause button and begin preheating. 2. In a bowl, mix all the except the cooking spray and the cilantro and whisk them well. Grease a pan that fits the air fryer with the cooking spray, pour the green beans and tomatoes mix into the pan, sprinkle the cilantro on top, put the pan into the machine and cook for 20 minutes. Serve right away.
Per Serving: Calories 222; Fat 11g; Sodium 314mg; Carbs 6g; Fiber 4g; Sugar 1g; Protein 12g

Spicy Hot Cups

Prep time: 10 minutes | Cook time: 3 minutes | Serves: 6

6 eggs, beaten
2 jalapeno, sliced
2 oz bacon, chopped, cooked

½ teaspoon salt
½ teaspoon chili powder
Cooking spray

1. Spay the silicone egg molds with cooking spray from inside. In the mixing bowl mix up beaten eggs, sliced jalapeno, salt, bacon, and chili powder. Stir the liquid gently and pour in the egg molds. 2. Select the "AIR FRY" function of Ninja Foodi digital air fry oven, set the temperature to 400 degrees F/ 200 degrees C and set the time to 10 minutes. Press the Start/Pause button and begin preheating. Place the molds with the egg mixture in the air fryer. 3. Cook the meal for 3 minutes. Then cool the cooked jalapeno & bacon cups for 2-3 minutes and remove from the silicone molds.
Per Serving: Calories 116; Fat 8.4g; Sodium 542mg; Carbs 0.9g; Fiber 0.2g; Sugar 0.1g; Protein 9.1g

Breakfast Parmesan Muffins

Prep time: 5 minutes | Cook time: 15 minutes | Serves: 4

2 eggs, whisked
Cooking spray
1 and ½ cups coconut milk
1 tablespoon baking powder

4 ounces baby spinach, chopped
2 ounces parmesan cheese, grated
3 ounces almond flour

1. Select the "AIR FRY" function of Ninja Foodi digital air fry oven, set the temperature to 380 degrees F/ 195 degrees C and set the time to 15 minutes. Press the Start/Pause button and begin preheating. In a bowl, mix all the ingredients except the cooking spray and whisk really well. 2. Grease a muffin pan that fits your air fryer with the cooking spray, divide the muffins mix, introduce the pan in the air fryer, cook for 15 minutes, divide between plates and serve.
Per Serving: Calories 210; Fat 12g; Sodium 174mg; Carbs 5g; Fiber 3g; Sugar 1g; Protein 8g

Chives Yogurt Eggs Omelet

Prep time: 5 minutes | Cook time: 20 minutes | Serves: 4

Cooking spray
Salt and black pepper to the taste
1 and ½ cups Greek yogurt

4 eggs, whisked
1 tablespoon chives, chopped
1 tablespoon cilantro, chopped

1. Select the "AIR FRY" function of Ninja Foodi digital air fry oven, set the temperature to 360 degrees F/ 180 degrees C and set the time to 20 minutes. Press the Start/Pause button and begin preheating. In a bowl, mix all the ingredients except the cooking spray and whisk well. Grease a pan that fits the air fryer with the cooking spray, pour the eggs mix, spread well, put the pan into the machine and cook the omelet for 20 minutes. 2. Divide between plates and serve for breakfast.
Per Serving: Calories 221; Fat 14g; Sodium 221mg; Carbs 6g; Fiber 4g; Sugar 1g; Protein 11g

Crispy Bacon Eggs

Prep time: 15 minutes | Cook time: 5 minutes | Serves: 2

2 eggs, hard-boiled, peeled
4 bacon slices

½ teaspoon avocado oil
1 teaspoon mustard

1. Select the "AIR FRY" function of Ninja Foodi digital air fry oven, set the temperature to 400 degrees F/ 200 degrees C and set the time to 5 minutes. Press the Start/Pause button and begin preheating. Then sprinkle the air fryer basket with avocado oil and place the bacon slices inside. Flatten them in one layer and cook for 2 minutes from each side. 2. After this, cool the bacon to the room temperature. Wrap every egg into 2 bacon slices. Secure the eggs with toothpicks and place them in the air fryer. Cook the wrapped eggs for 1 minute.
Per Serving: Calories 278; Fat 20.9g; Sodium 145mg; Carbs 1.5g; Fiber 0.3g; Sugar 0.1g; Protein 20g

Tangy Balsamic Asparagus Salad

Prep time: 5 minutes | Cook time: 10 minutes | Serves: 4

1 bunch asparagus, trimmed
1 cup baby arugula
1 tablespoon cheddar cheese, grated

1 tablespoon balsamic vinegar
A pinch of salt and black pepper
Cooking spray

1. Select the "AIR FRY" function of Ninja Foodi digital air fry oven, set the temperature to 360 degrees F/ 180 degrees C and set the time to 10 minutes. Press the Start/Pause button and begin preheating. Put the asparagus in your air fryer's basket, grease with cooking spray, season with salt and pepper and cook for 10 minutes. 2.In a bowl, mix the asparagus with the arugula and the vinegar, toss, divide between plates and serve hot with cheese sprinkled on top
Per Serving: Calories 200; Fat 5g; Sodium 269mg; Carbs 4g; Fiber 1g; Sugar 1g; Protein 5g

Healthy Ground Pork Pizza

Prep time: 10 minutes | Cook time: 12 minutes | Serves: 2

8 oz ground pork
1 tablespoon keto tomato sauce
½ teaspoon dried basil
⅓ cup Mozzarella, shredded

½ teaspoon butter, melted
¼ teaspoon dried oregano
Cooking spray

1. Select the "BAKE" function of Ninja Foodi digital air fry oven, set the temperature to 365 degrees F/ 185 degrees C and set the time to 12 minutes. Press the Start/Pause button and begin preheating. Spray the air fryer basket with cooking spray. 2. In the mixing bowl mix up ground pork, marinara sauce, dried basil, oregano, butter, and Mozzarella. Put the mixture in the air fryer basket and spread gently with the help of the spatula. Cook the morning pizza for 12 minutes.
Per Serving: Calories 191; Fat 6g; Sodium 298mg; Carbs 1.4g; Fiber 0.3g; Sugar 0.1g; Protein 31.2g

Cheesy Veggie Frittata

Prep time: 5 minutes | Cook time: 20 minutes | Serves: 4

2 eggs, whisked
1 tablespoon olive oil
1 avocado, pitted, peeled and cubed

2 spring onions, chopped
Salt and black pepper to the taste
1 ounce parmesan cheese, grated
½ cup coconut cream

1. Select the "AIR FRY" function of Ninja Foodi digital air fry oven, set the temperature to 360 degrees F/ 180 degrees C and set the time to 20 minutes. Press the Start/Pause button and begin preheating. 2. In a bowl, add eggs with the rest of the except the oil and whisk well. Grease a sheet pan that fits the air fryer with the oil, pour the avocado mix, spread, put the pan in the machine and cook for 20 minutes. Divide between plates and serve for breakfast.
Per Serving: Calories 271; Fat 14g; Sodium 288mg; Carbs 5g; Fiber 3g; Sugar 5g; Protein 11g

Baked Eggs Ramekins

Prep time: 5 minutes | Cook time: 6 minutes | Serves: 5

5 eggs
1 teaspoon coconut oil, melted

¼ teaspoon ground black pepper

1. Select the "BAKE" function of Ninja Foodi digital air fry oven, set the temperature to 355 degrees F/ 180 degrees C and set the time to 8 minutes. Press the Start/Pause button and begin preheating. Brush the ramekins with coconut oil and crack the eggs inside. Then sprinkle the eggs with ground black pepper and place it in the wire rack in the air fryer. Cook the baked eggs for 6 minutes.
Per Serving: Calories 138; Fat 10.6g; Sodium 102mg; Carbs 1g; Fiber 0g; Sugar 1g; Protein 9g

Chapter 2 Vegetable and Side Recipes

Smashed Baby Potatoes

Prep time: 5 minutes | Cook time: 18 minutes | Serves: 3 to 4

1½ pounds baby red or baby Yukon gold potatoes
¼ cup butter, melted
1 teaspoon olive oil
½ teaspoon paprika
1 teaspoon dried parsley
salt and freshly ground black pepper
2 scallions, finely chopped

1. Boil salted water. Boil potatoes for 18 minutes or until the potatoes are fork-tender. 2. Drain and place them to a cutting board to cool slightly. Spray or brush the bottom of a drinking glass with a little oil. Smash or flatten the potatoes by pressing the glass down on each potato slowly. Try not to completely flatten the potato or smash it so hard that it breaks apart. 3. Combine the melted butter, olive oil, paprika, and parsley together. 4. Select the "AIR FRY" function of Ninja Foodi digital air fry oven, set the temperature to 400 degrees F/ 200 degrees C and set the time to 18 minutes. Press the Start/Pause button and begin preheating. 5. Spray the air fryer basket with oil and transfer one layer of the smashed potatoes into the basket. Grease with butter mixture and spice generously with salt and freshly ground black pepper. 6. Air-fry for 10 minutes. Carefully flip the potatoes over and air-fry for an additional 8 minutes until crispy and lightly browned.7. Keep the potatoes warm. Sprinkle minced scallions over the potatoes and serve warm.
Per Serving: Calories 240; Fat 14g; Sodium 704mg; Carbs 28g; Fiber 2g; Sugar 2g; Protein 4g

Air Fried Cauliflower Rice

Prep time: 20 minutes | Cook time: 30 minutes | Serves: 2

Round 1:
1 teaspoon turmeric
1 cup diced carrot
½ cup diced onion
Round 2:
½ cup frozen peas
2 minced garlic cloves
½ cup chopped broccoli
1 tablespoon minced ginger
1 tablespoon rice vinegar
2 tablespoons low-sodium soy sauce
½ block of extra firm tofu

1 ½ teaspoons toasted sesame oil
2 tablespoons reduced-sodium soy sauce
3 cups riced cauliflower

1. Crumble tofu in a large bowl and toss with all the Round one ingredients. 2. Select the "AIR FRY" function of Ninja Foodi digital air fry oven, set the temperature to 370 degrees F/ 185 degrees C and set the time to 20 minutes. Press the Start/Pause button and begin preheating. Place the tofu in the greased Ninja sheet pan and cook 10 minutes, making sure to shake once. 3. In another bowl, toss from Round 2 together. 4. Add Round 2 mixture to air fryer Ninja sheet pan and cook another 10 minutes, ensuring to shake 5 minutes in. Enjoy!
Per Serving: Calories 293; Fat 13.8g; Sodium 855mg; Carbs 28g; Fiber 8g; Sugar 11g; Protein 19g

Healthy Potato Latkes

Prep time: 15 minutes | Cook time: 60 minutes | Serves: 6

1 russet potato
¼ onion
2 eggs, lightly beaten
⅓ cup flour
½ teaspoon baking powder
1 teaspoon salt
freshly ground black pepper
canola or vegetable oil, in a spray bottle
chopped chives, for garnish
apple sauce
sour cream

1. Shred the potato and onion with a coarse box grater or a food processor with a shredding blade. squeeze the excess water of shredded vegetables. 2. Transfer the onion and potato to a large bowl and add the eggs, flour, baking powder, salt and black pepper. Mix well and prepare patties, about ¼-cup of mixture each. Brush or spray both sides of the latkes with oil. 3. Select the "AIR FRY" function of Ninja Foodi digital air fry oven, set the temperature to 400 degrees F/ 200 degrees C and set the time to 13 minutes. Press the Start/Pause button and begin preheating. 4. Air-fry the latkes in batches. Transfer one layer of the latkes to the air fryer basket and Place the basket in the air fryer ; air-fry for 12 to 13 minutes, flipping them over halfway through the cooking time. Transfer the finished latkes to a platter and cover with aluminum foil, or place them in a warm oven to keep warm. 5. Garnish the latkes with chopped chives and serve with sour cream and applesauce.
Per Serving: Calories 60; Fat 1g; Sodium 123mg; Carbs 12g; Fiber 1g; Sugar 0g; Protein 2g

Air Fried Carrots, Yellow Squash & Zucchini

Prep time: 7 minutes | Cook time: 30 minutes | Serves: 4

1 tablespoon chopped tarragon leaves
½ teaspoon white pepper
1 teaspoon salt
1 pound yellow squash
1 pound zucchini
6 teaspoons olive oil
½ pound carrots

1. Stem and root the end of squash and zucchini and cut in ¾-inch half-moons. Peel and cut carrots into 1-inch cubes. 2. Combine carrot cubes with 2 teaspoons of olive oil, tossing to combine. Select the "AIR FRY" function of Ninja Foodi digital air fry oven, set the temperature to 400 degrees F/ 200 degrees C and set the time to 35 minutes. Press the Start/Pause button and begin preheating. Pour carrots into air fryer basket and cook 5 minutes. 3. As carrots cook, drizzle remaining olive oil over squash and zucchini pieces, then season with pepper and salt. Toss well to coat. 4. Add squash and zucchini when the timer for carrots goes off. Cook 30 minutes, making sure to toss 2-3 times during the cooking process. 5. Once done, take out veggies and toss with tarragon. Serve up warm!
Per Serving: Calories 151; Fat 7.5g; Sodium 621mg; Carbs 20g; Fiber 5g; Sugar 2g; Protein 5g

Goluptious Air Fried Kale Chips

Prep time: 5 minutes | Cook time: 5 minutes | Serves: 4

¼ teaspoon Himalayan salt
3 tablespoons yeast
Avocado oil
1 bunch of kale

1. Rinse kale and with paper towels, dry well. 2. Chop kale into large pieces. 3. Place kale pieces in a bowl and spritz with avocado oil till shiny. Sprinkle with salt and yeast. 4. With your hands, toss kale leaves well to combine. 5. Select the "AIR FRY" function of Ninja Foodi digital air fry oven, set the temperature to 350 degrees F/ 175 degrees C and set the time to 10 minutes. Press the Start/Pause button and begin preheating. Pour half of the mixture into air fryer basket. Cook 5 minutes at 350 degrees F/ 175 degrees C. Remove and repeat with another half of kale.
Per Serving: Calories 25; Fat 0.1g; Sodium 546mg; Carbs 3g; Fiber 1g; Sugar 0g; Protein 3g

Cheddar Cheese Cauliflower Fritters

Prep time: 5 minutes | Cook time: 15 minutes | Serves: 8

½ cup chopped parsley
1 cup Italian breadcrumbs
⅓ cup shredded mozzarella cheese
⅓ cup shredded sharp cheddar
cheese
1 egg
2 minced garlic cloves
3 chopped scallions
1 head of cauliflower

1. Cut cauliflower up into florets. Wash well and pat dry. Place into a food processor and pulse 20-30 seconds till it looks like rice. 2. Place cauliflower rice in a bowl and mix with pepper, salt, egg, cheeses, breadcrumbs, garlic, and scallions. 3. With hands, form 15 patties of the mixture. Add more breadcrumbs if needed. 4. Select the "AIR ROAST" function of Ninja Foodi digital air fry oven, set the temperature to 390 degrees F/ 200 degrees C and set the time to 15 minutes. Press the Start/Pause button and begin preheating. With olive oil, spritz patties, and place into air fryer basket in a single layer. 5. Cook 14 minutes, flipping after 7 minutes.
Per Serving: Calories 56; Fat 2.2g; Sodium 177mg; Carbs 5g; Fiber 1g; Sugar 1g; Protein 5g

Jicama Fries with Eggs

Prep time: 10 minutes | Cook time: 20 minutes | Serves: 8

1 tablespoon dried thyme
¾ cup arrowroot flour
½ large Jicama
2 eggs

1. Select the "AIR FRY" function of Ninja Foodi digital air fry oven, set the temperature to 350 degrees F/ 175 degrees C and set the time to 25 minutes. Press the Start/Pause button and begin preheating. 2. Sliced jicama into fries. Whisk eggs together and pour over fries. Toss to coat. 3. Mix a pinch of salt, thyme, and arrowroot flour together. Toss egg-coated jicama into dry mixture, tossing to coat well. 4. Spray air fryer basket with olive oil and add fries. Cook 20 minutes. Toss halfway into the cooking process.
Per Serving: Calories 104; Fat 2.5g; Sodium 29mg; Carbs 18g; Fiber 4g; Sugar 2g; Protein 3g

Spicy Sweet toasted Potato Fries

Prep time: 5 minutes | Cook time: 27 minutes | Serves: 4

2 tablespoons sweet potato fry
seasoning mix
Seasoning Mix:
2 tablespoons salt
1 tablespoon cayenne pepper
1 tablespoon dried oregano

2 tablespoons olive oil
2 sweet potatoes

1 tablespoon fennel
2 tablespoons coriander

1. Slice both ends off sweet potatoes and peel. Slice lengthwise in half and again crosswise to make four pieces from each potato. 2. Slice each potato piece into 2-3 slices, then slice into fries. 3. Grind together all of seasoning mix and mix in the salt. 4. Select the "AIR ROAST" function of Ninja Foodi digital air fry oven, set the temperature to 350 degrees F/ 175 degrees C and set the time to 30 minutes. Press the Start/Pause button and begin preheating. 5. Toss potato pieces in olive oil, sprinkling with seasoning mix and tossing well to coat thoroughly. 6. Add fries to air fryer basket and set time for 27 minutes. Press start and cook 15 minutes. 7. Take out the pan and turn fries. Turn on air fryer and let cook 10-12 minutes till fries are golden.
Per Serving: Calories 69; Fat 7.2g; Sodium 486mg; Carbs 2g; Fiber 1g; Sugar 0g; Protein 0g

Air Fried Avocado Fries

Prep time: 5 minutes | Cook time: 10 minutes | Serves: 6

1 avocado
½ teaspoon salt
½ cup panko breadcrumbs

Bean liquid (aquafaba) from
a 15-ounce can of white or
garbanzo beans

1. Peel, pit, and slice up avocado. 2. Toss salt and breadcrumbs together in a bowl. Place aquafaba into another bowl. 3. Dredge slices of avocado first in aquafaba and then in panko, making sure you get an even coating. 4. Select the "AIR FRY" function of Ninja Foodi digital air fry oven, set the temperature to 390 degrees F/ 200 degrees C and set the time to 10 minutes. Press the Start/Pause button and begin preheating. Place coated avocado slices into a single layer in the air fryer basket. 5. Cook 5 minutes, shaking at 5 minutes. 6. Serve with your favorite keto dipping sauce!
Per Serving: Calories 217; Fat 21.8g; Sodium 207mg; Carbs 7g; Fiber 4g; Sugar 3g; Protein 2g

Cheesy Zucchini Parmesan Chips

Prep time: 5 minutes | Cook time: 10 minutes | Serves: 10

½ teaspoon paprika
½ cup grated parmesan cheese
½ cup Italian breadcrumbs

1 lightly beaten egg
2 thinly sliced zucchinis

1. Select the "BAKE" function of Ninja Foodi digital air fry oven, set the temperature to 350 degrees F/ 175 degrees C and set the time to 9 minutes. Press the Start/Pause button and begin preheating. Use a very sharp knife or mandolin slicer to slice zucchini as thinly as you can. Pat off extra moisture. 2. Beat egg with a pinch of pepper and salt and a bit of water. 3. Combine paprika, cheese, and breadcrumbs in a bowl. 4. Dip slices of zucchini into the egg mixture and then into breadcrumb mixture. Press gently to coat. 5. With olive oil cooking spray, mist coated zucchini slices. Place into air fryer basket in a single layer. 6. Cook 8 minutes. 7. Sprinkle with salt and serve with salsa.
Per Serving: Calories 34; Fat 2.3g; Sodium 122mg; Carbs 1g; Fiber 0g; Sugar 0g; Protein 2g

Crispy Brussels Sprouts

Prep time: 5 minutes | Cook time: 10 minutes | Serves: 5

¼ teaspoon salt
1 tablespoon balsamic vinegar

1 tablespoon olive oil
2 cups Brussels sprouts

1. Select the "AIR FRY" function of Ninja Foodi digital air fry oven, set the temperature to 400 degrees F/ 200 degrees C and set the time to 10 minutes. Press the Start/Pause button and begin preheating. 2. Cut Brussels sprouts in half lengthwise. Toss with salt, vinegar, and olive oil till coated thoroughly. Add coated sprouts to air fryer Ninja basket, cooking 8-10 minutes. Shake after 5 minutes of cooking. 3. Brussels sprouts are ready to devour when brown and crisp!
Per Serving: Calories 42; Fat 2.8g; Sodium 126mg; Carbs 4g; Fiber 1g; Sugar 1g; Protein 1g

Crispy Roasted Broccoli with Yogurt

Prep time: 10 minutes | Cook time: 40 minutes | Serves: 2

¼ teaspoon Masala
½ teaspoon red chili powder
½ teaspoon salt
¼ teaspoon turmeric powder

1 tablespoon chickpea flour
2 tablespoons yogurt
1 pound broccoli

1. Select the "AIR ROAST" function of Ninja Foodi digital air fry oven, set the temperature to 390 degrees F/ 200 degrees C and set the time to 15 minutes. Press the Start/Pause button and begin preheating. Cut broccoli up into florets. Soak in water with 2 teaspoons of salt for at least half an hour to remove impurities. 2. Take out broccoli florets from water and let drain. Wipe down thoroughly. 3. Mix all other together to create a marinade. 4. Toss broccoli florets in the marinade. Cover and chill 15-30 minutes. 5. Place marinated broccoli florets into the air fryer Ninja basket and place in. Cook 10 minutes. 6. 5 minutes into cooking shake the pan. Florets will be crispy when done.
Per Serving: Calories 74; Fat 1.9g; Sodium 685mg; Carbs 9g; Fiber 7g; Sugar 2g; Protein 9g

Air Fried Crispy Jalapeno Coins

Prep time: 10 minutes | Cook time: 10 minutes | Serves: 8

1 egg
2-3 tablespoons coconut flour
1 sliced and seeded jalapeno
Pinch of garlic powder

Pinch of onion powder
Pinch of Cajun seasoning
(optional)
Pinch of pepper and salt

1. Select the "AIR FRY" function of Ninja Foodi digital air fry oven, set the temperature to 400 degrees F/ 200 degrees C and set the time to 10 minutes. Press the Start/Pause button and begin preheating. 2. Mix together all dry ingredients. 3. Pat jalapeno slices dry. Dip coins into egg wash and then into dry mixture. Toss to thoroughly coat. 4. Add coated jalapeno slices to air fryer basket in a singular layer. Spray with olive oil. 5. Cook just till crispy.
Per Serving: Calories 23; Fat 1.3g; Sodium 40mg; Carbs 2g; Fiber 1g; Sugar 1g; Protein 1g

Baked Buffalo Cauliflower

Prep time: 15 minutes | Cook time: 17 minutes | Serves: 8

Cauliflower:
1 cup panko breadcrumbs
1 teaspoon salt
Buffalo Coating:
¼ cup Vegan Buffalo sauce

4 cups cauliflower florets

¼ cup melted vegan butter

1. Select the "BAKE" function of Ninja Foodi digital air fry oven, set the temperature to 350 degrees F/ 175 degrees C and set the time to 30 minutes. Press the Start/Pause button and begin preheating. 2. Melt butter in microwave and whisk in buffalo sauce. Dip each cauliflower floret into buffalo mixture, ensuring it gets coated well. Hold over a bowl till floret is done dripping. 3. Mix breadcrumbs with salt. 4. Dredge dipped florets into breadcrumbs and place into air fryer basket. 5. Cook 14-17 minutes. When slightly browned, they are ready to eat! 6. Serve with your favorite keto dipping sauce!
Per Serving: Calories 80; Fat 6g; Sodium 444mg; Carbs 6g; Fiber 1g; Sugar 4g; Protein 1g

Air Fried Spaghetti Squash Tots

Prep time: 5 minutes | Cook time: 15 minutes | Serves: 8-10

¼ teaspoon pepper
½ teaspoon salt

1 thinly sliced scallion
1 spaghetti squash

1. Select the "AIR FRY" function of Ninja Foodi digital air fry oven, set the temperature to 350 degrees F/ 175 degrees C and set the time to 20 minutes. Press the Start/Pause button and begin preheating. 2. Wash and cut the squash in half lengthwise. Scrape out the seeds. With a fork, remove spaghetti meat by strands and throw out skins. 3. In a clean towel, toss in squash and wring out as much moisture as possible. Place in a bowl and with a knife slice through meat a few times to cut up smaller. 4. Add pepper, salt, and scallions to squash and mix well. 5. Create "tot" shapes with your hands and place in air fryer. Spray with olive oil. 6. Cook 15 minutes until golden and crispy!
Per Serving: Calories 1; Fat 0g; Sodium 114mg; Carbs 0g; Fiber 0g; Sugar 0g; Protein 0g

Buttery Sweet Potatoes

Prep time: 15 minutes | Cook time: 25 minutes | Serves: 2

2 sweet potatoes, peeled and halved	1 teaspoon dried dill weed
1 tablespoon butter, melted	Sea salt and red pepper flakes, crushed

1. Select the "AIR FRY" function of Ninja Foodi digital air fry oven, set the temperature to 380 degrees F/ 195 degrees C and set the time to 15 minutes. Press the Start/Pause button and begin preheating. Toss the sweet potatoes with the remaining ingredients. 2. Cook the sweet potatoes for 15 minutes, shaking the basket halfway through the cooking time. 3. Taste and adjust the seasonings. Bon appétit!
Per Serving: Calories 163; Fat 5.8g; Sodium 323mg; Carbs 26.2g; Fiber 3.6g; Sugar 5.4g; Protein 2g

Herbed Mushrooms and Tomatoes

Prep time: 5 minutes | Cook time: 10 minutes | Serves: 4

1 pound cremini mushrooms, sliced	1 teaspoon rosemary, minced
1 large tomato, sliced	1 teaspoon parsley, minced
2 tablespoons butter, melted	1 teaspoon garlic, minced
	Coarse sea salt and ground black pepper, to taste

1. Select the "AIR FRY" function of Ninja Foodi digital air fry oven, set the temperature to 400 degrees F/ 200 degrees C and then set the time to 7 minutes. Press the Start/Pause button and begin preheating. Toss the mushrooms and tomatoes with the remaining ingredients. Toss until they are well coated on all sides. 2. Arrange the mushrooms in the air fryer basket. 3. Place the basket into the air fryer, cook your mushrooms for about 7 minutes, shaking the basket halfway through the cooking time. Bon appétit!
Per Serving: Calories 84; Fat 6.3g; Sodium 132mg; Carbs 6.1g; Fiber 4.1g; Sugar 2g; Protein 2.8g

Colorful Vegetable and Egg Patties

Prep time: 5 minutes | Cook time: 15 minutes | Serves: 3

1 carrot, shredded	1 teaspoon cayenne pepper
1 parsnip, shredded	Sea salt and ground black pepper, to taste
1 onion, chopped	2 eggs, whisked
1 garlic clove, minced	
½ cup all-purpose flour	

1. Select the "AIR FRY" function of Ninja Foodi digital air fry oven, set the temperature to 380 degrees F/ 195 degrees C and set the time to 15 minutes. Press the Start/Pause button and begin preheating. Mix all of the ingredients until everything is well combined. Form the mixture into three patties. 2. Place the basket with patties into the air fryer; cook the patties for about 15 minutes or until cooked through. Bon appétit!
Per Serving: Calories 184; Fat 3.3g; Sodium 366mg; Carbs 8g; Fiber 4.3g; Sugar 5.6g; Protein 8g

Asian Balsamic Fennel

Prep time: 5 minutes | Cook time: 15 minutes | Serves: 4

1-pound fennel bulbs, trimmed and sliced	crushed
2 tablespoons sesame oil	1 tablespoon balsamic vinegar
Sea salt & ground black pepper, to taste	1 tablespoon soy sauce
1 teaspoon red pepper flakes,	1 tablespoon sesame seeds, lightly toasted

1. Select the "AIR FRY" function of Ninja Foodi digital air fry oven, set the temperature to 370 degrees F/ 185 degrees C and set the time to 15 minutes. Press the Start/Pause button and begin preheating. Toss the fennel with the sesame oil, salt, black pepper, and red pepper flakes. 2. Place the fennel in air fryer basket and cook the fennel for about 15 minutes or until cooked through; check your fennel halfway through the cooking time. 3.Toss the warm fennel with the vinegar, soy sauce, and sesame seeds. Bon appétit!
Per Serving: Calories 114; Fat 8.3g; Sodium 144mg; Carbs 9.1g; Fiber 3.8g; Sugar 5.2g; Protein 2g

Roasted Spicy Asparagus

Prep time: 5 minutes | Cook time: 10 minutes | Serves: 3

¾-pound fresh asparagus, trimmed	pepper, to taste
Coarse sea salt and ground black	1 teaspoon paprika
	2 tablespoons olive oil

1. Select the "AIR FRY" function of Ninja Foodi digital air fry oven, set the temperature to 400 degrees F/ 200 degrees C, then set the time to 6 minutes. Press the Start/Pause button and begin preheating. Toss the asparagus with the salt, black pepper, paprika, and olive oil. Place the asparagus spears in the air fry basket. Place the basket in the air fryer. 2. Cook the asparagus for about 6 minutes, tossing them halfway through the cooking time. Bon appétit!
Per Serving: Calories 110; Fat 6.3g; Sodium 304mg; Carbs 9.2g; Fiber 2.9g; Sugar 2.9g; Protein 2.9g

Buckwheat Bean Patties

Prep time: 5 minutes | Cook time: 15 minutes | Serves: 4

1 cup buckwheat, soaked overnight and rinsed	1 small onion, chopped.
1 cup canned kidney beans, drained and well rinsed	1 teaspoon smoked paprika
¼ cup walnuts, chopped	Sea salt and ground black pepper, to taste
1 tablespoon olive oil	½ cup bread crumbs

1. Select the "AIR FRY" function of Ninja Foodi digital air fry oven, set the temperature to 380 degrees F/ 195 degrees C and set the time to 15 minutes. Press the Start/Pause button and begin preheating. Mix all ingredients until everything is well combined. Form the mixture into four patties and arrange them in a lightly greased Air Fryer basket. 2. Place the basket in the air fryer. Cook the patties for about 15 minutes until cooked through. Turn them over halfway through the cooking time. Bon appétit!
Per Serving: Calories 198; Fat 8.7g; Sodium 236mg; Carbs 24.2g; Fiber 5.3g; Sugar 2.2g; Protein 8g

Asparagus with Cheese

Prep time: 5 minutes | Cook time: 10 minutes | Serves: 4

1-pound asparagus, trimmed	Sea salt and cayenne pepper, to taste
1 tablespoon sesame oil	
½ teaspoon onion powder	½ cup Pecorino cheese, preferably freshly grated
½ teaspoon granulated garlic	

1. Select the "AIR FRY" function of Ninja Foodi digital air fry oven, set the temperature to 400 degrees F/ 200 degrees C; set the time to 6 minutes. Press the Start/Pause button and begin preheating. Toss the asparagus with the sesame oil, onion powder, granulated garlic, salt, and cayenne pepper. Arrange the asparagus spears in the air fryer basket. 2. Place the basket in the air fryer. Cook the asparagus for about 6 minutes, tossing them halfway through the cooking time. 3. Top the asparagus with the cheese. Bon appétit!
Per Serving: Calories 120; Fat 8.5g; Sodium 244mg; Carbs 5.9g; Fiber 2.8g; Sugar 2.6g; Protein 6.9g

Cheesy Mushrooms

Prep time: 5 minutes | Cook time: 10 minutes | Serves: 4

1-pound chestnut mushrooms, quartered	Sea salt and ground black pepper, to taste
1 tablespoon olive oil	4 tablespoons Pecorino Romano cheese, shredded
1 garlic clove, pressed	

1. Select the "AIR FRY" function of Ninja Foodi digital air fry oven, set the temperature to 400 degrees F/ 200 degrees C and set the time to 7 minutes. Press the Start/Pause button and begin preheating. Toss the mushrooms with the oil, garlic, salt, and black pepper. Toss until they are well coated on all sides. 2. Arrange the mushrooms in the air fryer basket. 3. Cook your mushrooms for about 7 minutes, shaking the basket halfway through the cooking time. 4. Afterwards, toss the mushrooms with the cheese and serve immediately!
Per Serving: Calories 83; Fat 5.1g; Sodium 136mg; Carbs 6.4g; Fiber 1.7g; Sugar 3.4g; Protein 4g

Cheesy Green Beans

Prep time: 5 minutes | Cook time: 9 minutes | Serves: 2

½ pound green beans
1 tablespoon sesame oil
Sea salt and ground black pepper,

to taste
2 ounces cheddar cheese, grated

1. Select the "AIR FRY" function of Ninja Foodi digital air fry oven, set the temperature to 380 degrees F/ 195 degrees C and set the time to 7 minutes. Press the Start/Pause button and begin preheating. Toss the green beans with the sesame oil and arrange them in the air fry basket. 2. Place the basket in the air fryer. Cook the green beans for 7 minutes, tossing the basket halfway through the cooking time. 3. Toss the warm green beans with the salt, black pepper, and cheese; stir to combine well. Enjoy!
Per Serving: Calories 154; Fat 9.6g; Sodium 444mg; Carbs 13g; Fiber 3.4g; Sugar 6.9g; Protein 6.4g

Herby Italian Peppers

Prep time: 10 minutes | Cook time: 15 minutes | Serves: 3

3 Italian peppers, seeded and halved
1 tablespoon olive oil
Kosher salt and ground black pepper, to taste
1 teaspoon cayenne pepper

1 tablespoon fresh parsley, chopped
1 tablespoon fresh basil, chopped
1 tablespoon fresh chives, chopped

1. Select the "AIR FRY" function of Ninja Foodi digital air fry oven, set the temperature to 400 degrees F/ 200 degrees C; set the time to 13 minutes. Press the Start/Pause button and begin preheating. Toss the peppers with the olive oil, salt, black pepper, and cayenne pepper; place the peppers in the air fryer basket. 2. Place the basket in the air fryer .Cook the peppers for about 13 minutes, shaking the basket halfway through the cooking time. 3. Taste, adjust the seasonings, and serve with the fresh herbs. Bon appétit!
Per Serving: Calories 77; Fat 4.6g; Sodium 359mg; Carbs 7.2g; Fiber 2.4g; Sugar 5g; Protein 1.4g

Simple Brussels Sprouts with Ham

Prep time: 5 minutes | Cook time: 15 minutes | Serves: 4

1 pound Brussels sprouts, trimmed
1 tablespoon peanut oil

Sea salt and freshly ground black pepper, to season
2 ounces ham, diced

1. Select the "AIR FRY" function of Ninja Foodi digital air fry oven, set temperature to 380 degrees F/ 195 degrees C and time to 13 minutes. Select START/PAUSE to begin preheating. Toss the Brussels sprouts with the remaining ingredients; then, arrange the Brussels sprouts in the air fryer basket. 2. Place the basket into the air fryer; cook the Brussels sprouts for 13 minutes, shaking the basket halfway through the cooking time. 3. Serve warm and enjoy!
Per Serving: Calories 93; Fat 4.3g; Sodium 311mg; Carbs 10.2g; Fiber 4.3g; Sugar 2.4g; Protein 6.2g

Roasted Buttery Rainbow Carrots

Prep time: 5 minutes | Cook time: 12 minutes | Serves: 2

10 to 12 heirloom or rainbow carrots (about 1 pound), scrubbed but not peeled
1 teaspoon olive oil
salt and freshly ground black

pepper
1 tablespoon butter
1 teaspoon fresh orange zest
1 teaspoon chopped fresh thyme

1. Select the "AIR FRY" function of Ninja Foodi digital air fry oven, set the temperature to 400 degrees F/ 200 degrees C and set the time to 12 minutes. Press the Start/Pause button and begin preheating. 2. Scrub the carrots and halve them lengthwise. Toss them in the olive oil, season with salt and freshly ground black pepper and transfer to the air fryer. 3. Air-fry for 12 minutes, shaking the basket every once in a while to rotate the carrots as they cook. 4. As soon as the carrots have finished cooking, add the butter, orange zest and thyme and toss all the ingredients together in the air fryer basket to melt the butter and coat evenly. Serve warm.
Per Serving: Calories 170; Fat 8g; Sodium 345mg; Carbs 24g; Fiber 7g; Sugar 11g; Protein 2g

Buttery Garlicky Potatoes

Prep time: 10 minutes | Cook time: 15 minutes | Serves: 3

¾ pound potatoes, quartered
1 tablespoon butter, melted
1 teaspoon garlic, pressed

1 teaspoon dried oregano
Sea salt and ground black pepper, to taste

1. Select the "AIR FRY" function of Ninja Foodi digital air fry oven, set the temperature to 400 degrees F/ 200 degrees C; set the time to 18 minutes. Press the Start/Pause button and begin preheating. Toss the potatoes with the remaining ingredients until well coated on all sides. 2. Arrange the potatoes in the air fryer basket. 3. Place the basket in the air fryer; cook the potatoes for about 18 minutes, shaking the basket halfway through the cooking time. 4. Serve warm and enjoy!
Per Serving: Calories 123; Fat 4g; Sodium 213mg; Carbs 20.1g; Fiber 2.5g; Sugar 0.9g; Protein 2.3g

Mexican Sweet Potatoes with Salsa

Prep time: 15 minutes | Cook time: 25 minutes | Serves: 4

1 pound sweet potatoes, scrubbed, prick with a fork
1 tablespoon olive oil
Coarse sea salt and ground black

pepper, to taste
½ teaspoon cayenne pepper
4 tablespoons salsa

1. Select the "AIR FRY" function of Ninja Foodi digital air fry oven, set the temperature to 380 degrees F/ 195 degrees C and set the time to 35 minutes. Press the Start/Pause button and begin preheating. Sprinkle the sweet potatoes with olive oil, salt, black pepper, and cayenne pepper and place them on the air fryer basket. 2. Place the basket in the air fryer, cook the sweet potatoes for 35 minutes, checking them halfway through the cooking time. 3. Split the tops open with a knife. Top each potato with salsa and serve. Bon appétit!
Per Serving: Calories 128; Fat 3.5g; Sodium 146mg; Carbs 22.1g; Fiber 3g; Sugar 2.1g; Protein 3g

Cheese Mushroom Patties

Prep time: 5 minutes | Cook time: 15 minutes | Serves: 3

¾-pound brown mushrooms, chopped
1 large egg, whisked
½ cup breadcrumbs
½ cup parmesan cheese, grated

1 small onion, minced
1 garlic clove, minced
Sea salt and ground black pepper, to taste
1 tablespoon olive oil

1. Select the "BAKE" function of Ninja Foodi digital air fry oven, set the temperature to 380 degrees F/ 195 degrees C and set the time to 15 minutes. Press the Start/Pause button and begin preheating. In a bowl, mix all ingredients until everything is well combined. Form the mixture into three patties. 2. Place the patties in the air fryer and cook them for about 15 minutes or until cooked through. Bon appétit!
Per Serving: Calories 184; Fat 11.1g; Sodium 332mg; Carbs 14g; Fiber 1.5g; Sugar 4g; Protein 9.4g

Tasty Butter Corn

Prep time: 5 minutes | Cook time: 6 minutes | Serves: 4

1 teaspoon ground allspice
1 teaspoon dried thyme
½ teaspoon ground ginger
½ teaspoon ground cinnamon
¼ teaspoon ground nutmeg

⅛ teaspoon ground cayenne pepper
1 teaspoon salt
2 tablespoons butter, melted
4 ears of corn, husked

1. Select the "AIR FRY" function of Ninja Foodi digital air fry oven, set the temperature to 380 degrees F/ 195 degrees C and set the time to 6 minutes. Press the Start/Pause button and begin preheating. 2. Combine all the spices in a bowl. Grease the corn evenly with the melted butter and then sprinkle the spices generously on all sides of each ear of corn. 3. Transfer the ears of corn to the air fryer basket. It's ok if they are crisscrossed on top of each other. Place the basket in the air fryer, air-fry for 6 minutes, rotating the ears as they cook. 4. Brush more butter on at the end and sprinkle with any remaining spice mixture.
Per Serving: Calories 110; Fat 6g; Sodium 85mg; Carbs 15g; Fiber 2g; Sugar 2g; Protein 2g

Cheesy Summer Vegetables Drizzle with Balsamic

Prep time: 5 minutes | Cook time: 17 minutes | Serves: 2

1 cup balsamic vinegar
1 zucchini, sliced
1 yellow squash, sliced
2 tablespoons olive oil
1 clove garlic, minced
½ teaspoon Italian seasoning

salt and freshly ground black pepper
½ cup cherry tomatoes, halved
2 ounces crumbled goat cheese
2 tablespoons chopped fresh basil, plus more leaves for garnish

1. Place the balsamic vinegar in a small saucepot on the stovetop. Boil the vinegar to a boil, lower the heat and manage to simmer uncovered for 20 minutes, until the mixture reduces and thickens. Set aside to cool. 2. Select the "AIR FRY" function of Ninja Foodi digital air fry oven, set the temperature to 390 degrees F/ 200 degrees C and set the time to 5 minutes. Press the Start/Pause button and begin preheating. 3. Combine the zucchini and yellow squash in a large bowl. Add the olive oil, minced garlic, Italian seasoning, salt and pepper and toss to coat. 4. Air-fry the vegetables for 10 minutes, shaking the basket several times through the cooking time. Add the cherry tomatoes and continue to air-fry for another 5 minutes. Sprinkle the goat cheese over the vegetables and air-fry for 2 more minutes. 5. Drizzle with the balsamic reduction and season with freshly ground black pepper. Garnish with the fresh basil leaves.
Per Serving: Calories 360; Fat 19g; Sodium 114mg; Carbs 37g; Fiber 3g; Sugar 23g; Protein 8g

Roasted Fennel

Prep time: 5 minutes | Cook time: 15 minutes | Serves: 4

1-pound fennel bulbs, trimmed and sliced
2 tablespoons olive oil
1 teaspoon fresh garlic, minced

1 teaspoon dried parsley flakes
Kosher salt and ground black pepper, to taste

1. Select the "AIR FRY" function of Ninja Foodi digital air fry oven, set the temperature to 370 degrees F/ 185 degrees C and set the time to 15 minutes. Press the Start/Pause button and begin preheating. Toss all ingredients in a mixing bowl. 2. Place them in air fryer basket and cook the fennel for about 15 minutes or until cooked through; check basket halfway through the cooking time. Bon appétit!
Per Serving: Calories 97; Fat 6.9g; Sodium 211mg; Carbs 8.4g; Fiber 3.5g; Sugar 4.4g; Protein 1.4g

Moroccan Falafel

Prep time: 5 minutes | Cook time: 10 minutes | Serves: 4

1 cup dried chickpeas
½ onion, chopped
1 clove garlic
¼ cup fresh parsley leaves
1 teaspoon salt
¼ teaspoon crushed red pepper
Tomato Salad
2 tomatoes, seeds removed and diced
½ cucumber, finely diced
¼ red onion, finely diced and rinsed with water
1 teaspoon red wine vinegar

flakes
1 teaspoon ground cumin
½ teaspoon ground coriander
1 to 2 tablespoons flour
olive oil

1 tablespoon olive oil
salt and freshly ground black pepper
2 tablespoons chopped fresh parsley

1. Soak chickpeas overnight on the counter. Then drain them and place them in a food processor, along with the onion, garlic, parsley, spices and 1 tablespoon of flour. Pulse until coarse paste consistency appears in a processor. When pinch, the mix hold together. 2. Scoop portions of the mix and shape into balls. Place the balls on a plate and refrigerate for at least 30 minutes. You should have between 12 and 14 balls. 3. Select the "AIR FRY" function of Ninja Foodi digital air fry oven, set the temperature to 380 degrees F/ 195 degrees C and set the time to 10 minutes. Press the Start/Pause button and begin preheating. 4. Spray the falafel balls with oil and place them in the air fryer. Air-fry for 10 minutes, rolling them over and spraying them with oil again halfway through the cooking time so that they cook and brown evenly. 5. Serve with pita bread, hummus, cucumbers, hot peppers, tomatoes or any other fillings you might like.
Per Serving: Calories 203; Fat 10.9g; Sodium 402mg; Carbs 2g; Fiber 0g; Sugar 1g; Protein 23g

Refreshing Romaine Slaw

Prep time: 5 minutes | Cook time: 15 minutes | Serves: 4

5 cups shredded romaine lettuce
¼ cup slivered red onion
1½ tablespoons olive oil
1½ tablespoons apple cider

vinegar
4 teaspoons fresh lime juice
¼ teaspoon kosher salt
Freshly ground black pepper

In a bowl, mix the lettuce, onion, oil, vinegar, lime juice, salt, and pepper to taste. Toss well and serve right away.
Per Serving: Calories 60; Fat 5g; Sodium 76mg; Carbs 3g; Fiber 1.5g; Sugar 1g; Protein 1g

Spicy Chinese Asparagus

Prep time: 5 minutes | Cook time: 10 minutes | Serves: 4

1-pound asparagus
4 teaspoons Chinese chili oil
½ teaspoon garlic powder

1 tablespoon soy sauce
½ teaspoon red pepper flakes, crushed

1. Select the "AIR FRY" function of Ninja Foodi digital air fry oven, set the temperature to 400 degrees F/ 200 degrees C and set the time to 6 minutes. Press the Start/Pause button and begin preheating. Toss the asparagus with the remaining ingredients. Arrange the asparagus spears in the air fryer basket. 2. Place the basket in the air fryer, cook the asparagus at 400 degrees F/ 200 degrees C for about 6 minutes, tossing them halfway through the cooking time. Bon appétit!
Per Serving: Calories 75; Fat 6g; Sodium 111mg; Carbs 5.6g; Fiber 2.5g; Sugar 2.9g; Protein 2.8g

Spicy Gujarati Green Beans

Prep time: 5 minutes | Cook time: 10 minutes | Serves: 3

¾ pound fresh green beans, trimmed
1 garlic clove, minced
2 tablespoons olive oil
1 tablespoon soy sauce

1 teaspoon black mustard seeds
1 dried red chile pepper, crushed
Sea salt and ground black pepper, to taste

1. Select the "AIR FRY" function of Ninja Foodi digital air fry oven, set the temperature to 380 degrees F/ 195 degrees C and set the time to 8 minutes. Press the Start/Pause button and begin preheating. Toss the green beans with the remaining ingredients; then arrange them in the air fryer basket. 2. Place the basket in the air fryer; cook the green beans for 8 minutes, tossing the basket halfway through the cooking time. Enjoy!
Per Serving: Calories 136; Fat 9.8g; Sodium 239mg; Carbs 2.7g; Fiber 3.3g; Sugar 4.9g; Protein 2.7g

Fried Tomatoes with Sriracha Mayo

Prep time: 10 minutes | Cook time: 24 minutes | Serves: 4

3 green tomatoes
salt and freshly ground black pepper
⅓ cup all-purpose flour
2 eggs
½ cup buttermilk
1 cup panko breadcrumbs
1 cup cornmeal

olive oil, in a spray bottle
fresh thyme sprigs or chopped fresh chives
Sriracha Mayo
½ cup mayonnaise
1 to 2 tablespoons sriracha hot sauce
1 tablespoon milk

1. Cut the tomatoes in slices. Pat dry tomatoes slices and season generously with salt and pepper. 2. Place the flour in the first shallow dish, whisk the eggs and buttermilk together in the other dish, and combine the panko breadcrumbs and cornmeal in the third one. 3. Select the "AIR FRY" function of Ninja Foodi digital air fry oven, set the temperature to 400 degrees F/ 200 degrees C and set the time to 8 minutes. Press the Start/Pause button and begin preheating. 4. Dredge the spiced slices in flour. Then dip into the egg and finally press in the breadcrumbs .5. Spray the air-fryer basket with oil. Transfer prepared tomato slices in and spray with olive oil. Air-fry for 8 minutes. Flip them and grease with oil and air-fry for further 4 minutes until golden brown. 6. For sriracha mayo. mix the mayonnaise, sriracha hot sauce and milk in a bowl. Stir well until smooth. 7. Serve the fried tomatoes hot with the sriracha mayo on the side.
Per Serving: Calories 340; Fat 5g; Sodium 321mg; Carbs 62g; Fiber 5g; Sugar 9g; Protein 12g

Curried Cauliflower with Yogurt

Prep time: 5 minutes | Cook time: 12 minutes | Serves: 2

4 cups cauliflower florets (about half a large head)
1 tablespoon olive oil
Cool Yogurt Drizzle
¼ cup plain yogurt
2 tablespoons sour cream
1 teaspoon lemon juice
pinch cayenne pepper

salt
1 teaspoon curry powder
½ cup toasted, chopped cashews

salt
1 teaspoon honey
1 tablespoon chopped cilantro,

1. Select the "AIR FRY" function of Ninja Foodi digital air fry oven, set the temperature to 400 degrees F/ 200 degrees C and set the time to 12 minutes. Press the Start/Pause button and begin preheating. 2. Toss the cauliflower florets with the olive oil, salt and curry powder, coating evenly. 3. Transfer the cauliflower to the air fryer basket and place the basket in the air fryer, air-fry for 12 minutes, shaking the basket twice during the cooking process. 4. While the cauliflower is cooking, make the cool yogurt drizzle by combining all ingredients in a bowl. 5. Serve it warm with the cool yogurt either underneath or drizzled over the top. Scatter the cashews and cilantro leaves around.
Per Serving: Calories 270; Fat 21g; Sodium 478mg; Carbs 18g; Fiber 5g; Sugar 5g; Protein 9g

Egg-Stuffed Peppers

Prep time: 5 minutes | Cook time: 15 minutes | Serves: 3

3 bell peppers, seeded and halved
1 tablespoon olive oil
3 eggs

3 tablespoons green onion, chopped
Sea salt and ground black pepper

1. Select the "AIR FRY" function of Ninja Foodi digital air fry oven, set the temperature to 400 degrees F/ 200 degrees C and set the time to 10 minutes. Press the Start/Pause button and begin preheating. Toss the peppers with the oil; place them in the air fryer basket. 2. Crack an egg into each bell pepper half. Sprinkle your peppers with the salt and black pepper. 3. Place the basket in the air fryer, cook the peppers for about 10 minutes. Top the peppers with green onions. Continue to cook for 4 minutes more. Bon appétit!
Per Serving: Calories 143; Fat 9.1g; Sodium 203mg; Carbs 7.8g; Fiber 2.6g; Sugar 5.4g; Protein 6.4g

Brussels Sprouts with Cheese

Prep time: 5 minutes | Cook time: 13 minutes | Serves: 4

1 pound Brussels sprouts, trimmed
1 tablespoon olive oil
Sea salt and ground black pepper,

to taste
4 ounces Provolone cheese, crumbled

1. Select the "AIR FRY" function of Ninja Foodi digital air fry oven, set the temperature to 380 degrees F/ 195 degrees C and set the time to 10 minutes. Press the Start/Pause button and begin preheating. Toss the Brussels sprouts with the olive oil and spices until they are well coated on all sides; then, arrange the Brussels sprouts in the air fryer basket. 2. Place the basket in the air fryer; cook the Brussels sprouts for 10 minutes, shaking the basket halfway through the cooking time. 3. Toss the Brussels sprouts with the cheese and serve warm. Enjoy!
Per Serving: Calories 183; Fat 11.8g; Sodium 144mg; Carbs 11.8g; Fiber 4.5g; Sugar 3.2g; Protein 11.4g

Hot Fried Cabbage Patties

Prep time: 5 minutes | Cook time: 15 minutes | Serves: 4

4 eggs, beaten
2 cups, shredded purple cabbage
1 cup cornmeal
Pinch of sea salt

1 tablespoon onion powder
1 tablespoon olive oil
1 teaspoon black pepper

1. Select the "AIR FRY" function of Ninja Foodi digital air fry oven, set the temperature to 390 degrees F/ 200 degrees C and set the time to 15 minutes. Press the Start/Pause button and begin preheating. Blend all the except olive oil, in a bowl. Grease heat-safe dish with olive oil. 2. Spoon the mixture into dish and form patties. Add patties to heat-safe dish and cook in air fryer for 15-minutes. Serve as a vegetarian breakfast burger.
Per Serving: Calories 221; Fat 9.4g; Sodium 321mg; Carbs 8.6g; Fiber 2g; Sugar 1g; Protein 14.2g

Sweet Butternut Squash

Prep time: 5 minutes | Cook time: 15 minutes | Serves: 2 to 3

1 butternut squash, peeled
olive oil, in a spray bottle
salt and freshly ground black pepper
2 tablespoons butter, softened

2 tablespoons honey
pinch ground cinnamon
pinch ground nutmeg
chopped fresh sage

1. Select the "AIR FRY" function of Ninja Foodi digital air fry oven, set the temperature to 370 degrees F/ 185 degrees C and set the time to 5 minutes. Press the Start/Pause button and begin preheating. 2. Cut the neck of the butternut squash into disks about ½-inch thick. Brush or spray the disks with oil and season with salt and ground black pepper. 3. Transfer the butternut disks to the air fryer in one layer (or just ever so slightly overlapping). Air-fry for 5 minutes. 4. While the butternut squash is cooking, combine the butter, honey, cinnamon and nutmeg in a small bowl. Brush this mixture on the butternut squash, flip the disks over and brush the other side as well. Continue to air-fry for another 5 minutes. Flip the disks once more, brush with more of the honey butter and air-fry for another 5 minutes. The butternut should be browning nicely around the edges. 5. Remove the butternut squash from the air-fryer and repeat with additional batches if necessary. Transfer to a serving platter, sprinkle with the fresh sage and serve.
Per Serving: Calories 310; Fat 8g; Sodium 578mg; Carbs 63g; Fiber 9g; Sugar 20g; Protein 5g

Delicious Cauliflower Steaks

Prep time: 5 minutes | Cook time: 13 minutes | Serves: 2

1 head cauliflower
1 tablespoon olive oil
salt and freshly ground black pepper
½ teaspoon chopped fresh thyme

leaves
3 tablespoons grated Parmigiano-Reggiano cheese
2 tablespoons panko breadcrumbs

1. Select the "AIR FRY" function of Ninja Foodi digital air fry oven, set the temperature to 370 degrees F/ 185 degrees C and set the time to 10 minutes. Press the Start/Pause button and begin preheating. 2. Cut two steaks out of the center of the cauliflower. To do this, cut the cauliflower in half and then cut one slice about 1-inch thick off each. 3. Brush the cauliflower with olive oil and spice with salt, freshly ground black pepper and fresh thyme. Place the cauliflower steaks into the air fryer basket and air-fry for 6 minutes. Turn the steaks over and air-fry for another 4 minutes. Combine the Parmesan cheese and panko breadcrumbs and sprinkle the mixture over the tops of both steaks and air-fry for another 3 minutes until the cheese has melted and the breadcrumbs have browned. Serve this with some sautéed bitter greens and air-fried blistered tomatoes.
Per Serving: Calories 1646; Fat 146g; Sodium 498mg; Carbs 10g; Fiber 2g; Sugar 2g; Protein 77g

Elote Corn with Cilantro Salad

Prep time: 5 minutes | Cook time: 10 minutes | Serves: 2

2 ears of corn, shucked
1 tablespoon unsalted butter, at room temperature
1 teaspoon chili powder
¼ teaspoon garlic powder
Kosher salt and freshly ground black pepper
1 cup lightly packed fresh cilantro

leaves
1 tablespoon sour cream
1 tablespoon mayonnaise
1 teaspoon adobo sauce
2 tablespoons crumbled queso fresco
Lime wedges, for serving

1. Select the "AIR FRY" function of Ninja Foodi digital air fry oven, set the temperature to 400 degrees F/ 200 degrees C and set the time to 10 minutes. Press the Start/Pause button and begin preheating. Brush the corn all over with the butter, then sprinkle with the chili powder and garlic powder, and season with salt and pepper. Place the corn in the air fryer and cook, turning halfway through, until charred and tender, about 10 minutes. 2. Transfer to cutting board, cut the kernels off and move to a bowl. Add the cilantro and toss to combine well. 3. In a bowl, stir the sour cream, mayonnaise, and adobo sauce. Spoon the adobo dressing over the top of corn. Spice with the queso fresco and serve with lime wedges on the side.
Per Serving: Calories 218; Fat 2.4g; Sodium 641mg; Carbs 14g; Fiber 6g; Sugar 2g; Protein 19g

Caramelized Eggplant with Harissa Yogurt

Prep time: 10 minutes | Cook time: 20 minutes | Serves: 2

1 eggplant, cut crosswise into	½ cup plain yogurt
½-inch-thick slices	2 tablespoons harissa paste
2 tablespoons vegetable oil	1 garlic clove, grated
Kosher salt	2 teaspoons honey
Ground black pepper	

1. Select the "AIR FRY" function of Ninja Foodi digital air fry oven, set the temperature to 400 degrees F/ 200 degrees C and set the time to 15 minutes. Press the Start/Pause button and begin preheating. In a bowl, toss the eggplant and oil, spice with salt and pepper, and toss. Transfer to air fryer and cook, shaking every 5 minutes, until the eggplant caramelized and soft, about 15 minutes. 2. Meanwhile, in a bowl, whisk the yogurt, harissa, and garlic, spread onto a serving plate. 3. Place the warm eggplant over the yogurt and spread the honey just before serving.
Per Serving: Calories 18; Fat 0.3g; Sodium 7mg; Carbs 1g; Fiber 0g; Sugar 0g; Protein 2g

Vegetable Lasagna

Prep time: 10 minutes | Cook time: 45 minutes | Serves: 6

1 zucchini, sliced	divided
1 yellow squash, sliced	1 egg
8 ounces mushrooms, sliced	1 teaspoon salt
1 red bell pepper, cut into strips	freshly ground black pepper
1 tablespoon olive oil	¼ cup shredded carrots
2 cups ricotta cheese	½ cup chopped fresh spinach
2 cups grated mozzarella cheese,	8 lasagna noodles, cooked
Béchamel Sauce:	
3 tablespoons butter	½ teaspoon salt
3 tablespoons flour	freshly ground black pepper
2½ cups milk	pinch of ground nutmeg
½ cup grated Parmesan cheese	

1. Select the "AIR FRY" function of Ninja Foodi digital air fry oven, set the temperature to 400 degrees F/ 200 degrees C and set the time to 10 minutes. Press the Start/Pause button and begin preheating. 2.Toss the zucchini, yellow squash, mushrooms and red pepper in a large bowl with the olive oil and season with salt and pepper. Air-fry for 10 minutes, shaking the basket once or twice while the vegetables cook. 3. While the vegetables are cooking, make the béchamel sauce and cheese filling. Add flour in melted butter and whisk, cooking for a couple of minutes. Add in milk and whisk until smooth. Boil the mix and manage simmer until the sauce thickens. Stir in cheese and spice with the salt, pepper and nutmeg. Set the sauce aside. 4. Combine the ricotta cheese, 1¼ cups of the mozzarella cheese, egg, salt and pepper in a large bowl and stir until combined. Fold in the carrots and spinach. 5. When the vegetables have finished cooking, build the lasagna. Use a sheet pan that is 6 inches in diameter and 4 inches high. Spread béchamel sauce on the bottom of the sheet pan. Top with two lasagna noodles, cut to fit the dish and overlapping each other a little. Spoon a third of the ricotta cheese mixture and then a third of the roasted veggies on top of the noodles. Pour ½ cup of béchamel sauce on top and then repeat these layers two more times: noodles – cheese mixture – vegetables – béchamel sauce. Sprinkle the mozzarella cheese over the top. Cover with foil, loosely so the aluminum doesn't touch the cheese. 6. Air-fry for 45 minutes, removing the foil for the last 2 minutes, to slightly brown the cheese on top.
Per Serving: Calories 162; Fat 5.3g; Sodium 1006mg; Carbs 3g; Fiber 2g; Sugar 0g; Protein 25g

Butternut Squash Fries with Cinnamon

Prep time: 10 minutes | Cook time: 10 minutes | Serves: 2

1 pinch of salt	2 teaspoon cinnamon
1 tablespoon powdered	1 tablespoon coconut oil
unprocessed sugar	10 ounces pre-cut butternut
½ teaspoon nutmeg	squash fries

1. Select the "AIR FRY" function of Ninja Foodi digital air fry oven, set the temperature to 390 degrees F/ 200 degrees C and set the time to 10 minutes. Press the Start/Pause button and begin preheating. 2. In a plastic bag, pour in all ingredients. Coat fries with other components till coated and sugar is dissolved. Spread coated fries into a single layer in the air fryer. Cook 10 minutes until crispy.
Per Serving: Calories 175; Fat 8g; Sodium 326mg; Carbs 5g; Fiber 0.2g; Sugar 0.3g; Protein 1g

Green Tofu Quiche

Prep time: 10 minutes | Cook time: 31 minutes | Serves: 4

¾ cup whole-meal flour	4-ounces mushrooms, sliced
Dash of salt	1 yellow onion, chopped
Sprig of fresh parsley, chopped	2 tablespoons olive oil
2 tablespoons nutritional yeast	2 tablespoons cold water
½ tablespoon dried dill	½ cup coconut oil
1 lb. spinach, washed, chopped	Salt and pepper to taste
1 package of tofu, firm	

1. Select the "AIR FRY" function of Ninja Foodi digital air fry oven, set the temperature to 375 degrees F/ 190 degrees C and set the time to 30 minutes. Press the Start/Pause button and begin preheating. Create the pastry by sifting flour and salt together. Add coconut oil until flour crumbles. To bind dough add water gradually. Wrap dough in cling wrap and leave in the fridge for 30-minutes. Over medium heat, sauté the onion for 1-minute then add the mushroom and tofu in olive oil. 2. Add spinach; nutritional yeast dried dill and season with salt and pepper to taste. Add the parsley and set aside. On a floured surface roll dough until thin. Place the dough inside of greased baking dish that will fit into your air fryer. Pour the tofu mixture on top of dough and cook for 30-minutes. Serve warm.
Per Serving: Calories 242; Fat 12.2g; Sodium 222mg; Carbs 10.5g; Fiber 1.6g; Sugar 2g; Protein 11.6g

Vegetable Stromboli

Prep time: 9 minutes | Cook time: 20 minutes | Serves: 2

½ onion, thinly sliced	pepper
½ red pepper, julienned	1 (14-ounce) tube refrigerated
½ yellow pepper, julienned	pizza dough
olive oil	2 cups grated mozzarella cheese
1 small zucchini, thinly sliced	¼ cup grated Parmesan cheese
1 cup thinly sliced mushrooms	½ cup sliced black olives,
1½ cups chopped broccoli	optional
1 teaspoon Italian seasoning	dried oregano
salt and freshly ground black	pizza or marinara sauce

1. Select the "AIR FRY" function of Ninja Foodi digital air fry oven, set the temperature to 400 degrees F/ 200 degrees C and set the time to 7 minutes. Press the Start/Pause button and begin preheating. 2.Toss the onions and peppers with a little olive oil and air-fry the vegetables for 7 minutes, shaking the basket once or twice while the vegetables cook. Add the zucchini, mushrooms, broccoli and Italian seasoning to the basket. Add a little more olive oil and season with salt and freshly ground black pepper. Air-fry for an additional 7 minutes, shaking the basket halfway through. Let the vegetables cool slightly while you roll out the pizza dough. 3. Press the pizza dough into a 13-inch by 11-inch rectangle, with the long side closest to you. Spread the mozzarella and Parmesan cheeses on the dough leaving an empty 1-inch border from the edge farthest away from you. Spoon the roasted vegetables over the cheese, sprinkle the olives (if using) over everything and top with the remaining cheese. 4. Start rolling the stromboli toward the empty border. Tuck the dough ends and pinch to shut. Place the seam down and shape it to a U-shape to fit into the air fryer basket. Cut small slits with a sharp knife evenly in the top of the dough, lightly brush the stromboli with a little oil and sprinkle with some dried oregano. 5. Grease the air fryer sheet pan with oil and transfer the U-shaped stromboli to the air fryer. Air-fry for 15 minutes, flipping the stromboli over after the first 10 minutes. 6.To remove, carefully flip over. Cut it into 2-inch slices and serve with pizza or marinara sauce.
Per Serving: Calories 387; Fat 26.3g; Sodium 602mg; Carbs 12g; Fiber 8g; Sugar 1g; Protein 26g

Crispy Sweet Potato Chips

Prep time: 10 minutes | Cook time: 15 minutes | Serves: 2

2 large sweet potatoes, thinly	2 tablespoons olive oil
sliced with Mandoline	Salt to taste

1. Select the "AIR FRY" function of Ninja Foodi digital air fry oven, set the temperature to 350 degrees F/ 175 degrees C and set the time to 15 minutes. Press the Start/Pause button and begin preheating. 2. Stir the sweet potato slices, in a large bowl with the oil. Arrange slices in your air fryer and cook them until crispy, for about 15-minutes.
Per Serving: Calories 253; Fat 11.2g; Sodium 333mg; Carbs 8.4g; Fiber 2g; Sugar 1g; Protein 6.5g

Cheesy Spinach Calzones

Prep time: 10 minutes | Cook time: 20 minutes | Serves: 2

⅔ cup frozen chopped spinach, thawed
1 cup grated mozzarella cheese
1 cup ricotta cheese
½ teaspoon Italian seasoning
½ teaspoon salt
freshly ground black pepper
1 store-bought or homemade pizza dough
2 tablespoons olive oil
pizza or marinara sauce

1. Drain and squeeze all the water out of the thawed spinach and set it aside. Mix the mozzarella cheese, ricotta cheese, Italian seasoning, salt and freshly ground black pepper together in a bowl. Stir in the chopped spinach. 2. Divide the dough, stretch or roll one half of the dough into a 10-inch circle. Spread the cheese and spinach mixture on half of the dough, leaving about one inch of dough empty around the edge. 3. Fold the half of the dough over the cheese mixture, almost to the edge of the bottom in a half moon. Fold the edge up over the top edge and crimp the dough around the edges in order to make the crust and seal the calzone. Brush the dough with olive oil. 4. Select the "AIR FRY" function of Ninja Foodi digital air fry oven, set the temperature to 360 degrees F/ 180 degrees C and set the time to 10 minutes. Press the Start/Pause button and begin preheating. 5. Grease the air fryer basket with olive oil. Air-fry the calzones one at a time for 10 minutes, flipping the calzone over halfway through. Serve with warm pizza or marinara sauce if desired.
Per Serving: Calories 463; Fat 15.5g; Sodium 553mg; Carbs 366g; Fiber 3g; Sugar 3g; Protein 41g

Toffee Apple Upside-Down Cake

Prep time: 10 minutes | Cook time: 30 minutes | Serves: 9

½ cup walnuts, chopped
1 lemon, zest
1 teaspoon vinegar
¾ cup water
1 ½ teaspoons mixed spice
¼ cup sunflower oil
1 teaspoon baking soda
1 cup almond flour
3 baking apples, cored and sliced
2 tablespoon liquid Stevia, divided
¼ cup almond butter

1. Select the "AIR FRY" function of Ninja Foodi digital air fry oven, set the temperature to 390 degrees F/ 200 degrees C and set the time to 30 minutes. Press the Start/Pause button and begin preheating. Melt the butter in skillet, then remove from heat and add one tablespoon Stevia and stir. Pour the mixture into baking dish that will fit into your air fryer. Arrange the slices of apples on top and set aside. 2. Combine flour, baking soda, and mixed spice in a large mixing bowl. In another bowl add water, vinegar, remaining tablespoon of liquid Stevia, lemon zest and oil, mix well. Stir in the wet with dry and stir until well combined. Pour over apple slices and bake for 30-minutes.
Per Serving: Calories 252; Fat 11.3g; Sodium 321mg; Carbs 10.2g; Fiber 3g; Sugar 1g; Protein 12.2g

Charred Okra with nut Sauce

Prep time: 10 minutes | Cook time: 25 minutes | Serves: 2

¾ pound okra pods
2 tablespoons vegetable oil
Kosher salt and freshly ground black pepper
1 large shallot, minced
1 garlic clove, minced
½ Scotch bonnet chile, minced
(seeded if you want a milder sauce)
1 tablespoon tomato paste
1 cup vegetable stock or water
2 tablespoons natural peanut butter
Juice of ½ lime

1. Select the "AIR FRY" function of Ninja Foodi digital air fry oven, set the temperature to 400 degrees F/ 200 degrees C and set the time to 16 minutes. Press the Start/Pause button and begin preheating. In a bowl, toss the okra with 1 tablespoon of the oil and season with salt and pepper. Transfer the okra to the air fryer and cook, shaking the basket halfway through, until the okra is tender and lightly charred at the edges, about 16 minutes. 2. In a skillet, cook the shallot, garlic, and chile and cook, stirring, until soft, about 2 minutes. add tomato paste and cook for 30 seconds, then stir in the vegetable stock and peanut butter. Lower the heat to manage to simmer and cook until the sauce is reduced slightly and thickened, 3 to 4 minutes. Remove from the heat, stir in the lime juice, and season with salt and pepper. 3. Place the peanut sauce on a plate, then pile the okra on top and serve hot.
Per Serving: Calories 18; Fat 1g; Sodium 106mg; Carbs 2g; Fiber 0g; Sugar 2g; Protein 0g

Fried Cauliflower in Mole Sauce

Prep time: 5 minutes | Cook time: 35 minutes | Serves: 2

8 ounces medium cauliflower florets
1 tablespoon vegetable oil
Kosher salt and freshly ground black pepper
1½ cups vegetable broth
2 tablespoons New Mexico chile powder (or regular chili powder)
2 tablespoons salted roasted
peanuts
1 tablespoon sesame seeds
1 tablespoon finely chopped golden raisins
1 teaspoon kosher salt
1 teaspoon dark brown sugar
½ teaspoon dried oregano
¼ teaspoon cayenne pepper
⅛ teaspoon ground cinnamon

1. In a bowl, toss the cauliflower with the oil and season with salt and black pepper. Select the "AIR FRY" function of Ninja Foodi digital air fry oven, set the temperature to 375 degrees F/ 190 degrees C and set the time to 10 minutes. Press the Start/Pause button and begin preheating. Transfer the cauliflower into the air fryer and cook until the itis lightly browned , about 10 minutes, stirring halfway through. 2. Meanwhile, in a small blender, combine the broth, chile powder, peanuts, sesame seeds, raisins, salt, brown sugar, oregano, cayenne, and cinnamon and puree until smooth. Pour into a small saucepan or skillet and bring to a simmer over medium heat, then cook until reduced 3 to 5 minutes. 3. Pour the hot mole sauce over the cauliflower in the pan, stir to coat, then cook until the sauce is thickened and lightly charred on the cauliflower, about 5 minutes more. Sprinkle with more sesame seeds and serve warm.
Per Serving: Calories 205; Fat 5.8g; Sodium 1481mg; Carbs 1g; Fiber 0g; Sugar 0g; Protein 35g

Delicious Veggie Tofu Frittata

Prep time: 15 minutes | Cook time: 40 minutes | Serves: 4

1 flax egg (1 tablespoon flax meal + 3 tablespoons water)
1 ¾ cups brown rice, cooked
1 tablespoon olive oil
½ onion, chopped
4 spring onions, chopped
Handful of basil leaves, chopped
2 teaspoons arrowroot powder
⅔ cup almond milk
3 tablespoons nutritional yeast
2 tablespoons soy sauce
2 teaspoons Dijon mustard
1 package firm tofu
½ cup baby spinach, chopped
½ cup kale, chopped
1 yellow pepper, chopped
3 big mushrooms, chopped
½ teaspoon turmeric
4 cloves of garlic, crushed

1. Select the "AIR FRY" function of Ninja Foodi digital air fry oven, set the temperature to 375 degrees F/ 190 degrees C and set the time to 50 minutes. Press the Start/Pause button and begin preheating. Grease a pan that will fit into air fryer. Prepare the frittata crust by mixing the brown rice and flax egg. Press the rice mix onto baking dish until crust is formed. 2. Brush little olive oil on rice mix and cook for 10-minutes. Meanwhile, add the remaining olive oil to skillet and heat, then sautė the garlic and onions for 2-minutes. Add the mushrooms and pepper and continue to sautė for an additional 3-minutes. Stir in the spinach, kale, spring onions and basil. Remove from pan and set aside. 3. In a food processor, pulse the tofu, mustard, turmeric, nutritional yeast, soy sauce, almond milk and arrowroot powder. Pour into mixing bowl and stir in the sautéed vegetables. Pour veggie mix over the rice crust and cook in air fryer for 40-minutes. Serve warm.
Per Serving: Calories 232; Fat 11.2g; Sodium 554mg; Carbs 10.6g; Fiber 3g; Sugar 1g; Protein 13.2g

Crispy Pineapple Sticks with Yogurt Dip

Prep time: 10 minutes | Cook time: 10 minutes | Serves: 2

¼ cup dried coconut
Yogurt Dip:
1 cup vanilla yogurt
½ pineapple

1 sprig of fresh mint

1. Select the "AIR FRY" function of Ninja Foodi digital air fry oven, set the temperature to 390 degrees F/ 200 degrees C and set the time to 10 minutes. Press the Start/Pause button and begin preheating. Cut the pineapple into sticks. Dip pineapple sticks into the dried coconut. 2.Place the sticks covered with desiccated coconut into air fryer basket and cook for 10-minutes. 3.Prepare the yogurt dip. Dice the mint leaves and combine with vanilla yogurt and stir. Serve pineapple sticks with yogurt dip and enjoy!
Per Serving: Calories 246; Fat 8.4g; Sodium 298mg; Carbs 7.2g; Fiber 1g; Sugar 2g; Protein 6.3g

Spiced Stuffed Zucchini Boats

Prep time: 5 minutes | Cook time: 20 minutes | Serves: 2

olive oil
½ cup onion, finely chopped
1 clove garlic, finely minced
½ teaspoon dried oregano
¼ teaspoon dried thyme
¾ cup couscous
1½ cups chicken stock, divided
1 tomato, seeds removed and finely chopped
½ cup coarsely chopped Kalamata olives

½ cup grated Romano cheese
¼ cup pine nuts, toasted
1 tablespoon chopped fresh parsley
1 teaspoon salt
freshly ground black pepper
1 egg, beaten
1 cup grated mozzarella cheese, divided
2 thick zucchini

1.Pre-heat a sauté pan on the stovetop and add the oil and sauté the onion until it just starts to soften–about 4 minutes. Stir in the garlic, dried oregano and thyme. Add the couscous and sauté for just a minute. Add 1¼ cups of the chicken stock and simmer over low heat for 3 to 5 minutes, until liquid has been absorbed and the couscous is soft. Remove the pan from heat and set it aside to cool slightly. 2. Fluff the couscous and add the tomato, Kalamata olives, Romano cheese, pine nuts, parsley, salt and pepper. Mix well. Add the remaining chicken stock, the egg and ½ cup of the mozzarella cheese. Stir to ensure everything is combined. 3. Cut each zucchini in half lengthwise. Then, trim each half of the zucchini into four 5-inch lengths. Use a spoon to scoop out the center of the zucchini, leaving some flesh around the sides. Grease zucchini with olive oil and spice the cut side with salt and pepper. 4. Select the "AIR FRY" function of Ninja Foodi digital air fry oven, set the temperature to 380 degrees F/ 195 degrees C and set the time to 19 minutes. Press the Start/Pause button and begin preheating. 5.Divide the couscous filling between the four zucchini boats. Press the filling and fill the inside of the zucchini. The filling should be mounded into the boats and rounded on top. 6. Transfer the zucchini boats to the air fryer basket and drizzle the stuffed zucchini boats with olive oil. Air-fry for 19 minutes. Then, spread the mozzarella cheese on zucchini, pressing it down onto the filling lightly to prevent it from blowing around in the air fryer. Air-fry for one more minute to melt the cheese. Transfer the finished zucchini boats to a serving platter and garnish with the chopped parsley.
Per Serving: Calories 494; Fat 36g; Sodium 690mg; Carbs 17g; Fiber 11g; Sugar 2g; Protein 28g

Cheese Broccoli Stuffed Potatoes

Prep time: 12 minutes | Cook time: 50 minutes | Serves: 2

2 large russet potatoes, scrubbed
1 tablespoon olive oil
salt and freshly ground black pepper
2 tablespoons butter
¼ cup sour cream
3 tablespoons half-and-half (or

milk)
1¼ cups grated Cheddar cheese, divided
¾ teaspoon salt
freshly ground black pepper
1 cup frozen baby broccoli florets, thawed and drained

1. Select the "AIR FRY" function of Ninja Foodi digital air fry oven, set the temperature to 400 degrees F/ 200 degrees C and set the time to 30 minutes. Press the Start/Pause button and begin preheating. 2. Rub the potatoes all over with olive oil and season generously with salt and freshly ground black pepper. Place the spiced potatoes into the air fryer sheet pan and air-fry for 30 minutes, turning the potatoes over halfway through the cooking process. 3. Let them rest for 5 minutes. Cut a large oval out of the top of both potatoes. Leaving half an inch of potato flesh around the edge of the potato, scoop the inside of the potato out and into a large bowl to prepare the potato filling. Mash the scooped potato filling with a fork and add the butter, sour cream, half-and-half, 1 cup of the grated Cheddar cheese, salt and pepper to taste. Mix well and then fold in the broccoli florets. 4. Stuff the hollowed out potato shells with the potato and broccoli mixture. Mound the filling high in the potatoes – you will have more filling than room in the potato shells. 5. Transfer the stuffed potatoes back to the air fryer basket and air-fry at 360 degrees F/ 180 degrees C for 10 minutes. Spread the Cheddar cheese on top of each stuffed potato, lower the heat to 330 degrees F/ 165 degrees C and air-fry for an additional minute or two to melt cheese.
Per Serving: Calories 295; Fat 21.2g; Sodium 94mg; Carbs 3g; Fiber 1g; Sugar 1g; Protein 23g

Tangy Green Beans

Prep time: 5 minutes | Cook time: 12 minutes | Serves: 4

1 lb. green beans washed and destemmed
Sea salt and black pepper to taste

1 lemon
¼ teaspoon extra virgin olive oil

1. Select the "AIR FRY" function of Ninja Foodi digital air fry oven, set the temperature to 400 degrees F/ 200 degrees C and set the time to 15 minutes. Press the Start/Pause button and begin preheating. Place the beans in the air fryer. Squeeze lemon over beans and season with salt and pepper. Cover with oil and toss well. Cook green beans for 12-minutes and serve!
Per Serving: Calories 263; Fat 9.2g; Sodium 211mg; Carbs 8.6g; Fiber 2g; Sugar 1g; Protein 8.7g

Cheesy Eggplant

Prep time: 15 minutes | Cook time: 35 minutes | Serves: 4 to 6

1 medium eggplant, cut into slices
kosher salt
½ cup breadcrumbs
2 teaspoons dried parsley
½ teaspoon Italian seasoning
½ teaspoon garlic powder
½ teaspoon onion powder
½ teaspoon salt

freshly ground black pepper
2 tablespoons milk
½ cup mayonnaise
1 cup tomato sauce
1 (14-ounce) can diced tomatoes
1 teaspoon Italian seasoning
2 cups grated mozzarella cheese
½ cup grated Parmesan cheese

1. Lay the eggplant slices on a baking sheet and sprinkle kosher salt generously over the top. Let the eggplant sit for 15 minutes while you prepare the rest of the ingredients. 2. Combine the breadcrumbs with parsley, Italian seasoning, garlic and onion powder, salt and black pepper in a dish. Whisk the milk with mayonnaise in a bowl until smooth. 3. Select the "AIR FRY" function of Ninja Foodi digital air fry oven, set the temperature to 400 degrees F/ 200 degrees C and set the time to 15 minutes. Press the Start/Pause button and begin preheating. 4. Brush off salt from the eggplant slices and then coat both sides of each slice with the mayonnaise mixture. Dip the eggplant into the breadcrumbs. Place the eggplant on a Ninja sheet pan and grease both sides with olive oil. Air-fry the eggplant slices for 15 minutes, turning halfway through the cooking time. 5. While the eggplant is cooking, prepare the components of the eggplant Parmesan. Mix the tomato sauce, diced tomatoes and Italian seasoning in a bowl. Combine the mozzarella and Parmesan cheeses in a second bowl. 6. When all of the eggplant cooked build the dish with all the ingredient components. Cover the bottom of a 1½-quart round sheet pan (6-inches in diameter) with a few tablespoons of the tomato sauce mixture. Top with one third of the eggplant, tomato sauce and cheese. Repeat two more times, finishing with cheese on top. Cover with foil and Air-fry at 350 degrees F/ 175 degrees C for 30 minutes. Remove the foil and air-fry for an additional 5 minutes to brown the cheese on top. Let the eggplant Parmesan rest for a few minutes to set up and cool to an edible temperature before serving.
Per Serving: Calories 184; Fat 7.4g; Sodium 103mg; Carbs 7g; Fiber 1g; Sugar 1g; Protein 22g

Spicy Tahini Kale

Prep time: 5 minutes | Cook time: 15 minutes | Serves: 2 to 4

¼ cup tahini
¼ cup fresh lemon juice
2 tablespoons olive oil
1 teaspoon sesame seeds
½ teaspoon garlic powder

¼ teaspoon cayenne pepper
4 cups packed torn kale leaves
Kosher salt and freshly ground black pepper

1 Select the "AIR FRY" function of Ninja Foodi digital air fry oven, set the temperature to 350 degrees F/ 175 degrees C and set the time to 15 minutes. Press the Start/Pause button and begin preheating In a bowl, whisk the tahini, lemon juice, olive oil, sesame seeds, garlic powder, and cayenne until smooth. Add the kale leaves, season with salt and black pepper, and toss in the dressing until completely coated. Transfer the kale leaves to a 7-inch round cake or pizza pan, metal cake pan, or foil pan. 2. Place in the air fryer and cook stirring every 5 minutes, until the kale wilted and the top is lightly browned, about 15 minutes. Serve warm.
Per Serving: Calories 300; Fat 24g; Sodium 117mg; Carbs 3g; Fiber 3g; Sugar 2g; Protein 18g

Chia Oat Porridge

Prep time: 5 minutes | Cook time: 5 minutes | Serves: 4

2 tablespoons peanut butter
2 teaspoons liquid Stevia
1 tablespoon butter, melted
4 cups milk
2 cups oats
1 cup chia seeds

1. Select the "AIR FRY" function of Ninja Foodi digital air fry oven, set the temperature to 390 degrees F/ 200 degrees C and set the time to 5 minutes. Press the Start/Pause button and begin preheating. 2. Whisk the peanut butter, butter, milk and Stevia in a bowl. Stir in the oats and chia seeds. Pour the mixture into an oven-proof bowl and place in the air fryer and cook for 5-minutes.
Per Serving: Calories 228; Fat 11.4g; Sodium 389mg; Carbs 10.2g; Fiber 5g; Sugar 4g; Protein 14.5g

Mushroom, Zucchini and Bean Burgers

Prep time: 10 minutes | Cook time: 15 minutes | Serves: 4

1 cup diced zucchini, (about ½ medium zucchini)
1 tablespoon olive oil
salt and freshly ground black pepper
1 cup chopped brown mushrooms (about 3 ounces)
1 small clove garlic
1 (15-ounce) can black beans, drained and rinsed
1 teaspoon lemon zest
1 tablespoon chopped fresh cilantro
½ cup plain breadcrumbs
1 egg, beaten
½ teaspoon salt
freshly ground black pepper
whole-wheat pita bread, burger buns or brioche buns
mayonnaise, tomato, avocado and lettuce, for serving

1. Select the "AIR FRY" function of Ninja Foodi digital air fry oven, set the temperature to 400 degrees F/ 200 degrees C and set the time to 6 minutes. Press the Start/Pause button and begin preheating. 2. Toss the zucchini with the olive oil, season with salt and freshly ground black pepper and air-fry for 6 minutes, shaking the basket once or twice while it cooks. 3. Transfer the zucchini to a food processor with the mushrooms, garlic and black beans and process until still a little chunky but broken down and pasty. Transfer the mixture to a bowl. Add the lemon zest, cilantro, breadcrumbs and egg and mix well. Spice with salt and ground black pepper. Shape the mixture into four burger patties and refrigerate for at least 15 minutes. 4. Transfer two of the veggie burgers to the air fryer basket and air-fry for 12 minutes, flipping the burgers gently halfway through the cooking time. Keep the burgers warm by loosely tenting them with foil while you cook the remaining two burgers. Return the first batch of burgers back into the air fryer with the second batch for the last two minutes of cooking to re-heat. 5. Serve on toasted whole-wheat pita bread, burger buns or brioche buns with some mayonnaise, tomato, avocado and lettuce.
Per Serving: Calories 314; Fat 27.2g; Sodium 182mg; Carbs 0g; Fiber 0g; Sugar 0g; Protein 17g

Low-Carb Tofu Fried Cauliflower Rice

Prep time: 10 minutes | Cook time: 20 minutes | Serves: 3

For The Tofu
½ block firm tofu
½ cup chopped onion
1 teaspoon turmeric
For The Cauliflower
½ cup frozen peas
½ cup chopped broccoli
1 tablespoon rice vinegar
1 tablespoon ginger, minced
1 cup chopped carrot
2 tablespoons low salt soy sauce

1 ½ teaspoons sesame oil, toasted
2 minced garlic cloves
2 tablespoons low salt soy sauce
3 cups riced cauliflower

1. Select the "AIR FRY" function of Ninja Foodi digital air fry oven, set the temperature to 370 degrees F/ 185 degrees C and set the time to 12 minutes. Press the Start/Pause button and begin preheating. Using a mixing bowl, add in the tofu and crumble then pour in the remaining for the tofu and incorporate together. 2. Transfer the coated tofu into the fryer basket then fry for 10 minutes at 370 degrees F/ 185 degrees C. 3. In the meantime, add all the cauliflower together and incorporate until mixed the transfer into the fryer basket after the 10 minutes of initial cooking. 4. Shake the fryer basket together then continue to fry for an extra 10 minutes, shaking just once mid cook time. 5. Check for desired doneness and add an extra 2- minutes of cook time if required. 6. Serve and enjoy as desired.
Per Serving: Calories 263; Fat 6g; Sodium 200mg; Carbs 28.3g; Fiber 11g; Sugar 10g; Protein 13g

Potato & Cauliflower Stuffed Turnovers

Prep time: 10 minutes | Cook time: 35 minutes | Serves: 4

Dough:
2 cups all-purpose flour
½ teaspoon baking powder
1 teaspoon salt
Turnover Filling:
1 tablespoon canola or vegetable oil
1 onion, finely chopped
1 clove garlic, minced
1 tablespoon grated fresh ginger
½ teaspoon cumin seeds
½ teaspoon fennel seeds
1 teaspoon curry powder
2 russet potatoes, diced
freshly ground black pepper
¼ teaspoon dried thyme
¼ cup canola oil
½ to ⅔ cup water

2 cups cauliflower florets
½ cup frozen peas
2 tablespoons chopped fresh cilantro
salt and freshly ground black pepper
2 tablespoons butter, melted
mango chutney, for serving

1. Start by making the dough. Mix the flour along with baking powder, salt, pepper and dried thyme in a mixing bowl or the bowl of a stand mixer. Drizzle in the canola oil and pinch it together with your fingers to turn the flour into a crumby mixture. Stir in the water. Knead it for 5 minutes until it is smooth. Let the dough rest while you make the turnover filling. 2. Pre-heat a large skillet on the stovetop over medium-high heat. Add the oil and sauté the onion until it starts to become tender – about 4 minutes. Add the garlic, ginger and cook for another minute. Add the dried spices and toss everything to coat. Add the potatoes and cauliflower to the skillet and pour in 1½ cups of water. Simmer everything together for 20 to 25 minutes, or until the potatoes are soft and most of the water has evaporated. Stir well, crushing the potatoes and cauliflower a little as you do so. Stir in the peas and cilantro, season to taste with salt and freshly ground black pepper and set aside to cool. 3. Divide the dough into 4 balls. Roll the dough balls out into ¼-inch thick circles. Divide the cooled potato filling between the dough circles, placing an empty border around the edge of the dough. Wet the dough edges with water and fold one edge of the circle over to meet the other edge of the circle, creating a half moon. Pinch the edges together with your fingers and then press the edge with the tines of a fork to decorate and seal. 4. Select the "AIR FRY" function of Ninja Foodi digital air fry oven, set the temperature to 380 degrees F/ 195 degrees C and set the time to 15 minutes. Press the Start/Pause button and begin preheating. 5. Spray or brush the air fryer basket with oil. Brush the turnovers with the melted butter and place 2 turnovers into the air fryer basket. Air-fry for 15 minutes. Flip the turnovers over and air-fry for another 5 minutes. Repeat with the remaining 2 turnovers. 6. Serving warm with mango chutney.
Per Serving: Calories 144; Fat 6.6g; Sodium 171mg; Carbs 2g; Fiber 0g; Sugar 1g; Protein 19g

Hasselback Potatoes with Sour Cream and Pesto

Prep time: 15 minutes | Cook time: 40 minutes | Serves: 2

2 russet potatoes
5 tablespoons olive oil
Kosher salt and freshly ground black pepper
¼ cup roughly chopped fresh chives
2 tablespoons packed fresh flat-
leaf parsley leaves
1 tablespoon chopped walnuts
1 tablespoon grated parmesan cheese
1 teaspoon fresh lemon juice
1 small garlic clove, peeled
¼ cup sour cream

1. Place the potatoes on a hard surface and lay a chopstick or thin-handled wooden spoon to the side of each potato. Thinly slice the potatoes crosswise, letting the chopstick or spoon handle stop the blade of your knife, and stop ½ inch short of each end of the potato. Rub the potatoes with 1 tablespoon of the olive oil and season with salt and pepper. 2. Select the "AIR FRY" function of Ninja Foodi digital air fry oven, set the temperature to 375 degrees F/ 190 degrees C; set the time to 40 minutes. Press the Start/Pause button and begin preheating. Place the potatoes, cut-side up, in the air fryer and cook until golden brown and crisp on the outside and tender inside, about 40 minutes, drizzling the insides with olive oil and spice with salt and pepper halfway through. 3. Meanwhile, in a small blender or food processor, combine the remaining 3 tablespoons olive oil, the walnuts, parmesan, chives, parsley, lemon juice, and garlic and puree until smooth. Season the chive pesto with salt and pepper. 4. Transfer the potatoes to plates. Drizzle the potatoes with the pesto, letting it drip down into the grooves, then dollop each with sour cream and serve hot.
Per Serving: Calories 143; Fat 7.5g; Sodium 5mg; Carbs 19g; Fiber 3g; Sugar 3g; Protein 3g

Chili-Roasted Broccoli

Prep time: 5 minutes | Cook time: 15 minutes | Serves: 2

12 ounces broccoli florets
2 tablespoons Asian hot chili oil
1 teaspoon ground Sichuan peppercorns
2 garlic cloves, chopped

One ginger, peeled and finely chopped
Kosher salt and freshly ground black pepper

1. Select the "AIR FRY" function of Ninja Foodi digital air fry oven, set the temperature to 375 degrees F/ 190 degrees C and set the time to 10 minutes. Press the Start/Pause button and begin preheating. In a bowl, toss together the broccoli, chili oil, Sichuan peppercorns, garlic, ginger, and salt and black pepper to taste. 2. Transfer to the air fryer basket and cook, shaking the basket halfway through, until lightly charred and tender, about 10 minutes. Serve warm.
Per Serving: Calories 722; Fat 39g; Sodium 140mg; Carbs 7g; Fiber 2g; Sugar 4g; Protein 18g

Spicy-and-Sour Brussels Sprouts

Prep time: 10 minutes | Cook time: 25 minutes | Serves: 2

¼ cup Thai sweet chili sauce
2 tablespoons black vinegar or balsamic vinegar
½ teaspoon hot sauce, such as Tabasco
8 ounces Brussels sprouts, trimmed (large sprouts halved)

2 small shallots, cut into ¼-inch-thick slices
Kosher salt and freshly ground black pepper
2 teaspoons lightly packed fresh cilantro leaves

1. Select the "AIR FRY" function of Ninja Foodi digital air fry oven, set the temperature to 375 degrees F/ 190 degrees C and set the time to 20 minutes. Press the Start/Pause button and begin preheating. In a bowl, whisk the chili sauce, vinegar, and hot sauce. Add the Brussels sprouts and shallots, season with salt and pepper, and toss to combine. Scrape the Brussels sprouts and sauce into a 7-inch round cake pan, metal cake pan, or foil pan. 2. Place in the Ninja air fryer and cook, stirring every 5 minutes, until and the sauce reduced to a sticky glaze, about 20 minutes. 3. Transfer the Brussels sprouts to plates. Sprinkle with the cilantro and serve warm.
Per Serving: Calories 153; Fat 39g; Sodium 108mg; Carbs 25g; Fiber 6g; Sugar 2g; Protein 37g

Caesar Cauliflower

Prep time: 15 minutes | Cook time: 30 minutes | Serves: 2 to 4

3 tablespoons olive oil
2 tablespoons red wine vinegar
2 tablespoons Worcestershire sauce
2 tablespoons grated parmesan cheese
1 tablespoon Dijon mustard
4 garlic cloves, minced
4 oil-packed anchovy fillets,

drained and finely minced
Kosher salt and freshly ground black pepper
1 small head cauliflower (about 1 pound), green leaves trimmed and stem trimmed flush with the bottom of the head
1 tablespoon roughly chopped fresh flat-leaf parsley

1. Select the "AIR FRY" function of Ninja Foodi digital air fry oven, set the temperature to 340 degrees F/ 170 degrees C and set the time to 25 minutes. Press the Start/Pause button and begin preheating. In a liquid measuring cup, whisk together the olive oil, vinegar, Worcestershire, parmesan, mustard, garlic, anchovies, and salt and pepper to taste. Place the cauliflower head upside down on a cutting board and use a paring knife to make an "x" through the full length of the core. Transfer the cauliflower head to a large bowl and pour half the dressing over it. Turn the cauliflower head to coat it in the dressing, then let it rest, stem-side up, in the dressing for 10 minutes and up to 30 minutes to allow the dressing to seep into all its nooks and crannies. 2. Transfer the cauliflower head, stem-side down, to the air fryer in sheet pan and cook for 25 minutes. Drizzle the remaining dressing over the cauliflower and cook at 400 degrees F/ 200 degrees C until the top of the cauliflower is golden brown and the core is tender, about 5 minutes more. 3. Remove the basket from the air fryer and transfer the cauliflower to a large plate. Sprinkle with the parsley, if you like, and serve hot.
Per Serving: Calories 18; Fat 7.9g; Sodium 704mg; Carbs 6g; Fiber 3.6g; Sugar 6g; Protein 18g

Cheese Soufflés with Asparagus and Mushroom

Prep time: 7 minutes | Cook time: 14 minutes | Serves: 3

butter
grated Parmesan cheese
3 button mushrooms, thinly sliced
8 spears asparagus, sliced ½-inch long
1 teaspoon olive oil
1 tablespoon butter
4½ teaspoons flour
pinch paprika

pinch ground nutmeg
salt and freshly ground black pepper
½ cup milk
½ cup grated Gruyère cheese or other Swiss cheese (about 2 ounces)
2 eggs, separated

1. Butter three 6-ounce ramekins and dust with grated Parmesan cheese. 2. Select the "AIR FRY" function of Ninja Foodi digital air fry oven, set the temperature to 400 degrees F/ 200 degrees C and set the time to 7 minutes. Press the Start/Pause button and begin preheating. 3.Toss the mushrooms and asparagus in a bowl with the olive oil. Transfer the vegetables to the air fryer and air-fry for 7 minutes, shaking the basket once or twice to redistribute the ingredients while they cook .4. While the vegetables are cooking, make the soufflé base. Add the melted butter in flour, stir and cook for a minute or two. Add the paprika, nutmeg, salt and pepper. Whisk the milk in and manage to a simmer to thicken. Stir in the cheese, to melt. Let the mix cool for few minutes and then whisk the egg yolks in, one at a time. Stir in the cooked mushrooms and asparagus. Let this soufflé base cool. 5. In a bowl, whisk the egg whites till soft peak stage. Fold the whipped egg whites into the soufflé base, adding a little at a time. 6. Transfer the batter carefully to the buttered ramekins, leaving about ½-inch at the top. Place the ramekins in the air fryer and air-fry for 14 minutes. The soufflés should have risen nicely and be brown on top. Serve immediately.
Per Serving: Calories 543; Fat 38.1g; Sodium 134mg; Carbs 27g; Fiber 1g; Sugar 0g; Protein 23g

Charred Sweet Potatoes

Prep time: 5 minutes | Cook time: 20 minutes | Serves: 2

4 small sweet potatoes, scrubbed clean (3 ounces each)
2 tablespoons olive oil
Kosher salt and freshly ground black pepper

2 tablespoons honey
½ teaspoon smoked paprika
Smoked or regular sea salt, for serving

1. Select the "AIR FRY" function of Ninja Foodi digital air fry oven, set the temperature to 375 degrees F/ 190 degrees C and set the time to 20 minutes. Press the Start/Pause button and begin preheating. In a bowl, toss together the sweet potatoes and olive oil, spice with salt and pepper, and toss again to coat evenly. Transfer the sweet potatoes to the air fryer and cook, flipping halfway through, until tender on the inside and the skins are crisp and slightly blistered, about 20 minutes. 2. In a bowl, mix the honey and smoked paprika. 3. When the potatoes are done, split them down the middle like a baked potato and lightly press the ends toward the middle to expose the flesh. Transfer to plates, drizzle with the paprika honey, and sprinkle with the smoked salt before serving.
Per Serving: Calories 365; Fat 12.4g; Sodium 717mg; Carbs 29g; Fiber 3g; Sugar 10g; Protein 19g

Curried Cauliflower with Sultanas

Prep time: 10 minutes | Cook time: 10 minutes | Serves: 4

¼ cup sultanas or golden raisins
¼ teaspoon salt
1 tablespoon curry powder
1 head cauliflower, broken into

small florets
¼ cup pine nuts
½ cup olive oil

1. In a cup of boiling water, soak your sultanas to plump. Select the "AIR FRY" function of Ninja Foodi digital air fry oven, set the temperature to 350 degrees F/ 175 degrees C and set the time to 10 minutes. Press the Start/Pause button and begin preheating. 2. Add oil and pine nuts to air fryer and toast for a minute or so. In a bowl, toss the cauliflower and curry powder as well as salt, then add the mix to air fryer mixing well. Cook for 10-minutes. 3. Drain the sultanas, toss with cauliflower, and serve.
Per Serving: Calories 275; Fat 11.3g; Sodium 511mg; Carbs 8.6g; Fiber 2g; Sugar 1g; Protein 9.5g

Maitake Mushrooms with Sesame

Prep time: 10 minutes | Cook time: 15 minutes | Serves: 2

1 tablespoon soy sauce
3 teaspoons vegetable oil
2 teaspoons toasted sesame oil
1 garlic clove, minced
7 ounces maitake mushrooms

½ teaspoon flaky sea salt
½ teaspoon sesame seeds
½ teaspoon finely chopped fresh thyme leaves

1. Select the "AIR FRY" function of Ninja Foodi digital air fry oven, set the temperature to 300 degrees F/ 150 degrees C and set the time to 15 minutes. Press the Start/Pause button and begin preheating. In a bowl, mix soy sauce with 1 teaspoon of the vegetable oil, the sesame oil, and garlic. Place the maitake mushrooms in more or less a single layer in the air fryer, then drizzle with the soy sauce mixture. 2. Cook for 10 minutes. Sprinkle with the sea salt, sesame seeds, and thyme, then drizzle with the remaining 2 teaspoons vegetable oil. Cook until the mushrooms are crisp at the edges and tender inside, about 5 minutes more. 3. Remove the mushrooms from the air fryer, transfer to plates, and serve hot.
Per Serving: Calories 605; Fat 31g; Sodium 833mg; Carbs 51g; Fiber 6g; Sugar 5g; Protein 74g

Zucchini with Kimchi Sauce

Prep time: 10 minutes | Cook time: 20 minutes | Serves: 2

2 medium zucchini, ends trimmed (about 6 ounces each)
2 tablespoons olive oil
½ cup kimchi, finely chopped
¼ cup finely chopped fresh cilantro
¼ cup chopped parsley

2 tablespoons rice vinegar
2 teaspoons Asian chili-garlic sauce
1 teaspoon grated fresh ginger
Kosher salt and freshly ground black pepper

1. Select the "AIR FRY" function of Ninja Foodi digital air fry oven, set the temperature to 400 degrees F/ 200 degrees C and set the time to 15 minutes. Press the Start/Pause button and begin preheating. Brush the zucchini with half of the olive oil, place in the air fryer, and cook, turning halfway through, until lightly charred on the outside and tender, about 15 minutes. 2. In a bowl, mix the oil, with kimchi, cilantro, parsley, vinegar, chili-garlic sauce, and ginger. 3. Once the zucchini is finished cooking, transfer it to a colander and let it cool for 5 minutes. Using your fingers, pinch and break the zucchini into bite-size pieces, letting them fall back into the colander. Season the zucchini with salt and pepper, toss to combine, then let sit a further 5 minutes to allow some of its liquid to drain. Pile the zucchini atop the kimchi sauce on a plate and sprinkle with more parsley to serve.
Per Serving: Calories 718; Fat 23g; Sodium 964mg; Carbs 8g; Fiber 5g; Sugar 2g; Protein 37g

Vegetable Spring Rolls

Prep time: 10 minutes | Cook time: 23 minutes | Serves: 10

10 spring roll wrappers
2 tablespoons cornstarch
Water
3 green onions, thinly sliced
1 tablespoon black pepper
1 teaspoon soy sauce
Pinches of salt
2 tablespoons cooking oil
8-cloves of garlic, minced

½ bell pepper, cut into thin matchsticks
2 large onions, cut into thin matchsticks
1 large carrot, cut into thin matchsticks
2 cups cabbage, shredded
2-inch piece of ginger, grated

1. To prepare the filling: add to a large bowl the carrot, bell pepper, onion, cabbage, ginger, and garlic. Gently add two tablespoons of olive oil in a pan over high heat. Add the filling mixture and stir in salt and a dash of stevia sweetener if you like. Cook for 3-minutes. Add soy sauce, black pepper and mix well. 2. Add green onions, stir and set aside. In a small bowl, combine enough water and cornstarch to make a creamy paste. Fill the rolls with a tablespoon of filling in center of each wrapper and roll tightly, dampening the edges with cornstarch paste to ensure a good seal. Repeat until all done. 3.Select the "AIR FRY" function of Ninja Foodi digital air fry oven, set the temperature to 350 degrees F/ 175 degrees C and set the time to 20 minutes. Press the Start/Pause button and begin preheating. Brush the rolls with oil, and arrange them in the air fryer, and cook them until crisp and golden for about 20-minutes. Halfway through the cook time flip them over.
Per Serving: Calories 263; Fat 11.2g; Sodium 218mg; Carbs 8.6g; Fiber 1.6g; Sugar 2.3g; Protein 8.2g

Sweet Roasted Tomatoes

Prep time: 5 minutes | Cook time: 20 minutes | Serves: 2

10 ounces cherry tomatoes, halved
Kosher salt
2 tablespoons maple syrup
1 tablespoon vegetable oil

2 sprigs fresh thyme, stems removed
1 garlic clove, minced
Freshly ground black pepper

1. Select the "AIR FRY" function of Ninja Foodi digital air fry oven, set the temperature to 325 degrees F/ 160 degrees C and set the time to 20 minutes. Press the Start/Pause button and begin preheating. Place the tomatoes in a colander and sprinkle liberally with salt. Let stand for 10 minutes to drain. 2. Transfer the tomatoes cut-side up to a 7-inch round cake pan then drizzle with the maple syrup, followed by the oil. Sprinkle with the thyme leaves and garlic and season with pepper. Place it in the air fryer and cook until the tomatoes are soft, collapsed, and lightly caramelized on top, about 20 minutes. 3. Serve with the tomatoes to a plate and drizzle with the juices from the pan to serve.
Per Serving: Calories 240; Fat 4.3g; Sodium 278mg; Carbs 47g; Fiber 7g; Sugar 3g; Protein 6g

Sweet and Savory Roast Carrots

Prep time: 1 minutes | Cook time: 25 minutes | Serves: 2

1½ tablespoons agave syrup or honey
1 tablespoon soy sauce
1 tablespoon vegetable oil
¼ teaspoon crushed red chile flakes
¼ teaspoon ground coriander

¼ teaspoon freshly ground black pepper
1 pound carrots, peeled and cut on an angle into ½-inch-thick slices
1 tablespoon finely chopped fresh flat-leaf parsley

1. Select the "AIR FRY" function of Ninja Foodi digital air fry oven, set the temperature to 375 degrees F/ 190 degrees C and set the time to 20 minutes. Press the Start/Pause button and begin preheating. In a bowl, combine the agave syrup, soy sauce, oil, chile flakes, coriander, black pepper, and carrots and toss to coat evenly. Transfer the carrots and dressing to a 7-inch round cake pan. 2. Place in the air fryer and cook stirring every 5 minutes, until the dressing is reduced to a glaze and the carrots are lightly caramelized and tender, about 20 minutes. 3. Sprinkle with the parsley before serving.
Per Serving: Calories 232; Fat 8.5g; Sodium 465mg; Carbs 38g; Fiber 1g; Sugar 15g; Protein 2g

Tropical Coconut Chips

Prep time: 10 minutes | Cook time: 5 minutes | Serves: 2

2 cups large pieces of shredded coconut

⅓ teaspoon liquid Stevia
1 tablespoon chili powder

1. Select the "AIR FRY" function of Ninja Foodi digital air fry oven, set the temperature to 375 degrees F/ 190 degrees C and set the time to 5 minutes. Press the Start/Pause button and begin preheating. Combine the shredded coconut pieces with spices. Cook for 5-minutes in air fryer and enjoy!
Per Serving: Calories 261; Fat 9.2g; Sodium 784mg; Carbs 7.3g; Fiber 1g; Sugar 2g; Protein 6.2g

Cheese & Mushroom Frittata

Prep time: 10 minutes | Cook time: 30 minutes | Serves: 4

1 red onion, thinly sliced
4 cups button mushrooms, thinly sliced
Salt to taste
6 tablespoons feta cheese,

crumbled
6 medium eggs
Non-stick cooking spray
2 tablespoons olive oil

1. Sauté the onion and mushrooms in olive oil over medium heat until the vegetables are tender. 2. Remove the vegetables from pan and drain on a paper towel-lined plate. In a mixing bowl, whisk eggs and salt. Coat all sides of baking dish with cooking spray. Select the "BAKE" function of Ninja Foodi digital air fry oven, set the temperature to 325 degrees F/ 160 degrees C and set the time to 30 minutes. Press the Start/Pause button and begin preheating. 3. Pour the beaten eggs into prepared baking dish and scatter the sautéed vegetables and crumble feta on top. Bake in the air fryer for 30-minutes. Allow to cool slightly and serve!
Per Serving: Calories 226; Fat 9.3g; Sodium 324mg; Carbs 8.7g; Fiber 3g; Sugar 2g; Protein 12.6g

Crispy-Bottom Rice with Currants and Pistachios

Prep time: 10 minutes | Cook time: 25 minutes | Serves: 2

1 tablespoon olive oil
¼ teaspoon ground turmeric
2 cups cooked white basmati, jasmine, or other long-grain rice
¼ cup dried currants
¼ cup roughly chopped pistachios
Kosher salt and freshly ground black pepper
1 tablespoon thinly sliced fresh cilantro

1. Select the "AIR FRY" function of Ninja Foodi digital air fry oven, set the temperature to 300 degrees F/ 150 degrees C and set the time to 25 minutes. Press the Start/Pause button and begin preheating. Combine the olive oil and turmeric in the bottom of a 7-inch round cake pan. 2. In a bowl, combine the rice, currants, and pistachios, season with salt and pepper, then spoon the rice over the oil, making sure to not stir the oil up into the rice. Very gently press the rice into an even layer. 3. Place the pan in the air fryer and cook until the rice is warmed through and the bottom is toasted and crispy, 20 to 25 minutes. 4. Break up the crust on the bottom of the rice, sprinkle with the cilantro, and serve warm.
Per Serving: Calories 567; Fat 16.3g; Sodium 478mg; Carbs 19g; Fiber 14g; Sugar 6g; Protein 18g

Spring Onion Pancake

Prep time: 10 minutes | Cook time: 15 minutes | Serves: 6

1 cup almond flour
¾ cup boiling water
¼ cup cold water
½ cup spring onion, chopped
1 teaspoon sea salt
Olive oil as needed

1. Pour boiling water into a bowl and mix with almond flour using a spatula. Pour in cold water and knead the pancake mix. Brush oil over the dough and cover with cling wrap and leave to rest for 1 hour. 2. After resting the dough should have a smooth, shiny look to it. The gluten in the dough also makes it more elastic and stretchable. Divide the dough into four equal parts. 3. Flatten each part with hands. Brush oil over dough and sprinkle with onion and salt. Gently press the onion into dough. Roll dough into a barrel shape. Roll to elongate dough. 4. Coil the dough into a spiral and coat it with the last coating of coil. Leave it on a plate covered with cling wrap for an hour to rest. Gently press the spiral pancake flat. Select the "AIR FRY" function of Ninja Foodi digital air fry oven, set the temperature to 365 degrees F/ 185 degrees C and set the time to 15 minutes. Press the Start/Pause button and begin preheating. Cook the pancake for 15-minutes and serve warm.
Per Serving: Calories 228; Fat 11.2g; Sodium 541mg; Carbs 10.3g; Fiber 4g; Sugar 2g; Protein 13.2g

Asian Samosas

Prep time: 15 minutes | Cook time: 20 minutes | Serves: 4

2 cups all-purpose flour
½ teaspoon cumin seeds
2 tablespoons olive oil
1 teaspoon turmeric
1 teaspoon chili powder
1 teaspoon ginger-garlic paste
2 teaspoons garam masala powder
½ cup green peas
2 russet potatoes, peeled and cubed
1 teaspoon carom seeds
2 teaspoons ghee butter

1. Prepare the crust in a bowl, combining the carom seeds, flour, water as needed to make a dough. Knead dough and chill in the fridge for 30-minutes. Prepare the filling: in a saucepan, cover the potatoes with water and bring to a boil. Add peas and continue to boil until vegetables are tender. Drain and mash well. Add the garam masala, ginger-garlic paste, chili powder, and turmeric to potato mixture. Season with salt and mix well. In a small pan sauté oil over medium heat. Add the cumin seeds and toast they are sizzling and aromatic. Add the cumin to potato mixture, mix well, then set aside. Retrieve the dough out of the fridge, roll it out on the counter, and cut into several squares about 4-inches across. Place a spoonful of filling in each square and fold samosa to a triangle-like shape, carefully sealing edges. Select the "AIR FRY" function of Ninja Foodi digital air fry oven, set the temperature to 350 degrees F/ 175 degrees C and set the time to 20 minutes. Press the Start/Pause button and begin preheating. 3. Brush the samosas with oil, place them into air fryer, cook them until they are golden brown for about 20-minutes and serve warm or cold.
Per Serving: Calories 253; Fat 11.3g; Sodium 411mg; Carbs 8.6g; Fiber 1g; Sugar 2g; Protein 7.2g

Zucchini Carrot Muffins

Prep time: 5 minutes | Cook time: 14 minutes | Serves: 4

2 tablespoons butter, melted
¼ cup carrots, shredded
½ cup zucchini, shredded
1 ½ cups almond flour
1 tablespoon liquid Stevia
2 teaspoons baking powder
Pinch of salt
3 eggs
1 tablespoon yogurt
1 cup milk

1. Select the "AIR FRY" function of Ninja Foodi digital air fry oven, set the temperature to 350 degrees F/ 175 degrees C and set the time to 15 minutes. Press the Start/Pause button and begin preheating. Beat the eggs, yogurt, milk, salt, pepper, baking soda, and Stevia. Whisk in the flour gradually. 2. Add zucchini and carrots. Grease muffin tins with butter and pour muffin batter into tins. Cook for 14-minutes and serve.
Per Serving: Calories 224; Fat 12.3g; Sodium 458mg; Carbs 11.2g; Fiber 2g; Sugar 1g; Protein 14.2g

Vegetable Hash Browns

Prep time: 10 minutes | Cook time: 19 minutes | Serves: 8

4 large potatoes, peeled, shredded
1 teaspoon onion powder
1 teaspoon garlic powder
2 teaspoons chili flakes
Salt and pepper to taste
2 tablespoons corn flour
2 teaspoons olive oil
Cooking spray as needed

1. Wash potatoes thoroughly. Add a teaspoon of olive oil into skillet and cook potatoes over medium heat for 4-minutes. 2. Place potatoes on plate to cool once they are cooked. In a large mixing bowl, add flour, potatoes, salt, pepper and other seasonings and combine well. Place bowl in fridge for 20-minutes. 3. Select the "AIR FRY" function of Ninja Foodi digital air fry oven, set the temperature to 350 degrees F/ 175 degrees C and set the time to 15 minutes. Press the Start/Pause button and begin preheating. Remove hash browns from fridge and cut into size pieces you desire. Spray the wire basket of your air fryer with some oil, add the hash browns and fry them for 15-minutes. 4. Halfway through flip them to help cook them all over. Serve hot!
Per Serving: Calories 242; Fat 13.1g; Sodium 269mg; Carbs 9.6g; Fiber 2g; Sugar 1g; Protein 14.2g

Mushroom Croissant Bake

Prep time: 10 minutes | Cook time: 8 minutes | Serves: 1

1 croissant, sliced in half crosswise
½ sprig rosemary, chopped
1 large egg
Salt and pepper to taste
3 cherry tomatoes, halved
1 ½ ounces of cheddar cheese, shredded
4 small button mushrooms, quartered
Handful of salad greens
Butter for greasing baking dish

1. Prepare baking dish by greasing it with butter. Arrange all the ingredients in two layers in baking dish except for salad greens and croissant. 2. Crack egg into baking dish, add mushrooms and cheese on the top then season with salt, pepper, and rosemary. 3. Select the "BAKE" function of Ninja Foodi digital air fry oven, set the temperature to 325 degrees F/ 160 degrees C and set the time to 8 minutes. Press the Start/Pause button and begin preheating. Bake for 8-minutes and then assemble your breakfast sandwich and enjoy!
Per Serving: Calories 223; Fat 10.2g; Sodium 211mg; Carbs 9.4g; Fiber 2g; Sugar 2g; Protein 14.3g

Healthy Parsnip Fries

Prep time: 10 minutes | Cook time: 12 minutes | Serves: 2

2 tablespoons of olive oil
A pinch of sea salt
1 large bunch of parsnips

1. Wash and peel the parsnips, then cut them into strips. Place the parsnips in a bowl with the olive oil and sea salt and coat well. 2. Select the "AIR FRY" function of Ninja Foodi digital air fry oven, set the temperature to 360 degrees F/ 180 degrees C and set the time to 12 minutes. Press the Start/Pause button and begin preheating. Place the parsnip and oil mixture into the air fryer basket. Cook for 12-minutes. Serve with sour cream or ketchup.
Per Serving: Calories 262; Fat 11.3g; Sodium 369mg; Carbs 10.4g; Fiber 2g; Sugar 1g; Protein 7.2g

Spiced Squash

Prep time: 10 minutes | Cook time: 20 minutes | Serves: 4

1 medium butternut squash
1 bunch coriander
⅔ cup Greek yogurt
¼ cup pine nuts
1 tablespoon olive oil
1 pinch chili flakes
2 teaspoons cumin seeds
Salt and pepper to taste

1. Select the "AIR ROAST" function of Ninja Foodi digital air fry oven, set the temperature to 380 degrees F/ 195 degrees C and set the time to 20 minutes. Press the Start/Pause button and begin preheating. Slice the squash into small chunks. Mix the spices and oil in a baking pan. Roast the squash in your air fryer for 20-minutes. Toast the pine nuts and serve with Greek yogurt and sprinkle coriander on top.
Per Serving: Calories 252; Fat 10.3g; Sodium 277mg; Carbs 7.6g; Fiber 3g; Sugar 4g; Protein 8.7g

Veggie and Feta Frittata

Prep time: 10 minutes | Cook time: 30 minutes | Serves: 4

4 cups button mushrooms
1 red onion
2 tablespoons olive oil
6 tablespoons feta cheese,
crumbled
Pinch of salt
6 eggs
Cooking spray

1. Slice the onion into ¼ inch thin slices. Cut mushroom into ¼ inch thin slices. Add oil to pan and sauté mushrooms until tender. 2. Remove from heat and pan so that they can cool. Select the "AIR FRY" function of Ninja Foodi digital air fry oven, set the temperature to 330 degrees F/ 165 degrees C and set the time to 30 minutes. Press the Start/Pause button and begin preheating. Add cracked eggs into a bowl, and whisk them, adding a pinch of salt. Coat an 8-inch heat resistant baking dish with cooking spray. 3. Add the eggs into the small casserole dish, then veggies mixture, and then add cheese. Place the dish into air fryer for 30-minutes and serve warm.
Per Serving: Calories 246; Fat 12.3g; Sodium 114mg; Carbs 9.2g; Fiber 4g; Sugar 2g; Protein 10.3g

Bacon, & Tomato Sandwiches

Prep time: 10 minutes | Cook time: 5 minutes | Serves: 4

8-ounce package tempeh
1 cup warm vegetable broth
Tomato slices and lettuce, to serve
¼ teaspoon chipotle chili powder
½ teaspoon garlic powder
½ teaspoon onion powder
1 teaspoon Liquid smoke
3 tablespoons soy sauce

1. Select the "AIR FRY" function of Ninja Foodi digital air fry oven, set the temperature to 360 degrees F/ 180 degrees C and set the time to 5 minutes. Press the Start/Pause button and begin preheating. Begin by opening the packet of tempeh and slice into pieces about ¼ inch thick. Grab a medium bowl and add the remaining except for lettuce and tomato and stir well. 2. Place the pieces of tempeh onto a baking tray that will fit into your air fryer and pour over the flavor mix. Put the tray in air fryer and cook for 5-minutes. 3. Remove from air fryer and place on sliced bread with the tomato and lettuce and any other extra toppings you desire.
Per Serving: Calories 265; Fat 11.3g; Sodium 188mg; Carbs 9.2g; Fiber 1g; Sugar 1g; Protein 12.4g

Indian Onion Pakora

Prep time: 10 minutes | Cook time: 6 minutes | Serves: 6

1 cup graham flour
¼ teaspoon turmeric powder
Salt to taste
⅛ teaspoon chili powder
¼ teaspoon carom
1 tablespoon fresh coriander,
chopped
2 green chili peppers, finely chopped
4 onions, finely chopped
2 teaspoons vegetable oil
¼ cup rice flour

1. Combine the flours and oil in a mixing bowl. Add water as needed to create a dough-like consistency. Add peppers, onions, coriander, carom, chili powder, and turmeric. 2. Select the "AIR FRY" function of Ninja Foodi digital air fry oven, set the temperature to 350 degrees F/ 175 degrees C and set the time to 6 minutes. Press the Start/Pause button and begin preheating. Roll vegetable mixture into small balls, add to the fryer and cook for about 6-minutes. Serve with hot sauce!
Per Serving: Calories 253; Fat 12.2g; Sodium 245mg; Carbs 11.4g; Fiber 3g; Sugar 1g; Protein 7.6g

Semolina Cutlets

Prep time: 10 minutes | Cook time: 23 minutes | Serves: 2

1 cup semolina
Olive oil for frying
Salt and pepper to taste
1 ½ cups of your favorite veggies
5 cups milk

1. Stir and warm the milk in a saucepan over medium heat. Add vegetables when it becomes hot and cook until they are softened for about 3-minutes. Season with salt and pepper. Add the semolina to milk mixture and cook for another 10-minutes. 2. Remove from heat and spread thin across a piece of parchment on a baking sheet, and chill for about 4 hours. Take out the baking sheet from the fridge, cut semolina mixture into cutlets. Select the "AIR FRY" function of Ninja Foodi digital air fry oven, set the temperature to 350 degrees F/ 175 degrees C and set the time to 10 minutes. Press the Start/Pause button and begin preheating. your air fryer to 350 degrees F/ 175 degrees C ahrenheit. Brush the cutlets with oil and bake for 10-minutes in your air fryer and serve with hot sauce!
Per Serving: Calories 252; Fat 11.2g; Sodium 310mg; Carbs 10.3g; Fiber 3g; Sugar 1.5g; Protein 7.3g

Charred Peppers

Prep time: 10 minutes | Cook time: 5 minutes | Serves: 4

20 Shishito peppers
1 teaspoon vegetable oil
Sea salt to taste
1 lemon, juiced

1. Select the "AIR FRY" function of Ninja Foodi digital air fry oven, set the temperature to 390 degrees F/ 200 degrees C and set the time to 5 minutes. Press the Start/Pause button and begin preheating. 2. Toss Shishito peppers with salt and oil adding to the air basket. Air fry for 5-minutes and transfer peppers to bowl. Squeeze lemon juice over peppers and season with coarse sea salt. Serve as finger food.
Per Serving: Calories 243; Fat 8.4g; Sodium 404mg; Carbs 6.3g; Fiber 2g; Sugar 1.5g; Protein 6.2g

Baked Tomatoes with cheese& Pesto sauce

Prep time: 10 minutes | Cook time: 14 minutes | Serves: 4

Pesto:
½ cup fresh parsley and basil, chopped
½ cup Parmesan cheese, grated
Pinch of salt
1 tablespoon olive oil
1 clove garlic, toasted
3 tablespoons pine nuts, toasted

Tomatoes & Feta:
2 Heirloom tomatoes, cut into ½ inch slices
8-ounces feta cheese, cut into ½ inch slices
1 tablespoon olive oil
Pinch of salt
½ cup red onion, sliced paper-thin

1. Prepare the pesto sauce by combining all the pesto excluding olive oil and salt into a food processor. Run the food processor on slow until thick paste forms. Season with salt to taste. 2. Toss tomatoes, feta, and red onion with the olive oil. Briefly, Select the "AIR FRY" function of Ninja Foodi digital air fry oven, set the temperature to 350 degrees F/ 175 degrees C and set the time to 15 minutes. Press the Start/Pause button and begin preheating. 3. Arrange tomato mixture in food tray and cook for 14-minutes. Portion the tomato mixture onto individual serving plates and top with some pesto and serve!
Per Serving: Calories 246; Fat 10.4g; Sodium 368mg; Carbs 8.6g; Fiber 4g; Sugar 4g; Protein 8.4g

Low-Carb Zucchini Roll

Prep time: 5 minutes | Cook time: 5 minutes | Serves: 4

3 zucchinis, sliced thin, lengthwise
Sea salt to taste
1 cup goat cheese
¼ teaspoon black pepper
1 tablespoon olive oil

1. Select the "BAKE" function of Ninja Foodi digital air fry oven, set the temperature to 390 degrees F/ 200 degrees C and set the time to 5 minutes. Press the Start/Pause button and begin preheating. Brush each zucchini strips with olive oil. Mix sea salt and black pepper with goat cheese. Spoon the goat cheese into the middle of each strip of zucchini and roll it up and fasten with a toothpick. Place into air fryer and cook for 5-minutes.
Per Serving: Calories 243; Fat 8.7g; Sodium 647mg; Carbs 6.4g; Fiber 3g; Sugar 1g; Protein 6.5g

Crispy Zucchini Fries & Roasted Garlic Aioli

Prep time: 5 minutes | Cook time: 12 minutes | Serves: 4

Roasted Garlic Aioli:

½ cup mayonnaise	2 tablespoons olive oil
Sea salt and pepper to taste	½ lemon, juiced
1 teaspoon roasted garlic, pureed	

Zucchini Fries:

Sea salt and pepper to taste	1 large zucchini, cut into ½-inch
½ cup almond flour	sticks
2 eggs, beaten	1 tablespoon olive oil
1 cup breadcrumbs	Cooking spray

1. Take three bowls and line them up on the counter. In the first, combine flour, salt, and pepper. Place eggs in the second bowl. Place breadcrumbs combined with salt and pepper in the third bowl. Take zucchini sticks and dip first into flour, then in the eggs, and then into crumbs. Select the "AIR FRY" function of Ninja Foodi digital air fry oven, set the temperature to 400 degrees F/ 200 degrees C and set the time to 12 minutes. Press the Start/Pause button and begin preheating. 2. Cover sticks with cooking spray and layer in the basket. There should be two layers, pointing in opposite. Halfway through the 12-minute cook time rotate and turn the fries and spray with more cooking spray. Prepare the roasted garlic aioli in a medium bowl by mixing mayonnaise, pureed roasted garlic, olive oil and lemon juice. Stir in some pepper and salt. Serve the fries with the roasted garlic aioli and enjoy!
Per Serving: Calories 246; Fat 9.3g; Sodium 489mg; Carbs 8.1g; Fiber 2g; Sugar 3g; Protein 7.4g

Fryer Roasted Asian Broccoli

Prep time: 10 minutes | Cook time: 20 minutes | Serves: 4

⅛ teaspoon kosher salt	1 ½ tablespoons olive oil
⅓ cup roasted peanuts, salted	2 teaspoons honey
1 teaspoon rice vinegar	2 teaspoons sriracha
1-pound broccoli florets	2 tablespoons low-salt soy sauce
1 tablespoon minced garlic	juiced lemon, if desired

1. Select the "AIR FRY" function of Ninja Foodi digital air fry oven, set the temperature to 400 degrees F/ 200 degrees C and set the time to 20 minutes. Press the Start/Pause button and begin preheating. Using a mixing bowl, add in the garlic, olive oil, sea salt, broccoli florets and incorporate together until well coated. 2. Arrange the coated broccoli florets in a single layer in the fryer basket, ensuring enough space as possible. 3. Cook for 20 minutes until golden brown and crispy. 4. In the meantime, combine the rice vinegar, honey, sriracha and soy sauce together using a microwave safe bowl. 5. Once combined microwave the mixture for 15 seconds until mixed and the honey is melted. 6. Serve the prepared broccoli then coat with the vinegar mixture and toss together. 7. Add in the roasted peanuts and stir then top with the juiced lemon. 8. Serve and enjoy as desired.
Per Serving: Calories 187; Fat 12.4g; Sodium 110mg; Carbs 8.9g; Fiber 2g; Sugar 1g; Protein 4.7g

Roast Pumpkin with Balsamic Vinaigrette

Prep time: 10 minutes | Cook time: 20 minutes | Serves: 4

1 butternut pumpkin, cut into	2 ½ tablespoons toasted pine nuts
1-inch slices	Sea salt and pepper to taste
Sprigs of thyme for garnishing	1 ½ tablespoons olive oil
Vinaigrette:	
6 tablespoons olive oil	Sea salt and black pepper to taste
1 tablespoon Dijon mustard	2 tablespoons balsamic vinegar

1. Select the "AIR FRY" function of Ninja Foodi digital air fry oven, set the temperature to 390 degrees F/ 200 degrees C and set the time to 25 minutes. Press the Start/Pause button and begin preheating. Cover the slices of pumpkin with olive oil and season with thyme, salt, and pepper. 2. Select the "AIR FRY" function of Ninja Foodi digital air fry oven, set the temperature to 375 degrees F/ 190 degrees C and set the time to 15 minutes. Press the Start/Pause button and begin preheating. to cook for 20-minutes, and place seasoned pumpkin slices into air fryer. 3.Prepare the vinaigrette by combining all the vinaigrette in a bowl. Serve pumpkin covered with vinaigrette, sprinkle top with toasted pine nuts and sprigs of thyme.
Per Serving: Calories 257; Fat 11.3g; Sodium 256mg; Carbs 10.6g; Fiber 6g; Sugar 2g; Protein 8.3g

Spicy Black-Eyed Peas

Prep time: 10 minutes | Cook time: 10 minutes | Serves: 6

15-ounces black-eyed peas	½ teaspoon chili powder
⅛ teaspoon chipotle chili powder	⅛ teaspoon black pepper
¼ teaspoon salt	

1. Select the "AIR FRY" function of Ninja Foodi digital air fry oven, set the temperature to 360 degrees F/ 180 degrees C and set the time to 10 minutes. Press the Start/Pause button and begin preheating. Rinse the beans well with running water then set aside. 2. In a large bowl, mix the spices until well combined. Add the peas to spices and mix. Place the peas in the wire basket and cook for 10-minutes. Serve and enjoy!
Per Serving: Calories 262; Fat 9.4g; Sodium 312mg; Carbs 8.6g; Fiber 1g; Sugar 1g; Protein 9.2g

Spiced Brussels Sprouts

Prep time: 10 minutes | Cook time: 8 minutes | Serves: 4

¼ teaspoon salt	1 teaspoon parsley, dried
½ teaspoon dried thyme	1 teaspoon powdered garlic
1 pound brussels sprouts	2 teaspoons sesame oil

1. Select the "AIR FRY" function of Ninja Foodi digital air fry oven, set the temperature to 390 degrees F/ 200 degrees C and set the time to 8 minutes. Press the Start/Pause button and begin preheating. Using a large mixing bowl, add all the ingredients and toss together until the brussels are well coated. 2. Empty the bowl contents into the fryer basket then roast for 8 minutes 3. Once done, allow to cool for a bit then serve and enjoy as desired.
Per Serving: Calories 79; Fat 2g; Sodium 332mg; Carbs 12g; Fiber 2g; Sugar 4g; Protein 4g

Crispy Asparagus Drizzled with Lime

Prep time: 5 minutes | Cook time: 10 minutes | Serves: 4

1 bunch fresh asparagus	lime wedge
1 ½ teaspoons Herbes de	cooking spray oil
Provence	salt & pepper, to taste

1. Select the "AIR FRY" function of Ninja Foodi digital air fry oven, set the temperature to 360 degrees F/ 180 degrees C and set the time to 10 minutes. Press the Start/Pause button and begin preheating. Trim the asparagus hard ends off and wash then pat dry. 2. Drizzle the asparagus with the spray oil and coat with the seasonings. 3. Transfer the asparagus into the fryer basket then cook until crisp for 10 minutes .4. Serve, drizzled with the lime juice then enjoy as desired.
Per Serving: Calories 382; Fat 0.6g; Sodium 711mg; Carbs 62.6g; Fiber 12g; Sugar 14g; Protein 62.5g

Sweet Potato and Cauliflower Patties

Prep time: 15 minutes | Cook time: 20 minutes | Serves: 10

¼ teaspoon cumin	2 cups cauliflower florets
¼ cup sunflower seeds	2 tablespoons ranch seasoning
¼ cup ground flaxseed	mix
½ teaspoon chili powder	2 tablespoons plain gluten free
1 minced green onion	flour
1 cup packed cilantro	any dipping sauce
1 peeled large sweet potato	salt & pepper, to taste
1 teaspoon minced garlic cloves	

1. Select the "AIR FRY" function of Ninja Foodi digital air fry oven, set the temperature to 360 degrees F/ 180 degrees C and set the time to 20 minutes. Press the Start/Pause button and begin preheating. Dice the peeled potatoes into small chunks then process in a blender until chopped into smaller pieces. 2. Add the minced onion and cauliflower florets into the blender and pulse together again. 3. Add in the cilantro, plain flour, flaxseed, sunflower seeds and remaining seasonings then pulse together until a thick batter is achieved. 4. Transfer the batter out of the blender then use ¼ cup of the batter to mold 1 ½" thick patties then transfer in the freezer to set. 5. Once ready place the patties in the air fryer and fry for 18-20 minutes. 6. Once done, serve and enjoy as desired.
Per Serving: Calories 85; Fat 2.9g; Sodium 233mg; Carbs 9g; Fiber 4g; Sugar 2g; Protein 2.7g

Crispy Green Beans & Bacon

Prep time: 15 minutes | Cook time: 10 minutes | Serves: 4

3 cups frozen cut green beans
3 bacon slices
¼ cup water

kosher salt & black pepper, to taste

1. Select the "AIR FRY" function of Ninja Foodi digital air fry oven, set the temperature to 375 degrees F/ 190 degrees C and set the time to 15 minutes. Press the Start/Pause button and begin preheating. Using a small heatproof pan. add in the water, bacon slices, onion and green beans. 2. Place the pan into the fryer basket then air fry for 15 minutes 3. Increase the temperature to 400 degrees F/ 200 degrees C for another 5 minutes.4. Season with the salt, pepper and mix together. 5. Serve and enjoy as desired.
Per Serving: Calories 95; Fat 6g; Sodium 132mg; Carbs 6g; Fiber 1.8g; Sugar 0.6g; Protein 3g

Fried Pearl Onions

Prep time: 5 minutes | Cook time: 20 minutes | Serves: 3

2 tablespoons avocado oil
2 tablespoons balsamic vinegar
2 teaspoons chopped fresh rosemary

15 ounces frozen pearl onions
kosher salt & black pepper, to taste

1. Select the "AIR FRY" function of Ninja Foodi digital air fry oven, set the temperature to 400 degrees F/ 200 degrees C and set the time to 20 minutes. Press the Start/Pause button and begin preheating. Using a medium mixing bowl, add in the onions, rosemary, pepper, oil, salt, vinegar and toss around until combined. 2. Transfer the coated pearl onions into the fryer basket then air fry for 20 minutes. 3. Serve and enjoy as desired.
Per Serving: Calories 92; Fat 9g; Sodium 104mg; Carbs 2g; Fiber 0.2g; Sugar 0.1g; Protein 5g

Roasted Veggies

Prep time: 10 minutes | Cook time: 35 minutes | Serves: 4

½ lb carrots, diced
1 lime, cut into wedges
½ teaspoon ground white pepper
1 lb. zucchini, trim stem and root ends, cut into ¾ inch semicircles
1 lb. yellow squash, with roots

and stems, trimmed
6 teaspoons olive oil, divided
1 teaspoon sea salt
1 tablespoon tarragon leaves, chopped

1. Select the "AIR FRY" function of Ninja Foodi digital air fry oven, set the temperature to 400 degrees F/ 200 degrees C and set the time to 35 minutes. Press the Start/Pause button and begin preheating. In a bowl, add carrots and cover with 2 teaspoons of oil and stir. Put the carrots in fryer basket and cook for 5-minutes. Place the zucchini and yellow squash into a bowl. 2. Cover with the remaining 4 teaspoons of olive oil. Season with pepper and salt. When air fryer timer goes off, stir in zucchini and yellow squash with carrots. 3. Cook for 30-minutes. Stir from time to time. Garnish with lime wedges and tarragon leaves.
Per Serving: Calories 256; Fat 9.4g; Sodium 347mg; Carbs 8.6g; Fiber 5g; Sugar 2g; Protein 7.4g

Cheese stuffed Mushrooms

Prep time: 7 minutes | Cook time: 8 minutes | Serves: 5

⅛ cup shaved white cheddar cheese
⅛ cup shaved sharp cheddar cheese
¼ cup shaved parmesan cheese

1 teaspoon Worcestershire sauce
2 minced garlic cloves
4 ounces cream cheese
8 ounces mushrooms
salt & pepper, to taste

1. Select the "AIR FRY" function of Ninja Foodi digital air fry oven, set the temperature to 370 degrees F/ 185 degrees C and set the time to 8 minutes. Press the Start/Pause button and begin preheating. Chop the mushroom stem off then soften cream cheese in a microwave for about 15 seconds. 2. Using a medium mixing bowl, add in the Worcestershire sauce, pepper, salt, cream cheese, cheddar cheeses and combine together.3. Stuff the stemmed mushrooms with the cheese mixture and transfer into the fryer basket. 4. Fry the mushrooms for 8 minutes then allow to cool before serving and enjoying as desired.
Per Serving: Calories 195; Fat 18.3g; Sodium 278mg; Carbs 5.4g; Fiber 1g; Sugar 2g; Protein 5.8g

Cheesy Kale Chip

Prep time: 5 minutes | Cook time: 10 minutes | Serves: 12

¼ cup shredded parmesan cheese
1 tablespoon avocado oil
10 ounces chopped kale, ribs

removed
salt & pepper, to taste

1. Select the "AIR FRY" function of Ninja Foodi digital air fry oven, set the temperature to 270 degrees F/ 130 degrees C and set the time to 5 minutes. Press the Start/Pause button and begin preheating. Using a mixing bowl, add in the kale and coat with the salt, pepper and avocado oil. 2. Transfer the coated kale into the fryer basket the air fry for 5 minutes. 3. Open the fryer and shake the basket then cook for an extra 3 minutes. 4. Open the fryer again and sprinkle with the shredded parmesan cheese and cook for an extra 2 minutes. 5. Serve warm and enjoy as desired.
Per Serving: Calories 30; Fat 1.9g; Sodium 269mg; Carbs 2.4g; Fiber 1.9g; Sugar 0.9g; Protein 1.6g

Crispy tangy Onion Sprouts

Prep time: 10 minutes | Cook time: 10 minutes | Serves: 5

½ cup diced red onions
1 tablespoon balsamic vinegar
2 cups halved fresh brussels

sprouts
cooking oil spray
salt & pepper, to taste

1. Select the "AIR FRY" function of Ninja Foodi digital air fry oven, set the temperature to 350 degrees F/ 175 degrees C and set the time to 10 minutes. Press the Start/Pause button and begin preheating. Add the brussels and onions into a medium sized mixing bowl then drizzle with the vinegar and cooking spray. 2. Season the coated sprouts with salt & pepper, massaging the seasoning in. 3. Coat the fryer basket with the remaining spray then add in the seasoned brussels and onions. 4. Air fry for 5 minutes then toss the onion and brussels sprouts together and cook until crisp for an extra 5 minutes. 5. Allow the sprouts to cool off a bit then serve and enjoy as desired.
Per Serving: Calories 26; Fat 0.6g; Sodium 123mg; Carbs 3.4g; Fiber 0g; Sugar 0g; Protein 1.4g

Cheesy Spinach

Prep time: 10 minutes | Cook time: 15 minutes | Serves: 2

¼ cup parmesan cheese, shredded
½ cup diced onions
½ teaspoon ground nutmeg
1 teaspoon kosher salt
1 teaspoon ground black pepper

2 teaspoons minced garlic
4 ounces shaved cream cheese
10-ounce pack thawed frozen spinach

1. Select the "AIR FRY" function of Ninja Foodi digital air fry oven, set the temperature to 400 degrees F/ 200 degrees C and set the time to 10 minutes. Press the Start/Pause button and begin preheating. Using a medium mixing bowl, add in the shaved cream cheese, spinach, garlic, onion, nutmeg, salt & pepper then combine together. 2. Transfer the cream mixture into the greased fryer basket then air fry for 10 minutes. 3. Open the air fryer and stir the mixture together again then top with the parmesan cheese. 4. Air fry again until the cheese is browned and melted for 5 minutes. 5. Serve and enjoy as desired.
Per Serving: Calories 273; Fat 23g; Sodium 111mg; Carbs 8g; Fiber 2g; Sugar 1g; Protein 8g

Fried Vegetables

Prep time: 5 minutes | Cook time: 23 minutes | Serves: 4

2 cups diced radishes
1 cup diced onion
1 cup diced bell peppers
2 tablespoons melted butter

5 minced garlic cloves
kosher salt & black pepper, to taste

1. Select the "AIR FRY" function of Ninja Foodi digital air fry oven, set the temperature to 360 degrees F/ 180 degrees C and set the time to 20 minutes. Press the Start/Pause button and begin preheating. Using a mixing bowl, add in the pepper, salt, garlic, bell peppers, onions, radishes and combine together. 2. Cover the vegetable mixture with the melted butter and incorporate then transfer into the fryer basket. 3. Air fry the veggies for 20 minutes and cook for extra minutes if you want a crispier texture.4. Serve and enjoy as desired.
Per Serving: Calories 88; Fat 6g; Sodium 102mg; Carbs 9g; Fiber 2.3g; Sugar 1.2g; Protein 1g

Chapter 3 Poultry Recipes

Baked Hazelnut Crusted Chicken

Prep time: 10 minutes | Cook time: 10 minutes | Serves: 4

1-pound chicken fillet	½ teaspoon salt
3 oz hazelnuts, grinded	1 tablespoon coconut flour
2 egg whites, whisked	1 teaspoon avocado oil
½ teaspoon ground black pepper	

1. Select the "BAKE" function of Ninja Foodi digital air fry oven, set the temperature to 365 degrees F/ 185 degrees C and set the time to 10 minutes. Press the Start/Pause button and begin preheating. Cut the chicken on 4 tenders and sprinkle them with ground black pepper and salt. In the mixing bowl, mix up grinded hazelnuts and coconut flour. Then dip the chicken tenders in the whisked egg and coat in the hazelnut mixture. Sprinkle every chicken tender with avocado oil. Place the prepared chicken tenders in the preheated air fryer and cook for 10 minutes.
Per Serving: Calories 281; Fat 17.2g; Sodium 407mg; Carbs 4g; Fiber 2g; Sugar 1g; Protein 28g

Roasted Oregano Chicken and Green Beans

Prep time: 5 minutes | Cook time: 35 minutes | Serves: 4

4 chicken breasts, skinless, boneless and halved	and halved
10 ounces chicken stock	2 tablespoons olive oil
1 teaspoon oregano, dried	A pinch of salt and black pepper
10 ounces green beans, trimmed	1 tablespoon parsley, chopped

1. Select the "AIR ROAST" function of Ninja Foodi digital air fry oven, set the temperature to 380 degrees F/ 195 degrees C and set the time to 30 minutes. Press the Start/Pause button and begin preheating. 2. Heat up the air fryer Ninja sheet pan with the oil add the chicken and brown for 2 minutes on each side. Add the remaining ingredients, toss a bit, put the pan in the Ninja Foodi and cook for 30 minutes. Divide everything between plates and serve.
Per Serving: Calories 281; Fat 17.2g; Sodium 407mg; Carbs 4g; Fiber 2g; Sugar 1g; Protein 28g

Air Fried Chicken Nuggets

Prep time: 10 minutes | Cook time: 20 minutes | Serves: 4

4 (8-ounce) boneless, skinless chicken breasts, trimmed	¼ cup extra-virgin olive oil
Salt and pepper	3 large eggs
3 tablespoons sugar	3 tablespoons all-purpose flour
3 cups panko bread crumbs	1 tablespoon onion powder
	¾ teaspoon garlic powder

1. Select the "AIR FRY" function of Ninja Foodi digital air fry oven, set the temperature to 400 degrees F/ 200 degrees C and set the time to 16 minutes. Press the Start/Pause button and begin preheating. Pound chicken to desired uniform thickness as needed. Cut each breast diagonally into thirds, then cut each piece into thirds. Dissolve 3 tablespoons salt and sugar in 2 quarts cold water in large container. Add chicken, cover, and let sit for 15 minutes. 2. Meanwhile, toss panko with oil in bowl until evenly coated. Microwave, stirring frequently, until light golden brown, about 5 minutes. Transfer to shallow dish and let cool slightly. Whisk eggs, flour, onion powder, garlic powder, 1 teaspoon salt, and ¼ teaspoon pepper together in second shallow dish. 3. Set wire rack in rimmed baking sheet. Remove chicken from brine and pat dry with paper towels. Working with several chicken pieces at a time, dredge in egg mixture, letting excess drip off, then coat with panko mixture, pressing gently to adhere; transfer to prepared rack. Freeze until firm, about 4 hours. 4. To cook nuggets. Lightly spray air-fryer cooking pan with vegetable oil spray. Place up to 18 nuggets in prepared basket. Place in air fryer and cook for 6 minutes. Transfer nuggets to bowl and gently toss. Return nuggets to air fryer and cook until chicken is crisp and registers 160 degrees F/ 70 degrees C, 6 to 10 minutes. Serve.
Sweet-And-Sour Dipping Sauce
Whisk ¾ cup apple jelly, 1 tablespoon distilled white vinegar, ½ teaspoon soy sauce, ⅛ teaspoon garlic powder, pinch ground ginger, and pinch cayenne pepper together in bowl; season with salt and pepper to taste.
Honey-Dijon Dipping Sauce
Whisk ½ cup Dijon mustard and ¼ cup honey together in a bowl; season with salt and pepper to taste.
Per Serving: Calories 722; Fat 39g; Sodium 140mg; Carbs 7g; Fiber 2g; Sugar 4g; Protein 18g

Nut Crusted Butter Lemon Chicken Breasts

Prep time: 10 minutes | Cook time: 25 minutes | Serves: 2

½ cup slivered almonds, chopped fine	1 large egg
½ cup panko bread crumbs	1 tablespoon all-purpose flour
2 tablespoons unsalted butter, melted	1 teaspoon minced fresh thyme or ½ teaspoon dried
1 teaspoon grated lemon zest, plus lemon wedges for serving	Pinch cayenne pepper
Salt and pepper	2 (8-ounce) boneless, skinless chicken breasts, trimmed

1. Select the "AIR ROAST" function of Ninja Foodi digital air fry oven, set the temperature to 375 degrees F/ 190 degrees C and set the time to 16 minutes. Press the Start/Pause button and begin preheating. Combine almonds, panko, melted butter, lemon zest, and ¼ teaspoon salt in bowl and microwave, stirring occasionally, until panko is light golden brown and almonds are fragrant, about 4 minutes. Transfer to dish and set aside to cool slightly. Whisk egg, flour, thyme, and cayenne in second dish. 2. Spice chicken with salt and pepper. Dredge chicken in egg mixture, letting excess drip off, then coat with panko mixture, pressing gently to adhere. 3. Lightly spray air-fryer basket with vegetable oil spray. Place chicken on the basket and place in air fryer. Cook until chicken is crisp and registers 160 degrees, 12 to 16 minutes, flipping halfway through cooking. Serve with lemon wedges.
Per Serving: Calories 153; Fat 39g; Sodium 108mg; Carbs 25g; Fiber 6g; Sugar 2g; Protein 37g

Chicken Parmesan with Marinara Sauce

Prep time: 15 minutes | Cook time: 30 minutes | Serves: 2

¾ cup panko bread crumbs	Salt and pepper
2 tablespoons extra-virgin olive oil	2 (8-ounce) boneless, skinless chicken breasts, trimmed
¼ cup grated Parmesan cheese	2 ounces whole-milk mozzarella cheese, shredded (½ cup)
1 large egg	¼ cup jarred marinara sauce, warmed
1 tablespoon all-purpose flour	2 tablespoons chopped fresh basil
¾ teaspoon garlic powder	
½ teaspoon dried oregano	

1. Mix panko with oil evenly. Microwave, until light golden brown, 1 to 3 minutes. Place to shallow dish, cool slightly, then stir in Parmesan cheese. Whisk egg with flour, oregano, ⅛ teaspoon salt, and ⅛ teaspoon pepper, garlic powder in other shallow dish. 2. Pound chicken to desire thickness. Spice with salt and pepper. Dredge the ponded chicken in egg mixture, then coat with panko mixture, pressing gently. 3. Lightly grease the air-fryer pan with vegetable oil. Arrange breasts in prepared pan, spaced evenly apart, alternating ends. Select the "AIR ROAST" function of Ninja Foodi digital air fry oven, set the temperature to 400 degrees F/ 200 degrees C and set the time to 20 minutes. Press the Start/Pause button and begin preheating. Cook after 4 minutes of preheating, until chicken is crisp and registers 160 degrees F/ 70 degrees C, 12 to 16 minutes, flipping halfway through cooking. 4. Sprinkle chicken with mozzarella. Return basket to air fryer and cook until cheese is melted, about 1 minute. Transfer basket to serving plates. Top each breast with marinara sauce and sprinkle with basil. Serve.
Per Serving: Calories 365; Fat 12.4g; Sodium 717mg; Carbs 29g; Fiber 3g; Sugar 10g; Protein 19g

Air Fried Apricot Thyme Glazed Chicken Breats

Prep time: 5 minutes | Cook time: 12 minutes | Serves: 2

2 tablespoons apricot preserves	chicken breasts, trimmed
½ teaspoon minced fresh thyme or ⅛ teaspoon dried	1 teaspoon vegetable oil
2 (8-ounce) boneless, skinless	Salt and pepper

1. Select the "AIR FRY" function of Ninja Foodi digital air fry oven, set the temperature to 400 degrees F/ 200 degrees C and set the time to 15 minutes. Press the Start/Pause button and begin preheating. Microwave apricot preserves and thyme until fluid, about 30 seconds; set aside. Spice chicken with salt and pepper. 2. Place breasts skinned side down in air-fryer basket, spaced evenly apart. Place it in air fryer and cook chicken for 4 minutes. Flip chicken, then brush apricot-thyme mixture. Return basket to air fryer and cook until chicken registers 160 degrees, 8 to 12 minutes. 3. Transfer chicken to platter, coverloosely with foil, and let rest for 5 minutes. Serve.
Per Serving: Calories 605; Fat 31g; Sodium 833mg; Carbs 51g; Fiber 6g; Sugar 5g; Protein 74g

Spicy Fried Chicken Sandwich

Prep time: 5 minutes | Cook time: 25 minutes | Serves: 4

1 cup panko bread crumbs
2 tablespoons extra-virgin olive oil
1 large egg
3 tablespoons hot sauce
1 tablespoon all-purpose flour
½ teaspoon garlic powder
Salt and pepper

2 (8-ounce) boneless, skinless chicken breasts, trimmed
¼ cup mayonnaise
4 hamburger buns, toasted if desired
2 cups shredded iceberg lettuce
¼ cup jarred sliced jalapeños

1. Select the "AIR ROAST" function of Ninja Foodi digital air fry oven, set the temperature to 400 degrees F/ 200 degrees C and set the time to 16 minutes. Press the Start/Pause button and begin preheating. Toss panko with oil in bowl. Microwave, until light golden brown, 1 to 3 minutes. Transfer to dish and set aside to cool slightly. Whisk egg, 2. tablespoons hot sauce, flour, garlic powder, ⅛ teaspoon salt, and ⅛ teaspoon pepper in second dish.2 Spice chicken with salt and pepper. Dredge chicken in egg mixture, letting excess drip off, then coat with panko mixture. 3. Lightly spray air-fryer basket with vegetable oil spray. Place chicken on the basket and place in air fryer. Cook until chicken is crisp and registers 160 degrees F/ 70 degrees C, 12 to 16 minutes, flipping halfway through cooking. 4. Combine mayonnaise and hot sauce in a bowl. Spread mayonnaise mixture evenly over bun, then top with chicken, lettuce, jalapeños, and bun tops. Serve.
Per Serving: Calories 300; Fat 24g; Sodium 117mg; Carbs 3g; Fiber 3g; Sugar 2g; Protein 18g

Chicken Breasts with Mayonnaise & Cheese

Prep time: 10 minutes | Cook time: 16 minutes | Serves: 2

2 (8-ounce) boneless, skinless chicken breasts, trimmed
Salt and pepper
4 thick slices ham (4 ounces)
2 slices Swiss cheese (2 ounces)

2 tablespoons mayonnaise
1 tablespoon Dijon mustard
1 teaspoon water
1 tablespoon minced fresh chives

1. Select the "AIR ROAST" function of Ninja Foodi digital air fry oven, set the temperature to 375 degrees F/ 190 degrees C and set the time to 30 minutes. Press the Start/Pause button and begin preheating. Spice chicken with salt and pepper. For each chicken breast, shingle 2 slices of ham on the counter, overlapping edges slightly, and lay chicken, skinned side down, in center. Fold ham around chicken and secure overlapping ends by threading toothpick through ham and chicken. Flip chicken and thread toothpick through ham and chicken on second side. 2. Lightly spray air-fryer basket with vegetable oil spray. Place breasts skinned side down and place in air fryer. Cook until edges of ham begin to brown and chicken registers 160 degrees F/ 70 degrees C, 12 to 16 minutes, flipping halfway through cooking. Top with 1 slice Swiss, folding cheese. Return basket to air fryer and cook until cheese is melted, about 1 minute. 3. Transfer chicken to platter and tent loosely with foil and let rest for 5 minutes. Meanwhile, combine mayonnaise, mustard, and water in a s bowl. Drizzle chicken with sauce and sprinkle with chives. Serve.
Per Serving: Calories 218; Fat 2.4g; Sodium 641mg; Carbs 14g; Fiber 6g; Sugar 2g; Protein 19g

Peppery Chicken Fillets

Prep time: 10 minutes | Cook time: 20 minutes | Serves: 4

1-pound chicken fillets
2 tablespoons butter
2 bell peppers, seeded and sliced
1 teaspoon garlic, minced

Sea salt
Ground black pepper, to taste
1 teaspoon red pepper flakes

1. Select the "AIR ROAST" function of Ninja Foodi digital air fry oven, set the temperature to 380 degrees F/ 195 degrees C and set the time to 15 minutes. Press the Start/Pause button and begin preheating. Toss the chicken fillets with the butter and place them in the Air Fryer basket. Top the chicken with bell peppers, garlic, salt, black pepper, and red pepper flakes. 2. Cook the chicken and peppers for 15 minutes, tossing the basket halfway through the cooking time. Serve warm and enjoy!
Per Serving: Calories 305; Fat 22.8g; Sodium 642mg; Carbs 2.3g; Fiber 0.4g; Sugar 1.1g; Protein 21.6g

Spiced Roasted Chicken Breasts with Bean Salad

Prep time: 10 minutes | Cook time: 30 minutes | Serves: 2

1 cup canned cannellini beans, rinsed
2 tablespoons extra-virgin olive oil
1½ tablespoons red wine vinegar
1 garlic clove, minced
Salt and pepper
½ red onion, sliced thin

8 ounces asparagus, trimmed and cut into 1-inch lengths
½ teaspoon ground coriander
¼ teaspoon paprika
2 (8-ounce) boneless, skinless chicken breasts, trimmed
2 ounces (2 cups) baby arugula

1. Select the "AIR ROAST" function of Ninja Foodi digital air fry oven, set the temperature to 400 degrees F/ 200 degrees C and set the time to 20 minutes. Press the Start/Pause button and begin preheating. Microwave beans in bowl until warm, about 30 seconds. Stir in oil, vinegar, garlic, ¼ teaspoon salt, and pinch pepper; set aside. 2. Toss onion with oil, ⅛ teaspoon salt, and pinch pepper in a bowl to coat. Place onion in air-fryer basket, and cook for 2 minutes. Stir in asparagus, return back to air fryer, and cook until asparagus is tender, 6 to 8 minutes. Transfer veggies to bowl with beans and set aside. 3. Combine coriander, paprika, ¼ teaspoon salt, and ⅛ teaspoon pepper in bowl. Spice chicken evenly with spice mixture. Arrange breasts skinned side down in air-fryer cooking pan, spaced evenly apart, alternating ends. Place in air fryer and cook until chicken registers 160 degrees F/ 70 degrees C, 12 to 16 minutes, flipping halfway through cooking. 4. Transfer chicken to platter, tent loosely with foil, and let rest for 5 minutes. Add arugula to asparagus in bowl and toss to combine. Season with salt and pepper to taste. Serve chicken with salad.
Per Serving: Calories 718; Fat 23g; Sodium 964mg; Carbs 8g; Fiber 5g; Sugar 2g; Protein 37g

Roasted Bone-in Split Chicken Breasts

Prep time: 5 minutes | Cook time: 25 minutes | Serves: 2

2 (12-ounce) bone-in split chicken breasts, trimmed

1 teaspoon extra-virgin olive oil
Salt and pepper

1.Select the "AIR ROAST" function of Ninja Foodi digital air fry oven, set the temperature to 350 degrees F/ 175 degrees C and set the time to 30 minutes. Press the Start/Pause button and begin preheating. 2. Grease chicken with oil, and season with salt and pepper. Arrange breasts skin side down in air-fryer basket, spaced evenly apart, alternating ends. Place in air fryer and cook until chicken registers 160 degrees F/ 70 degrees C, 20 to 25 minutes, flipping halfway through cooking. 3. Transfer chicken to platter, and let rest for 5 minutes. Serve.
LEMON-BASIL SALSA VERDE
1. Whisk ¼ cup minced fresh parsley, ¼ cup chopped fresh basil, 3 tablespoons extra-virgin olive oil, 1 tablespoon rinsed and minced capers, 1 tablespoon water, 2 minced garlic cloves, 1 rinsed and minced anchovy fillet, ½ teaspoon grated lemon zest and 2 teaspoons juice, and ⅛ teaspoon salt together in bowl.
Per Serving: Calories 18; Fat 1g; Sodium 106mg; Carbs 2g; Fiber 0g; Sugar 2g; Protein 0g

Roasted Chicken and Cauliflower

Prep time: 5 minutes | Cook time: 35 minutes | Serves: 4

2 cups cauliflower florets, chopped
A pinch of salt and black pepper
A drizzle of olive oil
6 ounces coconut cream
2 tablespoons butter, melted

2 teaspoons thyme, chopped
1 garlic clove, minced
1 tablespoon parsley, chopped
4 chicken thighs, boneless and skinless

1. Select the "AIR ROAST" function of Ninja Foodi digital air fry oven, set the temperature to 380 degrees F/ 195 degrees C and set the time to 20 minutes. Press the Start/Pause button and begin preheating. Heat up a pan with the butter over medium heat, add the cream and the other ingredients except the cauliflower, oil and the chicken, whisk, bring to a simmer and cook for 5 minutes. 2. Heat up a pan with the oil over medium-high heat, add the chicken and brown for 2 minutes on each side. In an air fry basket, mix the chicken with the cauliflower, spread the coconut cream mix all over, put the pan in the air fryer and cook for 20 minutes. Divide between plates and serve hot.
Per Serving: Calories 505; Fat 38.1g; Sodium 264mg; Carbs 6g; Fiber 2g; Sugar 3g; Protein 34g

Paprika Duck Skin

Prep time: 5 minutes | Cook time: 28 minutes | Serves: 6

10 oz duck skin
1 teaspoon sunflower oil
½ teaspoon salt
½ teaspoon ground paprika

1. Select the "AIR FRY" function of Ninja Foodi digital air fry oven, set the temperature to 375 degrees F/ 190 degrees C and set the time to 18 minutes. Press the Start/Pause button and begin preheating. Then sprinkle the duck skin with sunflower oil, salt, and ground paprika. Put the duck skin in the air fryer and cook it for 18 minutes. Flip it and cook for 10 minutes more or until it is crunchy from both sides.
Per Serving: Calories 265; Fat 23.9g; Sodium 189mg; Carbs 0.1g; Fiber 0.1g; Sugar 0g; Protein 11.6g

Delicious Chicken Patties

Prep time: 10 minutes | Cook time: 10 minutes | Serves: 6

1-pound ground chicken
⅓ cup shredded cheddar cheese (omit for dairy-free)
2 tablespoons diced onions, or ¼
Coating:
1 cup pork dust (see here)
For Serving:
Cornichons
Mayonnaise

teaspoon onion powder
2 tablespoons mayonnaise
1 teaspoon dill pickle juice
1 teaspoon fine sea salt

Prepared yellow mustard

1. Spray the air fryer basket with avocado oil. Select the "AIR FRY" function of Ninja Foodi digital air fry oven, set the temperature to 375 degrees F/ 190 degrees C and set the time to 10 minutes. Press the Start/Pause button and begin preheating. 2. Place the ingredients for the patties in a medium-sized bowl and use your hands to combine well. Form the mixture into six 3½-inch patties. 3. Place the pork dust in a shallow bowl. Dredge each patty in the pork dust and use your hands to press the pork dust into a crust around the patty. 4. Working in batches if necessary, place the patties in the air fryer basket, leaving space between them, and cook for 5 minutes. Flip the patties with a spatula and cook for another 5 minutes, or until the coating is golden brown and the chicken is no longer pink inside. 5. Serve the patties with cornichons, mayo, and mustard, if desired.6. Store leftovers in an airtight container in the refrigerator for up to 3 days.
Per Serving: Calories 354; Fat 7.9g; Sodium 704mg; Carbs 6g; Fiber 3.6g; Sugar 6g; Protein 18g

Roasted Chicken Breasts and Potatoes with Tomato Relish

Prep time: 10 minutes | Cook time: 25 minutes | Serves: 2

1 pound fingerling potatoes, unpeeled
2 teaspoons extra-virgin olive oil, plus extra as needed
2 teaspoons minced fresh thyme or ¾ teaspoon dried
2 teaspoons minced fresh oregano or ¾ teaspoon dried
1 garlic clove, minced
Salt and pepper

2 (12-ounce) bone-in split chicken breasts, trimmed
¼ cup oil-packed sun-dried tomatoes, patted dry and chopped fine
1 small shallot, minced
1½ tablespoons red wine vinegar
1 tablespoon capers, rinsed and minced

1. Select the "AIR ROAST" function of Ninja Foodi digital air fry oven, set the temperature to 375 degrees F/ 190 degrees C and set the time to 30 minutes. Press the Start/Pause button and begin preheating. Toss potatoes with 1 teaspoon oil, 1 teaspoon thyme, 1 teaspoon oregano, garlic, ¼ teaspoon salt, and ¼ teaspoon pepper in bowl to coat; transfer to air-fryer basket. 2. Pat chicken dry with paper towels. Rub with remaining 1 teaspoon oil, season with salt and pepper, and sprinkle with remaining 1 teaspoon thyme and 1 teaspoon oregano. Arrange breasts skin side down on top of potatoes, spaced evenly apart, alternating ends. Place in air fryer and cook until potatoes are tender and chicken registers 160 degrees F/ 70 degrees C, 20 to 25 minutes, flipping and rotating breasts halfway through cooking. 3. Transfer chicken and potatoes to serving platter, tent loosely with aluminum foil, and let rest for 5 minutes. Pour off and reserve 1½ tablespoons juices from air-fryer drawer. Combine tomatoes, shallot, vinegar, capers, ⅛ teaspoon salt, ⅛ teaspoon pepper, and reserved chicken juices in bowl. Serve chicken and potatoes with tomato relish.
Per Serving: Calories 240; Fat 4.3g; Sodium 278mg; Carbs 47g; Fiber 7g; Sugar 3g; Protein 6g

Air Fried Chicken Breasts with Paprika

Prep time: 20 minutes | Cook time: 16 minutes | Serves: 2

Vegetable oil spray
2 (12-ounce) bone-in split chicken breasts, trimmed
Salt and pepper
⅓ cup buttermilk
½ teaspoon dry mustard
½ teaspoon garlic powder

¼ cup all-purpose flour
2 cups (2 ounces) cornflakes, finely crushed
1½ teaspoons poultry seasoning
½ teaspoon paprika
⅛ teaspoon cayenne pepper

1. Select the "AIR FRY" function of Ninja Foodi digital air fry oven, set the temperature to 400 degrees F/ 200 degrees C and set the time to 30 minutes. Press the Start/Pause button and begin preheating. Lightly spray base of air-fryer basket with oil spray. Remove skin from chicken and trim any excess fat. Halve each breast crosswise, pat dry with paper towels, and season with salt and pepper. Whisk buttermilk, mustard, garlic powder, ½ teaspoon salt, and ¼ teaspoon pepper together in a medium bowl. Spread flour in a shallow dish. Combine cornflakes, poultry seasoning, paprika, ¼ teaspoon salt, and cayenne in second shallow dish. 2. Working with 1 piece of chicken at a time, dredge in flour, dip in buttermilk mixture, letting excess drip off, then coat with cornflake mixture, pressing gently to adhere; transfer to large plate. Lightly spray chicken with oil spray. 3. Arrange chicken pieces in prepared basket, spaced evenly apart. Place basket in air fryer and set temperature to 400 degrees F/ 200 degrees C. Cook until chicken is crisp and registers 160 degrees F/ 70 degrees C, 16 to 24 minutes, flipping and rotating pieces halfway through cooking. Serve.
Per Serving: Calories 169; Fat 1.5g; Sodium 629mg; Carbs 36g; Fiber 6g; Sugar 14g; Protein 8g

Barbecued Chicken Breasts with Creamy Coleslaw

Prep time: 25 minutes | Cook time: 20 minutes | Serves: 2

3 cups (8 ounces) shredded coleslaw mix
Salt and pepper
2 (12-ounce) bone-in split chicken breasts, trimmed
1 teaspoon vegetable oil
2 tablespoons barbecue sauce,

plus extra for serving
2 tablespoons mayonnaise
2 tablespoons sour cream
1 teaspoon distilled white vinegar, plus extra for seasoning
¼ teaspoon sugar

1. Select the "ROAST" function of Ninja Foodi digital air fry oven, set the temperature to 350 degrees F/ 175 degrees C and set the time to 15 minutes. Press the Start/Pause button and begin preheating. Toss coleslaw mix and ¼ teaspoon salt in colander set over bowl. Let sit until wilted slightly, about 30 minutes. Rinse, drain, and dry well with a dish towel. 2. Meanwhile, pat chicken dry with paper towels, rub with oil, and season with salt and pepper. Arrange breasts skin side down in air-fryer basket, spaced evenly apart, alternating ends. Place basket in air fryer, set temperature to 350 degrees F/ 175 degrees C, and cook for 10 minutes. Flip and rotate breasts, then brush skin side with barbecue sauce. Return basket to air fryer and cook until well browned and chicken registers 160 degrees, 10 to 15 minutes. 3. Place chicken to platter, tent loosely with aluminum foil, and let rest for 5 minutes. While chicken rests, whisk mayonnaise, sour cream, vinegar, sugar, and pinch pepper together in a large bowl. Stir in coleslaw mix and season with salt, pepper, and additional vinegar to taste. Serve chicken with coleslaw, passing extra barbecue sauce separately.
Per Serving: Calories 232; Fat 8.5g; Sodium 465mg; Carbs 38g; Fiber 1g; Sugar 15g; Protein 2g

Air Fried Chicken with Pesto Sauce

Prep time: 10 minutes | Cook time: 25 minutes | Serves: 4

12 oz chicken legs
1 teaspoon sesame oil
½ teaspoon chili flakes
4 teaspoons pesto sauce

1. Select the "AIR FRY" function of Ninja Foodi digital air fry oven, set the temperature to 390 degrees F/ 200 degrees C and set the time to 30 minutes. Press the Start/Pause button and begin preheating. In the bowl mix up pesto sauce, chili flakes, and sesame oil. Rub the chicken with the pesto mix. Put the chicken legs in the air fryer basket and cook them for 25 minutes.
Per Serving: Calories 685; Fat 35g; Sodium 239mg; Carbs 4g; Fiber 2g; Sugar 1g; Protein 26g

Bone-in Chicken Breasts with Couscous Salad

Prep time: 30 minutes | Cook time: 20 minutes | Serves: 2

3 tablespoons plus 2 teaspoons pomegranate molasses
1 teaspoon minced fresh thyme
½ teaspoon ground cinnamon
Salt and pepper
2 (12-ounce) bone-in split chicken breasts, trimmed
2 tablespoons extra-virgin olive oil
¼ cup water

¼ cup chicken broth
½ cup couscous
1 scallion, white part minced, green part sliced thin on bias
2 ounces cherry tomatoes, quartered
1 tablespoon minced fresh parsley
1 ounce feta cheese, crumbled (¼ cup)

1. Select the "AIR ROAST" function of Ninja Foodi digital air fry oven, set the temperature to 350 degrees F/ 175 degrees C and set the time to 30 minutes. Press the Start/Pause button and begin preheating. Combine 3 tablespoons pomegranate molasses, thyme, cinnamon, and ⅛ teaspoon salt in small bowl. Pat chicken dry with paper towels, rub with 1 teaspoon oil, and season with salt and pepper. Arrange breasts skin side down in air-fryer basket, spaced evenly apart, alternating ends. Place basket in air fryer, set temperature to 350 degrees F/ 175 degrees C, and cook for 10 minutes. 2. Flip and rotate breasts, then brush skin with half of pomegranate molasses mixture. Return basket to air fryer and cook for 5 minutes. Brush breasts with remaining pomegranate molasses mixture, return basket to air fryer, and continue to cook until well browned and chicken registers 160 degrees F/ 70 degrees C, 5 to 10 minutes. Transfer chicken to serving platter, tent loosely with aluminum foil, and let rest for 5 minutes. Meanwhile, microwave water and broth in medium bowl until very hot, 3 to 5 minutes. Stir in couscous and ⅛ teaspoon salt. Cover and let sit until couscous is tender and all liquid has been absorbed, about 7 minutes. 4. Whisk remaining 5 teaspoons oil, remaining 2 teaspoons pomegranate molasses, and scallion whites together in clean bowl. Add tomatoes, parsley, scallion greens, and pomegranate-oil mixture to couscous and gently fluff with a fork to combine. Sprinkle with feta and serve with chicken.
Per Serving: Calories 567; Fat 16.3g; Sodium 478mg; Carbs 19g; Fiber 14g; Sugar 6g; Protein 18g

Cheesy Fried Chicken

Prep time: 10 minutes | Cook time: 20 minutes | Serves: 4

1 egg, whisked
½ cup parmesan cheese, preferably freshly grated
½ cup tortilla chips, crushed
½ teaspoon onion powder

½ teaspoon garlic powder
1 teaspoon red chili powder
1½ pounds chicken breasts, boneless skinless cut into strips

1. Select the "AIR ROAST" function of Ninja Foodi digital air fry oven, set the temperature to 380 degrees F/ 195 degrees C and set the time to 12 minutes. Press the Start/Pause button and begin preheating. Whisk the egg in a shallow bowl. In a separate bowl, whisk the parmesan cheese, tortilla chips, onion powder, garlic powder, and red chili powder. 2. Dip the chicken into the egg mixture. Then, roll the chicken pieces over the breadcrumb mixture. 3. Cook the chicken for 12 minutes, flipping them halfway through the cooking time. Bon appétit!
Per Serving: Calories 427; Fat 23.1g; Sodium 633mg; Carbs 11.1g; Fiber 0.9g; Sugar 0.6g; Protein 41.4g

Herbed Turkey Drumsticks

Prep time: 10 minutes | Cook time: 45 minutes | Serves: 5

2 pounds turkey drumsticks, bone-in
2 tablespoons olive oil
Kosher salt

Ground black pepper, to taste
1 teaspoon dried thyme
1 teaspoon dried rosemary
1 teaspoon garlic, minced

1. Select the "AIR ROAST" function of Ninja Foodi digital air fry oven, set the temperature to 400 degrees F/ 200 degrees C and set the time to 40 minutes. Press the Start/Pause button and begin preheating. Toss the turkey drumsticks with the remaining ingredients. 2. Cook the turkey drumsticks for 40 minutes, turning them over halfway through the cooking time. Bon appétit!
Per Serving: Calories 341; Fat 21.7g; Sodium 324mg; Carbs 0.5g; Fiber 0.1g; Sugar 0.1g; Protein 35.5g

Crispy Chicken Wings

Prep time: 5 minutes | Cook time: 18 minutes | Serves: 2

¾-pound chicken wings, boneless
1 tablespoon butter, room temperature

½ teaspoon garlic powder
½ teaspoon shallot powder
½ teaspoon mustard powder

1. Select the "AIR ROAST" function of Ninja Foodi digital air fry oven, set the temperature to 380 degrees F/ 195 degrees C and set the time to 18 minutes. Press the Start/Pause button and begin preheating. Toss the chicken wings with the remaining ingredients. 2. Cook the chicken wings for 18 minutes, turning over halfway through the cooking time.
Per Serving: Calories 265; Fat 11.7g; Sodium 322mg; Carbs 0.5g; Fiber 0.9g; Sugar 0.5g; Protein 37.5g

Easy Turkey Schnitzel

Prep time: 10 minutes | Cook time: 25 minutes | Serves: 3

1½ pounds turkey thighs, skinless, boneless
1 egg, beaten
½ cup all-purpose flour
½ cup seasoned breadcrumbs

½ teaspoon red pepper flakes, crushed
Sea salt
Ground black pepper, to taste
1 tablespoon olive oil

1. Select the "AIR ROAST" function of Ninja Foodi digital air fry oven, set the temperature to 380 degrees F/ 195 degrees C and set the time to 5 minutes. Press the Start/Pause button and begin preheating. Flatten the turkey thighs with a mallet. 2. Whisk the egg in a bowl. Place the flour in another bowl. 3. Then, in another bowl, place the breadcrumbs, red pepper, salt, and black pepper. Dip in the flour, then, in the egg, and roll them in the breadcrumb mixture. 4. Place the breaded turkey thighs in the Air Fryer basket. Mist your schnitzel with the olive oil and transfer them to the basket. 5. Cook the schnitzel for 22 minutes, turning them over halfway through the cooking time. Bon appétit!
Per Serving: Calories 579; Fat 27.4g; Sodium 456mg; Carbs 30.3g; Fiber 1.6g; Sugar 2g; Protein 51g

Spicy Marinated Chicken

Prep time: 10 minutes | Cook time: 15 minutes | Serves: 2

¾-pound chicken breasts, boneless, skinless
1 teaspoon garlic, minced
½ cup red wine

¼ cup hot sauce
1 tablespoon Dijon mustard
Sea salt and cayenne pepper, to taste

1. Select the "AIR ROAST" function of Ninja Foodi digital air fry oven, set the temperature to 380 degrees F/ 195 degrees C and set the time to 12 minutes. Press the Start/Pause button and begin preheating. Place the chicken, garlic, red wine, hot sauce, and mustard in a ceramic bowl. Cover and let it marinate for about 3 hours in your refrigerator. 2. Place the chicken in the Air Fryer basket. 3. Cook the chicken breasts for 12 minutes, turning them over halfway through the cooking time. 4. Spice it with the salt and cayenne pepper to taste. Bon appétit!
Per Serving: Calories 313; Fat 16g; Sodium 542mg; Carbs 3.7g; Fiber 0.9g; Sugar 2g; Protein 36.5g

Lemon Turkey with Parsley

Prep time: 10 minutes | Cook time: 35 minutes | Serves: 5

2 pounds turkey wings
2 tablespoons olive oil
½ teaspoon garlic powder
½ teaspoon onion powder

1 teaspoon poultry seasoning mix
2 tablespoons fresh parsley, roughly chopped
1 lemon, cut into slices

1. Select the "AIR ROAST" function of Ninja Foodi digital air fry oven, set the temperature to 400 degrees F/ 200 degrees C and set the time to 40 minutes. Press the Start/Pause button and begin preheating. Toss the turkey wings with the olive oil, garlic powder, onion powder, and poultry seasoning mix. 2. Cook the turkey wings for 40 minutes, turning them over halfway through the cooking time. 3. Let it rest for 10 minutes before carving and serving. Garnish the turkey wings with the parsley and lemon slices. Bon appétit!
Per Serving: Calories 411; Fat 27.8g; Sodium 411mg; Carbs 1.3g; Fiber 0.2g; Sugar 0.3g; Protein 36.5g

Traditional Orange Duck

Prep time: 15 minutes | Cook time: 45 minutes | Serves: 4

1-pound duck legs
¼ cup orange sauce

Sea salt and red pepper flakes, crushed

1. Select the "AIR FRY" function of Ninja Foodi digital air fry oven, set the temperature to 400 degrees F/ 200 degrees C and set the time to 40 minutes. Press the Start/Pause button and begin preheating. Toss the duck legs with the remaining ingredients. 2. Cook the duck legs for 40 minutes, flipping them over halfway through the cooking process. Bon appétit!
Per Serving: Calories 471; Fat 44.1g; Sodium 311mg; Carbs 2.9g; Fiber 0.3g; Sugar 2.1g; Protein 13.1g

Yummy Chicken Dinner Rolls

Prep time: 5 minutes | Cook time: 17 minutes | Serves: 4

1-pound chicken, ground
½ cup tortilla chips, crushed
2 ounces cheddar cheese, grated
1 teaspoon dried parsley flakes
1 teaspoon cayenne pepper

½ teaspoon paprika
Kosher salt
Ground black pepper
4 dinner rolls

1. Select the "AIR FRY" function of Ninja Foodi digital air fry oven, set the temperature to 380 degrees F/ 195 degrees C and set the time to 17 minutes. Press the Start/Pause button and begin preheating. Mix the chicken, tortilla chips, cheese, and spices until everything is well combined. Now, roll the mixture into four patties. 2. Cook the burgers for about 17 minutes or until cooked through; turn over halfway through the cooking time. 3. Serve your burgers in dinner rolls. Bon appétit!
Per Serving: Calories 575; Fat 25.3g; Sodium 369mg; Carbs 37g; Fiber 3.2g; Sugar 4.6g; Protein 49.7g

Cheesy Ham Stuffed Chicken

Prep time: 5 minutes | Cook time: 22 minutes | Serves: 4

1-pound chicken breasts, skinless, boneless and cut into 4 slices
4 ounces goat cheese, crumbled
4 ounces ham, chopped
1 egg

¼ cup all-purpose flour
¼ cup parmesan cheese, grated
½ teaspoon onion powder
½ teaspoon garlic powder

1. Pound the chicken breasts with a mallet. 2. Stuff each piece of chicken with cheese and ham. Roll them up and secure with toothpicks. 3. In a shallow bowl, mix the remaining ingredients until well combined. Dip the chicken rolls into the egg/flour mixture. 4. Place the stuffed chicken in the Air Fryer basket. Select the "AIR FRY" function of Ninja Foodi digital air fry oven, set the temperature to 400 degrees F/ 200 degrees C and set the time to 22 minutes. Press the Start/Pause button and begin preheating. Cook the stuffed chicken breasts for about 22 minutes, turning them over halfway through the cooking time. Bon appétit!
Per Serving: Calories 486; Fat 32.3g; Sodium 589mg; Carbs 7.9g; Fiber 0.2g; Sugar 0.8g; Protein 39.3g

Spicy Chicken

Prep time: 10 minutes | Cook time: 15 minutes | Serves: 4

1-pound chicken breasts, boneless, skinless
½ cup rice wine
1 tablespoon stone-ground mustard

1 teaspoon garlic, minced
1 teaspoon black peppercorns, whole
1 teaspoon chili powder
¼ teaspoon sea salt

1. Select the "AIR FRY" function of Ninja Foodi digital air fry oven, set the temperature to 380 degrees F/ 195 degrees C and set the time to 12 minutes. Press the Start/Pause button and begin preheating. Place the chicken, wine, mustard, garlic, and whole peppercorns in a ceramic bowl. Cover and let it marinate for about 3 hours in your refrigerator. 2. Discard the marinade and place the chicken breasts in the Air Fryer basket. 3. Cook the chicken breasts for 12 minutes, turning them over halfway through the cooking time. 4. Season the chicken with the chili powder and salt. Serve immediately and enjoy!
Per Serving: Calories 206; Fat 11g; Sodium 421mg; Carbs 1g; Fiber 0.2g; Sugar 0.4g; Protein 24.2g

Chicken Cutlets with steamed Broccoli

Prep time: 5 minutes | Cook time: 15 minutes | Serves: 4

1-pound chicken cutlets
1-pound broccoli florets
1 tablespoon olive oil

Sea salt
Ground black pepper, to taste

1. Select the "AIR ROAST" function of Ninja Foodi digital air fry oven, set the temperature to 380 degrees F/ 195 degrees C and set the time to 6 minutes. Press the Start/Pause button and begin preheating. Pat the chicken dry with kitchen towels. Place the chicken cutlets in a lightly greased Air Fryer basket. 2. Cook the chicken cutlets for 6 minutes, turning them over halfway through the cooking time. 3.Turn the heat to 400 degrees F/ 200 degrees C and add in the remaining ingredients. Continue to cook for 6 minutes more. Bon appétit!
Per Serving: Calories 313; Fat 20.8g; Sodium 444mg; Carbs 7.5g; Fiber 2g; Sugar 1.9g; Protein 24.5g

Creamy Chicken Salad

Prep time: 5 minutes | Cook time: 20 minutes | Serves: 4

1-pound chicken breasts, skinless and boneless
¼ cup mayonnaise
¼ cup sour cream

1 tablespoon lemon juice
Sea salt and ground black pepper
½ cup celery, chopped

1. Select the "AIR FRY" function of Ninja Foodi digital air fry oven, set the temperature to 380 degrees F/ 195 degrees C and set the time to 5 minutes. Press the Start/Pause button and begin preheating. Pat dry the chicken and place the chicken in a lightly oiled basket. 2. Cook the chicken breasts for 12 minutes, turning them over halfway through the cooking time. 3. Shred the chicken breasts using two forks; transfer it to a salad bowl and add in the remaining ingredients. 4. Toss to combine and serve well chilled. Bon appétit!
Per Serving: Calories 315; Fat 23g; Sodium 478mg; Carbs 2.8g; Fiber 0.4g; Sugar 0.9g; Protein 24.5g

Traditional Italian Chicken Tenders

Prep time: 10 minutes | Cook time: 8 minutes | Serves: 6

2 large eggs
1 cup pork dust
2 teaspoons Italian seasoning

1 pound boneless, skinless chicken tenders
½ cup marinara sauce, for serving

1. Spray the air fryer basket with avocado oil. Select the "AIR FRY" function of Ninja Foodi digital air fry oven, set the temperature to 390 degrees F/ 200 degrees C and set the time to 8 minutes. Press the Start/Pause button and begin preheating. 2. In a medium-sized bowl, lightly beat the eggs. In another medium-sized bowl, combine the pork dust and Italian seasoning. 3. One at a time, dip the chicken tenders in the eggs, shake off the excess egg, then dredge the tenders in the pork dust mixture. Using your hands, press the coating into each tender, coating it well. Place the tenders in the air fryer basket, leaving space between them. 4. Cook the tenders for 8 minutes, or until they are golden brown, flipping halfway through. Transfer the chicken tenders to a platter and serve with the marinara sauce. 5. Store leftovers in an airtight container in the refrigerator for up to 4 days.
Per Serving: Calories 354; Fat 7.9g; Sodium 704mg; Carbs 6g; Fiber 3.6g; Sugar 6g; Protein 18g

Simple Ranch Chicken Wings

Prep time: 10 minutes | Cook time: 25 minutes | Serves: 3

1-pound chicken wings, boneless
2 tablespoons olive oil
1 teaspoon Ranch seasoning mix

Kosher salt
Ground black pepper

1. Select the "AIR FRY" function of Ninja Foodi digital air fry oven, set the temperature to 380 degrees F/ 195 degrees C and set the time to 22 minutes. Press the Start/Pause button and begin preheating. Pat the chicken dry with kitchen towels. Toss the chicken with the remaining ingredients. 2. Cook the chicken wings for 22 minutes, turning them over halfway through the cooking time. Bon appétit!
Per Serving: Calories 273; Fat14.3g; Sodium 357mg; Carbs 0.5g; Fiber 0.5g; Sugar 0.4g; Protein 33.2g

Roasted Turkey with Scallions

Prep time: 10 minutes | Cook time: 40 minutes | Serves: 4

1½ pounds turkey legs
1 tablespoon butter, melted
1 teaspoon hot paprika
1 teaspoon garlic, pressed

Sea salt
Ground black pepper
2 tablespoons scallions, chopped

1. Select the "AIR FRY" function of Ninja Foodi digital air fry oven, set the temperature to 400 degrees F/ 200 degrees C and set the time to 40 minutes. Press the Start/Pause button and begin preheating. Toss the turkey legs with the remaining ingredients, except for the scallions. 2. Cook the turkey legs for 40 minutes, turning them over halfway through the cooking time. 3. Garnish the roasted turkey legs with the fresh scallions and enjoy!
Per Serving: Calories 279; Fat 14.4g; Sodium 678mg; Carbs 1.8g; Fiber 0.5g; Sugar 0.7g; Protein 33.6g

Turkey Sliders with Avocado

Prep time: 10 minutes | Cook time: 25 minutes | Serves: 4

1-pound turkey, ground
1 tablespoon olive oil
1 avocado, peeled, pitted and chopped
2 garlic cloves, minced

½ cup breadcrumbs
Kosher salt
Ground black pepper
8 small rolls

1. Select the "AIR FRY" function of Ninja Foodi digital air fry oven, set the temperature to 380 degrees F/ 195 degrees C and set the time to 20 minutes. Press the Start/Pause button and begin preheating. Mix the turkey, olive oil, avocado, garlic, breadcrumbs, salt, and black pepper until everything is well combined. Form the mixture into eight small patties. 2. Cook the patties for about 20 minutes or until cooked through; turn over halfway through the cooking time. 3. Serve your patties in the prepared rolls and enjoy!
Per Serving: Calories 519; Fat 22.4g; Sodium 711mg; Carbs 48g; Fiber 5g; Sugar 6.7g; Protein 31.6g

Homemade Chicken Salad Sandwich

Prep time: 10 minutes | Cook time: 20 minutes | Serves: 4

1-pound chicken breasts, boneless and skinless
1 stalks celery, chopped
1 carrot, chopped
1 small onion, chopped

1 cup mayonnaise
Sea salt
Ground black pepper, to taste
4 sandwich buns

1. Select the "AIR FRY" function of Ninja Foodi digital air fry oven, set the temperature to 380 degrees F/ 195 degrees C and set the time to 12 minutes. Press the Start/Pause button and begin preheating. Pat dry the chicken and place the chicken in a lightly oiled basket. 2. Cook the chicken breasts for 12 minutes, turning them over halfway through the cooking time. 3. Shred the chicken breasts using two forks; transfer it to a salad bowl and add in the celery, carrot, onion, mayo, salt, and pepper. 4. Toss to combine and serve in sandwich buns. Enjoy!
Per Serving: Calories 522; Fat 31.4g; Sodium 478mg; Carbs 27.1g; Fiber 2.5g; Sugar 5.2g; Protein 31.6g

Crispy Buttermilk Fried Chicken

Prep time: 10 minutes | Cook time: 15 minutes | Serves: 4

1-pound chicken breast halves
Sea salt
Ground black pepper, to taste
1 cup buttermilk

1 cup all-purpose flour
½ teaspoon onion powder
1 teaspoon garlic powder
1 teaspoon smoked paprika

1. Select the "AIR FRY" function of Ninja Foodi digital air fry oven, set the temperature to 380 degrees F/ 195 degrees C and set the time to 12 minutes. Press the Start/Pause button and begin preheating. Toss together the chicken pieces, salt, and black pepper in a large bowl to coat. Stir in the buttermilk until the chicken is coated on all sides. Place the chicken in your refrigerator for about 6 hours. 2. In a shallow bowl, thoroughly combine the flour, onion powder, garlic powder, and smoked paprika. 3. Dredge the chicken in the spiced flour; shake off any excess and transfer them to a lightly oiled Air Fryer basket. 4. Cook the chicken breasts for 12 minutes, turning them over halfway through the cooking time. Enjoy!
Per Serving: Calories 266; Fat 3.9g; Sodium 478mg; Carbs 26.7g; Fiber 0.8g; Sugar 3g; Protein 28.2g

Delicious Chicken Meatballs with Penne Pasta

Prep time: 5 minutes | Cook time: 15 minutes | Serves: 4

1 cup chicken meat, ground
1 sweet red pepper, minced
¼ cup green onions, chopped
1 green garlic, minced
4 tablespoons friendly bread crumbs
½ teaspoon cumin powder

1 tablespoon fresh coriander, minced
½ teaspoon sea salt
¼ teaspoon mixed peppercorns, ground
1 package penne pasta, cooked

1. Select the "AIR FRY" function of Ninja Foodi digital air fry oven, set the temperature to 350 degrees F/ 175 degrees C and set the time to 15 minutes. Press the Start/Pause button and begin preheating. 2. Put the chicken, red pepper, green onions, and garlic into a mixing bowl and stir together to combine. 3. Throw in the seasoned bread crumbs and all of the seasonings. Combine again. 4. Use your hands to mold equal amounts of the mixture into small balls, each one roughly the size of a golf ball. 5. Put them in the fryer and cook for 15 minutes. Shake once or twice throughout the cooking time for even results. 6. Serve with cooked penne pasta.
Per Serving: Calories 429; Fat 32g; Sodium 325mg; Carbs 5g; Fiber 1g; Sugar 3g; Protein 5g

Italian Chicken Drumsticks

Prep time: 10 minutes | Cook time: 25 minutes | Serves: 4

4 chicken drumsticks, bone-in
1 tablespoon butter
½ teaspoon cayenne pepper

1 teaspoon Italian herb mix
Sea salt
Ground black pepper, to taste

1. Select the "BAKE" function of Ninja Foodi digital air fry oven, set the temperature to 370 degrees F/ 185 degrees C and set the time to 20 minutes. Press the Start/Pause button and begin preheating. Pat the chicken drumsticks dry with paper towels. Toss the chicken with all ingredients. 2. Cook the chicken drumsticks for 20 minutes, turning them over halfway through the cooking time. Bon appétit!
Per Serving: Calories 235; Fat 14.8g; Sodium 422mg; Carbs 0.3g; Fiber 0.3g; Sugar 0.1g; Protein 23.3g

Thai-Style Hot Chicken Drumettes

Prep time: 5 minutes | Cook time: 25 minutes | Serves: 3

1-pound chicken drumettes, bone-in
Sea salt and freshly ground black pepper, to taste

¼ cup Thai hot sauce
2 tablespoons sesame oil
1 teaspoon tamari sauce

1. Select the "AIR FRY" function of Ninja Foodi digital air fry oven, set the temperature to 380 degrees F/ 195 degrees C and set the time to 22 minutes. Press the Start/Pause button and begin preheating. Toss the chicken drumettes with the remaining ingredients. 2. Cook the chicken drumettes for 22 minutes, turning them over halfway through the cooking time. Bon appétit!
Per Serving: Calories 260; Fat 13.3g; Sodium 432mg; Carbs 0.5g; Fiber 0.5g; Sugar 0.4g; Protein 31.2g

Southern Hot Fried Chicken

Prep time: 10 minutes | Cook time: 26 minutes | Serves: 2

2 x 6-oz. boneless skinless chicken breasts
2 tablespoons hot sauce

½ teaspoon onion powder
1 tablespoon chili powder
2 oz. pork rinds, finely ground

1. Select the "AIR FRY" function of Ninja Foodi digital air fry oven, set the temperature to 350 degrees F/ 175 degrees C and set the time to 26 minutes. Press the Start/Pause button and begin preheating. Cut the chicken in half lengthwise and rub in the hot sauce. Combine the onion powder with the chili powder, then rub into the chicken. Leave to marinate for at least a half hour. 2. Use the ground pork rinds to coat the chicken breasts in the ground pork rinds, covering them thoroughly. Place the chicken in your fryer. 3. Cook the chicken for 13 minutes. Flip it and cook for another 13 minutes or until golden. 4. Serve hot.
Per Serving: Calories 170; Fat 7.9g; Sodium 204mg; Carbs 3g; Fiber 0g; Sugar 2g; Protein 19g

Delicious Chicken Goulash

Prep time: 5 minutes | Cook time: 17 minutes | Serves: 2

2 chopped bell peppers
2 diced tomatoes
1 lb. ground chicken
½ cup chicken broth
Salt and pepper

1. Select the "AIR ROAST" function of Ninja Foodi digital air fry oven, set the temperature to 365 degrees F/ 185 degrees C and set the time to 17 minutes. Press the Start/Pause button and begin preheating. 2. Cook the bell pepper for five minutes. 3. Add in the diced tomatoes and ground chicken. Combine well, then allow to cook for a further six minutes. 4. Pour in broth, and spice to taste with salt and pepper. Cook for another six minutes before serving.
Per Serving: Calories 169; Fat 1.5g; Sodium 629mg; Carbs 36g; Fiber 6g; Sugar 14g; Protein 8g

Garlicky Nutty Meatballs

Prep time: 5 minutes | Cook time: 15 minutes | Serves: 2

½ lb. boneless chicken thighs
1 teaspoon minced garlic
1¼ cups roasted pecans
½ cup mushrooms
1 teaspoon extra virgin olive oil

1. Select the "AIR FRY" function of Ninja Foodi digital air fry oven, set the temperature to 375 degrees F/ 190 degrees C and set the time to 18 minutes. Press the Start/Pause button and begin preheating. Cube the chicken thighs. Place them in the food processor along with the garlic, pecans, and other seasonings as desired. Pulse until a smooth consistency is achieved. 2. Chop the mushrooms finely. Add to the chicken mixture and combine. 3. Shape the mix into balls and brush them with olive oil. 4. Put the balls into the fryer and cook for eighteen minutes. Serve hot.
Per Serving: Calories 505; Fat 38.1g; Sodium 264mg; Carbs 6g; Fiber 2g; Sugar 3g; Protein 34g

Lemony Chimichurri Chicken Drumsticks

Prep time: 10 minutes | Cook time: 20 minutes | Serves: 4

8 chicken drumsticks
½ cup chimichurri sauce
¼ cup lemon juice

1. Select the "AIR FRY" function of Ninja Foodi digital air fry oven, set the temperature to 400 degrees F/ 200 degrees C and set the time to 18 minutes. Press the Start/Pause button and begin preheating. Coat the chicken drumsticks with chimichurri sauce and refrigerate in an airtight container for no less than an hour, ideally overnight. 2. Remove the chicken from refrigerator and allow return to room temperature for roughly twenty minutes. 3. Cook for eighteen minutes in the fryer. Drizzle with lemon juice to taste and enjoy.
Per Serving: Calories 281; Fat 17.2g; Sodium 407mg; Carbs 4g; Fiber 2g; Sugar 1g; Protein 28g

Hot Jalapeno Chicken Breasts

Prep time: 5 minutes | Cook time: 20 minutes | Serves: 2

2 oz. full-fat cream cheese, softened
4 slices sugar-free bacon, cooked and crumbled
¼ cup pickled jalapenos, sliced
½ cup sharp cheddar cheese, shredded and divided
2 x 6-oz. boneless skinless chicken breasts

1. In a bowl, mix cream cheese, bacon, jalapeno slices, and half of the cheddar cheese until well-combined. 2. Cut parallel slits in the chicken breasts of about ¾ the length – make sure not to cut all the way down. You should be able to make between six and eight slices, depending on the size of the chicken breast. 3. Insert evenly sized dollops of the cheese mixture into the slits of the chicken breasts. Top the chicken with sprinkles of the rest of the cheddar cheese. Place the chicken in air fryer sheet pan. 4. Select the "AIR ROAST" function of Ninja Foodi digital air fry oven, set the temperature to 350 degrees F/ 175 degrees C and set the time to 20 minutes. Press the Start/Pause button and begin preheating. Cook the chicken breasts for twenty minutes. 5. Serve hot and enjoy!
Per Serving: Calories 216; Fat 10.4g; Sodium 311mg; Carbs 14g; Fiber 1g; Sugar 2g; Protein 18g

Popcorn Chicken

Prep time: 5 minutes | Cook time: 15 minutes | Serves: 1

1 lb. skinless, boneless chicken breast
1 teaspoon chili flakes
1 teaspoon garlic powder
½ cup coconut flour
1 tablespoon olive oil

1. Select the "AIR FRY" function of Ninja Foodi digital air fry oven, set the temperature to 365 degrees F/ 185 degrees C and set the time to 15 minutes. Press the Start/Pause button and begin preheating. Spray with olive oil. 2. Cut the chicken into 1-inches cubes and place in a bowl. Toss with the chili flakes, garlic powder, and additional seasonings to taste and make sure to coat entirely. 3. Add the coconut flour and toss once more. 4. Cook the chicken in the fryer for ten minutes. Turn over and cook for a further five minutes before serving.
Per Serving: Calories 281; Fat 17.2g; Sodium 407mg; Carbs 4g; Fiber 2g; Sugar 1g; Protein 28g

Crispy Fried Chicken Skin

Prep time: 5 minutes | Cook time: 6 minutes | Serves: 2

1 lb. chicken skin
1 teaspoon butter
½ teaspoon chili flakes
1 teaspoon dill

1. Select the "AIR FRY" function of Ninja Foodi digital air fry oven, set the temperature to 360 degrees F/ 180 degrees C and set the time to 6 minutes. Press the Start/Pause button and begin preheating. 2. Cut the chicken skin into slices. 3. Heat the butter until melted and pour it over the chicken skin. Toss with chili flakes, dill, and any additional seasonings to taste, making sure to coat well. 4. Cook the skins in the fryer for 3 minutes. Turn and cook for another 3 minutes. 5. Serve immediately or save them for later – they can be eaten hot or at room temperature.
Per Serving: Calories 685; Fat 35g; Sodium 239mg; Carbs 4g; Fiber 2g; Sugar 1g; Protein 26g

Chicken Fajita Rolls

Prep time: 10 minutes | Cook time: 25 minutes | Serves: 2

2 x 6-oz. boneless skinless chicken breasts
1 green bell pepper, sliced
¼ medium white onion, sliced
1 tablespoon coconut oil, melted
3 teaspoons taco seasoning mix

1. Cut chicken in half and place each one between two sheets of cooking parchment. Using a mallet, pound the chicken to flatten to a quarter-inch thick. 2. Place the chicken on a flat surface, with the short end facing you. Place four slices of pepper and three slices of onion at the end of each piece of chicken. Roll up the chicken tightly, making sure not to let any veggies fall out. Secure with some toothpicks or with butcher's string. 3. Coat the chicken with coconut oil and then with taco seasoning. Place into your air fryer. 4. Select the "AIR ROAST" function of Ninja Foodi digital air fry oven, set the temperature to 350 degrees F/ 175 degrees C and set the time to 25 minutes. Press the Start/Pause button and begin preheating. Cook the chicken for twenty-five minutes. 5. Serve the rolls immediately with your favorite dips and sides.
Per Serving: Calories 276; Fat 16g; Sodium 70mg; Carbs 1g; Fiber 0g; Sugar 0g; Protein 30g

Buttery Lemon Pepper Chicken

Prep time: 5 minutes | Cook time: 25 minutes | Serves: 4

½ teaspoon garlic powder
2 teaspoons baking powder
8 chicken legs
4 tablespoons salted butter,
melted
1 tablespoon lemon pepper seasoning

1. In a bowl mix the garlic powder and baking powder, then use this mixture to coat the chicken legs. Lay the chicken in the basket of your fryer. 2. Select the "AIR FRY" function of Ninja Foodi digital air fry oven, set the temperature to 375 degrees F/ 190 degrees C and set the time to 5 minutes. Press the Start/Pause button and begin preheating. Cook the chicken legs for twenty-five minutes. Halfway through, turn them over and allow to cook on the other side. 3. Remove from the fryer. Mix together the melted butter and lemon pepper seasoning and toss with the chicken legs until the chicken is coated all over. Serve hot.
Per Serving: Calories 145; Fat 7.2g; Sodium 66mg; Carbs 7g; Fiber 2g; Sugar 2g; Protein 15g

Greek Meatballs

Prep time: 5 minutes | Cook time: 12 minutes | Serves: 1

½ oz. finely ground pork rinds
1 lb. ground chicken
1 teaspoon Greek seasoning

⅓ cup feta, crumbled
⅓ cup frozen spinach, drained and thawed

1. In a bowl, place all ingredients and combine using your hands. Take equal-sized portions of this mixture and roll each into a 2-inch ball. Place the balls in your fryer. 2. Select the "AIR FRY" function of Ninja Foodi digital air fry oven, set the temperature to 350 degrees F/ 175 degrees C and set the time to 12 minutes. Press the Start/Pause button and begin preheating. Cook the meatballs for twelve minutes, in several batches if necessary. 3. Once they are golden, remove from the fryer. Keep each batch warm while you move on to the next one. Serve with Tzatziki if desired.
Per Serving: Calories 629; Fat 61g; Sodium 64mg; Carbs 3g; Fiber 1g; Sugar 1g; Protein 18g

Cheesy Buffalo Chicken Tenders

Prep time: 5 minutes | Cook time: 15 minutes | Serves: 4

1 egg
1 cup mozzarella cheese, shredded

¼ cup buffalo sauce
1 cup cooked chicken, shredded
¼ cup feta cheese

1. Combine all ingredients. Line the basket of your fryer with a suitably sized piece of parchment paper. Lay the mixture into the fryer and press it into a circle about half an inch thick. Crumble the feta cheese over it. 2. Select the "AIR FRY" function of Ninja Foodi digital air fry oven, set the temperature to 400 degrees F/ 200 degrees C and set the time to 8 minutes. Press the Start/Pause button and begin preheating. Cook for eight minutes. Turn the fryer off and allow the chicken to rest inside before removing with care. 3.Cut the mixture into slices and serve hot.
Per Serving: Calories 227; Fat 11.2g; Sodium 412mg; Carbs 1g; Fiber 0g; Sugar 1g; Protein 31g

Spicy Buffalo Chicken Tenders

Prep time: 10 minutes | Cook time: 20 minutes | Serves: 1

¼ cup hot sauce
1 lb. boneless skinless chicken tenders

1 teaspoon garlic powder
1½ oz. pork rinds, finely ground
1 teaspoon chili powder

1. Toss the hot sauce and chicken tenders together in a bowl, ensuring the chicken is completely coated. 2. In another bowl, combine the garlic powder, ground pork rinds, and chili powder. Use this mixture to coat the tenders, covering them well. Place the chicken into your fryer, taking care not to layer pieces on top of one another. 3. Select the "AIR FRY" function of Ninja Foodi digital air fry oven, set the temperature to 375 degrees F/ 190 degrees C and set the time to 20 minutes. Press the Start/Pause button and begin preheating. Cook the chicken for twenty minutes until cooked all the way through and golden. Serve warm with your favorite dips and sides.
Per Serving: Calories 342; Fat 11.8g; Sodium 683mg; Carbs 24g; Fiber 4g; Sugar 1g; Protein 38g

Chicken with Pepperoni Pizza

Prep time: 5 minutes | Cook time: 15 minutes | Serves: 6

2 cups cooked chicken, cubed
20 slices pepperoni
1 cup sugar-free pizza sauce

1 cup mozzarella cheese, shredded
¼ cup parmesan cheese, grated

1. Select the "AIR FRY" function of Ninja Foodi digital air fry oven, set the temperature to 375 degrees F/ 190 degrees C and set the time to 15 minutes. Press the Start/Pause button and begin preheating. Place the chicken into the base of a four-cup sheet pan and add the pepperoni and pizza sauce on top. Mix well so as to completely coat the meat with the sauce. 2. Add the parmesan and mozzarella on top of the chicken, then place the sheet pan into your fryer. 3. Cook for 15 minutes. 4. When everything is bubbling and melted, remove from the fryer. Serve hot.
Per Serving: Calories 191; Fat 13g; Sodium 574mg; Carbs 5g; Fiber 1g; Sugar 3g; Protein 13g

Italian Garlicky Chicken Thighs

Prep time: 10 minutes | Cook time: 20 minutes | Serves: 4

4 skin-on bone-in chicken thighs
2 tablespoons unsalted butter, melted

3 teaspoons Italian herbs
½ teaspoon garlic powder
¼ teaspoon onion powder

1. Select the "AIR ROAST" function of Ninja Foodi digital air fry oven, set the temperature to 380 degrees F/ 195 degrees C and set the time to 20 minutes. Press the Start/Pause button and begin preheating. Using a brush, coat the chicken thighs with the melted butter. Combine the herbs with the garlic powder and onion powder, then massage into the chicken thighs. Place the thighs in the fryer. 2. Cook for 20 minutes, turning the chicken halfway through to cook on the other side. 3. When the thighs have achieved a golden color, remove from the fryer and serve.
Per Serving: Calories 350; Fat 16.7g; Sodium 428mg; Carbs 22g; Fiber 1g; Sugar 3g; Protein 28g

Classic Teriyaki Chicken Wings

Prep time: 10 minutes | Cook time: 35 minutes | Serves: 4

¼ teaspoon ground ginger
2 teaspoons minced garlic
½ cup sugar-free teriyaki sauce

2 lb. chicken wings
2 teaspoons baking powder

1. Select the "AIR ROAST" function of Ninja Foodi digital air fry oven, set the temperature to 400 degrees F/ 200 degrees C and set the time to 25 minutes. Press the Start/Pause button and begin preheating. In a bowl, mix the ginger with garlic, and teriyaki sauce. Place the chicken wings in a larger bowl and pour the mixture over them. Toss to coat until the chicken is well covered. 2. Refrigerate for at least an hour. 3. Remove the marinated wings from the fridge and add the baking powder, tossing again to coat. Then place the chicken in the basket of your air fryer. 4. Cook for 25 minutes, giving the basket a shake intermittently throughout the cooking time. 5. When the wings are golden in color, remove from the fryer and serve immediately.
Per Serving: Calories 433; Fat 37g; Sodium 192mg; Carbs 14g; Fiber 1g; Sugar 4g; Protein 11g

Delicious Chicken Pizza Crusts

Prep time: 10 minutes | Cook time: 25 minutes | Serves: 1

½ cup mozzarella, shredded
¼ cup parmesan cheese, grated

1 lb. ground chicken

1. Select the "AIR FRY" function of Ninja Foodi digital air fry oven, set the temperature to 375 degrees F/ 190 degrees C and set the time to 25 minutes. Press the Start/Pause button and begin preheating. In a bowl, mix up all ingredients and then spread the mixture out, dividing it into four parts of equal size. 2. Cut a parchment paper into four circles, roughly six inches in diameter, and put the chicken mix onto the center of each piece, flattening the mixture to fill out the circle. 3. Cook for 25 minutes. Halfway through, turn the crust over to cook on the other side. Keep each batch warm while you move onto the next one. 4. Once all the crusts are cooked, top with cheese and the toppings of your choice. If desired, cook the topped crusts for an additional five minutes. 5. Serve hot, or freeze and save for later!
Per Serving: Calories 291; Fat 15.4g; Sodium 96mg; Carbs 3g; Fiber 1g; Sugar 2g; Protein 33g

Buttery Baked Chicken

Prep time: 10 minutes | Cook time: 60 minutes | Serves: 1

½ cup butter
1 teaspoon pepper

3 tablespoons garlic, minced
1 whole chicken

1. Select the "BAKE" function of Ninja Foodi digital air fry oven, set the temperature to 350 degrees F/ 175 degrees C and set the time to 60 minutes. Press the Start/Pause button and begin preheating. 2. Soft butter at room temperature, then mix well in a small bowl with the pepper and garlic. 3. Massage the butter into the chicken. Any remaining butter can go inside the chicken. 4. Cook the chicken in the fryer for half an hour. Flip, then cook on the other side for another thirty minutes. 5. Let sit for ten minutes before you carve it and serve.
Per Serving: Calories 381; Fat 36g; Sodium 2mg; Carbs 16g; Fiber 1g; Sugar 13g; Protein 0g

Crispy Chicken Thighs

Prep time: 10 minutes | Cook time: 25 minutes | Serves: 1

1 lb. chicken thighs
Salt and pepper
2 cups roasted pecans
1 cup water
1 cup flour

1. Select the "AIR FRY" function of Ninja Foodi digital air fry oven, set the temperature to 400 degrees F/ 200 degrees C and set the time to 22 minutes. Press the Start/Pause button and begin preheating. 2. Spice the chicken with salt and pepper, then set aside. 3. Pulse the roasted pecans in a food processor until a flour-like consistency is achieved. 4. Fill a dish with the water, another with the flour, and a third with the pecans. 5. Coat the thighs with the flour. Mix the remaining flour with the processed pecans. 6. Dredge the thighs in the water and then press into the -pecan mix, ensuring the chicken is completely covered. 7. Cook the chicken in the fryer for twenty-two minutes, with an extra five minutes added if you would like the chicken a darker-brown color. Serve.
Per Serving: Calories 426; Fat 22.6g; Sodium 357mg; Carbs 36g; Fiber 2g; Sugar 19g; Protein 20g

Sweet Strawberry Turkey

Prep time: 10 minutes | Cook time: 40 minutes | Serves: 2

2 lb. turkey breast
1 tablespoon olive oil
Salt and pepper
1 cup fresh strawberries

1. Select the "AIR FRY" function of Ninja Foodi digital air fry oven, set the temperature to 375 degrees F/ 190 degrees C and set the time to 30 minutes. Press the Start/Pause button and begin preheating. 2. Massage the turkey breast with olive oil, before seasoning with a generous amount of salt and pepper. 3. Cook the turkey in the fryer for fifteen minutes. Flip the turkey and cook for a further fifteen minutes. 4. During these last fifteen minutes, blend the strawberries in a food processor until a smooth consistency has been achieved. 5. Heap the strawberries over the turkey, then cook for a final seven minutes and enjoy.
Per Serving: Calories 253; Fat 13.4g; Sodium 663mg; Carbs 7g; Fiber 3g; Sugar 2g; Protein 26g

Chimichurri Turkey with Herbed Butter Sauce

Prep time: 15 minutes | Cook time: 55 minutes | Serves: 1

1 lb. turkey breast
½ cup chimichurri sauce
½ cup butter
¼ cup parmesan cheese, grated
¼ teaspoon garlic powder

1. Massage the chimichurri sauce into the turkey breast, then refrigerate in an airtight container for at least a half hour. 2. In the meantime, prepare the herbed butter. Mix together the butter, parmesan, and garlic powder, using a hand mixer if desired. 3. Select the "AIR ROAST" function of Ninja Foodi digital air fry oven, set the temperature to 350 degrees F/ 175 degrees C and set the time to 40 minutes. Press the Start/Pause button and begin preheating. 4. Place the turkey in the fryer and cook for twenty minutes. Flip and cook on the other side for a further twenty minutes. 5. Take care when removing the turkey from the fryer. Place it on a serving dish and enjoy with the herbed butter.
Per Serving: Calories 217; Fat 7.9g; Sodium 998mg; Carbs 17g; Fiber 4g; Sugar 8g; Protein 19g

Chicken & Spicy Tomatoes

Prep time: 5 minutes | Cook time: 35 minutes | Serves: 1

1 lb. boneless chicken breast
Salt and pepper
1 cup butter
1 cup tomatoes, diced
1½ teaspoons paprika
1 teaspoon pumpkin pie spices

1. Select the "AIR FRY" function of Ninja Foodi digital air fry oven, set the temperature to 375 degrees F/ 190 degrees C and set the time to 15 minutes. Press the Start/Pause button and begin preheating. 2. Cut the chicken into relatively thick slices and put them in the fryer. Sprinkle with salt and pepper to taste. Cook for fifteen minutes. 3. Melt the butter before adding the tomatoes, paprika, and pumpkin pie spices. Leave simmering while the chicken finishes cooking. 4. Pour the tomato mixture over the cooked chicken in serving plate. Serve hot.
Per Serving: Calories 106; Fat 6.9g; Sodium 1mg; Carbs 12g; Fiber 2g; Sugar 10g; Protein 0g

Coconut Chicken

Prep time: 5 minutes | Cook time: 35 minutes | Serves: 4

1½ cups coconut milk
2 tablespoons garam masala
1½ lbs. chicken thighs
¾ tablespoon coconut oil, melted

1. Combine the coconut oil and garam masala together in a bowl. Pour the mixture over the chicken thighs and leave to marinate for a half hour. 2. Select the "AIR FRY" function of Ninja Foodi digital air fry oven, set the temperature to 375 degrees F/ 190 degrees C and set the time to 15 minutes. Press the Start/Pause button and begin preheating. 3. Cook the chicken into the fryer for fifteen minutes. 4. Add in the coconut milk, giving it a good stir, then cook for an additional ten minutes. 5. Remove the chicken and place on a serving dish. Make sure to pour all of the coconut "gravy" over it and serve immediately.
Per Serving: Calories 118; Fat 7.2g; Sodium 232mg; Carbs 14g; Fiber 1g; Sugar 11g; Protein 2g

Roasted Whole Chicken

Prep time: 10 minutes | Cook time: 80 minutes | Serves: 6

6 lb. whole chicken
1 teaspoon olive oil
1 tablespoon minced garlic
1 white onion, peeled and halved
3 tablespoon butter

1. Select the "AIR FRY" function of Ninja Foodi digital air fry oven, set the temperature to 360 degrees F/ 180 degrees C and set the time to 75 minutes. Press the Start/Pause button and begin preheating. 2. Grease the chicken with oil and the minced garlic. 3. Place the peeled and halved onion, as well as the butter, inside of the chicken. 4. Cook the chicken in the fryer for seventy-five minutes. 5. Take care when removing the chicken from the fryer, then carve and serve.
Per Serving: Calories 87; Fat 5.6g; Sodium 42mg; Carbs 9g; Fiber 0g; Sugar 6g; Protein 0g

Sweet Saucy Chicken Sausages

Prep time: 5 minutes | Cook time: 15 minutes | Serves: 4

4 chicken sausages
2 tablespoons honey
¼ cup mayonnaise
2 tablespoons Dijon mustard
1 tablespoon balsamic vinegar
½ teaspoon dried rosemary

1. Select the "AIR FRY" function of Ninja Foodi digital air fry oven, set the temperature to 350 degrees F/ 175 degrees C and set the time to 13 minutes. Press the Start/Pause button and begin preheating. 2. Place the sausages on the air fry basket of your fryer and cook for about 13 minutes, flipping halfway. 3. Make the sauce by whisking the rest of the ingredients. 4. Pour the sauce over the warm sausages before serving.
Per Serving: Calories 350; Fat 22.5g; Sodium 166mg; Carbs 38g; Fiber 1g; Sugar 25g; Protein 1g

Traditional Tarragon Chicken

Prep time: 5 minutes | Cook time: 35 minutes | Serves: 4

2 cups roasted vegetable broth
2 chicken breasts, cut into halves
¾ teaspoon fine sea salt
¼ teaspoon mixed peppercorns, freshly cracked
1 teaspoon cumin powder
1½ teaspoons sesame oil
1½ tablespoons Worcester sauce
½ cup of spring onions, chopped
1 Serrano pepper, deveined and chopped
1 bell pepper, deveined and chopped
1 tablespoon tamari sauce
½ chopped fresh tarragon

1. Select the "AIR FRY" function of Ninja Foodi digital air fry oven, set the temperature to 380 degrees F/ 195 degrees C and set the time to 18 minutes. Press the Start/Pause button and begin preheating. Cook the vegetable broth and chicken breasts in a large saucepan for 10 minutes. 2. Lower the heat and simmer for another 10 minutes. 3. Let the chicken cool briefly. Then tear the chicken into shreds with a stand mixer or two forks. 4. Coat the shredded chicken with the salt, cracked peppercorns, cumin, sesame oil and the Worcester sauce. 5. Transfer to the Air Fryer and air fry for 18 minutes, or longer as needed. 6. In the meantime, cook the remaining ingredients over medium heat in a skillet, until the vegetables are tender and fragrant. 7. Take the skillet off the heat. Stir in the shredded chicken, incorporating all the ingredients well. Serve immediately.
Per Serving: Calories 173; Fat 13.6g; Sodium 281mg; Carbs 3g; Fiber 1g; Sugar 1g; Protein 10g

Pepperoni and Cheese Stuffed Chicken

Prep time: 5 minutes | Cook time: 15 minutes | Serves: 4

4 small boneless, skinless chicken breasts	16 slices pepperoni
¼ cup pizza sauce	Salt and pepper, to taste
½ cup Colby cheese, shredded	1½ tablespoons olive oil
	1½ tablespoons dried oregano

1. Select the "AIR FRY" function of Ninja Foodi digital air fry oven, set the temperature to 370 degrees F/ 185 degrees C and set the time to 15 minutes. Press the Start/Pause button and begin preheating. 2. Flatten the chicken breasts with a rolling pin. 3. Top the chicken with equal amounts of each ingredient and roll the fillets around the stuffing. Secure with a small skewer or two toothpicks. 4. Roast in the fryer on the basket for 13 - 15 minutes.
Per Serving: Calories 105; Fat 5g; Sodium 233mg; Carbs 7g; Fiber 2g; Sugar 4g; Protein 8g

Delicious Turkey Quinoa Skewers

Prep time: 5 minutes | Cook time: 10 minutes | Serves: 8

1 cup red quinoa, cooked	2 tablespoons seasoned friendly bread crumbs
1½ cups water	
14 oz. ground turkey	¾ teaspoon salt
2 small eggs, beaten	1 heaped teaspoon fresh rosemary, finely chopped
1 teaspoon ground ginger	
2½ tablespoons vegetable oil	½ teaspoon ground allspice
1 cup chopped fresh parsley	

1. In a bowl, mix ingredients together using your hands, kneading the mixture well. 2. Mold equal amounts of the mixture into small balls. 3. Select the "AIR FRY" function of Ninja Foodi digital air fry oven, set the temperature to 380 degrees F/ 195 degrees C and set the time to 10 minutes. Press the Start/Pause button and begin preheating. 4. Place the balls in the fryer basket and fry for 8 - 10 minutes. 5. Skewer them and serve with the dipping sauce of your choice.
Per Serving: Calories 76; Fat 5.7 g; Sodium 63mg; Carbs 2g; Fiber 0g; Sugar 2g; Protein 3g

Cheesy Chicken Caprese

Prep time: 5 minutes | Cook time: 20 minutes | Serves: 4

Tomatoes:

1-pint heirloom cherry tomatoes, halved	1 teaspoon olive oil
	¼ teaspoon kosher salt
4 large garlic cloves, slightly smashed	¼ teaspoon freshly ground black pepper

Chicken:

2 (8-ounce) boneless, skinless chicken breasts	2 tablespoons freshly grated Parmesan cheese
½ teaspoon kosher salt	Olive oil spray
Freshly ground black pepper	4 ounces fresh mozzarella cheese, thinly sliced
1 tablespoon prepared pesto	
1 large egg, beaten	2 tablespoons balsamic glaze
½ cup seasoned bread crumbs, whole wheat or gluten-free	Chopped fresh basil, for garnish

1. Select the "AIR FRY" function of Ninja Foodi digital air fry oven, set the temperature to 400 degrees F/ 200 degrees C and set the time to 5 minutes. Press the Start/Pause button and begin preheating. 2. For the tomatoes: In a medium bowl, combine the tomatoes, garlic, oil, salt, and pepper, tossing to coat. Place the air fryer basket and cook for 4 to 5 minutes, shaking the basket a few times, until the tomatoes are soft. 3. Meanwhile, for the chicken: Halve each chicken breast horizontally to make a total of 4 cutlets. Place the chicken between parchment paper. With meat mallet pound to a ¼-inch thickness. Spice with the salt and pepper to taste and evenly coat with the pesto. 4. Place the egg in a shallow bowl. Combine the bread crumbs with Parmesan in a separate shallow bowl. Dip the chicken into the egg, then coat in the bread crumb mixture, gently pressing to adhere. Spray both sides with oil. 5. Preheat the air fryer to 400 degrees F/ 200 degrees C again. 6. Place them in the air fryer basket. Cook for 7 minutes, flipping halfway, until golden and cooked through. Top each cutlet with 1 ounce of the mozzarella and one-quarter of the tomatoes. Return the cutlets to the air fryer basket, in batches, and cook for about 2 minutes to melt the cheese. Remove from the air fryer, drizzle with the balsamic glaze, and top with the basil. Serve immediately.
Per Serving: Calories 364; Fat 15.5g; Sodium 868mg; Carbs 20g; Fiber 3g; Sugar 10g; Protein 36g

Maple-Glazed Chicken

Prep time: 5 minutes | Cook time: 15 minutes | Serves: 4

2½ tablespoons maple syrup	1 teaspoon garlic puree
1 tablespoon tamari soy sauce	Seasoned salt
1 tablespoon oyster sauce	Ground pepper
1 teaspoon fresh lemon juice	2 boneless, skinless chicken breasts
1 teaspoon minced fresh ginger	

1. Select the "AIR FRY" function of Ninja Foodi digital air fry oven, set the temperature to 365 degrees F/ 185 degrees C and set the time to 15 minutes. Press the Start/Pause button and begin preheating. In a bowl, mix the maple syrup, tamari sauce, oyster sauce, lemon juice, fresh ginger and garlic puree. This is your marinade. 2. Sprinkle the chicken with salt and pepper. 3. Coat the chicken breasts with the marinade. Place some foil over the bowl and refrigerate for 3 hours, or overnight if possible. 4. Remove the chicken from the marinade. Place it in the Air Fryer and fry for 15 minutes flipping each one once or twice throughout. 5. Add the remaining marinade to a pan over medium heat. Allow the marinade to simmer for 3 - 5 minutes until it has reduced by half. 6. Pour over the cooked chicken and serve.
Per Serving: Calories 200; Fat 15.6g; Sodium 165mg; Carbs 5g; Fiber 1g; Sugar 2g; Protein 10g

Cabbage-Potato Cakes & Cajun Chicken Wings

Prep time: 10 minutes | Cook time: 30 minutes | Serves: 4

4 large-sized chicken wings	1 small-sized brown onion, coarsely grated
1 teaspoon Cajun seasoning	
1 teaspoon maple syrup	1 teaspoon garlic puree
¾ teaspoon sea salt flakes	1 medium whole egg, well whisked
¼ teaspoon red pepper flakes, crushed	
	½ teaspoon table salt
1 teaspoon onion powder	½ teaspoon ground black pepper
1 teaspoon porcini powder	1½ tablespoons flour
½ teaspoon celery seeds	¾ teaspoon baking powder
1 small-seized head of cabbage, shredded	1 heaped tablespoon cilantro
	1 tablespoon sesame oil
1 cup mashed potatoes	

1. Select the "BAKE" function of Ninja Foodi digital air fry oven, set the temperature to 390 degrees F/ 200 degrees C and set the time to 30 minutes. Press the Start/Pause button and begin preheating. 2. Pat the chicken wings dry. Place them in the fryer and cook for 25 - 30 minutes, ensuring they are cooked through. 3. Make the rub by combining the Cajun seasoning, maple syrup, sea salt flakes, red pepper, onion powder, porcini powder, and celery seeds. 4. Mix together the shredded cabbage, potato, onion, garlic puree, egg, table salt, black pepper, flour, baking powder and cilantro. 5. Separate the cabbage mixture into 4 portions and use your hands to mold each one into a cabbage-potato cake. 6. Douse each cake with the sesame oil. 7. Bake the cabbage-potato cakes in the fryer at 390 degrees F/ 200 degrees C for 10 minutes, turning them once through the cooking time. You will need to do this in multiple batches. 8. Serve the cakes and the chicken wings together.
Per Serving: Calories 138; Fat 10.6g; Sodium 102mg; Carbs 1g; Fiber 0g; Sugar 1g; Protein 9g

Traditional Provençal Chicken

Prep time: 5 minutes | Cook time: 25 minutes | Serves: 4

4 medium-sized skin-on chicken drumsticks	2 tablespoons olive oil
	2 garlic cloves, crushed
1½ teaspoons herbs de Provence	12 oz. crushed canned tomatoes
Salt and pepper to taste	1 small-size leek, thinly sliced
1 tablespoon rice vinegar	2 slices smoked bacon, chopped

1. Select the "AIR FRY" function of Ninja Foodi digital air fry oven, set the temperature to 360 degrees F/ 180 degrees C and set the time to 10 minutes. Press the Start/Pause button and begin preheating. Season the chicken drumsticks with herbs de Provence, salt and pepper. Pour over a light drizzling of the rice vinegar and olive oil. 2. Cook in the sheet pan for 8 - 10 minutes. 3. Pause the fryer. Add in the rest of ingredients, give them a stir, and resume cooking for 15 more minutes, checking them occasionally to ensure they don't overcook. 4. Serve with rice and lemon wedges.
Per Serving: Calories 288; Fat 23.3g; Sodium 308mg; Carbs 6g; Fiber 1g; Sugar 5g; Protein 2g

Parmesan-Crusted Turkey Cutlets with Arugula Salad

Prep time: 5 minutes | Cook time: 10 minutes | Serves: 4

4 turkey breast cutlets (18 ounces total)
Kosher salt and freshly ground black pepper
1 large egg, beaten
½ cup seasoned bread crumbs, regular or gluten-free
2 tablespoons grated Parmesan cheese
Olive oil spray
6 cups (4 ounces) baby arugula
1 tablespoon olive oil
1 tablespoon lemon juice
1 lemon cut into wedges for serving
Shaved Parmesan

1. One at a time, place a cutlet between two sheets of parchment paper or plastic wrap. Pound meat to a ¼-inch thickness. Season the cutlets with ½ teaspoon salt (total) and pepper to taste. 2. Place the egg in a shallow medium bowl. In a separate bowl, combine the bread crumbs and Parmesan. Dip the turkey cutlets in the egg, then in the bread crumb mixture, gently pressing to adhere. Shake off the excess bread crumbs and place on a work surface. Spray both sides with oil. 3. Select the "AIR FRY" function of Ninja Foodi digital air fry oven, set the temperature to 400 degrees F/ 200 degrees C and set the time to 8 minutes. Press the Start/Pause button and begin preheating. 4. Working in batches, place the turkey cutlets in the air fryer basket. Cook for 8 minutes, flipping halfway, until golden brown and the center is cooked. 5. Place the arugula in a bowl and toss with the oil, lemon juice, ¼ teaspoon salt, and pepper to taste. 6. To serve, place a cutlet on each plate and top with 1½ cups arugula salad. Serve with lemon wedges, and top with some shaved Parmesan, if desired.
Per Serving: Calories 244; Fat 6.5g; Sodium 534mg; Carbs 9g; Fiber 1g; Sugar 2g; Protein 36g

Herbed Cornish Hen

Prep time: 15 minutes | Cook time: 30 minutes | Serves: 2

1 Cornish hen (about 2 pounds)
½ teaspoon ground cumin
½ teaspoon dried oregano
½ teaspoon garlic powder
½ teaspoon kosher salt
⅛ teaspoon freshly ground black pepper
1 teaspoon unsalted butter, melted

1. Discard the giblets from the hen or reserve for another use. Using kitchen shears, cut off the neck and along both sides of the backbone to remove. Trim any excess fat, then cut the hen in half along the breastbone. Trim off the wing tips. 2. In a bowl, combine the cumin with oregano, garlic powder, salt, and pepper. 3. Place the hen skin side up on a work surface. Brush the skin with the melted butter, then season with the spices. 4. Select the "AIR FRY" function of Ninja Foodi digital air fry oven, set the temperature to 380 degrees F/ 195 degrees C and set the time to 30 minutes. Press the Start/Pause button and begin preheating. 5. Transfer the hen to the air fryer basket, skin side down. Cook for about 30 minutes, flipping halfway. Cover with foil for 5 minutes before serving. 6. To make this even lighter, remove the skin and you'll save around 250 calories and 25 grams of total fat per serving.
Per Serving: Calories 499; Fat 35.5g; Sodium 400mg; Carbs 1g; Fiber 0g; Sugar 0g; Protein 41g

Seasoned Chicken Tenders

Prep time: 5 minutes | Cook time: 10 minutes | Serves: 4

Seasoning:
1 teaspoon kosher salt
½ teaspoon garlic powder
½ teaspoon onion powder
½ teaspoon chili powder
¼ teaspoon sweet paprika
¼ teaspoon freshly ground black pepper
Chicken:
8 chicken breast tenders (1-pound total)
2 tablespoons mayonnaise

1. For the seasoning: In a bowl, combine the salt, garlic powder, onion powder, chili powder, paprika, and pepper. 2. For the chicken: Add the chicken in a bowl and add the mayonnaise. Mix well to coat all over, then sprinkle with the seasoning mix. 3. Select the "AIR FRY" function of Ninja Foodi digital air fry oven, set the temperature to 375 degrees F/ 190 degrees C and set the time to 7 minutes. Press the Start/Pause button and begin preheating. 4. Place a single layer of the chicken in the air fryer basket. Cook for 6 to 7 minutes, flipping halfway, until cooked through in the center. Serve immediately.
Per Serving: Calories 183; Fat 8.5g; Sodium 457mg; Carbs 0g; Fiber 0g; Sugar 0g; Protein 24g

Spiced Chicken with Avocado Salsa

Prep time: 10 minutes | Cook time: 15 minutes | Serves: 4

Chicken:
Kosher salt
4 (6-ounce) boneless, skinless chicken breasts
¾ teaspoon garlic powder
½ teaspoon onion powder
½ teaspoon ground cumin
½ teaspoon ancho chile powder
½ teaspoon sweet paprika
½ teaspoon dried oregano
⅛ teaspoon crushed red pepper flakes
Olive oil spray
Avocado Salsa:
½ cup finely diced red onion
3 tablespoons fresh lime juice
10 ounces avocado (2 medium Hass), diced
1 tablespoon chopped fresh cilantro
Kosher salt

1. For the chicken: Fill a large bowl with lukewarm water and add ¼ cup salt. Stir to dissolve. Let the water cool to room temperature. Add the chicken to the water and refrigerate for at least 1 hour to brine. Remove the chicken from the water and pat dry with paper towels. 2. In a small bowl, combine ¾ teaspoon salt, the garlic powder, onion powder, cumin, ancho powder, paprika, oregano, and pepper flakes. Spritz the chicken all over with oil, then rub with the spice mix. 3. Select the "AIR FRY" function of Ninja Foodi digital air fry oven, set the temperature to 380 degrees F/ 195 degrees C and set the time to 10 minutes. Press the Start/Pause button and begin preheating. 4. Place the chicken in the air fryer basket. Cook for about 10 minutes, flipping halfway, until browned and cooked through. 5. Meanwhile, for the avocado salsa: In a medium bowl, combine the onion and lime juice. Fold in avocado and cilantro and season with ¼ teaspoon salt. 6. Serve the chicken topped with the salsa.
Per Serving: Calories 324; Fat 15g; Sodium 490mg; Carbs 10g; Fiber 5.5g; Sugar 2g; Protein 38g

Crispy Pickle-Brined Chicken Tenders

Prep time: 5 minutes | Cook time: 22 minutes | Serves: 4

12 chicken tenders
1¼ cups dill pickle juice
1 large egg
1 large egg white
½ teaspoon kosher salt
Freshly ground black pepper
½ cup seasoned bread crumbs
½ cup seasoned panko bread crumbs
Olive oil spray

1. Add the chicken with the pickle juice in a bowl. Cover it and let it marinate for 8 hours in the refrigerator. 2. Drain and pat dry the chicken. 3. In a bowl, beat the whole egg, egg white, salt, and pepper to taste. In a shallow bowl, combine both bread crumbs. 4. Dredge the chicken in the egg, then into the bread crumbs. Generously spray both sides of the chicken with oil. 5. Select the "AIR FRY" function of Ninja Foodi digital air fry oven, set the temperature to 400 degrees F/ 200 degrees C and set the time to 12 minutes. Press the Start/Pause button and begin preheating. 6. Place the chicken in the air fryer basket. Cook for 10 to 12 minutes, flipping halfway, until cooked through, crispy, and golden. Serve immediately.
Per Serving: Calories 257; Fat 5.5g; Sodium 742mg; Carbs 14g; Fiber 1g; Sugar 1g; Protein 35g

Delicious Lemongrass Hens

Prep time: 20 minutes | Cook time: 65 minutes | Serves: 4

1 14 oz hen (chicken)
1 teaspoon lemongrass
1 teaspoon ground coriander
1 oz celery stalk, chopped
1 teaspoon dried cilantro
3 spring onions, diced
2 tablespoons avocado oil
2 tablespoons lime juice
½ teaspoon lemon zest, grated
1 teaspoon salt
1 tablespoon apple cider vinegar
1 teaspoon chili powder
½ teaspoon ground black pepper

1. In the mixing bowl mix up lemongrass, ground coriander, dried cilantro, lime juice, lemon zest, salt, apple cider vinegar, and ground black pepper. Then add spring onions and celery stalk. 2. After this, rub the hen with the spice mixture and leave for 10 minutes to marinate. 3.Meanwhile, Select the "AIR FRY" function of Ninja Foodi digital air fry oven, set the temperature to 375 degrees F/ 190 degrees C and set the time to 65 minutes. Press the Start/Pause button and begin preheating. Put the spiced hen in the air fryer and cook it for 55 minutes. Flip it and cook for 10 minutes more.
Per Serving: Calories 177; Fat 4.1g; Sodium 568mg; Carbs 4.4g; Fiber 1g; Sugar 1g; Protein 29.3g

Crispy Popcorn Chicken

Prep time: 10 minutes | Cook time: 15 minutes | Serves: 4

½ cup mayonnaise
1 teaspoon prepared yellow mustard
½ cup finely shredded cheddar cheese (about 2 ounces) (see Note, here)
½ cup pork dust (see here)
¼ teaspoon garlic powder
¼ teaspoon onion powder
¼ teaspoon smoked paprika
1 pound boneless, skinless chicken breasts, cut into ½-inch pieces
Chopped fresh parsley, for garnish
Ranch Dressing (here), for serving

1. Spray the air fryer basket with avocado oil. Select the "AIR FRY" function of Ninja Foodi digital air fry oven, set the temperature to 400 degrees F/ 200 degrees C and set the time to 15 minutes. Press the Start/Pause button and begin preheating. 2. In a large bowl, mix together the mayonnaise and mustard. In a separate medium-sized bowl, mix together the cheese, pork dust, garlic powder, onion powder, and paprika until well combined. 3. Add the chicken pieces to the mayonnaise mixture and stir well to coat. One at a time, roll the coated chicken pieces in the pork dust mixture and spray them with avocado oil, then place them in the air fryer basket, leaving space between them. 4. Cook the chicken for 12 to 15 minutes, until the coating is golden brown. 5. Garnish with fresh parsley, if desired, and serve with ranch dressing, if desired. Store leftovers in an airtight container in the fridge for up to 4 days. Serve leftovers chilled or reheat.
Per Serving: Calories 354; Fat 7.9g; Sodium 704mg; Carbs 6g; Fiber 3.6g; Sugar 6g; Protein 18g

Asian-Style Turkey Meatballs with Hoisin Sauce

Prep time: 5 minutes | Cook time: 20 minutes | Serves: 4

Meatballs:
1⅓ pounds 93% lean ground turkey
¼ cup panko bread crumbs, regular or gluten-free
3 chopped scallions, plus more for garnish
¼ cup chopped fresh cilantro
1 large egg
Hoisin Sauce:
2 tablespoons hoisin sauce
2 tablespoons fresh orange juice
1 tablespoon grated fresh ginger
1 garlic clove, minced
1 tablespoon reduced-sodium soy sauce or tamari
2 teaspoons toasted sesame oil
¾ teaspoon kosher salt
Olive oil spray

1 tablespoon reduced-sodium soy sauce or tamari

1. For the meatballs: In a bowl, combine the turkey, panko, scallions, cilantro, egg, ginger, garlic, sesame oil, soy sauce, and salt. Gently mix with until combined. Roll into 12 meatballs (¼ cup each) and spritz with oil. 2. Select the "AIR FRY" function of Ninja Foodi digital air fry oven, set the temperature to 380 degrees F/ 195 degrees C and set the time to 9 minutes. Press the Start/Pause button and begin preheating. 3. Place meatballs in the air fryer basket. Cook for about 9 minutes, flipping halfway, until cooked through in the center and browned. 4. Meanwhile, for the hoisin sauce: In a small saucepan, combine the hoisin sauce, orange juice, and soy sauce and boil over medium-low heat. Lower the heat and manage to simmer until reduced slightly, 2 to 3 minutes.
Per Serving: Calories 313; Fat 16.5g; Sodium 755mg; Carbs 10g; Fiber 1g; Sugar 4g; Protein 31g

Tangy Chicken with Peppers

Prep time: 5 minutes | Cook time: 25 minutes | Serves: 4

4 chicken breasts, skinless, boneless and halved
2 zucchinis, sliced
4 tomatoes, cut into wedges
2 yellow bell peppers, cut into wedges
2 tablespoons olive oil
1 teaspoon Italian seasoning

1. Select the "AIR FRY" function of Ninja Foodi digital air fry oven, set the temperature to 380 degrees F/ 195 degrees C and set the time to 25 minutes. Press the Start/Pause button and begin preheating. 2. In a dish, mix all the ingredients, toss, introduce in the fryer and cook for 25 minutes. Divide everything between plates and serve.
Per Serving: Calories 280; Fat 12g; Sodium 678mg; Carbs 6g; Fiber 4g; Sugar 2g; Protein 14g

Tasty Chicken Piccata

Prep time: 5 minutes | Cook time: 10 minutes | Serves: 4

Chicken:
2 (8-ounce) boneless, skinless chicken breasts
¼ teaspoon kosher salt
Freshly ground black pepper
Sauce:
1 tablespoon whipped butter
½ cup reduced-sodium chicken broth
¼ cup dry white wine
For Serving:
1 lemon, sliced
2 large egg whites
⅔ cup seasoned bread crumbs
Olive oil spray

Juice of 1 lemon, lemon halves reserved
Freshly ground black pepper
1 tablespoon capers, drained

Chopped fresh parsley leaves

1. Cut the chicken horizontally for 4 cutlets. Pound it to a ¼-inch thickness. Spice with the salt and pepper to taste. 2. In a bowl, beat the egg whites with little water. Place the bread crumbs on a deep plate. Dip chicken in the egg, then in the bread crumbs. Generously spray both sides of the chicken with olive oil. 3. Select the "AIR FRY" function of Ninja Foodi digital air fry oven, set the temperature to 370 degrees F/ 185 degrees C and set the time to 6 minutes. Press the Start/Pause button and begin preheating. 4. Working in batches, place the chicken cutlets in the air fryer. Cook for about 6 minutes, flipping halfway, until cooked through, crisp, and golden. 5. For the sauce: In a skillet, melt the butter and add the chicken broth along with wine, lemon juice, and pepper to taste. Boil until the liquid is reduced by half. Discard the lemon halves and stir in the capers.
Per Serving: Calories 232; Fat 6g; Sodium 691mg; Carbs 13g; Fiber 2g; Sugar 2g; Protein 29g

Cornflake-Crusted Chicken with Romaine Slaw

Prep time: 10 minutes | Cook time: 35 minutes | Serves: 4

Chicken:
8 bone-in chicken drumsticks (30 ounces total), skin removed
½ teaspoon kosher salt
2 large eggs
Crumb Coating:
1⅔ cups (3½ ounces)
Olive oil spray
1 teaspoon kosher salt
1 tablespoon dried parsley
1½ teaspoons sweet paprika
1 teaspoon dried marjoram
½ teaspoon sweet paprika
¼ teaspoon garlic powder
¼ teaspoon chili powder
Olive oil spray

1 teaspoon dried thyme
½ teaspoon garlic powder
½ teaspoon onion powder
¼ teaspoon chili powder
Romaine Slaw for serving

1. For the chicken: Season the chicken with the salt. Whisk the eggs with 1 teaspoon water, the paprika, garlic powder, and chili powder. Set aside. 2. For the crumb coating: Place the cornflakes in a zip-top bag and crush them. Place to a shallow bowl. Spritz the cornflakes with a little oil, then add the salt, parsley, paprika, marjoram, thyme, garlic powder, onion powder, and chili powder. Mix well to combine. 3. Dip drumstick in the egg mix, then in the crumbs. 4. Select the "AIR FRY" function of Ninja Foodi digital air fry oven, set the temperature to 350 degrees F/ 175 degrees C and set the time to 28 minutes. Press the Start/Pause button and begin preheating. Place the chicken in the air fryer basket. Cook for about 28 minutes, flipping halfway, until the chicken is cooked through and golden. Serve with the slaw.
Per Serving: Calories 346; Fat 11g; Sodium 693mg; Carbs 15g; Fiber 1g; Sugar 2g; Protein 45g

Spicy Chicken Breasts

Prep time: 5 minutes | Cook time: 20 minutes | Serves: 4

4 chicken breasts, skinless and boneless
1 teaspoon chili powder
A pinch of salt and black pepper
A drizzle of olive oil
1 teaspoon smoked paprika
1 teaspoon garlic powder
1 tablespoon parsley, chopped

1. Select the "AIR FRY" function of Ninja Foodi digital air fry oven, set the temperature to 350 degrees F/ 175 degrees C and set the time to 10 minutes. Press the Start/Pause button and begin preheating. Spice chicken with salt and pepper, and rub it with the oil and all the other instead of the parsley, Put the chicken breasts in your air fryer's basket and cook at for 10 minutes on each side. 2. Sprinkle the parsley on top and serve.
Per Serving: Calories 222; Fat 11g; Sodium 245mg; Carbs 6g; Fiber 4g; Sugar 1g; Protein 12g

Chicken Chimichangas

Prep time: 5 minutes | Cook time: 10 minutes | Serves: 4

Pico De Gallo:

½ cup tomato, diced	1 teaspoon fresh lime juice
3 tablespoons onion	¼ teaspoon kosher salt
1 tablespoon chopped cilantro	Freshly ground black pepper

Chimichangas:

12 ounces shredded chicken breast	drained
Juice of ½ orange	4 (7- to 8-inch) low-carb whole wheat tortillas
Juice of ½ lime	½ cup (2 ounces) shredded pepper Jack cheese
1 garlic clove, minced	
1 teaspoon ground cumin	Olive oil spray
1 (4-ounce) can green chiles,	

For Serving:

3 cups lettuce, shredded	4 ounces avocado, diced
4 tablespoons sour cream	

1. In a bowl, Add the tomato, onion along with cilantro, lime juice, salt, pepper, mix well to combine. 2. For the chimichangas: In a bowl, combine the chicken, orange juice, lime juice, garlic, cumin, and drained chiles. Mix well to incorporate. 3. Place the chicken mixture (almost ¾ cup) on. Sprinkle with cheese. Lift and wrap it around the filling. 4. Select the "AIR FRY" function of Ninja Foodi digital air fry oven, set the temperature to 400 degrees F/ 200 degrees C and set the time to 8 minutes. Press the Start/Pause button and begin preheating. 5. Lightly grease the chimichangas with oil. Place in the air fryer basket. Cook for 7 to 8 minutes, flipping halfway, until golden and crisp. 6. To serve: Place ¾ cup lettuce top with chimichanga along with pico de gallo, sour cream, and avocado. Garnish with cilantro. Serve immediately.
Per Serving: Calories 391; Fat 18.5g; Sodium 716mg; Carbs 30g; Fiber 16.5g; Sugar 5g; Protein 40g

Delicious Chicken Cordon Bleu

Prep time: 5 minutes | Cook time: 15 minutes | Serves: 4

8 (4 ounces each) thin-sliced chicken breast cutlets	lengthwise
¾ teaspoon kosher salt	1 large egg
Freshly ground black pepper	2 large egg whites
4 slices (1 ounce each) reduced-sodium deli ham, halved lengthwise	¾ cup bread crumbs, regular or gluten-free
4 slices (1 ounce each) low-sodium Swiss cheese, halved	2 tablespoons grated Parmesan cheese
	Olive oil spray

1. Season the chicken cutlets with ¾ teaspoon salt and pepper to taste. Working with one at a time, place a cutlet on a work surface and put a half-slice of ham and cheese on top. Roll the chicken up, then set aside, seam side down. 2. In a bowl, beat together the whole egg and egg whites. In a shallow bowl, mix the bread crumbs and Parmesan. 3. Dip the chicken into the egg mixture, then into the bread crumbs, gently pressing to adhere. Spray both sides with oil. 4. Select the "AIR FRY" function of Ninja Foodi digital air fry oven, set the temperature to 400 degrees F/ 200 degrees C and set the time to 12 minutes. Press the Start/Pause button and begin preheating. 5. Working in batches, place chicken rolls seam side down in the air fryer basket. Cook for 12 minutes, flipping halfway, until golden and cooked through. Serve immediately.
Per Serving: Calories 497; Fat 15.5g; Sodium 983mg; Carbs 16g; Fiber 1g; Sugar 2g; Protein 69g

Tropical Chicken

Prep time: 5 minutes | Cook time: 20 minutes | Serves: 4

4 chicken breasts, skinless, boneless and halved	2 tablespoons stevia
4 tablespoons coconut aminos	Salt and black pepper to the taste
1 teaspoon olive oil	¼ cup chicken stock
	1 tablespoon ginger, grated

1. Select the "AIR FRY" function of Ninja Foodi digital air fry oven, set the temperature to 380 degrees F/ 195 degrees C and set the time to 20 minutes. Press the Start/Pause button and begin preheating. In a pan, combine the chicken with the ginger and all the ingredients and toss. Put the pan in your air fryer and cook for 20 minutes, shaking the fryer halfway. Serve with a side salad.
Per Serving: Calories 256; Fat 12g; Sodium 311mg; Carbs 6g; Fiber 4g; Sugar 2g; Protein 14g

Turkey Meatloaves

Prep time: 5 minutes | Cook time: 20 minutes | Serves: 4

Meatloaves:

1 pound 93% lean ground turkey	¼ cup chopped scallions
⅓ cup bread crumbs, regular or gluten-free	2 tablespoons chopped fresh cilantro
⅓ cup canned black beans, rinsed and drained	1 large egg, beaten
⅓ cup frozen corn	1 tablespoon tomato paste
¼ cup jarred chunky mild salsa	1 teaspoon kosher salt
¼ cup minced onion	½ teaspoon ground cumin

Glaze:

2 tablespoons ketchup	2 tablespoons jarred mild salsa

1. For the meatloaves: In a medium bowl, combine the turkey, bread crumbs, beans, corn, salsa, onion, scallions, cilantro, egg, tomato paste, salt, and cumin and mix well. Divide the mixture into 4 equal portions and shape into 1-inch-thick round patties. 2. For the glaze: In a small bowl, stir together the ketchup and salsa. 3. Select the "AIR FRY" function of Ninja Foodi digital air fry oven, set the temperature to 350 degrees F/ 175 degrees C and set the time to 18 minutes. Press the Start/Pause button and begin preheating. 4. Working in batches, place the meatloaves in the air fryer basket. Cook for about 18 minutes, flipping halfway, until the center is cooked through. Brush the meatloaves with the glaze and return to the air fryer and cook for about 2 minutes to heat through. Serve immediately.
Per Serving: Calories 279; Fat 11.5g; Sodium 695mg; Carbs 18g; Fiber 3g; Sugar 4g; Protein 26g

Spiced Yogurt-Marinated Chicken Thighs with Vegetables

Prep time: 10 minutes | Cook time: 22 minutes | Serves: 4

¼ cup whole-milk yogurt (not Greek)	8 (4-ounce) boneless, skinless chicken thighs, trimmed
3 garlic cloves, minced	7 ounces shishito peppers
2 tablespoons fresh lemon juice	2 medium vine tomatoes, quartered
1 teaspoon grated fresh ginger	Olive oil spray
1 teaspoon garam masala	1 tablespoon chopped fresh cilantro, for garnish
¼ teaspoon ground turmeric	
¼ teaspoon cayenne pepper	1 lemon, cut into wedges
1¼ teaspoons kosher salt	

1. In a bowl, stir the yogurt, garlic, lemon juice, ginger, garam masala, turmeric, cayenne, and 1 teaspoon of the salt. Place the chicken and marinade in a zip-top bag. Marinate the chicken in the refrigerator for at least 2 hours, or overnight. 2. Select the "AIR FRY" function of Ninja Foodi digital air fry oven, set the temperature to 400 degrees F/ 200 degrees C and set the time to 14 minutes. Press the Start/ Pause button and begin preheating. 3. Remove the chicken from the marinade. Place chicken in the air fryer basket. Cook for about 14 minutes, flipping halfway, until slightly browned and cooked through. Set the cooked chicken aside and tent with foil. 4. Spritz the shishito and tomatoes all over with oil. Place in the air fryer basket and cook for 8 minutes, shaking halfway, until soft and slightly charred. Sprinkle with the remaining ¼ teaspoon salt. 5. Transfer the chicken and vegetables to plates. Garnish with cilantro and serve with the lemon wedges on the side.
Per Serving: Calories 321; Fat 10g; Sodium 563mg; Carbs 11g; Fiber 2g; Sugar 5g; Protein 46g

Buttery Parmesan Chicken Wings

Prep time: 5 minutes | Cook time: 30 minutes | Serves: 4

2 pounds chicken wings	½ cup heavy cream
Salt and black pepper to the taste	½ teaspoon basil, dried
3 garlic cloves, minced	½ teaspoon oregano, dried
3 tablespoons butter, melted	¼ cup parmesan, grated

1. Select the "AIR FRY" function of Ninja Foodi digital air fry oven, set the temperature to 380 degrees F/ 195 degrees C and set the time to 30 minutes. Press the Start/Pause button and begin preheating. In a dish, mix the chicken wings with all the except the parmesan and toss. 2. Put the dish to air fryer and cook for 30 minutes. Spread the cheese on top, leave the mix aside for 10 minutes, divide between plates and serve.
Per Serving: Calories 270; Fat 12g; Sodium 444mg; Carbs 6g; Fiber 3g; Sugar 1g; Protein 17g

Delicious Provolone Meatballs

Prep time: 10 minutes | Cook time: 12 minutes | Serves: 6

12 oz ground chicken	1 teaspoon salt
½ cup coconut flour	4 oz Provolone cheese, grated
2 egg whites, whisked	1 teaspoon ground oregano
1 teaspoon ground black pepper	½ teaspoon chili powder
1 egg yolk	1 tablespoon avocado oil

1. In the bowl mix up ground chicken, ground black pepper, egg yolk, salt, Provolone cheese, ground oregano, and chili powder. Stir the mixture until homogenous and make the small meatballs. 2. Dip the meatballs in the whisked egg whites and coat in the coconut flour. Select the "AIR FRY" function of Ninja Foodi digital air fry oven, set the temperature to 370 degrees F/ 185 degrees C and set the time to 12 minutes. Press the Start/Pause button and begin preheating. Put the chicken meatballs in the air fryer basket and cook them for 6 minutes from both sides.
Per Serving: Calories 234; Fat 11.7g; Sodium 411mg; Carbs 6.6g; Fiber 3.7g; Sugar 2g; Protein 24.3g

Herbed Okra Chicken Thighs

Prep time: 5 minutes | Cook time: 30 minutes | Serves: 4

4 chicken thighs, bone-in and skinless	Zest of 1 lemon, grated
	4 garlic cloves, minced
A pinch of salt and black pepper	1 tablespoon thyme, chopped
1 cup okra	1 tablespoon parsley, chopped
½ cup butter, melted	

1. Select the "AIR FRY" function of Ninja Foodi digital air fry oven, set the temperature to 370 degrees F/ 185 degrees C and set the time to 20 minutes. Press the Start/Pause button and begin preheating. Heat up a pan that fits your air fryer with half of the butter, add the chicken in and brown them for 2-3 minutes on each side. 2.Add the rest of the butter, the okra and all the remaining ingredients, toss, put it in the air fryer and cook for 20 minutes. Divide between plates and serve.
Per Serving: Calories 270; Fat 12g; Sodium 264mg; Carbs 6g; Fiber 4g; Sugar 1g; Protein 14g

Sour and Spicy Chicken Drumsticks

Prep time: 10 minutes | Cook time: 20 minutes | Serves: 6

6 chicken drumsticks	½ teaspoon chili flakes
1 teaspoon dried oregano	1 teaspoon garlic powder
1 tablespoon lemon juice	½ teaspoon ground coriander
½ teaspoon lemon zest, grated	1 tablespoon avocado oil
1 teaspoon ground cumin	

1. Select the "AIR FRY" function of Ninja Foodi digital air fry oven, set the temperature to 375 degrees F/ 190 degrees C and set the time to 20 minutes. Press the Start/Pause button and begin preheating. Rub the chicken drumsticks with dried oregano, lemon juice, lemon zest, ground cumin, chili flakes, garlic powder, and ground coriander. Then sprinkle them with avocado oil and put in the air fryer. Cook the chicken drumsticks for 20 minutes.
Per Serving: Calories 85; Fat 3.1g; Sodium 278mg; Carbs 0.9g; Fiber 0.3g; Sugar 0.1g; Protein 12.9g

Tomato Chicken

Prep time: 10 minutes | Cook time: 18 minutes | Serves: 4

1-pound chicken breast, skinless, boneless	1 teaspoon avocado oil
	½ teaspoon garlic powder
1 tablespoon keto tomato sauce	

1. In the small bowl mix up tomato sauce, avocado oil, and garlic powder. Then brush the chicken breast with the tomato sauce mixture well. Select the "AIR FRY" function of Ninja Foodi digital air fry oven, set the temperature to 385 degrees F/ 195 degrees C and set the time to 18 minutes. Press the Start/Pause button and begin preheating. Place the chicken in the air fryer and cook it for 15 minutes. Flip it and cook for 3 minutes more. Slice the cooked chicken breast into servings.
Per Serving: Calories 139; Fat 3g; Sodium 433mg; Carbs 2g; Fiber 0.2g; Sugar 0.8g; Protein 24.2g

Garlic lemon Chicken Wings

Prep time: 5 minutes | Cook time: 30 minutes | Serves: 4

2 pounds chicken wings	Zest of 1 lemon, grated
¼ cup olive oil	A pinch of salt and black pepper
Juice of 2 lemons	2 garlic cloves, minced

1. Select the "AIR FRY" function of Ninja Foodi digital air fry oven, set the temperature to 400 degrees F/ 200 degrees C and set the time to 30 minutes. Press the Start/Pause button and begin preheating. In a bowl, mix the chicken wings with the rest of the ingredients and toss well. Put the chicken wings in your air fryer's basket and cook for 30 minutes, shaking halfway. Serve with a salad.
Per Serving: Calories 263; Fat 14g; Sodium 547mg; Carbs 6g; Fiber 4g; Sugar 2g; Protein 15g

Creamy Chicken Mix

Prep time: 15 minutes | Cook time: 16 minutes | Serves: 4

1-pound chicken wings	½ teaspoon smoked paprika
¼ cup cream cheese	½ teaspoon ground nutmeg
1 tablespoon apple cider vinegar	1 teaspoon avocado oil
1 teaspoon Truvia	

1. In the mixing bowl mix up cream cheese, Truvia, apple cider vinegar, smoked paprika, and ground nutmeg. Then add the wings and coat them in the cream cheese mixture well. 2. Leave the chicken wings in the cream cheese mixture for 10-15 minutes to marinate. Meanwhile, Select the "AIR FRY" function of Ninja Foodi digital air fry oven, set the temperature to 380 degrees F/ 195 degrees C and set the time to 16 minutes. Press the Start/Pause button and begin preheating. Put the chicken wings in the air fryer and cook them for 8 minutes. 3. Then flip the chicken wings on another and brush with cream cheese marinade. Cook the chicken wings for 8 minutes more.
Per Serving: Calories 271; Fat 13.7g; Sodium 420mg; Carbs 1.2g; Fiber 0.2g; Sugar 0.3g; Protein 34g

Spicy Chicken with dill and Parmesan

Prep time: 15 minutes | Cook time: 20 minutes | Serves: 6

18 oz chicken breast, skinless, boneless	2 tablespoons avocado oil
	1 teaspoon Erythritol
5 oz pork rinds	¼ teaspoon onion powder
3 oz Parmesan, grated	1 teaspoon cayenne pepper
3 eggs, beaten	1 chili pepper, minced
1 teaspoon chili flakes	½ teaspoon dried dill
1 teaspoon ground paprika	

1. In the shallow bowl, mix up chili flakes, ground paprika, Erythritol. Onion powder, and cayenne pepper. Add dried dill and stir the mixture gently. Then rub the chicken breast in the spice mixture. 2. Then rub the chicken with minced chili pepper. Dip the chicken breast in the beaten eggs. After this, coat it in the Parmesan and dip in the eggs again. Then coat the chicken in the pork rinds and sprinkle with avocado oil. 3. Select the "AIR FRY" function of Ninja Foodi digital air fry oven, set the temperature to 380 degrees F/ 195 degrees C and set the time to 20 minutes. Press the Start/Pause button and begin preheating. Put the chicken breast in the air fryer and cook it for 16 minutes. Then flip the chicken breast on another side and cook it for 4 minutes more.
Per Serving: Calories 318; Fat 16.5g; Sodium 245mg; Carbs 1.5g; Fiber 0.5g; Sugar 0.5g; Protein 40.7g

Almond Chicken Tenders

Prep time: 5 minutes | Cook time: 20 minutes | Serves: 4

4 chicken breasts, skinless, boneless and cut into tenders	⅓ cup almond flour
	2 eggs, whisked
A pinch of salt and black pepper	9 ounces coconut flakes

1. Select the "AIR ROAST" function of Ninja Foodi digital air fry oven, set the temperature to 400 degrees F/ 200 degrees C and set the time to 20 minutes. Press the Start/Pause button and begin preheating. Spice the chicken tenders with salt and pepper, dredge them in almond flour, then dip in eggs and roll in coconut flakes. 2. Put the chicken tenders in your air fryer's basket and cook for 10 minutes on each side. Serve with a side salad.
Per Serving: Calories 250; Fat 12g; Sodium 178mg; Carbs 6g; Fiber 4g; Sugar 1g; Protein 14g

Chicken with veggies

Prep time: 15 minutes | Cook time: 25 minutes | Serves: 4

1 pound chicken thighs, boneless and skinless
Juice of 1 lemon
2 tablespoons olive oil
3 garlic cloves, minced
1 teaspoon oregano, dried
½ pound asparagus, trimmed and halved
A pinch of salt and black pepper
1 zucchini, halved lengthwise and sliced into half-moons

1. Select the "AIR FRY" function of Ninja Foodi digital air fry oven, set the temperature to 380 degrees F/ 195 degrees C and set the time to 25 minutes. Press the Start/Pause button and begin preheating. In a bowl, add the chicken with all the except the asparagus and the zucchinis, toss and leave aside for 15 minutes. 2. Add the zucchinis and the asparagus, toss, put everything into a pan that fits the air fryer, and cook for 25 minutes. Divide everything between plates and serve.
Per Serving: Calories 280; Fat 11g; Sodium 511mg; Carbs 6g; Fiber 4g; Sugar 2g; Protein 17g

Chicken Thighs and Olives Mix

Prep time: 10 minutes | Cook time: 30 minutes | Serves: 4

8 chicken thighs, boneless and skinless
A pinch of salt and black pepper
2 tablespoons olive oil
1 teaspoon oregano, dried
½ teaspoon garlic powder
1 cup pepperoncini, drained and sliced
½ cup black olives, pitted and sliced
½ cup kalamata olives, pitted and sliced
¼ cup parmesan, grated

1. Select the "AIR FRY" function of Ninja Foodi digital air fry oven, set the temperature to 370 degrees F/ 185 degrees C and set the time to 25 minutes. Press the Start/Pause button and begin preheating. Heat up a pan that fits the air fryer with the oil over medium-high heat, add the chicken and sear to brown for 2 minutes on each side. Add salt, pepper, and all the other except the parmesan and toss. 2. Put the pan in the air fryer, sprinkle the parmesan on top and cook for 25 minutes. Divide the chicken mix between plates and serve.
Per Serving: Calories 270; Fat 14g; Sodium 200mg; Carbs 6g; Fiber 1.3g; Sugar 0.9g; Protein 18g

Ghee Roast Chicken

Prep time: 15 minutes | Cook time: 30 minutes | Serves: 4

12 oz chicken legs
1 teaspoon nutritional yeast
1 teaspoon chili flakes
½ teaspoon ground cumin
½ teaspoon garlic powder
1 teaspoon ground turmeric
½ teaspoon ground paprika
1 teaspoon Splenda
¼ cup coconut flour
1 tablespoon ghee, melted

1. In the mixing bowl mix up nutritional yeast, chili flakes, ground cumin, garlic powder, ground turmeric, ground paprika, Splenda, and coconut flour. Then brush every chicken leg with ghee and coat well in the coconut flour mixture. 2. Select the "AIR FRY" function of Ninja Foodi digital air fry oven, set the temperature to 380 degrees F/ 195 degrees C and set the time to 30 minutes. Press the Start/Pause button and begin preheating. Place the chicken in the air fryer in one layer. Cook them for 15 minutes. Then flip the chicken legs on another side and cook them for 15 minutes more.
Per Serving: Calories 238; Fat 10.9g; Sodium 111mg; Carbs 6.8g; Fiber 3.5g; Sugar 2g; Protein 26.7g

Pesto Baked Chicken Wings

Prep time: 10 minutes | Cook time: 25 minutes | Serves: 4

1 cup basil pesto
2 tablespoons olive oil
A pinch of salt and black pepper
1 and ½ pounds chicken wings

1. Select the "BAKE" function of Ninja Foodi digital air fry oven, set the temperature to 380 degrees F/ 195 degrees C and set the time to 25 minutes. Press the Start/Pause button and begin preheating. In a bowl, add the chicken wings with all the ingredients and toss well. Put the meat in the air fryer's basket and cook for 25 minutes. Divide between plates and serve.
Per Serving: Calories 244; Fat 11g; Sodium 410mg; Carbs 6g; Fiber 4g; Sugar 2g; Protein 17g

Traditional Hoisin Chicken

Prep time: 25 minutes | Cook time: 22 minutes | Serves: 4

½ teaspoon hoisin sauce
½ teaspoon salt
½ teaspoon chili powder
½ teaspoon ground black pepper
½ teaspoon ground cumin
¼ teaspoon xanthan gum
1 teaspoon apple cider vinegar
1 tablespoon sesame oil
3 tablespoons coconut cream
½ teaspoon minced garlic
½ teaspoon chili paste
1-pound chicken drumsticks
2 tablespoons almond flour

1. Rub the chicken drumsticks with salt, chili powder, ground black pepper, ground cumin, and leave for 10 minutes to marinate. Meanwhile, in the mixing bowl mix up chili paste, minced garlic, coconut cream, apple cider vinegar, xanthan gum, and almond flour. 2. Coat the chicken drumsticks in the coconut cream mixture well, and leave to marinate for 10 minutes more. Select the "AIR FRY" function of Ninja Foodi digital air fry oven, set the temperature to 375 degrees F/ 190 degrees C and set the time to 25 minutes. Press the Start/Pause button and begin preheating. Put the chicken drumsticks in the air fryer and cook them for 22 minutes.
Per Serving: Calories 279; Fat 14.5g; Sodium 233mg; Carbs 3.4g; Fiber 1.7g; Sugar 1.6g; Protein 32.4g

Spiced Coconut Chicken

Prep time: 15 minutes | Cook time: 12 minutes | Serves: 4

12 oz chicken fillet (3 oz each fillet)
4 teaspoons coconut flakes
1 egg white, whisked
1 teaspoon salt
½ teaspoon ground black pepper
Cooking spray

1. Beat the chicken fillets with the kitchen hammer and sprinkle with salt and ground black pepper. Then dip every chicken chop in the whisked egg white and coat in the coconut flakes. 2. Select the "AIR FRY" function of Ninja Foodi digital air fry oven, set the temperature to 360 degrees F/ 180 degrees C and set the time to 12 minutes. Press the Start/Pause button and begin preheating. Put the chicken chops in the air fryer and spray with cooking spray. Cook the chicken chop for 7 minutes. 3. Then flip them on another side and cook for 5 minutes. The cooked chicken chops should have a golden brown color.
Per Serving: Calories 172; Fat 6.9g; Sodium 302mg; Carbs 0.5g; Fiber 0g; Sugar 0g; Protein 25.6g

Parmesan Chicken and Tomato Mix

Prep time: 5 minutes | Cook time: 25 minutes | Serves: 4

4 chicken thighs, skinless, boneless
1 tablespoon olive oil
A pinch of salt and black pepper
1 tablespoon thyme, chopped
1 cup chicken stock
3 garlic cloves, minced
½ cup coconut cream
1 cup sun-dried tomatoes, chopped
4 tablespoons parmesan, grated

1. Select the "AIR FRY" function of Ninja Foodi digital air fry oven, set the temperature to 370 degrees F/ 185 degrees C and set the time to 20 minutes. Press the Start/Pause button and begin preheating. Heat up a pan that fits the air fryer with the oil over medium-high heat, add the chicken, salt, pepper and the garlic, and brown for 2-3 minutes on each side. 2. Add the rest of except the parmesan, toss, put the pan in the air fryer and cook for 20 minutes. Sprinkle the parmesan on top, leave the mix aside for 5 minutes, divide everything between plates and serve.
Per Serving: Calories 275; Fat 12g; Sodium 336mg; Carbs 6g; Fiber 4g; Sugar 1g; Protein 17g

Simple Cinnamon Chicken Thighs

Prep time: 5 minutes | Cook time: 30 minutes | Serves: 4

2 pounds chicken thighs
A pinch of salt and black pepper
2 tablespoons olive oil
½ teaspoon cinnamon, ground

1. Select the "AIR FRY" function of Ninja Foodi digital air fry oven, set the temperature to 360 degrees F/ 180 degrees C and set the time to 15 minutes. Press the Start/Pause button and begin preheating. Spice the chicken with salt and pepper, and rub with the rest of the ingredients. 2. Put the chicken thighs in air fryer's basket, cook for 15 minutes on each side, Serve.
Per Serving: Calories 271; Fat 12g; Sodium 510mg; Carbs 6g; Fiber 4g; Sugar g; Protein 13g

Ginger Chicken with Lemon Sauce

Prep time: 5 minutes | Cook time: 25 minutes | Serves: 4

2 tablespoons spring onions, minced
1 tablespoon ginger, grated
4 garlic cloves, minced
2 tablespoons coconut aminos
8 chicken drumsticks

½ cup chicken stock
Salt and black pepper to the taste
1 teaspoon olive oil
¼ cup cilantro, chopped
1 tablespoon lemon juice

1. Select the "AIR FRY" function of Ninja Foodi digital air fry oven, set the temperature to 370 degrees F/ 185 degrees C and set the time to 20 minutes. Press the Start/Pause button and begin preheating. Heat up a pan with the oil, add the chicken drumsticks, brown them for 2 minutes and transfer the fryer. 2. Add all the other ingredients, toss everything, put the pan in the fryer and cook for 20 minutes. Divide the chicken and lemon sauce between plates and serve.
Per Serving: Calories 267; Fat 11g; Sodium 247mg; Carbs 6g; Fiber 4g; Sugar 2g; Protein 16g

Low-Carb Dill Chicken Quesadilla

Prep time: 15 minutes | Cook time: 10 minutes | Serves: 2

2 low carb tortillas
7 oz chicken breast, skinless, boneless, boiled
1 tablespoon cream cheese
1 teaspoon butter, melted
1 teaspoon minced garlic

1 teaspoon fresh dill, chopped
½ teaspoon salt
2 oz Monterey Jack cheese, shredded
Cooking spray

1. Select the "AIR FRY" function of Ninja Foodi digital air fry oven, set the temperature to 400 degrees F/ 200 degrees C and set the time to 5 minutes. Press the Start/Pause button and begin preheating. Shred the chicken breast with the help of the fork and put it in the bowl. Add cream cheese, butter, minced garlic, dill, and salt. Add shredded Monterey jack cheese and stir the shredded chicken. 2. Then put 1 tortilla in the air fryer baking pan. Top it with the shredded chicken mixture and cover with the second corn tortilla.
Per Serving: Calories 337; Fat 16.7g; Sodium 245mg; Carbs 13.1g; Fiber 7.1g; Sugar 2g; Protein 31.6g

Cheesy Chicken and Spinach

Prep time: 5 minutes | Cook time: 24 minutes | Serves: 6

6 chicken breasts, skinless, boneless and halved
A pinch of salt and black pepper
2 tablespoons olive oil
1 pound mozzarella, sliced

2 cups baby spinach
1 teaspoon Italian seasoning
2 tomatoes, sliced
1 tablespoon basil, chopped

1. Select the "AIR FRY" function of Ninja Foodi digital air fry oven, set the temperature to 370 degrees F/ 185 degrees C and set the time to 12 minutes. Press the Start/Pause button and begin preheating. Make slits in each chicken breast halves, season with salt, pepper and Italian seasoning and stuff with mozzarella, spinach and tomatoes. 2. Drizzle the oil over stuffed chicken, put it in your air fryer's basket and cook for 12 minutes on each side. Divide between plates and serve with basil sprinkled on top.
Per Serving: Calories 285; Fat 12g; Sodium 647mg; Carbs 7g; Fiber 4g; Sugar 2g; Protein 15g

Pepper Turkey Roast

Prep time: 10 minutes | Cook time: 8 minutes | Serves: 2

7 oz turkey bacon
1 teaspoon coconut oil, melted

½ teaspoon ground black pepper

1. Slice the turkey bacon if needed and sprinkle it with ground black pepper and coconut oil. 2. Select the "AIR FRY" function of Ninja Foodi digital air fry oven, set the temperature to 400 degrees F/ 200 degrees C and set the time to 8 minutes. Press the Start/Pause button and begin preheating. Arrange the turkey bacon in the air fryer in one layer and cook it for 4 minutes. Then flip the bacon on another side and cook for 4 minutes more.
Per Serving: Calories 149; Fat 5.5g; Sodium 362mg; Carbs 0.3g; Fiber 0.1g; Sugar 0g; Protein 19.3g

Spicy Chicken Wings

Prep time: 5 minutes | Cook time: 30 minutes | Serves: 4

1 tablespoon olive oil
2 pounds chicken wings
1 tablespoon lime juice
2 teaspoons smoked paprika

1 teaspoon red pepper flakes, crushed
Salt and black pepper to the taste

1. Select the "AIR FRY" function of Ninja Foodi digital air fry oven, set the temperature to 380 degrees F/ 195 degrees C and set the time to 15 minutes. Press the Start/Pause button and begin preheating. In a bowl, add the chicken wings with all the other ingredients and toss well. 2. Put the chicken wings in your air fryer's basket and cook for 15 minutes on each side. Serve with a side salad.
Per Serving: Calories 280; Fat 13g; Sodium 3mg; Carbs 6g; Fiber 3g; Sugar 6g; Protein 14g

Cheesy Cauliflower Stuffed Chicken

Prep time: 20 minutes | Cook time: 25 minutes | Serves: 5

1 ½-pound chicken breast, skinless, boneless
½ cup cauliflower, shredded
1 jalapeno pepper, chopped
1 teaspoon ground nutmeg
1 teaspoon salt

¼ cup Cheddar cheese, shredded
½ teaspoon cayenne pepper
1 tablespoon cream cheese
1 tablespoon sesame oil
½ teaspoon dried thyme

1. Make the horizontal cut in the chicken breast. In the mixing bowl mix up shredded cauliflower, chopped jalapeno pepper, ground nutmeg, salt, and cayenne pepper. Fill the chicken cut with the shredded cauliflower and secure the cut with toothpicks. 2. Then rub the chicken breast with cream cheese, dried thyme, and sesame oil. Select the "AIR FRY" function of Ninja Foodi digital air fry oven, set the temperature to 380 degrees F/ 195 degrees C and set the time to 25 minutes. Press the Start/Pause button and begin preheating. Put the chicken breast in the air fryer and cook it for 20 minutes. Then sprinkle it with Cheddar cheese and cook for 5 minutes more.
Per Serving: Calories 266; Fat 9.6g; Sodium 298mg; Carbs1.2g; Fiber 0.5g; Sugar 0.3g; Protein 41.3g

Spicy Chicken Cutlets

Prep time: 20 minutes | Cook time: 16 minutes | Serves: 4

15 oz chicken fillet
1 teaspoon white pepper
1 teaspoon ghee, melted

½ teaspoon onion powder
¼ teaspoon chili flakes

1. Chop the chicken fillet into the tiny pieces. Then sprinkle the chopped chicken with white pepper, onion powder, and chili flakes. Stir the mixture until homogenous. Make the medium-size cutlets from the mixture. 2. Select the "AIR FRY" function of Ninja Foodi digital air fry oven, set the temperature to 365 degrees F/ 185 degrees C and set the time to 16 minutes. Press the Start/Pause button and begin preheating. Brush the air fryer basket with ghee and put the chicken cutlets inside. Cook them for 8 minutes and then flip on another side with the help of the spatula. Transfer the cooked chicken cutlets on the serving plate.
Per Serving: Calories 214; Fat 9g; Sodium 123mg; Carbs 0.6g; Fiber 0.2g; Sugar 0g; Protein 30.9g

Spiced Chicken Drumsticks

Prep time: 10 minutes | Cook time: 30 minutes | Serves: 4

1 and ½ cups Keto tomato sauce
1 teaspoon onion powder
A pinch of salt and black pepper

1 tablespoon coconut aminos
½ teaspoon chili powder
2 pounds chicken drumsticks

1. Select the "AIR FRY" function of Ninja Foodi digital air fry oven, set the temperature to 380 degrees F/ 195 degrees C and set the time to 15 minutes. Press the Start/Pause button and begin preheating. In a bowl, mix the chicken drumsticks with all the other ingredients, toss and keep in the fridge for 10 minutes. 2. Drain the drumsticks, put them in your air fryer's basket and cook for 15 minutes on each side. Divide everything between plates and serve.
Per Serving: Calories 254; Fat 14g; Sodium 129mg; Carbs 6g; Fiber 4g; Sugar 1g; Protein 15g

Herbed Turkey Breasts

Prep time: 10 minutes | Cook time: 25 minutes | Serves: 4

2 turkey breasts, skinless, boneless and halved
4 tablespoons butter, melted
2 tablespoons thyme, chopped
2 tablespoons sage, chopped
1 tablespoon rosemary, chopped
2 tablespoons parsley, chopped
A pinch of salt and black pepper
2 cups chicken stock
2 celery stalks, chopped

1. Select the "AIR FRY" function of Ninja Foodi digital air fry oven, set the temperature to 390 degrees F/ 200 degrees C and set the time to 20 minutes. Press the Start/Pause button and begin preheating. Heat up a pan with the butter over medium-high heat, add the turkey and brown for 2-3 minutes on each side. 2. Add the herbs, stock, celery, salt and pepper, toss, put the pan in your air fryer, cook for 20 minutes. Divide between plates and serve.
Per Serving: Calories 284; Fat 14g; Sodium 477mg; Carbs 6g; Fiber 2g; Sugar 2g; Protein 20g

Chili and Paprika Chicken Wings

Prep time: 10 minutes | Cook time: 12 minutes | Serves: 5

1-pound chicken wings
1 teaspoon ground paprika
1 teaspoon chili powder
½ teaspoon salt
1 tablespoon sunflower oil

1. Pour the sunflower oil in the shallow bowl. Add chili powder and ground paprika. Gently stir the mixture. Sprinkle the chicken wings with red chili mixture and salt. 2. Select the "AIR FRY" function of Ninja Foodi digital air fry oven, set the temperature to 400 degrees F/ 200 degrees C and set the time to 15 minutes. Press the Start/Pause button and begin preheating. Place the chicken wings in the air fryer in one layer and cook for 6 minutes. Then flip the wings on another side and cook for 6 minutes more.
Per Serving: Calories 200; Fat 9.7g; Sodium 321mg; Carbs 0.5g; Fiber 0.3g; Sugar 0.2g; Protein 26.4g

Chicken Rolls with nutmeg

Prep time: 15 minutes | Cook time: 25 minutes | Serves: 5

1-pound chicken fillet
2 oz celery stalk, chopped
¼ teaspoon ground paprika
¼ teaspoon ground nutmeg
½ teaspoon garlic powder
1 teaspoon ghee, melted
½ teaspoon salt
1 teaspoon dried oregano
1 teaspoon cream cheese
1 teaspoon avocado oil
1 cup spinach, chopped

1. Cut the chicken fillet on 5 pieces and beat them gently with the help of the kitchen hammer. In the end, you should get 5 flat chicken fillets. Sprinkle the chicken fillets with ground paprika, nutmeg, garlic powder, salt, and dried oregano. Then put the ghee in the skillet and preheat it for 1-2 minutes over the medium heat. 2. Add spinach and cream cheese. Add chopped celery stalk and cook the greens over the low heat for 10 minutes. Then express the fluid from the spinach. With the help of the spoon put the expressed greens on the chicken fillets. 3. After this, roll the chicken into the rolls and secure with toothpicks or kitchen thread if needed. Select the "AIR ROAST" function of Ninja Foodi digital air fry oven, set the temperature to 375 degrees F/ 190 degrees C and set the time to 12 minutes. Press the Start/Pause button and begin preheating. Put the chicken rolls in the air fryer and sprinkle with avocado oil. Cook the rolls for 12 minutes.
Per Serving: Calories 189; Fat 8g; Sodium 489mg; Carbs 1.1g; Fiber 0.6g; Sugar 0g; Protein 26.7g

Lemon Chicken Tenders with Chives

Prep time: 5 minutes | Cook time: 20 minutes | Serves: 4

1 pound chicken tenders, boneless, skinless
A pinch of salt and black pepper
Juice of 1 lemon
1 tablespoon chives, chopped
A drizzle of olive oil

1. Select the "AIR FRY" function of Ninja Foodi digital air fry oven, set the temperature to 370 degrees F/ 185 degrees C and set the time to 10 minutes. Press the Start/Pause button and begin preheating. In a bowl, add the chicken tenders with all except the chives, toss, put the meat in your air fryer's basket and cook for 10 minutes on each side. 2. Divide between plates and serve with chives sprinkled on top.
Per Serving: Calories 230; Fat 13g; Sodium 456mg; Carbs 6g; Fiber 4g; Sugar 2g; Protein 16g

Sweet Turmeric Chicken Wings

Prep time: 15 minutes | Cook time: 15 minutes | Serves: 8

8 chicken wings
1 teaspoon Splenda
1 teaspoon ground turmeric
½ teaspoon cayenne pepper
1 tablespoon avocado oil

1. Mix up Splenda and avocado oil and stir the mixture until Splenda is dissolved. Then rub the chicken wings with ground turmeric and cayenne pepper. Brush the chicken wings with sweet avocado oil from both sides. 2. Select the "AIR FRY" function of Ninja Foodi digital air fry oven, set the temperature to 390 degrees F/ 200 degrees C and set the time to 15 minutes. Press the Start/Pause button and begin preheating. Place the wings in the air fryer and cook them for 15 minutes.
Per Serving: Calories 105; Fat 6.9g; Sodium 147mg; Carbs 0.8g; Fiber 0.2g; Sugar 0.1g; Protein 9.2g

Tangy Celery Chicken

Prep time: 20 minutes | Cook time: 15 minutes | Serves: 4

16 oz chicken thighs, skinless
1 teaspoon ground celery root
1 teaspoon dried celery leaves
1 teaspoon apple cider vinegar
½ teaspoon salt
1 tablespoon sunflower oil

1. Rub the chicken thighs with the celery root, dried celery leaves, and salt. Then sprinkle the chicken with apple cider vinegar and sunflower oil. Leave it for 15 minutes to marinate. 2. After this, Select the "AIR FRY" function of Ninja Foodi digital air fry oven, set the temperature to 385 degrees F/ 195 degrees C and set the time to 15 minutes. Press the Start/Pause button and begin preheating. Place the chicken in the air fryer and cook them for 12 minutes. Then flip the chicken on another side and cook for 3 minutes more. Transfer the cooked chicken thighs on the plate.
Per Serving: Calories 247; Fat 11.9g; Sodium 112mg; Carbs 0g; Fiber 0g; Sugar 0g; Protein 32.8g

Tasty Chicken Sausages

Prep time: 20 minutes | Cook time: 10 minutes | Serves: 4

1 garlic clove, diced
1 spring onion, chopped
1 cup ground chicken
½ teaspoon salt
½ teaspoon ground black pepper
4 sausage links
1 teaspoon olive oil

1. In the mixing bowl, mix up a diced garlic clove, onion, ground chicken, salt, and ground black pepper. Then fill the sausage links with the ground chicken mixture. Cut every sausage into halves and secure the endings. 2. Select the "BAKE" function of Ninja Foodi digital air fry oven, set the temperature to 365 degrees F/ 185 degrees C and set the time to 25 minutes. Press the Start/Pause button and begin preheating. Brush the sausages with olive oil and put it in the air fryer. Cook them for 10 minutes. Then flip the sausages on another side and cook for 5 minutes more. Increase the cooking time to 390 degrees F/ 200 degrees C and cook for 8 minutes for faster results.
Per Serving: Calories 130; Fat 8.3g; Sodium 130mg; Carbs 1g; Fiber 0.1g; Sugar 0g; Protein 12.2g

Lemon Chicken Drumsticks with oregano

Prep time: 15 minutes | Cook time: 21 minutes | Serves: 4

4 chicken drumsticks, with skin, bone-in
1 teaspoon dried cilantro
½ teaspoon dried oregano
½ teaspoon salt
1 teaspoon lemon juice
1 teaspoon butter, softened
2 garlic cloves, diced

1. In the mixing bowl, mix up dried cilantro, oregano, and salt. Then fill the chicken drumstick's skin with a cilantro mixture. Add butter and diced garlic. Sprinkle the chicken with lemon juice. 2. Select the "AIR FRY" function of Ninja Foodi digital air fry oven, set the temperature to 375 degrees F/ 190 degrees C and set the time to 21 minutes. Press the Start/Pause button and begin preheating. Put the chicken drumsticks in the air fryer and cook them for 21 minutes.
Per Serving: Calories 89; Fat 3.6g; Sodium 411mg; Carbs 0.7g; Fiber 0.1g; Sugar 0.1g; Protein 12.8g

Herbed Chicken Meatballs

Prep time: 20 minutes | Cook time: 11 minutes | Serves: 6

14 oz ground chicken
2 oz scallions, chopped
1 egg yolk
½ teaspoon dried thyme

½ teaspoon salt
1 tablespoon almond flour
1 teaspoon sesame oil

1. Whisk the egg yolk and mix it up with ground chicken. Add dried thyme, salt, and almond flour. Stir the mixture until smooth and add scallions. Mix up the mixture and make the medium-size meatballs. 2. Use the scooper or make them with the help of the fingertips. Select the "AIR FRY" function of Ninja Foodi digital air fry oven, set the temperature to 375 degrees F/ 190 degrees C and set the time to 11 minutes. Press the Start/Pause button and begin preheating. Put the chicken meatballs in the air fryer and sprinkle with sesame oil. Cook them for 7 minutes. 3. Then flip the chicken meatballs on another side and cook for 4 minutes more.
Per Serving: Calories 171; Fat 8.8g; Sodium 336mg; Carbs 1.8g; Fiber 0.8g; Sugar 0g; Protein 20.8g

Spicy Onion Chicken Tenders

Prep time: 15 minutes | Cook time: 10 minutes | Serves: 2

8 oz chicken fillet
1 teaspoon minced onion
¼ teaspoon onion powder

¼ teaspoon salt
½ teaspoon cayenne pepper
Cooking spray

1. Cut the chicken fillet on 2 tenders and sprinkle with salt, onion powder, and cayenne pepper. 2. Select the "AIR FRY" function of Ninja Foodi digital air fry oven, set the temperature to 365 degrees F/ 185 degrees C and set the time to 10 minutes. Press the Start/Pause button and begin preheating. Spray the basket with cooking spray from inside and place the chicken tenders in it. 3. Top the chicken with minced onion and cook for 10 minutes.
Per Serving: Calories 219; Fat 8.5g; Sodium 548mg; Carbs 0.7g; Fiber 0.2g; Sugar 0g; Protein 32.9g

Turkey with Butter Sauce

Prep time: 5 minutes | Cook time: 24 minutes | Serves: 4

1 turkey breast, skinless, boneless and cut into 4 pieces
A pinch of salt and black pepper

Juice of 1 lemon
2 tablespoons rosemary, chopped
2 tablespoons butter, melted

1. Select the "AIR FRY" function of Ninja Foodi digital air fry oven, set the temperature to 380 degrees F/ 195 degrees C and set the time to 12 minutes. Press the Start/Pause button and begin preheating. In a bowl, add the butter with the rosemary, lemon juice, salt and pepper and whisk really well. Brush the turkey pieces with the rosemary butter, put them your air fryer's basket, cook for 12 minutes on each side. 2. Divide between plates and serve with a side salad.
Per Serving: Calories 236; Fat 12g; Sodium 297mg; Carbs 6g; Fiber 4g; Sugar 3g; Protein 13g

Spicy Chicken with tangy Tomato Sauce

Prep time: 15 minutes | Cook time: 18 minutes | Serves: 8

8 chicken drumsticks
½ teaspoon cayenne pepper
½ teaspoon chili powder
¼ teaspoon jalapeno pepper, minced

½ teaspoon ground cumin
1 teaspoon dried thyme
1 teaspoon keto tomato sauce
1 tablespoon nut oil
½ teaspoon salt

1. In the bowl mix tomato sauce and nut oil. Then add minced jalapeno pepper and stir the mixture until homogenous. Rub the chicken drumsticks with chili powder, cayenne pepper, dried cumin, thyme, and sprinkle with salt. 2. Then brush the chicken with tomato sauce mixture and leave to marinate for overnight or for at least 8 hours. Select the "AIR FRY" function of Ninja Foodi air fry oven, set the temperature to 375 degrees F/ 190 degrees C and set the time to 18 minutes. Press the Start/Pause button and begin preheating. Put the marinated chicken drumsticks in the air fryer and cook them for 18 minutes.
Per Serving: Calories 95; Fat 4.4g; Sodium 430mg; Carbs 0.3g; Fiber 0.2g; Sugar 0g; Protein 12.7g

Delicious Chicken Pockets

Prep time: 15 minutes | Cook time: 4 minutes | Serves: 4

2 low carb tortillas
2 oz Cheddar cheese, grated
1 tomato, chopped
1 teaspoon fresh cilantro, chopped
½ teaspoon dried basil

2 teaspoons butter
6 oz chicken fillet, boiled
1 teaspoon sunflower oil
½ teaspoon salt

1. Cut the tortillas into halves. Shred the chicken fillet with the help of the fork and put it in the bowl. Add chopped tomato, grated cheese, basil, cilantro, and alt. Then grease the tortilla halves with butter from one side. Put the shredded chicken mixture on half of every tortilla piece and fold them into the pockets. 2. Select the "AIR FRY" function of Ninja Foodi digital air fry oven, set the temperature to 400 degrees F/ 200 degrees C and set the time to 4 minutes. Press the Start/ Pause button and begin preheating. Brush every tortilla pocket with sunflower oil and put it in the air fryer. Cook the meal for 4 minutes.
Per Serving: Calories 208; Fat 12g; Sodium 145mg; Carbs 6.8g; Fiber 3.7g; Sugar 0.6g; Protein 17.5g

Easy Red Vinegar Chicken Wings

Prep time: 5 minutes | Cook time: 30 minutes | Serves: 4

2 pounds chicken wings, halved
¼ cup red vinegar
4 garlic cloves, minced
Salt and black pepper to the taste

4 tablespoons olive oil
1 tablespoon garlic powder
1 teaspoon turmeric powder

1. Select the "AIR FRY" function of Ninja Foodi digital air fry oven, set the temperature to 370 degrees F/ 185 degrees C and set the time to 15 minutes. Press the Start/Pause button and begin preheating. 2. In a bowl, add the chicken with all the other ingredients and toss well. Put the chicken wings in your air fryer's basket and cook for 30 minutes, flipping the meat halfway. 3. Divide everything between plates and serve with a side salad.
Per Serving: Calories 250; Fat 12g; Sodium 663mg; Carbs 6g; Fiber 4g; Sugar 1g; Protein 15g

Paprika Turkey with Shallot Sauce

Prep time: 5 minutes | Cook time: 30 minutes | Serves: 4

1 big turkey breast, skinless, boneless and cubed
1 tablespoon olive oil
¼ teaspoon sweet paprika

Salt and black pepper to the taste
1 cup chicken stock
3 tablespoons butter, melted
4 shallots, chopped

1. Select the "AIR FRY" function of Ninja Foodi digital air fry oven, set the temperature to 370 degrees F/ 185 degrees C and set the time to 20 minutes. Press the Start/Pause button and begin preheating. Heat up a pan that fits the air fryer with the olive oil and the butter over medium high heat, add the turkey cubes, and brown for 3 minutes on each side. Add the shallots in and sauté for 5 minutes more. Add the paprika, stock, salt and pepper, toss, put the pan in the air fryer and cook for 20 minutes. 2. Divide into bowls and serve.
Per Serving: Calories 236; Fat 12g; Sodium 321mg; Carbs 6g; Fiber 4g; Sugar 2g; Protein 15g

Turkey with Lime Gravy

Prep time: 5 minutes | Cook time: 25 minutes | Serves: 4

1 big turkey breast, skinless, boneless, cubed and browned
Juice of 1 lime
Zest of 1 lime, grated
1 cup chicken stock

3 tablespoons parsley, chopped
4 tablespoons butter, melted
2 tablespoons thyme, chopped
A pinch of salt and black pepper

1. Select the "AIR FRY" function of Ninja Foodi digital air fry oven, set the temperature to 380 degrees F/ 195 degrees C and set the time to 20 minutes. Press the Start/Pause button and begin preheating. Heat up a pan that fits the air fryer with the butter over medium heat, add all the ingredients except the turkey, whisk, bring to a simmer and cook for 5 minutes. Add the turkey cubes, put the pan in the air fryer and cook for 20 minutes. Divide the meat between plates, drizzle the gravy all over and serve.
Per Serving: Calories 284; Fat 13g; Sodium 423mg; Carbs 5g; Fiber 3g; Sugar 2g; Protein 15g

Cheesy Stuffed Lemon Chicken Fillets

Prep time: 15 minutes | Cook time: 14 minutes | Serves: 2

1 lemon pepper
¼ cup Cheddar cheese, shredded
8 oz chicken fillets
½ teaspoon dried cilantro
1 teaspoon coconut oil, melted
¼ teaspoon smoked paprika

1. Cut the lemon pepper into halves and remove the seeds. Then cut the chicken fillet into 2 fillets. Make the horizontal cuts in every chicken fillet. Then sprinkle the chicken fillets with smoked paprika and dried cilantro. After this, fill them with lemon pepper halves and Cheddar cheese. 2. Select the "AIR FRY" function of Ninja Foodi digital air fry oven, set the temperature to 385 degrees F/ 195 degrees C and set the time to 15 minutes. Press the Start/Pause button and begin preheating. Put the chicken fillets in the air fryer and sprinkle with melted coconut oil. Cook the chicken for 14 minutes. Carefully transfer the chicken fillets in the serving plates.
Per Serving: Calories 293; Fat 15.4g; Sodium 222mg; Carbs 0.4g; Fiber 0.1g; Sugar 0.1g; Protein 36.4g

Creamy Ginger Turkey

Prep time: 5 minutes | Cook time: 25 minutes | Serves: 4

1 pound turkey breast, skinless, boneless and cubed
1 cup heavy cream
A pinch of salt and black pepper
4 ounces cherry tomatoes, halved
1 tablespoon ginger, grated
2 tablespoons red chili powder
2 teaspoons olive oil

1. Select the "AIR FRY" function of Ninja Foodi digital air fry oven, set the temperature to 380 degrees F/ 195 degrees C and set the time to 20 minutes. Press the Start/Pause button and begin preheating. Heat up a pan that fits the air fryer with the oil over medium heat, add the turkey and brown for 2 minutes on each side. 2. Add the rest of ingredients, toss, put the pan in the machine and cook for 20 minutes. Divide everything between plates and serve.
Per Serving: Calories 267; Fat 13g; Sodium 520mg; Carbs 6g; Fiber 4g; Sugar 2g; Protein 16g

Tangy Mustard and Garlic Turkey

Prep time: 5 minutes | Cook time: 20 minutes | Serves: 4

1 big turkey breast, skinless, boneless and cubed
4 garlic cloves, minced
Salt and black pepper to the taste
1 and ½ tablespoon olive oil
1 tablespoon mustard

1. Select the "AIR FRY" function of Ninja Foodi digital air fry oven, set the temperature to 360 degrees F/ 180 degrees C and set the time to 20 minutes. Press the Start/Pause button and begin preheating. In a bowl, add the chicken with the garlic and the other and toss. 2. Put the turkey in your air fryer's basket, cook for 20 minutes, divide between plates and serve with a side salad.
Per Serving: Calories 240; Fat 12g; Sodium 268mg; Carbs 6g; Fiber 4g; Sugar 2g; Protein 15g

Herbed Duck Liver Spread

Prep time: 15 minutes | Cook time: 10 minutes | Serves: 6

½ cup butter, softened
12 oz duck liver
1 tablespoon sesame oil
1 teaspoon salt
1 tablespoon dried oregano
½ onion, peeled

1. Select the "AIR FRY" function of Ninja Foodi digital air fry oven, set the temperature to 395 degrees F/ 200 degrees C and set the time to 10 minutes. Press the Start/Pause button and begin preheating. Chop the onion. Put the duck liver in the air fryer, add onion, and cook the for 10 minutes. Then transfer the duck pate in the food processor and process it for 2-3 minutes or until the liver is smooth. 2. Then add onion and blend the mixture for 2 minutes more. Transfer the liver mixture into the bowl. After this, add oregano, salt, sesame oil, and butter. Stir the duck liver with the help of the spoon and transfer it in the bowl. Refrigerate the pate for 10-20 minutes before serving.
Per Serving: Calories 227; Fat 20.4g; Sodium 365mg; Carbs 1.8g; Fiber 0.5g; Sugar 0g; Protein 9.9g

Balsamic Turkey

Prep time: 5 minutes | Cook time: 30 minutes | Serves: 4

1 big turkey breast, skinless, boneless and cut into 4 slices
3 tablespoons balsamic vinegar
2 garlic cloves, minced
3 tablespoons butter, melted
A pinch of salt and black pepper
1 tablespoon chives, chopped

1. Select the "AIR FRY" function of Ninja Foodi digital air fry oven, set the temperature to 380 degrees F/ 195 degrees C and set the time to 20 minutes. Press the Start/Pause button and begin preheating. Heat up a pan that fits the air fryer with the butter over medium-high heat, add the garlic and sauté for 2 minutes. Add the turkey, brown for 2 minutes on each side and take off the heat. Add the rest of the ingredients, toss, put the pan in your air fryer and cook for 20 minutes. 2. Divide everything between plates and serve.
Per Serving: Calories 283; Fat 12g; Sodium 322mg; Carbs 5g; Fiber 3g; Sugar 1g; Protein 15g

Easy Nutty Shallots Turkey

Prep time: 5 minutes | Cook time: 25 minutes | Serves: 2

1 big turkey breast, skinless, boneless and halved
⅓ cup almonds, chopped
Salt and black pepper to the taste
2 tablespoons olive oil
1 tablespoon sweet paprika
2 shallots, chopped

1. Select the "AIR FRY" function of Ninja Foodi digital air fry oven, set the temperature to 370 degrees F/ 185 degrees C and set the time to 25 minutes. Press the Start/Pause button and begin preheating. In a pan, combine the turkey with all the other ingredients, toss, put the pan in the machine and cook for 25 minutes. 2. Divide everything between plates and serve.
Per Serving: Calories 274; Fat 12g; Sodium 402mg; Carbs 5g; Fiber 3g; Sugar 1g; Protein 14g

Simple Turkey with Veggie

Prep time: 5 minutes | Cook time: 30 minutes | Serves: 4

1 turkey breast, skinless, boneless and cut into strips
A pinch of salt and black pepper
1 tablespoon olive oil
1 cup veggie stock
4 leeks, sliced
2 tablespoon chives, chopped

1. Select the "AIR FRY" function of Ninja Foodi digital air fry oven, set the temperature to 380 degrees F/ 195 degrees C and set the time to 25 minutes. Press the Start/Pause button and begin preheating. Heat up a pan with the oil, add the meat and brown for 2 minutes on each side. Add the remaining ingredients, toss, put the pan in the machine and cook for 25 minutes. 2. Divide everything between plates and serve with a side salad.
Per Serving: Calories 257; Fat 12g; Sodium 620mg; Carbs 5g; Fiber 4g; Sugar 1g; Protein 14g

Spiced Chicken Strips

Prep time: 15 minutes | Cook time: 14 minutes | Serves: 6

2-pound chicken breast, skinless, boneless
1 teaspoon salt
1 teaspoon ground turmeric
½ teaspoon cayenne pepper
1 egg, beaten
2 tablespoons coconut flour

1. Cut the chicken breast into the strips and sprinkle with salt, ground turmeric, and cayenne pepper. Then add beaten egg in the chicken strips and stir the mixture. After this, add coconut flour and stir it. 2. Select the "AIR FRY" function of Ninja Foodi digital air fry oven, set the temperature to 400 degrees F/ 200 degrees C and set the time to 7 minutes. Press the Start/Pause button and begin preheating. Put ½ part of all chicken strips in the air fryer basket in one layer and cook them for 7 minutes.
Per Serving: Calories 195; Fat 4.9g; Sodium 110mg; Carbs 1.7g; Fiber 1g; Sugar 0.7g; Protein 33.4g

Spiced Turkey and Celery

Prep time: 5 minutes | Cook time: 30 minutes | Serves: 4

1 big turkey breast, skinless, boneless and sliced
4 garlic cloves, minced
3 tablespoons olive oil
4 celery stalks, roughly chopped
1 teaspoon turmeric powder
1 teaspoon cumin, ground
1 tablespoon smoked paprika
1 tablespoon garlic powder

1. Select the "AIR FRY" function of Ninja Foodi digital air fry oven, set the temperature to 380 degrees F/ 195 degrees C and set the time to 30 minutes. Press the Start/Pause button and begin preheating. In a pan, combine the turkey and the other ingredients, toss, put the pan in the machine and cook for 30 minutes. 2. Divide everything between plates and serve.
Per Serving: Calories 285; Fat 12g; Sodium 541mg; Carbs 6g; Fiber 3g; Sugar 2g; Protein 16g

Bacon Chicken Thighs

Prep time: 15 minutes | Cook time: 25 minutes | Serves: 2

2 chicken legs
4 oz bacon, sliced
½ teaspoon salt
½ teaspoon ground black pepper
1 teaspoon sesame oil

1. Sprinkle the chicken legs with salt and ground black pepper and wrap in the sliced bacon. 2. After this, Select the "AIR FRY" function of Ninja Foodi digital air fry oven, set the temperature to 385 degrees F/ 195 degrees C and set the time to 25 minutes. Press the Start/Pause button and begin preheating. Place the chicken in the air fryer and sprinkle with sesame oil. Cook the bacon chicken legs for 25 minutes.
Per Serving: Calories 437; Fat 30.8g; Sodium 698mg; Carbs 1.2g; Fiber 0.1g; Sugar 0g; Protein 36.5g

Chapter 4 Beef, Pork, and Lamb Recipes

Marinated Flank Steak with Garlic

Prep time: 5 minutes | Cook time: 10 minutes | Serves: 4

¾ lb. flank steak
1 ½ tablespoons sake
1 tablespoon brown miso paste

1 teaspoon honey
2 cloves garlic, pressed
1 tablespoon olive oil

1. Select the "AIR FRY" function of Ninja Foodi digital air fry oven, set the temperature to 400 degrees F/ 200 degrees C and set the time to 12 minutes. Press the Start/Pause button and begin preheating. Put all of them in a Ziploc bag. Shake to cover the steak well with the seasonings and refrigerate for at least 1 hour. 2. Coat all sides of the steak with cooking spray. 3. Put the steak in the Air Fryer sheet pan. 4. Cook for 12 minutes, turning the steak twice during the cooking time, then serve immediately.
Per Serving: Calories 170; Fat 7.9g; Sodium 204mg; Carbs 3g; Fiber 0g; Sugar 2g; Protein 19g

Roasted Steak with Pepper

Prep time: 5 minutes | Cook time: 10 minutes | Serves: 1

3 cm-thick beef steak
Pepper and salt to taste

1. Select the "AIR ROAST" function of Ninja Foodi digital air fry oven, set the temperature to 400 degrees F/ 200 degrees C and set the time to 6 minutes. Press the Start/Pause button and begin preheating. 2. Place the beef steak in the sheet pan and sprinkle on pepper and salt. 3.Spritz the steak with cooking spray. 4.Allow to cook for 3 minutes. Flip and cook other side for 3 more minutes. Serve hot.
Per Serving: Calories 216; Fat 10.4g; Sodium 311mg; Carbs 14g; Fiber 1g; Sugar 2g; Protein 18g

Homemade Meatballs in Thai curry paste

Prep time: 5 minutes | Cook time: 15 minutes | Serves: 4

1 lb. ground beef
1 teaspoon red Thai curry paste
½ lime, rind and juice
1 teaspoon Chinese spice

2 teaspoons lemongrass, finely chopped
1 tablespoon sesame oil

1. Select the "AIR FRY" function of Ninja Foodi digital air fry oven, set the temperature to 380 degrees F/ 195 degrees C and set the time to 10 minutes. Press the Start/Pause button and begin preheating. Mix all ingredients in a bowl, combining well. 2. Take 24 equal amounts of the mixture and shape each one into a meatball. Put them in the Air Fryer basket. 3. Cook for 10 minutes. 4. Turn them over and cook for 5 minutes on the other side, ensuring they are well-cooked before serving with your favorite dipping sauce.
Per Serving: Calories 276; Fat 16g; Sodium 70mg; Carbs 1g; Fiber 0g; Sugar 0g; Protein 30g

Roasted Marinated Beef Chuck & Brussels Sprouts

Prep time: 5 minutes | Cook time: 20 minutes | Serves: 4

1 lb. beef chuck shoulder steak
2 tablespoons vegetable oil
1 tablespoon red wine vinegar
1 teaspoon fine sea salt
½ teaspoon ground black pepper
1 teaspoon smoked paprika
1 teaspoon onion powder

½ teaspoon garlic powder
½ lb. Brussels sprouts, cleaned and halved
½ teaspoon fennel seeds
1 teaspoon dried basil
1 teaspoon dried sage

1. Select the "AIR ROAST" function of Ninja Foodi digital air fry oven, set the temperature to 390 degrees F/ 200 degrees C and set the time to 10 minutes. Press the Start/Pause button and begin preheating. Massage the beef with the vegetable oil, wine vinegar, salt, black pepper, paprika, onion powder, and garlic powder, coating it well. 2. Allow to marinate for a minimum of 3 hours. 3. Air fry at 390 degrees F/ 200 degrees C for 10 minutes. 4. Put the prepared Brussels sprouts in the fryer along with the fennel seeds, basil, and sage. 5. Lower the heat to 380 degrees F/ 195 degrees C and cook everything for another 5 minutes. 6. Pause the Ninja Foodi and give the contents a good stir. Cook for an additional 10 minutes. 7. Take out the beef and allow the vegetables to cook for a few more minutes if necessary or desired. 8. Serve everything together with the sauce of your choice.
Per Serving: Calories 253; Fat 13.4g; Sodium 663mg; Carbs 7g; Fiber 3g; Sugar 2g; Protein 26g

Spiced Creamy Beef & Kale Omelet

Prep time: 5 minutes | Cook time: 15 minutes | Serves: 4

Cooking spray
½ lb. leftover beef, coarsely chopped
2 garlic cloves, pressed
1 cup kale, torn into pieces and wilted
1 tomato, chopped

¼ teaspoon sugar
4 eggs, beaten
4 tablespoons heavy cream
½ teaspoon turmeric powder
Salt and ground black pepper to taste
⅛ teaspoon ground allspice

1. Grease four ramekins with cooking spray. Select the "BAKE" function of Ninja Foodi digital air fry oven, set the temperature to 360 degrees F/ 180 degrees C and set the time to 16 minutes. Press the Start/Pause button and begin preheating. 2. Place equal amounts of each of them into each ramekin and mix well. 3. Air-fry for 16 minutes, or longer if necessary. Serve immediately.
Per Serving: Calories 191; Fat 13g; Sodium 574mg; Carbs 5g; Fiber 1g; Sugar 3g; Protein 13g

Crumbed Filet Mignon with Black Pepper

Prep time: 5 minutes | Cook time: 15 minutes | Serves: 4

½ lb. filet mignon
Sea salt and ground black pepper, to taste
½ teaspoon cayenne pepper
1 teaspoon dried basil

1 teaspoon dried rosemary
1 teaspoon dried thyme
1 tablespoon sesame oil
1 small-sized egg, well-whisked
½ cup friendly breadcrumbs

1. Select the "AIR ROAST" function of Ninja Foodi digital air fry oven, set the temperature to 360 degrees F/ 180 degrees C and set the time to 15 minutes. Press the Start/Pause button and begin preheating. Cover the filet mignon with the salt, black pepper, cayenne pepper, basil, rosemary, and thyme. Coat with a light brushing of sesame oil. 2. Put the egg in a shallow plate. 3. Pour the breadcrumbs in another plate. 4. Dip the filet mignon into the egg. Roll it into the crumbs. 5. Transfer the steak to the Air Fryer and cook for 10 to 13 minutes until it turns golden. Serve with a salad.
Per Serving: Calories 145; Fat 7.2g; Sodium 66mg; Carbs 7g; Fiber 2g; Sugar 2g; Protein 15g

Pork Schnitzel with Dill Sauce

Prep time: 10 minutes | Cook time: 24 minutes | Serves: 4 to 6

6 boneless, center cut pork chops (about 1 ½ pounds)
½ cup flour
1 ½ teaspoons salt
freshly ground black pepper
2 eggs
½ cup milk
Dill Sauce:
1 cup chicken stock
1 ½ tablespoons cornstarch
⅓ cup sour cream

1 ½ cups toasted fine breadcrumbs
1 teaspoon paprika
3 tablespoons butter, melted
2 tablespoons vegetable or olive oil
lemon wedges

1 ½ tablespoons chopped fresh dill
salt and pepper

1. Pound each chop until they are ½-inch thick. 2. Mix the flour, salt, and black pepper in a shallow dish. Whisk the eggs and milk together in a second shallow dish. Finally, combine the breadcrumbs and paprika in a third shallow dish. 3. Dip each flattened pork chop in the flour. Dip each chop into the egg mixture. Finally dip them into the breadcrumbs and press the breadcrumbs onto the meat firmly. Place each finished chop on a baking sheet until they are all coated. 4. Select the "AIR FRY" function of Ninja Foodi digital air fry oven, set the temperature to 400 degrees F/ 200 degrees C and set the time to 4 minutes. Press the Start/Pause button and begin preheating. 5. Combine the melted butter and the oil in a small bowl and lightly brush both sides of the coated pork chops. Do not brush the chops too heavily or the breading will not be as crispy. 6. Air-fry one schnitzel at a time for 4 minutes, turning it over halfway through the cooking time. Hold the cooked schnitzels warm on a baking pan in a 170 degrees F/ 75 degrees C oven while you finish air-frying the rest. 7. While the schnitzels are cooking, whisk the chicken stock and cornstarch together in a small saucepan over medium-high heat on the stovetop. Boil and manage to simmer for 2 minutes. Add the dill and spice with salt and pepper. 8. Transfer the pork schnitzel to a platter and serve with dill sauce and lemon wedges. For a traditional meal, serve this alongside some egg noodles, spätzle or German potato salad.
Per Serving: Calories 414; Fat 21g; Sodium 369mg; Carbs 24g; Fiber 1g; Sugar 3g; Protein 30g

Beef Burgers with Cheddar Cheese

Prep time: 5 minutes | Cook time: 60 minutes | Serves: 4

10.5 oz. beef, minced	1 teaspoon mixed herbs
1 onion, diced	Salt to taste
1 teaspoon garlic, minced or pureed	Pepper to taste
1 teaspoon tomato, pureed	1 oz. cheddar cheese
1 teaspoon mustard	4 buns
1 teaspoon basil	Salad leaves

1. Select the "BAKE" function of Ninja Foodi digital air fry oven, set the temperature to 390 degrees F/ 200 degrees C and set the time to 5 minutes. Press the Start/Pause button and begin preheating. Drizzle the Air Fryer Ninja sheet pan with one teaspoon of olive oil and allow it to warm up. 2. Place the diced onion in the fryer and fry until they turn golden brown. 3. Mix in all of the seasoning and cook for 25 minutes at 390 degrees F/ 200 degrees C. 4. Lay 2 – 3 onion rings and pureed tomato on two of the buns. Place one slice of cheese and the layer of beef on top. Top with salad leaves and any other condiments you desire before closing off the sandwich with the other buns. 5. Serve with ketchup, cold drink and French fries.
Per Serving: Calories 426; Fat 22.6g; Sodium 357mg; Carbs 36g; Fiber 2g; Sugar 19g; Protein 20g

Roasted Steak Cubes with Broccoli and Mushrooms

Prep time: 2 minutes | Cook time: 15 minutes | Serves: 4

1 lb. top round steak, cut into cubes	pepper
2 tablespoons olive oil	½ teaspoon garlic powder
1 tablespoon apple cider vinegar	¼ teaspoon ground cumin
1 teaspoon fine sea salt	¼ lb. broccoli, cut into florets
½ teaspoon ground black pepper	¼ lb. mushrooms, sliced
1 teaspoon shallot powder	1 teaspoon dried basil
¾ teaspoon smoked cayenne	1 teaspoon celery seeds

1. Select the "AIR ROAST" function of Ninja Foodi digital air fry oven, set the temperature to 365 degrees F/ 185 degrees C and set the time to 12 minutes. Press the Start/Pause button and begin preheating. Massage the olive oil, vinegar, salt, black pepper, shallot powder, cayenne pepper, garlic powder, and cumin into the cubed steak, ensuring to coat each piece evenly. 2. Allow to marinate for a minimum of 3 hours. 3. Put the beef cubes in the Air Fryer sheetpan and allow to cook at 365 degrees F/ 185 degrees C for 12 minutes. 4. When the steak is cooked through, place it in a bowl. 5. Wipe the grease from the cooking pan and pour in the vegetables. Season them with basil and celery seeds and cook the veggies at 400 degrees F/ 200 degrees C for 6 minutes. 6. When the vegetables are hot, serve them with the steak.
Per Serving: Calories 342; Fat 11.8g; Sodium 683mg; Carbs 24g; Fiber 4g; Sugar 1g; Protein 38g

Fried Beef Taco Egg Rolls

Prep time: 15 minutes | Cook time: 12 minutes | Serves: 4

1 teaspoon cilantro	½ can cilantro lime rotel
2 chopped garlic cloves	½ chopped onion
1 tablespoon olive oil	16 egg roll wrappers
1 cup shredded Mexican cheese	1-pound lean ground beef
½ packet taco seasoning	

1. Select the "AIR FRY" function of Ninja Foodi digital air fry oven, set the temperature to 400 degrees F/ 200 degrees C; set the time to 12 minutes. Press the Start/Pause button and begin preheating. 2. Add onions and garlic to a skillet, cooking till fragrant. Then add taco seasoning, pepper, salt, and beef, cooking till beef is broken up into tiny pieces and cooked thoroughly. Add Rotel and stir well. Lay out egg wrappers and brush with water to soften a bit. Load wrappers with beef filling and add cheese to each. Fold diagonally to close and use water to secure edges. 3. Brush filled egg wrappers with olive oil and add to the air fryer. Cook 8 minutes, flip, and cook another 4 minutes. Served sprinkled with cilantro.
Per Serving: Calories 1052; Fat 50g; Sodium 438mg; Carbs 7g; Fiber 0g; Sugar 7g; Protein 132g

Grilled Spicy Beef Ribs

Prep time: 5 minutes | Cook time: 15 minutes | Serves: 4

1 lb. meaty beef ribs	1 chipotle powder
3 tablespoons apple cider vinegar	1 teaspoon fennel seeds
1 cup coriander, finely chopped	1 teaspoon hot paprika
1 heaped tablespoon fresh basil leaves, chopped	Kosher salt and black pepper, to taste
2 garlic cloves, finely chopped	½ cup vegetable oil

1. Select the "AIR ROAST" function of Ninja Foodi digital air fry oven, set the temperature to 360 degrees F/ 180 degrees C and set the time to 10 minutes. Press the Start/Pause button and begin preheating. 2. Wash and dry the ribs. Coat the ribs with the rest of the and refrigerate for a minimum of 3 hours. 3. Separate the ribs from the marinade and put them on an Air Fryer sheet pan. 4. Cook at 360 degrees F/ 180 degrees C for 8 minutes, or longer as needed. 5. Pour the remaining marinade over the ribs before serving immediately.
Per Serving: Calories 629; Fat 61g; Sodium 64mg; Carbs 3g; Fiber 1g; Sugar 1g; Protein 18g

Roasted Spicy London Broil

Prep time: 5 minutes | Cook time: 25 minutes | Serves: 8

2 lb. London broil	2 tablespoons olive oil
3 large garlic cloves, minced	Sea salt and ground black pepper, to taste
3 tablespoons balsamic vinegar	
3 tablespoons whole-grain mustard	½ teaspoon dried hot red pepper flakes

1. Select the "AIR ROAST" function of Ninja Foodi digital air fry oven, set the temperature to 400 degrees F/ 200 degrees C and set the time to 15 minutes. Press the Start/Pause button and begin preheating. Wash and dry the London broil. Score its sides with a knife. 2. Mix the remaining ingredients. Rub this mixture into the broil, coating it well. Allow to marinate for a minimum of 3 hours. 3. Cook the meat for 15 minutes. 4. Turn it over and cook for an additional 10 - 12 minutes before serving.
Per Serving: Calories 282; Fat 13.7g; Sodium 50mg; Carbs 4g; Fiber 0g; Sugar 1g; Protein 35g

Spicy Smoked Beef Roast with Paprika

Prep time: 5 minutes | Cook time: 40 minutes | Serves: 8

2 lbs. roast beef, at room temperature	1 teaspoon black pepper, preferably freshly ground
2 tablespoons extra-virgin olive oil	1 teaspoon smoked paprika
	Few dashes of liquid smoke
1 teaspoon sea salt flakes	2 jalapeño peppers, thinly sliced

1. Select the "AIR ROAST" function of Ninja Foodi digital air fry oven, set the temperature to 330 degrees F/ 165 degrees C and set the time to 30 minutes. Press the Start/Pause button and begin preheating. 2. With kitchen towels, pat the beef dry. 3. Massage the extra-virgin olive oil and seasonings into the meat. Cover with liquid smoke. 4.Place the beef in the Air Fryer and roast for 30 minutes. Flip the roast over and allow to cook for another 15 minutes. 5.When cooked through, serve topped with sliced jalapeños.
Per Serving: Calories 227; Fat 11.2g; Sodium 412mg; Carbs 1g; Fiber 0g; Sugar 1g; Protein 31g

Beef and Mushroom Meatloaf

Prep time: 5 minutes | Cook time: 25 minutes | Serves: 4

1 lb. ground beef	1 small onion, chopped
1 egg, beaten	3 tablespoons breadcrumbs
1 mushrooms, sliced	Pepper to taste
1 tablespoon thyme	

1. Select the "AIR ROAST" function of Ninja Foodi digital air fry oven, set the temperature to 400 degrees F/ 200 degrees C and set the time to 30 minutes. Press the Start/Pause button and begin preheating. 2. Place all the ingredients into a large bowl and combine entirely. 3. Transfer the meatloaf mixture into the loaf pan, and move it to the Air Fryer. 4. Cook for 25 minutes. Slice up before serving.
Per Serving: Calories 291; Fat 15.4g; Sodium 96mg; Carbs 3g; Fiber 1g; Sugar 2g; Protein 33g

Air Fried Cheeseburgers with Salad

Prep time: 5 minutes | Cook time: 10 minutes | Serves: 4

¾ lb. ground chuck
1 envelope onion soup mix
Kosher salt
Ground black pepper, to taste
1 teaspoon paprika

4 slices Monterey-Jack cheese
4 ciabatta rolls
Mustard and pickled salad, to serve

1. Select the "AIR FRY" function of Ninja Foodi digital air fry oven, set the temperature to 385 degrees F/ 195 degrees C and set the time to 30 minutes. Press the Start/Pause button and begin preheating. 2. In a bowl, stir together the ground chuck, onion soup mix, salt, black pepper, and paprika to combine well. 3. Take four equal portions of the mixture and mold each one into a patty. Transfer to the fryer and air fry for 10 minutes. 4. Put the slices of cheese on the top of the burgers. 5. Cook for another minute before serving on ciabatta rolls along with mustard and the pickled salad of your choosing.
Per Serving: Calories 350; Fat 16.7g; Sodium 428mg; Carbs 22g; Fiber 1g; Sugar 3g; Protein 28g

Simple Air Fried Beef with Bread Crumbs, Pepper

Prep time: 5 minutes | Cook time: 20 minutes | Serves: 1

1 thin beef schnitzel
1 egg, beaten
½ cup friendly bread crumbs

2 tablespoons olive oil
Pepper and salt to taste

1. Select the "AIR FRY" function of Ninja Foodi digital air fry oven, set the temperature to 350 degrees F/ 175 degrees C and set the time to 12 minutes. Press the Start/Pause button and begin preheating. 2. In a shallow dish, combine the bread crumbs, oil, pepper, and salt. 3. In a second dish, place the beaten egg. 4. Dredge the schnitzel in the egg before rolling it in the bread crumbs. 5. Put the coated schnitzel in the fryer basket and air fry for 12 minutes.
Per Serving: Calories 433; Fat 37g; Sodium 192mg; Carbs 14g; Fiber 1g; Sugar 4g; Protein 11g

Swedish Meatballs with Tomato Sauce

Prep time: 5 minutes | Cook time: 20 minutes | Serves: 8

1 lb. ground beef
2 friendly bread slices, crumbled
1 small onion, minced
½ teaspoon garlic salt
1 cup tomato sauce

2 cups pasta sauce
1 egg, beaten
2 carrots, shredded
Pepper and salt to taste

1. Select the "AIR ROAST" function of Ninja Foodi digital air fry oven, set the temperature to 400 degrees F/ 200 degrees C and set the time to 15 minutes. Press the Start/Pause button and begin preheating. 2. In a bowl, combine the ground beef, egg, carrots, crumbled bread, onion, garlic salt, pepper and salt. 3. Divide the mixture into equal amounts and shape each one into a small meatball. 4. Put them in the Air Fryer sheet pan and cook for 7 minutes. 5.Top with the tomato sauce. 6. Set the pan back into the Air Fryer and allow to cook at 320 degrees F/ 160 degrees C for 5 more minutes. Serve hot.
Per Serving: Calories 217; Fat 7.9g; Sodium 998mg; Carbs 17g; Fiber 4g; Sugar 8g; Protein 19g

Delicious Corned Beef Egg Rolls

Prep time: 5 minutes | Cook time: 8 minutes | Serves: 2 to 3

Swiss cheese
Can of sauerkraut

Sliced deli corned beef
Egg roll wrappers

1. Select the "AIR FRY" function of Ninja Foodi digital air fry oven, set the temperature to 400 degrees F/ 200 degrees C and set the time to 8 minutes. Press the Start/Pause button and begin preheating. Cut corned beef and Swiss cheese into thin slices. Drain sauerkraut and dry well. 2. Take egg roll wrapper and moisten edges with water. Stack center with corned beef and cheese till you reach desired thickness. Top off with sauerkraut. Fold the corner over the edge of filling. Bring up sides and glue with water. Add to air fryer basket and spritz with olive oil. Cook 4 minutes, then flip and cook another 4 minutes.
Per Serving: Calories 227; Fat 9.8g; Sodium 525mg; Carbs 7g; Fiber 2g; Sugar 4g; Protein 28g

Easy Roast Beef

Prep time: 10 minutes | Cook time: 45 minutes | Serves: 6 to 8

Roast beef
1 tablespoon olive oil

Seasonings of choice

Select the "AIR ROAST" function of Ninja Foodi digital air fry oven, set the temperature to 390 degrees F/ 200 degrees C and set the time to 30 minutes. Press the Start/Pause button and begin preheating. Place roast in a bowl and toss with olive oil and desired seasonings. Put seasoned roast into air fryer and cook 30 minutes. Turn over the roast when the timer sounds and cook another 15 minutes.
Per Serving: Calories 429; Fat 32.4g; Sodium 325mg; Carbs 5g; Fiber 1g; Sugar 3g; Protein 28g

Beef and Cheese Egg Rolls

Prep time: 15 minutes | Cook time: 10 minutes | Serves: 3

6 egg roll wrappers
6 chopped dill pickle chips
1 tablespoon yellow mustard
3 tablespoons cream cheese
3 tablespoons shredded cheddar cheese

½ cup chopped onion
½ cup chopped bell pepper
¼ teaspoon onion powder
¼ teaspoon garlic powder
8 ounces of raw lean ground beef

1. Select the "AIR ROAST" function of Ninja Foodi digital air fry oven, set the temperature to 390 degrees F/ 200 degrees C and set the time to 9 minutes. Press the Start/Pause button and begin preheating. 2. In a skillet, add seasonings, beef, onion, and bell pepper. Stir and crumble beef till fully cooked and vegetables are soft. 3. Take skillet off the heat and add cream cheese, mustard, and cheddar cheese, stirring till melted. Pour beef mixture into a bowl and fold in pickles. Lay out egg wrappers and place one sixth of beef mixture into each one. 4. Moisten egg roll wrapper edges with water. Fold sides to the middle and seal with water. Repeat with all other egg rolls. Place rolls into the air fryer, one batch at a time. Cook for 7-9 minutes.
Per Serving: Calories 112; Fat 2g; Sodium 12mg; Carbs 8g; Fiber 1g; Sugar 6g; Protein 0g

Beef-Stuffed Tortillas

Prep time: 5 minutes | Cook time: 5 minutes | Serves: 6

6 wheat tostadas
2 cups sour cream
2 cups Mexican blend cheese
2 cups shredded lettuce
12 ounces low-sodium nacho cheese

3 Roma tomatoes
6 12-inch wheat tortillas
1 ⅓ cups water
2 packets low-sodium taco seasoning
2 pounds of lean ground beef

1. Select the "AIR FRY" function of Ninja Foodi digital air fry oven, set the temperature to 400 degrees F/ 200 degrees C and set the time to 5 minutes. Press the Start/Pause button and begin preheating. 2. Make beef according to taco seasoning packets. Place ⅔ cup prepared beef, 4 tablespoons cheese, 1 tostada, ⅓ cup sour cream, ⅓ cup lettuce, one sixth of tomatoes and ⅓ cup cheese on each tortilla. Fold up tortillas edges and repeat with the remaining ingredients. 3. Lay the folded sides of tortillas down into the air fryer and spray with olive oil. Cook 2 minutes till browned.
Per Serving: Calories 311; Fat 6g; Sodium 112mg; Carbs 15g; Fiber 6g; Sugar 12g; Protein 2g

Delicious Beef Burgers

Prep time: 5 minutes | Cook time: 20 minutes | Serves: 3

¾-pound ground beef
2 cloves garlic, minced
1 small onion, chopped

Kosher salt
Ground black pepper
3 hamburger buns

1. Select the "AIR FRY" function of Ninja Foodi digital air fry oven, set the temperature to 380 degrees F/ 195 degrees C and set the time to 15 minutes. Press the Start/Pause button and begin preheating. 2. Mix the beef, garlic, onion, salt, and black pepper until everything is well combined. Form the mixture into three patties. Cook the burgers for about 15 minutes or until cooked through; Serve your burgers on the prepared buns and enjoy!
Per Serving: Calories 392; Fat 16.6g; Sodium 222mg; Carbs 32.3g; Fiber 1.8g; Sugar 5.3g; Protein 28.8g

Pork Strips with Basil

Prep time: 10 minutes | Cook time: 25 minutes | Serves: 6

2 pounds pork belly, cut into strips
2 tablespoons olive oil
2 teaspoons fennel seeds
A pinch of salt and black pepper
A pinch of basil, dried

Select the "AIR FRY" function of Ninja Foodi digital air fry oven, set the temperature to 425 degrees F/ 220 degrees C and set the time to 25 minutes. Press the Start/Pause button and begin preheating. In a bowl, mix all the ingredients, toss and put the pork strips in your air fryer's basket and cook for 25 minutes. Serve and enjoy.
Per Serving: Calories 251; Fat 14g; Sodium 122mg; Carbs 5g; Fiber 3g; Sugar 2g; Protein 18g

Fried Steak with Sausage Gravy

Prep time: 10 minutes | Cook time: 15 minutes | Serves: 2

1 teaspoon pepper
2 cups almond milk
2 tablespoons almond flour
6 ounces ground sausage meat
1 teaspoon pepper
1 teaspoon salt
1 teaspoon garlic powder
1 teaspoon onion powder
1 cup panko breadcrumbs
1 cup almond flour
3 beaten eggs
6 ounces sirloin steak, pounded till thin

1. Select the "AIR FRY" function of Ninja Foodi digital air fry oven, set the temperature to 370 degrees F/ 185 degrees C and set the time to 12 minutes. Press the Start/Pause button and begin preheating. 2. Season panko breadcrumbs with spices. Dredge steak in flour, then egg, and then seasoned panko mixture. Place into air fryer basket. Cook 12 minutes. 3. To make sausage gravy, cook sausage and drain off fat, but reserve 2 tablespoons. Add flour to sausage and mix until incorporated. Gradually mix in milk over medium to high heat till it becomes thick. Season mixture with pepper and cook 3 minutes longer. 4. Serve steak topped with gravy and enjoy!
Per Serving: Calories 30; Fat 13g; Sodium 12mg; Carbs 49g; Fiber 4g; Sugar 6g; Protein 3g

Delicious Mongolian-Style Beef

Prep time: 10 minutes | Cook time: 12 minutes | Serves: 6 to 10

Olive oil
½ cup almond flour
Sauce:
½ cup chopped green onion
1 teaspoon red chili flakes
1 teaspoon almond flour
½ cup brown sugar
1 teaspoon hoisin sauce
½ cup water
2 pounds beef tenderloin or beef chuck, sliced into strips

½ cup rice vinegar
½ cup low-sodium soy sauce
1 tablespoon chopped garlic
1 tablespoon finely chopped ginger
2 tablespoons olive oil

Select the "AIR FRY" function of Ninja Foodi digital air fry oven, set the temperature to 300 degrees F/ 150 degrees C and set the time to 10 minutes. Press the Start/Pause button and begin preheating. Toss strips of beef in almond flour, ensuring they are coated well. Add to air fryer and cook 10 minutes. Meanwhile, add all sauce ingredients to the pan and bring to a boil. Mix well. Add beef strips to the sauce and cook 2 minutes. Serve over cauliflower rice!
Per Serving: Calories 173; Fat 13.6g; Sodium 281mg; Carbs 3g; Fiber 1g; Sugar 1g; Protein 10g

Spicy Herbed Roast Beef

Prep time: 15 minutes | Cook time: 30 minutes | Serves: 5 to 6

½ teaspoon fresh rosemary
1 teaspoon dried thyme
¼ teaspoon pepper
1 teaspoon salt
4-pound top round roast beef
2 teaspoons olive oil

1. Select the "AIR ROAST" function of Ninja Foodi digital air fry oven, set the temperature to 360 degrees F/ 180 degrees C and set the time to 20 minutes. Press the Start/Pause button and begin preheating. Rub olive oil all over beef. Mix rosemary, thyme, pepper, and salt together and proceed to rub all sides of beef with spice mixture. Place seasoned beef into air fryer and cook 20 minutes. Allow it to rest for at least 10 minutes before slicing to serve.
Per Serving: Calories 248; Fat 21.1g; Sodium 429mg; Carbs 2g; Fiber 0g; Sugar 1g; Protein 12g

Beef Egg Rolls with Brandy Mustard Sauce

Prep time: 5 minutes | Cook time: 20 minutes | Serves: 5

Olive oil
½ cup orange marmalade
5 slices of Swiss cheese
Brandy Mustard Sauce:
1/16th teaspoon pepper
2 tablespoons whole-grain mustard
1 teaspoon dry mustard powder
1 cup heavy cream
½ cup chicken stock
¼ cup brandy
4 cups corned beef and cabbage
1 egg
10 egg roll wrappers

¾ cup dry white wine
¼ teaspoon curry powder
½ tablespoon cilantro
1 minced shallot
2 tablespoons ghee

1. For mustard sauce, Cook shallots in ghee until softened. Add brandy along with wine, boil on low heat. Cook until liquids reduce. Add stock and seasonings. Manage to Simmer 5 minutes. Low the heat and whisk in heavy cream. Cook on low flame till sauce thicken. Place it in the fridge. 2. Select the "AIR FRY" function of Ninja Foodi digital air fry oven, set the temperature to 390 degrees F/ 200 degrees C and set the time to 10 minutes. Press the Start/Pause button and begin preheating. Whisk the egg and set to the side. Lay out an egg wrapper and brush the edges with egg wash. Place corned beef mix into the center along with marmalade and Swiss cheese. Fold the bottom corner over filling. 3. Fold gently and make sure filling is completely sealed. Place rolls into air fryer basket. Grease rolls with olive oil. Cook 10 minutes shaking halfway through cooking. Serve with Brandy Mustard sauce and devour!
Per Serving: Calories 134; Fat 9.8g; Sodium 394mg; Carbs 2g; Fiber 0g; Sugar 1g; Protein 9g

Regular Beef Empanadas

Prep time: 15 minutes | Cook time: 10 minutes | Serves: 4

1 teaspoon water
1 egg white
1 cup picadillo
8 Goya empanada discs (thawed)

1. Select the "AIR FRY" function of Ninja Foodi digital air fry oven, set the temperature to 325 degrees F/ 160 degrees C and set the time to 8 minutes. Press the Start/Pause button and begin preheating. Spray basket with olive oil. 2. Place 2 tablespoons of picadillo into the center of each disc Fold disc in half and use a fork to seal edges. Repeat with all ingredients. Whisk egg white with water and brush tops of empanadas with egg wash. Add 2-3 empanadas to the air fryer, cooking 8 minutes until golden. Repeat till you cook all filled empanadas.
Per Serving: Calories 200; Fat 15.6g; Sodium 165mg; Carbs 5g; Fiber 1g; Sugar 2g; Protein 10g

Regular Cheeseburger Meatballs

Prep time: 10 minutes | Cook time: 16 minutes | Serves: 4

1-pound ground beef
¼ cup diced onions
1 large egg
1½ teaspoons smoked paprika
½ teaspoon fine sea salt
½ teaspoon garlic powder
For Serving:
Prepared yellow mustard
Sugar-free or reduced-sugar
½ teaspoon ground black pepper
1 cup mushrooms (about 8 ounces), finely chopped
½ cup tomato sauce
1 dozen (½-inch) cubes cheddar cheese

ketchup

1. Spray the air fryer basket with avocado oil. Select the "AIR FRY" function of Ninja Foodi digital air fry oven, set the temperature to 375 degrees F/ 190 degrees C and set the time to 8 minutes. Press the Start/Pause button and begin preheating. 2. In a large bowl, mix together the ground beef, onions, egg, paprika, salt, garlic powder, and pepper until well combined. Add the mushrooms and slowly stir in the tomato sauce. The meat mixture should be very moist but still hold its shape when rolled into meatballs. 3. Divide the meat mixture into 12 equal portions. Place 1 cube of cheese in the center of each portion and form the meat around the cheese into a 2-inch meatball. Arrange the meatballs in a single layer in the air fryer basket, leaving space between them. 4. Cook the meatballs for 8 minutes, flip them over, and lower the temperature to 325 degrees F/ 160 degrees C. Cook for another 6 to 8 minutes, until cooked through. 5. Serve with mustard and ketchup, if desired. Store leftovers in an airtight container in the refrigerator for up to 4 days or in the freezer for up to 2 months.
Per Serving: Calories 354; Fat 7.9g; Sodium 704mg; Carbs 6g; Fiber 3.6g; Sugar 6g; Protein 18g

Beef Patties

Prep time: 10 minutes | Cook time: 10 minutes | Serves: 4

1-pound lean ground beef
1 teaspoon dried parsley
½ teaspoon dried oregano
½ teaspoon pepper
½ teaspoon salt
½ teaspoon onion powder
½ teaspoon garlic powder
Few drops of liquid smoke
1 teaspoon Worcestershire sauce

1. Select the "AIR FRY" function of Ninja Foodi digital air fry oven, set the temperature to 350 degrees F/ 175 degrees C and set the time to 10 minutes. Press the Start/Pause button and begin preheating. 2. Mix all seasonings together till combined. Place beef in a bowl and add seasonings. Mix well, but do not overmix. Make 4 patties from the mixture and, using your thumb, make an indent in the center of each patty. Add patties to air fryer basket and cook 10 minutes. No need to turn!
Per Serving: Calories 76; Fat 5.7g; Sodium 63mg; Carbs 1g; Fiber 0g; Sugar 1g; Protein 5g

Roasted Beef Stuffed Peppers

Prep time: 5 minutes | Cook time: 25 minutes | Serves: 4

4 ounces shredded cheddar cheese
½ teaspoon pepper
½ teaspoon salt
1 teaspoon Worcestershire sauce
½ cup tomato sauce
8 ounces lean ground beef
1 teaspoon olive oil
1 minced garlic clove
½ chopped onion
2 green peppers

1. Select the "AIR ROAST" function of Ninja Foodi digital air fry oven, set the temperature to 390 degrees F/ 200 degrees C and set the time to 20 minutes. Press the Start/Pause button and begin preheating. 2. Spray with olive oil. Cut stems off bell peppers and remove seeds. Cook in boiling salted water for 3 minutes. Sauté garlic and onion together in a skillet until golden in color. Take skillet off the heat. 3. Mix pepper, salt, Worcestershire sauce, ¼ cup of tomato sauce, half of cheese and beef together. Divide meat mixture into pepper halves. Top filled peppers with remaining cheese and tomato sauce. Place filled peppers in air fryer and roast 15-20 minutes.
Per Serving: Calories 509; Fat 40.6g; Sodium 525mg; Carbs 8g; Fiber 2g; Sugar 5g; Protein 28g

Tasty Steak and Broccoli

Prep time: 10 minutes | Cook time: 15 minutes | Serves: 4

1 minced garlic clove
1 sliced ginger root
1 tablespoon olive oil
1 teaspoon almond flour
1 teaspoon sweetener of choice
1 teaspoon low-sodium soy sauce
⅓ cup sherry
2 teaspoons sesame oil
⅓ cup oyster sauce
1 pound of broccoli
¾ pound round steak

1. Select the "AIR FRY" function of Ninja Foodi digital air fry oven, set the temperature to 400 degrees F/ 200 degrees C and set the time to 12 minutes. Press the Start/Pause button and begin preheating. 2. Remove stems from broccoli and slice into florets. Slice steak into thin strips. Combine sweetener, soy sauce, sherry, almond flour, sesame oil, and oyster sauce together, stirring till sweetener dissolves. Put strips of steak into the mixture and allow to marinate 45 minutes to 2 hours. 3. Add broccoli and marinated steak to air fryer. Place garlic, ginger, and olive oil on top. Cook 12 minutes. Serve with cauliflower rice!
Per Serving: Calories 288; Fat 23.3g; Sodium 308mg; Carbs 6g; Fiber 1g; Sugar 5g; Protein 14g

Herbed Strip Steak

Prep time: 10 minutes | Cook time: 20 minutes | Serves: 4

1½ pounds New York strip steak
2 tablespoons butter, melted
Sea salt
Ground black pepper, to taste
1 teaspoon paprika
1 teaspoon dried thyme
1 teaspoon dried rosemary

Select the "AIR FRY" function of Ninja Foodi digital air fry oven, set the temperature to 400 degrees F/ 200 degrees C and set the time to 15 minutes. Press the Start/Pause button and begin preheating. Toss the beef with the remaining ingredients; place the beef in the Air Fryer basket. Cook the beef for 15 minutes, turning it over halfway through the cooking time. Enjoy!
Per Serving: Calories 218; Fat 12.6g; Sodium 456mg; Carbs 1.4g; Fiber 0.4g; Sugar 0.6g; Protein 23.6g

Sweet Honey Mesquite Pork Chops

Prep time: 5 minutes | Cook time: 10 minutes | Serves: 2

2 tablespoons mesquite seasoning
¼ cup honey
1 tablespoon olive oil
1 tablespoon water
freshly ground black pepper
2 bone-in center pork chops

1. In a shallow glass dish, whisk the mesquite seasoning, honey, olive oil, water and ground black pepper together. Pierce the chops all over and on both sides with a fork or meat tenderizer. Add the pork chops to the marinade. Massage the marinade into the chops. Cover and marinate for 30 minutes. 2. Select the "AIR FRY" function of Ninja Foodi digital air fry oven, set the temperature to 400 degrees F/ 200 degrees C and set the time to 6 minutes. Press the Start/Pause button and begin preheating. 3. Transfer the pork chops to the air fryer basket. Pour half of the marinade over the chops, reserving the remaining marinade. Air-fry the pork chops for 6 minutes. Flip and pour the marinade on top. Air-fry for 3 more minutes at 330 degrees F/ 165 degrees C. Then, increase the air fryer temperature to 400 degrees F/ 200 degrees C and air-fry the pork chops for an additional minute. 4. Let them rest for 5 minutes before serving. If you'd like a sauce for these chops, pour the cooked marinade from the bottom of the air fryer over the top.
Per Serving: Calories 69; Fat 7.2g; Sodium 486mg; Carbs 2g; Fiber 1g; Sugar 0g; Protein 0g

Roasted Rib Eye Steak

Prep time: 10 minutes | Cook time: 21 minutes | Serves: 4

2 lb. rib eye steak
1 tablespoon olive oil
1 tablespoon steak rub

1. Select the "AIR ROAST" function of Ninja Foodi digital air fry oven, set the temperature to 400 degrees F/ 200 degrees C and set the time to 15 minutes. Press the Start/Pause button and begin preheating. Massage the olive oil and steak rub into both sides of the steak. 2. Put the steak in the fryer's basket and cook for 14 minutes. Turn the steak over and cook on the other side for another 7 minutes. Serve hot.
Per Serving: Calories 311; Fat 6g; Sodium 112mg; Carbs 15g; Fiber 6g; Sugar 12g; Protein 2g

Cheesy Bacon and Pear Stuffed Chops

Prep time: 5 minutes | Cook time: 6 to 18 minutes | Serves: 3

4 slices bacon, chopped
1 tablespoon butter
½ cup finely diced onion
⅓ cup chicken stock
1½ cups seasoned stuffing cubes
1 egg, beaten
½ teaspoon dried thyme
½ teaspoon salt
⅛ teaspoon black pepper
1 pear, finely diced
⅓ cup crumbled blue cheese
3 boneless center-cut pork chops (2-inch thick)
olive oil
salt and freshly ground black pepper

1. Select the "AIR FRY" function of Ninja Foodi digital air fry oven, set the temperature to 400 degrees F/ 200 degrees C and set the time to 6 minutes. Press the Start/Pause button and begin preheating. 2. Place the bacon into the air fryer basket and air-fry for 6 minutes, stirring halfway through the cooking time. Pour out the grease from the bottom of the air fryer. 3. To make the stuffing, melt the butter in a medium saucepan over medium heat on the stovetop. Cook the onion for a few minutes, until it starts to soften. Add the chicken stock and simmer for 1 minute. Add the stuffing cubes. Stir until the stock has been absorbed. Add the bacon, egg, dried thyme, salt and freshly ground black pepper, and stir until combined. Fold in the diced pear and crumbled blue cheese. 4. Place the chops on a cutting board. Using the palm of your hand to hold the chop flat and steady, slice into the side of the pork chop to make a pocket in the center of the chop. Leave about an inch of chop uncut and make sure you don't cut all the way through the pork chop. Brush chops with olive oil and season with salt and freshly ground black pepper. Stuff each pork chop with a third of the stuffing, packing the stuffing tightly inside the pocket. 5. Preheat the air fryer to 360 degrees F/ 180 degrees C. 6. Spray or brush the sides of the air fryer basket with oil. Place the chops in the air fryer basket with the open stuffed edge of the pork chop facing the outside edges of the basket. 7. Air-fry the pork chops for 18 minutes, turning the pork chops over halfway through the cooking time. Let rest and then transfer to a serving platter.
Per Serving: Calories 151; Fat 7.5g; Sodium 621mg; Carbs 20g; Fiber 5g; Sugar 2g; Protein 5g

Mustard and Rosemary Tenderloin with Fried Apples

Prep time: 5 minutes | Cook time: 23 minutes | Serves: 2 to 3

1 pork tenderloin (about 1-pound)
2 tablespoons coarse brown mustard
salt and freshly ground black pepper
1½ teaspoons finely chopped

fresh rosemary, plus sprigs for garnish
2 apples, cored and cut into 8 wedges
1 tablespoon butter, melted
1 teaspoon brown sugar

1. Select the "AIR FRY" function of Ninja Foodi digital air fry oven, set the temperature to 370 degrees F/ 185 degrees C and set the time to 10 minutes. Press the Start/Pause button and begin preheating. 2. Cut the pork tenderloin in half so that you have two pieces that fit into the air fryer basket. Brush the mustard onto both halves of the pork tenderloin and then season with salt, pepper and the fresh rosemary. Place the pork tenderloin halves into the air fryer basket and air-fry for 10 minutes. Turn the pork over and air-fry for an additional 5 to 8 minutes. If your pork tenderloin is especially thick, you may need to add a minute or two, but it's better to check the pork and add time, than to overcook it. 3. Let the pork rest for 5 minutes. In the meantime, toss the apple wedges with the butter and brown sugar and air-fry at 400 degrees F/ 200 degrees C for 8 minutes, shaking the basket once or twice during the cooking process so the apples cook and brown evenly. 4. Slice the pork on the bias. Serve with the fried apples scattered over the top and a few sprigs of rosemary as garnish.
Per Serving: Calories 25; Fat 0.1g; Sodium 546mg; Carbs 3g; Fiber 1g; Sugar 0g; Protein 3g

Hoisin BBQ Pork Chops

Prep time: 5 minutes | Cook time: 12 minutes | Serves: 2 to 3

3 tablespoons hoisin sauce
¼ cup honey
1 tablespoon soy sauce
3 tablespoons rice vinegar
2 tablespoons brown sugar
1½ teaspoons grated fresh ginger

2 teaspoons Sriracha sauce
2 to 3 bone-in center cut pork chops, 1-inch thick (about 1¼ pounds)
chopped scallions, for garnish

1. Combine the hoisin sauce, honey, soy sauce, rice vinegar, brown sugar, ginger, and Sriracha sauce in a small saucepan. Whisk the ingredients and boil over medium-high heat on the stovetop. Lower the heat and manage to simmer the sauce until it has reduced in volume and thickened slightly – about 10 minutes. 2. Select the "AIR FRY" function of Ninja Foodi digital air fry oven, set the temperature to 400 degrees F/ 200 degrees C and set the time to 6 minutes. Press the Start/Pause button and begin preheating. 3. Place the pork chops into the air fryer basket and pour half the hoisin BBQ sauce over the top. Air-fry for 6 minutes. Then, flip the chops over, pour the remaining hoisin BBQ sauce on top and air-fry for 5 to 6 more minutes, depending on the thickness of the pork chops. 4. You can spoon a little of the sauce from the bottom drawer of the air fryer over the top if desired. Sprinkle with chopped scallions and serve.
Per Serving: Calories 293; Fat 13.8g; Sodium 855mg; Carbs 28g; Fiber 8g; Sugar 11g; Protein 19g

Roasted Beef & Broccoli

Prep time: 10 minutes | Cook time: 12 minutes | Serves: 4

1 lb. broccoli, cut into florets
¾ lb. round steak, cut into strips
1 garlic clove, minced
1 teaspoon ginger, minced
1 tablespoon olive oil
1 teaspoon cornstarch

1 teaspoon sugar
1 teaspoon soy sauce
⅓ cup sherry wine
2 teaspoons sesame oil
⅓ cup oyster sauce

1. Select the "AIR FRY" function of Ninja Foodi digital air fry oven, set the temperature to 350 degrees F/ 175 degrees C and set the time to 12 minutes. Press the Start/Pause button and begin preheating. 2. In a bowl, combine the sugar, soy sauce, sherry wine, cornstarch, sesame oil, and oyster sauce. 3. Place the steak strips in the bowl, coat each one with the mixture and allow to marinate for 45 minutes. 4. Put the broccoli in and lay the steak on top. Top with the olive oil, garlic and ginger. Cook for 12 minutes. Serve hot with rice if desired.
Per Serving: Calories 217; Fat 21.8g; Sodium 207mg; Carbs 7g; Fiber 4g; Sugar 3g; Protein 2g

Asian Spring Rolls

Prep time: 14 minutes | Cook time: 16 minutes | Serves: 20

⅓ cup noodles
1 cup beef minced
2 tablespoons cold water
1 packet spring roll sheets
1 teaspoon soy sauce

1 cup fresh mix vegetables
3 garlic cloves, minced
1 small onion, diced
1 tablespoon sesame oil

1. Cook the noodle in hot water to soften them up, drain them and snip them to make them shorter. 2. In a frying pan, cook the minced beef, soy sauce, mixed vegetables, garlic, and onion in a little oil until the beef minced is cooked through. 3. Take the pan off the heat and throw in the noodles. Mix well to incorporate everything. 4. Unroll a spring roll sheet and lay it flat. Scatter the filling diagonally across it and roll it up, brushing the edges lightly with water to act as an adhesive. 5. Select the "AIR ROAST" function of Ninja Foodi digital air fry oven, set the temperature to 350 degrees F/ 175 degrees C and set the time to 8 minutes. Press the Start/Pause button and begin preheating. 6. Coat each spring roll with a light brushing of oil and transfer to the fryer. Cook for 8 minutes and serve hot.
Per Serving: Calories 509; Fat 40.6g; Sodium 525mg; Carbs 8g; Fiber 2g; Sugar 5g; Protein 28g

Pork Loin Filets with Blue Cheese

Prep time: 5 minutes | Cook time: 20 minutes | Serves: 4

1½ pounds pork loin filets
Sea salt and ground black pepper, to taste

2 tablespoons olive oil
1 pound mushrooms, sliced
2 ounces blue cheese

1. Select the "AIR FRY" function of Ninja Foodi digital air fry oven, set the temperature to 400 degrees F/ 200 degrees C and set the time to 10 minutes. Press the Start/Pause button and begin preheating. 2. Place the pork, salt, black pepper, and olive oil in a lightly greased Air Fryer basket. Cook the pork loin filets for 10 minutes, turning them over halfway through the cooking time. 3. Top the pork loin filets with the mushrooms. Continue cooking for 5 minutes. Top the warm pork with blue cheese. Bon appétit!
Per Serving: Calories 408; Fat 18.3g; Sodium 236mg; Carbs 5g; Fiber 1.3g; Sugar 2.8g; Protein 53.4g

Herbed Roast Beef

Prep time: 10 minutes | Cook time: 55 minutes | Serves: 4

1½ pounds bottom round roast
2 tablespoons olive oil
2 garlic cloves, minced
1 teaspoon rosemary

1 teaspoon parsley
1 teaspoon oregano
Sea salt and freshly ground black pepper

1. Select the "AIR FRY" function of Ninja Foodi digital air fry oven, set the temperature to 390 degrees F/ 200 degrees C and set the time to 50 minutes. Press the Start/Pause button and begin preheating. 2. Toss the beef with the spices, garlic, and olive oil; place the beef in the Air Fryer basket. Cook the roast beef for 50 minutes, turning it over halfway through the cooking time. 3. Cut the beef into slices and serve them with dinner rolls. Bon appétit!
Per Serving: Calories 301; Fat 16.7g; Sodium 411mg; Carbs 0.4g; Fiber 0.1g; Sugar 0.1g; Protein 35.4g

Fried Porterhouse Steak

Prep time: 5 minutes | Cook time: 15 minutes | Serves: 4

1½ pounds Porterhouse steak
1 tablespoon olive oil
Kosher salt
Ground black pepper
½ teaspoon cayenne pepper

1 teaspoon dried parsley
1 teaspoon dried oregano
½ teaspoon dried basil
2 tablespoons butter
2 garlic cloves, minced

1. Select the "AIR FRY" function of Ninja Foodi digital air fry oven, set the temperature to 400 degrees F/ 200 degrees C and set the time to 12 minutes. Press the Start/Pause button and begin preheating. 2. Toss the steak with the remaining ingredients; place the steak in the Air Fryer basket. Cook the steak for 12 minutes, turning it over halfway through the cooking time. Bon appétit!
Per Serving: Calories 326; Fat 19.6g; Sodium 458mg; Carbs 1.9g; Fiber 0.4g; Sugar 0.6g; Protein 35.6g

Pistachio-Crusted Rack of Lamb

Prep time: 5 minutes | Cook time: 19 minutes | Serves: 2

½ cup finely chopped pistachios
3 tablespoons panko breadcrumbs
1 teaspoon chopped fresh rosemary
2 teaspoons chopped fresh oregano

salt and freshly ground black pepper
1 tablespoon olive oil
1 rack of lamb, bones trimmed of fat
1 tablespoon Dijon mustard

1. Select the "AIR FRY" function of Ninja Foodi digital air fry oven, set the temperature to 380 degrees F/ 195 degrees C and set the time to 12 minutes. Press the Start/Pause button and begin preheating. 2. Combine the pistachios, breadcrumbs, rosemary, oregano, salt and pepper in a small bowl. Grease in the oil and stir to combine. 3. Season the rack of lamb with salt and pepper on all sides and transfer it to the air fryer basket with the fat side facing up. Air-fry the lamb for 12 minutes. Remove the lamb and brush the fat side of the lamb rack with the Dijon mustard. Coat the rack with the pistachio mixture, pressing the breadcrumbs onto the lamb with your hands and rolling the bottom of the rack in any of the crumbs that fall off. 4. Return the rack of lamb to the air fryer and air-fry for another 3 to 7 minutes. Add or subtract a couple of minutes for lamb that is more or less well cooked. 5. Let the lamb rest for at least 5 minutes. Then, slice into chops and serve.
Per Serving: Calories 56; Fat 2.2g; Sodium 177mg; Carbs 5g; Fiber 1g; Sugar 1g; Protein 5g

Lamb Koftas with Cucumber-Yogurt Dip

Prep time: 5 minutes | Cook time: 8 minutes | Serves: 3 to 4

For the Lamp:
1-pound ground lamb
1 teaspoon ground cumin
1 teaspoon ground coriander
2 tablespoons chopped fresh mint

1 egg, beaten
½ teaspoon salt
freshly ground black pepper

For the Cucumber-Yogurt Dip:
½ English cucumber, grated (1 cup)
salt
½ clove garlic, finely minced

1 cup plain yogurt
1 tablespoon olive oil
1 tablespoon chopped fresh dill
freshly ground black pepper

1. Combine ingredients and mix well. Divide the mixture into 10 portions. Make ball from portions and then by cupping the meatball in your hand, shape it into an oval. 2. Select the "AIR ROAST" function of Ninja Foodi digital air fry oven, set the temperature to 400 degrees F/ 200 degrees C and set the time to 8 minutes. Press the Start/Pause button and begin preheating. 3. Air-fry the koftas for 8 minutes. 4. Place the grated cucumber in a strainer and sprinkle with salt. Let this drain while the koftas are cooking. Meanwhile, combine the garlic, yogurt, oil and fresh dill in a bowl. Just before serving, stir the cucumber into the yogurt sauce and season to taste with freshly ground black pepper. 5. Serve warm with the cucumber-yogurt dip.
Per Serving: Calories 217; Fat 21.8g; Sodium 207mg; Carbs 7g; Fiber 4g; Sugar 3g; Protein 2g

Delicious Chicken Sausage Balls

Prep time: 5 minutes | Cook time: 8 minutes | Serves: 5

8-ounces ground chicken
1 egg white
1 teaspoon paprika
1 tablespoon olive oil

2 tablespoons almond flour
½ teaspoon ground black pepper
½ teaspoon salt
1 tablespoon parsley, dried

1. Whisk the egg white and combine it with the ground chicken in a mixing bowl. Add parsley and salt to the mixture. 2. Add paprika and ground black pepper to mixture and stir with wet hands, make small sausage balls from the ground chicken mixture. Sprinkle each sausage ball with almond flour. 3. Select the "AIR FRY" function of Ninja Foodi digital air fry oven, set the temperature to 380 degrees F/ 195 degrees C and set the time to 8 minutes. Press the Start/Pause button and begin preheating. 4. Spray the air fryer basket tray with olive oil. Place the sausage balls into the basket and cook for 8-minutes. Turn the balls to brown all sides during the cooking process. 5. Transfer the cooked sausage balls into serving plates. Serve warm.
Per Serving: Calories 180; Fat 11.8g; Sodium 248mg; Carbs 2.9g; Fiber 1g; Sugar 1g; Protein 16.3g

Herbed Beef Roast with Onion

Prep time: 15 minutes | Cook time: 55 minutes | Serves: 4

1½ pounds beef eye round roast
1 tablespoon olive oil
Sea salt
Ground black pepper, to taste

1 onion, sliced
1 rosemary sprig
1 thyme sprig

1. Select the "AIR FRY" function of Ninja Foodi digital air fry oven, set the temperature to 390 degrees F/ 200 degrees C and set the time to 45 minutes. Press the Start/Pause button and begin preheating. 2. Toss the beef with the olive oil, salt, and black pepper; place the beef in the Air Fryer basket. Cook the beef eye round roast for 45 minutes, turning it over halfway through the cooking time. 3. Top the beef with the onion, rosemary, and thyme. Continue to cook an additional 10 minutes. Enjoy!
Per Serving: Calories 268; Fat 13.6g; Sodium 348mg; Carbs 1.2g; Fiber 0.2g; Sugar 0.6g; Protein 35.2g

Cheesy Lamb Hamburgers

Prep time: 5 minutes | Cook time: 16 minutes | Serves: 3 to 4

2 teaspoons olive oil
⅓ onion, finely chopped
1 clove garlic, minced
1-pound ground lamb
2 tablespoons fresh parsley, finely chopped
1½ teaspoons fresh oregano, finely chopped

½ cup black olives, finely chopped
⅓ cup crumbled feta cheese
½ teaspoon salt
freshly ground black pepper
4 thick pita bread
toppings and condiments

1. Preheat a skillet on the stovetop. Cook the onion in olive oil until tender, but not browned. Add in the garlic and cook. Place the cooked onion and garlic in a bowl and add the lamb, parsley, oregano, olives, cheese, salt and pepper. Mix the ingredients. 2. Divide the mix into 4 portions and form the hamburgers. 3. Select the "AIR FRY" function of Ninja Foodi digital air fry oven, set the temperature to 370 degrees F/ 185 degrees C and set the time to 13 minutes. Press the Start/Pause button and begin preheating. 4. Air-fry the burgers for 5 minutes. Flip the burgers over and air-fry for another 8 minutes. Toast the bread in the air fryer for 2 minutes. Place the burgers into the toasted bread, and serve with a tzatziki sauce or some mayonnaise.
Per Serving: Calories 74; Fat 1.9g; Sodium 685mg; Carbs 9g; Fiber 7g; Sugar 2g; Protein 9g

The London Broil

Prep time: 10 minutes | Cook time: 30 minutes | Serves: 3

1 pound London broil
¼ cup soy sauce
¼ cup fresh lemon juice
2 garlic cloves, minced

1 tablespoon paprika
Sea salt and ground black pepper, to taste

1. Select the "AIR FRY" function of Ninja Foodi digital air fry oven, set the temperature to 400 degrees F/ 200 degrees C and set the time to 28 minutes. Press the Start/Pause button and begin preheating. 2. Toss the beef with the remaining ingredients and let it marinate for an hour. Place the beef in a lightly oiled Air Fryer basket and discard the marinade. Cook the beef for 28 minutes, turning it over halfway through the cooking time. Bon appétit!
Per Serving: Calories 220; Fat 9.6g; Sodium 369mg; Carbs 6.3g; Fiber 1g; Sugar 3.6g; Protein 24.2g

Easy Italian Herb Filet Mignon

Prep time: 5 minutes | Cook time: 20 minutes | Serves: 4

1½ pounds filet mignon
2 tablespoons olive oil
2 cloves garlic, pressed
1 tablespoon Italian herb mix

1 teaspoon cayenne pepper
Kosher salt and freshly ground black pepper, to taste

1. Select the "AIR FRY" function of Ninja Foodi digital air fry oven, set the temperature to 400 degrees F/ 200 degrees C and set the time to 14 minutes. Press the Start/Pause button and begin preheating. 2. Toss the beef with the remaining ingredients; place the beef in the Air Fryer basket. Cook the beef for 14 minutes, turning it over halfway through the cooking time. Enjoy!
Per Serving: Calories 218; Fat 12.6g; Sodium 289mg; Carbs 1.4g; Fiber 0.4g; Sugar 0.6g; Protein 23.6g

Fragrant Ribeye Steak

Prep time: 5 minutes | Cook time: 20 minutes | Serves: 4

1-pound ribeye steak, bone-in
2 tablespoons butter, room temperature
2 garlic cloves, minced

Sea salt and ground black pepper, to taste
2 rosemary sprigs, leaves picked, chopped

1. Select the "AIR ROAST" function of Ninja Foodi digital air fry oven, set the temperature to 350 degrees F/ 175 degrees C and set the time to 15 minutes. Press the Start/Pause button and begin preheating. 2. Toss the ribeye steak with the butter, garlic, salt, black pepper, and rosemary; place the steak in the Air Fryer basket. Cook the ribeye steak for 15 minutes, turning it over halfway through the cooking time. Bon appétit!
Per Serving: Calories 263; Fat 17.6g; Sodium 259mg; Carbs 3.7g; Fiber 0.2g; Sugar 0.6g; Protein 22.7g

Mustardy Steak Sliders

Prep time: 10 minutes | Cook time: 20 minutes | Serves: 4

1½ pounds skirt steak
1 teaspoon steak dry rub
½ teaspoon cayenne pepper
Sea salt and ground black pepper,

to taste
2 tablespoons olive oil
2 tablespoons Dijon mustard
8 Hawaiian buns

1. Select the "AIR FRY" function of Ninja Foodi digital air fry oven, set the temperature to 400 degrees F/ 200 degrees C and set the time to 15 minutes. Press the Start/Pause button and begin preheating. 2. Toss the beef with the spices and olive oil; place the beef in the Air Fryer basket. Cook the beef for 15 minutes, turning it over halfway through the cooking time. Cut the beef into slices and serve them with mustard and Hawaiian buns. Bon appétit!
Per Serving: Calories 541; Fat 20.7g; Sodium 436mg; Carbs 44g; Fiber 2.3g; Sugar 6.1g; Protein 44g

Marinated London Broil

Prep time: 10 minutes | Cook time: 30 minutes | Serves: 4

1 pound London broil
Kosher salt
Ground black pepper
2 tablespoons olive oil
1 small lemon, freshly squeezed

3 cloves garlic, minced
1 tablespoon fresh parsley, chopped
1 tablespoon fresh coriander, chopped

1. Select the "AIR FRY" function of Ninja Foodi digital air fry oven, set the temperature to 400 degrees F/ 200 degrees C and set the time to 28 minutes. Press the Start/Pause button and begin preheating. 2. Toss the beef with the remaining ingredients and let it marinate for an hour. Place the beef in a lightly oiled Air Fryer basket and discard the marinade. Cook the beef for 28 minutes, turning it over halfway through the cooking time. Bon appétit!
Per Serving: Calories 227; Fat 13.6g; Sodium 417mg; Carbs 2.7g; Fiber 0.3g; Sugar 0.9g; Protein 23.8g

Sticky Glazed Ham

Prep time: 10 minutes | Cook time: 60 minutes | Serves: 4

1½ pounds smoked and cooked ham
¼ cup honey
1 small-sized orange, freshly squeezed
1 tablespoon balsamic vinegar

1 tablespoon stone-ground mustard
½ teaspoon red pepper flakes, crushed
Freshly ground black pepper, to taste

1. Select the "AIR ROAST" function of Ninja Foodi digital air fry oven, set the temperature to 375 degrees F/ 190 degrees C and set the time to 30 minutes. Press the Start/Pause button and begin preheating. 2. In a mixing bowl, whisk all the remaining ingredients to make the glaze. Wrap the ham in a piece of aluminum foil and lower it into the Air Fryer basket and cook the ham for about 30 minutes. 3. Remove the foil, turn the temperature to 400 degrees F/ 200 degrees C, and continue to cook for an additional 15 minutes, coating the ham with the glaze every 5 minutes.
Per Serving: Calories 368; Fat 27.8g; Sodium 114mg; Carbs 28.9g; Fiber 3g; Sugar 20.3g; Protein 28.9g

Beef Brisket

Prep time: 10minutes | Cook time: 1 hour 10 minutes | Serves: 4

1½ pounds beef brisket
2 tablespoons olive oil
1 teaspoon onion powder
1 teaspoon garlic powder

Sea salt
Ground black pepper
1 teaspoon dried parsley flakes
1 teaspoon dried thyme

1. Select the "AIR FRY" function of Ninja Foodi digital air fry oven, set the temperature to 390 degrees F/ 200 degrees C and set the time to 15 minutes. Press the Start/Pause button and begin preheating. 2. Toss the beef with the remaining ingredients; place the beef in the Air Fryer basket. Cook the beef for 15 minutes, turn the beef over and turn the temperature to 360 degrees F/ 180 degrees C. Continue to cook the beef for 55 minutes more. Bon appétit!
Per Serving: Calories 401; Fat 32.1g; Sodium 236mg; Carbs 2.4g; Fiber 0.4g; Sugar 0.6g; Protein 25.4g

Spicy Herbed Top Round Roast

Prep time: 10 minutes | Cook time: 55 minutes | Serves: 5

2 pounds top round roast
2 tablespoons extra-virgin olive oil
2 cloves garlic, pressed
1 tablespoon fresh rosemary, chopped

1 tablespoon fresh parsley, chopped
1 teaspoon red chili powder
Kosher salt and freshly ground black pepper, to taste

1. Select the "AIR ROAST" function of Ninja Foodi digital air fry oven, set the temperature to 390 degrees F/ 200 degrees C and set the time to 55 minutes. Press the Start/Pause button and begin preheating. 2. Toss the beef with the remaining ingredients; place the beef in the Air Fryer basket. Cook the beef for 55 minutes, turning it over halfway through the cooking time. Enjoy!
Per Serving: Calories 270; Fat 10.9g; Sodium 236mg; Carbs 0.5g; Fiber 0.2g; Sugar 0.1g; Protein 42.2g

Italian-Style Pork Burgers

Prep time: 5 minutes | Cook time: 20 minutes | Serves: 4

1-pound ground pork
Sea salt
Ground black pepper
1 tablespoon Italian herb mix
1 small onion, chopped
1 teaspoon garlic, minced

¼ cup parmesan cheese, grated
¼ cup seasoned breadcrumbs
1 egg
4 hamburger buns
4 teaspoons Dijon mustard
4 tablespoons mayonnaise

1. Select the "AIR FRY" function of Ninja Foodi digital air fry oven, set the temperature to 380 degrees F/ 195 degrees C and set the time to 15 minutes. Press the Start/Pause button and begin preheating. 2. In a mixing bowl, thoroughly combine the pork, spices, onion, garlic, parmesan, breadcrumbs, and egg. Form the mixture into four patties. Cook the burgers for about 15 minutes or until cooked through. Serve your burgers with hamburger buns, mustard, and mayonnaise. Enjoy!
Per Serving: Calories 593; Fat 38.9g; Sodium 235mg; Carbs 30.2g; Fiber 2.7g; Sugar 5g; Protein 27.6g

Herbed Meatloaf

Prep time: 10 minutes | Cook time: 30 minutes | Serves: 4

1½ pounds ground chuck
1 egg, beaten
2 tablespoons olive oil
4 tablespoons crackers, crushed
½ cup shallots, minced
2 garlic cloves, minced

1 tablespoon fresh rosemary, chopped
1 tablespoon fresh thyme, chopped
Sea salt and ground black pepper, to taste

1. Select the "AIR FRY" function of Ninja Foodi digital air fry oven, set the temperature to 390 degrees F/ 200 degrees C and set the time to 25 minutes. Press the Start/Pause button and begin preheating. 2. Thoroughly combine all ingredients until everything is well combined. Scrape the beef mixture into a lightly oiled baking pan and transfer it to the Air Fryer basket. Cook your meatloaf for 25 minutes. Bon appétit!
Per Serving: Calories 373; Fat 23.1g; Sodium 258mg; Carbs 5g; Fiber 0.6g; Sugar 1.4g; Protein 36.8g

Homemade Skirt Steak

Prep time: 5 minutes | Cook time: 15 minutes | Serves: 4

1½ pounds skirt steak	¼ teaspoon cumin powder
Kosher salt and freshly cracked	2 tablespoons olive oil
black pepper, to taste	2 garlic cloves, minced
1 teaspoon cayenne pepper	

1. Select the "AIR FRY" function of Ninja Foodi digital air fry oven, set the temperature to 400 degrees F/ 200 degrees C and set the time to 12 minutes. Press the Start/Pause button and begin preheating. 2. Toss the steak with the other ingredients; place the steak in the Air Fryer basket. Cook for 12 minutes, turning it over halfway through the cooking time. Bon appétit!
Per Serving: Calories 305; Fat 17.5g; Sodium 369mg; Carbs 1.8g; Fiber 0.3g; Sugar 0.6g; Protein 35.2g

French Chateaubriand

Prep time: 5 minutes | Cook time: 15 minutes | Serves: 4

1-pound beef filet mignon	3 tablespoons olive oil
Sea salt	1 tablespoon Dijon mustard
Ground black pepper	4 tablespoons dry French wine
1 teaspoon cayenne pepper	

1. Select the "AIR FRY" function of Ninja Foodi digital air fry oven, set the temperature to 400 degrees F/ 200 degrees C and set the time to 14 minutes. Press the Start/Pause button and begin preheating. 2. Toss the filet mignon with the rest of the ingredients; place the filet mignon in the Air Fryer basket. Cook the filet mignon for 14 minutes, turning it over halfway through the cooking time. Enjoy!
Per Serving: Calories 249; Fat 15.5g; Sodium 423mg; Carbs 1.8g; Fiber 0.4g; Sugar 0.8g; Protein 26.6g

Tasty Montreal Ribeye Steak

Prep time: 5 minutes | Cook time: 20 minutes | Serves: 4

1½ pounds ribeye steak, bone-in	Sea salt and ground black pepper,
2 tablespoons butter	to taste
1 Montreal seasoning mix	

1. Select the "AIR FRY" function of Ninja Foodi digital air fry oven, set the temperature to 400 degrees F/ 200 degrees C and set the time to 15 minutes. Press the Start/Pause button and begin preheating. 2. Toss the ribeye steak with the remaining ingredients; place the ribeye steak in a lightly oiled Air Fryer basket. Cook the ribeye steak for 15 minutes, turning it over halfway through the cooking time. Bon appétit!
Per Serving: Calories 357; Fat 23.5g; Sodium 247mg; Carbs 33.5g; Fiber 0.4g; Sugar 0.2g; Protein 33.5g

Asian Ground Beef Burgers

Prep time: 8 minutes | Cook time: 12 minutes | Serves: 4

¾ lb. lean ground beef	¼ cup scallions, minced
1 tablespoon soy sauce	⅓ teaspoon sea salt flakes
1 teaspoon Dijon mustard	⅓ teaspoon freshly cracked mixed
Few dashes of liquid smoke	peppercorns
1 teaspoon shallot powder	1 teaspoon celery seeds
1 clove garlic, minced	1 teaspoon parsley flakes
½ teaspoon cumin powder	

1. Mix together all of the in a bowl using your hands, combining everything well. 2. Take four equal amounts of the mixture and mold each one into a patty. 3. Create a shallow dip in the center of each patty. Lightly coat all sides of the patties with cooking spray. 4. Select the "AIR ROAST" function of Ninja Foodi digital air fry oven, set the temperature to 360 degrees F/ 180 degrees C and set the time to 12 minutes. Press the Start/Pause button and begin preheating. Place each in the air fryer and cook for 12 minutes. 5. Test with a meat thermometer, the patties are ready once they have reached 160 degrees F/ 70 degrees C. Serve them on top of butter rolls with any sauces and toppings you desire.
Per Serving: Calories 134; Fat 9.8g; Sodium 394mg; Carbs 2g; Fiber 0g; Sugar 1g; Protein 9g

Delicious Italian Rump Roast

Prep time: 10 minutes | Cook time: 55 minutes | Serves: 4

1½ pounds rump roast	1 teaspoon Italian seasoning mix
2 tablespoons olive oil	1 onion, sliced
Sea salt	2 cloves garlic, peeled
Ground black pepper, to taste	¼ cup red wine

1. Select the "AIR ROAST" function of Ninja Foodi digital air fry oven, set the temperature to 390 degrees F/ 200 degrees C and set the time to 55 minutes. Press the Start/Pause button and begin preheating. 2. Toss the rump roast with the rest of the ingredients; place the rump roast in a lightly oiled Air Fryer basket. Cook the rump roast for 55 minutes, turning it over halfway through the cooking time. Bon appétit!
Per Serving: Calories 297; Fat 16.9g; Sodium 358mg; Carbs 0.7g; Fiber 0.1g; Sugar 0.2g; Protein 35.2g

Spicy Beef Burgers

Prep time: 10 minutes | Cook time: 20 minutes | Serves: 3

¾-pound ground beef	Sea salt
2 tablespoons onion, minced	Ground black pepper
1 teaspoon garlic, minced	1 teaspoon red chili powder
1 teaspoon cayenne pepper	3 hamburger buns

1. Select the "AIR FRY" function of Ninja Foodi digital air fry oven, set the temperature to 380 degrees F/ 195 degrees C and set the time to 15 minutes. Press the Start/Pause button and begin preheating. 2. Mix the beef, onion, garlic, cayenne pepper, salt, black pepper, and red chili powder until everything is well combined. Form the mixture into three patties. Cook the burgers for about 15 minutes or until cooked through. Serve your burgers on the prepared buns and enjoy!
Per Serving: Calories 270; Fat 10.9g; Sodium 369mg; Carbs 0.5g; Fiber 0.2g; Sugar 0.1g; Protein 42.2g

Tenderloin Steaks with Crispy Mushrooms

Prep time: 5 minutes | Cook time: 20 minutes | Serves: 4

1½ pounds tenderloin steaks	Sea salt
2 tablespoons butter, melted	Ground black pepper
1 teaspoon garlic powder	½ pound cremini mushrooms,
½ teaspoon mustard powder	sliced
1 teaspoon cayenne pepper	

1. Select the "AIR FRY" function of Ninja Foodi digital air fry oven, set the temperature to 400 degrees F/ 200 degrees C and set the time to 10 minutes. Press the Start/Pause button and begin preheating. 2. Toss the beef with 1 tablespoon of the butter and spices; place the beef in the Air Fryer basket. Cook the beef for 10 minutes, turning it over halfway through the cooking time. 3. Add in the mushrooms along with the remaining 1 tablespoon of the butter. Continue to cook an additional 5 minutes. Serve warm. Bon appétit!
Per Serving: Calories 310; Fat 17g; Sodium 369mg; Carbs 3.7g; Fiber 1.7g; Sugar 1.6g; Protein 41.2g

Delicious German Beef Schnitzel

Prep time: 5 minutes | Cook time: 12 minutes | Serves: 4

4 thin beef schnitzel	4 tablespoons flour
1 tablespoon sesame seeds	2 eggs, beaten
2 tablespoons paprika	1 cup friendly bread crumbs
3 tablespoons olive oil	Pepper and salt to taste

1. Select the "AIR ROAST" function of Ninja Foodi digital air fry oven, set the temperature to 350 degrees F/ 175 degrees C and set the time to 12 minutes. Press the Start/Pause button and begin preheating. Sprinkle the pepper and salt on the schnitzel. In a shallow dish, combine the paprika, flour, and salt in a second shallow dish, mix the bread crumbs with the sesame seeds. Place the beaten eggs in a bowl. Coat the schnitzel in the flour mixture. Dip it into the egg before rolling it in the bread crumbs. 2. Put the coated schnitzel in the Air Fryer basket and allow to cook for 12 minutes before serving hot.
Per Serving: Calories 112; Fat 2g; Sodium 12mg; Carbs 8g; Fiber 1g; Sugar 6g; Protein 0g

Healthy Keto Turtles

Prep time: 15 minutes | Cook time: 15 minutes | Serves: 4

1-pound ground beef
1 teaspoon fine sea salt
½ teaspoon ground black pepper
4 hot dogs
For Serving:
Prepared yellow mustard

8 whole peppercorns
2 large dill pickles
2 slices bacon

Cornichons

1. Spray the air fryer basket with avocado oil. Select the "AIR FRY" function of Ninja Foodi digital air fry oven, set the temperature to 390 degrees F/ 200 degrees C and set the time to 15 minutes. Press the Start/Pause button and begin preheating. 2. Create the turtle shells: Form the ground beef into 4 equal-sized patties. Season the outside of the patties with the salt and pepper. 3. Make the turtle heads: Slice 1½ inches off one end of each hot dog. Use your thumb to make an indent in the side of each ground beef patty and press in a hot dog end for the head. Use the tip of a sharp knife to score 2 spots in each hot dog end for the eyes. Place a whole peppercorn in each slot. 4. Make the turtle legs: Cut the rest of the hot dogs in half lengthwise, then cut each half in half crosswise (you should have sixteen 1½-inch pieces). Place one-piece flat side down under each front corner of the patties. (You will have 8 hot dog pieces left over.) 5. Decorate the shells: Cut the dill pickles into ⅛-inch-thick slices that are about 3 inches long. Place the pickle slices parallel to each other on top of the ground beef patties, spaced about half an inch apart. 6. Slice the bacon into ¼-inch-wide and 5- to 6-inch-long strips. Place the strips on the patties, on top of and perpendicular to the pickle slices, spaced about half an inch apart. Tuck the ends of the bacon strips underneath the turtle so they don't curl up. 7. Place the turtles in the air fryer basket, leaving space between them. Cook for 10 to 15 minutes, until the beef is cooked to your liking. 8. Remove from the air fryer and serve with mustard and cornichons. Store leftovers in an airtight container in the refrigerator for up to 4 days or in the freezer for up to 2 months.
Per Serving: Calories 354; Fat 7.9g; Sodium 704mg; Carbs 6g; Fiber 3.6g; Sugar 6g; Protein 18g

Smoked Paprika Pork Loin Chops

Prep time: 5 minutes | Cook time: 20 minutes | Serves: 4

1-pound pork loin chops
1 tablespoon olive oil
Sea salt and ground black pepper,

to taste
1 tablespoon smoked paprika

Select the "AIR FRY" function of Ninja Foodi digital air fry oven, set the temperature to 400 degrees F/ 200 degrees C and set the time to 5 minutes. Press the Start/Pause button and begin preheating. Place all ingredients in a lightly greased Air Fryer basket. Cook the pork loin chops for 15 minutes, turning them over halfway through the cooking time.
Per Serving: Calories 332; Fat 1.9g; Sodium 378mg; Carbs 1.9g; Fiber 0.8g; Sugar 0.7g; Protein 23.4g

Cheesy Chicken & Bacon Casserole

Prep time: 5 minutes | Cook time: 18 minutes | Serves: 6

9-ounces ground chicken
5-ounces bacon, sliced
1 tablespoon butter
1 tablespoon almond flour
½ cup cream
1 egg
6-ounces cheddar cheese,

shredded
1 teaspoon turmeric
1 teaspoon paprika
½ teaspoon ground black pepper
1 teaspoon sea salt
½ yellow onion, diced

1. Spread the inside of the air fryer basket with butter. 2. Place the ground chicken in a bowl with salt and pepper. Add the paprika, turmeric and mix well. 3. Add the shredded cheese to mix. Beat the egg into the ground chicken and mix until well blended. 4. Whisk together the cream and almond flour in a small bowl. Dice up the yellow onion. 5. Place the ground chicken into the bottom of your air fryer tray. 6. Sprinkle top of ground chicken with diced onion and cream mixture. Add layers of bacon and shredded cheese. 7. Select the "BAKE" function of Ninja Foodi digital air fry oven, set the temperature to 380 degrees F/ 195 degrees C and set the time to 18 minutes. Press the Start/Pause button and begin preheating. When the casserole is cooked, allow it to chill briefly before serving.
Per Serving: Calories 396; Fat 28.6g; Sodium 452mg; Carbs 3.8g; Fiber 1g; Sugar 1g; Protein 30.4g

Pork Belly Roast

Prep time: 10 minutes | Cook time: 1 hour 32 minutes | Serves: 4

1 ½ lbs. of pork belly roast
1 teaspoon white pepper
1 ½ teaspoons rosemary
For Rubbing on Skin Only:
½ a teaspoon salt

1 ½ teaspoons five-spice
2 teaspoons garlic and onion seasoning

2 tablespoons lemon juice

1. Wash the pork belly under running water and pat it dry. In a large-sized pot, boil some water and blanch the pork belly for about 12-minutes. Pat dry with kitchen paper towel. Let it air-dry for about 3-hours. Prepare the rub. 2. Mix all the ingredients except the lemon juice. Turn the pork belly around and make 3-4 straight cuts into the meat, about ½ an inch deep. Massage dry rub all over meat. Turn it over and rub salt on the surface of the skin and squeeze lemon all over it. 3. Select the "AIR ROAST" function of Ninja Foodi digital air fry oven, set the temperature to 320 degrees F/ 160 degrees C and set the time to 100 minutes. Press the Start/Pause button and begin preheating. Cook for 30-minutes. Then turn over to other side and cook for another 30-minutes. Increase the temperature to 355 degrees F/ 180 degrees C ahrenheit and cook for another 20-minutes. Serve warm.
Per Serving: Calories 286; Fat 12.7g; Sodium 444mg; Carbs 11.5g; Fiber 3g; Sugar 3g; Protein 16.4g

Easy Beef Patties

Prep time: 5 minutes | Cook time: 10 minutes | Serves: 6

1 lb. ground beef
6 cheddar cheese slices

Pepper and salt to taste

1. Select the "AIR FRY" function of Ninja Foodi digital air fry oven, set the temperature to 350 degrees F/ 175 degrees C and set the time to 10 minutes. Press the Start/Pause button and begin preheating. 2. Sprinkle the salt and pepper on the ground beef. 3. Shape six equal portions of the ground beef into patties and put each one in the air fryer basket. Air fry the patties for 10 minutes. 4. Top with the cheese slices and air fry for one more minute. Serve the patties on top of dinner rolls.
Per Serving: Calories 227; Fat 9.8g; Sodium 525mg; Carbs 7g; Fiber 2g; Sugar 4g; Protein 28g

Center Cut Pork Roast

Prep time: 10 minutes | Cook time: 55 minutes | Serves: 4

1½ pounds center-cut pork roast
1 tablespoon olive oil
Sea salt
Ground black pepper

1 teaspoon garlic powder
1 teaspoon hot paprika
½ teaspoon dried parsley flakes
½ teaspoon dried rosemary

1. Select the "AIR FRY" function of Ninja Foodi digital air fry oven, set the temperature to 360 degrees F/ 180 degrees C and set the time to 55 minutes. 2. Press the Start/Pause button and begin preheating. 3. Toss all ingredients in a lightly greased Air Fryer basket. Cook the pork for 55 minutes, turning it over halfway through the cooking time. Serve warm and enjoy!
Per Serving: Calories 330; Fat 14.3g; Sodium 347mg; Carbs 1g; Fiber 0.3g; Sugar 0g; Protein 37.4g

Classic Pork Spareribs

Prep time: 10 minutes | Cook time: 40 minutes | Serves: 4

2 pounds pork spareribs
1 teaspoon coarse sea salt
⅓ teaspoon freshly ground black pepper

1 tablespoon brown sugar
1 teaspoon cayenne pepper
1 teaspoon garlic powder
1 teaspoon mustard powder

1. Select the "AIR FRY" function of Ninja Foodi digital air fry oven, set the temperature to 350 degrees F/ 175 degrees C and set the time to 35 minutes. Press the Start/Pause button and begin preheating. 2. Toss all ingredients in a lightly greased Air Fryer basket. Cook the pork ribs for 35 minutes, turning them over halfway through the cooking time.
Per Serving: Calories 301; Fat 8.5g; Sodium 147mg; Carbs 2.8g; Fiber 0.2g; Sugar 2g; Protein 50.1g

Delicious Pork Belly

Prep time: 5 minutes | Cook time: 20 minutes | Serves: 6

1½ pounds pork belly, cut into pieces
¼ cup tomato sauce
1 tablespoon tamari sauce

2 tablespoons dark brown sugar
1 teaspoon garlic, minced
Sea salt and ground black pepper, to season

1. Select the "AIR FRY" function of Ninja Foodi digital air fry oven, set the temperature to 400 degrees F/ 200 degrees C and set the time to 17 minutes. Press the Start/Pause button and begin preheating. 2. Toss all ingredients in your Air Fryer basket. Cook the pork belly for about 17 minutes, shaking the basket halfway through the cooking time.
Per Serving: Calories 603; Fat 60.1g; Sodium 578mg; Carbs 3.3g; Fiber 0.8g; Sugar 1.7g; Protein 11.1g

Pork Sausage with Crunchy Brussels Sprouts

Prep time: 5 minutes | Cook time: 20 minutes | Serves: 4

1-pound sausage links, uncooked
1 pound Brussels sprouts, halved
1 teaspoon dried thyme

1 teaspoon dried rosemary
1 teaspoon dried parsley flakes
1 teaspoon garlic powder

1. Select the "AIR FRY" function of Ninja Foodi digital air fry oven, set the temperature to 380 degrees F/ 195 degrees C and set the time to 15 minutes. Press the Start/Pause button and begin preheating. 2. Place the sausage and Brussels sprouts in a lightly greased Air Fryer basket. Air fry the sausage and Brussels sprouts for 15 minutes tossing the basket halfway through the cooking time. Bon appétit!
Per Serving: Calories 444; Fat 35.8g; Sodium 225mg; Carbs 11.5g; Fiber 4.4g; Sugar 2.5g; Protein 20.1g

Garlicky Rosemary Pork Butt

Prep time: 10 minutes | Cook time: 60 minutes | Serves: 4

1½ pounds pork butt
1 teaspoon butter, melted
2 garlic cloves, pressed
2 tablespoons fresh rosemary,

chopped
Coarse sea salt and freshly ground black pepper, to taste

1. Select the "AIR FRY" function of Ninja Foodi digital air fry oven, set the temperature to 360 degrees F/ 180 degrees C and set the time to 55 minutes. Press the Start/Pause button and begin preheating. 2. Toss all ingredients in a lightly greased Air Fryer basket. Cook the pork for 55 minutes, turning it over halfway through the cooking time. Serve warm and enjoy!
Per Serving: Calories 338; Fat 22g; Sodium 522mg; Carbs 0.7g; Fiber 0.2g; Sugar 0.2g; Protein 29.7g

Beef Stuffed Pepper with Cheese

Prep time: 5 minutes | Cook time: 20 minutes | Serves: 4

4 bell peppers, cut top of bell pepper
16 oz. ground beef
⅔ cup cheese, shredded
½ cup rice, cooked
1 teaspoon basil, dried
½ teaspoon chili powder

1 teaspoon black pepper
1 teaspoon garlic salt
2 teaspoons Worcestershire sauce
8 oz. tomato sauce
2 garlic cloves, minced
1 small onion, chopped

1. Grease a frying pan with oil and fry the onion and garlic over a medium heat. 2. Stir in the beef, basil, chili powder, black pepper, and garlic salt, combining everything well. Allow to cook until the beef is nicely browned, before taking the pan off the heat. 3. Add in half of the cheese, the rice, Worcestershire sauce, and tomato sauce and stir to combine. 4. Spoon equal amounts of the beef mixture into the four bell peppers, filling them entirely. 5. Select the "AIR FRY" function of Ninja Foodi digital air fry oven, set the temperature to 400 degrees F/ 200 degrees C and set the time to 20 minutes. Press the Start/Pause button and begin preheating. 6. Grease the basket with cooking spray. 7. Put the stuffed bell peppers in the basket and allow to cook for 11 minutes. 8. Add the cheese on top of bell pepper with remaining cheese and cook for a further 2 minutes. When the cheese is melted and the bell peppers are piping hot, serve immediately.
Per Serving: Calories 152; Fat 50g; Sodium 438mg; Carbs 7g; Fiber 0g; Sugar 7g; Protein 132g

Ham Omelet with mushroom

Prep time: 5 minutes | Cook time: 12 minutes | Serves: 9

1 tablespoon flax seeds
¼ teaspoon sea salt
½ teaspoon paprika
1 teaspoon ground black pepper
1 teaspoon olive oil

4-ounces white mushrooms, sliced
½ cup cream cheese
7 eggs
½ cup diced cooked ham

1. Slice the mushrooms and sprinkle them with paprika, sea salt, and ground black pepper. 2. Select the "AIR FRY" function of Ninja Foodi digital air fry oven, set the temperature to 400 degrees F/ 200 degrees C and set the time to 12 minutes. Press the Start/Pause button and begin preheating. 3. Spray the air fryer basket tray with olive oil inside and place the sliced mushrooms there. Cook the mushrooms for 3-minutes. 4. Meanwhile, add eggs to a small bowl along with ham and whisk them. Add the cream cheese and flax seeds and mix egg mixture carefully. 5. Pour the omelet into the air fryer basket tray over the mushrooms. Stir omelet gently and cook for 7-minutes. 6. When omelet is cooked, remove it from the air fryer basket tray with the use of a wooden spatula. Slice it into servings and serve warm.
Per Serving: Calories 106; Fat 8.7g; Sodium 332mg; Carbs 1.5g; Fiber 0.3g; Sugar 0.1g; Protein 5.9g

Pork Ribs with Zucchini

Prep time: 10 minutes | Cook time: 40 minutes | Serves: 4

1½ pounds pork loin ribs
2 cloves garlic, minced
1 tablespoon olive oil
4 tablespoons whiskey

1 teaspoon onion powder
Sea salt and ground black pepper, to taste
½-pound zucchini, sliced

1. Select the "AIR FRY" function of Ninja Foodi digital air fry oven, set the temperature to 350 degrees F/ 175 degrees C and set the time to 25 minutes. Press the Start/Pause button and begin preheating. 2. Toss the pork ribs with the garlic, olive oil, whiskey and spices; place the ingredients in a lightly greased Air Fryer basket. Cook the pork ribs for 25 minutes, turning them over halfway through the cooking time. 3. Top the pork ribs with the sliced zucchini and continue cooking for an additional 12 minutes. Serve immediately.
Per Serving: Calories 303; Fat 13.5g; Sodium 471mg; Carbs 7.2g; Fiber 0.9g; Sugar 4.1g; Protein 37.1g

Dijon Pork Loin Roast

Prep time: 5 minutes | Cook time: 20 minutes | Serves: 4

1½ pounds top loin roasts, sliced into four pieces
2 tablespoons olive oil
1 teaspoon hot paprika

Sea salt and ground black pepper
1 tablespoon Dijon mustard
1 teaspoon garlic, pressed

1. Select the "AIR ROAST" function of Ninja Foodi digital air fry oven, set the temperature to 400 degrees F/ 200 degrees C and set the time to 15 minutes. Press the Start/Pause button and begin preheating. 2. Place all ingredients in a lightly greased Air Fryer basket. Cook the pork for 15 minutes, turning it over halfway through the cooking time.
Per Serving: Calories 352; Fat 1.9g; Sodium 414mg; Carbs 1.9g; Fiber 0.6g; Sugar 0.6g; Protein 36.4g

Hot and Spicy Rib Roast

Prep time: 10 minutes | Cook time: 55 minutes | Serves: 4

1½ pounds pork center cut rib roast
2 teaspoons butter, melted
1 teaspoon red chili powder
1 teaspoon paprika

1 teaspoon garlic powder
½ teaspoon onion powder
Sea salt and ground black pepper, to taste
2 tablespoons tamari sauce

1. Select the "AIR ROAST" function of Ninja Foodi digital air fry oven, set the temperature to 350 degrees F/ 175 degrees C and set the time to 55 minutes. Press the Start/Pause button and begin preheating. 2. Toss all ingredients in a lightly greased Air Fryer basket. Cook the pork for 55 minutes, turning it over halfway through the cooking time. Serve warm and enjoy!
Per Serving: Calories 383; Fat 17.9g; Sodium 269mg; Carbs 3.2g; Fiber 1.1g; Sugar 1g; Protein 49.9g

Creamy Bacon Scrambled Eggs

Prep time: 5 minutes | Cook time: 10 minutes | Serves: 4

6-ounces bacon, chopped into
small pieces
4 eggs
5 tablespoons heavy cream
1 teaspoon ground black pepper

1 teaspoon salt
½ teaspoon nutmeg
1 teaspoon paprika
1 tablespoon butter

1. Dice bacon into small pieces and sprinkle with salt. Stir the bacon gently and put in the air fryer basket. 2. Select the "AIR FRY" function of Ninja Foodi digital air fry oven, set the temperature to 360 degrees F/ 180 degrees C and set the time to 10 minutes. Press the Start/Pause button and begin preheating. Cook for 5-minutes. 3. Meanwhile, beat the eggs in a bowl and whisk them with a hand whisker. Sprinkle paprika, nutmeg, ground black pepper into the egg mixture and whisk. Toss the butter in with the chopped bacon and pour the egg mixture over it. Add the heavy cream and cook for 2-minutes. 4. After this, stir the mixture with a spatula until you get scrambled eggs and cook dish for an additional 3-minutes. Transfer the dish into serving plates and serve warm.
Per Serving: Calories 387; Fat 32.1g; Sodium 145mg; Carbs 2.3g; Fiber 0.5g; Sugar 0.6g; Protein 21.9g

Spicy St. Louis-Style Ribs

Prep time: 10 minutes | Cook time: 40 minutes | Serves: 4

1½ pounds St. Louis-style ribs
1 teaspoon hot sauce
1 tablespoon canola oil

Kosher salt and ground black
pepper, to taste
2 garlic cloves, minced

1. Select the "AIR ROAST" function of Ninja Foodi digital air fry oven, set the temperature to 350 degrees F/ 175 degrees C and set the time to 35 minutes. Press the Start/Pause button and begin preheating. 2. Toss all ingredients in a lightly greased Air Fryer basket. Cook the pork ribs for 35 minutes, turning them over halfway through the cooking time.
Per Serving: Calories 360; Fat 23.6g; Sodium 478mg; Carbs 33.4g; Fiber 0.2g; Sugar 0.6g; Protein 33.4g

Spiced Ground Pork Dinner Rolls

Prep time: 5 minutes | Cook time: 20 minutes | Serves: 4

1-pound ground pork
Sea salt and freshly ground black
pepper, to taste
1 teaspoon red pepper flakes,
crushed

½ cup scallions, chopped
2 garlic cloves, minced
1 tablespoon olive oil
1 tablespoon soy sauce
8 dinner rolls, split

1. Select the "AIR FRY" function of Ninja Foodi digital air fry oven, set the temperature to 380 degrees F/ 195 degrees C and set the time to 15 minutes. Press the Start/Pause button and begin preheating. 2. In a mixing bowl, thoroughly combine the pork, spices, scallions, garlic, olive oil, and soy sauce. Form the mixture into four patties. Cook the patties for about 15 minutes or until cooked through. Serve the patties in dinner rolls and enjoy!
Per Serving: Calories 499; Fat 31.6g; Sodium 478mg; Carbs 28.2g; Fiber 2.6g; Sugar 2g; Protein 24.5g

Pork Tacos

Prep time: 10 minutes | Cook time: 60 minutes | Serves: 4

2 ancho chiles, seeded and
minced
2 garlic cloves, chopped
1 tablespoon olive oil
Kosher salt

Ground black pepper, to season
1 teaspoon dried Mexican
oregano
1½ pounds pork butt
4 corn tortillas, warmed

1. Select the "AIR FRY" function of Ninja Foodi digital air fry oven, set the temperature to 360 degrees F/ 180 degrees C and set the time to 55 minutes. Press the Start/Pause button and begin preheating. 2. Toss all ingredients, except for the tortillas, in a lightly greased Air Fryer basket. Air fry the pork butt for 55 minutes, turning it over halfway through the cooking time. Using two forks, shred the pork and serve in tortillas with toppings of choice. Serve immediately!
Per Serving: Calories 538; Fat 34.2g; Sodium 455mg; Carbs 11.3g; Fiber 1.6g; Sugar 0.2g; Protein 44.1g

Beef and Spinach Rolls

Prep time: 15 minutes | Cook time: 15 minutes | Serves: 2

2 lb. beef flank steak
3 teaspoons pesto
1 teaspoon black pepper
6 slices of provolone cheese

3 oz. roasted red bell peppers
¾ cup baby spinach
1 teaspoon sea salt

1. Select the "AIR FRY" function of Ninja Foodi digital air fry oven, set the temperature to 400 degrees F/ 200 degrees C and set the time to 15 minutes. Press the Start/Pause button and begin preheating. 2. Spoon equal amounts of the pesto onto each flank steak and spread it across evenly. 3. Place the cheese, roasted red peppers and spinach on top of the meat, about three-quarters of the way down. Roll the steak up, holding it in place with toothpicks. Sprinkle on the sea salt and pepper. 4. Place in the air fryer basket and cook for 14 minutes, turning halfway through the cooking time. Let it rest a while before slicing up and serving.
Per Serving: Calories 248; Fat 21.1g; Sodium 429mg; Carbs 2g; Fiber 0g; Sugar 1g; Protein 12g

Pork Loin Chops with Onions

Prep time: 5 minutes | Cook time: 20 minutes | Serves: 4

1½ pounds pork loin chops,
boneless
2 tablespoons olive oil
½ teaspoon cayenne pepper

1 teaspoon garlic powder
Sea salt
Ground black pepper
1 onion, cut into wedges

1. Select the "AIR FRY" function of Ninja Foodi digital air fry oven, set the temperature to 400 degrees F/ 200 degrees C and set the time to 15 minutes. Press the Start/Pause button and begin preheating. 2. Place all ingredients in a lightly greased Air Fryer basket. Cook the pork loin chops for 15 minutes, turning them over halfway through the cooking time.
Per Serving: Calories 358; Fat 18.6g; Sodium 633mg; Carbs 8g; Fiber 1g; Sugar 4.7g; Protein 37.3g

Spiced Roast Beef

Prep time: 10 minutes | Cook time: 55 minutes | Serves: 6

2 lb. beef
1 tablespoon olive oil
1 teaspoon dried rosemary
1 teaspoon dried thyme
½ teaspoon black pepper

½ teaspoon oregano
½ teaspoon garlic powder
1 teaspoon salt
1 teaspoon onion powder

1. Select the "AIR ROAST" function of Ninja Foodi digital air fry oven, set the temperature to 330 degrees F/ 165 degrees C and set the time to 55 minutes. Press the Start/Pause button and begin preheating. In a bowl, mix all spices. Coat the beef with a brushing of olive oil. Massage the spice mixture into the beef. 2. Transfer the meat to the air fryer and cook for 30 minutes. Turn it over and cook on the other side for another 25 minutes.
Per Serving: Calories 429; Fat 32.4g; Sodium 325mg; Carbs 5g; Fiber 1g; Sugar 3g; Protein 28g

Easy Meatloaf

Prep time: 5 minutes | Cook time: 25 minutes | Serves: 4

¾ lb. ground chuck
¼ lb. ground pork sausage
1 cup shallots, finely chopped
2 eggs, well beaten
3 tablespoons plain milk
1 tablespoon oyster sauce
1 teaspoon porcini mushrooms

½ teaspoon cumin powder
1 teaspoon garlic paste
1 tablespoon fresh parsley
Seasoned salt
Crushed red pepper flakes
1 cup crushed saltines

1. Select the "AIR ROAST" function of Ninja Foodi digital air fry oven, set the temperature to 360 degrees F/ 180 degrees C and set the time to 25 minutes. Press the Start/Pause button and begin preheating. Mix together all of the ingredients in a bowl, combining everything well. 2. Transfer to the air fryer baking dish and cook for 25 minutes. Serve hot.
Per Serving: Calories 173; Fat 13.6g; Sodium 281mg; Carbs 3g; Fiber 1g; Sugar 1g; Protein 10g

Delicious Cheesy Schnitzel

Prep time: 15 minutes | Cook time: 15 minutes | Serves: 1

1 thin beef schnitzel	3 tablespoons pasta sauce
1 egg, beaten	¼ cup parmesan cheese, grated
½ cup friendly bread crumbs	Pepper and salt to taste
2 tablespoons olive oil	

1. Select the "AIR FRY" function of Ninja Foodi digital air fry oven, set the temperature to 350 degrees F/ 175 degrees C and set the time to 20 minutes. Press the Start/Pause button and begin preheating. 2. In a shallow dish, combine the bread crumbs, olive oil, pepper, and salt. 3. In another shallow dish, put the beaten egg. Cover the schnitzel in the egg before pressing it into the breadcrumb mixture and placing it in the Air Fryer basket. Cook for 15 minutes. 4. Pour the pasta sauce over the schnitzel and top with the grated cheese. Cook for an additional 5 minutes until the cheese melts. Serve hot.
Per Serving: Calories 288; Fat 23.3g; Sodium 308mg; Carbs 6g; Fiber 1g; Sugar 5g; Protein 14g

Yummy Beef Schnitzel

Prep time: 15 minutes | Cook time: 14 minutes | Serves: 1

1 egg	2 tablespoons olive oil
1 thin beef schnitzel	1 parsley, roughly chopped
3 tablespoons friendly bread crumbs	½ lemon, cut in wedges

1. Select the "AIR ROAST" function of Ninja Foodi digital air fry oven, set the temperature to 360 degrees F/ 180 degrees C and set the time to 15 minutes. Press the Start/Pause button and begin preheating. 2. In a bowl combine the bread crumbs and olive oil to form a loose, crumbly mixture. 3. Beat the egg with a whisk. Coat the schnitzel first in the egg and then in the bread crumbs, ensuring to cover it fully. 4. Place the schnitzel in the air fryer and cook for 12 – 14 minutes. 5. Garnish the schnitzel with the lemon wedges and parsley before serving.
Per Serving: Calories 138; Fat 10.6g; Sodium 102mg; Carbs 1g; Fiber 0g; Sugar 1g; Protein 9g

Simple Meatballs

Prep time: 5 minutes | Cook time: 15 minutes | Serves: 4

1 egg	2 tablespoons raisins
½ lb. beef minced	1 cup onion, chopped and fried
½ cup friendly breadcrumbs	½ tablespoon pepper
1 tablespoon parsley, chopped	½ teaspoon salt

1. Select the "AIR FRY" function of Ninja Foodi digital air fry oven, set the temperature to 350 degrees F/ 175 degrees C and set the time to 15 minutes. Press the Start/Pause button and begin preheating. 2. Place all of the ingredients in a bowl and combine well. 3. Use your hands to shape equal amounts of the mixture into small balls. 4. Place in the greased air fryer basket. Air fry the meatballs for 15 minutes. Serve with the sauce of your choice.
Per Serving: Calories 293; Fat 13.8g; Sodium 855mg; Carbs 28g; Fiber 8g; Sugar 11g; Protein 19g

Crunchy Bacon

Prep time: 15 minutes | Cook time: 1 minutes | Serves: 4

10-ounces Canadian bacon, sliced	¼ teaspoon ground black pepper
1 teaspoon cream	½ teaspoon ground coriander
½ teaspoon salt	½ teaspoon ground thyme

1. In a mixing bowl, combine the thyme, coriander, black pepper, and salt. Sprinkle this spice mix on top of the bacon slices on each side. 2. Select the "AIR FRY" function of Ninja Foodi digital air fry oven, set the temperature to 360 degrees F/ 180 degrees C and set the time to 10 minutes. Press the Start/Pause button and begin preheating. 3. Place prepared bacon inside the air fryer and cook it for 5-minutes. 4. After this, turn the sliced bacon over and cook for an additional 5-minutes more. When cooked, remove it from the air fryer and sprinkle it with cream and serve immediately!
Per Serving: Calories 150; Fat 6.7g; Sodium 336mg; Carbs 1.9g; Fiber 0.2g; Sugar 0.1g; Protein 19.6g

Quick Beef Steak

Prep time: 8 minutes | Cook time: 6 minutes | Serves: 1

1 steak, 1-inch thick	Black pepper to taste
1 tablespoon olive oil	Sea salt to taste

1. Select the "AIR FRY" function of Ninja Foodi digital air fry oven, set the temperature to 390 degrees F/ 200 degrees C and set the time to 10 minutes. Press the Start/Pause button and begin preheating. 2. Brush both sides of the steak with the oil. Season both sides with salt and pepper. 3. Take care when placing the steak in the baking tray and allow to cook for 3 minutes. Flip over, and cook for 3 minutes. 4. Take it out of the fryer and allow to sit for roughly 3 minutes before serving.
Per Serving: Calories 151; Fat 7.5g; Sodium 621mg; Carbs 20g; Fiber 5g; Sugar 2g; Protein 5g

Herbed Beef Meatloaf

Prep time: 10 minutes | Cook time: 25 minutes | Serves: 4

1 large onion, peeled and diced	1 tablespoon oregano
2 kg. minced beef	1 tablespoon mixed herbs
1 teaspoon Worcester sauce	1 tablespoon friendly bread
3 tablespoons tomato ketchup	crumbs
1 tablespoon basil	Salt & pepper to taste

1. Select the "AIR FRY" function of Ninja Foodi digital air fry oven, set the temperature to 350 degrees F/ 175 degrees C and set the time to 25 minutes. Press the Start/Pause button and begin preheating. 2. In a large bowl, combine the minced beef with the herbs, Worcester sauce, onion and tomato ketchup, incorporating every component well. 3. Pour in the breadcrumbs and give it another stir. 4. Transfer the mixture to a small dish and cook for 25 minutes in the air fryer.
Per Serving: Calories 326; Fat 19.6g; Sodium 458mg; Carbs 1.9g; Fiber 0.4g; Sugar 0.6g; Protein 35.6g

Herbed Cheddar Bacon

Prep time: 5 minutes | Cook time: 10 minutes | Serves: 4

8-ounces bacon, sliced	½ teaspoon ground black pepper
½ teaspoon oregano, dried	½ teaspoon salt
4-ounces cheddar cheese, shredded	½ teaspoon ground thyme

1. Slice the bacon and rub it with the dried oregano, ground black pepper, salt and ground thyme on each side. 2. Leave the bacon for 3-minutes to soak in the spices. 3. Meanwhile, Select the "AIR FRY" function of Ninja Foodi digital air fry oven, set the temperature to 360 degrees F/ 180 degrees C and set the time to 10 minutes. Press the Start/Pause button and begin preheating. Place the sliced bacon in the air fryer rack and cook for 5-minutes. 4. Meanwhile, shred the cheddar cheese. When the bacon is cooked—sprinkle it with the shredded cheddar cheese and cook for 30-seconds more. Transfer to serving plates and serve warm.
Per Serving: Calories 423; Fat 33.1g; Sodium 668mg; Carbs 1.5g; Fiber 0.3g; Sugar 0g; Protein 28g

Crunchy Tuna with Bacon

Prep time: 5 minutes | Cook time: 10 minutes | Serves: 4

6-ounces bacon, sliced	6-ounces tuna
1 teaspoon butter	½ teaspoon ground black pepper
4-ounces parmesan cheese, shredded	¼ teaspoon turmeric
1 teaspoon cream	¼ teaspoon sea salt

1. Place bacon inside of four ramekins. Add a small amount of butter in each ramekin. 2. Mix the sea salt, turmeric, and ground black pepper. Combine chopped tuna with spice mix. Place some tuna mix into each ramekin on top of bacon. 3. Add the cream and shredded cheese on top of tuna mix. 4. Select the "AIR FRY" function of Ninja Foodi digital air fry oven, set the temperature to 360 degrees F/ 180 degrees C and set the time to 10 minutes. Press the Start/Pause button and begin preheating. 5. Put the tuna boards into the air fryer basket and cook for 10-minutes. When the tuna boards are done cooking, they will have a sweet, crunchy taste with a light brown color to them. Serve hot!
Per Serving: Calories 411; Fat 28.3g; Sodium 398mg; Carbs 1.9g; Fiber 0.2g; Sugar 0.3g; Protein 36.2g

Delicious Breakfast Cookies

Prep time: 5 minutes | Cook time: 15 minutes | Serves: 6

½ cup coconut flour
1 egg
1 tablespoon cream
3 tablespoons butter
4-ounces bacon, chopped, cooked

1 teaspoon apple cider vinegar
1 teaspoon baking powder
⅓ teaspoon salt
½ cup almond flour

1. Beat the egg and whisk it. Add the baking powder, cream, and apple cider vinegar. Add the butter stirring gently. Add the almond flour, coconut flour, and salt. Sprinkle the mixture with chopped cooked bacon and knead the dough. 2. Select the "AIR FRY" function of Ninja Foodi digital air fry oven, set the temperature to 360 degrees F/ 180 degrees C and set the time to 15 minutes. Press the Start/Pause button and begin preheating. 3. Cover the air fryer tray with foil. Make 6 medium-sized meatballs and place them in the air fryer basket. 4. Cook the cookies for 15-minutes. Once cooked, Cool them for a brief time. Then transfer them onto a serving plate.
Per Serving: Calories 219; Fat 16.7g; Sodium 665mg; Carbs 8g; Fiber 2g; Sugar 4g; Protein 9.8g

Delicious Bacon Omelet

Prep time: 5 minutes | Cook time: 13 minutes | Serves: 6

6 eggs
1 teaspoon butter
4-ounces bacon
1 tablespoon dill, dried

½ teaspoon salt
½ teaspoon turmeric
¼ cup almond milk

1. In a bowl, whisk eggs, then add the almond milk. Add the turmeric, dried dill, salt and mix well. Slice the bacon. 2. Select the "AIR FRY" function of Ninja Foodi digital air fry oven, set the temperature to 360 degrees F/ 180 degrees C and set the time to 13 minutes. Press the Start/Pause button and begin preheating. 3. Place the bacon in the air fryer sheet pan. Cook the bacon for 5-minutes. 4. Turn the bacon over and pour the egg mixture on top of it. Cook the omelet for 8-minutes. When the omelet is cooked, transfer it to a plate and slice into servings. Serve warm.
Per Serving: Calories 196; Fat 15.3g; Sodium 423mg; Carbs 1.6g; Fiber 0.1g; Sugar 0.3g; Protein 12.9g

Air Fryer Beef & Mushrooms

Prep time: 15 minutes | Cook time: 1 minutes | Serves: 1

6 oz. beef
¼ onion, diced

½ cup mushroom slices
2 tablespoons favorite marinade

1. Select the "AIR FRY" function of Ninja Foodi digital air fry oven, set the temperature to 350 degrees F/ 175 degrees C and set the time to 10 minutes. Press the Start/Pause button and begin preheating. 2. Slice or cube the beef and put it in a bowl. 3. Cover the meat with the marinade, place a layer of aluminum foil or saran wrap over the bowl, and put in the refrigerator for 3 hours. 4. Put the meat in a baking dish along with the onion and mushrooms. Air fry for 10 minutes. Serve hot.
Per Serving: Calories 268; Fat 13.6g; Sodium 348mg; Carbs 1.2g; Fiber 0.2g; Sugar 0.6g; Protein 35.2g

Rack of Lamb with Garlic Sauce

Prep time: 5 minutes | Cook time: 15 minutes | Serves: 2

2 racks of lamb
1 bunch of fresh mint
Salt and pepper to taste

⅓ cup extra-virgin olive oil
1 tablespoon honey
2 garlic cloves

1. Select the "AIR FRY" function of Ninja Foodi digital air fry oven, set the temperature to 390 degrees F/ 200 degrees C and set the time to 15 minutes. Press the Start/Pause button and begin preheating. 2. Add all the ingredients in a blender except the lamb. Puree into a sauce. 3. Make small cuts in lamb racks, from top between bones, and then tie rack into crown shape using kitchen twine. Smear rack generously with sauce. 4. Place pan with lamb rack into air fryer and cook for 15-minutes. Open the air fryer every 5-minutes to layer more sauce onto rack. Serve with mashed potatoes and fresh vegetables.
Per Serving: Calories 322; Fat 13.2g; Sodium 444mg; Carbs 10.8g; Fiber 1g; Sugar 2g; Protein 17.5g

Country Style Roasted Pork Ribs

Prep time: 5 minutes | Cook time: 12 minutes | Serves: 4

4 country-style pork ribs, trimmed
of excess fat
Salt and black pepper to taste
1 teaspoon dried marjoram
1 teaspoon garlic powder

1 teaspoon thyme
2 teaspoons dry mustard
3 tablespoons coconut oil
3 tablespoons cornstarch

1. Select the "BAKE" function of Ninja Foodi digital air fry oven, set the temperature to 400 degrees F/ 200 degrees C and set the time to 15 minutes. Press the Start/Pause button and begin preheating. 2. Place all ingredients in a bowl except pork ribs, mix. Soak the ribs in the mixture and rub in. 3. Place the ribs into the air fryer for 12-minutes. Serve and enjoy!
Per Serving: Calories 265; Fat 12.6g; Sodium 365mg; Carbs 12.2g; Fiber 4g; Sugar 3g; Protein 16.5g

Spiced Pork Sticks

Prep time: 5 minutes | Cook time: 10 minutes | Serves: 4

10-ounce pork fillet
1 tablespoon olive oil
½ teaspoon salt
1 teaspoon paprika
1 teaspoon apple cider vinegar
1 teaspoon oregano

1 teaspoon nutmeg
¼ teaspoon ground ginger
1 teaspoon basil, dried
5-ounces Parmesan cheese, shredded

1. Cut the pork fillet into thick strips. Combine the nutmeg, ginger, oregano, paprika, and salt in a shallow bowl and stir. 2. Sprinkle the pork strips with the spice mixture. Sprinkle the pork strips with apple cider vinegar. 3. Select the "AIR FRY" function of Ninja Foodi digital air fry oven, set the temperature to 380 degrees F/ 195 degrees C and set the time to 10 minutes. Press the Start/Pause button and begin preheating. 4. Sprinkle the inside of the air fryer basket with olive oil and place the pork strips inside of it. Cook pork strips for 5-minutes, then turn strips over and cook for 4-minutes more. 5. Cover the pork strips with parmesan cheese and cook for 1-minute more. Remove the pork strips from air fryer and serve immediately.
Per Serving: Calories 315; Fat 20.4g; Sodium 333mg; Carbs 2.2g; Fiber 0.2g; Sugar 0.3g; Protein 31.3g

Herbed Lamb Chops

Prep time: 5 minutes | Cook time: 32 minutes | Serves: 4

1 tablespoon + 2 tablespoons
olive oil, divided
4 lamb chops

Pinch of black pepper
1 tablespoon dried thyme
1 garlic clove

1. Select the "AIR FRY" function of Ninja Foodi digital air fry oven, set the temperature to 390 degrees F/ 200 degrees C and set the time to 25 minutes. Press the Start/Pause button and begin preheating. 2. Cook the garlic with 1 teaspoon olive oil for 10-minutes in air fryer. 3. Combine thyme and pepper with rest of olive oil. Squeeze the roasted garlic and stir into thyme and oil mixture. Brush mixture over lamb chops. 4. Cook for 12-minutes in air fryer.
Per Serving: Calories 312; Fat 12.3g; Sodium 354mg; Carbs 10.2g; Fiber 3g; Sugar 1g; Protein 16.5g

Fried Pork Balls

Prep time: 10 minutes | Cook time: 14 minutes | Serves: 4

¾ lb. minced pork
Salt and pepper to taste
1 small onion, diced
1 teaspoon mustard

1 teaspoon honey
1 teaspoon garlic, minced
1 tablespoon cheddar cheese, grated

1. Select the "AIR FRY" function of Ninja Foodi digital air fry oven, set the temperature to 400 degrees F/ 200 degrees C and set the time to 15 minutes. Press the Start/Pause button and begin preheating. 2. Place the ingredients into a mixing bowl and combine well. Spray air fryer basket with cooking spray. Make some balls from the mixture and place them into air fryer basket. Air fry pork balls for 14-minutes.
Per Serving: Calories 288; Fat 12.2g; Sodium 339mg; Carbs 11.6g; Fiber 3g; Sugar 2g; Protein 16.5g

Pork Satay with nutty Sauce

Prep time: 5 minutes | Cook time: 21 minutes | Serves: 4

1 teaspoon ground ginger
2 teaspoons hot pepper sauce
2 cloves garlic, crushed
3 tablespoons sweet soy sauce
3 ½ ounces unsalted peanuts, ground

¾ cup coconut milk
1 teaspoon ground coriander
2 tablespoons vegetable oil
14-ounces lean pork chops, in cubes of 1-inch

1. In a mixing bowl, mix hot sauce, ginger, half garlic, oil and soy sauce. Place the meat into the mixture and leave for 15-minutes to marinate. 2. Select the "AIR FRY" function of Ninja Foodi digital air fry oven, set the temperature to 390 degrees F/ 200 degrees C and set the time to 25 minutes. Press the Start/Pause button and begin preheating. Place the meat into the basket of your air fryer. Cook for 12-minutes. Turn over halfway through cook time. 3. For the peanut sauce, place the oil into a skillet and heat it up. Add the garlic and cook for 5-minutes, stirring often. Add the coconut milk, peanuts, hot pepper sauce and soy sauce to the pan and bring to boil. Stir often. Remove the pork when cooked and pour sauce over it and serve warm.
Per Serving: Calories 262; Fat 12.3g; Sodium 269mg; Carbs 11.4g; Fiber 2g; Sugar 2g; Protein 17.3g

Pork Ribs with Hoisin Sauce

Prep time: 5 minutes | Cook time: 40 minutes | Serves: 2

1lb. baby pork ribs
1 tablespoon olive oil
1 tablespoon hoisin sauce

½ tablespoon honey
½ tablespoon soy sauce
3 garlic cloves, minced

1. Select the "AIR FRY" function of Ninja Foodi digital air fry oven, set the temperature to 320 degrees F/ 160 degrees C and set the time to 40 minutes. Press the Start/Pause button and begin preheating. 2. In a bowl, add all of the ingredients and mix well, Coat the ribs with mixture. Place the marinated ribs in the fridge for 2-hours. Place marinated ribs in air fryer basket for 40-minutes.
Per Serving: Calories 287; Fat 12.5g; Sodium 364mg; Carbs 11.5g; Fiber 3g; Sugar 2g; Protein 16.2g

Traditional Pork Roast

Prep time: 10 minutes | Cook time: 15 minutes | Serves: 4

2 lbs. pork shoulder, chopped
½ tablespoon salt
⅓ cup soy sauce

1 tablespoon honey
1 tablespoon liquid Stevia

1. Select the "AIR FRY" function of Ninja Foodi digital air fry oven, set the temperature to 350 degrees F/ 175 degrees C and set the time to 15 minutes. Press the Start/Pause button and begin preheating. 2. Place all the ingredients into a mixing bowl and combine well. Place marinated pork in fridge for 2-hours. 3. Spray air fryer basket with cooking spray. Add marinated pork pieces into an air fryer basket and cook for 10-minutes. Now increase temperature to 400 degrees F/ 200 degrees C and cook for an additional 5-minutes.
Per Serving: Calories 283; Fat 12.3g; Sodium 444mg; Carbs 11.5g; Fiber 2g; Sugar 2g; Protein 16.7g

Sweet & Sour Pork Chunks

Prep time: 10 minutes | Cook time: 10 minutes | Serves: 4

1 cup cornstarch
½ teaspoon spice mix
¼ cup sweet and sour sauce
2 lbs. pork, chunked

3 tablespoons olive oil
2 large eggs, beaten
½ teaspoon sea salt
¼ teaspoon black pepper

1. In a bowl, combine spice mix, cornstarch, pepper, and salt. 2. In another bowl add beaten eggs. 3. Coat pork chunks with cornstarch mixture, then dip in eggs and again into cornstarch. 4. Grease air fryer basket with olive oil. Select the "AIR FRY" function of Ninja Foodi digital air fry oven, set the temperature to 340 degrees F/ 170 degrees C and set the time to 10 minutes. Press the Start/Pause button and begin preheating. Place the coated pork chunks into an air fryer basket and cook for 10-minutes. Shake the basket. Place the air fried pork chunks on serving dish and drizzle with sweet and sour sauce.
Per Serving: Calories 282; Fat 12.6g; Sodium 269mg; Carbs 11.5g; Fiber 2g; Sugar 2g; Protein 17.3g

Delicious Sweet & Sour Pork

Prep time: 10 minutes | Cook time: 22 minutes | Serves: 4

¾ lb. pork, chunked
1 slice of pineapple, cut into pieces
1 medium tomato, chopped
2 tablespoons oyster sauce
2 tablespoons tomato sauce
1 tablespoon Worcestershire sauce

1 medium onion, sliced
1 tablespoon garlic, minced
1 teaspoon olive oil
Almond flour
1 egg, beaten
1 tablespoon liquid Stevia

1. Select the "AIR FRY" function of Ninja Foodi digital air fry oven, set the temperature to 250 degrees F/ 120 degrees C and set the time to 20 minutes. Press the Start/Pause button and begin preheating. 2. Dip pork pieces in egg then coat with flour and place into air fryer basket. Air fry pork pieces in air fryer for 20-minutes. 3. Heat oil in pan over medium heat. Add onion and garlic into pan and sauté for 2-minutes. 4. Place all remaining into pan and stir. Add pork to pan and stir well. Serve hot!
Per Serving: Calories 286; Fat 12.5g; Sodium 711mg; Carbs 11.6g; Fiber 3g; Sugar 1.3g; Protein 16.3g

Roasted Pork Loin with Potatoes

Prep time: 5 minutes | Cook time: 25 minutes | Serves: 2

2 lbs. pork loin
½ teaspoon garlic powder
½ teaspoon red pepper flakes

½ teaspoon black pepper
2 large potatoes, chunked

1. Sprinkle the pork loin with garlic powder, red pepper flakes, parsley, salt, and pepper. 2. Select the "AIR ROAST" function of Ninja Foodi digital air fry oven, set the temperature to 370 degrees F/ 185 degrees C and set the time to 25 minutes. Press the Start/Pause button and begin preheating. Place pork loin and potatoes to one side in basket of air fryer. Cook for 25-minutes. 3. Remove the pork loin and potatoes from air fryer. Allow pork loin to cool before slicing and enjoy!
Per Serving: Calories 268; Fat 12.3g; Sodium 358mg; Carbs 11g; Fiber 3g; Sugar 2g; Protein 16.2g

Chinese Pork Ribs Roast

Prep time: 5 minutes | Cook time: 40 minutes | Serves: 6

4 garlic cloves, minced
1 tablespoon honey
2 lbs. pork ribs
2 tablespoons sesame oil

2 tablespoons ginger, minced
2 tablespoons hoisin sauce
2 tablespoons char Siu sauce
1 tablespoon soy sauce

1. Select the "AIR ROAST" function of Ninja Foodi digital air fry oven, set the temperature to 330 degrees F/ 165 degrees C and set the time to 50 minutes. Press the Start/Pause button and begin preheating. Place the in a bowl except for meat and combine well. Place the ribs in a bowl and pour the sauce over them and coat well. Place in the fridge for 4-hours. Place ribs into air fryer for 40-minutes. Increase the temperature to 350 degrees F/ 175 degrees C ahrenheit and cook for an additional 10-minutes. Serve warm.
Per Serving: Calories 287; Fat 12.3g; Sodium 254mg; Carbs 10.6g; Fiber 3g; Sugar 3g; Protein 16.2g

Spiced Pork Loin Chops

Prep time: 10 minutes | Cook time: 10 minutes | Serves: 2

6 pork loin chops
Pepper to taste
1 garlic clove
¼ teaspoon ground ginger

1 teaspoon balsamic vinegar
2 tablespoons soy sauce
2 tablespoons honey

1. Select the "AIR FRY" function of Ninja Foodi digital air fry oven, set the temperature to 350 degrees F/ 175 degrees C and set the time to 10 minutes. Press the Start/Pause button and begin preheating. 2. Season pork chops with pepper. In a mixing bowl, add soy sauce, honey, ground ginger, garlic, vinegar and mix well. 3. Add the pork chops with mixture to bowl and coat well. Place pork chops in the fridge for 2 hours. Place marinated pork chops into air fryer basket and air fry for 10-minutes.
Per Serving: Calories 287; Fat 12.4g; Sodium 333mg; Carbs 11.6g; Fiber 7g; Sugar 2g; Protein 16.5g

Fried Pork Ribs with BBQ Sauce

Prep time: 10 minutes | Cook time: 27 minutes | Serves: 2

1 lb. pork ribs
Salt and pepper to taste
½ cup BBQ sauce
1 teaspoon liquid Stevia

1 teaspoon spice mix
1 medium onion, chopped
1 tablespoon olive oil

1. Select the "AIR FRY" function of Ninja Foodi digital air fry oven, set the temperature to 320 degrees F/ 160 degrees C and set the time to 25 minutes. Press the Start/Pause button and begin preheating. 2. In a pan warm the oil. Add onion to pan and sauté for 2-minutes. Add spice mix, stevia, and BBQ sauce into the pan and stir well. Remove pan from heat and set aside. 3. Spice pork ribs with salt and pepper and place inside of air fryer basket. Air Fry the ribs for 10-minutes. 4. Brush BBQ sauce on both sides of pork. Air fry pork for an additional 15-minutes, cut into slices and serve.
Per Serving: Calories 284; Fat 12.5g; Sodium 412mg; Carbs 11.2g; Fiber 3g; Sugar 3g; Protein 16.5g

Fried Apple Pork Balls

Prep time: 10 minutes | Cook time: 15 minutes | Serves: 8

2 teaspoons Dijon mustard
5 basil leaves, chopped
Salt and pepper to taste
2 tablespoons cheddar cheese, grated

4 garlic cloves, minced
1 small apple, chopped
1 large onion, chopped
1 1b. pork, minced

1. Select the "AIR FRY" function of Ninja Foodi digital air fry oven, set the temperature to 400 degrees F/ 200 degrees C and set the time to 15 minutes. Press the Start/Pause button and begin preheating. 2. Add the minced pork, onion, and apple into mixing bowl and stir. Add mustard, honey, garlic, cheese, basil, pepper, salt and mix well. 3. Make small balls and place them inside of air fryer basket. Cook for 15-minutes.
Per Serving: Calories 267; Fat 12.3g; Sodium 432mg; Carbs 11.6g; Fiber 2g; Sugar 3g; Protein 16.4g

Fried Pork Loin with Sweet Potatoes

Prep time: 5 minutes | Cook time: 25 minutes | Serves: 8

2 lbs. pork loin
2 large Sweet potatoes, diced
1 teaspoon salt

1 teaspoon pepper
½ teaspoon garlic powder
½ teaspoon parsley flakes

1. Select the "AIR FRY" function of Ninja Foodi digital air fry oven, set the temperature to 350 degrees F/ 175 degrees C and set the time to 25 minutes. Press the Start/Pause button and begin preheating. 2. Add all the ingredients into mixing bowl and mix well. Add bowl with pork and sweet potato mixture into air fryer basket. Cook in air fryer for 25-minutes. Carve up the pork into slices and serve with sweet potatoes.
Per Serving: Calories 286; Fat 12.6g; Sodium 399mg; Carbs 11.4g; Fiber 5g; Sugar 6g; Protein 16.6g

Roasted lamb rack with Macadamia Crust

Prep time: 5 minutes | Cook time: 35 minutes | Serves: 4

1 garlic clove, minced
1 ⅓ lbs. rack of lamb
Macadamia Crust:
3-ounces macadamia nuts, raw and unsalted
1 egg, beaten

1 tablespoon olive oil
Salt and pepper to taste

1 tablespoon fresh rosemary, chopped
1 tablespoon breadcrumbs

1. In a small mixing bowl, mix garlic and olive oil. Brush all over lamb and season with salt and pepper. 2. In your food processor, chop macadamia nuts and mix with breadcrumbs and rosemary. Be careful not to make the nuts into a paste. Stir in egg. Coat lamb with nut mixture. 3. Select the "AIR ROAST" function of Ninja Foodi digital air fry oven, set the temperature to 220 degrees F/ 105 degrees C and set the time to 40 minutes. Press the Start/Pause button and begin preheating. Place the lamb in the air fryer and cook for 30-minutes. Raise the temperature to 390 degrees F/ 200 degrees C and cook for an additional 5-minutes. 4. Remove the meat, cover it loosely with foil for 10-minutes. Serve warm.
Per Serving: Calories 306; Fat 11g; Sodium 288mg; Carbs 10.7g; Fiber 2g; Sugar 2g; Protein 16.5g

Crispy Pork Cutlets

Prep time: 5 minutes | Cook time: 20 minutes | Serves: 2

½ cup milk
1 egg
1 cup breadcrumbs
1 tablespoon parmesan cheese, grated
¼ bunch of thyme, chopped
1 teaspoon pine nuts

¼ cup semi-dried tomatoes
½ cup almond flour
2 pork cutlets
1 lemon, zested
6 basil leaves
1 tablespoon olive oil

1. Combine and whisk milk and egg in a bowl, then set aside. Mix in another bowl, breadcrumbs, parmesan, thyme, lemon zest, salt, and pepper. 2. Add flour to another bowl. Dip pork cutlet in flour, then into egg and milk mixture, and finally into breadcrumb mixture. 3. Select the "AIR FRY" function of Ninja Foodi digital air fry oven, set the temperature to 360 degrees F/ 180 degrees C and set the time to 20 minutes. Press the Start/Pause button and begin preheating. Spray basket with cooking spray. Place pork inside of basket and cook until golden and crisp. 4. Prepare the pesto, add the tomatoes, pine nuts, olive oil, and basil leaves into a food processor. Blend for 20-seconds. When the pork is ready, serve with pesto and a salad of your choice.
Per Serving: Calories 264; Fat 13.2g; Sodium 578mg; Carbs 11.7g; Fiber 2g; Sugar 2g; Protein 16.3g

Spiced Pork Ribs

Prep time: 10 minutes | Cook time: 30 minutes | Serves: 2

2 garlic cloves, chopped
1 lb. pork ribs, chunked
3 tablespoons BBQ sauce
1 tablespoon honey

½ teaspoon mix spice
1 teaspoon sesame oil
Salt and black pepper to taste
1 teaspoon soy sauce

1. Combine soy sauce, garlic, pepper, salt, sesame oil, mix spice, BBQ sauce, and honey in a mixing bowl. Add pork ribs in bowl and mix well. Place marinated pork into fridge for 2-hours. 2. Select the "AIR FRY" function of Ninja Foodi digital air fry oven, set the temperature to 350 degrees F/ 175 degrees C and set the time to 30 minutes. Press the Start/Pause button and begin preheating. Add marinated pork ribs into air fryer basket and cook for 15-minutes. Toss ribs over and cook for an additional 15-minutes.
Per Serving: Calories 283; Fat 12.3g; Sodium 432mg; Carbs 11.5g; Fiber 3g; Sugar 3g; Protein 16.5g

Delicious Baked Meatballs

Prep time: 10 minutes | Cook time: 20 minutes | Serves: 4

¾ lb. ground pork
2 tablespoons mozzarella cheese, cubed
Salt and pepper to taste

3 tablespoons breadcrumbs
½ tablespoon Italian herbs
1 onion, chopped
1 egg

1. Place all the ingredients in a bowl and mix well. Place marinated mixture into fridge for 1-hour. 2. Select the "AIR FRY" function of Ninja Foodi digital air fry oven, set the temperature to 350 degrees F/ 175 degrees C and set the time to 20 minutes. Press the Start/Pause button and begin preheating. Grease the air fryer basket with oil. Make small meatballs from mixture and place them in air fryer basket. Air fry meatballs in air fryer for 20-minutes. Shake the basket halfway. Serve and enjoy!
Per Serving: Calories 279; Fat 12.3g; Sodium 520mg; Carbs 10.4g; Fiber 2g; Sugar 2g; Protein 15.2g

Easy Fried Pork Chops

Prep time: 5 minutes | Cook time: 15 minutes | Serves: 2

2 pork chops
½ cup breadcrumbs
1 tablespoon olive oil

1 egg, beaten
1 tablespoon almond flour
Salt and pepper to taste

1. Select the "AIR FRY" function of Ninja Foodi digital air fry oven, set the temperature to 400 degrees F/ 200 degrees C and set the time to 15 minutes. Press the Start/Pause button and begin preheating. 2. Season pork chops with salt and pepper. Add flour to mixing bowl. 3. In another small bowl, add beaten egg. 4. In a third bowl, combine breadcrumbs with olive oil. Coat the pork chops with flour, dip in egg, and coat with breadcrumbs. 5. Place chops into air fryer basket and cook for 10-minutes. Flip chops over and cook on the other side for an additional 5-minutes. Serve warm.
Per Serving: Calories 279; Fat 11.6g; Sodium 741mg; Carbs 9.3g; Fiber 2g; Sugar 2g; Protein 16.2g

Chapter 5 Fish and Seafood Recipes

Calamari with Paprika, Garlic and Sherry Wine

Prep time: 5 minutes | Cook time: 5 minutes | Serves: 4

1 pound calamari, sliced into rings
2 tablespoons butter, melted
4 garlic cloves, smashed
2 tablespoons sherry wine

2 tablespoons fresh lemon juice
Coarse sea salt
Ground black pepper, to taste
1 teaspoon paprika
1 teaspoon dried oregano

1. Select the "AIR ROAST" function of Ninja Foodi digital air fry oven, set the temperature to 400 degrees F/ 200 degrees C and set the time to 5 minutes. Press the Start/Pause button and begin preheating. Toss all in a lightly greased Air Fryer basket. 2. Cook your calamari for 5 minutes, tossing halfway through the cooking time. Bon appétit!
Per Serving: Calories 1646; Fat 146g; Sodium 498mg; Carbs 10g; Fiber 2g; Sugar 2g; Protein 77g

Lemon Shrimp with Broccoli Florets

Prep time: 4 minutes | Cook time: 6 minutes | Serves: 4

1 pound raw shrimp, peeled and deveined
½ pound broccoli florets
1 tablespoon olive oil
1 garlic clove, minced

2 tablespoons freshly squeezed lemon juice
Coarse sea salt
Ground black pepper, to taste
1 teaspoon paprika

1. Select the "AIR FRY" function of Ninja Foodi digital air fry oven, set the temperature to 400 degrees F/ 200 degrees C and set the time to 6 minutes. Press the Start/Pause button and begin preheating. Toss all in a lightly greased Air Fryer basket. 2. Cook the shrimp and broccoli for 6 minutes, tossing halfway through the cooking time. Bon appétit!
Per Serving: Calories 162; Fat 5.3g; Sodium 1006mg; Carbs 3g; Fiber 2g; Sugar 0g; Protein 25g

Air Fried Easy Prawn Salad

Prep time: 5 minutes | Cook time: 6 minutes | Serves: 4

1 ½ pounds king prawns, peeled and deveined
Coarse sea salt
Ground black pepper, to taste
1 tablespoon fresh lemon juice
1 cup mayonnaise

1 teaspoon Dijon mustard
1 tablespoon fresh parsley, roughly chopped
1 teaspoon fresh dill, minced
1 shallot, chopped

1. Select the "AIR FRY" function of Ninja Foodi digital air fry oven, set the temperature to 400 degrees F/ 200 degrees C and set the time to 6 minutes. Press the Start/Pause button and begin preheating. Toss the prawns with the salt and black pepper in a lightly greased Air Fryer basket. 2. Cook the prawns for 6 minutes, tossing halfway through the cooking time. 3. Add the prawns to a salad bowl; add in the remaining and stir to combine well. Bon appétit!
Per Serving: Calories 203; Fat 10.9g; Sodium 402mg; Carbs 2g; Fiber 0g; Sugar 1g; Protein 23g

Fried Fish Fillets

Prep time: 4 minutes | Cook time: 6 minutes | Serves: 4

2 eggs
¼ cup all-purpose flour
Sea salt
Ground black pepper, to taste
½ teaspoon onion powder

¼ teaspoon garlic powder
¼ cup plain breadcrumbs
1 ½ tablespoons olive oil
1 pound cod fish fillets, slice into pieces

1. Select the "BAKE" function of Ninja Foodi digital air fry oven, set the temperature to 400 degrees F/ 200 degrees C and set the time to 10 minutes. Press the Start/Pause button and begin preheating. In a bowl, mix the eggs and flour, and spices. In a separate bowl, thoroughly combine the breadcrumbs and olive oil. Mix to combine well. 2. Now, dip the fish pieces into the flour mixture to coat; roll the fish pieces over the breadcrumb mixture until they are well coated on all sides. 3. Place the fish in air fryer basket and cook the fish fingers for 10 minutes, turning them over halfway through the cooking time. Bon appétit!
Per Serving: Calories 463; Fat 15.5g; Sodium 553mg; Carbs 366g; Fiber 3g; Sugar 3g; Protein 41g

Cheesy English Muffin Tuna Melts

Prep time: 5 minutes | Cook time: 10 minutes | Serves: 4

1 pound tuna, boneless and chopped
½ cup all-purpose flour
½ cup breadcrumbs
2 tablespoons buttermilk
2 eggs, whisked

Kosher salt and ground black pepper, to taste
½ teaspoon cayenne pepper
1 tablespoon olive oil
4 mozzarella cheese slices
4 English muffins

1. Select the "BAKE" function of Ninja Foodi digital air fry oven, set the temperature to 375 degrees F/ 190 degrees C and set the time to 14 minutes. Press the Start/Pause button and begin preheating. Mix all ingredients, except for the cheese and English muffins, in a bowl. Shape the mixture into four patties and place them in a lightly oiled Air Fryer basket. 2. Cook the fish patties for about 14 minutes, turning them over halfway through the cooking time. 3. Place the cheese slices on the warm patties and serve on hamburger buns and enjoy!
Per Serving: Calories 387; Fat 26.3g; Sodium 602mg; Carbs 12g; Fiber 8g; Sugar 1g; Protein 26g

Butter Lemon Mahi-Mahi Fillets

Prep time: 5 minutes | Cook time: 14 minutes | Serves: 4

1 pound mahi-mahi fillets
2 tablespoons butter, at room temperature
2 tablespoons fresh lemon juice
Kosher salt

Ground black pepper, to taste
1 teaspoon smoked paprika
1 teaspoon garlic, minced
1 teaspoon dried basil
1 teaspoon dried oregano

1. Select the "BAKE" function of Ninja Foodi digital air fry oven, set the temperature to 400 degrees F/ 200 degrees C and set the time to 14 minutes. Press the Start/Pause button and begin preheating. Toss the fish fillets with the remaining ingredients and place them in a lightly oiled Air Fry basket. 2. Cook the fish fillets for about 14 minutes, turning them over halfway through the cooking time. Bon appétit!
Per Serving: Calories 494; Fat 36g; Sodium 690mg; Carbs 17g; Fiber 11g; Sugar 2g; Protein 28g

Classic Fish Tacos with Corn Tortillas

Prep time: 5 minutes | Cook time: 14 minutes | Serves: 4

1 pound codfish fillets
1 tablespoon olive oil
1 avocado, pitted, peeled and mashed
4 tablespoons mayonnaise

1 teaspoon mustard
1 shallot, chopped
1 habanero pepper, chopped
8 small corn tortillas

1. Select the "AIR FRY" function of Ninja Foodi digital air fry oven, set the temperature to 400 degrees F/ 200 degrees C and set the time to 14 minutes. Press the Start/Pause button and begin preheating. Toss the fish fillets with the olive oil; place them in a lightly oiled Air fry basket. 2. Cook the fish fillets for about 14 minutes, turning them over halfway through the cooking time. 3. Assemble your tacos with the chopped fish and remaining and serve warm. Bon appétit!
Per Serving: Calories 184; Fat 7.4g; Sodium 103mg; Carbs 7g; Fiber 1g; Sugar 1g; Protein 22g

Roasted Cilantro Garlic Swordfish

Prep time: 5 minutes | Cook time: 10 minutes | Serves: 4

1 pound swordfish steaks
4 garlic cloves, peeled
4 tablespoons olive oil
2 tablespoons fresh lemon juice, more for later

1 tablespoon fresh cilantro, roughly chopped
1 teaspoon Spanish paprika
Sea salt and ground black pepper, to taste

1. Select the "AIR ROAST" function of Ninja Foodi digital air fry oven, set the temperature to 400 degrees F/ 200 degrees C and set the time to 10 minutes. Press the Start/Pause button and begin preheating. Toss the swordfish steaks with the remaining and place them in a lightly oiled Air Fry basket. 2. Cook the swordfish steaks for about 10 minutes, turning them over halfway through the cooking time. Bon appétit!
Per Serving: Calories 314; Fat 27.2g; Sodium 182mg; Carbs 0g; Fiber 0g; Sugar 0g; Protein 17g

Roasted Peppercorn Butter Halibut Steaks

Prep time: 5 minutes | Cook time: 10 minutes | Serves: 4

1 pound halibut steaks	chopped
¼ cup butter	1 teaspoon garlic, minced
Sea salt, to taste	1 teaspoon mixed peppercorns,
2 tablespoons fresh chives,	ground

1. Select the " AIR ROAST" function of Ninja Foodi digital air fry oven, set the temperature to 400 degrees F/ 200 degrees C and set the time to 12 minutes. Press the Start/Pause button and begin preheating. Toss the halibut steaks with the rest of the and place them in a lightly oiled Air Fry basket. 2. Cook the halibut steaks for about 12 minutes, turning them over halfway through the cooking time. Bon appétit!
Per Serving: Calories 144; Fat 6.6g; Sodium 171mg; Carbs 2g; Fiber 0g; Sugar 1g; Protein 19g

Chili and Sweet Paprika Squid

Prep time: 5 minutes | Cook time: 5 minutes | Serves: 5

1 ½ pounds squid, cut into pieces	1 tablespoon coriander, chopped
1 chili pepper, chopped	2 tablespoons parsley, chopped
1 small lemon, squeezed	1 teaspoon sweet paprika
2 tablespoons olive oil	Sea salt
1 tablespoon capers, drained	Ground black pepper, to taste
2 garlic cloves, minced	

1. Select the "AIR FRY" function of Ninja Foodi digital air fry oven, set the temperature to 400 degrees F/ 200 degrees C and set the time to 5 minutes. Press the Start/Pause button and begin preheating. Toss all in a lightly greased Air fry basket. 2. Cook your squid for 5 minutes, tossing the squid halfway through the cooking time. Bon appétit!
Per Serving: Calories 295; Fat 21.2g; Sodium 94mg; Carbs 3g; Fiber 1g; Sugar 1g; Protein 23g

Butter Garlic Orange Roughy Fillets

Prep time: 5 minutes | Cook time: 10 minutes | Serves: 4

1 pound orange roughy fillets	Sea salt and red pepper flak es, to
2 tablespoons butter	taste
2 cloves garlic, minced	

1. Select the "BAKE" function of Ninja Foodi digital air fry oven, set the temperature to 400 degrees F/ 200 degrees C and set the time to 10 minutes. Press the Start/Pause button and begin preheating. Toss the fish fillets with the remaining and place them in a lightly oiled sheet pan. 2. Cook the fish fillets for about 10 minutes, turning them over halfway through the cooking time. Bon appétit!
Per Serving: Calories 543; Fat 38.1g; Sodium 134mg; Carbs 27g; Fiber 1g; Sugar 0g; Protein 23g

Delicious Fish Taco

Prep time: 5 minutes | Cook time: 8 minutes | Serves: 2

1½ cups almond flour	small strips
1 can of beer	Corn tortillas
1 teaspoon baking powder	Cilantro, chopped
1 teaspoon sea salt	Cholula sauce to taste
½ cup salsa	2 tablespoons olive oil
8-ounces fresh halibut, sliced into	2 chili peppers, sliced
Avocado Cream:	
1 large avocado	½ lime juiced
¾ cup buttermilk	

1. Make your batter by mixing baking powder, 1 cup of flour, beer, and salt. Stir well. Cover the halibut with the remaining ½ cup of flour and dip it into the batter to coat well. 2. Select the "AIR FRY" function of Ninja Foodi digital air fry oven, set the temperature to 390 degrees F/ 200 degrees C and set the time to 8 minutes. Press the Start/ Pause button and begin preheating. Grease air fry basket with olive oil. Cook the fish for 8-minutes. 3. Mix the avocado cream ingredients in a blender until smooth. Place the corn tortillas on a plate and cover with salsa. Set aside. 4. Put the fish on top of tortillas and cover with avocado cream. Add Cholula sauce, sprinkle with cilantro and top with chili slices and serve.
Per Serving: Calories 354; Fat 7.9g; Sodium 704mg; Carbs 6g; Fiber 3.6g; Sugar 6g; Protein 18g

Fried Calamari with Tortilla Chips

Prep time: 5 minutes | Cook time: 5 minutes | Serves: 4

1 cup all-purpose flour	pepper, to taste
½ cup tortilla chips, crushed	1 teaspoon cayenne pepper
1 teaspoon mustard powder	2 tablespoons olive oil
1 tablespoon dried parsley	1 pound calamari, sliced into
Sea salt and freshly ground black	rings

1. Select the "AIR FRY" function of Ninja Foodi digital air fry oven, set the temperature to 400 degrees F/ 200 degrees C and set the time to 5 minutes. Press the Start/Pause button and begin preheating. In a bowl, combine the flour, tortilla chips, spices, and olive oil. Mix to combine well. 2. Now, dip your calamari into the flour mixture to coat. Place it in the greased air fry basket. 3. Cook your calamari for 5 minutes, turning them over halfway through the cooking time. Bon appétit!
Per Serving: Calories 205; Fat 5.8g; Sodium 1481mg; Carbs 1g; Fiber 0g; Sugar 0g; Protein 35g

Air Fried Classic Garlic Shrimp

Prep time: 5 minutes | Cook time: 6 minutes | Serves: 4

1 ½ pounds raw shrimp, peeled	1 teaspoon cayenne pepper
and deveined	½ teaspoon lemon pepper
1 tablespoon olive oil	Sea salt, to taste
1 teaspoon garlic, minced	

1. Select the "AIR FRY" function of Ninja Foodi digital air fry oven, set the temperature to 400 degrees F/ 200 degrees C and set the time to 6 minutes. Press the Start/Pause button and begin preheating. Toss all in a lightly greased Air Fry basket. 2. Cook the shrimp for 6 minutes, tossing the basket halfway through the cooking time. Bon appétit!
Per Serving: Calories 143; Fat 7.5g; Sodium 5mg; Carbs 19g; Fiber 3g; Sugar 3g; Protein 3g

Spicy and Sweet Exotic Fried Prawns

Prep time: 5 minutes | Cook time: 5 minutes | Serves: 4

1 ½ pounds prawns, peeled and	½ teaspoon sweet paprika
deveined	1 teaspoon hot paprika
2 garlic cloves, minced	Salt
2 tablespoons fresh chives,	Ground black pepper, to taste
chopped	2 tablespoons coconut oil
½ cup whole-wheat flour	2 tablespoons lemon juice

1. Select the "AIR FRY" function of Ninja Foodi digital air fry oven, set the temperature to 400 degrees F/ 200 degrees C and set the time to 9 minutes. Press the Start/Pause button and begin preheating. Toss all in a lightly greased Air Fry basket. 2. Cook the prawns for 9 minutes, tossing the prawns halfway through the cooking time. Bon appétit!
Per Serving: Calories 18; Fat 7.9g; Sodium 704mg; Carbs 6g; Fiber 3.6g; Sugar 6g; Protein 18g

Mom's Famous Garlic Pepper Fish Sticks

Prep time: 5 minutes | Cook time: 10 minutes | Serves: 4

½ cup all-purpose flour	Sea salt and ground black pepper,
1 large egg	to taste
2 tablespoons buttermilk	½ teaspoon cayenne pepper
½ cup crackers, crushed	1 pound tilapia fillets, cut into
1 teaspoon garlic powder	strips

1. Select the "AIR FRY" function of Ninja Foodi digital air fry oven, set the temperature to 400 degrees F/ 200 degrees C and set the time to 10 minutes. Press the Start/Pause button and begin preheating. 2. In a bowl, Add the flour. Whisk the egg and buttermilk in a other bowl, and mix the crushed crackers and spices in a third bowl. Dip the fish strips in the flour mixture, then in the whisked eggs; finally, roll the fish strips over the cracker mixture until they are well coated on all sides. 3. Place the coated fish in the Ninja Foodi Air Fryer basket. 4. Cook the fish sticks for about 10 minutes, shaking the basket halfway through the cooking time. Bon appétit!
Per Serving: Calories 18; Fat 0.3g; Sodium 7mg; Carbs 1g; Fiber 0g; Sugar 0g; Protein 2g

Calamari with Tangy Tomato Sauce

Prep time: 5 minutes | Cook time: 8 minutes | Serves: 4

3 lbs. calamari
⅓ cup olive oil
1 tablespoon fresh oregano
1 teaspoon lemon juice
1 tablespoon garlic, minced
Sauce:
1 lb. fresh whole tomatoes
3 cloves garlic, minced
1 stalk of celery, chopped
1 tablespoon olive oil

¼ teaspoon chopped fresh lemon peel
¼ teaspoon crushed red pepper
¼ cup vinegar

½ green bell pepper
Salt and pepper to taste
½ cup onion, chopped

1. Select the "AIR FRY" function of Ninja Foodi digital air fry oven, set the temperature to 390 degrees F/ 200 degrees C and set the time to 6 minutes. Press the Start/Pause button and begin preheating. 2. Clean the calamari and slice it into ½-inch rings. Season calamari with vinegar, red pepper, lemon peel, garlic, lemon juice, and oregano. Add oil to air fryer sheet pan. Add calamari with its juice. Air fry for about 6-minutes. Stir once and air fry for another 2-minutes. 3. To make the sauce, mix all the sauce ingredients and add to blender. Blend until mixture is smooth. Serve hot with sauce.
Per Serving: Calories 298; Fat 11g; Sodium 336mg; Carbs 10.2g; Fiber g; Sugar 6g; Protein 18g

Delicious Salmon & Eggs

Prep time: 5 minutes | Cook time: 10 minutes | Serves: 2

2 eggs
1 lb. salmon, seasoned and cooked
1 cup celery, chopped

1 onion, chopped
1 tablespoon olive oil
Salt and pepper to taste

1. Select the "AIR FRY" function of Ninja Foodi digital air fry oven, set the temperature to 300 degrees F/ 150 degrees C and set the time to 10 minutes. Press the Start/Pause button and begin preheating. 2. Whisk the eggs in a bowl. Add celery, onion, salt, and pepper. Add the oil to a round baking tray and pour in the egg mixture, then place them in the air fryer. Let it cook for 10-minutes. When done, serve with cooked salmon.
Per Serving: Calories 354; Fat 7.9g; Sodium 704mg; Carbs 6g; Fiber 3.6g; Sugar 6g; Protein 18g

Clam and Veggie Balls

Prep time: 5 minutes | Cook time: 30 minutes | Serves: 4

2 cups clam meat
2 tablespoons olive oil
¾ cup water
1 cup chickpea flour

¼ teaspoon black pepper
½ cup shredded zucchini
1 cup shredded carrot

1. Select the "AIR FRY" function of Ninja Foodi digital air fry oven, set the temperature to 390 degrees F/ 200 degrees C and set the time to 30 minutes. Press the Start/Pause button and begin preheating. 2. Mix clam meat, olive oil, shredded carrot and zucchini along with black pepper in a bowl. Form small balls using your hands. 3. Mix chickpea flour and water to form batter. Coat balls with batter. Place in air fryer and cook for 30-minutes.
Per Serving: Calories 354; Fat 7.9g; Sodium 704mg; Carbs 6g; Fiber 3.6g; Sugar 6g; Protein 18g

Crispy Nacho-Crusted Shrimp

Prep time: 5 minutes | Cook time: 8 minutes | Serves: 8

18 jumbo shrimps, peeled and deveined
1 egg, beaten

8-9-ounce nacho-flavored chips, crushed
Salt and pepper to taste

1. Prepare two shallow dishes, one with egg and one with crushed chips. Spice the shrimp with salt and pepper. Dip shrimp in the egg and then coat in nacho crumbs. 2. Select the "AIR FRY" function of Ninja Foodi digital air fry oven, set the temperature to 350 degrees F/ 175 degrees C and set the time to 8 minutes. Press the Start/Pause button and begin preheating. Arrange the shrimp in the air fryer and cook for 8-minutes.
Per Serving: Calories 354; Fat 7.9g; Sodium 704mg; Carbs 6g; Fiber 3.6g; Sugar 6g; Protein 18g

Bread Crusted Fish

Prep time: 5 minutes | Cook time: 12 minutes | Serves: 4

4 fish fillets
1 egg

5-ounces breadcrumbs
4 tablespoons olive oil

1. Select the "AIR FRY" function of Ninja Foodi digital air fry oven, set the temperature to 350 degrees F/ 175 degrees C and set the time to 12 minutes. Press the Start/Pause button and begin preheating. 2. In a bowl mix oil and breadcrumbs. Whisk egg. Gently dip the fish into egg and then into crumb mixture. Put into air fryer and cook for 12-minutes.
Per Serving: Calories 354; Fat 7.9g; Sodium 704mg; Carbs 6g; Fiber 3.6g; Sugar 6g; Protein 18g

Tuna Stuffed Potatoes

Prep time: 5 minutes | Cook time: 30 minutes | Serves: 2

4 medium potatoes
1 teaspoon olive oil
½ tablespoon capers
Salt and pepper to taste
1 green onion, sliced

1 tablespoon Greek yogurt
½ teaspoon chili powder
½ can of tuna in oil, drained
2 boiled eggs, sliced

1. Select the "AIR FRY" function of Ninja Foodi digital air fry oven, set the temperature to 355 degrees F/ 180 degrees C and set the time to 30 minutes. Press the Start/Pause button and begin preheating. Soak the potatoes in water for 30-minutes. Pat dry with kitchen towel. Brush the potatoes with olive oil. Place potatoes in air fryer and air fry for 30-minutes. 2. Put tuna in a bowl with yogurt and chili powder, mix well. Add half of the green onion plus salt and pepper. Slit potatoes length-wise. Stuff tuna mixture in middle of potatoes and place on a serving plate. Sprinkle with chili powder and remaining green onions over potatoes. Serve with capers and a salad of your choice and topped with boiled egg slices.
Per Serving: Calories 354; Fat 7.9g; Sodium 704mg; Carbs 6g; Fiber 3.6g; Sugar 6g; Protein 18g

Sticky Glazed Halibut Steak

Prep time: 5 minutes | Cook time: 12 minutes | Serves: 3

1 lb. halibut steak
⅔ cup soy sauce
¼ teaspoon ginger, ground
1 garlic clove, minced
¼ cup orange juice

¼ teaspoon crushed red pepper flakes
2 tablespoons lime juice
1 teaspoon liquid stevia
½ cup mirin

1. Prepare teriyaki glaze by combining all ingredients except halibut steak in a saucepan. Bring mixture to a boil and then reduce heat by half. Set aside and allow to cool. Pour half of the glaze into a re-sealable bag with halibut and place in the fridge for 30-minutes. 2. Select the "AIR FRY" function of Ninja Foodi digital air fry oven, set the temperature to 390 degrees F/ 200 degrees C and set the time to 12 minutes. Press the Start/Pause button and begin preheating. Place marinated halibut in air fryer and cook for 12-minutes. When finished, brush some of the remaining glaze over halibut steak.
Per Serving: Calories 354; Fat 7.9g; Sodium 704mg; Carbs 6g; Fiber 3.6g; Sugar 6g; Protein 18g

Crispy Salmon with Dill Sauce

Prep time: 5 minutes | Cook time: 23 minutes | Serves: 4

1½ lbs. of salmon
4 teaspoons olive oil
Dill Sauce:
½ cup non-fat Greek yogurt
½ cup light sour cream

Pinch of sea salt

2 tablespoons dill, finely chopped
Pinch of sea salt

1. Select the "AIR FRY" function of Ninja Foodi digital air fry oven, set the temperature to 270 degrees F/ 130 degrees C and set the time to 23 minutes. Press the Start/Pause button and begin preheating. 2. Cut salmon into four 6-ounce portions and drizzle 1 teaspoon of olive oil over each piece and season with sea salt. Place salmon into basket and cook for 23-minutes. 3. Make dill sauce. In a mixing bowl, mix sour cream, yogurt, chopped dill and sea salt. Top cooked salmon with sauce and garnish with additional dill and serve.
Per Serving: Calories 354; Fat 7.9g; Sodium 704mg; Carbs 6g; Fiber 3.6g; Sugar 6g; Protein 18g

Sweet and Spicy Tossed Calamari

Prep time: 5 minutes | Cook time: 13 minutes | Serves: 2

½ lb. calamari tubes, about ¼ inch wide, rinsed and patted dry
1 cup club soda
½ cup honey

Red pepper flakes to taste
1 cup almond flour
Salt and black pepper to taste
2 tablespoons sriracha

1. Select the "AIR FRY" function of Ninja Foodi digital air fry oven, set the temperature to 380 degrees F/ 195 degrees C and set the time to 11 minutes. Press the Start/Pause button and begin preheating. 2. Cover calamari rings with club soda in a bowl. Set aside for 10-minutes. 3. In another bowl, mix flour, salt, and black pepper. In a third bowl, combine honey, sriracha, and red pepper flakes. Drain the calamari, pat dry, and cover with flour mixture. 4. Grease your air fryer basket with cooking spray. Add calamari in one layer, leaving little space in between. Cook for 11-minutes. Shake basket a couple of times during the process. 5. Remove the calamari from the air fryer and cover with half of the honey sauce and place inside the air fryer again. Cook for an additional 2-minutes. When ready to serve, cover with remaining sauce.
Per Serving: Calories 354; Fat 7.9g; Sodium 704mg; Carbs 6g; Fiber 3.6g; Sugar 6g; Protein 18g

Kataifi Shrimp with Garlic Butter Sauce

Prep time: 5 minutes | Cook time: 22 minutes | Serves: 5

20 large green shrimps, peeled and deveined
7 tablespoons unsalted butter
12-ounces of kataifi pastry

Wedges of lemon or lime
Salt and pepper to taste
5 cloves of garlic, crushed
2 lemons, zested and juiced

1. In a pan, heat butter. Add the garlic and lemon zest, and sauté for about 2-minutes. Season with salt, pepper and lemon juice. Cover the shrimp with half of garlic butter sauce and set aside the remaining half of sauce. 2. Select the "AIR FRY" function of Ninja Foodi digital air fry oven, set the temperature to 360 degrees F/ 180 degrees C and set the time to 10 minutes. Press the Start/Pause button and begin preheating. Remove the pastry from the bag and tease out strands. On the countertop lay 6-inch strands. Roll shrimp and butter into pastry. Shrimp tail should be exposed. Repeat the process for all shrimp. 3. Place the shrimp into air fryer for 10-minutes. Flip shrimp over and place them back into air fryer for another 10-minutes. 4. Serve with a salad and lime or lemon wedges. Dip the shrimp into the remaining garlic butter sauce.
Per Serving: Calories 354; Fat 7.9g; Sodium 704mg; Carbs 6g; Fiber 3.6g; Sugar 6g; Protein 18g

Tuna Croquettes

Prep time: 10 minutes | Cook time: 8 minutes | Serves: 2

2 (5-ounce) cans tuna, drained
1 (8-ounce) package cream cheese, softened
½ cup finely shredded cheddar cheese
2 tablespoons diced onions
For Serving:
Cherry tomatoes
Mayonnaise

2 teaspoons prepared yellow mustard
1 large egg
1½ cups pork dust
Fresh dill, for garnish

Prepared yellow mustard

1. Select the "AIR FRY" function of Ninja Foodi digital air fry oven, set the temperature to 400 degrees F/ 200 degrees C and set the time to 8 minutes. Press the Start/Pause button and begin preheating. 2. Make the patties: In a large bowl, stir together the tuna, cream cheese, cheddar cheese, onions, mustard, and egg until well combined. 3. Place the pork dust in a shallow bowl. 4. Form the tuna mixture into twelve 1½-inch balls. Roll the balls in the pork dust and use your hands to press it into a thick crust around each ball. Flatten the balls into ½-inch-thick patties. 5. Working in batches to avoid overcrowding, place the patties in the air fryer basket, leaving space between them. Cook for 8 minutes, or until golden and crispy, flipping halfway through. 6. Garnish the croquettes with fresh dill, if desired, and serve with cherry tomatoes and dollops of mayo and mustard on the side.
Per Serving: Calories 354; Fat 7.9g; Sodium 704mg; Carbs 6g; Fiber 3.6g; Sugar 6g; Protein 18g

Grilled Barramundi with Tangy Butter

Prep time: 5 minutes | Cook time: 40 minutes | Serves: 2

1 lb. small potatoes
7-ounces barramundi fillets
1 teaspoon olive oil
Lemon Butter Sauce:
1 scallion, chopped
½ cup thickened cream
½ cup white wine
1 bay leaf
10 black peppercorns

¼ bunch of fresh thyme, chopped
Green beans, cooked, optional

1 clove garlic, chopped
8-ounces unsalted butter
1 lemon, juiced
Salt and pepper to taste

1. Select the "AIR FRY" function of Ninja Foodi digital air fry oven, set the temperature to 390 degrees F/ 200 degrees C and set the time to 40 minutes. Press the Start/Pause button and begin preheating. 2. In a bowl, add potatoes, salt, thyme and olive oil. Mix ingredients well. Put potatoes into air fryer basket and cook for 20-minutes. Layer the fish fillets in a basket on top of potatoes. Cook for another 20-minutes. 3. In a skillet, heat garlic over medium-high heat and add the peppercorns and bay leaf. Pour the wine in and reduce heat to low. Add the thickened cream and stir to blend. Add the butter and whisk over low heat. When butter has melted, add salt, pepper, and lemon juice. 4. Strain the sauce to remove peppercorns and bay leaf. Place the fish and potatoes on a serving plate and add sauce and serve with green beans.
Per Serving: Calories 354; Fat 7.9g; Sodium 704mg; Carbs 6g; Fiber 3.6g; Sugar 6g; Protein 18g

Tropical Shrimp with Spicy Mayo

Prep time: 10 minutes | Cook time: 6 minutes | Serves: 4

1-pound large shrimp (about 2 dozen), peeled and deveined, tails on
Fine sea salt and ground black pepper
Spicy Mayo:
½ cup mayonnaise
2 tablespoons beef or chicken broth
For Serving:
Microgreens

2 large eggs
1 tablespoon water
½ cup unsweetened coconut flakes
½ cup pork dust

½ teaspoon hot sauce
½ teaspoon cayenne pepper

Thinly sliced radishes

1. Spray the air fryer basket with avocado oil. Select the "AIR FRY" function of Ninja Foodi digital air fry oven, set the temperature to 350 degrees F/ 175 degrees C and set the time to 6 minutes. Press the Start/Pause button and begin preheating. 2. Season the shrimp well on all sides with salt and pepper. 3. Crack the eggs into a shallow sheet pan, add the water and a pinch each of salt and pepper, and whisk to combine. In the sheet pan, stir the coconut flakes and pork dust until well combined. 4. Dip one shrimp in the eggs and let any excess egg drip off, then dredge both sides of the shrimp in the coconut mixture. Spray the shrimp with avocado oil and place it in the air fryer basket. Repeat with the remaining shrimp, leaving space between them in the air fryer basket. 5. Cook the shrimp in the air fryer for 6 minutes, or until cooked through and no longer translucent, flipping halfway through. 6. While the shrimp cook, make the spicy mayo: In a medium-sized bowl, stir together all the spicy mayo ingredients until well combined. 7. Serve the shrimp on a bed of microgreens and thinly sliced radishes, if desired. Serve the spicy mayo on the side for dipping.
Per Serving: Calories 354; Fat 7.9g; Sodium 704mg; Carbs 6g; Fiber 3.6g; Sugar 6g; Protein 18g

Tangy Cranberry Cod

Prep time: 5 minutes | Cook time: 20 minutes | Serves: 2

3 filets cod
1 tablespoon olive oil

3 tablespoons cranberry jam

Select the "AIR FRY" function of Ninja Foodi digital air fry oven, set the temperature to 390 degrees F/ 200 degrees C and set the time to 20 minutes. Press the Start/Pause button and begin preheating. Brush the cod filets with olive oil. Spoon a tablespoon of cranberry jam on each filet. Cook for 20-minutes.
Per Serving: Calories 354; Fat 7.9g; Sodium 704mg; Carbs 6g; Fiber 3.6g; Sugar 6g; Protein 18g

Cod Fish and Oysters Teriyaki with Mushrooms & Veggies

Prep time: 5 minutes | Cook time: 10 minutes | Serves: 2

1 tablespoon olive oil
6 pieces mini king oyster mushrooms, thinly sliced
2 slices (1-inch) codfish
1 Napa cabbage leaf, sliced
Teriyaki Sauce:
1 teaspoon liquid stevia
2 tablespoons mirin

1 clove garlic, chopped
Salt to taste
1 green onion, minced
Veggies, steamed of your choice

2 tablespoons soy sauce

1. Make teriyaki sauce by mixing well all the ingredients then set aside. Grease the air fryer basket with oil. Place the mushrooms, garlic, Napa cabbage leaf, and salt inside. Layer the fish and king oysters on top. 2. Select the "AIR FRY" function of Ninja Foodi digital air fry oven, set the temperature to 360 degrees F/ 180 degrees C and set the time to 10 minutes. Press the Start/Pause button and begin preheating. 3. Place the basket in air fryer and cook for 5-minutes. Stir. Pour the teriyaki sauce over the ingredients in the basket. Cook for an additional 5-minutes. Serve with your choice of steamed veggies.
Per Serving: Calories 354; Fat 7.9g; Sodium 704mg; Carbs 6g; Fiber 3.6g; Sugar 6g; Protein 18g

Herbed Salmon

Prep time: 10 minutes | Cook time: 7 minutes | Serves: 2

10 oz. salmon fillet
1 teaspoon dried oregano
1 teaspoon sesame oil

2 oz. Parmesan, grated
¼ teaspoon chili flakes

1. Sprinkle the salmon fillet with dried oregano and chili flakes. Then brush it with sesame oil. Select the "AIR FRY" function of Ninja Foodi digital air fry oven, set the temperature to 385 degrees F/ 195 degrees C and set the time to 5 minutes. Press the Start/Pause button and begin preheating. 2. Place the salmon in the air fryer basket and cook it for 5 minutes. Then flip the fish on another side and top with Parmesan. Cook the fish for 2 minutes more.
Per Serving: Calories 354; Fat 7.9g; Sodium 704mg; Carbs 6g; Fiber 3.6g; Sugar 6g; Protein 18g

Crispy Crab Patties with Sweet 'n' Sour Sauce

Prep time: 10 minutes | Cook time: 24 minutes | Serves: 8

Patties:
1 pound canned lump crabmeat, drained
1 (8-ounce) package cream cheese, softened
Coating:
1½ cups pork dust
Dipping Sauce:
½ cup chicken broth
⅓ cup coconut aminos or wheat-free tamari
⅓ cup Swerve sweetener
¼ cup tomato sauce

1 tablespoon chopped fresh chives
1 large egg
1 teaspoon grated fresh ginger
1 clove garlic, minced

1 tablespoon coconut vinegar
¼ teaspoon grated fresh ginger
1 clove garlic, smashed to a paste
Sliced green onions, for garnish
Fried Cauliflower Rice, for serving

1. Select the "AIR FRY" function of Ninja Foodi digital air fry oven, set the temperature to 400 degrees F/ 200 degrees C and set the time to 12 minutes. Press the Start/Pause button and begin preheating. 2. In a medium-sized bowl, gently mix all the ingredients for the patties, without breaking up the crabmeat. 3. Form the crab mixture into 8 patties that are 2½ inches in diameter and ¾ inch thick. 4. Place the pork dust in a shallow dish. Place each patty in the pork dust and use your hands to press the pork dust into the patties to form a crust. Place the patties in the air fryer, leaving space between them. Cook for 12 minutes, or until the crust is golden and crispy. 5. While the patties cook, make the dipping sauce: In a large saucepan, whisk together all the sauce ingredients. Simmer, then turn the heat down to medium until the sauce thickens, about 5 minutes. 6. Place the patties on a serving platter, drizzle with the dipping sauce, and garnish with sliced green onions, if desired. Serve the dipping sauce on the side. Serve with fried cauliflower rice, if desired.
Per Serving: Calories 354; Fat 7.9g; Sodium 704mg; Carbs 6g; Fiber 3.6g; Sugar 6g; Protein 18g

Crispy Cheesy Cod Fillets

Prep time: 10 minutes | Cook time: 10 minutes | Serves: 4

1 large egg
½ cup powdered Parmesan cheese
1 teaspoon smoked paprika
¼ teaspoon celery salt
¼ teaspoon ground black pepper

4 (4-ounce) cod fillets
Chopped fresh oregano or parsley, for garnish
Lemon slices, for serving

1. Spray the air fryer basket with avocado oil. Select the "AIR FRY" function of Ninja Foodi digital air fry oven, set the temperature to 400 degrees F/ 200 degrees C and set the time to 10 minutes. Press the Start/Pause button and begin preheating. 2. Crack the egg in a shallow bowl and beat it lightly with a fork. Combine the Parmesan cheese, paprika, celery salt, and pepper in a separate shallow bowl. 3. Dip the fillets in egg, then dredge them in the Parmesan mixture. Using your hands, press the Parmesan onto the fillets to form a nice crust. As you finish, place the fish in the air fryer basket. 4. Cook the fish for 10 minutes, or until it is cooked through and flakes easily with a fork. Garnish with parsley and serve with lemon slices, if desired.
Per Serving: Calories 354; Fat 7.9g; Sodium 704mg; Carbs 6g; Fiber 3.6g; Sugar 6g; Protein 18g

Nut-Crusted Catfish

Prep time: 5 minutes | Cook time: 12 minutes | Serves: 4

½ cup pecan meal
1 teaspoon fine sea salt
For Garnish:
Fresh oregano

¼ teaspoon ground black pepper
4 (4-ounce) catfish fillets

Pecan halves

1. Spray the air fryer basket with avocado oil. Select the "AIR FRY" function of Ninja Foodi digital air fry oven, set the temperature to 375 degrees F/ 190 degrees C and set the time to 12 minutes. Press the Start/Pause button and begin preheating. 2. In a bowl, mix the pecan meal, salt, and pepper. One at a time, dredge the catfish fillets in the mixture, coating them well. Use your hands to press the pecan meal into the fillets. Spray the fish with avocado oil and place them in the air fryer basket. 3. Cook the coated catfish for 12 minutes, or until it flakes easily and is no longer translucent in the center, flipping halfway through. 4. Garnish with oregano sprigs and pecan halves, if desired.
Per Serving: Calories 354; Fat 7.9g; Sodium 704mg; Carbs 6g; Fiber 3.6g; Sugar 6g; Protein 18g

Marinated Salmon with Sweet Sauce

Prep time: 5 minutes | Cook time: 6 minutes | Serves: 2

Marinade:
¼ cup wheat-free tamari or coconut aminos
2 tablespoons lime or lemon juice
2 tablespoons sesame oil
2 tablespoons Swerve confectioners'-style sweetener, or a few drops liquid stevia
Sauce:
¼ cup beef broth
¼ cup wheat-free tamari
3 tablespoons Swerve confectioners'-style sweetener or equivalent amount of liquid or

2 teaspoons grated fresh ginger
2 cloves garlic, minced
½ teaspoon ground black pepper
2 (4-ounce) salmon fillets (about 1¼ inches thick)
Sliced green onions, for garnish

powdered sweetener
1 tablespoon tomato sauce
1 teaspoon stevia glyceride
⅛ teaspoon guar gum or xanthan gum

1. Make the marinade: In a medium-sized shallow dish, stir together all the ingredients for the marinade until well combined. Place the salmon in the marinade. Cover and refrigerate for at least 2 hours or overnight. 2. Select the "AIR FRY" function of Ninja Foodi digital air fry oven, set the temperature to 400 degrees F/ 200 degrees C and set the time to 6 minutes. Press the Start/Pause button and begin preheating. 3. Place the marinated salmon in the air fryer, leaving space between them. Cook for 6 minutes, until cooked through and flakes easily with a fork. 4. While the salmon cooks, make the sauce, if using: Place all the sauce ingredients except the guar gum in a medium-sized bowl and stir until well combined. Taste and adjust the sweetness to your liking. While whisking slowly, add the guar gum. Allow the sauce to thicken for 3 to 5 minutes. Drizzle the sauce over the salmon before serving. 5. Garnish the salmon with sliced green onions before serving.
Per Serving: Calories 354; Fat 7.9g; Sodium 704mg; Carbs 6g; Fiber 3.6g; Sugar 6g; Protein 18g

Delicious BLT Crab Cakes

Prep time: 10 minutes | Cook time: 19 minutes | Serves: 4

4 slices bacon
Crab Cakes:

1 pound canned lump crabmeat, drained well	½ teaspoon dried parsley
	½ teaspoon dried dill weed
¼ cup plus 1 tablespoon powdered Parmesan cheese	¼ teaspoon garlic powder
	¼ teaspoon onion powder
3 tablespoons mayonnaise	⅛ teaspoon ground black pepper
1 large egg	1 cup pork dust
½ teaspoon dried chives	

For Serving:

Leaves from 1 small head Boston lettuce	4 slices tomato
	¼ cup mayonnaise

1. Spray the air fryer basket with avocado oil. Select the "AIR FRY" function of Ninja Foodi digital air fry oven, set the temperature to 350 degrees F/ 175 degrees C and set the time to 9 minutes. Press the Start/Pause button and begin preheating. 2. Place the bacon slices in the air fryer, leaving space between them, and cook for 7 to 9 minutes, until crispy. Remove the bacon and increase the heat to 400 degrees F/ 200 degrees C. Set the bacon aside. 3. Make the crab cakes: Place all the crab cake ingredients except the pork dust in a bowl and mix until well blended. Divide the mixture into 4 equal-sized crab cakes (they should each be about 1 inch thick). 4. Place the pork dust in a small bowl. Dredge the crab cakes in the pork dust to coat them well and use your hands to press the pork dust into the cakes. 5. Place them in the air fryer basket, leaving space between them, and cook for 10 minutes, or until crispy .6. To serve, place 4 lettuce leaves on a serving platter and top each leaf with a slice of tomato, then a crab cake, then a dollop of mayo, and finally a slice of bacon.
Per Serving: Calories 354; Fat 7.9g; Sodium 704mg; Carbs 6g; Fiber 3.6g; Sugar 6g; Protein 18g

Delicious Shrimp Scampi

Prep time: 5 minutes | Cook time: 8 minutes | Serves: 4

¼ cup unsalted butter	leaves
2 tablespoons fish stock or chicken broth	1 tablespoon parsley
	1 teaspoon red pepper flakes
1 tablespoon lemon juice	1-pound shrimp,
2 cloves garlic, minced	Fresh basil sprigs, for garnish
2 tablespoons chopped fresh basil	

1. Select the "AIR FRY" function of Ninja Foodi digital air fry oven, set the temperature to 350 degrees F/ 175 degrees C and set the time to 5 minutes. Press the Start/Pause button and begin preheating. 2. Place the butter, fish stock, lemon juice, garlic, basil, parsley, and red pepper flakes in a 6 by 3-inch pan, stir to combine, and place in the air fryer. Cook until fragrant and the garlic has softened. 3. Add the shrimp and stir to coat the shrimp in the sauce. Cook until the shrimp are pink, stirring after 3 minutes. Garnish with fresh basil sprigs and chopped parsley before serving.
Per Serving: Calories 354; Fat 7.9g; Sodium 704mg; Carbs 6g; Fiber 3.6g; Sugar 6g; Protein 18g

Squid Stuffed with Cauliflower Mix

Prep time: 20 minutes | Cook time: 6 minutes | Serves: 4

4 squid tubes, trimmed	1 egg, beaten
1 teaspoon ground paprika	½ teaspoon salt
½ teaspoon ground turmeric	½ teaspoon ground ginger
½ teaspoon garlic, diced	Cooking spray
½ cup cauliflower, shredded	

1. Clean the squid tubes if needed. After this, in the mixing bowl mix up ground paprika, turmeric, garlic, shredded cauliflower, salt, and ground ginger. Stir the mixture gently and add a beaten egg. Mix the mixture up. Then fill the squid tubes with shredded cauliflower mixture. Secure the edges of the squid tubes with toothpicks. 2. Select the "AIR FRY" function of Ninja Foodi digital air fry oven, set the temperature to 390 degrees F/ 200 degrees C and set the time to 6 minutes. Press the Start/Pause button and begin preheating. 3. Place the stuffed squid tubes in the air fryer and spray with cooking spray. Cook the meal for 6 minutes.
Per Serving: Calories 354; Fat 7.9g; Sodium 704mg; Carbs 6g; Fiber 3.6g; Sugar 6g; Protein 18g

Healthy Scallops

Prep time: 5 minutes | Cook time: 4 minutes | Serves: 2

12 medium sea scallops	¾ teaspoon ground black pepper
1 teaspoon fine sea salt	Fresh thyme leaves, for garnish

1. Spray the air fryer basket with avocado oil. Select the "AIR FRY" function of Ninja Foodi digital air fry oven, set the temperature to 390 degrees F/ 200 degrees C and set the time to 4 minutes. Press the Start/Pause button and begin preheating. 2. Rinse the scallops and pat completely dry. Spray avocado oil on the scallops and season them with the salt and pepper. Place them in the air fryer basket, spacing them apart. Cook for 2 minutes, then flip the scallops and cook for another 2 minutes, or until cooked through and no longer translucent. Garnish with ground black pepper and thyme leaves, if desired.
Per Serving: Calories 354; Fat 7.9g; Sodium 704mg; Carbs 6g; Fiber 3.6g; Sugar 6g; Protein 18g

Parmesan-Crusted Shrimp over Pesto Zoodles

Prep time: 10 minutes | Cook time: 14 minutes | Serves: 4

2 large eggs	½ cup powdered Parmesan cheese (about 1½ ounces)
3 cloves garlic, minced	
2 teaspoons dried basil, divided	1-pound jumbo shrimp, peeled, deveined, butterflied, tails removed
½ teaspoon fine sea salt	
½ teaspoon ground black pepper	

Pesto:

1 packed cup fresh basil	3 cloves garlic, peeled
¼ cup extra-virgin olive oil or avocado oil	1 tablespoon lemon juice
	½ teaspoon fine sea salt
¼ cup grated Parmesan cheese	¼ teaspoon ground black pepper
¼ cup roasted, salted walnuts (omit for nut-free)	2 recipes Perfect Zoodles, warm for serving

1. Spray the air fryer basket with avocado oil. Select the "AIR FRY" function of Ninja Foodi digital air fry oven, set the temperature to 400 degrees F/ 200 degrees C and set the time to 7 minutes. Press the Start/Pause button and begin preheating. 2. In a large bowl, whisk together the eggs, garlic, 1 teaspoon of the dried basil, the salt, and the pepper. In a bowl, mix the remaining teaspoon of dried basil and the Parmesan cheese. 3. Place the shrimp in the bowl with the egg mixture and use your hands to coat the shrimp. Roll one shrimp in the Parmesan mixture and press the coating onto the shrimp with your hands. Place the coated shrimp in the air fryer basket. Repeat with the remaining shrimp, leaving space between them in the air fryer basket. 4. Cook the shrimp in the air fryer for 7 minutes, or until cooked through and no longer translucent, flipping after 4 minutes. 5. While the shrimp cook, make the pesto: Place all the ingredients for the pesto in a food processor and pulse until smooth, with a few rough pieces of basil. 6. Just before serving, toss the warm zoodles with the pesto and place the shrimp on top.
Per Serving: Calories 354; Fat 7.9g; Sodium 704mg; Carbs 6g; Fiber 3.6g; Sugar 6g; Protein 18g

Creamy Tilapia Bowls

Prep time: 15 minutes | Cook time: 10 minutes | Serves: 4

7 oz. tilapia fillet or flathead fish	1 teaspoon lemon juice
1 teaspoon arrowroot powder	4 oz. purple cabbage, shredded
1 teaspoon ground paprika	1 jalapeno pepper, sliced
½ teaspoon salt	1 tablespoon heavy cream
½ teaspoon ground black pepper	½ teaspoon minced garlic
¼ teaspoon ground cumin	Cooking spray
½ teaspoon garlic powder	

1. Sprinkle the tilapia fillet with arrowroot powder, ground paprika, salt, ground black pepper, ground cumin, and garlic powder. 2. Select the "AIR FRY" function of Ninja Foodi digital air fry oven, set the temperature to 385 degrees F/ 195 degrees C and set the time to 10 minutes. Press the Start/Pause button and begin preheating. 3. Spray the tilapia fillet with cooking spray and place it in the air fryer. Cook the fish for 10 minutes. Meanwhile, in the bowl mix up shredded cabbage, jalapeno pepper, and lemon juice. When the tilapia fillet is cooked, chop it roughly. Put the shredded cabbage mixture in the serving bowls. Top them with chopped tilapia. 4. After this, in a shallow bowl mix up minced garlic and heavy cream. Sprinkle the meal with a heavy cream mixture.
Per Serving: Calories 354; Fat 7.9g; Sodium 704mg; Carbs 6g; Fiber 3.6g; Sugar 6g; Protein 18g

Cod over Creamy Leek Noodles

Prep time: 10 minutes | Cook time: 24 minutes | Serves: 4

1 small leek, sliced into long thin noodles
½ cup heavy cream
2 cloves garlic, minced
Coating:
¼ cup grated Parmesan cheese
2 tablespoons mayonnaise
2 tablespoons unsalted butter, softened

1 teaspoon fine sea salt, divided
4 (4-ounce) cod fillets
½ teaspoon ground black pepper

1 tablespoon chopped fresh thyme, or ½ teaspoon dried thyme leaves, plus more for garnish

1. Select the "AIR FRY" function of Ninja Foodi digital air fry oven, set the temperature to 350 degrees F/ 175 degrees C and set the time to 10 minutes. Press the Start/Pause button and begin preheating. 2. Place the leek noodles in a 6-inch casserole dish or a pan that will fit in your air fryer. 3. In a bowl, stir the cream, garlic, and ½ teaspoon of the salt. Pour the mixture over the leeks and cook in the air fryer for 10 minutes, or until the leeks are very tender. 4. Pat dry the fish and spice with the salt and the pepper. When the leeks are ready, open the air fryer and place the fish fillets on top of the leeks. Cook for 10 minutes, until the fish flakes easily with a fork. 5. While the fish cooks, make the coating: In a small bowl, combine the Parmesan, mayo, butter, and thyme. 6. When the fish is cooked; remove from fryer and increase the heat to 425 degrees F/ 220 degrees C. Spread the fillets with a ½-inch-thick to ¾-inch-thick layer of the coating. 7. Place the fish back in the air fryer and cook for 3 to 4 minutes, until the coating browns. 8. Garnish with fresh or dried thyme, if desired.
Per Serving: Calories 354; Fat 7.9g; Sodium 704mg; Carbs 6g; Fiber 3.6g; Sugar 6g; Protein 18g

Delicious Popcorn Shrimp

Prep time: 10 minutes | Cook time: 9 minutes | Serves: 4

4 large egg yolks
1 teaspoon prepared yellow mustard
1-pound small shrimp, peeled, deveined, and tails removed
For Serving/Garnish:
Prepared yellow mustard
Ranch Dressing

½ cup finely shredded Gouda or Parmesan cheese
½ cup pork dust
1 tablespoon Cajun seasoning

Tomato sauce
Sprig of fresh parsley

1. Spray the air fryer basket with avocado oil. Select the "AIR FRY" function of Ninja Foodi digital air fry oven, set the temperature to 400 degrees F/ 200 degrees C and set the time to 9 minutes. Press the Start/Pause button and begin preheating. 2. Place the egg yolks in a bowl, add the mustard, and whisk until well combined. Add in the shrimp and toss to coat. 3. In a medium-sized bowl, mix together the cheese, pork dust, and Cajun seasoning until well combined. 4. One at a time, roll the coated shrimp in the pork dust mixture and use your hands to press it onto the shrimp. Spray the coated shrimp with avocado oil and place them in the air fryer basket, leaving space between them 5. Cook in the air fryer for 9 minutes, or until cooked through and no longer translucent, flipping after 4 minutes. 6. Serve with your dipping sauces of choice and garnish with a sprig of fresh parsley.
Per Serving: Calories 354; Fat 7.9g; Sodium 704mg; Carbs 6g; Fiber 3.6g; Sugar 6g; Protein 18g

Tasty Salmon and Cauliflower Rice

Prep time: 5 minutes | Cook time: 25 minutes | Serves: 4

4 salmon fillets, boneless
Salt and black pepper to the taste
1 cup cauliflower, riced

½ cup chicken stock
1 teaspoon turmeric powder
1 tablespoon butter, melted

1. Select the "AIR FRY" function of Ninja Foodi digital air fry oven, set the temperature to 360 degrees F/ 180 degrees C and set the time to 25 minutes. Press the Start/Pause button and begin preheating. 2. In a pan that fits your air fryer, mix the cauliflower rice with the other ingredients except the salmon and toss. Arrange the salmon fillets over the cauliflower rice, put the pan in the fryer and cook for 25 minutes, flipping the fish after 15 minutes. Divide everything between plates and serve.
Per Serving: Calories 354; Fat 7.9g; Sodium 704mg; Carbs 6g; Fiber 3.6g; Sugar 6g; Protein 18g

Bread Crusted Shrimp with Lettuce

Prep time: 10 minutes | Cook time: 9 minutes | Serves: 2

2 large eggs
1 teaspoon prepared yellow mustard
1-pound small shrimp, peeled,
For Serving:
8 large Boston lettuce leaves
¼ cup pico de gallo
¼ cup shredded purple cabbage

deveined, and tails removed
½ cup finely shredded Gouda or Parmesan cheese
½ cup pork dust

1 lemon, sliced
Guacamole

1. Select the "AIR FRY" function of Ninja Foodi digital air fry oven, set the temperature to 400 degrees F/ 200 degrees C and set the time to 9 minutes. Press the Start/Pause button and begin preheating. 2. Crack the eggs into a large bowl, add the mustard, and whisk until well combined. Add in the shrimp and toss to coat. 3. In a medium-sized bowl, mix together the cheese and pork dust until well combined. 4. One at a time, roll the coated shrimp in the pork dust mixture and use your hands to press it onto each shrimp. Spray the coated shrimp with avocado oil and place them in the air fryer basket, leaving space between them. 5. Cook the shrimp for 9 minutes, or until cooked through and no longer translucent, flipping after 4 minutes. 6. Place a lettuce on a serving plate, place several shrimp on top, and top with 1½ teaspoons each of pico de gallo and purple cabbage. Squeeze some lemon juice on top and serve with guacamole, if desired.
Per Serving: Calories 354; Fat 7.9g; Sodium 704mg; Carbs 6g; Fiber 3.6g; Sugar 6g; Protein 18g

Cumin Paprika Shrimp

Prep time: 10 minutes | Cook time: 10 minutes | Serves: 4

1 teaspoon chili flakes
1 teaspoon ground cumin
½ teaspoon salt
½ teaspoon dried oregano
10 oz. shrimps, peeled

1 green bell pepper
2 spring onions, chopped
1 teaspoon apple cider vinegar
1 tablespoon olive oil
1 teaspoon smoked paprika

1. In the mixing bowl, mix up chili flakes, ground cumin, salt, dried oregano, and shrimp. Shake the mixture well. 2. Select the "AIR FRY" function of Ninja Foodi digital air fry oven, set the temperature to 400 degrees F/ 200 degrees C and set the time to 5 minutes. Press the Start/Pause button and begin preheating. 3. Put the spring onions in the air fryer and cook it for 3 minutes. Meanwhile, slice the bell pepper. Add it in the air fryer and cook the vegetables for 2 minutes more. 4. Then add shrimps and sprinkle the mixture with smoked paprika, olive oil, and apple cider vinegar. Shake it gently and cook for 5 minutes more. Transfer the cooked fajita in the serving plates.
Per Serving: Calories 354; Fat 7.9g; Sodium 704mg; Carbs 6g; Fiber 3.6g; Sugar 6g; Protein 18g

Fish Sticks with delicious Tartar Sauce

Prep time: 5 minutes | Cook time: 6 minutes | Serves: 2

12 ounces cod or flounder
½ cup flour
½ teaspoon paprika
1 teaspoon salt
lots of freshly ground black pepper
2 eggs, lightly beaten
1½ cups panko breadcrumbs
1 teaspoon salt

vegetable oil
Tartar Sauce:
¼ cup mayonnaise
2 teaspoons lemon juice
2 tablespoons finely chopped sweet pickles
salt and freshly ground black pepper

1. Cut the fish into strips. Mix the flour, paprika with salt and pepper in a dish. Beat the eggs in another shallow dish. Mix the crumbs and salt in a third dish. Coat the fish by dipping into the flour, then egg and the breadcrumbs, and pressing firmly onto the fish. Place the finished sticks on a plate or baking sheet while you finish all the sticks. 2. Select the "AIR FRY" function of Ninja Foodi digital air fry oven, set the temperature to 400 degrees F/ 200 degrees C and set the time to 6 minutes. Press the Start/Pause button and begin preheating. 3. Spray the fish with the oil and place in the air fryer basket. Place it into the basket and air-fry for 4 minutes, turn over, and air-fry for another 2 minutes. 4. While the fish is cooking, mix the tartar sauce together. 5. Serve warm with the tartar sauce and some French fries on the side.
Per Serving: Calories 420; Fat 23g; Sodium 369mg; Carbs 31g; Fiber 1g; Sugar 4g; Protein 20g

Minty Trout and Crunchy Pine Nuts

Prep time: 5 minutes | Cook time: 16 minutes | Serves: 4

4 rainbow trout
1 cup olive oil + 3 tablespoons
Juice of 1 lemon
A pinch of salt and black pepper
1 cup parsley, chopped
3 garlic cloves, minced
½ cup mint, chopped
Zest of 1 lemon
⅓ pine nuts
1 avocado, peeled, pitted and
roughly chopped

1. Select the "AIR FRY" function of Ninja Foodi digital air fry oven, set the temperature to 350 degrees F/ 175 degrees C and set the time to 8 minutes. Press the Start/Pause button and begin preheating. 2. Pat dry the trout, season with salt and pepper and rub with 3 tablespoons oil. Put the fish in your air fryer's basket and cook for 8 minutes on each side. Divide the fish between plates and drizzle half of the lemon juice all over. 3. In a blender, combine the oil with the remaining lemon juice, parsley, garlic, mint, lemon zest, pine nuts and the avocado and pulse well. Spread this over the trout and serve.
Per Serving: Calories 354; Fat 7.9g; Sodium 704mg; Carbs 6g; Fiber 3.6g; Sugar 6g; Protein 18g

Crispy Fried Anchovies

Prep time: 20 minutes | Cook time: 6 minutes | Serves: 4

1-pound anchovies
¼ cup coconut flour
2 eggs, beaten
1 teaspoon salt
1 teaspoon ground black pepper
1 tablespoon lemon juice
1 tablespoon sesame oil

1. Trim and wash anchovies if needed and put in the big bowl. Add salt and ground black pepper. Mix up the anchovies. 2. Then add eggs and lemon juice, stir the fish until you get a homogenous mixture. After this coat every anchovies fish in the coconut flour. Brush the air fryer basket with sesame oil. Place the anchovies in the basket in one layer. Select the "AIR FRY" function of Ninja Foodi digital air fry oven, set the temperature to 400 degrees F/ 200 degrees C and set the time to 6 minutes. Press the Start/Pause button and begin preheating. 3. Put the basket with anchovies in the air fryer and cook them for 6 minutes or until anchovies are golden brown.
Per Serving: Calories 354; Fat 7.9g; Sodium 704mg; Carbs 6g; Fiber 3.6g; Sugar 6g; Protein 18g

Trout with Crispy Asparagus

Prep time: 5 minutes | Cook time: 20 minutes | Serves: 4

4 trout fillets, boneless and
skinless
1 tablespoon lemon juice
2 tablespoons olive oil
A pinch of salt and black pepper
1 bunch asparagus, trimmed
2 tablespoons ghee, melted
¼ cup mixed chives and tarragon

1. Select the "AIR FRY" function of Ninja Foodi digital air fry oven, set the temperature to 380 degrees F/ 195 degrees C and set the time to 6 minutes. Press the Start/Pause button and begin preheating. 2. Mix the asparagus with half of the oil, salt and pepper, put it in your air fryer's basket, cook at 380 degrees F/ 195 degrees C for 6 minutes and divide between plates. 3. In a bowl, mix the trout with salt, pepper, lemon juice, the rest of the oil, chives and tarragon and toss, Put the fillets in your air fryer's basket and cook at 380 degrees F/ 195 degrees C for 7 minutes on each side. 4. Divide the fish next to the asparagus, drizzle the melted ghee all over and serve.
Per Serving: Calories 354; Fat 7.9g; Sodium 704mg; Carbs 6g; Fiber 3.6g; Sugar 6g; Protein 18g

Garlicky Shrimp with Olives

Prep time: 5 minutes | Cook time: 12 minutes | Serves: 4

1-pound shrimp, peeled and
deveined
4 garlic clove, minced
1 cup black olives, pitted and
chopped
3 tablespoons parsley
1 tablespoon olive oil

Select the "AIR FRY" function of Ninja Foodi digital air fry oven, set the temperature to 380 degrees F/ 195 degrees C and set the time to 12 minutes. Press the Start/Pause button and begin preheating. Combine all the ingredients in a Ninja sheet pan, toss, put the pan in the air fryer and cook for 12 minutes. Divide between plates and serve.
Per Serving: Calories 354; Fat 7.9g; Sodium 704mg; Carbs 6g; Fiber 3.6g; Sugar 6g; Protein 18g

Refreshing Cilantro Salmon

Prep time: 5 minutes | Cook time: 12 minutes | Serves: 4

4 salmon fillets, boneless
Juice of ½ lemon
¼ cup chives, chopped
4 cilantro springs, chopped
3 tablespoons olive oil
Salt and black pepper to the taste

1. Select the "AIR FRY" function of Ninja Foodi digital air fry oven, set the temperature to 370 degrees F/ 185 degrees C and set the time to 12 minutes. Press the Start/Pause button and begin preheating. 2. In a bowl, mix the salmon with all the other ingredients and toss. Put the fillets in your air fryer's basket and cook for 12 minutes, flipping the fish halfway. 3. Divide everything between plates and serve with a side salad.
Per Serving: Calories 354; Fat 7.9g; Sodium 704mg; Carbs 6g; Fiber 3.6g; Sugar 6g; Protein 18g

Mahi Mahi Cakes with Broccoli

Prep time: 15 minutes | Cook time: 11 minutes | Serves: 4

½ cup broccoli, shredded
1 tablespoon flax meal
1 egg, beaten
1 teaspoon ground coriander
1 oz. Monterey Jack cheese,
shredded
½ teaspoon salt
6 oz. Mahi Mahi, chopped
Cooking spray

1. In the mixing bowl mix up flax meal, egg, ground coriander, salt, broccoli, and chopped Mahi Mahi. Stir the ingredients gently with the help of the fork and add shredded Monterey Jack cheese. Stir the mixture until homogenous. Then make 4 cakes. 2. Select the "AIR FRY" function of Ninja Foodi digital air fry oven, set the temperature to 390 degrees F/ 200 degrees C and set the time to 11 minutes. Press the Start/Pause button and begin preheating. Place the Mahi Mahi cakes in the air fryer and spray them gently with cooking spray. Cook the fish cakes for 5 minutes and then flip on another side. Cook the fish cakes for 6 minutes more.
Per Serving: Calories 354; Fat 7.9g; Sodium 704mg; Carbs 6g; Fiber 3.6g; Sugar 6g; Protein 18g

Balsamic Trout with Charred Tomatoes and Pepper

Prep time: 5 minutes | Cook time: 16 minutes | Serves: 2

2 trout fillets, boneless
2 tomatoes, cubed
1 red bell pepper, chopped
2 garlic cloves, minced
1 tablespoon olive oil
1 tablespoon balsamic vinegar
A pinch of salt and black pepper
2 tablespoons almond flakes

1. Select the "AIR FRY" function of Ninja Foodi digital air fry oven, set the temperature to 370 degrees F/ 185 degrees C and set the time to 16 minutes. Press the Start/Pause button and begin preheating. 2. Arrange the fish in a pan that fits your air fryer, add the rest of the ingredients and toss gently. Cook for 16 minutes, divide between plates and serve.
Per Serving: Calories 354; Fat 7.9g; Sodium 704mg; Carbs 6g; Fiber 3.6g; Sugar 6g; Protein 18g

Sea Bass with Tropical Sauce

Prep time: 5 minutes | Cook time: 20 minutes | Serves: 4

4 sea bass fillets, boneless
A pinch of salt and black pepper
2 spring onions, chopped
Juice of 1 lime
1 garlic clove, minced
2 tomatoes, cubed
2 cups coconut cream
½ cup okra
A handful coriander, chopped
2 red chilies, minced

1. Select the "AIR FRY" function of Ninja Foodi digital air fry oven, set the temperature to 380 degrees F/ 195 degrees C and set the time to 15 minutes. Press the Start/Pause button and begin preheating. 2. Put the coconut cream in a pan that fits the air fryer, add garlic, spring onions, lime juice, tomatoes, okra, chilies and the coriander, toss, bring to a simmer and cook for 5-6 minutes. Add the fish, toss gently, introduce in the fryer and cook for 15 minutes. Divide between plates and serve.
Per Serving: Calories 354; Fat 7.9g; Sodium 704mg; Carbs 6g; Fiber 3.6g; Sugar 6g; Protein 18g

Nutty Trout

Prep time: 5 minutes | Cook time: 15 minutes | Serves: 2

2 trout fillets, boneless
2 tablespoons almonds, crushed
Zest of ½ lemon, grated
1 tablespoon olive oil
1 tablespoon ghee, melted
A pinch of salt and black pepper
1 tablespoon parsley, chopped

1. Select the "AIR FRY" function of Ninja Foodi digital air fry oven, set the temperature to 370 degrees F/ 185 degrees C and set the time to 15 minutes. Press the Start/Pause button and begin preheating. 2. In a bowl, mix the trout with all the other ingredients except the parsley and toss. Put the fish in your air fryer's basket and cook for 15 minutes, flipping the fillets halfway. Divide between serving plates, sprinkle the parsley on top and serve.
Per Serving: Calories 354; Fat 7.9g; Sodium 704mg; Carbs 6g; Fiber 3.6g; Sugar 6g; Protein 18g

Sea Bass and Olives

Prep time: 5 minutes | Cook time: 20 minutes | Serves: 2

2 sea bass, fillets
1 fennel bulb, sliced
Juice of 1 lemon
¼ cup black olives, pitted and
sliced
1 tablespoon olive oil
A pinch of salt and black pepper
¼ cup basil, chopped

1. Select the "AIR FRY" function of Ninja Foodi digital air fry oven, set the temperature to 380 degrees F/ 195 degrees C and set the time to 20 minutes. Press the Start/Pause button and begin preheating. 2. In a pan that fits the air fryer, combine all the ingredients, introduce the pan in the Ninja Foodi air fryer and cook for 20 minutes, shaking the fryer halfway. Divide between plates and serve.
Per Serving: Calories 354; Fat 7.9g; Sodium 704mg; Carbs 6g; Fiber 3.6g; Sugar 6g; Protein 18g

Creole Crab Hushpuppies

Prep time: 15 minutes | Cook time: 6 minutes | Serves: 6

1 teaspoon Creole seasonings
4 tablespoons almond flour
¼ teaspoon baking powder
1 teaspoon apple cider vinegar
¼ teaspoon onion powder
1 teaspoon dried dill
1 teaspoon ghee
13 oz. crab meat, finely chopped
1 egg, beaten
Cooking spray

1. In the mixing bowl, mix up crab meat, egg, dried dill, ghee, onion powder, apple cider vinegar, baking powder, and Creole seasonings. 2. Then add almond flour and stir the mixture with the help of the fork until it is homogenous. Make the small balls (hushpuppies). 3. Select the "AIR FRY" function of Ninja Foodi digital air fry oven, set the temperature to 390 degrees F/ 200 degrees C and set the time to 6 minutes. Press the Start/Pause button and begin preheating. Put the hushpuppies in the air fryer basket and spray with cooking spray. Cook them for 3 minutes. Then flip them on another side and cook for 3 minutes more or until the hushpuppies are golden brown.
Per Serving: Calories 354; Fat 7.9g; Sodium 704mg; Carbs 6g; Fiber 3.6g; Sugar 6g; Protein 18g

Sea Bass with Cauliflower Rice

Prep time: 5 minutes | Cook time: 25 minutes | Serves: 4

4 sea bass fillets, boneless
A pinch of salt and black pepper
1 tablespoon ghee, melted
1 garlic clove, minced
1 cup cauliflower rice
½ cup chicken stock
1 tablespoon parmesan, grated
1 tablespoon chervil, chopped
1 tablespoon parsley, chopped
1 tablespoon tarragon, chopped

1. Select the "AIR FRY" function of Ninja Foodi digital air fry oven, set the temperature to 380 degrees F/ 195 degrees C and set the time to 12 minutes. Press the Start/Pause button and begin preheating. 2. In a pan that fits your air fryer, mix the cauliflower rice with the stock, parmesan, chervil, tarragon and parsley, toss, introduce the pan in the air fryer and cook for 12 minutes. 3. In a bowl, mix the fish with salt, pepper, garlic and melted ghee and toss gently. Put the fish over the cauliflower rice, cook for 12 minutes more, divide everything between plates and serve.
Per Serving: Calories 354; Fat 7.9g; Sodium 704mg; Carbs 6g; Fiber 3.6g; Sugar 6g; Protein 18g

Refreshing Taco Lobster

Prep time: 10 minutes | Cook time: 6 minutes | Serves: 4

4 lettuce leaves
½ teaspoon taco seasonings
4 lobster tails
1 teaspoon Splenda
½ teaspoon ground cumin
½ teaspoon chili flakes
1 tablespoon ricotta cheese
1 teaspoon avocado oil

1. Select the "AIR FRY" function of Ninja Foodi digital air fry oven, set the temperature to 380 degrees F/ 195 degrees C and set the time to 6 minutes. Press the Start/Pause button and begin preheating. 2. Peel the lobster tails and sprinkle with ground cumin, taco seasonings, and chili flakes. Arrange the lobster tails in the air fryer basket and sprinkle with avocado oil. Cook them for 6 minutes. 3. After this, remove the cooked lobster tails from the air fryer and chop them roughly. Transfer the lobster tails into the bowl. Add ricotta cheese and Splenda. Mix them up. 4. Place the lobster mixture on the lettuce leaves and fold them.
Per Serving: Calories 354; Fat 7.9g; Sodium 704mg; Carbs 6g; Fiber 3.6g; Sugar 6g; Protein 18g

Clams with Coconut Lime Sauce

Prep time: 5 minutes | Cook time: 20 minutes | Serves: 4

15 small clams
1 tablespoon spring onions, chopped
Juice of 1 lime
10 ounces coconut cream
2 tablespoons cilantro, chopped
1 teaspoon olive oil

1. Select the "AIR FRY" function of Ninja Foodi digital air fry oven, set the temperature to 390 degrees F/ 200 degrees C and set the time to 15 minutes. Press the Start/Pause button and begin preheating. 2. Heat up a pan that fits your air fryer with the oil over medium heat, add the spring onions and sauté for 2 minutes. Add lime juice, coconut cream and the cilantro, stir and cook for 2 minutes more. Add the clams, toss, introduce in the fryer and cook for 15 minutes. Divide into bowls and serve hot.
Per Serving: Calories 354; Fat 7.9g; Sodium 704mg; Carbs 6g; Fiber 3.6g; Sugar 6g; Protein 18g

Fried Coconut Tilapia

Prep time: 10 minutes | Cook time: 12 minutes | Serves: 2

8 oz. tilapia fillet
1 teaspoon coconut cream
1 teaspoon coconut flour
½ teaspoon salt
¼ teaspoon smoked paprika
½ teaspoon dried oregano
½ teaspoon coconut oil, melted
¼ teaspoon ground cumin

1. Rub the tilapia fillet with ground cumin, dried oregano, smoked paprika, and salt. Then dip it in the coconut cream. Cut the tilapia fillet on 2 servings. After this, sprinkle every tilapia fillet with coconut flour gently. 2. Select the "AIR FRY" function of Ninja Foodi digital air fry oven, set the temperature to 385 degrees F/ 195 degrees C and set the time to 12 minutes. Press the Start/Pause button and begin preheating. Sprinkle the air fryer basket with coconut oil and put the tilapia fillets inside. Cook the fillets for 6 minutes from every side.
Per Serving: Calories 354; Fat 7.9g; Sodium 704mg; Carbs 6g; Fiber 3.6g; Sugar 6g; Protein 18g

Italian-Style Peppercorn Fennel Cod

Prep time: 5 minutes | Cook time: 15 minutes | Serves: 4

4 cod fillets, boneless
A pinch of salt and black pepper
1 tablespoon thyme, chopped
½ teaspoon black peppercorns
2 tablespoons olive oil
1 fennel, sliced
2 garlic cloves, minced
1 red bell pepper, chopped
2 teaspoons Italian seasoning

1. Select the "AIR FRY" function of Ninja Foodi digital air fry oven, set the temperature to 380 degrees F/ 195 degrees C and set the time to 15 minutes. Press the Start/Pause button and begin preheating. 2. In a bowl, mix the fennel with bell pepper and the other ingredients except the fish fillets and toss. Put this into a pan that fits the air fryer, add the fish on top, introduce the pan in your air fryer and cook for 15 minutes. Divide between plates and serve.
Per Serving: Calories 354; Fat 7.9g; Sodium 704mg; Carbs 6g; Fiber 3.6g; Sugar 6g; Protein 18g

Fried Coconut Cod Strips

Prep time: 10 minutes | Cook time: 6 minutes | Serves: 4

10 oz. cod fillet
1 tablespoon coconut flour
1 tablespoon coconut flakes
1 egg, beaten

1 teaspoon ground turmeric
½ teaspoon salt
1 tablespoon heavy cream
1 teaspoon olive oil

1. Cut the cod fillets on the fries strips. After this, in the mixing bowl mix up coconut flour, coconut flakes, ground turmeric, and salt. In the other bowl mix up egg and heavy cream. After this, dip the fish fries in the egg mixture. Coat in the coconut flour mixture. Repeat the steps again. 2. Select the "AIR FRY" function of Ninja Foodi digital air fry oven, set the temperature to 400 degrees F/ 200 degrees C and set the time to 6 minutes. Press the Start/Pause button and begin preheating. 3. Put the fish fries in the air fryer basket in one layer and sprinkle them with olive oil. Cook the meal for 3 minutes. Then flip the fish fries on another side and cook for 3 minutes more.
Per Serving: Calories 354; Fat 7.9g; Sodium 704mg; Carbs 6g; Fiber 3.6g; Sugar 6g; Protein 18g

Chili Sea Bass

Prep time: 5 minutes | Cook time: 15 minutes | Serves: 4

4 sea bass fillets, boneless
4 garlic cloves, minced
Juice of 1 lime
1 cup veggie stock
A pinch of salt and black pepper
1 tablespoon black peppercorns,

crushed
1-inch ginger, grated
4 lemongrasses, chopped
4 small chilies, minced
1 bunch coriander, chopped

Select the "AIR FRY" function of Ninja Foodi digital air fry oven, set the temperature to 380 degrees F/ 195 degrees C and set the time to 15 minutes. Press the Start/Pause button and begin preheating. In a blender, mix all the ingredients instead of the fish and pulse well. Pour the mix in a pan that fits the air fryer, add the fish, toss, introduce in the fryer and cook for 15 minutes. Divide between plates and serve.
Per Serving: Calories 354; Fat 7.9g; Sodium 704mg; Carbs 6g; Fiber 3.6g; Sugar 6g; Protein 18g

Sausage Shrimp Gumbo

Prep time: 10 minutes | Cook time: 12 minutes | Serves: 4

10 oz. shrimps, peeled
5 oz. smoked sausages, chopped
1 teaspoon olive oil
1 teaspoon ground black pepper
3 spring onions, diced

1 jalapeno pepper, chopped
½ cup chicken broth
1 teaspoon chili flakes
½ teaspoon dried cilantro
½ teaspoon salt

1. Select the "AIR FRY" function of Ninja Foodi digital air fry oven, set the temperature to 400 degrees F/ 200 degrees C and set the time to 4 minutes. Press the Start/Pause button and begin preheating. 2. In the mixing bowl mix up smoked sausages, ground black pepper, and chili flakes. Put the smoked sausages in the air fryer and cook them for 4 minutes. Meanwhile, in the mixing bowl mix up onion, jalapeno pepper, and salt. Put the ingredients in the air fryer sheet pan and sprinkle with olive oil. 3. After this, remove the sausages from the air fryer. Put the pan with onion in the air fryer and cook it for 2 minutes. After this, add smoked sausages, dried cilantro, and shrimps. Add chicken broth. Stir the ingredients gently and cook the meal for 6 minutes.
Per Serving: Calories 354; Fat 7.9g; Sodium 704mg; Carbs 6g; Fiber 3.6g; Sugar 6g; Protein 18g

Shrimp with Scallions

Prep time: 3 minutes | Cook time: 10 minutes | Serves: 4

1-pound shrimp, peeled and deveined
2 tablespoons olive oil

1 tablespoon scallions, chopped
1 cup chicken stock

Select the "AIR FRY" function of Ninja Foodi digital air fry oven, set the temperature to 380 degrees F/ 195 degrees C and set the time to 10 minutes. Press the Start/Pause button and begin preheating. In a pan that fits your air fryer, mix the shrimp with the oil, scallions and the stock, introduce the pan in the fryer and cook for 10 minutes. Divide into bowls and serve.
Per Serving: Calories 354; Fat 7.9g; Sodium 704mg; Carbs 6g; Fiber 3.6g; Sugar 6g; Protein 18g

Buttery Haddock with Parsley

Prep time: 10 minutes | Cook time: 16 minutes | Serves: 2

7 oz. haddock fillet
2 tablespoons butter, melted
1 teaspoon minced garlic

½ teaspoon salt
1 teaspoon fresh parsley, chopped
½ teaspoon ground celery root

Cut the fish fillet on 2 servings. In the shallow bowl mix up butter and minced garlic. Then add salt, celery root, and fresh parsley. After this, carefully brush the fish fillets with the butter mixture. Then wrap every fillet in the foil. Select the "AIR FRY" function of Ninja Foodi digital air fry oven, set the temperature to 385 degrees F/ 195 degrees C and set the time to 16 minutes. Press the Start/Pause button and begin preheating. Put the wrapped haddock fillets in the air fryer and cook for 16 minutes.
Per Serving: Calories 354; Fat 7.9g; Sodium 704mg; Carbs 6g; Fiber 3.6g; Sugar 6g; Protein 18g

Italian Garlicky Shrimp

Prep time: 5 minutes | Cook time: 10 minutes | Serves: 4

2 pounds shrimp, peeled and deveined
A drizzle of olive oil
¼ cup chicken stock
1 tablespoon Italian seasoning

Salt and black pepper to the taste
1 teaspoon red pepper flakes, crushed
8 garlic cloves, crushed

Select the "AIR FRY" function of Ninja Foodi digital air fry oven, set the temperature to 390 degrees F/ 200 degrees C and set the time to 10 minutes. Press the Start/Pause button and begin preheating. Grease a pan that fits your air fryer with the oil, add the shrimp and the rest of the ingredients, toss, introduce the pan in the fryer and cook for 10 minutes. Divide into bowls and serve.
Per Serving: Calories 354; Fat 7.9g; Sodium 704mg; Carbs 6g; Fiber 3.6g; Sugar 6g; Protein 18g

Tarragon and Spring Onions Salmon

Prep time: 15 minutes | Cook time: 15 minutes | Serves: 4

12 oz. salmon fillet
2 spring onions, chopped
1 tablespoon ghee, melted
1 teaspoon peppercorns

½ teaspoon salt
½ teaspoon ground black pepper
1 teaspoon tarragon
½ teaspoon dried cilantro

1. Cut the salmon fillet on 4 servings. Then make the parchment pockets and place the fish fillets in the parchment pockets. Sprinkle the salmon with salt, ground black pepper, tarragon, and dried cilantro. After this, top the fish with spring onions, peppercorns, and ghee. 2. Select the "AIR FRY" function of Ninja Foodi digital air fry oven, set the temperature to 385 degrees F/ 195 degrees C and set the time to 15 minutes. Press the Start/Pause button and begin preheating. Arrange the salmon pockets in the air fryer in one layer and cook them for 15 minutes.
Per Serving: Calories 354; Fat 7.9g; Sodium 704mg; Carbs 6g; Fiber 3.6g; Sugar 6g; Protein 18g

Easy Salmon Salad

Prep time: 10 minutes | Cook time: 15 minutes | Serves: 4

1 pound salmon fillets
Sea salt Ground black pepper, to taste
2 tablespoons olive oil
2 garlic cloves, minced
1 bell pepper, sliced

1 shallot, chopped
½ cup olives, pitted and sliced
½ lemon, juiced
1 teaspoon Aleppo pepper, minced

1. Select the "AIR FRY" function of Ninja Foodi digital air fry oven, set the temperature to 380 degrees F/ 195 degrees C and set the time to 15 minutes. Press the Start/Pause button and begin preheating. 2. Toss the salmon fillets with the salt, black pepper, and olive oil; place them in a lightly oiled air fryer cooking basket. Cook the salmon fillets for about 12 minutes, turning them over halfway through the cooking time. 3. Chop the salmon fillets using two forks and add them to a salad bowl; add in the remaining and toss to combine. Bon appétit!
Per Serving: Calories 243; Fat 13.3g; Sodium 269mg; Carbs 5.5g; Fiber 1.2g; Sugar 2g; Protein 24.4g

Spicy Octopus

Prep time: 10 minutes | Cook time: 26 minutes | Serves: 4

11 oz. octopus
1 teaspoon chili flakes
1 chili pepper, chopped
1 tablespoon coconut oil, melted
½ teaspoon salt
1 cup of water
1 tablespoon lemon juice

1. Select the "AIR FRY" function of Ninja Foodi digital air fry oven, set the temperature to 390 degrees F/ 200 degrees C and set the time to 1 minute. Press the Start/Pause button and begin preheating. Boil water in a saucepan. Chop the octopus and put it in the boiling water. Close and cook the seafood for 25 minutes. After this, remove the octopus from the water and sprinkle with chili flakes, chili pepper, coconut oil, salt, and lemon juice. Transfer them in the air fryer and cook for 1 minute.
Per Serving: Calories 354; Fat 7.9g; Sodium 704mg; Carbs 6g; Fiber 3.6g; Sugar 6g; Protein 18g

Sea Bass and Tangy Balsamic Salsa

Prep time: 5 minutes | Cook time: 15 minutes | Serves: 4

4 sea bass fillets, boneless
1 tablespoon olive oil
3 tomatoes, roughly chopped
2 spring onions, chopped
¼ cup chicken stock
A pinch of salt and black pepper
3 garlic cloves, minced
1 tablespoon balsamic vinegar

Select the "AIR FRY" function of Ninja Foodi digital air fry oven, set the temperature to 380 degrees F/ 195 degrees C and set the time to 15 minutes. Press the Start/Pause button and begin preheating. In a blender, mix all the ingredients instead of the fish and pulse well. Put the mix in a pan that fits the air fryer, add the fish, toss gently, introduce the pan in the fryer and cook for 15 minutes. Divide between plates and serve.
Per Serving: Calories 354; Fat 7.9g; Sodium 704mg; Carbs 6g; Fiber 3.6g; Sugar 6g; Protein 18g

Tasty Swordfish Steaks

Prep time: 5 minutes | Cook time: 15 minutes | Serves: 4

1 pound swordfish steaks
2 tablespoons olive oil
2 teaspoons tamari sauce
Salt and freshly ground pepper, to taste
¼ cup dry red wine
2 sprigs rosemary
1 sprig thyme
1 tablespoon grated lemon rind

1. Select the "BAKE" function of Ninja Foodi digital air fry oven, set the temperature to 400 degrees F/ 200 degrees C and set the time to 10 minutes. Press the Start/Pause button and begin preheating. 2. Toss the swordfish steaks with the remaining in a ceramic dish; cover and let it marinate in your refrigerator for about 2 hours. 3. Then, discard the marinade and place the fish in a lightly oiled air fryer cooking basket. Cook the swordfish steaks for about 10 minutes, turning them over halfway through the cooking time. Bon appétit!
Per Serving: Calories 230; Fat 14.3g; Sodium 258mg; Carbs 0.8g; Fiber 0.2g; Sugar 0.2g; Protein 22.3g

Fried Shrimp

Prep time: 5 minutes | Cook time: 10 minutes | Serves: 4

½ cup flour
Sea salt and lemon pepper, to taste
2 large eggs
1 cup seasoned breadcrumbs
2 tablespoons olive oil
1 pound shrimp, peeled and deveined

1. Select the "AIR FRY" function of Ninja Foodi digital air fry oven, set the temperature to 400 degrees F/ 200 degrees C and set the time to 10 minutes. Press the Start/Pause button and begin preheating. 2. In a bowl, mix the flour along with salt, and lemon pepper. Beat the eggs in a second bowl, and place the breadcrumbs in a third bowl. Dredge in the flour, then in the whisked eggs; finally, roll the shrimp over the breadcrumbs until well coated on all sides. 3. Place them in the air fryer basket. Drizzle the olive oil over the shrimp. Cook the shrimp for about 10 minutes, shaking the basket halfway through the cooking time. Bon appétit!
Per Serving: Calories 358; Fat 9.8g; Sodium 561mg; Carbs 31.5g; Fiber 5g; Sugar 3.7g; Protein 29.1g

Easy Fried Mackerel Fillets

Prep time: 10 minutes | Cook time: 15 minutes | Serves: 4

1 tablespoon olive oil, or more to taste
1 ½ pounds mackerel fillets
Sea salt and ground black pepper,
taste
2 tablespoons parsley
2 garlic cloves, minced
2 tablespoons fresh lime juice

1. Select the "AIR FRY" function of Ninja Foodi digital air fry oven, set the temperature to 400 degrees F/ 200 degrees C and set the time to 15 minutes. Press the Start/Pause button and begin preheating. 2. Toss the fish fillets with the remaining ingredients and place them in a lightly oiled Air Fryer cooking basket. Cook the fish fillets for about 14 minutes, turning them over halfway through the cooking time. Bon appétit!
Per Serving: Calories 218; Fat 6.8g; Sodium 268mg; Carbs 2.3g; Fiber 0.3g; Sugar 0.7g; Protein 34.6g

Greek Monkfish Pita

Prep time: 10 minutes | Cook time: 15 minutes | Serves: 4

1 pound monkfish fillets
1 tablespoon olive oil
Sea salt
Ground black pepper, to taste
1 teaspoon cayenne pepper
4 tablespoons coleslaw
1 avocado, pitted, peeled and diced
1 tablespoon fresh parsley, chopped
4 (6-½ inch) Greek pitas, warmed

1. Select the "AIR FRY" function of Ninja Foodi digital air fry oven, set the temperature to 400 degrees F/ 200 degrees C and set the time to 15 minutes. Press the Start/Pause button and begin preheating. 2. Toss the fish fillets with the olive oil; place them in a lightly oiled air fryer cooking basket. Cook the fish fillets for about 14 minutes, turning them over halfway through the cooking time. 3. Assemble your pitas with the chopped fish and remaining and serve warm. Bon appétit!
Per Serving: Calories 494; Fat 24.3g; Sodium 257mg; Carbs 43.8g; Fiber 8.3g; Sugar 3.7g; Protein 28.8g

Cheesy Monkfish Fillets

Prep time: 5 minutes | Cook time: 15 minutes | Serves: 4

1 pound monkfish fillets
Coarse sea salt
Ground black pepper, to taste
2 tablespoons butter
2 tablespoons lemon juice
4 tablespoon Parmesan cheese, grated

1. Select the "AIR FRY" function of Ninja Foodi digital air fry oven, set the temperature to 400 degrees F/ 200 degrees C and set the time to 15 minutes. Press the Start/Pause button and begin preheating. 2. Toss the fish fillets with the remaining ingredients, except for the Parmesan cheese; place them in a lightly oiled air fryer cooking basket. Cook the fish fillets for about 14 minutes, turning them over halfway through the cooking time. Top the fish fillets with the grated Parmesan cheese and serve immediately. Bon appétit!
Per Serving: Calories 168; Fat 8.9g; Sodium 269mg; Carbs 2.2g; Fiber 0.2g; Sugar 0.7g; Protein 18.2g

Herbed Tilapia Fillets Nuggets

Prep time: 10 minutes | Cook time: 15 minutes | Serves: 4

1 ½ pounds tilapia fillets, cut into 1 ½-inch pieces
1 tablespoon dried thyme
1 tablespoon dried oregano
1 tablespoon Dijon mustard
2 tablespoons olive oil
1 ½ cups all-purpose flour
Sea salt
Ground black pepper, to taste
½ teaspoon baking powder

1. Select the "AIR FRY" function of Ninja Foodi digital air fry oven, set the temperature to 400 degrees F/ 200 degrees C and set the time to 10 minutes. Press the Start/Pause button and begin preheating. 2. Pat the fish dry with kitchen towels. In a mixing bowl, thoroughly combine all remaining ingredients until well mixed. 3. Now, dip the fish pieces into the batter to coat. Cook the fish nuggets for 10 minutes, shaking the basket halfway through the cooking time. Bon appétit!
Per Serving: Calories 404; Fat 10.3g; Sodium 347mg; Carbs 37.2g; Fiber 1.7g; Sugar 0.7g; Protein 39g

Parsley Shrimp and Olives

Prep time: 5 minutes | Cook time: 12 minutes | Serves: 4

1-pound shrimp, peeled and deveined
4 garlic clove, minced
1 cup black olives, pitted and

chopped
3 tablespoons parsley
1 tablespoon olive oil

Select the "AIR FRY" function of Ninja Foodi digital air fry oven, set the temperature to 380 degrees F/ 195 degrees C and set the time to 12 minutes. Press the Start/Pause button and begin preheating. In a pan that fits the air fryer, combine all the ingredients, toss, put the pan in the Ninja Foodi air fryer and cook for 12 minutes. Divide between plates and serve.
Per Serving: Calories 354; Fat 7.9g; Sodium 704mg; Carbs 6g; Fiber 3.6g; Sugar 6g; Protein 18g

Coconut Sea Bass

Prep time: 10 minutes | Cook time: 20 minutes | Serves: 4

1 ½ pounds sea bass fillet
2 tablespoons lemon juice
2 garlic cloves, minced
½ cup coconut, shredded

½ cup all-purpose flour
Coarse sea salt
Ground black pepper, to taste
2 tomatoes, sliced

1. Select the "AIR FRY" function of Ninja Foodi digital air fry oven, set the temperature to 400 degrees F/ 200 degrees C and set the time to 10 minutes. Press the Start/Pause button and begin preheating. 2. Toss the fillets with the lemon juice, garlic, coconut, flour, salt, and black pepper; place them in a lightly oiled air fryer cooking basket. Cook the fish fillets for about 8 minutes. 3. Turn them over and top with the tomatoes. Continue to cook for a further 8 minutes. Bon appétit!
Per Serving: Calories 237; Fat 3.6g; Sodium 354mg; Carbs 15.4g; Fiber 1.2g; Sugar 1.8g; Protein 33.3g

Sweet Garlic Trout

Prep time: 5 minutes | Cook time: 15 minutes | Serves: 4

1 pound trout, cut into sticks
1 tablespoon olive oil
2 tablespoons liquid honey
2 teaspoons apple cider vinegar

2 cloves garlic, minced
Sea salt
Ground black pepper, to taste
½ teaspoon cayenne pepper

1. Select the "AIR FRY" function of Ninja Foodi digital air fry oven, set the temperature to 390 degrees F/ 200 degrees C and set the time to 12 minutes. Press the Start/Pause button and begin preheating. 2. Toss all in a lightly greased air fryer cooking basket. Cook your fish for 12 minutes, tossing the basket halfway through the cooking time. On appétit!
Per Serving: Calories 238; Fat 10.3g; Sodium 268mg; Carbs 10.3g; Fiber 0.3g; Sugar 9.2g; Protein 23.6g

Soft Crab Cakes

Prep time: 5 minutes | Cook time: 10 minutes | Serves: 2

1 teaspoon butter
⅓ cup finely diced onion
⅓ cup finely diced celery
¼ cup mayonnaise
1 teaspoon Dijon mustard
1 egg

pinch ground cayenne pepper
1 teaspoon salt
freshly ground black pepper
16 ounces lump crabmeat
½ cup + 2 tablespoons panko breadcrumbs, divided

1. Melt the butter and sauté the onion and celery until soften, but not brown – about 4 minutes. Transfer the vegetables to a bowl. Add the mayonnaise, Dijon mustard, egg, cayenne pepper, salt and freshly ground black pepper to the bowl. Gently fold in crabmeat and panko breadcrumbs. 2. Select the "BAKE" function of Ninja Foodi digital air fry oven, set the temperature to 400 degrees F/ 200 degrees C and set the time to 10 minutes. Press the Start/Pause button and begin preheating. 3. Place the breadcrumbs in a dish. Divide the mixture and shape into a round patty. Dredge the crab patties in the breadcrumbs, coating both sides as well as the edges with the crumbs. 4. Air-fry the cakes for 5 minutes. Flip gently and cook for another 5 minutes. Serve with tartar sauce(optional).
Per Serving: Calories 180; Fat 4g; Sodium 321mg; Carbs 5g; Fiber 2g; Sugar 3g; Protein 7g

Fried Squid with Paprika and Garlic

Prep time: 5 minutes | Cook time: 10 minutes | Serves: 4

1 ½ pounds small squid tubes
Sea salt
Ground black pepper, to taste
1 teaspoon paprika

½ cup parsley, minced
2 cloves garlic, minced
¼ cup olive oil

1. Select the "AIR FRY" function of Ninja Foodi digital air fry oven, set the temperature to 400 degrees F/ 200 degrees C and set the time to 5 minutes. Press the Start/Pause button and begin preheating. 2. Toss the squid, salt, black pepper, and paprika in a lightly greased air fryer cooking basket. Cook your squid for 5 minutes, tossing the basket halfway through the cooking time. Bon appétit!
Per Serving: Calories 311; Fat 16.3g; Sodium 257mg; Carbs 8.3g; Fiber 0.6g; Sugar 0.7g; Protein 31.3g

Simple Beer-Battered Calamari

Prep time: 5 minutes | Cook time: 10 minutes | Serves: 4

2 cups all-purpose flour
1 cup beer
Sea salt
Ground black pepper, to taste

2 teaspoons garlic powder
1 teaspoon dried parsley flakes
1 tablespoon olive oil
1 pound calamari rings

1. Select the "AIR FRY" function of Ninja Foodi digital air fry oven, set the temperature to 400 degrees F/ 200 degrees C and set the time to 5 minutes. Press the Start/Pause button and begin preheating. 2. In a bowl, combine the flour, beer, spices, and olive oil. Mix to combine well. 3. Now, dip your calamari into the flour mixture to coat. Cook your calamari for 5 minutes, turning them over halfway through the cooking time. Bon appétit!
Per Serving: Calories 397; Fat 5.5g; Sodium 256mg; Carbs 55.5g; Fiber 2g; Sugar 0.7g; Protein 24.8g

Cod Patties

Prep time: 5 minutes | Cook time: 15 minutes | Serves: 4

1 pound cod fish, boneless and chopped
½ cup breadcrumbs
2 medium eggs
1 teaspoon Dijon mustard
2 garlic cloves, minced

Sea salt
Ground black pepper, to taste
½ teaspoon onion powder
1 teaspoon hot paprika
1 tablespoon olive oil
4 hamburger buns

1. Select the "AIR FRY" function of Ninja Foodi digital air fry oven, set the temperature to 400 degrees F/ 200 degrees C and set the time to 15 minutes. Press the Start/Pause button and begin preheating. Mix all ingredients except for the hamburger buns in a bowl. 2. Shape into four patties and place in a lightly oiled air fryer cooking basket. Cook the fish patties for about 14 minutes, turning them over halfway through the cooking time. Serve on hamburger buns and enjoy!
Per Serving: Calories 308; Fat 10.2g; Sodium 456mg; Carbs 23.5g; Fiber 1.5g; Sugar 3.3g; Protein 27.3g

Sweet Balsamic Glazed Salmon

Prep time: 5 minutes | Cook time: 10 minutes | Serves: 4

4 (6-ounce) fillets of salmon
salt and freshly ground black pepper
vegetable oil

¼ cup pure maple syrup
3 tablespoons balsamic vinegar
1 teaspoon Dijon mustard

1. Select the "AIR ROAST" function of Ninja Foodi digital air fry oven, set the temperature to 400 degrees F/ 200 degrees C and set the time to 10 minutes. Press the Start/Pause button and begin preheating. 2. Season the salmon well with salt and freshly ground black pepper. Grease the basket with oil and place the salmon fillets inside. Air-fry the salmon for 5 minutes. 3. While the salmon is air-frying, combine the maple syrup, balsamic vinegar and Dijon mustard in a small saucepan over medium heat and stir to blend well. Let the mixture simmer while the fish is cooking. It should start to thicken slightly, but keep your eye on it so it doesn't burn. 4. Brush the glaze on the salmon fillets and air-fry for an additional 5 minutes. The salmon should feel firm to the touch when finished and the glaze should be nicely browned on top. Brush a little more glaze on top before removing and serving with rice and vegetables, or a nice green salad.
Per Serving: Calories 334; Fat 29.1g; Sodium 177mg; Carbs 10.8g; Fiber 5.2g; Sugar 5g; Protein 13.4g

Crispy Shrimp with Sweet Chili Mayo

Prep time: 5 minutes | Cook time: 15 minutes | Serves: 4

Sweet Chili Mayo
3 tablespoons mayonnaise
3 tablespoons Thai sweet chili
Shrimp
⅔ cup sweetened shredded
coconut
⅔ cup panko bread crumbs,
regular or gluten-free
Kosher salt
2 tablespoons all-purpose or

sauce
1 tablespoon Sriracha sauce

gluten-free flour
2 large eggs
24 extra-jumbo shrimp (about 1
pound), peeled and deveined
Olive oil spray

1. For the sweet chili mayo: In a medium bowl, combine the mayonnaise, Thai sweet chili sauce, and Sriracha and mix well. For the shrimp: In a medium bowl, combine the coconut, panko, and ¼ teaspoon salt. Place the flour in a shallow bowl. Whisk the eggs in another shallow bowl. Season the shrimp with ⅛ teaspoon salt. Dip the shrimp in the flour, shaking off any excess, then into the egg. Coat in the coconut-panko mixture, gently pressing to adhere, then transfer to a large plate. Spray both sides of the shrimp with oil. Select the "AIR FRY" function of Ninja Foodi digital air fry oven, set the temperature to 360 degrees F/ 180 degrees C and set the time to 8 minutes. Press the Start/Pause button and begin preheating. Working in batches, arrange a single layer of the shrimp in the air fryer basket. Cook for about 8 minutes, flipping halfway, until the crust is golden brown and the shrimp are cooked through. Serve with the sweet chili mayo for dipping.
Per Serving: Calories 355; Fat 16g; Sodium 750mg; Carbs 25g; Fiber 1g; Sugar 13g; Protein 25g

Crispy Salmon Strips

Prep time: 10 minutes | Cook time: 15 minutes | Serves: 4

1 egg, beaten
½ cup all-purpose flour
Sea salt
Ground black pepper, to taste

1 teaspoon hot paprika
½ cup seasoned breadcrumbs
1 tablespoon olive oil
1 pound salmon strips

1. Select the "AIR FRY" function of Ninja Foodi digital air fry oven, set the temperature to 400 degrees F/ 200 degrees C and set the time to 10 minutes. Press the Start/Pause button and begin preheating. 2. In a mixing bowl, thoroughly combine the egg, flour, and spices. In a separate bowl, thoroughly combine the breadcrumbs and olive oil. Mix to combine well. 3. Now, dip the salmon strips into the flour mixture to coat; roll the fish pieces over the breadcrumb until well coated on all sides. Cook the salmon strips for 10 minutes, turning them over halfway through the cooking time. Bon appétit!
Per Serving: Calories 354; Fat 23.3g; Sodium 236mg; Carbs 23.3g; Fiber 3.1g; Sugar 2.5g; Protein 27.3g

Classic Fish and Chips

Prep time: 5 minutes | Cook time: 10 minutes | Serves: 2

½ cup flour
½ teaspoon paprika
¼ teaspoon ground white pepper
1 egg
¼ cup mayonnaise
2 cups salt & vinegar kettle

cooked potato chips, coarsely
crushed
12 ounces cod
tartar sauce
lemon wedges

1. Set up a dredging station. Combine the flour along with paprika and pepper in a shallow dish. Combine the egg and mayonnaise in a second shallow dish. Place the crushed potato chips in a third shallow dish. 2. Cut the cod into 6 pieces. Dredge in the flour, then dip it into the egg mixture and then place it into the crushed potato chips. Make sure all sides of the fish are covered and pat the chips gently onto the fish so they stick well. 3. Select the "AIR ROAST" function of Ninja Foodi digital air fry oven, set the temperature to 370 degrees F/ 185 degrees C and set the time to 10 minutes. Press the Start/Pause button and begin preheating. 4. Place the coated fish fillets into the air fry basket. 5. Air-fry for 10 minutes, gently turning the fish over halfway through the cooking time. 6. Place the fish to a platter and serve with tartar sauce and lemon wedges.
Per Serving: Calories 221; Fat 4g; Sodium 159mg; Carbs 3g; Fiber 1g; Sugar 2g; Protein 3g

Prawns in Sherry Wine

Prep time: 10 minutes | Cook time: 10 minutes | Serves: 4

1 ½ pounds tiger prawns, peeled
and deveined
1 tablespoon coconut oil
1 teaspoon garlic, crushed
1 teaspoon Old Bay seasoning

Coarse sea salt
Ground black pepper, to taste
¼ cup sherry wine
1 teaspoon Dijon mustard

1. Select the "AIR FRY" function of Ninja Foodi digital air fry oven, set the temperature to 400 degrees F/ 200 degrees C and set the time to 15 minutes. Press the Start/Pause button and begin preheating. 2. Toss all in a lightly greased air fryer cooking basket. Cook the prawns for 9 minutes, tossing the basket halfway through the cooking time. Bon appétit!
Per Serving: Calories 182; Fat 1.6g; Sodium 258mg; Carbs 1.6g; Fiber 0.3g; Sugar 0.7g; Protein 34.5g

Black Cod with veggies

Prep time: 10 minutes | Cook time: 15 minutes | Serves: 2

2 (6- to 8-ounce) fillets of black
cod (or sablefish)
salt and freshly ground black
pepper
olive oil
1 cup grapes, halved
1 small bulb fennel, sliced ¼-inch

thick
½ cup pecans
3 cups shredded kale
2 teaspoons white balsamic
vinegar
2 tablespoons extra virgin olive
oil

1. Select the "AIR FRY" function of Ninja Foodi digital air fry oven, set the temperature to 400 degrees F/ 200 degrees C and set the time to 15 minutes. Press the Start/Pause button and begin preheating. 2. Season the cod fillets with salt and pepper and drizzle, brush or spray a little olive oil on top. Place the fish, presentation side up, into the air fryer basket. Air-fry for 10 minutes. 3. When the fish cooked, place in a plate and cover with foil to rest. 4. Toss the grapes, fennel and pecans in a bowl with a drizzle of olive oil and season with salt and pepper. Add the grapes, fennel and pecans to the air fryer basket and air-fry for 5 minutes, shaking the basket once during the cooking time. 5. Place the veggies in bowl. Add the balsamic vinegar along with olive oil, spice with salt and pepper and serve alongside the cooked fish.
Per Serving: Calories 354; Fat 7.9g; Sodium 704mg; Carbs 6g; Fiber 3.6g; Sugar 6g; Protein 18g

Asian Barramundi with tangy Mustard

Prep time: 10 minutes | Cook time: 15 minutes | Serves: 4

1 pound Barramundi fillets
Sea salt and ground Szechuan
pepper, to taste
1 tablespoon sesame oil

2 tablespoons rice wine vinegar
½ cup seasoned breadcrumbs
1 tablespoon grain mustard

1. Select the "AIR FRY" function of Ninja Foodi digital air fry oven, set the temperature to 400 degrees F/ 200 degrees C and set the time to 15 minutes. Press the Start/Pause button and begin preheating. 2. Toss the fish with the remaining ingredients; place them in a lightly oiled Air Fryer cooking basket. Cook the fish for about 12 minutes, turning them over halfway through the cooking time. Bon appétit!
Per Serving: Calories 194; Fat 4.3g; Sodium 369mg; Carbs 11.2g; Fiber 2.6g; Sugar 2.4g; Protein 22.6g

Lemon and herbed Sea bass

Prep time: 10 minutes | Cook time: 15 minutes | Serves: 3

8 oz sea bass, trimmed, peeled
4 lemon slices
1 tablespoon thyme

2 teaspoons sesame oil
1 teaspoon salt

1. Fill the sea bass with lemon slices and rub with thyme, salt, and sesame oil. 2. Then Select the "AIR FRY" function of Ninja Foodi digital air fry oven, set the temperature to 385 degrees F/ 195 degrees C and set the time to 15 minutes. Press the Start/Pause button and begin preheating. Put the fish in the air fryer basket. Cook it for 12 minutes. 3. Then flip the fish on another side and cook it for 3 minutes more.
Per Serving: Calories 216; Fat 7.9g; Sodium 147mg; Carbs 6.3g; Fiber 0.6g; Sugar 0.6g; Protein 0.2g

Spicy Fish Tacos with Sriracha Slaw

Prep time: 5 minutes | Cook time: 5 minutes | Serves: 2

Sriracha Slaw:

½ cup mayonnaise	¼ cup shredded carrots
2 tablespoons rice vinegar	2 scallions, chopped
1 teaspoon sugar	salt and freshly ground black
2 tablespoons sriracha chili sauce	pepper
5 cups shredded green cabbage	

Tacos:

½ cup flour	1 cup breadcrumbs
1 teaspoon chili powder	1 pound mahi-mahi or snapper
½ teaspoon ground cumin	fillets
1 teaspoon salt	1 tablespoon canola or vegetable
freshly ground black pepper	oil
½ teaspoon baking powder	6 (6-inch) flour tortillas
1 egg, beaten	1 lime, cut into wedges
¼ cup milk	

1. Combine the mayonnaise along with rice vinegar, sugar, and sriracha sauce in a bowl. Mix well and add the cabbage, carrots, and chopped scallions. Toss until well coated with the dressing and spice with salt and pepper. Chilled the slaw till serving. 2. Combine the flour with chili powder, cumin, salt, pepper and baking powder. Add the egg with milk and mix until the batter is smooth. Place the breadcrumbs in a shallow dish. 3. Cut the fish into 1-inch sticks. Dip the fish into the prepared batter, coating all sides. 4. Select the "AIR FRY" function of Ninja Foodi digital air fry oven, set the temperature to 400 degrees F/ 200 degrees C and set the time to 5 minutes. Press the Start/Pause button and begin preheating. 5. Spray the fish sticks with oil. Grease the air fryer basket with oil and Place it to the basket. 6. Air-fry the fish for 3 minutes. Turn over and air-fry for an additional 2 minutes. 7. Warm the tortilla shells in a skillet with a little oil. Fold the tortillas in half. 8. Place two pieces of the fish in tortilla shell and top with the chilled sriracha slaw. enjoy.
Per Serving: Calories 180; Fat 13.7g; Sodium 147mg; Carbs 9.6g; Fiber 3g; Sugar 6g; Protein 5.8g

Tropical Flounder

Prep time: 5 minutes | Cook time: 12 minutes | Serves: 2

2 flounder fillets, boneless	A pinch of salt and black pepper
2 garlic cloves, minced	½ teaspoon stevia
2 teaspoons coconut aminos	2 tablespoons olive oil
2 tablespoons lemon juice	

1. Select the "AIR FRY" function of Ninja Foodi digital air fry oven, set the temperature to 390 degrees F/ 200 degrees C and set the time to 12 minutes. Press the Start/Pause button and begin preheating. 2. In a pan, mix all the ingredients, toss, introduce in the fryer and cook for 12 minutes. Divide into bowls and serve.
Per Serving: Calories 251; Fat 13g; Sodium 225mg; Carbs 5g; Fiber 3g; Sugar 2g; Protein 10g

Tangy Salmon Burgers

Prep time: 5 minutes | Cook time: 8 minutes | Serves: 4

2 (6-ounce) fillets of salmon, finely chopped by hand or in a food processor	2 tablespoons chopped fresh dill weed
1 cup fine breadcrumbs	1 teaspoon salt
1 teaspoon freshly grated lemon zest	freshly ground black pepper
	2 eggs, lightly beaten
	4 brioche or hamburger buns

lettuce, tomato, red onion, avocado, mayonnaise or mustard, to serve
1. Select the "AIR FRY" function of Ninja Foodi digital air fry oven, set the temperature to 400 degrees F/ 200 degrees C and set the time to 10 minutes. Press the Start/Pause button and begin preheating. 2. Combine all the ingredients in a bowl. Mix together well and divide into four balls. Flatten the balls into patties, making an indentation in the center of each patty with your thumb and flattening the sides of the burgers so that they fit nicely into the air fryer basket. 3. Transfer the burgers to the air fryer basket and air-fry for 4 minutes. Flip the burgers over and air-fry for another 3 to 4 minutes, until nicely browned and firm to the touch. 4. Serve on soft brioche buns with your choice of topping lettuce, tomato, red onion, avocado, mayonnaise or mustard.
Per Serving: Calories 192; Fat 4g; Sodium 322mg; Carbs 5g; Fiber 2g; Sugar 3g; Protein 7g

Flounder with Mushrooms

Prep time: 5 minutes | Cook time: 15 minutes | Serves: 4

4 flounder fillets, boneless	2 teaspoons olive oil
2 tablespoons coconut aminos	2 green onions, chopped
A pinch of salt and black pepper	2 cups mushrooms, sliced
1 and ½ teaspoons ginger, grated	

1. Select the "AIR FRY" function of Ninja Foodi digital air fry oven, set the temperature to 390 degrees F/ 200 degrees C and set the time to 10 minutes. Press the Start/Pause button and begin preheating. 2. Heat a pan that fits your air fryer with the oil over medium-high heat, add the mushrooms and all the other ingredients except the fish, toss and sauté for 5 minutes. 3. Add the fish, toss gently, introduce the pan in the fryer and cook for 10 minutes. Divide between plates and serve.
Per Serving: Calories 271; Fat 12g; Sodium 354mg; Carbs 6g; Fiber 4g; Sugar 2g; Protein 11g

Nutty Shrimp with Amaretto Glaze

Prep time: 10 minutes | Cook time: 40-50 minutes | Serves: 10

1 cup flour	oil
½ teaspoon baking powder	2 cups sliced almonds
1 teaspoon salt	2 pounds large shrimp (about
2 eggs, beaten	32 to 40 shrimp), peeled and
½ cup milk	deveined, tails left on
2 tablespoons olive or vegetable	2 cups amaretto liqueur

1. Combine the flour, baking powder and salt in a large bowl. Add the eggs, milk and oil and stir until it forms a smooth batter. Coarsely crush the sliced almonds into a second shallow dish with your hands. 2. Dry the shrimp well with paper towels. Dip the shrimp into the batter and shake off any excess batter, leaving just enough to lightly coat the shrimp. Transfer the shrimp to the dish with the almonds and coat completely. Place the coated shrimp on a plate or baking sheet and when all the shrimp have been coated, freeze the shrimp for 1 hour, or as long as a week before air-frying. 3. Select the "AIR FRY" function of Ninja Foodi digital air fry oven, set the temperature to 400 degrees F/ 200 degrees C and set the time to 10 minutes. Press the Start/Pause button and begin preheating. 4. Transfer 8 frozen shrimp at a time to the air fryer basket. Air-fry for 6 minutes. Turn the shrimp over and air-fry for an additional 4 minutes. Repeat with the remaining shrimp. 5. While the shrimp are cooking, bring the Amaretto to a boil in a small saucepan on the stovetop. Lower the heat and simmer until it has reduced and thickened into a glaze – about 10 minutes. 6. Remove the shrimp from the air fryer and brush both sides with the warm amaretto glaze. Serve warm.
Per Serving: Calories 224; Fat 16.8g; Sodium 211mg; Carbs 7.7g; Fiber 2.3g; Sugar 5g; Protein 11.4g

Crispy Shrimp Empanadas

Prep time: 10 minutes | Cook time: 8 minutes | Serves: 5

½ pound peeled and deveined raw shrimp, chopped	½ tablespoon fresh lime juice
¼ cup chopped red onion	¼ teaspoon sweet paprika
1 scallion, chopped	⅛ teaspoon kosher salt
2 garlic cloves, minced	⅛ teaspoon crushed red pepper
2 tablespoons minced red bell pepper	flakes (optional)
2 tablespoons chopped fresh cilantro	1 large egg, beaten
	10 frozen Goya Empanada Discos (for baking), thawed
	Cooking spray

1. In a medium bowl, combine the shrimp, red onion, scallion, garlic, bell pepper, cilantro, lime juice, paprika, salt, and pepper flakes (if using). 2. In a bowl, beat the egg until smooth. Place an empanada disc on a work surface and put 2 tablespoons of the shrimp mixture in the center. Brush the outer edges of the disc with the egg wash. 3. Fold the disc over and gently press the edges to seal. Use a fork and press around the edges to crimp and seal completely. Brush the tops of the empanadas with the egg wash. 4. Select the "AIR FRY" function of Ninja Foodi digital air fry oven, set the temperature to 380 degrees F/ 195 degrees C and set the time to 8 minutes. Press the Start/Pause button and begin preheating. Spray the bottom of the air fryer basket with cooking spray to prevent sticking. Cook for about 8 minutes, flipping halfway, until golden brown and crispy. Serve hot.
Per Serving: Calories 262; Fat 11g; Sodium 482mg; Carbs 26g; Fiber 1.5g; Sugar 1g; Protein 13g

Sea Bass with Roast Potatoes and Caper Aïoli

Prep time: 5 minutes | Cook time: 10 minutes | Serves: 2

2 (6- to 8-ounce) fillets of sea bass
salt and freshly ground black pepper
¼ cup mayonnaise
2 teaspoons finely chopped lemon zest
1 teaspoon chopped fresh thyme
2 fingerling potatoes, very thinly

sliced into rounds
olive oil
½ clove garlic, crushed into a paste
1 tablespoon capers, drained and rinsed
1 tablespoon olive oil
1 teaspoon lemon juice, to taste

1. Select the "AIR FRY" function of Ninja Foodi digital air fry oven, set the temperature to 400 degrees F/ 200 degrees C and set the time to 10 minutes. Press the Start/Pause button and begin preheating. 2. Spice the fish well with salt and freshly ground black pepper. Mix the mayonnaise, lemon zest and thyme in a bowl. Spread the mayonnaise mixture on both fillets. Start layering rows of potato slices onto the fish fillets to simulate the fish scales. The second row should overlap the first row slightly. Dabbing a little more mayonnaise along the upper edge of the row of potatoes where the next row overlaps will help the potato slices stick. Press the potatoes onto the fish to secure them well and season again with salt. Brush or spray the potato layer with olive oil. 3. Place the fish in air fryer and air-fry for 8 to 10 minutes. 4. While the fish is cooking, add the garlic, capers, olive oil and lemon juice to the remaining mayonnaise mixture to make the caper aïoli. 5. Serve the fish warm with a dollop of the aïoli on top or on the side.
Per Serving: Calories 354; Fat 7.9g; Sodium 704mg; Carbs 6g; Fiber 3.6g; Sugar 6g; Protein 18g

Spicy Fried Shrimp

Prep time: 5 minutes | Cook time: 6 minutes | Serves: 2

12 ounces uncooked medium shrimp, peeled and deveined
1 teaspoon cayenne pepper
1 teaspoon Old Bay seasoning

½ teaspoon smoked paprika
2 tablespoons olive oil
1 teaspoon salt

1. Select the "AIR FRY" function of Ninja Foodi digital air fry oven, set the temperature to 390 degrees F/ 200 degrees C and set the time to 6 minutes. Press the Start/Pause button and begin preheating. 2. Meanwhile, in a medium mixing bowl, combine the shrimp, cayenne pepper, Old Bay, paprika, olive oil, and salt. Toss the shrimp in the oil and spices until the shrimp is thoroughly coated with both. 3. Place them in the air fryer basket. Set the timer and steam for 3 minutes. 4. Remove the drawer and shake, so the shrimp redistribute in the basket for even cooking. 5. Reset the timer and steam for another 3 minutes. 6. Check that the shrimp are done. When they are cooked through, the flesh will be opaque. Add additional time if needed. 7. Plate, serve, and enjoy!
Per Serving: Calories 286; Fat 16g; Sodium 1868mg; Carbs 1g; Fiber 0g; Sugar 0g; Protein 37g

Homemade Crab Cake Sliders

Prep time: 5 minutes | Cook time: 10 minutes | Serves: 4

1 pound crabmeat, shredded
¼ cup bread crumbs
2 teaspoons dried parsley
1 teaspoon salt
½ teaspoon freshly ground black pepper

1 large egg
2 tablespoons mayonnaise
1 teaspoon dry mustard
4 slider buns
Sliced tomato, lettuce leaves, and rémoulade sauce, for topping

1. Select the "AIR FRY" function of Ninja Foodi digital air fry oven, set the temperature to 400 degrees F/ 200 degrees C and set the time to 5 minutes. Press the Start/Pause button and begin preheating. Spray the air fryer basket with olive oil or spray an air fryer–size baking sheet with olive oil or cooking spray. 2. In a medium mixing bowl, combine the crabmeat, bread crumbs, parsley, salt, pepper, egg, mayonnaise, and dry mustard. Mix well. 3. Form the crab mixture into 4 equal patties. 4. Place the crab cakes directly into the greased air fryer basket, or on the greased baking sheet set into the air fryer basket. 5. Flip the crab cakes. Reset the timer and fry the crab cakes for 5 minutes more. 6. Serve on slider buns with sliced tomato, lettuce, and rémoulade sauce.
Per Serving: Calories 294; Fat 11g; Sodium 1766mg; Carbs 20g; Fiber 1g; Sugar 3g; Protein 27g

Crab Cake with Cajun Mayo

Prep time: 5 minutes | Cook time: 5 minutes | Serves: 4

Crab Cakes
½ cup panko bread crumbs, regular or gluten-free
1 large egg, beaten
1 large egg white
1 tablespoon mayonnaise
1 teaspoon Dijon mustard
¼ cup minced fresh parsley
Cajun Mayo
¼ cup mayonnaise
1 tablespoon minced dill pickle
For Serving
4 Boston lettuce leaves
4 whole wheat potato buns or

1 tablespoon fresh lemon juice
½ teaspoon Old Bay seasoning
⅛ teaspoon sweet paprika
⅛ teaspoon kosher salt
Freshly ground black pepper
10 ounces lump crabmeat
Olive oil spray

1 teaspoon fresh lemon juice
¾ teaspoon Cajun seasoning

gluten-free buns

1. For the crab cakes: In a large bowl, combine the panko, whole egg, egg white, mayonnaise, mustard, parsley, lemon juice, Old Bay, paprika, salt, and pepper to taste and mix well. Fold in the crabmeat. Gently shape into 4 round patties, about ½ cup each, ¾ inch thick. Spray both sides with oil. 2. Select the "AIR FRY" function of Ninja Foodi digital air fry oven, set the temperature to 370 degrees F/ 185 degrees C and set the time to 10 minutes. Press the Start/Pause button and begin preheating. Cook about 10 minutes, flipping halfway, until the edges are golden. 3. Meanwhile, for the Cajun mayo: In a small bowl, combine the mayonnaise, pickle, lemon juice, and Cajun seasoning. 4. Place a lettuce on each bun bottom and top with a crab cake and a generous tablespoon of Cajun mayonnaise. Add the bun top and serve.
Per Serving: Calories 354; Fat 18.5g; Sodium 914mg; Carbs 25g; Fiber 3.5g; Sugar 5g; Protein 25g

Fried Butter Lobster Tails

Prep time: 5 minutes | Cook time: 8 minutes | Serves: 2

2 tablespoons unsalted butter, melted
1 tablespoon minced garlic
1 teaspoon salt

1 tablespoon minced fresh chives
2 (4- to 6-ounce) frozen lobster tails

1. In a small mixing bowl, combine the butter, garlic, salt, and chives. 2. Butterfly the lobster tail: Starting at the meaty end of the tail, use kitchen shears to cut down the center of the top shell. Stop when you reach the fanned, wide part of the tail. Carefully spread apart the meat and the shell along the cut line, but keep the meat attached where it connects to the wide part of the tail. Use your hand to gently disconnect the meat from the bottom of the shell. Lift the meat up and out of the shell. Close the shell under the meat, so the meat rests on top of the shell. 3. Place the lobster in the air fryer basket and generously brush the butter mixture over the meat. 4. Select the "AIR FRY" function of Ninja Foodi digital air fry oven, set the temperature to 380 degrees F/ 195 degrees C and set the time to 8 minutes. Press the Start/Pause button and begin preheating. 5. Open the air fryer and rotate the lobster tails. Brush them with more of the butter mixture. 6. Reset the timer and steam for 4 minutes more. The lobster is done when the meat is opaque.
Per Serving: Calories 255; Fat 13g; Sodium 1453mg; Carbs 2g; Fiber 0g; Sugar 0g; Protein 32g

Bacon Wrapped Sea Scallops

Prep time: 5 minutes | Cook time: 10 minutes | Serves: 4

16 sea scallops
8 slices bacon, cut in half
8 toothpicks

Salt
Freshly ground black pepper

1. Using a paper towel, pat dry the scallops. 2. Wrap each scallop with a half slice of bacon. Secure the bacon with a toothpick. 3. Place the scallops into the air fryer in a single layer. 4. Spray the scallops with olive oil, and season them with salt and pepper. 5. Select the "AIR FRY" function of Ninja Foodi digital air fry oven, set the temperature to 370 degrees F/ 185 degrees C and set the time to 5 minutes. Press the Start/Pause button and begin preheating. 6. Flip the scallops. 7. Reset your timer and cook the scallops for 5 minutes more. 8. Using tongs, remove the scallops from the air fryer basket. Plate, serve, and enjoy!
Per Serving: Calories 311; Fat 17g; Sodium 1110mg; Carbs 3g; Fiber 0g; Sugar 0g; Protein 34g

Spicy Paprika Prawns

Prep time: 15 minutes | Cook time: 5 minutes | Serves: 5

3-pound prawns, peeled
1 tablespoon ground turmeric
1 teaspoon smoked paprika

1 tablespoon coconut milk
1 teaspoon avocado oil
½ teaspoon salt

1. Put the prawns in the bowl and sprinkle them with ground turmeric, smoked paprika, and salt. Then add coconut milk and leave them for 10 minutes to marinate. 2. Meanwhile, Select the "AIR FRY" function of Ninja Foodi digital air fry oven, set the temperature to 400 degrees F/ 200 degrees C and set the time to 5 minutes. Press the Start/Pause button and begin preheating. Put the marinated prawns in the air fryer basket and sprinkle with avocado oil. Cook the prawns for 3 minutes. 3. Then shake them well and cook for 2 minutes more.
Per Serving: Calories 338; Fat 5.6g; Sodium 239mg; Carbs 5.5g; Fiber 0.6g; Sugar 0.6g; Protein 62.2g

Lemon Cajun Cod

Prep time: 5 minutes | Cook time: 12 minutes | Serves: 12

2 (8-ounce) cod fillets, cut to fit into the air fryer basket
1 tablespoon Cajun seasoning
½ teaspoon lemon pepper
1 teaspoon salt

½ teaspoon freshly ground black pepper
2 tablespoons unsalted butter, melted
1 lemon, cut into 4 wedges

1. Spray the air fryer basket with olive oil. 2. Place the fillets on a plate. 3. In a small mixing bowl, combine the Cajun seasoning, lemon pepper, salt, and pepper. 4. Rub the seasoning mix onto the fish. 5. Place the cod into the greased air fryer basket. Brush the top of each fillet with melted butter. 6. Select the "BAKE" function of Ninja Foodi digital air fry oven, set the temperature to 360 degrees F/ 180 degrees C and set the time to 12 minutes. Press the Start/Pause button and begin preheating. 7.After 6 minutes, open up your air fryer drawer and flip the fish. Brush the top of each fillet with more melted butter. 8. Squeeze fresh lemon juice over the fillets.
Per Serving: Calories 283; Fat 14g; Sodium 1460mg; Carbs 0g; Fiber 0g; Sugar 0g; Protein 40g

Salmon Patties

Prep time: 5 minutes | Cook time: 10 minutes | Serves: 4

1 (14.75-ounce) can wild salmon, drained
1 large egg
¼ cup diced onion
½ cup bread crumbs

1 teaspoon dried dill
½ teaspoon freshly ground black pepper
1 teaspoon salt
1 teaspoon Old Bay seasoning

1. Spray the air fryer basket with olive oil. 2. Put the salmon in a medium bowl and remove any bones or skin. 3. Add the egg, onion, bread crumbs, dill, pepper, salt, and Old Bay seasoning and mix well. 4. Form the salmon mixture into 4 equal patties. 5. Place the patties in the greased air fryer basket. 6. Select the "AIR FRY" function of Ninja Foodi digital air fry oven, set the temperature to 370 degrees F/ 185 degrees C and set the time to 10 minutes. Press the Start/Pause button and begin preheating. 7. Cook the patties for 5 minutes, flip the patties. Reset the timer and grill the patties for 5 minutes more. 8. Plate, serve, and enjoy!
Per Serving: Calories 239; Fat 9g; Sodium 901mg; Carbs 11g; Fiber 1g; Sugar 1g; Protein 27g

Easy French Clams

Prep time: 5 minutes | Cook time: 3 minutes | Serves: 5

2-pounds clams, raw, shells removed
1 tablespoon Herbs de Provence

1 tablespoon sesame oil
1 garlic clove, diced

1. Put the clams in the bowl and sprinkle with Herbs de Provence, sesame oil, and diced garlic. Shake the seafood well. 2. Select the "AIR FRY" function of Ninja Foodi digital air fry oven, set the temperature to 390 degrees F/ 200 degrees C and set the time to 5 minutes. Press the Start/Pause button and begin preheating. Put the clams in the air fryer and cook them for 3 minutes. 3. When the clams are cooked, shake them well and transfer to the serving plates.
Per Serving: Calories 45; Fat 3g; Sodium 100mg; Carbs 0.9g; Fiber 0g; Sugar 0g; Protein 3.5g

Lemony Shrimp and Zucchini

Prep time: 5 minutes | Cook time: 8 minutes | Serves: 4

1¼ pounds peeled and deveined extra-large raw shrimp
2 medium zucchini (about 8 ounces each), halved lengthwise and cut into ½-inch-thick slices
1½ tablespoons olive oil
½ teaspoon garlic salt

1½ teaspoons dried oregano
⅛ teaspoon crushed red pepper flakes (optional)
Juice of ½ lemon
1 tablespoon chopped fresh mint
1 tablespoon chopped fresh dill

1. Select the "AIR FRY" function of Ninja Foodi digital air fry oven, set the temperature to 350 degrees F/ 175 degrees C and set the time to 8 minutes. Press the Start/Pause button and begin preheating. 2. In a bowl, add the shrimp, zucchini, oil, garlic salt, oregano, and pepper flakes (if using) and toss to coat. Cook, shaking the basket halfway, until the zucchini is golden and the shrimp are cooked through, 7 to 8 minutes. 3. Transfer to dish and tent with foil while you cook the remaining shrimp and zucchini. Top with the lemon juice, mint, and dill and serve.
Per Serving: Calories 194; Fat 6g; Sodium 481mg; Carbs 6g; Fiber 1.5g; Sugar 3g; Protein 27g

Tasty Salmon with Garlic Butter Sauce

Prep time: 5 minutes | Cook time: 10 minutes | Serves: 4

3 tablespoons unsalted butter
1 garlic clove, minced, or ½ teaspoon garlic powder
1 teaspoon salt
2 tablespoons freshly squeezed lemon juice

1 tablespoon minced fresh parsley
1 teaspoon minced fresh dill
1 teaspoon salt
½ teaspoon freshly ground black pepper
4 (4-ounce) salmon fillets

1. Line the air fryer basket with parchment paper. 2. In a small microwave-safe mixing bowl, combine the butter, garlic, salt, lemon juice, parsley, dill, salt, and pepper. 3. Place the bowl in the microwave and cook on low heat until the butter is completely melted, about 45 seconds. 4. Meanwhile, place the salmon fillets in the parchment-lined air fryer basket. 5. Spoon the sauce over the salmon. 6. Select the "BAKE" function of Ninja Foodi digital air fry oven, set the temperature to 400 degrees F/ 200 degrees C and set the time to 8 minutes. Press the Start/Pause button and begin preheating. Since you don't want to overcook the salmon, begin checking for doneness at about 8 minutes. Salmon is done when the flesh is opaque and flakes easily when tested with a fork.
Per Serving: Calories 346; Fat 22g; Sodium 1300mg; Carbs 1g; Fiber 0g; Sugar 0g; Protein 32g

Shrimp Tacos with Cilantro-Lime Slaw

Prep time: 5 minutes | Cook time: 6 minutes | Serves: 4

Spicy Mayo
3 tablespoons mayonnaise
1 tablespoon Louisiana-style hot

pepper sauce

Cilantro-Lime Slaw
2 cups shredded green cabbage
½ small red onion, thinly sliced
1 small jalapeño, thinly sliced
2 tablespoons chopped fresh

cilantro
Juice of 1 lime
¼ teaspoon kosher salt

Shrimp
1 large egg, beaten
1 cup crushed tortilla chips (4 ounces)
24 jumbo shrimp (about 1 pound),

peeled and deveined
⅛ teaspoon kosher salt
Olive oil spray
8 corn tortillas, for serving

1. For the spicy mayo: In a bowl, mix together the mayonnaise and hot pepper sauce. 2. For the cilantro-lime slaw: In a large bowl, toss together the cabbage, onion, jalapeño, cilantro, lime juice, and salt to combine. Cover and refrigerate to chill. 3. For the shrimp: Place the egg in a shallow bowl and the crushed tortilla chips in another. Season the shrimp with the salt. Dip in the egg, then in the crumbs, pressing gently to adhere. Spray both sides with oil. 4. Select the "AIR FRY" function of Ninja Foodi digital air fry oven, set the temperature to 360 degrees F/ 180 degrees C and set the time to 6 minutes. Press the Start/Pause button and begin preheating. Cook for 6 minutes, flipping halfway, until golden and cooked through in the center. 5. Place 2 tortillas on plate and top each with 3 shrimp. Top each taco with ¼ cup slaw, then drizzle with spicy mayo.
Per Serving: Calories 440; Fat 17g; Sodium 590mg; Carbs 44g; Fiber 6g; Sugar 3g; Protein 27g

Salmon Burgers with Lemon-Caper Rémoulade

Prep time: 5 minutes | Cook time: 12 minutes | Serves: 5

Lemon-Caper Rémoulade
½ cup mayonnaise
2 tablespoons drained capers, minced
2 tablespoons chopped fresh parsley
2 teaspoons fresh lemon juice

Salmon Patties
1 pound wild salmon fillet, skinned and pin bones removed
6 tablespoons panko bread crumbs, regular or gluten-free
¼ cup minced red onion plus ¼ cup slivered for assembly
1 garlic clove, minced
1 large egg, lightly beaten
1 tablespoon Dijon mustard
1 teaspoon fresh lemon juice
1 tablespoon chopped fresh parsley
½ teaspoon kosher salt

For Serving
5 whole wheat potato buns or gluten-free buns
10 butter lettuce leaves

1. For the lemon-caper rémoulade: In a small bowl, combine the mayonnaise, capers, parsley, and lemon juice and mix well. 2. For the salmon patties: Cut off a 4-ounce piece of the salmon and transfer to a food processor. Pulse until it becomes pasty. With a sharp knife, chop the remaining salmon into small cubes. 3. In a medium bowl, combine the chopped and processed salmon with the panko, minced red onion, garlic, egg, mustard, lemon juice, parsley, and salt. Toss gently to combine. 4. Form the mixture into 5 patties about ¾ inch thick. Refrigerate for at least 30 minutes. 5. Select the "AIR FRY" function of Ninja Foodi digital air fry oven, set the temperature to 400 degrees F/ 200 degrees C and set the time to 12 minutes. Press the Start/Pause button and begin preheating. Cook for about 12 minutes, gently flipping halfway, until golden and cooked through. 6. To serve: Transfer each patty to a bun. Top each with 2 lettuce leaves, 2 tablespoons of the rémoulade, and the slivered red onions.
Per Serving: Calories 436; Fat 26.5g; Sodium 616mg; Carbs 24g; Fiber 4g; Sugar 5g; Protein 28g

Blackened Salmon with Salsa

Prep time: 5 minutes | Cook time: 7 minutes | Serves: 4

Salmon
1 tablespoon sweet paprika
½ teaspoon cayenne pepper
1 teaspoon garlic powder
1 teaspoon dried oregano
1 teaspoon dried thyme
¾ teaspoon kosher salt
⅛ teaspoon freshly ground black pepper
Olive oil spray
4 (6 ounces each) wild salmon fillets

Cucumber-Avocado Salsa
2 tablespoons chopped red onion
1½ tablespoons fresh lemon juice
1 teaspoon extra-virgin olive oil
¼ teaspoon plus ⅛ teaspoon kosher salt
Freshly ground black pepper
4 Persian (mini) cucumbers, diced
6 ounces Hass avocado (from 1 large), diced

1. In a bowl, add the paprika, cayenne, garlic powder, oregano, thyme, salt, and black pepper. Spray the fish with oil and rub the spice mix. 2. For the cucumber-avocado salsa: In a bowl, add the red onion with lemon juice, olive oil, salt, and pepper. Let rest for 5 minutes, then add the cucumbers and avocado. 3. Select the "AIR FRY" function of Ninja Foodi digital air fry oven, set the temperature to 400 degrees F/ 200 degrees C and set the time to 7 minutes. Press the Start/Pause button and begin preheating. Cook until the fish flakes easily, 5 to 7 minutes. 4. Serve topped with the salsa.
Per Serving: Calories 340; Fat 18.5g; Sodium 396mg; Carbs 8g; Fiber 4g; Sugar 2g; Protein 35g

Shrimp with Balsamic Okra

Prep time: 5 minutes | Cook time: 10 minutes | Serves: 4

1 pound shrimp, peeled and deveined
2 tablespoons coconut aminos
1 and ½ cups okra
3 tablespoons balsamic vinegar
½ cup chicken stock
A pinch of salt and black pepper
1 tablespoon parsley, chopped

1. Select the "AIR FRY" function of Ninja Foodi digital air fry oven, set the temperature to 380 degrees F/ 195 degrees C and set the time to 10 minutes. Press the Start/Pause button and begin preheating. 2. In a pan, mix all the ingredients, toss, introduce in the fryer and cook for 10 minutes. 3. Divide into bowls and serve.
Per Serving: Calories 251; Fat 10g; Sodium 233mg; Carbs 4g; Fiber 3g; Sugar 1g; Protein 8g

Roasted Fish with Lemon-Almond Crumbs

Prep time: 15 minutes | Cook time: 15 minutes | Serves: 4

½ cup raw whole almonds
1 scallion, finely chopped
Grated zest and juice of 1 lemon
½ tablespoon extra-virgin olive oil
¾ teaspoon kosher salt
Freshly ground black pepper
4 (6 ounces each) skinless fish fillets, such as halibut, black cod, or sea bass
Olive oil spray
1 teaspoon Dijon mustard

1. Coarsely chop the almonds in food processor. 2. Transfer to a small bowl and add the scallion, lemon zest, and olive oil. Season with ¼ teaspoon of the salt and pepper to taste and mix to combine. 3. Spray the top of the fish with oil and squeeze the lemon juice over the fish. Season with the remaining ½ teaspoon salt and pepper to taste. 4. Spread the mustard on top of the fish. Dividing evenly, press the almond mixture onto the top of the fillets to adhere. 5. Select the "AIR FRY" function of Ninja Foodi digital air fry oven, set the temperature to 375 degrees F/ 190 degrees C and set the time to 8 minutes. Press the Start/Pause button and begin preheating. Cook until the crumbs start to brown and the fish is cooked through, 7 to 8 minutes. Serve immediately.
Per Serving: Calories 282; Fat 13g; Sodium 359mg; Carbs 6g; Fiber 2.5g; Sugar 1g; Protein 36g

Delicious Sea Bream Steaks

Prep time: 15 minutes | Cook time: 10 minutes | Serves: 3

1-pound sea bream steaks
1 egg, beaten
1 tablespoon coconut flour
1 teaspoon garlic powder
1 tablespoon almond butter,
melted
½ teaspoon Erythritol
½ teaspoon chili powder
1 teaspoon apple cider vinegar

1. In the shallow bowl mix up garlic powder, coconut flour, chili powder, and Erythritol. Sprinkle the sea bream steaks with apple cider vinegar and dip in the beaten egg. 2. After this, coat every fish steak in the coconut flour mixture. 3. Select the "AIR FRY" function of Ninja Foodi digital air fry oven, set the temperature to 390 degrees F/ 200 degrees C and set the time to 10 minutes. Press the Start/Pause button and begin preheating. Place the fish steak in the air fryer in one layer and sprinkle with almond butter. Cook them for 5 minutes from each side.
Per Serving: Calories 273; Fat 9.9g; Sodium 258mg; Carbs 3.4g; Fiber 1.6g; Sugar 0.3g; Protein 39.8g

Fish Croquettes

Prep time: 5 minutes | Cook time: 10 minutes | Serves: 4

Croquettes
3 large eggs
12 ounces raw cod fillet, flaked apart with two forks
¼ cup 1% milk
½ cup boxed instant mashed potatoes (such as Idahoan)
2 teaspoons olive oil
⅓ cup chopped fresh dill
1 shallot, minced
1 large garlic clove, minced
¾ cup plus 2 tablespoons bread crumbs, regular or gluten-free
1 teaspoon fresh lemon juice
1 teaspoon kosher salt
½ teaspoon dried thyme
¼ teaspoon freshly ground black pepper
Olive oil spray

Lemon-Dill Aioli
5 tablespoons mayonnaise
Juice of ½ lemon
1 tablespoon chopped fresh dill

1. For the croquettes: In a bowl, beat 2 eggs. Add the fish, milk, mashed potatoes, olive oil, dill, shallot, garlic, 2 tablespoons of the bread crumbs, the lemon juice, salt, thyme, and pepper. Mix to thoroughly combine. Place in the refrigerator for 30 minutes. 2. For the lemon-dill aioli: In a small bowl, combine the mayonnaise, lemon juice, and dill. 3. Measure out about 3½ tablespoons of the fish mixture and gently roll in your hands to form a log about 3 inches long. Repeat to make a total of 12 logs. 4. Beat the remaining egg in a small bowl. Place the remaining ¾ cup bread crumbs in a separate bowl. 5. Dip the croquettes in the egg, then coat in the bread crumbs, gently pressing to adhere. Place on a work surface and spray both sides with oil. 6. Select the "BAKE" function of Ninja Foodi digital air fry oven, set the temperature to 350 degrees F/ 175 degrees C and set the time to 10 minutes. Press the Start/Pause button and begin preheating. Cook for about 10 minutes, flipping halfway, until golden. 7. Serve with the aioli for dipping.
Per Serving: Calories 461; Fat 21.5g; Sodium 652mg; Carbs 41g; Fiber 3.5g; Sugar 5g; Protein 26g

Parmesan Butter Flounder Fillets

Prep time: 5 minutes | Cook time: 20 minutes | Serves: 4

4 flounder fillets, boneless
A pinch of salt and black pepper
1 cup parmesan, grated
4 tablespoons butter, melted
2 tablespoons olive oil

1. Select the "AIR FRY" function of Ninja Foodi digital air fry oven, set the temperature to 400 degrees F/ 200 degrees C and set the time to 20 minutes. Press the Start/Pause button and begin preheating. 2. In a bowl, mix the parmesan with salt, pepper, butter and the oil and stir well. 3. Arrange the fish in a pan that fits the air fryer, spread the parmesan mix all over, introduce in the fryer and cook for 20 minutes. 4. Divide between plates and serve with a side salad.
Per Serving: Calories 251; Fat 14g; Sodium 411mg; Carbs 6g; Fiber 5g; Sugar 1g; Protein 12g

Buttery Trout

Prep time: 10 minutes | Cook time: 12 minutes | Serves: 4

4 trout fillets, boneless
4 tablespoons butter, melted
Salt and black pepper to the taste
Juice of 1 lime
1 tablespoon chives, chopped
1 tablespoon parsley, chopped

1. Select the "AIR FRY" function of Ninja Foodi digital air fry oven, set the temperature to 390 degrees F/ 200 degrees C and set the time to 12 minutes. Press the Start/Pause button and begin preheating. 2. Mix the fish fillets with the melted butter, salt and pepper, rub gently, put the fish in your air fryer's basket and cook for 6 minutes on each side. 3. Divide between plates and serve with lime juice drizzled on top and with parsley and chives sprinkled at the end.
Per Serving: Calories 221; Fat 11g; Sodium 256mg; Carbs 6g; Fiber 4g; Sugar 2g; Protein 9g

Herbed Sea bass

Prep time: 10 minutes | Cook time: 15 minutes | Serves: 4

15 oz sea bass, trimmed, cleaned, washed
1 teaspoon salt
1 teaspoon dried rosemary
½ teaspoon lemon zest, grated
2 tablespoons sesame oil
1 tablespoon apple cider vinegar
2 oz Parmesan, grated

1. In the shallow bowl mix up apple cider vinegar and sesame oil. Sprinkle the sea bass with salt, dried rosemary, and lemon zest. 2. After this, brush the fish with sesame oil mixture. 3. Select the "AIR FRY" function of Ninja Foodi digital air fry oven, set the temperature to 400 degrees F/ 200 degrees C and set the time to 15 minutes. Press the Start/Pause button and begin preheating. Put the spiced fish in the air fryer basket and cook it for 14 minutes. 4. Then flip the fish on another side and top with grated Parmesan. Cook it for 1 minute more.
Per Serving: Calories 366; Fat 16.6g; Sodium 256mg; Carbs 7.5g; Fiber 0.2g; Sugar 0.3g; Protein 4.6g

Italian Halibut with Asparagus

Prep time: 10 minutes | Cook time: 7 minutes | Serves: 2

2 halibut fillets
4 oz asparagus, trimmed
1 tablespoon avocado oil
½ teaspoon garlic powder
1 teaspoon Italian seasonings
1 teaspoon butter
1 teaspoon salt
1 tablespoon lemon juice

1. Chop the halibut fillet roughly and sprinkle with garlic powder and Italian seasonings. 2. Select the "AIR FRY" function of Ninja Foodi digital air fry oven, set the temperature to 400 degrees F/ 200 degrees C and set the time to 10 minutes. Press the Start/Pause button and begin preheating. Place the asparagus in basket and sprinkle it with salt. Then put the fish over the asparagus and sprinkle it with avocado oil and lemon juice. Cook the meal for 8 minutes. 3. Then transfer it in the serving plates and top with butter.
Per Serving: Calories 367; Fat 10.3g; Sodium 222mg; Carbs 3.5g; Fiber 1.6g; Sugar 2.3g; Protein 62.1g

Chapter 6 Snack and Appetizer Recipes

Spiced Crispy Cauliflower Florets

Prep time: 5 minutes | Cook time: 15 minutes | Serves: 4

2 eggs, whisked	1 teaspoon chili powder
1 cup breadcrumbs	½ teaspoon onion powder
Sea salt	½ teaspoon cumin powder
ground black pepper, to taste	½ teaspoon garlic powder
1 teaspoon cayenne pepper	1 pound cauliflower florets

1. Select the "AIR FRY" function of Ninja Foodi digital air fry oven, set the temperature to 350 degrees F/ 175 degrees C and set the time to 15 minutes. Press the Start/Pause button and begin preheating. Mix the eggs, breadcrumbs, and spices until well combined. Dip the cauliflower florets in the batter. Place the cauliflower in air fry basket and place in it. 2. Cook the cauliflower florets for about 15 minutes, turning them over halfway through the cooking time. Bon appétit!
Per Serving: Calories 101; Fat 5.4g; Sodium 106mg; Carbs 8g; Fiber 3g; Sugar 3g; Protein 7g

Air Fried Spicy and Sticky Brussels Sprouts

Prep time: 5 minutes | Cook time: 10 minutes | Serves: 4

1 pound Brussels sprouts, trimmed	1 teaspoon chili flakes
2 tablespoons sesame oil	1 teaspoon garlic powder
2 tablespoons agave syrup	½ teaspoon paprika
2 tablespoons rice wine	Sea salt
	Ground black pepper, to taste

1. Select the "AIR FRY" function of Ninja Foodi digital air fry oven, set the temperature to 380 degrees F/ 195 degrees C and set the time to 10 minutes. Press the Start/Pause button and begin preheating. Toss the Brussels sprouts with the remaining ingredients; then, place the Brussels sprouts in the Air Fryer basket. 2. Cook the Brussels sprouts for 10 minutes, shaking the sprouts halfway through the cooking time. 3. Serve warm and enjoy!
Per Serving: Calories 147; Fat 7.3g; Sodium 56mg; Carbs 20g; Fiber 5g; Sugar 11g; Protein 4g

Glazed and Soft Baby Carrots

Prep time: 5 minutes | Cook time: 15 minutes | Serves: 3

¾ pound baby carrots, halved lengthwise	½ teaspoon cumin powder
2 tablespoons coconut oil	2 tablespoons honey
	2 tablespoons white wine

1. Select the "AIR FRY" function of Ninja Foodi digital air fry oven, set the temperature to 380 degrees F/ 195 degrees C and set the time to 15 minutes. Press the Start/Pause button and begin preheating. Toss the carrots with the remaining ingredients; then, arrange the carrots in the Air Fryer basket and place in the fryer. 2. Cook the carrots for 15 minutes, shaking the basket halfway through the cooking time. Bon appétit!
Per Serving: Calories 162; Fat 9.4g; Sodium 68mg; Carbs 21g; Fiber 4g; Sugar 16g; Protein 1g

Tomato and Basil Bruschetta

Prep time: 5 minutes | Cook time: 3 minutes | Serves: 6

4 tomatoes, diced	1 teaspoon olive oil
⅓ cup fresh basil, shredded	1 teaspoon salt
¼ cup shredded Parmesan cheese	1 teaspoon freshly ground black pepper
1 tablespoon minced garlic	
1 tablespoon balsamic vinegar	1 loaf French bread

1. In a bowl, add the tomatoes and basil. 2. Mix in the Parmesan cheese, garlic, vinegar, olive oil, salt, and pepper. 3. Let the tomato mixture sit and marinate while you prepare the bread. 4. Select the "AIR FRY" function of Ninja Foodi digital air fry oven, set the temperature to 250 degrees F/ 120 degrees C and set the time to 3 minutes. Press the Start/Pause button and begin preheating. Grease the air fryer basket with olive oil. 5. Cut the bread into 1-inch-thick slices. 6. Place the slices in the greased air fryer basket in a single layer. 7. Spray the top of the bread with olive oil. 8. Set the temperature to 250 degrees F/ 120 degrees C. Set the timer and toast for 3 minutes. 9. Using tongs, remove the bread slices from the air fryer and place a spoonful of the bruschetta topping on each piece.
Per Serving: Calories 258; Fat 3g; Sodium 826mg; Carbs 47g; Fiber 3g; Sugar 4g; Protein 11g

Spicy Chicken Cheese Balls

Prep time: 10 minutes | Cook time: 16 minutes | Serves: 8

8 ounces cream cheese, softened	3 cups shredded cooked chicken
2 cups grated pepper jack cheese	¼ cup all-purpose flour
1 Jalapeño pepper, diced	2 eggs, lightly beaten
2 scallions, minced	1 cup panko breadcrumbs
1 teaspoon paprika	olive oil, in a spray bottle
2 teaspoons salt, divided	salsa

1. Beat the cream cheese and add the pepper jack cheese, Jalapeño pepper, scallions, paprika and salt. Fold in the shredded chicken and combine well. Roll this mixture into 1-inch balls. 2. Place the flour into a shallow dish. Place the eggs into another shallow dish. Finally, combine the panko breadcrumbs and salt in a third dish. 3. Coat the chicken cheese balls with flour first, then dip them into the eggs and finally roll them in the panko breadcrumbs to coat all sides. Refrigerate for at least 30 minutes. 4. Select the "AIR FRY" function of Ninja Foodi digital air fry oven, set the temperature to 400 degrees F/ 200 degrees C and set the time to 8 minutes. Press the Start/Pause button and begin preheating. 5. Spray the chicken cheese balls with oil and air-fry in batches for 8 minutes. Shake the basket a few times throughout the cooking process to help the balls brown evenly. 6. Serve hot with salsa on the side.
Per Serving: Calories 310; Fat 20g; Sodium 614mg; Carbs 6g; Fiber 0g; Sugar 1g; Protein 25g

Mediterranean Herb Potato Chips

Prep time: 5 minutes | Cook time: 15 minutes | Serves: 3

2 large-sized potatoes, thinly sliced	mix
2 tablespoons olive oil	1 teaspoon cayenne pepper
1 teaspoon Mediterranean herb	Coarse sea salt
	Ground black pepper, to taste

1. Select the "AIR FRY" function of Ninja Foodi digital air fry oven, set the temperature to 360 degrees F/ 180 degrees C and set the time to 30 minutes. Press the Start/Pause button and begin preheating. 2. Toss the potatoes with the spices and place them in the Air Fryer cooking basket. 3. Air fry the potato chips for 16 minutes, shaking the basket halfway through the cooking time and working in batches. Enjoy!
Per Serving: Calories 271; Fat 9.3g; Sodium 15mg; Carbs 43g; Fiber 6g; Sugar 2g; Protein 5g

Baked Classic Mustard Broccoli Florets

Prep time: 5 minutes | Cook time: 10 minutes | Serves: 4

1 pound broccoli florets	1 tablespoon soy sauce
2 tablespoons butter, room temperature	Sea salt and freshly ground black pepper, to taste
¼ teaspoon mustard seeds	

1. Select the "BAKE" function of Ninja Foodi digital air fry oven, set the temperature to 370 degrees F/ 185 degrees C and set the time to 10 minutes. Press the Start/Pause button and begin preheating. Toss all the ingredients in a lightly oiled Ninja air fryer basket. 2. Cook the broccoli florets at 370 degrees F/ 185 degrees C for about 10 minutes, shaking the basket halfway through the cooking time. Bon appétit!
Per Serving: Calories 88; Fat 7.1g; Sodium 143mg; Carbs 4g; Fiber 3g; Sugar 1g; Protein 4g

Sweet Cinnamon Apple Chips

Prep time: 5 minutes | Cook time: 10 minutes | Serves: 4

2 large sweet, crisp apples, cored and sliced	½ teaspoon grated nutmeg
1 teaspoon ground cinnamon	A pinch of salt

1. Select the "AIR FRY" function of Ninja Foodi digital air fry oven, set the temperature to 390 degrees F/ 200 degrees C and set the time to 10 minutes. Press the Start/Pause button and begin preheating. 2. Toss the apple slices with the remaining ingredients and place in air fryer basket in a single layer. 3. Cook the apple chips for about 9 minutes, shaking them halfway through the cooking time. Work in batches. Bon appétit!
Per Serving: Calories 4; Fat 0.1g; Sodium 0mg; Carbs 1g; Fiber 1g; Sugar 0g; Protein 0g

Crispy Sweet Potato Fries with Mediterranean herb

Prep time: 5 minutes | Cook time: 15 minutes | Serves: 3

2 large-sized sweet potatoes, peeled and cut into ¼-inch sticks
2 teaspoons olive oil
1 teaspoon garlic powder
1 tablespoon Mediterranean herb mix
Kosher salt and freshly ground black pepper, to taste

1. Select the "AIR FRY" function of Ninja Foodi digital air fry oven, set the temperature to 360 degrees F/ 180 degrees C and set the time to 15 minutes. Press the Start/Pause button and begin preheating. 2. Toss the sweet potato with the remaining and place them in the Air Fryer basket. 3. Air fry the sweet potato sticks for 15 minutes, tossing halfway through the cooking time and working in batches. Enjoy!
Per Serving: Calories 139; Fat 3.2g; Sodium 45mg; Carbs 26g; Fiber 4g; Sugar 8g; Protein 3g

Air Fried Sticky Pork Ribs

Prep time: 5 minutes | Cook time: 40 minutes | Serves: 4

2 pounds pork ribs
2 tablespoons honey
2 tablespoons butter
1 teaspoon sweet paprika
1 teaspoon hot paprika
1 teaspoon granulated garlic
Sea salt
Ground black pepper, to taste
1 teaspoon brown mustard
1 teaspoon ground cumin

1. Select the "AIR FRY" function of Ninja Foodi digital air fry oven, set the temperature to 350 degrees F/ 175 degrees C and set the time to 35 minutes. Press the Start/Pause button and begin preheating. Toss all in a lightly greased Air Fryer basket. Place the ribs in the single layer. 2. Cook the pork ribs for 35 minutes, turning them over halfway through the cooking time. Bon appétit!
Per Serving: Calories 409; Fat 18.9g; Sodium 214mg; Carbs 10g; Fiber 1g; Sugar 9g; Protein 48g

Spiced Autumn Pumpkin Chips

Prep time: 5 minutes | Cook time: 15 minutes | Serves: 4

1 pound pumpkin, peeled and sliced
2 tablespoons coconut oil
1 teaspoon ground allspice
½ teaspoon chili powder
½ teaspoon garlic powder
½ teaspoon ground cumin
Sea salt
Ground black pepper, to taste

1. Select the "AIR FRY" function of Ninja Foodi digital air fry oven, set the temperature to 375 degrees F/ 190 degrees C and set the time to 13 minutes. Press the Start/Pause button and begin preheating. Toss the pumpkin with the remaining until well coated on all sides. 2. Place them in air fryer basket and cook for about 13 minutes, tossing once or twice. Bon appétit!
Per Serving: Calories 716; Fat 62.6g; Sodium 302mg; Carbs 18g; Fiber 8g; Sugar 2g; Protein 34g

Lemony Ricotta with Capers

Prep time: 5 minutes | Cook time: 10 minutes | Serves: 4 to6

1½ cups ricotta cheese
zest of 1 lemon,
1 teaspoon chopped rosemary
pinch red pepper flakes
2 tablespoons capers, rinsed
2 tablespoons extra-virgin olive
oil
salt and freshly ground black pepper
1 tablespoon grated Parmesan cheese

1. Select the "AIR FRY" function of Ninja Foodi digital air fry oven, set the temperature to 380 degrees F/ 195 degrees C and set the time to 10 minutes. Press the Start/Pause button and begin preheating. 2. Combine the cheese with lemon zest, rosemary, red pepper flakes, capers, olive oil, salt and pepper and whisk together well. Transfer the cheese mixture to a 7-inch pie dish and place the pie dish in the air fryer basket. 3. Air-fry the ricotta for 8 to 10 minutes, or until the top is nicely browned in spots. 4. Remove the pie dish from the air fryer and immediately sprinkle the Parmesan cheese on top. Drizzle with a little olive oil and add some freshly ground black pepper and lemon zest as garnish. Serve warm with pita bread or crostini.
Per Serving: Calories 150; Fat 13g; Sodium 398mg; Carbs 2g; Fiber 0g; Sugar 0g; Protein 7g

Parmesan Eggplant Fries

Prep time: 5 minutes | Cook time: 18 minutes | Serves: 6

½ cup all-purpose flour
salt and freshly ground black pepper
2 eggs, beaten
1 cup seasoned breadcrumbs
1 large eggplant
8 ounces mozzarella cheese
olive oil, in a spray bottle
grated Parmesan cheese
1 (14-ounce) jar marinara sauce

1. Place the flour in a shallow dish and spice with salt and freshly ground black pepper. Put the eggs in the second shallow dish. Place the breadcrumbs in the third shallow dish. 2. Peel the eggplant and then slice it vertically into long ½-inch thick slices. Slice the mozzarella cheese into ½-inch thick slices and make a mozzarella sandwich, using the eggplant as the bread. Slice the eggplant-mozzarella sandwiches into rectangular strips about 1-inch by 3½-inches. 3. Coat the eggplant strips carefully, holding the sandwich together with your fingers. Dredge with flour first, then dip them into the eggs, and finally place them into the breadcrumbs. Pat the crumbs onto the eggplant strips and then coat them in the egg and breadcrumbs one more time, pressing gently with your hands so the crumbs stick evenly. 4. Select the "AIR FRY" function of Ninja Foodi digital air fry oven, set the temperature to 400 degrees F/ 200 degrees C and set the time to 9 minutes. Press the Start/Pause button and begin preheating. 5. Spray the eggplant fries on all sides with olive oil, and transfer one layer at a time to the air-fryer basket. Air-fry in batches at for 9 minutes, turning and rotating halfway through the cooking time. Spray the eggplant strips with additional oil when you turn them over. 6. While the fries are cooking, gently warm the marinara sauce on the stovetop in a small saucepan. 7. Serve eggplant fries fresh out of the air fryer with a little Parmesan cheese grated on top and the warmed marinara sauce on the side.
Per Serving: Calories 210; Fat 11g; Sodium 268mg; Carbs 16g; Fiber 4g; Sugar 7g; Protein 12g

Fried Cheesy Ravioli with Marinara Sauce

Prep time: 7 minutes | Cook time: 14 minutes | Serves: 4 to 6

1-pound cheese ravioli, fresh or frozen
2 eggs, lightly beaten
1 cup plain breadcrumbs
½ teaspoon paprika
½ teaspoon dried oregano
½ teaspoon salt
grated Parmesan cheese
chopped fresh parsley
1 to 2 cups marinara sauce

1. Boil the salted water. Boil the ravioli and then drain. Let the cooked ravioli cool to a temperature where you can comfortably handle them. 2. Place the eggs into one dish. Combine the breadcrumbs, paprika, dried oregano and salt in the other dish. 3. Select the "AIR FRY" function of Ninja Foodi digital air fry oven, set the temperature to 380 degrees F/ 195 degrees C and set the time to 7 minutes. Press the Start/Pause button and begin preheating. 4. Working with one at a time, dip the cooked ravioli into the egg, coating all sides. Then press the ravioli into the breadcrumbs, ensuring that all sides are covered. Transfer the ravioli to the air fryer basket, cooking in batches, one layer at a time. Air-fry F for 7 minutes. 5. While the ravioli is air-frying, bring the marinara sauce to a simmer on the stovetop. Transfer to a small bowl. 6. Sprinkle a little Parmesan cheese and chopped parsley on top of the fried ravioli and serve warm with the marinara sauce on the side for dipping.
Per Serving: Calories 60; Fat 1g; Sodium 154mg; Carbs 9g; Fiber 1g; Sugar 3g; Protein 3g

Cheddar Tomato Platter

Prep time: 5 minutes | Cook time: 20 minutes | Serves: 6

6 tomatoes, halved
3 teaspoons sugar-free apricot jam
2 ounces watercress
2 teaspoons oregano, dried
1 tablespoon olive oil
A pinch of salt and black pepper
3 ounces cheddar cheese, grated

Select the "AIR FRY" function of Ninja Foodi digital air fry oven, set the temperature to 360 degrees F/ 180 degrees C and set the time to 20 minutes. Press the Start/Pause button and begin preheating. Spread the jam on each tomato half, sprinkle oregano, salt and pepper, and drizzle the oil all over them Introduce them in the fryer's basket, sprinkle the cheese on top and cook for 20 minutes. Arrange the tomatoes on a platter, top each half with some watercress and serve as an appetizer.
Per Serving: Calories 131; Fat 7g; Sodium 147mg; Carbs 4g; Fiber 2g; Sugar 2g; Protein 7g

Herb Crispy Sweet Potato Chips

Prep time: 5 minutes | Cook time: 15 minutes | Serves: 3

2 large-sized sweet potatoes, peeled and cut into thin slices
2 teaspoons butter, melted
Sea salt

ground black pepper, to taste
½ teaspoon dried oregano
½ teaspoon dried basil
½ teaspoon dried rosemary

1. Select the "AIR FRY" function of Ninja Foodi digital air fry oven, set the temperature to 360 degrees F/ 180 degrees C and set the time to 15 minutes. Press the Start/Pause button and begin preheating. 2. Toss the sweet potato with the remaining ingredients and place them in the Air Fryer cooking basket 3. Air fry the sweet potato chips for 14 minutes, tossing halfway through the cooking time and working in batches. Enjoy!
Per Serving: Calories 134; Fat 2.8g; Sodium 64mg; Carbs 26g; Fiber 4g; Sugar 8g; Protein 3g

Classic Crispy Onion Rings

Prep time:10 minutes | Cook time: 8 minutes | Serves: 4

1 cup all-purpose flour
Sea salt and black pepper, to taste
1 teaspoon red pepper flakes, crushed

½ teaspoon cumin powder
1 egg
1 cup breadcrumbs
1 medium yellow onion, sliced

1. Select the "AIR FRY" function of Ninja Foodi digital air fry oven, set the temperature to 380 degrees F/ 195 degrees C and set the time to 10 minutes. Press the Start/Pause button and begin preheating. 2. In a bowl, mix the flour with salt, black pepper, red pepper flakes, and cumin powder. 3. Whisk the egg in another shallow bowl. Place the breadcrumbs in a separate bowl. 4. Dip the onion rings in the flour, then in the eggs, then in the breadcrumbs. Place the onion rings in the Air Fryer basket. 5. Cook the onion rings for about 8 minutes or until golden brown and cooked through. Bon appétit!
Per Serving: Calories 153; Fat 2.8g; Sodium 28mg; Carbs 26g; Fiber 1g; Sugar 1g; Protein 6g

Air Fried Spicy Tortilla Chips

Prep time: 10 minutes | Cook time: 5 minutes | Serves: 4

9 corn tortillas, cut into wedges
1 tablespoon olive oil
1 teaspoon hot paprika

Sea salt
Ground black pepper, to taste

1. Select the "AIR FRY" function of Ninja Foodi digital air fry oven, set the temperature to 360 degrees F/ 180 degrees C and set the time to 6 minutes. Press the Start/Pause button and begin preheating. Toss the tortilla wedges with the remaining ingredients. 2. Place the wedges in wire rack and Cook your tortilla chips at 360 degrees F/ 180 degrees C for about 5 minutes or until crispy. Work in batches.
Per Serving: Calories 33; Fat 3.5g; Sodium 1mg; Carbs 1g; Fiber 0g; Sugar 0g; Protein 0g

Sweet Potato Fries with Dipping Sauce

Prep time: 10 minutes | Cook time: 20 minutes | Serves: 2 to 3

1 large sweet potato (about 1 pound)
Sweet & Spicy Dipping Sauce:
¼ cup light mayonnaise
1 tablespoon spicy brown mustard
1 tablespoon sweet Thai chili

1 teaspoon vegetable or canola oil
salt

sauce
½ teaspoon sriracha sauce

1. Scrub the sweet potato well and then cut it into ¼-inch French fries. Select the "AIR FRY" function of Ninja Foodi digital air fry oven, set the temperature to 250 degrees F/ 120 degrees C and set the time to 10 minutes. Press the Start/Pause button and begin preheating. 2. Toss the sweet potato sticks with the oil and transfer them to the air fryer basket. Air-fry for 10 minutes, shaking the basket several times during the cooking process for even cooking. Toss the fries with salt, increase the air fryer temperature to 400 degrees F/ 200 degrees C and air-fry for another 10 minutes, shaking the basket several times during the cooking process. 3. For dipping mix all the ingredients in a bowl and stir until combined. 4. Serve the sweet potato fries warm with the dipping sauce on the side.
Per Serving: Calories 130; Fat 1g; Sodium 336mg; Carbs 28g; Fiber 4g; Sugar 9g; Protein 3g

Cheesy Jalapeno Poppers

Prep time: 5 minutes | Cook time: 10 minutes | Serves: 4

4 ounces Cottage cheese, crumbled
4 ounces cheddar cheese, shredded
1 teaspoon mustard seeds

8 jalapenos, seeded and sliced in half lengthwise
8 slices bacon, sliced in half lengthwise

1. Select the "AIR FRY" function of Ninja Foodi digital air fry oven, set the temperature to 370 degrees F/ 185 degrees C and set the time to 8 minutes. Press the Start/Pause button and begin preheating. 2. Thoroughly combine the cheese and mustard seeds. Spoon the mixture into the jalapeno halves.Wrap jalapeno with bacon and secure with toothpicks. 3. Place the jalapeno in the Air fry basket and cook for about 7 minutes or until golden brown. Bon appétit!
Per Serving: Calories 292; Fat 24.3g; Sodium 660mg; Carbs 5g; Fiber 0g; Sugar 3g; Protein 14g

Roasted Easy Chicken Wings

Prep time: 5 minutes | Cook time: 15 minutes | Serves: 3

¾ pound chicken wings
1 tablespoon olive oil
1 teaspoon mustard seeds
1 teaspoon cayenne pepper

1 teaspoon garlic powder
Sea salt
Ground black pepper, to taste

1. Select the "AIR ROAST" function of Ninja Foodi digital air fry oven, set the temperature to 380 degrees F/ 195 degrees C and set the time to 20 minutes. Press the Start/Pause button and begin preheating. Toss the chicken wings with the remaining ingredients and place in the air fryer basket. 2. Cook the chicken wings for 18 minutes, turning them over halfway through the cooking time. Bon appétit!
Per Serving: Calories 193; Fat 8.9g; Sodium 93mg; Carbs 2g; Fiber 1g; Sugar 0g; Protein 25g

Crispy Fried Green Beans with Egg & Flour

Prep time: 5 minutes | Cook time: 10 minutes | Serves: 4

½ cup flour
2 eggs, beaten
½ cup bread crumbs
½ cup Parmesan cheese, grated

½ teaspoon onion powder
¼ teaspoon cumin powder
½ teaspoon garlic powder
1 pound fresh green beans

1. Select the "AIR FRY" function of Ninja Foodi digital air fry oven, set the temperature to 390 degrees F/ 200 degrees C and set the time to 6 minutes. Press the Start/Pause button and begin preheating. 2. In a shallow bowl, thoroughly combine the flour and eggs; mix to combine well. Then, in another bowl, mix the remaining ingredients. 3. Dip the green beans in the egg mixture, then, in the breadcrumb mixture. Place them in air fryer basket. 4. Air fry the green beans for about 6 minutes, tossing halfway through the cooking time. Enjoy!
Per Serving: Calories 427; Fat 18.3g; Sodium 603mg; Carbs 44g; Fiber 6g; Sugar 3g; Protein 23g

Sweet and Salty Snack

Prep time: 10 minutes | Cook time: 20 minutes | Serves: 10

1 teaspoon salt
2 cups sesame sticks
½ cup honey
3 tablespoons butter, melted
1 cup pepitas

2 cups granola
1 cup cashews
2 cups crispy corn puff cereal
2 cups mini pretzel crisps
1 cup dried cherries

1. Combine the honey, butter and salt in a small bowl or measuring cup and stir until combined. 2. Mix the sesame sticks, cashews, pepitas, granola, corn puff cereal and pretzel crisps in a large bowl. Pour the honey mixture and toss to combine. 3. Select the "AIR FRY" function of Ninja Foodi digital air fry oven, set the temperature to 370 degrees F/ 185 degrees C and set the time to 12 minutes. Press the Start/Pause button and begin preheating. 4. Place half the mixture in the air fryer basket and air-fry for 10 to 12 minutes, or until the snack mix is lightly toasted. Toss the basket several times throughout the process so that the mix cooks evenly and doesn't get too dark on top. 5. Transfer the snack mix to a cookie sheet and let it cool completely. Mix in the dried cherries and store the mix in an airtight container for up to a week or two.
Per Serving: Calories 270; Fat 12g; Sodium 633mg; Carbs 35g; Fiber 3g; Sugar 15g; Protein 6g

Ranch Roasted Chickpeas

Prep time: 4 minutes | Cook time: 10 minutes | Serves: 4

1 (15-ounce) can chickpeas, drained and rinsed
1 tablespoon olive oil
3 tablespoons ranch seasoning mix
1 teaspoon salt
2 tablespoons freshly squeezed lemon juice

1. Grease the air fryer basket with olive oil. 2. Using paper towels, pat the chickpeas dry. 3. In a bowl, add the chickpeas, oil, seasoning mix, salt, and lemon juice. 4. Put the chickpeas in the air fryer basket and spread them out in a single layer. Select the "AIR ROAST" function of Ninja Foodi digital air fry oven, set the temperature to 350 degrees F/ 175 degrees C and set the time to 4 minutes. Press the Start/Pause button and begin preheating. 5. Set the timer and roast for 4 minutes. Remove the drawer and shake vigorously to redistribute the chickpeas so they cook evenly. Reset the timer and roast for 6 minutes more. 6. When the time is up, release the air fryer basket from the drawer and pour the chickpeas into a bowl. Season with additional salt, if desired. Enjoy!
Per Serving: Calories 144; Fat 5g; Sodium 891mg; Carbs 19g; Fiber 5g; Sugar 3g; Protein 6g

Stuffed Mushrooms

Prep time: 5 minutes | Cook time: 10 minutes | Serves: 4

12 medium button mushrooms
½ cup bread crumbs
1 teaspoon salt
½ teaspoon freshly ground black pepper
5 to 6 tablespoons olive oil

1. Spray the air fryer basket with olive oil. 2. Separate the cap from the stem of each mushroom. Discard the stems. 3. In a mixing bowl, mix the bread crumbs, salt, pepper, and olive oil until you have a wet mixture. 4. Rub the mushrooms with olive oil on all sides. 5. Using a spoon, fill each mushroom with the bread crumb stuffing. 6. Place the mushrooms in the greased air fryer basket in a single layer. 7. Select the "AIR FRY" function of Ninja Foodi digital air fry oven, set the temperature to 360 degrees F/ 180 degrees C and set the time to 10 minutes. Press the Start/Pause button and begin preheating. Set the timer and cook for 10 minutes. 8. Using tongs, remove the mushrooms from the air fryer, place them on a platter, and serve.
Per Serving: Calories 216; Fat 18g; Sodium 683mg; Carbs 12g; Fiber 1g; Sugar 2g; Protein 4g

Crispy Ham 'n' Cheese Ravioli

Prep time: 15 minutes | Cook time: 10 minutes | Serves: 6

8 ounces thinly sliced ham (12 very large slices)
1 cup shredded cheddar cheese (about 4 ounces)
6 ounces cream cheese (¾ cup), softened
1 large egg
1 cup pork dust (see here)
Fresh parsley leaves, for garnish
Ranch Dressing (here), for serving

1. Spray the air fryer basket with avocado oil. Select the "AIR FRY" function of Ninja Foodi digital air fry oven, set the temperature to 400 degrees F/ 200 degrees C and set the time to 10 minutes. Press the Start/Pause button and begin preheating. 2. In a small bowl, stir together the cheddar cheese and cream cheese until well combined. 3. Assemble the ravioli: Lay one slice of ham on a sheet of parchment paper. Spoon about 2 heaping tablespoons of the filling into the center of the ham. Fold one end of the ham over the filling, making sure the ham completely covers the filling and meets the ham on the other side. Fold the ends around the filling to make a square, making sure that the filling is covered well. Using your fingers, press down around the filling to even the ravioli out into a square shape. Repeat with the rest of the ham and filling; you should have 12 raviolis. 4. Crack the egg into a shallow bowl and beat well with a fork. Place the pork dust in another shallow bowl. 5. Gently dip each ravioli into the egg, then dredge it in the pork dust. Use your hands to press the pork dust into the ravioli, coating it well. Spray the ravioli with avocado oil and place it in the air fryer basket. Make sure to leave space between the ravioli. 6. Cook the ravioli in the air fryer for 10 minutes, or until crispy, flipping after 6 minutes. 7. Serve warm, garnished with fresh parsley and with ranch dressing for dipping if desired. 8. Store leftovers in an airtight container in the fridge for up to 4 days.
Per Serving: Calories 354; Fat 7.9g; Sodium 704mg; Carbs 6g; Fiber 3.6g; Sugar 6g; Protein 18g

Ham 'n' Cheese Pies

Prep time: 10 minutes | Cook time: 12 minutes | Serves: 1

1¾ cups shredded mozzarella cheese (about 7 ounces)
2 tablespoons unsalted butter
Filling:
8 thin slices ham
4 slices provolone or cheddar cheese
1 large egg
¾ cup blanched almond flour
⅛ teaspoon fine sea salt

¼ cup mayonnaise
Prepared yellow mustard, for serving

1. Make the dough: Place the mozzarella cheese and butter in a large bowl and microwave for 2 minutes, until the cheese is entirely melted. Stir well. Add in the egg and combine well. Add the almond flour and salt and combine well with the mixer. 2. Lay a piece of parchment paper on the countertop, spray it with avocado oil, and place the dough on it. Knead for about 3 minutes. The dough should be thick yet pliable. 3. Spray the air fryer basket with avocado oil. Select the "AIR FRY" function of Ninja Foodi digital air fry oven, set the temperature to 350 degrees F/ 175 degrees C and set the time to 10 minutes. Press the Start/Pause button and begin preheating. 4. Separate the dough into 4 equal portions. Pat each portion out with your hands to form a small circle, about 4 inches in diameter. 5. Place 2 slices of ham and one slice of cheese in the center of each dough circle and smear a tablespoon of mayo on top. Seal each pie closed by folding the dough circle in half and crimping the edges with your fingers. 6. Transfer the pies to the air fryer basket, leaving space between them. Cook for 10 minutes, or until golden brown. Drizzle with mustard before serving, if desired. 7. Store leftovers in an airtight container in the refrigerator for up to 3 days.
Per Serving: Calories 354; Fat 7.9g; Sodium 704mg; Carbs 6g; Fiber 3.6g; Sugar 6g; Protein 18g

Homemade Roasted Mixed Nuts

Prep time: 5 minutes | Cook time: 20 minutes | Serves: 6

2 cups mixed nuts (walnuts, pecans, and/or almonds)
2 tablespoons egg white
1 teaspoon ground cinnamon
2 tablespoons sugar
1 teaspoon paprika

1. Select the "AIR ROAST" function of Ninja Foodi digital air fry oven, set the temperature to 300 degrees F/ 150 degrees C and set the time to 10 minutes. Press the Start/Pause button and begin preheating. Spray the sheet pan with olive oil. 2. In a mixing bowl, mix the nuts, egg white, cinnamon, sugar, and paprika, until the nuts are thoroughly coated. 3. Place the nuts in the greased sheet pan; set the timer and roast for 10 minutes. 4. Pour the nuts into a bowl, and serve.
Per Serving: Calories 232; Fat 21g; Sodium 6mg; Carbs 10g; Fiber 3g; Sugar 5g; Protein 6g

Seasoned Sausage Rolls

Prep time: 5 minutes | Cook time: 5 minutes | Serves: 6

For the Seasoning:
2 tablespoons sesame seeds
1½ teaspoons poppy seeds
1½ teaspoons dried minced onion
1 teaspoon salt
1 teaspoon dried minced garlic
For the Sausages:
1 (8-ounce) package crescent roll dough
1 (12-ounce) package mini smoked sausages (cocktail franks)

To Make the Seasoning: In a bowl, combine the sesame seeds, poppy seeds, onion, salt, and garlic and set aside.
To Make the Sausages: 1. Select the "AIR FRY" function of Ninja Foodi digital air fry oven, set the temperature to 330 degrees F/ 165 degrees C and set the time to 5 minutes. Press the Start/Pause button and begin preheating. Grease the air fryer basket with olive oil. 2. Remove the crescent dough from the package and lay it out on a cutting board. Separate the dough at the perforations. With a sharp knife, cut each triangle of dough into fourths. 3. Drain the sausages and pat them dry with a paper towel. 4. Roll each sausage in a piece of dough. 5. Sprinkle seasoning on top of each roll. 6. Place the seasoned sausage rolls into the greased air fryer basket in a single layer, cook for 5 minutes. Serve hot.
Per Serving: Calories 344; Fat 26g; Sodium 1145mg; Carbs 17g; Fiber 1g; Sugar 3g; Protein 10g

Delicious Hot Dog Buns

Prep time: 10 minutes | Cook time: 25 minutes | Serves: 1

1½ cups blanched almond flour
¼ cup plus 1 tablespoon psyllium husk powder
2 teaspoons baking powder
1 teaspoon fine sea salt
2½ tablespoons apple cider vinegar
3 large egg whites
1 cup boiling water

1. Spray a 7-inch pie pan or a casserole dish that will fit inside your air fryer with avocado oil. Select the "AIR FRY" function of Ninja Foodi digital air fry oven, set the temperature to 325 degrees F/ 160 degrees C and set the time to 25 minutes. Press the Start/Pause button and begin preheating. 2. In a medium-sized bowl, mix together the flour, psyllium husk powder, baking powder, and salt until well combined. Add the vinegar and egg whites and stir until a thick dough forms. Add the boiling water and mix until well combined. Let sit for 1 to 2 minutes, until the dough firms up. 3. Divide the dough into 8 equal-sized balls. Form each ball into a hot dog shape that's about 1-inch-wide and 3½ inches long. Place the buns in the greased pie pan, spacing them about 1 inch apart. 4. Place the buns in the air fryer and cook for 15 minutes, then flip the buns over. Cook for another 5 to 10 minutes, until the buns are puffed up and cooked through and a toothpick inserted in the center of a bun comes out clean. 5. Store leftovers in an airtight container in the fridge for up to 5 days or in the freezer for up to one month.
Per Serving: Calories 354; Fat 7.9g; Sodium 704mg; Carbs 6g; Fiber 3.6g; Sugar 6g; Protein 18g

Japanese BLT Sushi

Prep time: 15 minutes | Cook time: 8 minutes | Serves: 4

8 slices thin-cut bacon
¼ cup mayonnaise
1½ cups shredded lettuce
1 cup diced tomatoes

1. Select the "AIR FRY" function of Ninja Foodi digital air fry oven, set the temperature to 400 degrees F/ 200 degrees C and set the time to 8 minutes. Press the Start/Pause button and begin preheating. 2. Remove the air fryer basket from the air fryer and place the bacon in it. Weave the bacon slices together in a square, 4 slices per side, threading each slice over and under the others. Make sure the grid is tight; if there are gaps, the mayo will leak through. 3. Return the air fryer basket to the air fryer and cook the bacon for 8 minutes, or until slightly crisp yet still flexible. 4. Place the bacon square on a cutting board crispy side down. Spread the mayo over the bacon. Place the shredded lettuce and tomatoes on the mayo. Roll the bacon square up tightly. Slice into 4 thick rolls and serve. 5. Best served fresh. Store leftovers in an airtight container in the fridge for up to 4 days. Serve leftovers chilled or reheat.
Per Serving: Calories 354; Fat 7.9g; Sodium 704mg; Carbs 6g; Fiber 3.6g; Sugar 6g; Protein 18g

Mozzarella Sticks

Prep time: 10 minutes | Cook time: 8 minutes | Serves: 6

1 (12-count) package mozzarella sticks
1 (8-ounce) package crescent roll dough
3 tablespoons unsalted butter, melted
¼ cup panko bread crumbs
Marinara sauce, for dipping

1. Grease the air fryer basket with olive oil. 2. Cut each cheese stick into thirds. 3. Unroll the crescent roll dough. With a sharp knife, cut the dough into 36 even pieces. 4. Wrap each small cheese stick in a piece of dough. Make sure that the dough is wrapped tightly around the cheese. Close the dough by pinching them together at both ends, and pinch along the seam to ensure that the dough is completely sealed. 5. Using tongs, dip the wrapped cheese sticks in the melted butter, then dip the cheese sticks in the panko bread crumbs. 6. Place the cheese sticks in the greased air fryer basket in a single layer. (You may have to cook the cheese sticks in more than one batch.) 7. Select the "AIR FRY" function of Ninja Foodi digital air fry oven, set the temperature to 370 degrees F/ 185 degrees C and set the time to 8 minutes. Press the Start/Pause button and begin preheating. Set the timer and cook for 5 minutes. After 5 minutes, the tops should be golden brown. 8. Using tongs, flip the cheese sticks and cook for another 3 minutes, or until golden brown on all sides. 9. Plate, serve with the marinara sauce and enjoy!
Per Serving: Calories 348; Fat 23g; Sodium 811mg; Carbs 21g; Fiber 1g; Sugar 3g; Protein 17g

No-Corn Cheesy Dogs

Prep time: 10 minutes | Cook time: 10 minutes | Serves: 4

1¾ cups shredded mozzarella cheese (about 7 ounces)
2 tablespoons unsalted butter
1 large egg
¾ cup blanched almond flour
⅛ teaspoon fine sea salt
4 hot dogs
For Serving:
Prepared yellow mustard
No-sugar or reduced-sugar
ketchup

1. Make the dough: Place the mozzarella cheese and butter in a large bowl and microwave for 2 minutes, until the cheese melted. Stir well. Add the egg and, using a hand mixer, combine well. Add the almond flour and salt and combine well with the mixer. 2. Lay a piece of parchment paper on the countertop, spray it with avocado oil, and place the dough on it. Knead for about 3 minutes. The dough should be thick yet pliable. 3. Spray the air fryer basket with avocado oil. Select the "AIR FRY" function of Ninja Foodi digital air fry oven, set the temperature to 390 degrees F/ 200 degrees C and set the time to 8 minutes. Press the Start/Pause button and begin preheating. 4. Separate the dough into 4 equal portions. Pat each portion out with your hands to form a small oval, about 6 inches long and 2 inches wide. 5. Place one hot dog in each oval and form the dough around each hot dog using your hands. Place the dogs in the air fryer basket, leaving space between them, and cook for 8 minutes, or until golden brown, flipping halfway through. Drizzle with yellow mustard and serve with ketchup on the side, if desired. 6. Store leftovers in an airtight container in the refrigerator for up to 3 days.
Per Serving: Calories 354; Fat 7.9g; Sodium 704mg; Carbs 6g; Fiber 3.6g; Sugar 6g; Protein 18g

Air Fryer Pita Chips

Prep time: 5 minutes | Cook time: 6 minutes | Serves: 4

2 pieces' whole wheat pita bread
3 tablespoons olive oil
1 teaspoon freshly squeezed lemon juice
1 teaspoon salt
1 teaspoon dried basil
1 teaspoon garlic powder

1. Grease the air fryer basket with olive oil. 2. Using a pair of kitchen shears or a pizza cutter, cut the pita bread into small wedges. 3. Place the wedges in a small mixing bowl and add the olive oil, lemon juice, salt, dried basil, and garlic powder. 4. Mix well, coating each wedge. 5. Place the seasoned pita wedges in the greased air fryer basket in a single layer, being careful not to overcrowd them. (You may have to bake the pita chips in more than one batch.) 6. Select the "AIR FRY" function of Ninja Foodi digital air fry oven, set the temperature to 350 degrees F/ 175 degrees C and set the time to 6 minutes. Press the Start/Pause button and begin preheating. Set the timer and cook for 6 minutes. Every 2 minutes or so, remove the drawer and shake the pita chips so they redistribute in the basket for even cooking. 7. Serve with your choice of dip or alone as a tasty snack.
Per Serving: Calories 178; Fat 11g; Sodium 752mg; Carbs 18g; Fiber 3g; Sugar 1g; Protein 3g

Crispy Carrot Chips

Prep time: 5 minutes | Cook time: 6 to 8 minutes | Serves: 6

1 pound carrots, peeled and sliced ⅛ inch thick
2 tablespoons olive oil
1 teaspoon sea salt

1. In a bowl, combine the carrots, olive oil, and salt. Toss them together until the carrot slices are thoroughly coated with oil. 2. Place the carrot chips in the air fryer basket in a single layer. (You may have to bake the carrot chips in more than one batch.) 3. Select the "AIR FRY" function of Ninja Foodi digital air fry oven, set the temperature to 360 degrees F/ 180 degrees C and set the time to 3 minutes. Press the Start/Pause button and begin preheating. Set the timer and cook for 3 minutes. Remove the air fryer drawer and shake to redistribute the chips for even cooking. Reset the timer and cook for 3 minutes more. 4. Check the carrot chips for doneness. If you like them extra crispy, give the basket another shake and cook for another 1 to 2 minutes. 5. When the chips are done, release the air fryer basket from the drawer, pour the chips into a bowl, and serve.
Per Serving: Calories 71; Fat 5g; Sodium 364mg; Carbs 7g; Fiber 2g; Sugar 4g; Protein 1g

Healthy Cheesy Spinach Triangles

Prep time: 6 minutes | Cook time: 20 minutes | Serves: 6

3 cups mozzarella, shredded
4 tablespoons coconut flour
½ cup almond flour
2 eggs, whisked
A pinch of salt and black pepper

6 ounces spinach, chopped
¼ cup parmesan, grated
4 ounces cream cheese, soft
2 tablespoons ghee, melted

1. Select the "AIR FRY" function of Ninja Foodi digital air fry oven, set the temperature to 360 degrees F/ 180 degrees C and set the time to 20 minutes. Press the Start/Pause button and begin preheating. In a bowl, mix the mozzarella with coconut and almond flour, eggs, salt and pepper, stir well until you obtain a dough and roll it well on a parchment paper. 2. Cut into triangles and leave them aside for now. In a bowl, mix the spinach with parmesan, cream cheese, salt and pepper and stir really well. Divide this into the center of each dough triangle, roll and seal the edges. 3. Brush the rolls with the ghee, place them in your air fryer's basket and cook for 20 minutes. Serve as an appetizer.
Per Serving: Calories 210; Fat 8g; Sodium 100mg; Carbs 3g; Fiber 1g; Sugar 1g; Protein 8g

Scallions and Spinach Pie

Prep time: 15 minutes | Cook time: 15 minutes | Serves: 6

½ cup almond flour
6 eggs
2 cups spinach, chopped
1 oz. scallions, chopped
1 teaspoon sesame oil

1 tablespoon cream cheese
½ teaspoon baking powder
1 tablespoon butter, softened
1 teaspoon ground black pepper

1. In the mixing bowl put almond flour, baking powder, and butter. Then crack 2 eggs and mix up the mixture gently. After this, knead the non-sticky dough. Transfer the dough in the air fryer sheet pan and flatten well to get the shape of the pie crust. Select the "BAKE" function of Ninja Foodi digital air fry oven, set the temperature to 365 degrees F/ 185 degrees C and set the time to 10 minutes. Press the Start/Pause button and begin preheating. Put the pan with the pie crust inside. 2. Cook it for 10 minutes. Meanwhile, pour sesame oil in the skillet and heat it over the medium heat. 3. Cook scallions for 2 minutes. Then stir the vegetables and add chopped spinach and cream cheese. Cook the greens for 5 minutes over medium heat. Then sprinkle it with ground black pepper. 4. Transfer the spinach mixture in the pie crust and flatten gently. Bake the pie for 5 minutes at 365 degrees F/ 185 degrees C in the air fryer.
Per Serving: Calories 111; Fat 8.9g; Sodium 145mg; Carbs 2g; Fiber 0.7g; Sugar 0.9g; Protein 6.6g

Sesame Tofu

Prep time: 5 minutes | Cook time: 35 minutes | Serves: 4

1x 12 oz. package low-fat and extra firm tofu
2 tablespoons low-sodium soy sauce
2 tablespoons fish sauce

1 tablespoon coriander paste
1 teaspoon sesame oil
1 teaspoon duck fat or coconut oil
1 teaspoon Maggi sauce

1. Remove the liquid from the package of tofu and chop the tofu into 1-inch cubes. Place paper towels in plate and spread the tofu out on top in one layer. Place another paper towel on top, followed by another plate, weighting it down with a heavier object if necessary. This is to dry the tofu out completely. Leave for a minimum of 30 minutes or a maximum of 24 hours, replacing the paper towels once or twice throughout the duration. 2. In a medium bowl, mix together the sesame oil, Maggi sauce, coriander paste, fish sauce, and soy sauce. Stir to combine fully. 3. Coat the tofu cubes with this mixture and allow to marinate for at least a half-hour, tossing the cubes a few times throughout to ensure even coating. Add another few drops of fish sauce or soy sauce to thin out the marinade if necessary. 4. Select the "AIR FRY" function of Ninja Foodi digital air fry oven, set the temperature to 350 degrees F/ 175 degrees C and set the time to 20 minutes. Press the Start/Pause button and begin preheating. Melt the duck fat/coconut oil in your Air Fryer for about 2 minutes. Place the tofu cubes in the basket and cook for about 20 minutes or longer to achieve a crispier texture. Flip the tofu over or shake the basket every 10 minutes. 5. Serve hot with the dipping sauce of your choosing.
Per Serving: Calories 88; Fat 7.1g; Sodium 143mg; Carbs 4g; Fiber 3g; Sugar 1g; Protein 4g

Cheesy Bacon Fries

Prep time: 5 minutes | Cook time: 60 minutes | Serves: 2

2 large russet potatoes, peeled and cut into ½ inch sticks
5 slices of bacon, diced
2 tablespoons vegetable oil
2 ½ cups cheddar cheese, shredded

3 oz. cream cheese, melted
Salt and freshly ground black pepper
¼ cup chopped scallions
Ranch dressing

1. Boil water. 2. Briefly cook the potato sticks in the boiling water for 4 minutes. 3. Drain the potatoes and run some cold water over them in order to wash off the starch. Pat dry with a kitchen towel. 4. Select the "AIR FRY" function of Ninja Foodi digital air fry oven, set the temperature to 400 degrees F/ 200 degrees C and set the time to 60 minutes. Press the Start/Pause button and begin preheating. 5. Put the chopped bacon in the Air Fryer and air-fry for 4 minutes. Shake the basket at the halfway point. 6. Place the bacon on paper towels to drain any excess fat and remove the grease from the Air Fryer drawer. 7. Coat the dried potatoes with oil and put them in the Air Fryer basket. Air-fry at 360 degrees F/ 180 degrees C for 25 minutes, giving the basket the occasional shake throughout the cooking time and sprinkling the fries with salt and freshly ground black pepper at the halfway point. 8. Take a casserole dish or sheet pan that is small enough to fit inside your Air Fryer and place the fries inside. 9. Mix together the 2 cups of the Cheddar cheese and the melted cream cheese. 10. Pour the cheese mixture over the fries and top them with the rest of the Cheddar cheese and the cooked bacon crumbles. 11. Take absolute care when placing the sheet pan inside the cooker. Use a foil sling. 12. Cook the fries at 340 degrees F/ 170 degrees C for 5 minutes, ensuring the cheese melts. 13. Garnish the fries with the chopped scallions and serve straight from in the baking dish with some ranch dressing.
Per Serving: Calories 184; Fat 7.4g; Sodium 103mg; Carbs 7g; Fiber 1g; Sugar 1g; Protein 22g

Cheese and Bacon Potato Skins

Prep time: 10 minutes | Cook time: 12 minutes | Serves: 4

4 medium russet potatoes, baked
Olive oil
Salt
Freshly ground black pepper
2 cups shredded Cheddar cheese

4 slices cooked bacon, chopped
Finely chopped scallions, for topping
Sour cream, for topping
Finely chopped olives, for topping

1. Spray the air fryer basket with oil. 2. Cut each baked potato in half. 3. Using a large spoon, scoop out the center of each potato half, leaving about 1 inch of the potato flesh around the edges and the bottom. 4. Rub olive oil over the inside of each baked potato half and season with salt and pepper, then place the potato skins in the greased air fryer basket. 5. Select the "AIR FRY" function of Ninja Foodi digital air fry oven, set the temperature to 400 degrees F/ 200 degrees C and set the time to 10 minutes. Press the Start/Pause button and begin preheating. Set the timer and air fry for 10 minutes. 6. After 10 minutes, remove the potato skins and fill them with the shredded Cheddar cheese and bacon, then cook in the air fryer for another 2 minutes, just until the cheese is melted. 7. Garnish the potato skins with the scallions, sour cream, and olives.
Per Serving: Calories 487; Fat 31g; Sodium 986mg; Carbs 29g; Fiber 5g; Sugar 1g; Protein 24g

Tangy Olives Dip

Prep time: 5 minutes | Cook time: 5 minutes | Serves: 6

1 cup black olives, pitted and chopped
¼ cup capers
½ cup olive oil
3 tablespoons lemon juice

2 garlic cloves, minced
2 teaspoon apple cider vinegar
1 cup parsley leaves
1 cup basil leaves
A pinch of salt and black pepper

Select the "AIR FRY" function of Ninja Foodi digital air fry oven, set the temperature to 350 degrees F/ 175 degrees C and set the time to 5 minutes. Press the Start/Pause button and begin preheating. In a blender, blend all ingredients and transfer to a ramekin. Place the ramekin in your air fryer's basket and cook for 5 minutes. Serve as a snack.
Per Serving: Calories 120; Fat 5g; Sodium 147mg; Carbs 3g; Fiber 2g; Sugar 1g; Protein 7g

Fresh Potato Wedges

Prep time: 5 minutes | Cook time: 20 to 25 minutes | Serves: 4

4 russet potatoes
2 teaspoons salt, divided
1 teaspoon freshly ground black pepper
1 teaspoon paprika
1 to 3 tablespoons olive oil, divided

1. Cut the potatoes into ½-inch-thick wedges. Try to make the wedges uniform in size, so they cook at an even rate. 2. In a mixing bowl, Spice the potato wedges with 1 teaspoon of salt, pepper, paprika, and 1 tablespoon of olive oil. Toss until potatoes are coated with oil. Add additional oil, if needed. 3. Place the potato wedges in the air fryer basket in a single layer. (You may have to roast them in batches.) 4. Select the "AIR FRY" function of Ninja Foodi digital air fry oven, set the temperature to 400 degrees F/ 200 degrees C and set the time to 5 minutes. Press the Start/Pause button and begin preheating. 5. After 5 minutes, remove the air fryer drawer and shake the potatoes to keep them from sticking. Reset the timer and roast the potatoes for another 5 minutes, then shake again. Repeat this process until the potatoes have cooked for a total of 20 minutes. 6. Check and see if the potatoes are cooked. If they are not fork-tender, roast for 5 minutes more. 7. Using tongs, remove the potato wedges from the air fryer basket and transfer them to a bowl. Toss with the remaining salt.
Per Serving: Calories 210; Fat 7g; Sodium 1176mg; Carbs 34g; Fiber 6g; Sugar 3g; Protein 4g

Easy Potato Chips

Prep time: 5 minutes | Cook time: 15 to 20 minutes | Serves: 4

4 yellow potatoes
1 tablespoon olive oil
1 tablespoon salt (plus more for topping)

1. Using a mandolin or sharp knife, slice the potatoes into ⅛-inch-thick slices. 2. In a medium mixing bowl, toss the potato slices with the olive oil and salt until the potatoes are thoroughly coated with oil. 3. Place the potatoes in the air fryer basket in a single layer. (You may have to fry the potato chips in more than one batch.) 4. Select the "AIR FRY" function of Ninja Foodi digital air fry oven, set the temperature to 375 degrees F/ 190 degrees C and set the time to 15 minutes. Press the Start/Pause button and begin preheating. Set the timer and fry for 15 minutes. 5. Shake the basket several times during cooking, so the chips crisp evenly and don't burn. 6. Check to see if they are fork-tender; if not, add another 5 to 10 minutes, checking frequently. They will crisp up after they are removed from the air fryer. 7. Season with additional salt, if desired.
Per Serving: Calories 177; Fat 4g; Sodium 1757mg; Carbs 34g; Fiber 5g; Sugar 3g; Protein 4g

Crispy Parmesan Dill Pickles

Prep time: 5 minutes | Cook time: 8 minutes | Serves: 4

1 (16-ounce) jar sliced dill pickles
⅔ cup panko bread crumbs
⅓ cup grated Parmesan cheese
¼ teaspoon dried dill
2 large eggs

1. Line a platter with a double thickness of paper towels. Spread the pickles out in a single layer on the paper towels. Let the pickles drain on the towels for 20 minutes. After 20 minutes, pat the pickles again with a clean paper towel to get them as dry as possible before breading. 2. Select the "AIR FRY" function of Ninja Foodi digital air fry oven, set the temperature to 390 degrees F/ 200 degrees C and set the time to 4 minutes. Press the Start/Pause button and begin preheating. Grease the air fryer basket with olive oil. 3. In a mixing bowl, combine the panko bread crumbs, Parmesan cheese, and dried dill. Mix well. 4. In a bowl, Whisk the eggs until frothy. 5. Dip each pickle into the egg mixture, then into the breadcrumb mixture. Make sure the pickle is fully coated in breading. 6. Place the breaded pickle slices in the greased air fryer basket in a single layer. 7. Spray the pickles with a generous amount of olive oil. 8. Set the timer and fry for 4 minutes. 9. Open the air fryer drawer and use tongs to flip the pickles. Spray them again with olive oil. Reset the timer and fry for another 4 minutes. 10. Using tongs, remove the pickles from the drawer. Plate, serve, and enjoy!
Per Serving: Calories 153; Fat 6g; Sodium 1634mg; Carbs 16g; Fiber 2g; Sugar 3g; Protein 9g

Bacon-Wrapped Jalapeño Poppers

Prep time: 5 minutes | Cook time: 12 minutes | Serves: 12

12 jalapeño peppers
1 (8-ounce) cream cheese
1 cup shredded Cheddar cheese
1 teaspoon onion powder
1 teaspoon salt
½ teaspoon freshly ground black pepper
12 slices bacon, cut in half

1. Spray the air fryer basket with olive oil. 2. Cut each pepper in half, then use a spoon to scrape out the veins and seeds. 3. In a bowl, mix the cream cheese, Cheddar cheese, onion powder, salt, and pepper. 4. Using a small spoon, fill each pepper half with the cheese mixture. 5. Wrap stuffed pepper with a slice of bacon. 6. Place the bacon-wrapped peppers into the greased air fryer basket in a single layer. Select the "AIR FRY" function of Ninja Foodi digital air fry oven, set the temperature to 320 degrees F/ 160 degrees C and set the time to 12 minutes. Press the Start/Pause button and begin preheating. Set the timer and cook for 12 minutes. 7. Using tongs, remove the peppers from the air fryer, place them on a platter, and serve.
Per Serving: Calories 212; Fat 18g; Sodium 747mg; Carbs 2g; Fiber 0g; Sugar 1g; Protein 11g

Herbed Bacon Asparagus Wraps

Prep time: 5 minutes | Cook time: 15 minutes | Serves: 8

16 asparagus spears, trimmed
16 bacon strips
2 tablespoons olive oil
1 tablespoon lemon juice
1 teaspoon thyme, chopped
1 teaspoon oregano, chopped
A pinch of salt and black pepper

1. Select the "AIR FRY" function of Ninja Foodi digital air fry oven, set the temperature to 390 degrees F/ 200 degrees C and set the time to 15 minutes. Press the Start/Pause button and begin preheating. In a bowl, mix the oil with lemon juice, the herbs, salt and pepper and whisk well. Brush the asparagus spears with this mix and wrap each in a bacon strip. 2. Arrange the asparagus wraps in your air fryer's basket and cook for 15 minutes. Serve as an appetizer.
Per Serving: Calories 173; Fat 4g; Sodium 322mg; Carbs 3g; Fiber 2g; Sugar 1g; Protein 6g

Crispy Pickles Chips

Prep time: 10 minutes | Cook time: 10 minutes | Serves: 4

1 cup pickles, sliced
2 eggs, beaten
½ cup coconut flakes
1 teaspoon dried cilantro
¼ cup Provolone cheese, grated

1. Mix up coconut flakes, dried cilantro, and Provolone cheese. Then dip the sliced pickles in the egg and coat in coconut flakes mixture. 2. Select the "AIR FRY" function of Ninja Foodi digital air fry oven, set the temperature to 400 degrees F/ 200 degrees C and set the time to 5 minutes. Press the Start/Pause button and begin preheating. Arrange the pickles in the air fryer in one layer and cook them for 5 minutes. Then flip the pickles on another side and cook for another 5 minutes.
Per Serving: Calories 100; Fat 7.8g; Sodium 111mg; Carbs 2.8g; Fiber 1.4g; Sugar 1.2g; Protein 5.4g

Herbed Meat Skewers

Prep time: 10 minutes | Cook time: 20 minutes | Serves: 4

½ pound pork shoulder, cubed
¼ teaspoon sweet paprika
1 tablespoon coconut oil, melted
¼ teaspoon cumin, ground
¼ cup olive oil
¼ cup green bell peppers, chopped
1 and ½ tablespoons lemon juice
1 tablespoon cilantro, chopped
2 tablespoons parsley, chopped
2 garlic cloves, minced
A pinch of salt and black pepper

1. Select the "AIR FRY" function of Ninja Foodi digital air fry oven, set the temperature to 370 degrees F/ 185 degrees C and set the time to 20 minutes. Press the Start/Pause button and begin preheating. In a blender, blend the olive oil with bell peppers, lemon juice, cilantro, parsley, garlic, salt and pepper and pulse well. Thread the meat onto the skewers, sprinkle cumin and paprika all over and rub with the coconut oil. 2. In a bowl, mix the pork skewers with the herbed mix and rub well. Place the skewers in your air fryer's basket, cook for 10 minutes on each side and serve as an appetizer.
Per Serving: Calories 249; Fat 16g; Sodium 211mg; Carbs 3g; Fiber 2g; Sugar 2g; Protein 17g

Easy Radish Chips

Prep time: 5 minutes | Cook time: 15 minutes | Serves: 4

16 ounces radishes, thinly sliced   2 tablespoons coconut oil, melted
A pinch of salt and black pepper

1. Select the "AIR FRY" function of Ninja Foodi digital air fry oven, set the temperature to 400 degrees F/ 200 degrees C and set the time to 15 minutes. Press the Start/Pause button and begin preheating. 2. In a bowl, mix the radish slices with salt, pepper and the oil, toss well, place them in your air fryer's basket and cook for 15 minutes, flipping them halfway. Serve as a snack.
Per Serving: Calories 174; Fat 5g; Sodium 112mg; Carbs 3g; Fiber 1g; Sugar 1g; Protein 6g

Simple Cashew Bowls

Prep time: 5 minutes | Cook time: 5 minutes | Serves: 4

4 oz. cashew   1 teaspoon sesame oil
1 teaspoon ranch seasoning

1. Select the "AIR FRY" function of Ninja Foodi digital air fry oven, set the temperature to 375 degrees F/ 190 degrees C and set the time to 5 minutes. Press the Start/Pause button and begin preheating. Mix up cashew with ranch seasoning and sesame oil and put in the air fryer. 2. Cook the cashew for 4 minutes. Then shake well and cook for 1 minute more.
Per Serving: Calories 6; Fat 117g; Sodium 213mg; Carbs 6.2g; Fiber 0.5g; Sugar 1g; Protein 2.9g

Refreshing Lime Tomato Salsa

Prep time: 5 minutes | Cook time: 8 minutes | Serves: 4

4 tomatoes, cubed   2 tablespoons lime juice
3 chili peppers, minced   2 teaspoons cilantro, chopped
2 spring onions, chopped   2 teaspoons parsley, chopped
1 garlic clove, minced   Cooking spray

1. Select the "AIR FRY" function of Ninja Foodi digital air fry oven, set the temperature to 360 degrees F/ 180 degrees C and set the time to 8 minutes. Press the Start/Pause button and begin preheating. Grease a pan that fits your air fryer with the cooking spray, and mix all the ingredients inside. 2. Introduce the pan in the Ninja Foodi air fryer and cook for 8 minutes. Divide into bowls and serve as an appetizer.
Per Serving: Calories 148; Fat 1g; Sodium 159mg; Carbs 3g; Fiber 2g; Sugar 1g; Protein 5g

Easy Fried Beetroot Chips

Prep time: 5 minutes | Cook time: 30 minutes | Serves: 4

6 oz. beetroot, sliced   1 teaspoon salt

1. Sprinkle the beetroot slices with salt and mix up well. Select the "AIR FRY" function of Ninja Foodi digital air fry oven, set the temperature to 320 degrees F/ 160 degrees C and set the time to 30 minutes. Press the Start/Pause button and begin preheating. Put the beetroot slices in the air fryer basket. 2. Cook them for 30 minutes. Shake the beetroot chips every 5 minutes.
Per Serving: Calories 19; Fat 0.1g; Sodium 3mg; Carbs 64.2; Fiber 0.9g; Sugar 0.5g; Protein 0.7g

Creamy Chives Salmon Dip

Prep time: 5 minutes | Cook time: 6 minutes | Serves: 4

8 ounces cream cheese, soft   skinless, boneless and minced
2 tablespoons lemon juice   A pinch of salt and black pepper
½ cup coconut cream   1 tablespoon chives, chopped
4 ounces smoked salmon,

1. Select the "AIR FRY" function of Ninja Foodi digital air fry oven, set the temperature to 360 degrees F/ 180 degrees C and set the time to 6 minutes. Press the Start/Pause button and begin preheating. 2. In a bowl, mix all the ingredients and whisk them really well. Transfer the mix to a ramekin, place it in your air fryer's basket and cook for 6 minutes. Serve as a party spread.
Per Serving: Calories 180; Fat 7g; Sodium 12mg; Carbs 5g; Fiber 1g; Sugar 1g; Protein 7g

Yellow Jicama Wedges

Prep time: 10 minutes | Cook time: 3 minutes | Serves: 4

8 oz. Jicama, peeled   ¼ teaspoon dried dill
½ teaspoon ground turmeric   1 tablespoon avocado oil

1. Cut the Jicama on the wedges and sprinkle them with turmeric and dried dill. Then sprinkle the vegetables with avocado oil. 2. Select the "AIR FRY" function of Ninja Foodi digital air fry oven, set the temperature to 400 degrees F/ 200 degrees C and set the time to 3 minutes. Press the Start/Pause button and begin preheating. Place the Jicama wedges in the air fryer basket in one layer and cook them for 3 minutes.
Per Serving: Calories 27; Fat 0.5g; Sodium 11mg; Carbs 5.4g; Fiber 3g; Sugar 2g; Protein 0.5g

Spicy Kale Chips

Prep time: 5 minutes | Cook time: 5 minutes | Serves: 4

1 teaspoon nutritional yeast   ½ teaspoon chili flakes
1 teaspoon salt   1 teaspoon sesame oil
2 cups kale, chopped

1. Mix kale leaves with nutritional yeast, salt, chili flakes, and sesame oil. Shake the greens well. Select the "AIR FRY" function of Ninja Foodi digital air fry oven, set the temperature to 400 degrees F/ 200 degrees C and set the time to 5 minutes. Press the Start/Pause button and begin preheating. 2. Put the kale leaves in the air fryer basket. Cook them for 3 minutes and then give a good shake. Cook the kale leaves for 2 minutes more.
Per Serving: Calories 30; Fat 1.2g; Sodium 11mg; Carbs 3.9g; Fiber 0.7g; Sugar 0.4g; Protein 1.4g

Fried Cheese Slices

Prep time: 10 minutes | Cook time: 6 minutes | Serves: 4

8 oz. goat cheese   ¼ cup coconut flour
1 egg, beaten   ¼ cup almond flour
1 tablespoon heavy cream   1 teaspoon sesame oil

1. Slice the goat cheese on 4 slices. Then mix up beaten egg and heavy cream. In the separated bowl mix up coconut flour and almond flour. 2. Select the "AIR FRY" function of Ninja Foodi digital air fry oven, set the temperature to 400 degrees F/ 200 degrees C and set the time to 6 minutes. Press the Start/Pause button and begin preheating. Dip the cheese in the egg mix and then coat in the almond flour mixture. 3. Repeat the last 2 steps two times. Transfer the goat cheese slices to the air fryer basket and cook them for 3 minutes from each side or until the cheese slices are light brown.
Per Serving: Calories 340; Fat 25.4g; Sodium 110mg; Carbs 6.3g; Fiber 3.2g; Sugar 3g; Protein 20.6g

Tropical Shrimp

Prep time: 5 minutes | Cook time: 20 minutes | Serves: 16

½ teaspoon salt   shredded
1 lb. large shrimp [about 16 to 20   Zest of 1 lime
peeled/de-veined]   ¼ teaspoon cayenne pepper
½ cup flour   Spray can of vegetable or canola
2 egg whites   oil
½ cup friendly (panko) bread   Sweet chili sauce or duck sauce,
crumbs   to serve
½ cup unsweetened coconut,

1. In a dish, whisk the eggs with a whisk. 2. Combine the bread crumbs, coconut, lime zest, salt and cayenne pepper in a separate dish. 3. Select the "AIR FRY" function of Ninja Foodi digital air fry oven, set the temperature to 400 degrees F/ 200 degrees C and set the time to 6 minutes. Press the Start/Pause button and begin preheating. 4. Coat the shrimp in the flour. Dip them into the egg mixture, and then into the breadcrumb coconut mixture, ensuring to coat the shrimp all over. 5. Place the shrimp on a plate and spritz with oil. Move the shrimp to the basket of your fryer, taking care not to overlap the fish. 6. Air fry the shrimp for 5 - 6 minutes, ensuring that each shrimp is cooked through and firm before serving.
Per Serving: Calories 205; Fat 5.8g; Sodium 1481mg; Carbs 1g; Fiber 0g; Sugar 0g; Protein 35g

Mixed Cheesy Veggie Bites

Prep time: 10 minutes | Cook time: 10 minutes | Serves: 6

1 cup zucchinis, cubed
1 cup eggplant, cubed
3 oz. Parmesan

1 tablespoon coconut cream
1 egg, beaten
½ tablespoon avocado oil

Select the "AIR FRY" function of Ninja Foodi digital air fry oven, set the temperature to 400 degrees F/ 200 degrees C and set the time to 10 minutes. Press the Start/Pause button and begin preheating. In the mixing bowl mix up beaten egg and coconut cream. Then dip the veggie cubes in the egg mixture and sprinkle with Parmesan. Place the coated vegetables in the oiled air fryer basket in one layer and cook for 10 minutes. Serve as a snack.
Per Serving: Calories 75; Fat 4.6g; Sodium 33mg; Carbs 3.6g; Fiber 0.6g; Sugar 0.9g; Protein 5.9g

Parmesan Fried Green Beans

Prep time: 5 minutes | Cook time: 12 minutes | Serves: 4

12 ounces green beans, trimmed
1 cup parmesan, grated
1 egg, whisked

A pinch of salt and black pepper
¼ teaspoon sweet paprika

Select the "AIR FRY" function of Ninja Foodi digital air fry oven, set the temperature to 380 degrees F/ 195 degrees C and set the time to 12 minutes. Press the Start/Pause button and begin preheating. In a bowl, mix the parmesan with salt, pepper and the paprika and stir. Put the egg in a separate bowl, Dredge the green beans in egg and then in the parmesan mix. Arrange the green beans in your air fryer's basket and cook for 12 minutes. Serve as a snack.
Per Serving: Calories 112; Fat 6g; Sodium 85mg; Carbs 2g; Fiber 1g; Sugar 1g; Protein 9g

Herbed Balsamic Mushroom

Prep time: 5 minutes | Cook time: 12 minutes | Serves: 4

2 tablespoons balsamic vinegar
2 tablespoons olive oil
½ teaspoon basil, dried
½ teaspoon tarragon, dried
½ teaspoon rosemary, dried

½ teaspoon thyme, dried
A pinch of salt and black pepper
12 ounces Portobello mushrooms, sliced

Select the "AIR FRY" function of Ninja Foodi digital air fry oven, set the temperature to 380 degrees F/ 195 degrees C and set the time to 12 minutes. Press the Start/Pause button and begin preheating. In a bowl, mix all the ingredients and toss well. Arrange the mushroom slices in your air fryer's basket and cook for 12 minutes. Arrange the mushroom slices on a platter and serve.
Per Serving: Calories 147; Fat 8g; Sodium 333mg; Carbs 2g; Fiber 2g; Sugar 0g; Protein 3g

Chicken Wings with Barbecue Sauce

Prep time: 5 minutes | Cook time: 20 minutes | Serves: 6

For the Sauce:
1 tablespoon yellow mustard
1 tablespoon apple cider vinegar
1 tablespoon olive oil
¼ cup unsulfured blackstrap molasses
¼ cup ketchup
For the Wings
2 lb. chicken wings
¼ teaspoon celery salt

2 tablespoons sugar
1 garlic clove, minced
Salt and ground black pepper, to taste
⅛ teaspoon ground allspice
¼ cup water

¼ cup habanero hot sauce
Chopped fresh parsley, or garnish

1. Put all the for the sauce in a pan over a medium-to-high heat and bring the mixture to a boil. 2. Lower the heat and allow to simmer and thicken. 3. In the meantime, Select the "AIR FRY" function of Ninja Foodi digital air fry oven, set the temperature to 400 degrees F/ 200 degrees C and set the time to 15 minutes. Press the Start/Pause button and begin preheating. 4. Place the chicken in the fryer and cook for 6 minutes. 5. Turn the wings and cook for another 6 minutes on the other side. Sprinkle some celery salt over them. 6. Serve the chicken wings with the prepared sauce, along with habanero sauce or any other accompaniment of your choice.
Per Serving: Calories 144; Fat 6.6g; Sodium 171mg; Carbs 2g; Fiber 0g; Sugar 1g; Protein 19g

Crispy Pumpkin Seeds

Prep time: 5 minutes | Cook time: 25 minutes | Serves: 4

1 ½ cups pumpkin seeds [cut a whole pumpkin & scrape out the insides
using a large spoon, separating

the seeds from the flesh]
1 teaspoon smoked paprika
1 ½ teaspoon salt
Olive oil

1. Run the pumpkin seeds under some cold water. 2. Over a medium heat, boil two quarts of salted water in a pot. 3. Add in the pumpkin seeds and cook in the water for 8 to 10 minutes. 4. Dump the contents of the pot into a sieve to drain the seeds. Place them on paper towels and allow them to dry for at least 20 minutes. 5. Select the "AIR ROAST" function of Ninja Foodi digital air fry oven, set the temperature to 350 degrees F/ 175 degrees C and set the time to 15 minutes. Press the Start/Pause button and begin preheating. 6. In a medium bowl coat the pumpkin seeds with olive oil, smoked paprika and salt. 7. Put them in the fryer's basket and air fry for at least 30 minutes until slightly browned and crispy. Shake the basket during the cooking time. 8. Allow the seeds to cool. Serve with a salad or keep in an airtight container for snacking.
Per Serving: Calories 295; Fat 21.2g; Sodium 94mg; Carbs 3g; Fiber 1g; Sugar 1g; Protein 23g

Lemony Shrimp Bowls

Prep time: 5 minutes | Cook time: 10 minutes | Serves: 4

1-pound shrimp, peeled and deveined
3 garlic cloves, minced
¼ cup olive oil

Juice of ½ lemon
A pinch of salt and black pepper
¼ teaspoon cayenne pepper

Select the "AIR FRY" function of Ninja Foodi digital air fry oven, set the temperature to 370 degrees F/ 185 degrees C and set the time to 10 minutes. Press the Start/Pause button and begin preheating. In a pan that fits your air fryer, mix all the ingredients, toss, introduce in the fryer and cook for 10 minutes. Serve as a snack.
Per Serving: Calories 242; Fat 14g; Sodium 322mg; Carbs 3g; Fiber 2g; Sugar 3g; Protein 17g

Moroccan Eggplant Dip

Prep time: 10 minutes | Cook time: 15 minutes | Serves: 4

1 eggplant, peeled
1 garlic clove, peeled
1 tablespoon sesame oil
¼ teaspoon ginger, grated
1 chili pepper, minced
½ tablespoon spring onions,

chopped
½ teaspoon chili powder
¼ teaspoon ground coriander
¼ teaspoon turmeric
½ teaspoon fresh cilantro, chopped

1. Select the "AIR FRY" function of Ninja Foodi digital air fry oven, set the temperature to 400 degrees F/ 200 degrees C and set the time to 15 minutes. Press the Start/Pause button and begin preheating. Chop the eggplant into the cubes and put it in the air fryer. Add garlic and cook the vegetables for 15 minutes. Shake the vegetables every 5 minutes. 2. After this, transfer the soft eggplants and garlic in the bowl and mash them with the help of the fork. Add sesame oil, ginger, minced chili pepper, onion, chili powder, ground coriander, and turmeric. Stir the mixture until homogenous and top with cilantro.
Per Serving: Calories 63; Fat 3.7g; Sodium 11mg; Carbs 7.5g; Fiber 4.3g; Sugar 3g; Protein 1.3g

Spicy Onion Rings

Prep time: 10 minutes | Cook time: 10 minutes | Serves: 2

1 pound onion rings
1 teaspoon black pepper

½ teaspoon avocado oil
¼ teaspoon chili powder

Select the "AIR FRY" function of Ninja Foodi digital air fry oven, set the temperature to 400 degrees F/ 200 degrees C and set the time to 10 minutes. Press the Start/Pause button and begin preheating. In the air fryer, mix the onion rings with black pepper and the other ingredients and toss. Cook the onion rings 10 minutes.
Per Serving: Calories 127; Fat 8.2g; Sodium 62mg; Carbs 5.7g; Fiber 1.3g; Sugar 1g; Protein 7.7g

Yogurt Marinated Endive

Prep time: 5 minutes | Cook time: 20 minutes | Serves: 6

6 heads endive
½ cup plain and fat-free yogurt
3 tablespoons lemon juice
1 teaspoon garlic powder
½ teaspoon curry powder
Salt and ground black pepper to taste

1. Wash the endives, and slice them in half lengthwise. 2. In a bowl, mix together the yogurt, lemon juice, garlic powder [or minced garlic], curry powder, salt and pepper. If you would like your marinade to be thinner, add some more lemon juice. 3. Brush the endive halves with the marinade, coating them completely. Allow to sit for a minimum of a half-hour and a maximum of one day. 4. Select the "AIR FRY" function of Ninja Foodi digital air fry oven, set the temperature to 320 degrees F/ 160 degrees C and set the time to 10 minutes. Press the Start/Pause button and begin preheating. Allow the endives to cook for 10 minutes and serve hot.
Per Serving: Calories 271; Fat 9.3g; Sodium 15mg; Carbs 43g; Fiber 6g; Sugar 2g; Protein 5g

Cheesy Shrimp Dip

Prep time: 5 minutes | Cook time: 20 minutes | Serves: 4

1-pound shrimp, peeled, deveined and minced
2 tablespoons ghee, melted
¼ pound mushrooms, minced
½ cup mozzarella, shredded
4 garlic cloves, minced
1 tablespoon parsley, chopped
Salt and black pepper to the taste

Select the "AIR FRY" function of Ninja Foodi digital air fry oven, set the temperature to 360 degrees F/ 180 degrees C and set the time to 20 minutes. Press the Start/Pause button and begin preheating. In a bowl, mix all the ingredients, stir well, divide into small ramekins and place them in your air fryer's basket. Cook for 20 minutes and serve as a party dip.
Per Serving: Calories 271; Fat 15g; Sodium 366mg; Carbs 4g; Fiber 3g; Sugar 1g; Protein 14g

Healthy Tuna Bowls

Prep time: 5 minutes | Cook time: 10 minutes | Serves: 2

1-pound tuna, skinless, boneless and cubed
3 scallion stalks, minced
1 chili pepper, minced
2 tablespoons olive oil
1 tablespoon coconut cream
1 tablespoon coconut aminos
2 tomatoes, cubed
1 teaspoon sesame seeds

Select the "AIR FRY" function of Ninja Foodi digital air fry oven, set the temperature to 360 degrees F/ 180 degrees C and set the time to 10 minutes. Press the Start/Pause button and begin preheating. In a pan that fits your air fryer, mix all the ingredients except the sesame seeds, toss, introduce in the fryer and cook for 10 minutes. Serve as an appetizer with sesame seeds sprinkled on top.
Per Serving: Calories 231; Fat 18g; Sodium 147mg; Carbs 4g; Fiber 3g; Sugar 1g; Protein 18g

Turkey Patties

Prep time: 5 minutes | Cook time: 20 minutes | Serves: 6

1 lb. lean ground turkey
1 teaspoon olive oil
1 tablespoon chopped chives
1 small onion, diced
1 large garlic clove, chopped
¾ teaspoon paprika
Kosher salt and pepper to taste
Pinch of raw sugar
1 tablespoon vinegar
1 teaspoon fennel seed
Pinch of nutmeg

1. Select the "AIR FRY" function of Ninja Foodi digital air fry oven, set the temperature to 375 degrees F/ 190 degrees C and set the time to 20 minutes. Press the Start/Pause button and begin preheating. 2. Add a half-teaspoon of the oil to the fryer, along with the onion and garlic. Air fry for 30 seconds before adding in the fennel. Place everything on a plate. 3. In a bowl, combine the ground turkey with the sugar, paprika, nutmeg, vinegar, chives and the onion mixture. Divide and shape each one into a patty. 4. Add another teaspoon of oil to the fryer. Put the patties in yond cook for roughly 3 minutes. 5. Serve with salad or on hamburger buns.
Per Serving: Calories 494; Fat 36g; Sodium 690mg; Carbs 17g; Fiber 11g; Sugar 2g; Protein 28g

Tangy Tofu Cubes

Prep time: 10 minutes | Cook time: 7 minutes | Serves: 2

½ teaspoon ground coriander
1 tablespoon avocado oil
1 teaspoon lemon juice
½ teaspoon chili flakes
6 oz. tofu

1.In the shallow bowl mix up ground coriander, avocado oil, lemon juice, and chili flakes. Chop the tofu into cubes and sprinkle with coriander mixture. 2. Shake the tofu. Select the "AIR FRY" function of Ninja Foodi digital air fry oven, set the temperature to 400 degrees F/ 200 degrees C and set the time to 7 minutes. Press the Start/Pause button and begin preheating. Put the tofu cubes in it. Cook the tofu for 4 minutes. Then flip the tofu on another side and cook for 3 minutes more.
Per Serving: Calories 70; Fat 4.5g; Sodium 147mg; Carbs 1.9g; Fiber 1.1g; Sugar 0.3g; Protein 7.1g

Cheese and Chives Stuffed Mushrooms

Prep time: 5 minutes | Cook time: 10 minutes | Serves: 4

1 tablespoon butter
6 ounces Pecorino Romano cheese, grated
2 tablespoons chives, chopped
1 tablespoon minced garlic
½ teaspoon cayenne pepper
Sea salt
Ground black pepper, to taste
1 pound button mushrooms, stems removed

1. Select the "AIR FRY" function of Ninja Foodi digital air fry oven, set the temperature to 400 degrees F/ 200 degrees C and set the time to 7 minutes. Press the Start/Pause button and begin preheating. 2. In a mixing bowl, thoroughly combine the butter, cheese, chives, garlic, cayenne pepper, salt, and black pepper. 3. Divide the filling between your mushrooms. Place the mushrooms in the basket. Cook your mushrooms at for about 7 minutes, shaking the basket halfway through the cooking time. Bon appétit!
Per Serving: Calories 225; Fat 14.8g; Sodium 366mg; Carbs 7.2g; Fiber 1.4g; Sugar 3.2g; Protein 17.6g

Crispy Avocado Wedges

Prep time: 5 minutes | Cook time: 8 minutes | Serves: 2

4 avocados, peeled, pitted and cut into wedges
1 egg, whisked
1 and ½ cups almond meal
A pinch of salt and black pepper
Cooking spray

Select the "AIR FRY" function of Ninja Foodi digital air fry oven, set the temperature to 400 degrees F/ 200 degrees C and set the time to 8 minutes. Press the Start/Pause button and begin preheating. Put the egg in a bowl, and the almond meal in another. Season avocado wedges with salt and pepper, coat them in egg and then in meal almond. Arrange the avocado bites in your air fryer's basket, grease them with cooking spray and cook for 8 minutes. Serve as a snack right away.
Per Serving: Calories 200; Fat 12g; Sodium 325mg; Carbs 5g; Fiber 3g; Sugar 2g; Protein 16g

Easy Cheesy Cauliflower

Prep time: 5 minutes | Cook time: 20 minutes | Serves: 4

½ cup milk
1 cup all-purpose flour
1 teaspoon garlic powder
1 teaspoon onion powder
1 teaspoon hot paprika
Sea salt
Ground black pepper, to taste
2 tablespoons olive oil
1 pound cauliflower florets
4 ounces parmesan cheese, preferably freshly grated

1. Select the "AIR FRY" function of Ninja Foodi digital air fry oven, set the temperature to 350 degrees F/ 175 degrees C and set the time to 15 minutes. Press the Start/Pause button and begin preheating. 2. In a mixing bowl, thoroughly combine the milk, flour, spices, and olive oil. 3. Dip the cauliflower florets in the flour mixture. 4. Cook the cauliflower florets for about 10 minutes, turning them over halfway through the cooking time. 5. Top the cauliflower florets with cheese and continue to cook an additional 5 minutes. Bon appétit!
Per Serving: Calories 358; Fat 37.3g; Sodium 745mg; Carbs 14.9g; Fiber 3.6g; Sugar 4.5g; Protein 14.9g

Salami Wrapped Banana Peppers

Prep time: 5 minutes | Cook time: 20 minutes | Serves: 8

1 cup full-fat cream cheese
Cooking spray
16 avocado slices
16 slices salami
Salt and pepper to taste
16 banana peppers

1. Select the "BAKE" function of Ninja Foodi digital air fry oven, set the temperature to 400 degrees F/ 200 degrees C and set the time to 10 minutes. Press the Start/Pause button and begin preheating. 2. Spritz a baking tray with cooking spray. 3. Remove the stems from the banana peppers with a knife. 4. Cut a slit into one side of each banana pepper. 5. Season the cream cheese with the salt and pepper and combine well. 6. Fill each pepper with one spoonful of the cream cheese, followed by one slice of avocado. 7. Wrap the banana peppers in the slices of salami and secure with a toothpick. 8. Place the banana peppers in the baking tray and transfer it to the Air Fryer. Bake for roughly 8 - 10 minutes.
Per Serving: Calories 314; Fat 27.2g; Sodium 182mg; Carbs 0g; Fiber 0g; Sugar 0g; Protein 17g

Cheesy Bacon Dip

Prep time: 5 minutes | Cook time: 20 minutes | Serves: 12

2 tablespoons ghee, melted
3 cups spring onions, chopped
A pinch of salt and black pepper
2 ounces cheddar cheese,
shredded
⅓ cup coconut cream
6 bacon slices, cooked and crumbled

1. Select the "AIR FRY" function of Ninja Foodi digital air fry oven, set the temperature to 380 degrees F/ 195 degrees C and set the time to 13 minutes. Press the Start/Pause button and begin preheating. Heat up a pan that fits the fryer with the ghee over medium-high heat, add the onions, stir and sauté for 7 minutes. Add the remaining ingredients instead of the bacon and stir well. 2. Sprinkle the bacon on top, introduce the pan in the Ninja Foodi air fryer and cook for 13 minutes. Divide into bowls and serve as a party dip.
Per Serving: Calories 220; Fat 12g; Sodium 74mg; Carbs 4g; Fiber 2g; Sugar 2g; Protein 15g

Fried Green Tomatoes

Prep time: 10 minutes | Cook time: 20 minutes | Serves: 4

½ cup all-purpose flour
Sea salt
Ground black pepper, to taste
1 teaspoon garlic powder
1 teaspoon cayenne pepper
2 eggs
½ cup milk
2 tablespoons olive oil
1 cup breadcrumbs
1 pound green tomatoes, sliced

1. Select the "AIR FRY" function of Ninja Foodi digital air fry oven, set the temperature to 390 degrees F/ 200 degrees C and set the time to 15 minutes. Press the Start/Pause button and begin preheating. 2. In a shallow bowl, mix the flour with salt, pepper along with garlic powder, and cayenne pepper. 3. Whisk the egg and milk in shallow bowl. 4. Mix the olive oil and breadcrumbs in a separate bowl. 5. Dip the green tomatoes in the flour, then in the eggs, then in the breadcrumbs. 6. Place the green tomatoes in the air fryer basket. Cook the green tomatoes for about 15 minutes or until golden brown and cooked through. 7. Serve with toothpicks. Bon appétit!
Per Serving: Calories 215; Fat 10.4g; Sodium 214mg; Carbs 23.1g; Fiber 1.8g; Sugar 2.8g; Protein 7.6g

Herbed Eggplant Sticks

Prep time: 10 minutes | Cook time: 8 minutes | Serves: 3

6 oz. eggplant, trimmed
½ teaspoon dried oregano
½ teaspoon dried cilantro
½ teaspoon dried thyme
½ teaspoon ground cumin
½ teaspoon salt
1 tablespoon olive oil
¼ teaspoon garlic powder

Cut the eggplant into the fries and sprinkle with dried oregano, cilantro, thyme, cumin, salt, and garlic powder. Then sprinkle the eggplant fries with olive oil and shake well. Select the "AIR FRY" function of Ninja Foodi digital air fry oven, set the temperature to 400 degrees F/ 200 degrees C and set the time to 8 minutes. Press the Start/ Pause button and begin preheating. Place the eggplant in the air fryer and cook them for 4 minutes from each side.
Per Serving: Calories 58; Fat 4.9g; Sodium 112mg; Carbs 3.9g; Fiber 2.2g; Sugar 1.2g; Protein 0.7g

Roasted Nuts

Prep time: 5 minutes | Cook time: 10 minutes | Serves: 4

¼ cup almonds
½ cup hazelnuts
¼ cup peanuts

1. Select the "AIR ROAST" function of Ninja Foodi digital air fry oven, set the temperature to 330 degrees F/ 165 degrees C and set the time to 6 minutes. Press the Start/Pause button and begin preheating. Air fry the nuts for 6 minutes, shaking the basket halfway and working in batches. Enjoy!
Per Serving: Calories 210; Fat 19.2g; Sodium 410mg; Carbs 6.2g; Fiber 3.5g; Sugar 1.5g; Protein 6.7g

Ham and Cheese Stuffed Serrano Peppers

Prep time: 5 minutes | Cook time: 10 minutes | Serves: 4

8 Serrano peppers
4 ounces ham cubes
4 ounces goat cheese, crumbled

Select the "AIR FRY" function of Ninja Foodi digital air fry oven, set the temperature to 370 degrees F/ 185 degrees C and set the time to 7 minutes. Press the Start/Pause button and begin preheating. Stuff the peppers with ham and cheese; transfer them to a lightly oiled Air Fryer basket. Air fry the peppers for about 7 minutes or until golden brown. Bon appétit!
Per Serving: Calories 169; Fat 11.1g; Sodium 347mg; Carbs 1.7g; Fiber 0.6g; Sugar 1.1g; Protein 13.6g

Cheesy Crab Dip

Prep time: 5 minutes | Cook time: 20 minutes | Serves: 4

8 ounces cream cheese, soft
1 tablespoon lemon juice
1 cup coconut cream
1 tablespoon lemon juice
1 bunch green onions, minced
1-pound artichoke hearts, drained
and chopped
12 ounces jumbo crab meat
A pinch of salt and black pepper
1 and ½ cups mozzarella, shredded

1. Select the "AIR FRY" function of Ninja Foodi digital air fry oven, set the temperature to 400 degrees F/ 200 degrees C and set the time to 15 minutes. Press the Start/Pause button and begin preheating. In a bowl, mix all ingredients instead of half of the cheese and whisk them really well. Transfer this to a pan that fits your air fryer, introduce in the Ninja Foodi air fryer and cook for 15 minutes. 2. Sprinkle the rest of the mozzarella on top and cook for 5 minutes more. Divide and serve as a party dip.
Per Serving: Calories 240; Fat 8g; Sodium 144mg; Carbs 4g; Fiber 2g; Sugar 2g; Protein 14g

Bacon Butter

Prep time: 30 minutes | Cook time: 8 minutes | Serves: 5

½ cup butter
3 oz. bacon, chopped

Select the "AIR FRY" function of Ninja Foodi digital air fry oven, set the temperature to 400 degrees F/ 200 degrees C and set the time to 8 minutes. Press the Start/Pause button and begin preheating. Put the bacon inside. Cook it for 8 minutes. Stir the bacon every 2 minutes. Meanwhile, soften the butter in the oven and put it in the butter mold. Add cooked bacon and churn the butter. Refrigerate the butter for 30 minutes.
Per Serving: Calories 255; Fat 25.5g; Sodium 110mg; Carbs 0.3g; Fiber 0g; Sugar 0g; Protein 6.5g

Crispy Sage Radish Chips

Prep time: 10 minutes | Cook time: 35 minutes | Serves: 6

2 cups radish, sliced
½ teaspoon sage
2 teaspoons avocado oil
½ teaspoon salt

In the mixing bowl mix up radish, sage, avocado oil, and salt. Select the "AIR FRY" function of Ninja Foodi digital air fry oven, set the temperature to 320 degrees F/ 160 degrees C and set the time to 35 minutes. Press the Start/Pause button and begin preheating. Put the sliced radish in the air fryer basket and cook it for 35 minutes. Shake the vegetables every 10 minutes.
Per Serving: Calories 8; Fat 0.3g; Sodium 5mg; Carbs 1.4g; Fiber 0.7g; Sugar 0.6g; Protein 0.3g

Fried Eggplant Chips

Prep time: 5 minutes | Cook time: 20 minutes | Serves: 4

1 pound eggplant, sliced	Sea salt
2 tablespoons olive oil	Ground black pepper, to taste
1 teaspoon garlic, minced	2 tablespoons lemon juice

1. Select the "AIR FRY" function of Ninja Foodi digital air fry oven, set the temperature to 400 degrees F/ 200 degrees C and set the time to 15 minutes. Press the Start/Pause button and begin preheating. 2. Toss the eggplant pieces with the remaining ingredients until they are well coated on all sides. 3. Arrange the eggplant in the air fryer basket. Cook the eggplant for about 15 minutes, shaking the basket halfway through the cooking time. Bon appétit!
Per Serving: Calories 95; Fat 7g; Sodium 210mg; Carbs 8.4g; Fiber 3.6g; Sugar 4.7g; Protein 1.5g

Herbed Tomato Chips

Prep time: 5 minutes | Cook time: 20 minutes | Serves: 2

1 beefsteak tomato, thinly sliced	Ground pepper, to taste
2 tablespoons extra-virgin olive oil	1 teaspoon dried basil
	1 teaspoon dried thyme
Sea salt	1 teaspoon dried rosemary

1. Select the "AIR FRY" function of Ninja Foodi digital air fry oven, set the temperature to 360 degrees F/ 180 degrees C and set the time to 15 minutes. Press the Start/Pause button and begin preheating. 2. Toss the tomato slices with the remaining ingredients until they are well coated on all sides. 3. Arrange the tomato slices in the air fryer cooking basket. Cook the tomato slices for about 10 minutes. 4. Turn the temperature to 330 degrees F/ 165 degrees C and continue to cook for a further 5 minutes. Bon appétit!
Per Serving: Calories 145; Fat 13.7g; Sodium 411mg; Carbs 6g; Fiber 1.7g; Sugar 3.5g; Protein 1.3g

Cheddar Brussels Sprouts

Prep time: 5 minutes | Cook time: 15 minutes | Serves: 4

1 pound Brussels sprouts, trimmed	1 teaspoon garlic, minced
2 tablespoons butter, melted	2 tablespoons red wine vinegar
Sea salt	2 ounces cheddar cheese, shredded
Ground black pepper, to taste	

Select the "AIR FRY" function of Ninja Foodi digital air fry oven, set the temperature to 380 degrees F/ 195 degrees C and set the time to 10 minutes. Press the Start/Pause button and begin preheating. Toss the Brussels sprouts with the other ingredients; then, arrange the Brussels sprouts in the air fryer cooking basket. Cook the Brussels sprouts for 10 minutes, shaking the basket halfway through the cooking time. Serve warm and enjoy!
Per Serving: Calories 127; Fat 7.3g; Sodium 269mg; Carbs 5.8g; Fiber 4.3g; Sugar 3.5g; Protein 5.8g

Crunchy Carrots & Rhubarb

Prep time: 5 minutes | Cook time: 30 minutes | Serves: 4

1 lb. heritage carrots	2 teaspoons walnut oil
1 lb. rhubarb	½ teaspoon sugar or a few drops of sugar extract
1 medium orange	
½ cup walnuts, halved	

1. Select the "AIR FRY" function of Ninja Foodi digital air fry oven, set the temperature to 320 degrees F/ 160 degrees C and set the time to 20 minutes. Press the Start/Pause button and begin preheating. Rinse the carrots to wash. Dry and chop them into 1-inch pieces. 2. Transfer them to the air fryer basket and drizzle over the walnut oil. 3. Cook for about 20 minutes. 4. In the meantime, wash the rhubarb and chop it into ½-inch pieces. 5. Coarsely dice the walnuts. 6. Wash the orange and grate its skin into a small bowl. Peel the rest of the orange and cut it up into wedges. 7. Place the rhubarb, walnuts and sugar in the fryer and allow to cook for an additional 5 minutes. 8. Add in 2 tablespoons of the orange zest, along with the orange wedges. Serve immediately.
Per Serving: Calories 101; Fat 5.4g; Sodium 106mg; Carbs 8g; Fiber 3g; Sugar 3g; Protein 7g

Chicken Pizza

Prep time: 5 minutes | Cook time: 25 minutes | Serves: 4

10 ½ oz. minced chicken	2 tablespoons tomato basil sauce
1 teaspoon garlic powder	5 button mushrooms, sliced thinly
1 teaspoon black pepper	Handful of spinach

1. Select the "BAKE" function of Ninja Foodi digital air fry oven, set the temperature to 450 degrees F/ 230 degrees C and set the time to 25 minutes. Press the Start/Pause button and begin preheating. 2. Add parchment paper onto your baking tray. 3. In a large bowl add the chicken with the black pepper and garlic powder. 4. Add one spoonful of the chicken mix onto your baking tray. 5. Flatten them into 7-inch rounds. 6. Bake in the Air Fryer for about 10 minutes. 7. Take out the air fryer and add the tomato basil sauce onto each round. 8. Add the mushroom on top. Bake again for 5 minutes. 9. Serve immediately.
Per Serving: Calories 387; Fat 26.3g; Sodium 602mg; Carbs 12g; Fiber 8g; Sugar 1g; Protein 26g

Roasted Broccoli

Prep time: 5 minutes | Cook time: 30 minutes | Serves: 4

1 large head broccoli	1 tablespoon white sesame seeds
½ lemon, juiced	2 teaspoons Maggi sauce or other seasonings to taste
3 cloves garlic, minced	
1 tablespoon coconut oil	

1. Select the "AIR ROAST" function of Ninja Foodi digital air fry oven, set the temperature to 320 degrees F/ 160 degrees C and set the time to 20 minutes. Press the Start/Pause button and begin preheating. Wash and dry the broccoli. Chop it up into small florets. 2. Place the minced garlic in your air fryer basket, along with the coconut oil and lemon juice and Maggi sauce. 3. Heat for 2 minutes at 320 degrees F/ 160 degrees C and give it a stir. Put the garlic and broccoli in the basket and cook for another 13 minutes. 4. Top the broccoli with the white sesame seeds and resume cooking for 5 more minutes, ensuring the seeds become nice and toasty.
Per Serving: Calories 147; Fat 7.3g; Sodium 56mg; Carbs 20g; Fiber 5g; Sugar 11g; Protein 4g

Tasty Eggplant Cubes

Prep time: 5 minutes | Cook time: 45 minutes | Serves: 6

3 eggplants, medium	1 teaspoon sumac
½ lemon, juiced	1 teaspoon garlic powder
1 tablespoon duck fat, or coconut oil	1 teaspoon onion powder
	1 teaspoon extra virgin olive oil
1 tablespoon Maggi sauce	2 bay leaves
3 teaspoons za'atar	

1. Wash, dry and destem the eggplants. Chop them into 1-inch cubes. 2. In the air fryer basket, combine duck fat Maggi sauce, za'atar, onion powder, garlic powder, sumac and bay leaves. 3. Select the "AIR FRY" function of Ninja Foodi digital air fry oven, set the temperature to 320 degrees F/ 160 degrees C and set the time to 25 minutes. Press the Start/Pause button and begin preheating. Melt the for 2 minutes at 320 degrees F/ 160 degrees C, stirring well. 4. Place the eggplant in the basket and allow to cook for 25 minutes. 5. In a bowl, mix together the lemon juice and extra virgin olive oil. Add the eggplant and stir to coat evenly. 6. Serve immediately with grated parmesan or fresh chopped basil if desired.
Per Serving: Calories 203; Fat 10.9g; Sodium 402mg; Carbs 2g; Fiber 0g; Sugar 1g; Protein 23g

Broccoli Bites with Cheese

Prep time: 5 minutes | Cook time: 10 minutes | Serves: 4

1 pound broccoli florets	crushed
1 teaspoon granulated garlic	2 tablespoons olive oil
1 tablespoon onion flakes, dried	½ cup Pecorino Romano cheese, grated
1 teaspoon red pepper flakes,	

Select the "AIR FRY" function of Ninja Foodi digital air fry oven, set the temperature to 370 degrees F/ 185 degrees C and set the time to 10 minutes. Press the Start/Pause button and begin preheating. Toss all in a lightly oiled air fryer basket. Cook the broccoli florets for about 10 minutes, shaking the basket halfway through the cooking time. Enjoy!
Per Serving: Calories 156; Fat 10.6g; Sodium 236mg; Carbs 6.5g; Fiber 3.1g; Sugar 2.4g; Protein 6.5g

Herbed Tomatoes

| Prep time: 5 minutes | Cook time: 20 minutes | Serves: 2 |

2 tomatoes, medium to large
Herbs of your choice, to taste
Pepper to taste
High quality cooking spray

1. Select the "AIR FRY" function of Ninja Foodi digital air fry oven, set the temperature to 320 degrees F/ 160 degrees C and set the time to 20 minutes. Press the Start/Pause button and begin preheating. Wash and dry the tomatoes, before chopping them in half. 2. Lightly spritz them all over with cooking spray. 3. Season each half with herbs (oregano, basil, parsley, rosemary, thyme, sage, etc.) as desired and black pepper. 4. Put the halves in the tray of your air fryer. Cook for 20 minutes, or longer if necessary. Larger tomatoes will take longer to cook.
Per Serving: Calories 193; Fat 8.9g; Sodium 93mg; Carbs 2g; Fiber 1g; Sugar 0g; Protein 25g

Sweet Glazed Beets

| Prep time: 5 minutes | Cook time: 60 minutes | Serves: 8 |

3 ½ lb. beetroots
4 tablespoons maple syrup
1 tablespoon coconut oil

1. Select the "AIR FRY" function of Ninja Foodi digital air fry oven, set the temperature to 320 degrees F/ 160 degrees C and set the time to 40 minutes. Press the Start/Pause button and begin preheating. Wash and peel the beets. Cut them up into 1-inch pieces. 2. Put the coconut oil in the Air Fryer and melt for 1 minute. 3. Place the beet cubes to the Air Fryer Basket and allow to cook for 40 minutes. Coat the beetroots in two tablespoons of the maple syrup and cook for another 10 minutes, ensuring the beets become soft. 4. Toss the cooked beets with the remaining two tablespoons of maple syrup and serve right away.
Per Serving: Calories 162; Fat 9.4g; Sodium 68mg; Carbs 21g; Fiber 4g; Sugar 16g; Protein 1g

Fried Green Beans

| Prep time: 5 minutes | Cook time: 10 minutes | Serves: 4 |

1 pound green beans
4 tablespoons all-purpose flour
2 eggs, whisked
½ cup breadcrumbs
½ cup grated parmesan cheese
1 teaspoon cayenne pepper
½ teaspoon mustard seeds
1 teaspoon garlic powder
Sea salt
Ground black pepper, to taste

1. Select the "AIR FRY" function of Ninja Foodi digital air fry oven, set the temperature to 390 degrees F/ 200 degrees C and set the time to 6 minutes. Press the Start/Pause button and begin preheating. 2. In a shallow bowl, thoroughly combine the flour and eggs; mix to combine well. 3. Then, in another bowl, mix the remaining ingredients. 4. Dip the beans in the egg, then in the breadcrumb mixture. 5. Air fry the green beans for about 6 minutes, tossing the basket halfway through the cooking time. Enjoy!
Per Serving: Calories 181; Fat 8.8g; Sodium 230mg; Carbs 17g; Fiber 3.5g; Sugar 4.1g; Protein 11.1g

Tasty Cheesy Garlic Bread

| Prep time: 5 minutes | Cook time: 15 minutes | Serves: 2 |

1 friendly baguette
4 teaspoons butter, melted
3 chopped garlic cloves
5 teaspoons sundried tomato pesto
1 cup mozzarella cheese, grated

1. Select the "AIR FRY" function of Ninja Foodi digital air fry oven, set the temperature to 180 degrees F/ 80 degrees C and set the time to 8 minutes. Press the Start/Pause button and begin preheating. Cut your baguette into 5 thick round slices. 2. Add the garlic cloves to the melted butter and brush onto each slice of bread. 3. Spread a teaspoon of sun dried tomato pesto onto each slice. 4. Top each slice with the grated mozzarella. 5. Transfer the bread slices to the air fryer and cook them for 6 – 8 minutes. 6. Top with some freshly chopped basil leaves, chili flakes and oregano if desired.
Per Serving: Calories 33; Fat 3.5g; Sodium 1mg; Carbs 1g; Fiber 0g; Sugar 0g; Protein 0g

Tasty Cauliflower with Mayo Dipping

| Prep time: 10 minutes | Cook time: 15 minutes | Serves: 4 |

4 cups bite-sized cauliflower florets
1 cup friendly bread crumbs, mixed with 1 teaspoon salt
¼ cup melted butter
¼ cup buffalo sauce
Mayo or creamy dressing for dipping

1. Select the "AIR FRY" function of Ninja Foodi digital air fry oven, set the temperature to 350 degrees F/ 175 degrees C and set the time to 15 minutes. Press the Start/Pause button and begin preheating. In a bowl, add the butter and buffalo sauce to create a creamy paste. 2. Completely cover each floret with the sauce. 3. Coat the florets with the bread crumb mixture. Cook the florets in the air fryer for 15 minutes, shaking the basket occasionally. 4. Serve with a raw vegetable salad, mayo or creamy dressing.
Per Serving: Calories 134; Fat 2.8g; Sodium 64mg; Carbs 26g; Fiber 4g; Sugar 8g; Protein 3g

Onion and Bread Crumbs Stuffed Mushrooms

| Prep time: 5 minutes | Cook time: 20 minutes | Serves: 4 |

6 small mushrooms
1 tablespoon onion, peeled and diced
1 tablespoon friendly bread crumbs
1 tablespoon olive oil
1 teaspoon garlic, pureed
1 teaspoon parsley
Salt and pepper to taste

1. Select the "AIR FRY" function of Ninja Foodi digital air fry oven, set the temperature to 350 degrees F/ 175 degrees C and set the time to 10 minutes. Press the Start/Pause button and begin preheating. Combine the bread crumbs, oil, onion, parsley, salt, pepper and garlic in a bowl. 2. Scoop the stalks out of the mushrooms and spoon equal portions of the crumb mixture in the caps. Place to the air fryer and cook for 10 minutes. 3. Serve with mayo dip if desired.
Per Serving: Calories 292; Fat 24.3g; Sodium 660mg; Carbs 5g; Fiber 0g; Sugar 3g; Protein 14g

Cheesy Zucchini Chips

| Prep time: 5 minutes | Cook time: 15 minutes | Serves: 4 |

1 pound zucchini, sliced
1 cup Pecorino Romano cheese, grated
Sea salt and cayenne pepper, to taste

1. Select the "AIR FRY" function of Ninja Foodi digital air fry oven, set the temperature to 390 degrees F/ 200 degrees C and set the time to 10 minutes. Press the Start/Pause button and begin preheating. 2. Toss the zucchini slices with the remaining ingredients and arrange them in a single layer in the air fryer cooking basket. 3. Cook the zucchini slices for about 10 minutes, shaking the basket halfway through the cooking time. Work in batches. Bon appétit!
Per Serving: Calories 133; Fat 7g; Sodium 236mg; Carbs 8.1g; Fiber 1.4g; Sugar 0.5g; Protein 10.5g

Cheesy Zucchini Boats

| Prep time: 5 minutes | Cook time: 30 minutes | Serves: 2 |

1 cup ground chicken
1 zucchini
1 ½ cups crushed tomatoes
½ teaspoon salt
¼ teaspoon pepper
½ teaspoon garlic powder
2 tablespoons butter or olive oil
½ cup cheese, grated
¼ teaspoon dried oregano

1. Select the "AIR FRY" function of Ninja Foodi digital air fry oven, set the temperature to 400 degrees F/ 200 degrees C and set the time to 10 minutes. Press the Start/Pause button and begin preheating. Peel and halve the zucchini. Scoop out the flesh. 2. In a bowl, combine the ground chicken, tomato, garlic powder, butter, cheese, oregano, salt, and pepper. Fill in the hollowed-out zucchini with this mixture. 3. Transfer to the Air Fryer and bake for about 10 minutes. Serve warm.
Per Serving: Calories 162; Fat 5.3g; Sodium 1006mg; Carbs 3g; Fiber 2g; Sugar 0g; Protein 25g

Spicy Ribs

Prep time: 5 minutes | Cook time: 40 minutes | Serves: 4

1 ½ pounds spare ribs
Kosher salt and ground black
pepper, to taste
2 teaspoons brown sugar

1 teaspoon paprika
1 teaspoon chile powder
1 teaspoon garlic powder

Select the "AIR ROAST" function of Ninja Foodi digital air fry oven, set the temperature to 350 degrees F/ 175 degrees C and set the time to 35 minutes. Press the Start/Pause button and begin preheating. Toss all the ingredients in a lightly greased air fryer cooking basket. Cook the pork ribs for 35 minutes, turning them over halfway through the cooking time. Bon appétit!
Per Serving: Calories 442; Fat 33g; Sodium 411mg; Carbs 32.3g; Fiber 0.5g; Sugar 1.9g; Protein 32.3g

Roasted Baby Carrots

Prep time: 5 minutes | Cook time: 20 minutes | Serves: 4

1 pound baby carrots
2 tablespoons butter
Kosher salt

Ground white pepper, to taste
1 teaspoon paprika
1 teaspoon dried oregano

Select the "AIR FRY" function of Ninja Foodi digital air fry oven, set the temperature to 380 degrees F/ 195 degrees C and set the time to 15 minutes. Press the Start/Pause button and begin preheating. Toss the carrots with the remaining ingredients; then, arrange the carrots in the air fryer cooking basket. Cook the carrots for 15 minutes, shaking the basket halfway through the cooking time. Bon appétit!
Per Serving: Calories 104; Fat 6.3g; Sodium 154mg; Carbs 1.8g; Fiber 3.7g; Sugar 6g; Protein 1.8g

Spicy Potato Chips

Prep time: 5 minutes | Cook time: 20 minutes | Serves: 3

1 pound potatoes, thinly sliced
2 tablespoons olive oil
1 teaspoon paprika

Coarse salt and cayenne pepper,
to taste

1. Select the "AIR FRY" function of Ninja Foodi digital air fry oven, set the temperature to 360 degrees F/ 180 degrees C and set the time to 16 minutes. Press the Start/Pause button and begin preheating. 2. Toss the potatoes with the remaining ingredients and place them in the air fryer cooking basket. Air fry the potato chips for 16 minutes, shaking the basket halfway through the cooking time and work in batches. Enjoy!
Per Serving: Calories 198; Fat 9.2g; Sodium 258mg; Carbs 26.5g; Fiber 3.6g; Sugar 1.2g; Protein 3.1g

Spicy Drumettes

Prep time: 5 minutes | Cook time: 20 minutes | Serves: 5

2 pounds chicken drumettes
1 teaspoon ancho chile pepper
1 teaspoon smoked paprika
1 teaspoon onion powder
1 teaspoon garlic powder

Kosher salt
Ground black pepper, to taste
¼ tsp black pepper
2 tablespoons olive oil

1. Select the "AIR FRY" function of Ninja Foodi digital air fry oven, set the temperature to 380 degrees F/ 195 degrees C and set the time to 18 minutes. Press the Start/Pause button and begin preheating. 2. Toss the chicken drumettes with the remaining ingredients. 3. Cook the chicken drumettes for 18 minutes, turning them over halfway through the cooking time. Bon appétit!
Per Serving: Calories 404; Fat 25.8g; Sodium 358mg; Carbs 3.7g; Fiber 1.3g; Sugar 0.5g; Protein 37.5g

Delicious Fried Mushrooms

Prep time: 5 minutes | Cook time: 35 minutes | Serves: 4

2 lb. button mushrooms
3 tablespoons white or French
vermouth [optional]

1 tablespoon coconut oil
2 teaspoons herbs of your choice
½ teaspoon garlic powder

1. Wash and dry the mushrooms. Slice them into quarters. 2. Select the "AIR FRY" function of Ninja Foodi digital air fry oven, set the temperature to 320 degrees F/ 160 degrees C and set the time to 30 minutes. Press the Start/Pause button and begin preheating. Add the coconut oil, garlic powder, and herbs to the basket. 3. Briefly cook the for 2 minutes and give them a stir. Put the mushrooms in and cook for 25 minutes, stirring occasionally throughout. 4. Pour in the white vermouth and mix. Cook for an additional 5 minutes. 5. Serve hot.
Per Serving: Calories 153; Fat 2.8g; Sodium 28mg; Carbs 26g; Fiber 1g; Sugar 1g; Protein 6g

Sweet Roasted Parsnip

Prep time: 5 minutes | Cook time: 55 minutes | Serves: 5

2 lb. parsnips [about 6 large
parsnips]
2 tablespoons maple syrup

1 tablespoon coconut oil
1 tablespoon parsley, dried flakes

1. Select the "AIR ROAST" function of Ninja Foodi digital air fry oven, set the temperature to 320 degrees F/ 160 degrees C and set the time to 35 minutes. Press the Start/Pause button and begin preheating. Melt the duck fat or coconut oil in your air fryer for 2 minutes. 2. Rinse the parsnips to clean them and dry them. Chop into 1-inch cubes. Transfer to the fryer. 3. Cook the parsnip cubes in the fat/oil for 35 minutes, tossing them regularly. 4. Season the parsnips with parsley and maple syrup and allow to cook for another 5 minutes or longer to achieve a soft texture throughout. Serve straight away.
Per Serving: Calories 409; Fat 18.9g; Sodium 214mg; Carbs 10g; Fiber 1g; Sugar 9g; Protein 48g

Chapter 7 Dessert Recipes

No-sugar-Added Apple Hand Pies

Prep time: 5 minutes | Cook time: 8 minutes | Serves: 6

15-ounces no-sugar-added apple pie filling

1 store-bought crust

1. Select the "AIR FRY" function of Ninja Foodi digital air fry oven, set the temperature to 390 degrees F/ 200 degrees C and set the time to 10 minutes. Press the Start/Pause button and begin preheating. Lay out pie crust and slice into equal-sized squares. 2. Place 2 tablespoons filling into each square and seal the crust with a fork. 3. Place into the fryer. Cook 8 minutes until golden in color.
Per Serving: Calories 429; Fat 32g; Sodium 325mg; Carbs 5g; Fiber 1g; Sugar 3g; Protein 5g

Blueberry Lemon Muffins with Monk Fruit

Prep time: 10 minutes | Cook time: 10 minutes | Serves: 12

1 teaspoon vanilla
Juice and zest of 1 lemon
2 eggs
1 cup blueberries

½ cup cream
¼ cup avocado oil
½ cup monk fruit
2 ½ cups almond flour

1. Select the "AIR FRY" function of Ninja Foodi digital air fry oven, set the temperature to 320 degrees F/ 160 degrees C and set the time to 10 minutes. Press the Start/Pause button and begin preheating. Mix monk fruit and flour together. 2. In another bowl, mix vanilla, egg, lemon juice, and cream together. Add mixtures together and blend well. 3. Spoon batter into cupcake holders. Place in air fryer. Bake 10 minutes, checking at 6 minutes to ensure you don't overbake them.
Per Serving: Calories 173; Fat 13.6g; Sodium 281mg; Carbs 3g; Fiber 1g; Sugar 1g; Protein 10g

Sweet Cream Cheese Wontons

Prep time: 10 minutes | Cook time: 5 minutes | Serves: 5

1 egg mixed with a bit of water
Wonton wrappers
½ cup powdered erythritol

8 ounces softened cream cheese
Olive oil

1. Select the "AIR FRY" function of Ninja Foodi digital air fry oven, set the temperature to 400 degrees F/ 200 degrees C and set the time to 5 minutes. Press the Start/Pause button and begin preheating. Mix sweetener and cream cheese together. 2. Lay out 4 wontons at a time and cover with a dish towel to prevent drying out. 3. Place ½ of a teaspoon of cream cheese mixture into each wrapper. 4. Dip finger into egg/water mixture and fold diagonally to form a triangle. Seal edges well. 5. Repeat with remaining ingredients. 6. Place filled wontons into air fryer and cook 5 minutes, shaking halfway through cooking.
Per Serving: Calories 105; Fat 5g; Sodium 233mg; Carbs 7g; Fiber 2g; Sugar 4g; Protein 8g

Chocolate Coconut Brownies

Prep time: 7 minutes | Cook time: 15 minutes | Serves: 8

½ cup coconut oil
2 oz. dark chocolate
1 cup sugar
2½ tablespoons water
4 whisked eggs
¼ teaspoon ground cinnamon
½ teaspoon ground anise star

¼ teaspoon coconut extract
½ teaspoon vanilla extract
1 tablespoon honey
½ cup flour
½ cup desiccated coconut
sugar, to dust

1. Select the "BAKE" function of Ninja Foodi digital air fry oven, set the temperature to 355 degrees F/ 180 degrees C and set the time to 15 minutes. Press the Start/Pause button and begin preheating. Melt the chocolate and coconut oil in the microwave. 2. Combine with the sugar, water, eggs, cinnamon, anise, coconut extract, vanilla, and honey in a large bowl. 3. Stir in the flour and desiccated coconut. Incorporate everything well. 4. Lightly grease a sheet pan with butter. Transfer the mixture to the dish. 5. Place the dish in the Air Fryer and bake at 355 degrees F/ 180 degrees C for 15 minutes. 6. Remove from the fryer and allow to cool slightly. 7.Take care when taking it out of the sheet pan. Slice it into squares. 8. Dust with sugar before serving.
Per Serving: Calories 80; Fat 6g; Sodium 444mg; Carbs 6g; Fiber 1g; Sugar 4g; Protein 1g

Baked Cheesy Cinnamon Rolls

Prep time: 15 minutes | Cook time: 5 minutes | Serves: 8

1 ½ tablespoons cinnamon
¾ cup brown sugar
¼ cup melted coconut oil
Glaze:
½ teaspoon vanilla
1 ¼ cups powdered erythritol

1 pound frozen bread dough, thawed

2 tablespoons softened ghee
4 ounces softened cream cheese

1. Select the "BAKE" function of Ninja Foodi digital air fry oven, set the temperature to 350 degrees F/ 175 degrees C and set the time to 5 minutes. Press the Start/Pause button and begin preheating. Lay out bread dough and roll out into a rectangle. Brush melted ghee over dough and leave a 1-inch border along the edges. 2. Mix cinnamon and sweetener together and then sprinkle over dough. 3. Roll dough tightly and slice into 8 pieces. Let sit 1-2 hours to rise. 4. To make the glaze, simply mix together till smooth. 5. Once rolls rise, place into air fryer and cook 5 minutes. 6. Serve rolls drizzled in cream cheese glaze. Enjoy!
Per Serving: Calories 200; Fat 15.6g; Sodium 165mg; Carbs 5g; Fiber 1g; Sugar 2g; Protein 10g

French Cinnamon Toast Bites

Prep time: 5 minutes | Cook time: 15 minutes | Serves: 8

Almond milk
Cinnamon
Sweetener

3 eggs
4 pieces wheat bread

1. Select the "AIR FRY" function of Ninja Foodi digital air fry oven, set the temperature to 360 degrees F/ 180 degrees C and set the time to 15 minutes. Press the Start/Pause button and begin preheating. 2. Whisk eggs and thin out with almond milk. 3. Mix ⅓ cup of sweetener with lots of cinnamon. 4. Tear bread in half, ball up pieces and press together to form a ball. 5. Soak bread balls in egg and then roll into cinnamon sugar, making sure to thoroughly coat. 6. Place coated bread balls into air fryer and bake 15 minutes.
Per Serving: Calories 76; Fat 5.7g; Sodium 63mg; Carbs 2g; Fiber 0g; Sugar 2g; Protein 3g

Baked Apple with Raisins and Walnuts

Prep time: 10 minutes | Cook time: 20 minutes | Serves: 4

¼ cup water
¼ teaspoon nutmeg
¼ teaspoon cinnamon
1 ½ teaspoons melted ghee

2 tablespoons raisins
2 tablespoons chopped walnuts
1 medium apple

1. Select the "BAKE" function of Ninja Foodi digital air fry oven, set the temperature to 350 degrees F/ 175 degrees C and set the time to 20 minutes. Press the Start/Pause button and begin preheating. 2. Slice the apple in half and discard some of the flesh from the center. 3. Place into sheet pan. 4. Mix remaining together except water. Spoon mixture to the middle of apple halves. 5. Pour water overfilled apples. 6. Place pan with apple halves into air fryer, bake 20 minutes.
Per Serving: Calories 138; Fat 10.6g; Sodium 102mg; Carbs 1g; Fiber 0g; Sugar 1g; Protein 9g

Crispy Sweet Bananas

Prep time: 10 minutes | Cook time: 10 minutes | Serves: 4

4 ripe bananas, peeled and halved
1 tablespoon meal
1 tablespoon cashew, crushed
1 egg, beaten

1½ tablespoons coconut oil
¼ cup flour
1½ tablespoons sugar
½ cup friendly bread crumbs

1. Select the "AIR FRY" function of Ninja Foodi digital air fry oven, set the temperature to 350 degrees F/ 175 degrees C and set the time to 10 minutes. Press the Start/Pause button and begin preheating. In a saucepan, Heat the coconut oil. toast in the bread crumbs and cook, stirring continuously, for 4 minutes. 2. Transfer the bread crumbs to a bowl. 3. Add in the meal and crushed cashew. Mix well. 4. Coat each of the banana halves in the corn flour, before dipping it in the beaten egg and lastly coating it with the bread crumbs. 5. Put the coated banana halves in the Air Fryer basket. Season with the sugar. 6. Air fry for 10 minutes.
Per Serving: Calories 153; Fat 2.8g; Sodium 28mg; Carbs 26g; Fiber 1g; Sugar 1g; Protein 6g

Air Fried Cinnamon Bananas

Prep time: 5 minutes | Cook time: 10 minutes | Serves: 2

1 cup panko breadcrumbs
3 tablespoons cinnamon
½ cup almond flour
3 egg whites
8 ripe bananas
3 tablespoons vegan coconut oil

1. Select the "AIR FRY" function of Ninja Foodi digital air fry oven, set the temperature to 300 degrees F/ 150 degrees C and set the time to 8 minutes. Press the Start/Pause button and begin preheating. Heat coconut oil and add breadcrumbs. Mix around 2-3 minutes until golden. Pour into bowl. 2. Peel and cut bananas in half. Roll each banana half into flour, eggs, and crumb mixture. Place into air fryer. 3. Cook 10 minutes. 4. A great addition to a healthy banana split!
Per Serving: Calories 112; Fat 2g; Sodium 12mg; Carbs 8g; Fiber 1g; Sugar 6g; Protein 0g

Super Easy Jelly Doughnuts

Prep time: 10 minutes | Cook time: 15 minutes | Serves: 2

1 package (16.3 ounces) large refrigerator biscuits
Oil in mister
1¼ cups good-quality raspberry jam
Confectioners' sugar for dusting

1. Separate biscuits into 8 rounds. Spray both sides of rounds lightly with oil. 2. Select the "BAKE" function of Ninja Foodi digital air fry oven, set the temperature to 350 degrees F/ 175 degrees C and set the time to 5 minutes. Press the Start/Pause button and begin preheating. Spray Ninja sheet pan with oil and place 3 to 4 rounds in basket. Air-fry for 5 minutes, or until golden brown. Transfer to a wire rack; let cool. Repeat with the remaining rounds. 3. Fill a pastry bag, fitted with a small plain tip, with raspberry jam; use the tip to poke a small hole in the side of each doughnut, then fill the centers with the jam. Dust doughnuts with confectioners' sugar.
Per Serving: Calories 311; Fat 6g; Sodium 112mg; Carbs 15g; Fiber 6g; Sugar 12g; Protein 2g

Delicious Mini Strawberry Pies

Prep time: 7 minutes | Cook time: 10 minutes | Serves: 8

1 cup sugar
¼ teaspoon ground cloves
⅛ teaspoon cinnamon powder
1 teaspoon vanilla extract
1 [12-oz.] can biscuit dough
12 oz. strawberry pie filling
¼ cup butter, melted

1. Select the "BAKE" function of Ninja Foodi digital air fry oven, set the temperature to 340 degrees F/ 170 degrees C and set the time to 10 minutes. Press the Start/Pause button and begin preheating. In a bowl, mix together the sugar, cloves, cinnamon, and vanilla. 2. With a rolling pin, roll each piece of the biscuit dough into a flat, round circle. 3. Spoon an equal amount of the strawberry pie filling onto the center of each biscuit. 4. Roll up the dough. Dip the biscuits into the melted butter and coat them with the sugar mixture. 5. Coat with a light brushing of non-stick cooking spray on all sides. 6. Transfer the cookies to the Air Fryer and bake them at 340 degrees F/ 170 degrees C for roughly 10 minutes, or until a golden-brown color is achieved. 7. Allow to cool for 5 minutes before serving.
Per Serving: Calories 23; Fat 1.3g; Sodium 40mg; Carbs 2g; Fiber 1g; Sugar 1g; Protein 1g

Tropical Pineapple Cake

Prep time: 15 minutes | Cook time: 35 minutes | Serves: 4

2 cups flour
¼ lb. butter
¼ cup sugar
½ lb. pineapple, chopped
½ cup pineapple juice
1 oz. dark chocolate, grated
1 large egg
2 tablespoons skimmed milk

1. Select the "AIR FRY" function of Ninja Foodi digital air fry oven, set the temperature to 370 degrees F/ 185 degrees C and set the time to 35 minutes. Press the Start/Pause button and begin preheating. 2. Grease a cake tin with a little oil or butter. 3. In a bowl, combine the butter and flour to create a crumbly consistency. 4. Add in the sugar, diced pineapple, juice, and crushed dark chocolate and mix well. 5. In a separate bowl, combine the egg and milk. Add this mix to the flour and stir well until a soft dough forms. 6. Pour the batter into the cake tin and transfer to the Air Fryer. Cook for 35 - 40 minutes.
Per Serving: Calories 203; Fat 10.9g; Sodium 402mg; Carbs 2g; Fiber 0g; Sugar 1g; Protein 23g

Banana & Vanilla Puffs

Prep time: 7 minutes | Cook time: 8 minutes | Serves: 8

1 package [8-oz.] crescent dinner rolls, refrigerated
1 cup milk
4 oz. instant vanilla pudding
4 oz. cream cheese, softened
2 bananas, peeled and sliced
1 egg, lightly beaten

1. Select the "BAKE" function of Ninja Foodi digital air fry oven, set the temperature to 355 degrees F/ 180 degrees C and set the time to 10 minutes. Press the Start/Pause button and begin preheating. Roll out the crescent dinner rolls and slice each one into 8 squares. 2. Mix together the milk, pudding, and cream cheese using a whisk. 3. Scoop equal amounts of the mixture into the pastry squares. Add the banana slices on top. 4. Fold the squares around the filling, pressing down on the edges to seal them. 5. Apply a light brushing of the egg to each pastry puff before placing them in the Air Fryer. 6. Bake for 10 minutes.
Per Serving: Calories 104; Fat 2.5g; Sodium 29mg; Carbs 18g; Fiber 4g; Sugar 2g; Protein 3g

Chocolate Cake

Prep time: 20 minutes | Cook time: 45 minutes | Serves: 8

½ cup sugar
1¼ cups flour
1 teaspoon baking powder
⅓ cup cocoa powder
¼ teaspoon ground cloves
⅛ teaspoon freshly grated nutmeg
Pinch of table salt
1 egg
¼ cup soda of your choice
¼ cup milk
½ stick butter, melted
2 oz. bittersweet chocolate, melted
½ cup hot water

1. Select the "BAKE" function of Ninja Foodi digital air fry oven, set the temperature to 320 degrees F/ 160 degrees C and set the time to 35 minutes. Press the Start/Pause button and begin preheating. In a bowl, thoroughly combine the dry ingredients. 2. In another bowl, mix together the egg, soda, milk, butter, and chocolate. 3. Combine the two mixtures. Add in the water and stir well. 4. Take a cake pan that is small enough to fit inside your Air Fryer and transfer the mixture to the pan. 5. Place a sheet of foil on top and bake for 35 minutes. 6. Remove the foil and bake for further 10 minutes. 7. Frost the cake with buttercream if desired before serving.
Per Serving: Calories 42; Fat 2.8g; Sodium 126mg; Carbs 4g; Fiber 1g; Sugar 1g; Protein 1g

Tasty Apple Turnovers

Prep time: 5 minutes | Cook time: 30 minutes | Serves: 4

3½ ounces (100g) dried apples (about 2½ cups)
¼ cup (35g) golden raisins
1 tablespoon (13g) granulated sugar
1 tablespoon (15ml) freshly squeezed lemon juice
½ teaspoon cinnamon
1 pound (455g) frozen puff pastry, defrosted according to package instructions
1 egg beaten with 1 tablespoon (15ml) water
Turbinado or demerara sugar for sprinkling

1. Select the "BAKE" function of Ninja Foodi digital air fry oven, set the temperature to 325 degrees F/ 160 degrees C and set the time to 30 minutes. Press the Start/Pause button and begin preheating. Place the dried apples in a medium saucepan and cover with about 2 cups (480ml) of water. Bring the mixture to a boil over medium-high heat, then reduce the heat to low, cover, and simmer until the apples have absorbed most of the liquid, about 20 minutes. Remove the apples from the heat and allow to cool. Add the raisins, sugar, lemon juice, and cinnamon to the rehydrated apples and set aside. 2. On a well-floured board, roll the puff pastry out to a 12-inch (30cm) square. Cut the square into 4 equal quarters. Divide the filling equally among the 4 squares, mounding it in the middle of each square. Brush the edges of each square with water and fold the pastry diagonally over the apple mixture, creating a triangle. Seal the edges by pressing them with the tines of a fork. Transfer the turnovers to a sheet pan lined with parchment paper. 3. Brush the top of 2 turnovers with egg wash and sprinkle with turbinado sugar. Make 2 small slits in the top of the turnovers for venting and bake for 25 to 30 minutes, until the top is browned and puffed and the pastry is cooked through. Remove the cooked turnovers to a cooling rack and cook the remaining 2 turnovers in the same manner. Serve warm or at room temperature.
Per Serving: Calories 354; Fat 7.9g; Sodium 704mg; Carbs 6g; Fiber 3.6g; Sugar 6g; Protein 18g

Perfect Sweet Cinnamon Toast

Prep time: 5 minutes | Cook time: 5 minutes | Serves: 6

2 teaspoons pepper
1 ½ teaspoons vanilla extract
1 ½ teaspoons cinnamon
½ cup sweetener of choice
1 cup coconut oil
12 slices whole wheat bread

1. Select the "AIR FRY" function of Ninja Foodi digital air fry oven, set the temperature to 400 degrees F/ 200 degrees C and set the time to 5 minutes. Press the Start/Pause button and begin preheating. Melt coconut oil and mix with sweetener until dissolved. Mix in remaining minus bread till incorporated. 2. Spread mixture onto bread, covering all area. Place coated pieces of bread directly in wire rack of air fryer. 3. Cook 5 minutes at 400 degrees F/ 200 degrees C. 4. Remove and cut diagonally. Enjoy!
Per Serving: Calories 381; Fat 36g; Sodium 2mg; Carbs 16g; Fiber 1g; Sugar 13g; Protein 0g

Baked Apple Dumplings with Raisins

Prep time: 15 minutes | Cook time: 25 minutes | Serves: 4

2 tablespoons melted coconut oil
2 puff pastry sheets
1 tablespoon brown sugar
2 tablespoons raisins
2 small apples of choice

1. Select the "BAKE" function of Ninja Foodi digital air fry oven, set the temperature to 355 degrees F/ 180 degrees C and set the time to 30 minutes. Press the Start/Pause button and begin preheating. 2. Core and peel apples and mix with raisins and sugar. 3. Place a bit of apple mixture into puff pastry sheets and brush sides with melted coconut oil. 4. Place into air fryer. Cook 25 minutes, turning halfway through. Will be golden when done.
Per Serving: Calories 106; Fat 6.9g; Sodium 1mg; Carbs 12g; Fiber 2g; Sugar 10g; Protein 0g

Air Fried Chocolate Vanilla Cake

Prep time: 5 minutes | Cook time: 10 minutes | Serves: 10

½ cup hot water
1 teaspoon vanilla
¼ cup olive oil
½ cup almond milk
1 egg
½ teaspoon salt
¾ teaspoon baking soda
¾ teaspoon baking powder
½ cup unsweetened cocoa powder
2 cups almond flour
1 cup brown sugar

1. Select the "BAKE" function of Ninja Foodi digital air fry oven, set the temperature to 355 degrees F/ 180 degrees C and set the time to 45 minutes. Press the Start/Pause button and begin preheating. 2. Stir all dry together. Then stir in wet ingredients. Add hot water last. 3. The batter will be thin, no worries. 4. Pour cake batter into a pan that fits into the fryer. Cover with foil and poke holes into the foil. 5. Bake 35 minutes. 6. Discard foil and then bake another 10 minutes.
Per Serving: Calories 118; Fat 7.2g; Sodium 232mg; Carbs 14g; Fiber 1g; Sugar 11g; Protein 2g

Crunchy Shortbread Finger Cookies

Prep time: 10 minutes | Cook time: 12 minutes | Serves: 10

1 ½ cups butter
1 cup flour
¾ cup sugar
Cooking spray

1. Select the "AIR FRY" function of Ninja Foodi digital air fry oven, set the temperature to 350 degrees F/ 175 degrees C and set the time to 12 minutes. Press the Start/Pause button and begin preheating. 2. In a bowl. combine the flour and sugar. 3. Cut each stick of butter into small chunks. Add the chunks into the flour and the sugar. 4. Blend the butter into the mixture to combine everything well. 5. Use your hands to knead the mixture, forming a smooth consistency. 6. Shape the mixture into 10 equal-sized finger shapes, marking them with the tines of a fork for decoration if desired. 7. Lightly spritz the Air Fryer basket with the cooking spray. Place the cookies inside, spacing them out well. 8. Cook the cookies for 12 minutes. Let cool slightly before serving. Alternatively, you can store the cookies in an airtight container for up to 3 days.
Per Serving: Calories 292; Fat 24.3g; Sodium 660mg; Carbs 5g; Fiber 0g; Sugar 3g; Protein 14g

Sweet Apple or Pear Crumble

Prep time: 10 minutes | Cook time: 45 minutes | Serves: 2

1 ½ pounds baking apples (such as Gala) or firm-ripe pears
2 tablespoons brown sugar
½ teaspoon pie spice
Crumb Topping
½ cup old-fashioned oats
¼ cup packed brown sugar
1 teaspoon finely grated lemon peel
1 teaspoon grated fresh ginger
2 teaspoons fresh lemon juice
½ cup all-purpose flour

¾ teaspoon apple pie spice
⅛ teaspoon salt
5 tablespoons butter, cut up
Whipped cream, for topping

1. Select the "BAKE" function of Ninja Foodi digital air fry oven, set the temperature to 375 degrees F/ 190 degrees C and set the time to 25 minutes. Press the Start/Pause button and begin preheating. Fold a 20-inch piece of foil lengthwise into a 2-inch-wide strip to use as a sling. In a bowl, toss fruit with sugar, pie spice, ginger, and lemon juice. Place in cooking pan. Air-fry for 25 minutes, stirring twice. Press fruit down with the back of a wooden spoon to compact. 2. Prepare topping: Meanwhile, combine flour, oats, sugar, lemon peel, pie spice, and salt in a bowl. Blend in butter until evenly crumbly. 3. Pull out pan and spoon topping onto hot fruit mixture. 4. Reduce temperature to 300 degrees F/ 150 degrees C. Air-fry for 20 minutes until golden and fruit is tender.5. Serve with a scoop of vanilla ice cream or whipped cream.
Per Serving: Calories 30; Fat 13g; Sodium 12mg; Carbs 49g; Fiber 4g; Sugar 6g; Protein 3g

Easy Air Fryer Busicuits Donuts

Prep time: 5 minutes | Cook time: 5 minutes | Serves: 8

Pinch of allspice
4 tablespoons dark brown sugar
½ - 1 teaspoon cinnamon
⅓ cup granulated sweetener
3 tablespoons melted coconut oil
1 can of biscuits

1. Select the "AIR FRY" function of Ninja Foodi digital air fry oven, set the temperature to 350 degrees F/ 175 degrees C and set the time to 5 minutes. Press the Start/Pause button and begin preheating. Mix allspice, sugar, sweetener, and cinnamon together. 2. Take out biscuits from can and with a circle cookie cutter, cut holes from centers and place into air fryer. 3. Cook 5 minutes. As batches are cooked, use a brush to coat with melted coconut oil and dip each into sugar mixture. 4. Serve warm!
Per Serving: Calories 87; Fat 5.6g; Sodium 42mg; Carbs 9g; Fiber 0g; Sugar 6g; Protein 0g

Baked Chocolate Soufflé for Two

Prep time: 15 minutes | Cook time: 14 minutes | Serves: 2

2 tablespoons almond flour
½ teaspoon vanilla
3 tablespoons sweetener
2 separated eggs
¼ cup melted coconut oil
3 ounces of semi-sweet chocolate, chopped

1.Brush coconut oil and sweetener onto ramekins. 2. Melt coconut oil and chocolate together. Beat egg yolks well, adding vanilla and sweetener. Stir in flour and ensure there are no lumps. 3. Select the "BAKE" function of Ninja Foodi digital air fry oven, set the temperature to 350 degrees F/ 175 degrees C and set the time to 15 minutes. Press the Start/Pause button and begin preheating. 4. Whisk egg whites till they reach peak state and fold them into chocolate mixture. 5. Pour batter into ramekins and place into the fryer. 6. Cook 14 minutes. 7. Serve with powdered sugar dusted on top.
Per Serving: Calories 350; Fat 22.5g; Sodium 166mg; Carbs 38g; Fiber 1g; Sugar 25g; Protein 1g

Cinnamon Sugar Roasted Chickpeas

Prep time: 10 minutes | Cook time: 10 minutes | Serves: 2

1 tablespoon sweetener
1 tablespoon cinnamon
1 cup chickpeas

1. Select the "BAKE" function of Ninja Foodi digital air fry oven, set the temperature to 390 degrees F/ 200 degrees C and set the time to 10 minutes. Press the Start/Pause button and begin preheating. 2. Rinse and drain chickpeas. 3. Mix all together and add to the air fryer. 4.Cook 10 minutes.
Per Serving: Calories 288; Fat 23.3g; Sodium 308mg; Carbs 6g; Fiber 1g; Sugar 5g; Protein 2g

Buttery Sugar Fritters

Prep time: 15 minutes | Cook time: 15 minutes | Serves: 16

For the Dough:

4 cups flour	temperature
1 teaspoon kosher salt	1 packet instant yeast
1 teaspoon sugar	1¼ cups lukewarm water
3 tablespoons butter, at room	

For the Cakes:

1 cup sugar	1 teaspoon cinnamon powder
Pinch of cardamom	1 stick butter, melted

1. Select the "AIR FRY" function of Ninja Foodi digital air fry oven, set the temperature to 360 degrees F/ 180 degrees C and set the time to 10 minutes. Press the Start/Pause button and begin preheating. Place all ingredients in a bowl and combine well. 2. Add in the lukewarm water and mix until a soft, elastic dough forms. 3. Place the dough on a lightly floured surface and lay a greased sheet of aluminum foil on top of the dough. Refrigerate for 5 to 10 minutes. 4. Remove it from the refrigerator and divide it in two. Mold each half into a log and slice it into 20 pieces. 5. In a shallow bowl, combine the sugar, cardamom and cinnamon. 6. Coat the slices with a light brushing of melted butter and the sugar. 7. Spray Air Fryer basket with cooking spray. 8. Transfer the slices to the fryer and air fry for roughly 10 minutes. Turn each slice once during the baking time. 9. Dust each slice with the sugar before serving.

Per Serving: Calories 134; Fat 2.8g; Sodium 64mg; Carbs 26g; Fiber 4g; Sugar 8g; Protein 3g

Nutty Pear & Apple Crisp with Walnuts

Prep time: 10 minutes | Cook time: 20 minutes | Serves: 6

½ lb. apples, cored and chopped	1 teaspoon ground cinnamon
½ lb. pears, cored and chopped	¼ teaspoon ground cloves
1 cup flour	1 teaspoon vanilla extract
1 cup sugar	¼ cup chopped walnuts
1 tablespoon butter	Whipped cream, to serve

1. Select the "AIR FRY" function of Ninja Foodi digital air fry oven, set the temperature to 340 degrees F/ 170 degrees C and set the time to 20 minutes. Press the Start/Pause button and begin preheating. Lightly grease a sheet pan and place the apples and pears inside. 2. Combine the rest of the ingredients, minus the walnuts and the whipped cream, until a coarse, crumbly texture is achieved. 3. Pour the mixture over the fruits and spread it evenly. Top with the chopped walnuts. 4. Air fry at 340 degrees F/ 170 degrees C for 20 minutes or until the top turns golden brown. 5. When cooked through, serve at room temperature with whipped cream.

Per Serving: Calories 134; Fat 2.8g; Sodium 64mg; Carbs 26g; Fiber 4g; Sugar 8g; Protein 3g

Healthy Banana Oatmeal Cookies

Prep time: 10 minutes | Cook time: 15 minutes | Serves: 6

2 cups quick oats	4 ripe bananas, mashed
¼ cup milk	¼ cup coconut, shredded

1. Select the "BAKE" function of Ninja Foodi digital air fry oven, set the temperature to 350 degrees F/ 175 degrees C and set the time to 15 minutes. Press the Start/Pause button and begin preheating. 2. Combine all of the ingredients in a bowl. 3. Scoop equal amounts of the cookie dough onto a baking sheet and put it in the Air Fryer sheet pan. 4. Bake the cookies for 15 minutes.

Per Serving: Calories 1; Fat 0g; Sodium 114mg; Carbs 0g; Fiber 0g; Sugar 0g; Protein 0g

Pineapple Sticks

Prep time: 10 minutes | Cook time: 10 minutes | Serves: 4

½ fresh pineapple, cut into sticks	¼ cup desiccated coconut

1. Select the "AIR FRY" function of Ninja Foodi digital air fry oven, set the temperature to 400 degrees F/ 200 degrees C and set the time to 10 minutes. Press the Start/Pause button and begin preheating. 2.Coat the pineapple sticks in the desiccated coconut and put each one in the Air Fryer basket. Cook for 10 minutes. Air fry for 10 minutes.

Per Serving: Calories 147; Fat 7.3g; Sodium 56mg; Carbs 20g; Fiber 5g; Sugar 11g; Protein 4g

Banana & Walnuts Cake

Prep time: 15 minutes | Cook time: 60 minutes | Serves: 5

⅔ cup sugar, shaved	1 ripe banana, mashed
⅔ cup unsalted butter	½ teaspoon vanilla extract
3 eggs	⅛ teaspoon baking soda
1¼ cups flour	Sea salt to taste

Topping:

sugar to taste, shaved	Bananas to taste, sliced
Walnuts to taste, roughly chopped	

1. Select the "AIR FRY" function of Ninja Foodi digital air fry oven, set the temperature to 360 degrees F/ 180 degrees C and set the time to 48 minutes. Press the Start/Pause button and begin preheating. 2. Mix together the flour, baking soda, and a pinch of sea salt. 3. In a separate bowl, combine the butter, vanilla extract and sugar using an electrical mixer or a blender, to achieve a fluffy consistency. 4. Beat in the eggs one at a time. 5. Throw in half of the flour mixture and stir thoroughly. Add in the mashed banana and continue to mix. Lastly, throw in the remaining half of the flour mixture and combine until a smooth batter is formed. 6. Transfer the batter to a baking tray and top with the banana slices. 7. Scatter the chopped walnuts on top before dusting with the sugar. 8. Place a sheet of foil over the tray and pierce several holes in it. 9. Put the covered tray in the Air Fryer. Cook for 48 minutes. 10. Decrease the temperature to 320 degrees F/ 160 degrees C, take off the foil, and allow to cook for an additional 10 minutes until golden brown.

Per Serving: Calories 193; Fat 8.9g; Sodium 93mg; Carbs 2g; Fiber 1g; Sugar 0g; Protein 25g

Roasted Cinnamon Pumpkin Seeds

Prep time: 15 minutes | Cook time: 20 minutes | Serves: 2

1 cup pumpkin raw seeds	1 cup water
1 tablespoon ground cinnamon	1 tablespoon olive oil
2 tablespoons sugar	

1. In a frying pan, combine the pumpkin seeds, cinnamon and water. 2. Boil the mixture over a high heat for 2 - 3 minutes. 3. Pour out the water and place the seeds on a clean kitchen towel, allowing them to dry for 20 - 30 minutes. 4. In a bowl, mix together the sugar, dried seeds, a pinch of cinnamon and one tablespoon of olive oil. 5. Select the "BAKE" function of Ninja Foodi digital air fry oven, set the temperature to 340 degrees F/ 170 degrees C and set the time to 15 minutes. Press the Start/Pause button and begin preheating. 6. Place the seed mixture in the fryer sheet pan and allow to cook for 15 minutes, shaking the basket periodically throughout.

Per Serving: Calories 101; Fat 5.4g; Sodium 106mg; Carbs 8g; Fiber 3g; Sugar 3g; Protein 7g

Peanut Butter Doughnut Holes

Prep time: 5 minutes | Cook time: 4 minutes | Serves: 12

1½ cups bread flour	½ teaspoon vanilla extract
1 teaspoon active dry yeast	2 egg yolks
1 tablespoon sugar	2 tablespoons melted butter
¼ teaspoon salt	24 miniature peanut butter cups
½ cup warm milk	vegetable oil, in a spray bottle

Doughnut Topping:

1 cup chocolate chips	2 tablespoons milk

1. Combine the flour with yeast, sugar and salt in a bowl. Add the milk along with vanilla, egg yolks and butter. Mix well until dough formed. knead the dough on floured surface by hand for about 2 minutes. Shape the dough and place it to an oiled bowl. Cover and let it rise in a warm place for 1 to 1½ hours, until doubled in size. 2. Punch the risen dough down and roll the flattened dough into a 24-inch log. Cut it into 24 pieces. a peanut butter into the center of each piece, Close the dough side with and roll in a ball shape. Place the balls on a sheet and let them rise in a warm place for 30 minutes. 3. Select the "AIR FRY" function of Ninja Foodi digital air fry oven, set the temperature to 400 degrees F/ 200 degrees C and set the time to 4 minutes. Press the Start/ Pause button and begin preheating. 4. Spray the dough balls lightly with oil. Air-fry eight at a time, at 400 degrees F/ 200 degrees C for 4 minutes, turning them over halfway through the cooking process. 5. Prepare the topping. in a bowl, Place the chocolate chips and milk. Microwave on high temp for 1 minute. Stir until melted and smooth. 6. Dip the half of the balls into the melted chocolate.

Per Serving: Calories 184; Fat 7.4g; Sodium 103mg; Carbs 7g; Fiber 1g; Sugar 1g; Protein 22g

Pakistani Gulab Jamun

Prep time: 10 minutes | Cook time: 10 minutes | Serves: 2 to 3

Fritters:

1 cup (128g) dried milk powder	lemon juice
¼ cup (31g) all-purpose flour	¼ cup (60ml) milk, slightly
1 teaspoon powdered sugar	warmed
⅛ teaspoon baking soda	Vegetable oil for brushing
1 teaspoon ghee or vegetable oil	Sliced almonds for garnish
1 teaspoon freshly squeezed	

Syrup:

1 cup (200g) granulated sugar	crushed
1 cup (240ml) water	½ teaspoon rose water
3 or 4 cardamom pods, lightly	½ teaspoon lemon juice

1. Whisk together the milk powder, flour, powdered sugar, and baking soda. Add the ghee and lemon juice and stir with a fork to combine. Gradually add the milk and stir with a fork just until the dough comes together. Let the dough rest and absorb the liquids for 10 to 15 minutes while you prepare the sugar syrup. 2. To make the syrup, combine the sugar, water, and cardamom pods in a small saucepan and bring to a boil over medium-high heat, stirring to dissolve the sugar. Lower the heat and manage to simmer for 5 minutes. The syrup should be thin and only slightly sticky. Add the rose water and lemon juice, cover, and keep warm over very low heat. 3. To make the fritters, divide the dough into 6 equal pieces. Gently roll each piece into a smooth ball with your hands, then roll into a 3- to 4-inch (7.5 to 10 cm) cylinder. Select the "AIR FRY" function of Ninja Foodi digital air fry oven, set the temperature to 285 degrees F/ 140 degrees C and set the time to 5 minutes. Press the Start/Pause button and begin preheating. Brush the fritters on all sides with oil. Place the fritters in the basket of the air fryer and cook for 5 minutes until firm but still pale. Increase the heat to 350 degrees F/ 175 degrees C and cook until browned but not dark, 3 to 4 minutes. 4. Remove the fritters to a shallow bowl and poke them several times with a skewer to create holes. Pour the warm syrup over the fritters and turn to coat. Allow the fritters to absorb the syrup for at least 15 minutes prior to serving. Garnish with sliced almonds or chopped pistachios if desired.
Per Serving: Calories 295; Fat 21.2g; Sodium 94mg; Carbs 3g; Fiber 1g; Sugar 1g; Protein 23g

Soft Sponge Cake

Prep time: 15 minutes | Cook time: 35 minutes | Serves: 8

For the Cake:

9 oz. sugar	1 teaspoon vanilla extract
9 oz. butter	Zest of 1 lemon
3 eggs	1 teaspoon baking powder
9 oz. flour	

For the Frosting:

Juice of 1 lemon	7 oz. sugar
Zest of 1 lemon	4 egg whites
1 teaspoon yellow food coloring	

1. Select the "AIR FRY" function of Ninja Foodi digital air fry oven, set the temperature to 320 degrees F/ 160 degrees C and set the time to 15 minutes. Press the Start/Pause button and begin preheating. 2. Use an electric mixer to combine all of the cake ingredients. 3. Grease the insides of two round cake pans. 4. Pour an equal amount of the batter into each pan. 5. Place one pan in the fryer and cook for 15 minutes, before repeating with the second pan. 6. Mix all of the frosting ingredients. 7. Allow the cakes to cool. Spread the frosting and stack the other cake on top.
Per Serving: Calories 162; Fat 9.4g; Sodium 68mg; Carbs 21g; Fiber 4g; Sugar 16g; Protein 1g

Berries Stew

Prep time: 10 minutes | Cook time: 20 minutes | Serves: 4

1 pound strawberries, halved	1 tablespoon lemon juice
4 tablespoons stevia	1 and ½ cups water

1. Select the "AIR FRY" function of Ninja Foodi digital air fry oven, set the temperature to 340 degrees F/ 170 degrees C and set the time to 20 minutes. Press the Start/Pause button and begin preheating. 2. In a pan, mix all the ingredients, toss, put it in the fryer and cook for 20 minutes. 3. Divide the stew into cups and serve cold.
Per Serving: Calories 176; Fat 2g; Sodium 102mg; Carbs 3g; Fiber 1g; Sugar 2g; Protein 5g

Homemade Cherry Pie

Prep time: 15 minutes | Cook time: 20 minutes | Serves: 8

1 tablespoon milk	21 oz. cherry pie filling
2 ready-made pie crusts	1 egg yolk

1. Select the "AIR FRY" function of Ninja Foodi digital air fry oven, set the temperature to 310 degrees F/ 155 degrees C and set the time to 15 minutes. Press the Start/Pause button and begin preheating. 2. Coat the inside of a pie pan with a little oil or butter and lay one of the pie crusts inside. Use a fork to pierce a few holes in the pastry. 3. Spread the pie filling and egg yolk evenly over the crust. 4. Slice the other crust into strips and place them on top of the pie filling to make the pie look more homemade. 5. Place in the Air Fryer and cook for 15 minutes.
Per Serving: Calories 427; Fat 18.3g; Sodium 603mg; Carbs 44g; Fiber 6g; Sugar 3g; Protein 23g

Crispy Apple Wedges

Prep time: 10 minutes | Cook time: 15 minutes | Serves: 4

4 large apples	1–2 tablespoons sugar
2 tablespoons olive oil	½ teaspoon ground cinnamon
½ cup dried apricots, chopped	

1. Select the "AIR FRY" function of Ninja Foodi digital air fry oven, set the temperature to 350 degrees F/ 175 degrees C and set the time to 15 minutes. Press the Start/Pause button and begin preheating. Peel the apples and slice them into eight wedges. Throw away the cores. 2. Coat the apple wedges with the oil. 3. Place each wedge in the Air Fryer and cook for 12 - 15 minutes. 4. Add in the apricots and allow to cook for a further 3 minutes. 5. Stir together the sugar and cinnamon. Sprinkle this mixture over the cooked apples before serving.
Per Serving: Calories 271; Fat 9.3g; Sodium 15mg; Carbs 43g; Fiber 6g; Sugar 2g; Protein 5g

Lemon Tarts

Prep time: 15 minutes | Cook time: 15 minutes | Serves: 4

½ cup butter	1 large lemon, juiced and zested
½ lb. flour	2 tablespoons lemon curd
2 tablespoons sugar	Pinch of nutmeg

1. In a large bowl, combine the butter, flour and sugar until a crumbly consistency is achieved. 2. Add in the lemon zest and juice, followed by a pinch of nutmeg. Continue to combine. 3. Sprinkle the insides of a few small pastry tins with flour. Pour equal portions of the dough into each one and add sugar or lemon zest on top. 4. Select the "AIR FRY" function of Ninja Foodi digital air fry oven, set the temperature to 360 degrees F/ 180 degrees C and set the time to 15 minutes. Press the Start/Pause button and begin preheating. 5. Place the lemon tarts inside the fryer and allow to cook for 15 minutes.
Per Serving: Calories 4; Fat 0.1g; Sodium 0mg; Carbs 1g; Fiber 1g; Sugar 0g; Protein 0g

Tasty Blueberry Pancakes

Prep time: 10 minutes | Cook time: 10 minutes | Serves: 4

½ teaspoon vanilla extract	3 eggs, beaten
2 tablespoons honey	1 cup milk
½ cup blueberries	1 teaspoon baking powder
½ cup sugar	Pinch of salt
2 cups + 2 tablespoons flour	

1. Select the "BAKE" function of Ninja Foodi digital air fry oven, set the temperature to 390 degrees F/ 200 degrees C and set the time to 10 minutes. Press the Start/Pause button and begin preheating. 2. In a bowl, mix together all of the dry ingredients. 3. Pour in the wet ingredients and combine with a whisk, ensuring the mixture becomes smooth. 4. Roll each blueberry in some flour to lightly coat it before folding it into the mixture. This is to ensure they do not change the color of the batter. 5. Coat the inside of a sheet pan with a little oil or butter. 6. Spoon several equal amounts of the batter onto the sheet pan, spreading them into pancake-shapes and ensuring to space them out well. This may have to be completed in two batches. 7. Place the dish in the fryer and bake for about 10 minutes.
Per Serving: Calories 139; Fat 3.2g; Sodium 45mg; Carbs 26g; Fiber 4g; Sugar 8g; Protein 3g

Lemony-Lavender Doughnuts

Prep time: 20 minutes | Cook time: 75 minutes | Serves: 3 to 4

½ cup (120ml) milk, warmed to between 100°F and 110°F (38°C to 43°C)
1 teaspoon yeast
¼ cup (50g) granulated sugar, divided
2 cups (250g) all-purpose flour
½ teaspoon kosher salt

Zest and juice of 1 lemon
4 tablespoons (55g) unsalted butter, melted
1 egg
Vegetable oil for spraying
1½ cups (150g) powdered sugar, sifted
Dried lavender for culinary use

1. Combine the warm milk, yeast, and a pinch of the sugar in a small bowl and whisk to combine. Allow to sit until the yeast blooms and looks bubbly, about 5 to 10 minutes. Meanwhile, whisk together the remaining sugar, flour, and salt. Add the zest of the lemon to the dry ingredients. 2. When the yeast has bloomed, add the milk mixture to the dry ingredients and stir to combine. Add the melted butter and the egg and stir to form a thick dough. Turn out onto a well-floured board and knead until smooth, 1 to 2 minutes. Place the dough in an oiled bowl, cover, and allow to rise in the refrigerator overnight. 3. The following day, remove the dough from the refrigerator and allow it to come to room temperature. Turn out onto a well-floured board. Roll the dough out to¼ inch (6mm) thick. Using a 3- or 4-inch (7.5 or 10 cm) circular cookie cutter, cut out as many doughnuts as possible. Use a 1-inch (2.5 cm) round cookie cutter to cut out holes from the center of each doughnut. With the dough scraps, you can either cut out additional doughnut holes using the 1-inch (2.5cm) cutter or, if desired, gather the scraps and roll them out again to cut out more doughnuts. 4. Transfer the doughnuts and doughnut holes to a lined baking sheet. Proof in a warm until puffy and, when pressed with a finger, the dough slowly springs back, 30 minutes to 1 hour. 5. While the dough is proofing, prepare the glaze. In a bowl, whisk the powdered sugar and the juice from the lemon. Set aside. 6. Select the "AIR FRY" function of Ninja Foodi digital air fry oven, set the temperature to 360 degrees F/ 180 degrees C and set the time to 5 minutes. Press the Start/Pause button and begin preheating. When the doughnuts have proofed, spray the basket of the air fryer with oil. Transfer no more than 3 or 4 of the doughnuts and 2 or 3 of the holes to the air fryer basket. Spray the doughnuts lightly with oil. Cook for 5 to 6 minutes, flipping once halfway through, until browned and cooked through. Transfer the cooked doughnuts and holes to a cooling rack and repeat with the remaining doughnuts and holes. 7. Once the doughnuts are cool enough to handle, dip the tops into the glaze. Return the dipped doughnuts to the rack to allow the excess glaze to drip off. Once the glaze has hardened, dip each doughnut again to create a nice opaque finish. While the second glaze is still wet, if desired, sprinkle a few buds of lavender on top of each doughnut.
Per Serving: Calories 543; Fat 38.1g; Sodium 134mg; Carbs 27g; Fiber 1g; Sugar 0g; Protein 23g

Delicious Chocolate Hazelnut Cookies

Prep time: 5 minutes | Cook time: 10 to 12 minutes | Serves: 12

1 cup butter, softened
1 cup brown sugar
½ cup granulated sugar
2 eggs, lightly beaten
1½ teaspoons vanilla extract
1½ cups all-purpose flour

½ cup rolled oats
1 teaspoon baking soda
½ teaspoon salt
2 cups chocolate chunks
½ cup toasted chopped hazelnuts

1. Cream the butter along with sugars until light and fluffy using a stand mixer or electric hand mixer. Add the eggs along with vanilla, and mix until well combined. 2. Combine the flour, rolled oats, baking soda and salt in a second bowl. Add the dry and wet ingredients in a bowl and mix with a wooden spoon or spatula. Stir in the chocolate chunks and hazelnuts until distributed throughout the dough. 3. Shape the cookies into small balls about the size of golf balls and place them on a baking sheet. Freeze the cookie balls for at least 30 minutes, or package them in as airtight a package as you can and keep them in your freezer. 4. When you're ready for a delicious snack or dessert, Select the "AIR FRY" function of Ninja Foodi digital air fry oven, set the temperature to 350 degrees F/ 175 degrees C and set the time to 10 minutes. Press the Start/Pause button and begin preheating. Place the parchment down in the air fryer basket and place the frozen cookie ball or balls on top. 5. Air-fry the cookies for 10 to 12 minutes, or until they are done to your liking. Enjoy your freshly baked cookie.
Per Serving: Calories 210; Fat 12g; Sodium 311mg; Carbs 24g; Fiber 1g; Sugar 15g; Protein 3g

Delicious Chocolate Lava Cake

Prep time: 10 minutes | Cook time: 12 minutes | Serves: 4

1 cup dark cocoa candy melts
1 stick butter
2 eggs
4 tablespoons sugar
1 tablespoon honey

4 tablespoons flour
Pinch of kosher salt
Pinch of ground cloves
¼ teaspoon grated nutmeg
¼ teaspoon cinnamon powder

1. Select the "BAKE" function of Ninja Foodi digital air fry oven, set the temperature to 350 degrees F/ 175 degrees C and set the time to 12 minutes. Press the Start/Pause button and begin preheating. Spritz the insides of four custard cups with cooking spray. 2. Melt the cocoa candy melts and butter in the microwave for 30 seconds to 1 minute. 3. In a large bowl, combine the eggs, sugar and honey with a whisk until frothy. Pour in the melted chocolate mix. 4. Throw in the rest of the ingredients and combine well with an electric mixer or a manual whisk. 5. Transfer equal portions of the mixture into the prepared custard cups. 6. Place in the Air Fryer and bake for 12 minutes. 7. Cool for 5 to 6 minutes. 8. Place each cup upside-down on a dessert plate and let the cake slide out. Serve with fruits and chocolate syrup if desired.
Per Serving: Calories 88; Fat 7.1g; Sodium 143mg; Carbs 4g; Fiber 3g; Sugar 1g; Protein 4g

Healthy Hasselback Apple Crisp

Prep time: 10 minutes | Cook time: 20 minutes | Serves: 4

2 large Gala apples, peeled, cored and cut in half
¼ cup butter, melted
Topping:
3 tablespoons butter, melted
2 tablespoons brown sugar
¼ cup chopped pecans
2 tablespoons rolled oats

½ teaspoon ground cinnamon
2 tablespoons sugar

1 tablespoon flour
vanilla ice cream
caramel sauce

1. Place the cut side down apples on a cutting board. Slicing from stem end to blossom end, make 8 to 10 slits down the apple halves but only slice three quarters of the way through the apple, not all the way through to the cutting board. 2. Select the "AIR FRY" function of Ninja Foodi digital air fry oven, set the temperature to 330 degrees F/ 165 degrees C and set the time to 15 minutes. Press the Start/Pause button and begin preheating. 3. Transfer the apples to the air fryer basket, flat side down. Combine ¼ cup of melted butter, cinnamon and sugar in a small bowl. Brush this butter mixture onto the apples and air-fry at 330 degrees F/ 165 degrees C for 15 minutes. Baste the apples several times with the butter mixture during the cooking process. 4. While the apples are air-frying, make the filling. Combine 3 tablespoons of melted butter with the brown sugar, pecans, rolled oats and flour in a bowl. Stir until resembles small crumbles. 5. When the timer is up, spoon the topping down the center of the apples. Air-fry at 330 degrees F/ 165 degrees C for an additional 5 minutes. 6. Serve with ice cream and caramel sauce.
Per Serving: Calories 330; Fat 24g; Sodium 158mg; Carbs 28g; Fiber 5g; Sugar 18g; Protein 2g

Apple Pies

Prep time: 15 minutes | Cook time: 25 minutes | Serves: 3

1 refrigerated piecrust (store-bought or see below)
1 pound McIntosh apples
2 tablespoons packed brown sugar
2 tablespoons dried cranberries

2 teaspoons all-purpose flour
½ teaspoon ground cinnamon
⅛ teaspoon grated nutmeg
¼ teaspoon grated orange rind
Pinch salt

1. Roll piecrust out on a floured surface. Cut out three (4½-inch) rounds with a glass and refrigerate on a baking sheet. 2. Select the "AIR FRY" function of Ninja Foodi digital air fry oven, set the temperature to 350 degrees F/ 175 degrees C and set the time to 15 minutes. Press the Start/Pause button and begin preheating. Peel, core, and cut apples into half-slices. In a microwave-safe bowl, toss apples, brown sugar, cranberries, flour, cinnamon, nutmeg, orange rind, and a pinch of salt. Microwave for 2½ minutes until softened, stirring once. Divide filling among 3 (6-ounce/3½-inch-diameter) ramekins or custard cups. Place piecrust rounds on top, form a fluted edge, and cut a slit in the center. Place in the air fryer basket and air-fry for 10 to 12 minutes, or until golden brown. 3. Serve warm
Per Serving: Calories 345; Fat 14g; Sodium 336mg; Carbs 58g; Fiber 2g; Sugar 15g; Protein 3g

Pumpkin Cake

Prep time: 15 minutes | Cook time: 15 minutes | Serves: 4

1 large egg
½ cup skimmed milk
7 oz. flour
2 tablespoons sugar

5 oz. pumpkin puree
Pinch of salt
Pinch of cinnamon [if desired]
Cooking spray

1. Stir together the pumpkin puree and sugar in a bowl. Crack in the egg and combine using a whisk until smooth. 2. Add in the flour and salt, stirring constantly. Pour in the milk, ensuring to combine everything well. 3. Spritz a baking tin with cooking spray. 4. Transfer the batter to the baking tin. 5. Select the "BAKE" function of Ninja Foodi digital air fry oven, set the temperature to 350 degrees F/ 175 degrees C and set the time to 15 minutes. Press the Start/Pause button and begin preheating. 6. Put the tin in the Air Fryer sheet pan and bake for 15 minutes.
Per Serving: Calories 409; Fat 18.9g; Sodium 214mg; Carbs 10g; Fiber 1g; Sugar 9g; Protein 48g

Mixed Berry Puffed Pastry

Prep time: 10 minutes | Cook time: 15 minutes | Serves: 3

3 pastry dough sheets
½ cup mixed berries, mashed
1 tablespoon honey

2 tablespoons cream cheese
3 tablespoons chopped walnuts
¼ teaspoon vanilla extract

1. Select the "BAKE" function of Ninja Foodi digital air fry oven, set the temperature to 375 degrees F/ 190 degrees C and set the time to 15 minutes. Press the Start/Pause button and begin preheating. 2. Roll out the pastry sheets and spread the cream cheese over each one. 3. In a bowl, combine the berries, vanilla extract and honey. 4. Cover a baking sheet with parchment paper. 5. Spoon equal amounts of the berry mixture into the center of each sheet of pastry. Scatter the chopped walnuts on top. 6. Fold up the pastry around the filling and press down the edges with the back of a fork to seal them. 7. Transfer the baking sheet to the Air Fryer and cook for approximately 15 minutes.
Per Serving: Calories 716; Fat 62.6g; Sodium 302mg; Carbs 18g; Fiber 8g; Sugar 2g; Protein 34g

Crispy Apple Pie

Prep time: 10 minutes | Cook time: 15 minutes | Serves: 7

2 large apples
½ cup flour
2 tablespoons unsalted butter

1 tablespoon sugar
½ teaspoon cinnamon

1. Select the "AIR FRY" function of Ninja Foodi digital air fry oven, set the temperature to 360 degrees F/ 180 degrees C and set the time to 15 minutes. Press the Start/Pause button and begin preheating. 2. In a large bowl, combine the flour and butter. Pour in the sugar, continuing to mix. 3. Add in a 3 tablespoons water and combine everything to create a smooth dough. 4. Grease the insides of a few small pastry tins with butter. Divide the dough between each tin and lay each portion flat inside. 5. Peel, core and dice up the apples. Put the diced apples on top of the pastry and top with a sprinkling of sugar and cinnamon. 6. Place the pastry tins in your Air Fryer and cook for 15 - 17 minutes. Serve with ice cream if desired.
Per Serving: Calories 1646; Fat 146g; Sodium 498mg; Carbs 10g; Fiber 2g; Sugar 2g; Protein 77g

Delicious Glazed Donuts

Prep time: 10 minutes | Cook time: 15 minutes | Serves: 2 to 4

1 can [8oz.] refrigerated croissant dough
Cooking spray
1 can [16oz.] vanilla frosting

1. Select the "AIR FRY" function of Ninja Foodi digital air fry oven, set the temperature to 400 degrees F/ 200 degrees C and set the time to 5 minutes. Press the Start/Pause button and begin preheating. Cut the croissant dough into 1-inch-round slices. Create a donut. 2. Put the donuts in the Air Fryer basket, taking care not to overlap any, and spritz with cooking spray. 3. You may need to cook everything in multiple batches. 4. Cook for 2 minutes. Turn and cook for 3 minutes. 5. Place the rolls on a paper plate. 6. Microwave a half-cup of frosting for 30 seconds and pour a drizzling of the frosting over the donuts before serving.
Per Serving: Calories 463; Fat 15.5g; Sodium 553mg; Carbs 366g; Fiber 3g; Sugar 3g; Protein 41g

Traditional Apple Dumplings

Prep time: 15 minutes | Cook time: 25 minutes | Serves: 2

2 tablespoons sultanas
2 sheets puff pastry
2 tablespoons butter, melted

2 small apples
1 tablespoon sugar

1. Select the "BAKE" function of Ninja Foodi digital air fry oven, set the temperature to 350 degrees F/ 175 degrees C and set the time to 25 minutes. Press the Start/Pause button and begin preheating. 2. Peel the apples and remove the cores. 3. In a bowl, stir together the sugar and the sultanas. 4. Lay one apple on top of each pastry sheet and stuff the sugar and sultanas into the holes where the cores used to be. 5. Wrap the pastry around the apples, covering them completely. 6. Put them on a sheet of aluminum foil and coat each dumpling with a light brushing of melted butter. 7. Transfer to the Air Fryer and bake for 25 minutes until a golden brown color is achieved and the apples have softened inside.
Per Serving: Calories 387; Fat 26.3g; Sodium 602mg; Carbs 12g; Fiber 8g; Sugar 1g; Protein 26g

Plum Cream

Prep time: 5 minutes | Cook time: 20 minutes | Serves: 4

1 pound plums, pitted and chopped
¼ cup swerve

1 tablespoon lemon juice
1 and ½ cups heavy cream

Select the "AIR FRY" function of Ninja Foodi digital air fry oven, set the temperature to 340 degrees F/ 170 degrees C and set the time to 20 minutes. Press the Start/Pause button and begin preheating. In a bowl, mix all the ingredients and whisk really well. Divide this into 4 ramekins, put them in the air fryer and cook for 20 minutes. Serve cold.
Per Serving: Calories 170; Fat 4g; Sodium 66mg; Carbs 4g; Fiber 2g; Sugar 3g; Protein 4g

Bamiyeh

Prep time: 10 minutes | Cook time: 35 minutes | Serves: 6

Doughnuts:
3 tablespoons (45g) unsalted butter
1 tablespoon (13g) granulated sugar
Syrup:
1 cup (200g) granulated sugar
¾ cup (180ml) water
1 teaspoon rose water

1 cup (240ml) water
1 cup (125g) all-purpose flour
2 eggs
Vegetable oil for spraying

Pinch saffron threads dissolved in ¼ cup (60ml) boiling water

1. Combine the butter, sugar, and water in a medium saucepan and melt the butter over low heat. Add in the flour to form a cohesive dough. Cook over medium-low heat for 2 minutes to get rid of the raw flour taste. Remove from cooking and cool to room temperature. Beat the eggs in one at a time, ensuring the first egg is fully incorporated before the adding the second. The dough will curdle but keep beating vigorously until the dough becomes smooth. Once the eggs are fully incorporated, let the dough rest for 30 minutes. 2. Prepare the rose water syrup. Add the sugar with water in a saucepan and bring to a boil, stirring to dissolve the sugar. Turn down the heat and simmer for 5 minutes until thickened. Remove from the heat and add the rose water and 1 tablespoon (15ml) of the saffron water, reserving the remaining saffron water for another use, such as rice pilaf. Keep warm. 3. Once the dough has rested, place the dough in a piping bag outfitted with a large, star-shaped tip. Lightly grease the air fryer basket. Pipe the dough directly onto the basket of the air fryer, forming doughnuts approximately 3 inches (7.5cm) long and 1 inch (2.5cm) wide. Cut the dough when you have achieved the desired length. Work in batches so as not to overcrowd the basket. Spray lightly with oil. Select the "AIR FRY" function of Ninja Foodi digital air fry oven, set the temperature to 360 degrees F/ 180 degrees C and set the time to 12 minutes. Press the Start/Pause button and begin preheating. Cook at 360 degrees F/ 180 degrees C shaking the basket once or twice, for 10 to 12 minutes until the outside of the doughnuts is golden brown and the inside is fully cooked and airy. 4. Pour the warm syrup in a shallow bowl and place the first batch of doughnuts in the syrup. Soak for 5 minutes then remove to a plate or platter. Repeat the process with the remaining dough and syrup. Serve warm or at room temperature.
Per Serving: Calories 314; Fat 27.2g; Sodium 182mg; Carbs 0g; Fiber 0g; Sugar 0g; Protein 17g

Churros with Chocolate Sauce

Prep time: 10 minutes | Cook time: 30 minutes | Serves: 4

Chocolate Sauce:

4 ounces (115g) semisweet chocolate, finely chopped
½ cup (120ml) heavy cream

¼ cup (85g) light corn syrup
½ teaspoon cinnamon
¼ teaspoon cayenne pepper

Churros:

3 tablespoons (45g) unsalted butter, divided
1 cup (240ml) water
½ cup (100g) granulated sugar plus 1 tablespoon (13g)

Pinch kosher salt
1 cup (125g) all-purpose flour
2 eggs
Vegetable oil for spraying
2 teaspoons cinnamon

1. For chocolate sauce, place the chopped chocolate in a heat-proof bowl. Combine the cream with corn syrup in a saucepan and bring to a simmer. Pour the warm cream mixture over the chocolate and stir until the chocolate is melted. Add the cinnamon and cayenne pepper. Set aside. 2. To make the churros, combine 1 tablespoon (14g) of the butter, the water, 1 tablespoon (13g) of the sugar, and the salt in a medium saucepan. Melt the butter over low heat. Add the flour and stir vigorously to form a dough ball. Continue to cook, stirring until the mixture looks dry and thick, 2 minutes. Remove from the heat and allow to cool to room temperature. Once cool, beat in the eggs one at a time, ensuring the first egg is fully incorporated before adding the second. Continue beating until the mixture is smooth. Let the dough rest for 30 minutes. 3. Place the churros batter into a piping bag outfitted with an extra-large tip, round or star-shaped. Spray the air fryer basket with oil. Working in batches, pipe churros that are 5 to 6 inches (13 to 15 cm) long and ¾ to 1 inch (2 to 2.5 cm) in diameter directly onto the air fryer basket. Do not crowd the basket. Cut the dough when you've reached the desired length. Spray the churros with oil. 4. Select the "AIR FRY" function of Ninja Foodi digital air fry oven, set the temperature to 360 degrees F/ 180 degrees C and set the time to 14 minutes. Press the Start/Pause button and begin preheating. Cook for 12 to 14 minutes until the outside is firm and brown and the inside is soft. While the churros are cooking, combine the remaining ½ cup (100g) sugar with the cinnamon on a plate and whisk to combine. Melt the butter and place in a small dish. 5. Remove the cooked churros from the air fryer and immediately brush with melted butter and dredge in the cinnamon sugar. Repeat the process with the remaining churros. Serve hot with the chocolate sauce.

Per Serving: Calories 144; Fat 6.6g; Sodium 171mg; Carbs 2g; Fiber 0g; Sugar 1g; Protein 19g

Chocolaty Croissants

Prep time: 15 minutes | Cook time: 50 minutes | Serves: 8

1 sheet frozen puff pastry, thawed
⅓ cup chocolate-hazelnut spread

1 large egg, beaten

1. On floured surface, roll pastry into a 14-inch square. Cut pastry into quarters to form 4 squares. Cut diagonally to form triangles. 2. Spread 2 teaspoons chocolate-hazelnut spread on each triangle; from wider end, roll up pastry. Brush egg on top of each roll. 3. Select the "BAKE" function of Ninja Foodi digital air fry oven, set the temperature to 375 degrees F/ 190 degrees C and set the time to 8 minutes. Press the Start/Pause button and begin preheating. Air-fry rolls in batches, 3 or 4 at a time, 8 minutes per batch, or until pastry is golden brown. 4. Cool; serve warm or at room temperature.

Per Serving: Calories 200; Fat 12g; Sodium 163mg; Carbs 18g; Fiber 1g; Sugar 8g; Protein 4g

Fried Bananas with Ice Cream

Prep time: 10 minutes | Cook time: 15 minutes | Serves: 2

2 large bananas
1 tablespoon butter
1 tablespoon sugar

2 tablespoons friendly bread crumbs
Vanilla ice cream for serving

1. Select the "AIR FRY" function of Ninja Foodi digital air fry oven, set the temperature to 350 degrees F/ 175 degrees C and set the time to 15 minutes. Press the Start/Pause button and begin preheating. Place the butter in the Air Fryer basket and allow it to melt for 1 minute. 2. Combine the sugar and bread crumbs in a bowl. 3. Slice the bananas into 1-inch-round pieces. Drop them into the sugar mixture and coat them well. 4. Place the bananas in the Air Fryer and cook for 10–15 minutes. 5. Serve warm, with ice cream on the side if desired.

Per Serving: Calories 494; Fat 36g; Sodium 690mg; Carbs 17g; Fiber 11g; Sugar 2g; Protein 28g

Tasty S'mores Pockets

Prep time: 10 minutes | Cook time: 10 minutes | Serves: 6

12 sheets phyllo dough, thawed
1½ cups butter, melted
¾ cup graham cracker crumbs

1 (7-ounce) milk chocolate bar
12 marshmallows, cut in half

1. Place one sheet of the phyllo on a large cutting board. Keep the rest of the phyllo sheets covered with a slightly damp, clean kitchen towel. Brush the phyllo sheet generously with some melted butter. Place other phyllo sheet on top of the first and brush it with more butter. Repeat with one more phyllo sheet until you have a stack of 3 phyllo sheets with butter brushed between the layers. Cover the phyllo sheets with one quarter of the graham cracker crumbs leaving a 1-inch border the rectangle. Cut the phyllo sheets lengthwise into 3 strips. 2. Take 2 of the strips and crisscross them to form a cross with the empty borders at the top and to the left. Place 2 of the chocolate rectangles in the center of the cross. Place 4 of the marshmallow halves on top of the chocolate. Now fold the pocket together by folding the bottom phyllo strip up over the chocolate and marshmallows. Then fold the right side over, then the top strip down and finally the left side over. Brush all the edges generously with melted butter to seal shut. Repeat with the next three sheets of phyllo, until all the sheets have been used. You will be able to make 2 pockets with every second batch because you will have an extra graham cracker crumb strip from the previous set of sheets. 3. Select the "AIR FRY" function of Ninja Foodi digital air fry oven, set the temperature to 350 degrees F/ 175 degrees C and set the time to 5 minutes. Press the Start/Pause button and begin preheating. 4. Transfer 3 pockets at a time to the air fryer basket. Air-fry at 350 degrees F/ 175 degrees C for 4 to 5 minutes, until the phyllo dough is light brown in color. Flip the pockets over halfway through the cooking process. Repeat with the remaining 3 pockets. 5. Serve warm.

Per Serving: Calories 710; Fat 50g; Sodium 358mg; Carbs 61g; Fiber 1g; Sugar 30g; Protein 6g

Profiteroles

Prep time: 20 minutes | Cook time: 55 minutes | Serves: 4 to 5

Choux Puffs:

3 tablespoons (45g) unsalted butter
1 tablespoon (13g) granulated sugar

1 cup (235ml) water
1 cup (125g) all-purpose flour
2 eggs
Vegetable oil for brushing

Chocolate Sauce:

4 ounces semisweet chocolate, finely chopped
2 tablespoons unsalted butter
1 cup (240ml) heavy cream

¼ cup (85g) corn syrup
1 pint (285g) vanilla ice cream for serving

1. Combine the butter, sugar, and water in a medium saucepan and melt the butter over low heat. Add in the flour to form a cohesive dough. Cook over medium-low heat for 2 minutes to get rid of the raw flour taste. Remove from cooking and cool to room temperature. Beat the eggs in one at a time, making sure the first egg is fully incorporated before adding the second. The dough will curdle but keep beating vigorously until the dough becomes smooth. Once the eggs are fully incorporated, let the dough rest for 30 minutes. 2. Heat the chocolate and butter in a heat-proof bowl. Heat the cream and corn syrup in a small saucepan over medium heat until the cream is simmering. Remove from the heat and pour the cream mixture over the chocolate in the bowl. Stir until sauce is smooth. Set aside. 3. Place it in a piping bag outfitted with a large, round tip. Lightly oil the basket of the air fryer. Working in 2 batches, pipe round puffs of dough approximately 2 inches (5 cm) wide and 1 inch (2.5cm) tall directly onto the basket of the air fryer. Cut the dough when you have achieved the desired size. With a damp finger, press down on the swirl at the top of each puff to round it. Select the "AIR FRY" function of Ninja Foodi digital air fry oven, set the temperature to 360 degrees F/ 180 degrees C and set the time to 20 minutes. Press the Start/Pause button and begin preheating. Cook for 18 to 20 minutes until the outside of the puffs is golden brown and crisp and the inside is fully cooked and airy. 4. To serve, halve the choux puffs crosswise and place a scoop of ice cream inside each one. Replace the top of the puff and spoon chocolate sauce over the top. Serve immediately.

Per Serving: Calories 143; Fat 7.5g; Sodium 5mg; Carbs 19g; Fiber 3g; Sugar 3g; Protein 3g

Delicious Chocolate Chip Pan Cookie Sundae

Prep time: 10 minutes | Cook time: 15 minutes | Serves: 4

1 stick (4 ounces, or 112g) unsalted butter, softened	¼ teaspoon baking soda
3 tablespoons (39g) granulated sugar	¼ teaspoon kosher salt
3 tablespoons (28.5g) brown sugar	½ cup (88g) semisweet chocolate chips
1 egg	Vegetable oil for spraying
1 teaspoon vanilla extract	Vanilla ice cream for serving
½ cup (63g) all-purpose flour	Hot fudge or caramel sauce for serving

1. In a medium bowl, cream the butter and sugars together by using a handheld mixer until light and fluffy. Add the egg and vanilla and mix until they are well combined. In a bowl, whisk the flour, baking soda, and salt. Add the dry ingredients to the batter and mix until combined. Add the chocolate chips and mix a final time. 2. Select the "AIR FRY" function of Ninja Foodi digital air fry oven, set the temperature to 325 degrees F/ 160 degrees C and set the time to 15 minutes. Press the Start/Pause button and begin preheating. Lightly grease a 7-inch (18 cm) pizza pan for the air fryer. Spread the batter evenly in the pan. Place in the air fryer and cook for 12 to 15 minutes, until the top of the cookie is browned and the middle is gooey but cooked. Remove the pan from the air fryer. 3. Place 1 to 2 scoops of vanilla ice cream in the center of the cookie and top with hot fudge or caramel sauce, if desired. Pass around spoons and eat the cookie sundae right out of the pan.
Per Serving: Calories 365; Fat 12.4g; Sodium 717mg; Carbs 29g; Fiber 3g; Sugar 10g; Protein 19g

Chouquettes

Prep time: 15 minutes | Cook time: 45 minutes | Serves: 4 to 5

3 tablespoons (45g) unsalted butter	1 cup (125g) all-purpose flour
1 tablespoon (13g) granulated sugar	3 eggs
	1½ tablespoons (25ml) milk
1 cup (240ml) water	Vegetable oil for brushing
	½ cup (96g) pearl sugar

1. Combine the butter, granulated sugar, and water in a medium saucepan and melt the butter over low heat. Add in the flour to form a cohesive dough. Cook over medium-low heat for 2 minutes to get rid of the raw flour taste. Remove from the heat and allow to cool to room temperature. Beat in 2 of the eggs, one at a time, making sure the first egg is fully incorporated before the adding the second. The dough will curdle, but keep beating vigorously until the dough becomes smooth. Once the eggs are fully incorporated, let the dough rest for 30 minutes. 2. Beat the remaining egg together with the milk in a small bowl. Lightly brush the basket of the air fryer with oil. Using a small, spring-loaded cookie scoop or a tablespoon, scoop 6 to 8 circles of dough directly onto the basket of the air fryer. Brush top with the egg wash and sprinkle on pearl sugar. Select the "AIR FRY" function of Ninja Foodi digital air fry oven, set the temperature to 360 degrees F/ 180 degrees C and set the time to 17 minutes. Press the Start/Pause button and begin preheating. 3. Cook for 15 to 17 minutes until the outside of the chouquettes is golden brown and the inside fully cooked and airy. Serve immediately.
Per Serving: Calories 205; Fat 5.8g; Sodium 1481mg; Carbs 1g; Fiber 0g; Sugar 0g; Protein 35g

Plum Cake

Prep time: 10 minutes | Cook time: 30 minutes | Serves: 8

½ cup butter, soft	1 and ½ cups almond flour
3 eggs	½ cup coconut flour
½ cup swerve	2 teaspoons baking powder
¼ teaspoon almond extract	¾ cup almond milk
1 tablespoon vanilla extract	4 plums, pitted and chopped

1. Select the "AIR FRY" function of Ninja Foodi digital air fry oven, set the temperature to 370 degrees F/ 185 degrees C and set the time to 30 minutes. Press the Start/Pause button and begin preheating. In a bowl, mix all the and whisk well. 2. Pour this into a cake pan that fits the air fryer after you've lined it with parchment paper, put the pan in the machine and cook for 30 minutes. 3. Cool the cake down, slice and serve.
Per Serving: Calories 183; Fat 4g; Sodium 269mg; Carbs 4g; Fiber 3g; Sugar 2g; Protein 7g

Cinnamon Plums

Prep time: 5 minutes | Cook time: 20 minutes | Serves: 6

6 plums, cut into wedges	Zest of 1 lemon, grated
1 teaspoon ginger, ground	2 tablespoons water
½ teaspoon cinnamon powder	10 drops stevia

Select the "AIR FRY" function of Ninja Foodi digital air fry oven, set the temperature to 360 degrees F/ 180 degrees C and set the time to 20 minutes. Press the Start/Pause button and begin preheating. In a pan, combine the plums with the rest of the ingredients, toss gently, put the pan in the air fryer and cook for 20 minutes. Serve cold.
Per Serving: Calories 170; Fat 5g; Sodium 215mg; Carbs 3g; Fiber 1g; Sugar 3g; Protein 5g

Pecan-Stuffed Apples

Prep time: 15 minutes | Cook time: 40 minutes | Serves: 4

4 Gala or Empire apples (about 1¼ pounds)	3 tablespoons brown sugar
¼ cup chopped pecans	¼ teaspoon allspice
⅓ cup dried tart cherries	Pinch salt
1 tablespoon melted butter	Ice cream, for serving

1. Cut off the top ½ inch from each apple; reserve tops. With a melon baller, core through stem ends without breaking through the bottom. 2. Select the "BAKE" function of Ninja Foodi digital air fry oven, set the temperature to 350 degrees F/ 175 degrees C and set the time to 20 minutes. Press the Start/Pause button and begin preheating. Combine pecans, cherries, butter, brown sugar, allspice, and a pinch of salt. Stuff mixture into the hollow centers of the apples. Cover with apple tops. Place in the air fryer basket, using tongs. Air-fry for 20 to 25 minutes, or just until tender. 3. Serve warm, with ice cream.
Per Serving: Calories 225; Fat 8g; Sodium 56mg; Carbs 39g; Fiber 4g; Sugar 14g; Protein 1g

Charred Caramelized Peach Shortcakes

Prep time: 10 minutes | Cook time: 25 minutes | Serves: 4

Shortcakes:

1 cup (125g) self-rising flour	2 peaches, preferably freestone
½ cup (120ml) plus 1 tablespoon (15ml) heavy cream	1 tablespoon (14g) unsalted butter, melted
Vegetable oil for spraying	2 teaspoons brown sugar
Caramelized Peaches	1 teaspoon cinnamon

Whipped Cream:

1 cup (240ml) cold heavy cream	½ teaspoon vanilla extract
1 tablespoon (13g) granulated sugar	Zest of 1 lime

1. To make the shortcakes, place the flour in a medium bowl and whisk to remove any lumps. Make a hole in the flour like a well. While stirring with a fork, slowly pour in ½ cup (120ml) plus 1 tablespoon (15ml) of the heavy cream. Continue to stir until the dough has mostly come together. With your hands, gather the dough, incorporating any dry flour, and form into a ball. 2. Place the dough on floured board and pat into a rectangle that is ½ to ¾ inch (1.3 to 2 cm) thick. Fold in half. Turn and repeat. Pat the dough into a ¾-inch-thick (2cm) square. Cut dough into 4 equally sized square biscuits. 3. Select the "AIR FRY" function of Ninja Foodi digital air fry oven, set the temperature to 325 degrees F/ 160 degrees C and set the time to 15 minutes. Press the Start/Pause button and begin preheating. Spray the air fryer basket with oil to prevent sticking. Place the biscuits in the air fryer basket. Cook for 15 to 18 minutes until the tops are browned and the insides fully cooked. 4. To make the peaches, cut the peaches in half and remove the pit. Brush the peach with the butter and sprinkle ½ teaspoon of the brown sugar and ¼ teaspoon of the cinnamon on each peach half. Arrange the peaches in a single layer in the air fryer basket. Cook at 375 degrees F/ 190 degrees C for 8 to 10 minutes until the peaches are soft and the tops caramelized. 5. While the peaches are cooking, whip the cream. Pour the cold heavy cream, sugar, and vanilla (if using) into the bowl of a stand mixer or a metal mixing bowl. Beat with the whisk attachment for your stand mixer or a handheld electric mixer on high speed until stiff peaks form, about 1 minute. 6. To assemble the shortcakes, cut each biscuit in half horizontally. Place a peach on the bottom half of each biscuit and place the top half on top of the peach. Top each shortcake with whipped cream and a sprinkle of lime zest. Serve immediately.
Per Serving: Calories 722; Fat 39g; Sodium 140mg; Carbs 7g; Fiber 2g; Sugar 4g; Protein 18g

Creamy Rhubarb Crumble

Prep time: 15 minutes | Cook time: 20 minutes | Serves: 4

4 oz rhubarb, chopped
¼ cup heavy cream
1 teaspoon ground cinnamon
¼ cup Erythritol
1 cup almond flour
1 egg, beaten
1 teaspoon avocado oil
4 teaspoons butter, softened

1. Select the "AIR FRY" function of Ninja Foodi digital air fry oven, set the temperature to 375 degrees F/ 190 degrees C and set the time to 20 minutes. Press the Start/Pause button and begin preheating. In the bowl, mix up heavy cream, ground cinnamon, almond flour, egg, and butter, Stir the mixture until you get the crumbly texture. 2. Then mix up rhubarb and Erythritol. Brush the air fryer mold with avocado oil. 3. Separate the crumbled dough on 4 parts. Put 1 part of the dough in the air fryer mold. 4. Then sprinkle it with a small amount of rhubarb. Repeat the same steps till you use all ingredients. 5. Put the crumble in the air fryer. Cook it for 20 minutes.
Per Serving: Calories 124; Fat 11.4g; Sodium 147mg; Carbs 4.1g; Fiber 1g; Sugar 3g; Protein 3.4g

Charred Caramelized Pineapple with Mint and Lime

Prep time: 10 minutes | Cook time: 25 minutes | Serves: 4

1 pineapple
4 tablespoons (55g) unsalted butter, melted
2 tablespoons (30g) plus 2
1 lime
teaspoons brown sugar
2 tablespoons (12g) fresh mint, cut into ribbons

1. Cut off the top and bottom of the pineapple and stand it on a cut end. Slice off the outer skin, cutting deeply enough to remove the eyes of the pineapple. Cut off any pointy edges to make the pineapple nice and round. Cut the peeled pineapple into 8 circles, approximately ½ to ¾ inch (1.3 to 2 cm) thick. Remove the core of each slice using a small, circular cookie or biscuit cutter, or simply cut out the core using a paring knife. Place the pineapple rings on a plate. Select the "AIR FRY" function of Ninja Foodi digital air fry oven, set the temperature to 400 degrees F/ 200 degrees C and set the time to 10 minutes. Press the Start/Pause button and begin preheating. 2. Brush both sides of the pineapple rings with the melted butter. Working in 2 batches, arrange 4 slices in a single layer in the basket of the air fryer. Sprinkle ½ teaspoon brown sugar on the top of each ring. Cook at until the top side is browned and caramelized, about 10 minutes. With tongs, carefully flip each ring and sprinkle brown sugar on the second side. Cook for 5 minutes until the second side is browned and caramelized. Remove the cooked pineapple and repeat with the remaining pineapple rings. 3. Arrange all the cooked pineapple rings on a serving plate or platter. Sprinkle with mint and spritz with the juice of the lime. Serve warm.
Per Serving: Calories 153; Fat 39g; Sodium 108mg; Carbs 25g; Fiber 6g; Sugar 2g; Protein 37g

Delicious Black and Blueberry Clafoutis

Prep time: 10 minutes | Cook time: 30 minutes | Serves: 4

6-inch pie pan
3 large eggs
½ cup sugar
1 teaspoon vanilla extract
2 tablespoons butter, melted 1 cup
milk
½ cup all-purpose flour
1 cup blackberries
1 cup blueberries
2 tablespoons confectioners' sugar

1. Select the "AIR FRY" function of Ninja Foodi digital air fry oven, set the temperature to 320 degrees F/ 160 degrees C and set the time to 15 minutes. Press the Start/Pause button and begin preheating. 2. Combine the eggs along with sugar and whisk vigorously until smooth, lighter in color and well combined. Add the vanilla extract, butter and milk and whisk together well. Add in the flour and mix well until no streaks of white remain. 3. Scatter half the blueberries and blackberries in a greased (6-inch) pie pan or cake pan. Pour half of the batter (about 1¼ cups) on top of the berries and transfer the tart pan to the air fryer basket. 4. Air-fry for 12 to 15 minutes or until the clafoutis has puffed up and is still a little jiggly in the center. Remove the clafoutis from the air fryer, invert it onto a plate and let it cool while you bake the second batch. Serve the clafoutis warm (not hot), dusted with confectioners' sugar on top.
Per Serving: Calories 340; Fat 11g; Sodium 149mg; Carbs 53g; Fiber 3g; Sugar 9g; Protein 9g

Baked Apples with Nut Filling

Prep time: 5 minutes | Cook time: 20 minutes | Serves: 4

4 to 6 tablespoons chopped walnuts
4 to 6 tablespoons raisins
4 tablespoons (½ stick) unsalted butter, melted
1 teaspoon ground cinnamon
½ teaspoon ground nutmeg
4 apples, cored but with the bottoms left intact
Vanilla ice cream, for topping
Maple syrup, for topping

1. Select the "AIR FRY" function of Ninja Foodi digital air fry oven, set the temperature to 350 degrees F/ 175 degrees C and set the time to 20 minutes. Press the Start/Pause button and begin preheating. In a mixing bowl, make the filling. Mix together the walnuts, raisins, melted butter, cinnamon, and nutmeg. 2. Scoop a quarter of the filling into each apple. 3. Place the apples in an air fryer–safe pan and set the pan in the air fryer basket. 4. Bake for 20 minutes. 5. Serve with vanilla ice cream and a drizzle of maple syrup.
Per Serving: Calories 382; Fat 19g; Sodium 100mg; Carbs 57g; Fiber 7g; Sugar 44g; Protein 4g

Strawberry Tart with Sweet and Sour Sauce

Prep time: 10 minutes | Cook time: 25 minutes | Serves: 2

1 pound (455g) strawberries, hulled and thinly sliced
1 tablespoon (15ml) balsamic vinegar
1 tablespoon (20g) honey
1 sprig basil
1 sheet frozen puff pastry, thawed according to package instructions
1 egg beaten

1. Place the strawberries in a 7-inch (18cm) round pizza pan for the air fryer and mound them slightly in the center. In a small bowl, whisk together the balsamic vinegar and honey. Drizzle the mixture over the strawberries. Slice the leaves from the sprig of basil into ribbons and sprinkle them over the strawberries. 2. Cut out an 8-inch (20cm) square from the sheet of puff pastry. Drape the pastry over the strawberries in the pan. Poke holes in the puff pastry with the tines of a fork. Brush the top of the pastry with the egg wash. Place the pan in the basket of the air fryer. Select the "BAKE" function of Ninja Foodi digital air fry oven, set the temperature to 350 degrees F/ 175 degrees C and set the time to 25 minutes. Press the Start/Pause button and begin preheating. 3. Bake for 25 to 30 minutes until the top of the pastry is golden brown and glossy and the underside of the pastry is cooked. Remove the pan from the basket of the air fryer. If desired, cut the pastry in half and divide the dessert among 2 plates. Alternatively, for less mess, two people can enjoy this tart right out of the pan.
Per Serving: Calories 300; Fat 24g; Sodium 117mg; Carbs 3g; Fiber 3g; Sugar 2g; Protein 18g

Coconut Crusted Bananas with Pineapple Sauce

Prep time: 10 minutes | Cook time: 10 minutes | Serves: 4

Pineapple Sauce:
1½ cups puréed fresh pineapple
2 tablespoons sugar
juice of 1 lemon
¼ teaspoon ground cinnamon
3 firm bananas
¼ cup sweetened condensed milk
1¼ cups shredded coconut
⅓ cup crushed graham crackers (crumbs)
vegetable oil, in a spray bottle
vanilla frozen yogurt or ice cream

1. Make the pineapple sauce by combining the pineapple, sugar, lemon juice and cinnamon in a saucepan. Simmer the mixture on the stovetop for 20 minutes, and then set it aside. 2. Slice the bananas diagonally into ½-inch thick slices and place them in a bowl. Pour the condensed milk into the bowl and toss the bananas gently to coat. Combine the coconut and graham cracker crumbs together in a shallow dish. Remove the banana slices from the condensed milk and let any excess milk drip off. Dip the banana slices in the coconut and crumb mixture to coat both sides. Spray the coated slices with oil. 3. Select the "AIR FRY" function of Ninja Foodi digital air fry oven, set the temperature to 400 degrees F/ 200 degrees C and set the time to 5 minutes. Press the Start/Pause button and begin preheating. 4. Grease the bottom of the air fryer basket with a little oil. Air-fry the bananas in batches for 5 minutes, turning them over halfway through the cooking time. Air-fry until the bananas are golden brown on both sides. 5. Serve warm over vanilla frozen yogurt with some of the pineapple sauce spooned over top.
Per Serving: Calories 290; Fat 4g; Sodium 100mg; Carbs 48g; Fiber 5g; Sugar 29g; Protein 3g

Nutty Peanut Butter Topping

¼ cup peanut butter | 1 tablespoon powdered sugar
3 tablespoons milk

1. Add the milk and peanut butter into a bowl. Microwave for 30 seconds. Add in the powdered sugar and mix well until smooth. 2. Place the sauce in a bag and make a small hole. Drizzle over the chocolate layer on the doughnut holes.
Per Serving: Calories 170; Fat 9.5g; Sodium 158mg; Carbs 20g; Fiber 1g; Sugar 21g; Protein 5g

Honey Struffoli

Prep time: 10 minutes | Cook time: 20 minutes | Serves: 10

¼ cup butter, softened | ¼ teaspoon salt
⅔ cup sugar | 16 ounces honey
5 eggs | 1 teaspoon ground cinnamon
2 teaspoons vanilla extract | zest of 1 orange
zest of 1 lemon | 2 tablespoons water
4 cups all-purpose flour | nonpareils candy sprinkles
2 teaspoons baking soda

1. Cream the butter along with sugar in a bowl until light and fluffy using a hand mixer. Add the eggs along with vanilla and lemon zest and mix. In a separate bowl, combine the flour, baking soda and salt. Mix the dry ingredients to the wet ingredients and mix until you have a soft dough. Shape the dough and wrap it in plastic and let it rest for 30 minutes. 2. Divide the dough ball into four pieces. Roll each piece into a long rope. Cut each rope into about 25 (½-inch) pieces. Roll each piece into a tight ball. You should have 100 little balls when finished. 3. Select the "AIR FRY" function of Ninja Foodi digital air fry oven, set the temperature to 370 degrees F/ 185 degrees C and set the time to 4 minutes. Press the Start/Pause button and begin preheating. 4. In batches of about 20, transfer the dough balls to the air fryer basket, leaving a small space in between them. Air-fry the dough balls at 370 degrees F/ 185 degrees C for 3 to 4 minutes, shaking the basket when one minute of cooking time remains. 5. After all the dough balls are air-fried, make the honey topping. Melt the honey in a small saucepan on the stovetop. Add the cinnamon, orange zest, and water. Simmer for one minute. Place the air-fried dough balls in a large bowl and drizzle the honey mixture over top. Gently toss to coat all the dough balls evenly. Transfer the coated struffoli to a platter and sprinkle the nonpareil candy sprinkles over top. You can dress the presentation up by piling the balls into the shape of a wreath or pile them high in a cone shape to resemble a Christmas tree. 6. Struffoli can be made ahead. Store covered tightly.
Per Serving: Calories 180; Fat 3g; Sodium 68mg; Carbs 35g; Fiber 1g; Sugar 20g; Protein 3g

Blueberry Tartlets

Prep time: 5 minutes | Cook time: 12 minutes | Serves: 4

8 ounces cream cheese, softened | shells
¼ cup sugar | 2 cups blueberries
1 egg | ½ teaspoon ground cinnamon
½ teaspoon vanilla extract | juice of ½ lemon
zest of 2 lemons, divided | ¼ cup apricot preserves
9 mini graham cracker tartlet

1. Select the "BAKE" function of Ninja Foodi digital air fry oven, set the temperature to 330 degrees F/ 165 degrees C and set the time to 6 minutes. Press the Start/Pause button and begin preheating. 2. Combine the cream cheese, sugar, egg, vanilla and the zest of one lemon in a medium bowl and blend until smooth by hand or with an electric hand mixer. Pour the cream cheese mixture into the tartlet shells. 3. Air-fry 3 tartlets at a time for 6 minutes, rotating them in halfway through the cooking time. 4. Combine the blueberries, cinnamon, zest of one lemon and juice of half a lemon in a bowl. Melt the apricot preserves in the microwave or over low heat in a saucepan. Pour the apricot preserves over the blueberries and gently toss to coat. 5. Allow the cheesecakes to cool completely and then top each one with some of the blueberry mixture. Garnish the tartlets with a little sugared lemon peel and refrigerate until you are ready to serve.
Per Serving: Calories 12; Fat 12g; Sodium 147mg; Carbs 25g; Fiber 1g; Sugar 16g; Protein 3g

Sugared Pizza Dough with Raspberry Cream Cheese Dip

Prep time: 12 minutes | Cook time: 16 minutes | Serves: 10 to 15

1-pound pizza dough | ¾ to 1 cup sugar
½ cup butter, melted
Raspberry Cream Cheese Dip:
4 ounces cream cheese, softened | 1½ tablespoons milk
2 tablespoons powdered sugar | ¼ cup raspberry preserves
½ teaspoon almond extract or | fresh raspberries
almond paste

1. Cut the ingredients in half or save half of the dough for another recipe. 2. When you're ready to make your sugared dough dippers, at least 1 hour before baking, remove the pizza dough from the refrigerator and place it on the counter, lightly covered with plastic wrap. 3. Roll the dough into two 15-inch logs. Cut each log into 20 slices and roll each slice so that it is 3- to 3½-inches long. Twist the dough halves 3 to 4 times. Place the it on a cookie sheet, grease with melted butter and sprinkle sugar over the dough twists. 4. Select the "AIR FRY" function of Ninja Foodi digital air fry oven, set the temperature to 350 degrees F/ 175 degrees C and set the time to 6 minutes. Press the Start/Pause button and begin preheating. 5. Grease the air fryer basket with a little melted butter. Air-fry the dough twists in batches. Place 8 to 12 in the air fryer basket. 6. Air-fry for 6 minutes. Turn the dough strips over and brush the other side with butter. Air-fry for an additional 2 minutes. 7. While the dough twists are cooking, make the cream cheese and raspberry dip. Whip the cream cheese until fluffy. Add the powdered sugar, almond extract and milk, and beat until smooth. Fold in the raspberry preserves and transfer to a serving dish. 8. As the batches of dough twists are complete, place them into a shallow dish. Brush with more melted butter and generously coat with sugar, shaking the dish to cover both sides. Serve the sugared dough dippers warm with the raspberry cream cheese dip on the side. Garnish with fresh raspberries.
Per Serving: Calories 250; Fat 11.5g; Sodium 178mg; Carbs 34g; Fiber 0g; Sugar 17g; Protein 4g

Chocolaty Nutella Banana Sandwich

Prep time: 10 minutes | Cook time: 8 minutes | Serves: 2

4 slices white bread | 1 banana
¼ cup chocolate hazelnut spread

1. Select the "AIR FRY" function of Ninja Foodi digital air fry oven, set the temperature to 370 degrees F/ 185 degrees C and set the time to 5 minutes. Press the Start/Pause button and begin preheating. 2. Butter one side of bread and place the slices buttered side down. Spread the chocolate spread on the other side of the bread. Cut the banana lengthwise. Place the banana and top with the remaining slices of bread to make two sandwiches. Cut the sandwiches in half. Transfer the sandwiches to the air fryer. 3. Air-fry for 5 minutes. Flip the sandwiches over and air-fry for another 2 to 3 minutes, or until the top bread slices are nicely browned.
Per Serving: Calories 430; Fat 21g; Sodium 233mg; Carbs 57g; Fiber 4g; Sugar 31g; Protein 6g

Peppermint Bars

Prep time: 15 minutes | Cook time: 16 minutes | Serves: 8

1 teaspoon peppermint | ½ teaspoon baking powder
1 cup almond flour | 1 teaspoon lemon juice
⅓ cup peanut butter | ½ teaspoon orange zest, grated

1. In the bowl, mix up almond flour, peppermint, baking powder, and orange zest. 2. Then add peanut butter and lemon juice. Knead the non-sticky dough. Divide dough into 8 pieces and roll the balls. Press them gently to get the shape of the bars. 3. Select the "AIR FRY" function of Ninja Foodi digital air fry oven, set the temperature to 365 degrees F/ 185 degrees C and set the time to 8 minutes. Press the Start/ Pause button and begin preheating. Line the basket with baking paper. Put 4 cookies in the air fryer in one layer. Cook them for 8 minutes. 4. Remove the cooked bars from the air fryer. Repeat the same steps with uncooked bars.
Per Serving: Calories 84; Fat 7.g; Sodium 38mg; Carbs 3.1g; Fiber 1.1g; Sugar 2g; Protein 3.5g

Strawberry Hand Tarts

Prep time: 10 minutes | Cook time: 18 minutes | Serves: 4

½ cup butter, softened
½ cup sugar
2 eggs
1 teaspoon vanilla extract
2 tablespoons lemon zest
2½ cups all-purpose flour

1 teaspoon baking powder
¼ teaspoon salt
1¼ cups strawberry jam, divided
1 egg white, beaten
1 cup powdered sugar
2 teaspoons milk

1. Combine the butter and sugar in a bowl and beat with an electric mixer until the mixture is light and fluffy. Add the eggs one at a time. Add the vanilla extract with lemon zest and mix well. In a separate bowl, combine the flour, baking powder and salt. Add the dry and wet ingredients, mixing until dough form. Transfer the dough to a floured surface and knead by hand for 10 minutes. Cover and let rest for 30 minutes. 2. Divide the dough and roll each half out into a ¼-inch thick rectangle that measures 12-inches x 9-inches. Cut each rectangle of dough into nine 4-inch x 3-inch rectangles. You should have 18 rectangles. Spread two teaspoons of strawberry jam in the center of nine of the rectangles leaving a ¼-inch border around the edges. Brush the egg white around the edges of each rectangle and top with the remaining nine rectangles of dough. Press the back of a fork around the edges to seal the tarts shut. Brush the top of the tarts with the beaten egg white and pierce the dough three or four times down the center of the tart with a fork. 3. Select the "AIR FRY" function of Ninja Foodi digital air fry oven, set the temperature to 350 degrees F/ 175 degrees C and set the time to 6 minutes. Press the Start/Pause button and begin preheating. 4. Air-fry the tarts in batches at 350 degrees F/ 175 degrees C for 6 minutes. Flip the tarts over and air-fry for an additional 3 minutes. 5. While the tarts are air-frying, make the icing. Combine the powdered sugar, ¼ cup strawberry jam and milk in a bowl, whisking until the icing is smooth. Spread the icing, leaving an empty border around the edges. Decorate with sprinkles if desired.
Per Serving: Calories 420; Fat 12g; Sodium 179mg; Carbs 73g; Fiber 1g; Sugar 39g; Protein 6g

Baked Beignets

Prep time: 10 minutes | Cook time: 10 minutes | Serves: 12

¾ cup lukewarm water
¼ cup sugar
1 teaspoon active dry yeast
3½ to 4 cups all-purpose flour
½ teaspoon salt
2 tablespoons unsalted butter

1 egg, lightly beaten
½ cup evaporated milk
¼ cup melted butter
1 cup confectioners' sugar
chocolate sauce or raspberry
sauce, to dip

1. In a bowl add pinch of sugar, yeast and lukewarm water. Allow yeast to poof for 5 minutes. 2. In a bowl, Combine 3½ cups flour, salt, butter and sugar. Add the egg along with evaporated milk and yeast to the flour and mix with a wooden spoon until the dough form in a sticky ball. Transfer the dough to greased bowl, cover with kitchen towel and let it proof in a warm place until it has doubled in size. 3. Roll the dough to ½-inch thickness. Cut it into rectangular shaped pieces. 4. Select the "BAKE" function of Ninja Foodi digital air fry oven, set the temperature to 350 degrees F/ 175 degrees C and set the time to 5 minutes. Press the Start/Pause button and begin preheating. 5. Brush the beignets on both sides with some of the melted butter and bake in batches for 5 minutes, turning them over halfway through if desired. 6. As soon as the beignets are finished, transfer them to a plate or baking sheet and dust with the confectioners' sugar. Serve warm with a chocolate or raspberry sauce.
Per Serving: Calories 130; Fat 3.5g; Sodium 169mg; Carbs 22g; Fiber 1g; Sugar 7g; Protein 3g

Butter Cinnamon Plums

Prep time: 5 minutes | Cook time: 20 minutes | Serves: 4

2 teaspoons cinnamon powder
4 plums, halved

4 tablespoons butter, melted
3 tablespoons swerve

1. Select the "AIR FRY" function of Ninja Foodi digital air fry oven, set the temperature to 300 degrees F/ 150 degrees C and set the time to 20 minutes. Press the Start/Pause button and begin preheating. 2. In a pan, mix the plums with the rest of the ingredients, toss, put the pan in the air fryer and cook for 20 minutes. 3. Divide into cups and serve cold.
Per Serving: Calories 162; Fat 3g; Sodium 248mg; Carbs 4g; Fiber 2g; Sugar 1g; Protein 5g

Blueberry Cookies

Prep time: 10 minutes | Cook time: 30 minutes | Serves: 2

3 oz blueberries

½ teaspoon avocado oil

1. Select the "AIR FRY" function of Ninja Foodi digital air fry oven, set the temperature to 300 degrees F/ 150 degrees C and set the time to 30 minutes. Press the Start/Pause button and begin preheating. Put the blueberries in the blender and grind them until smooth. 2. Then line the air fryer basket with baking paper. Brush it with the avocado oil. 3. After this, pour the blended blueberries on the prepared baking paper and flatten it in one layer with the help of the spatula. 4. Cook the blueberry leather for 30 minutes. Cut into cookies and serve.
Per Serving: Calories 26; Fat 0.3g; Sodium 56mg; Carbs 6.3g; Fiber 1g; Sugar 5g; Protein 0.3g

Sweet 'n' Salty Granola Bark

Prep time: 10 minutes | Cook time: 45 minutes | Serves: 6

1 large egg white
⅓ cup maple syrup
1 teaspoon vanilla extract
¼ cup olive oil
¼ teaspoon salt
1½ cups old-fashioned oats
½ cup roasted, salted almonds,

coarsely chopped
¼ cup sunflower seeds
¼ cup almond flour
¾ teaspoon ground cinnamon
Milk and fresh fruit for serving
(optional)

1. In a bowl, lightly whisk egg white with a fork; measure out 1 tablespoon of the beaten egg white and set aside. Discard the remaining egg white or save for another use. 2. Line with parchment paper and halfway up the sides of the air fryer, pressing parchment against the sides and the bottom. 3. In a bowl, combine maple syrup with vanilla, olive oil, salt, and 1 tablespoon beaten egg white. In a bowl, Add oats, almonds, sunflower seeds, almond flour, and cinnamon. Add the maple syrup mixture to the dry and mix thoroughly. 4. Evenly press half the mixture (1⅓ cups) into the prepared air fryer basket, using the back of a spoon or wet hands. Place basket in air fryer pan. 5. Select the "BAKE" function of Ninja Foodi digital air fry oven, set the temperature to 325 degrees F/ 160 degrees C and set the time to 16 minutes. Press the Start/Pause button and begin preheating. Air-fry for 12 to 16 minutes, or until golden brown all over, not just at the edges. Do not stir. 6. Carefully lift granola out of the air fryer by grabbing the parchment at the sides; let it cool on the parchment on a wire rack for 1 hour before breaking it into chunks. Repeat with the remaining oat mixture. 7. Serve with milk and fruit, if desired.
Per Serving: Calories 335; Fat 22g; Sodium 146mg; Carbs 30g; Fiber 4g; Sugar 12g; Protein 7g

Chocolate Molten Cakes

Prep time: 20 minutes | Cook time: 45 minutes | Serves: 4

¼ cup butter (½ stick), cut into pieces, plus more for greasing the custard cups
2 tablespoons granulated sugar, plus more for dusting
2 ounces semisweet chocolate, chopped
2 tablespoons heavy or whipping

cream
¼ teaspoon vanilla extract
2 tablespoons all-purpose flour
1 large egg
1 large egg yolk
Confectioners' sugar, for dusting
Whipped cream for serving
(optional)

1. Grease four 6-ounce custard cups. Dust with granulated sugar. 2. In a heavy 2-quart saucepan, heat chocolate, butter, and cream over low heat, stirring occasionally, until chocolate has melted and mixture is smooth. Remove pan from heat. Add vanilla. Whisk in flour until mixture is smooth. 3. Select the "AIR FRY" function of Ninja Foodi digital air fry oven, set the temperature to 300 degrees F/ 150 degrees C and set the time to 45 minutes. Press the Start/Pause button and begin preheating. In a small bowl, with mixer at high speed, beat 2 tablespoons granulated sugar, whole egg, and egg yolk until thick and pale yellow, about 5 minutes. Fold egg mixture, one-third at a time, into chocolate mixture until blended. 4. Divide batter evenly among prepared custard cups. Air-fry in batches, 2 cups at a time, for 8 to 10 minutes, until firm from edges and soft from center when pressed lightly. 5. Cool for 5 minutes. loosen cakes with knife; invert onto plates. Dust with confectioners' sugar. 6. Serve with whipped cream.
Per Serving: Calories 290; Fat 22g; Sodium 113mg; Carbs 22g; Fiber 1g; Sugar 17g; Protein 113g

Easy Cocoa Bombs

Prep time: 5 minutes | Cook time: 8 minutes | Serves: 12

2 cups macadamia nuts, chopped
4 tablespoons coconut oil, melted
1 teaspoon vanilla extract
¼ cup cocoa powder
⅓ cup swerve

1. Select the "AIR FRY" function of Ninja Foodi digital air fry oven, set the temperature to 300 degrees F/ 150 degrees C and set the time to 8 minutes. Press the Start/Pause button and begin preheating. 2. In a bowl, mix all of the ingredients and whisk well. Shape medium balls out of this mix, place them in your air fryer and cook for 8 minutes. Serve cold.
Per Serving: Calories 120; Fat 12g; Sodium 100mg; Carbs 2g; Fiber 1g; Sugar 1g; Protein 1g

Sweet French Toast

Prep time: 15 minutes | Cook time: 45 minutes | Serves: 2

2 large eggs
¾ cup unsweetened coconut milk
2 tablespoons brown sugar
¼ teaspoon pumpkin pie spice
Pinch salt
4 (1-inch thick) slices brioche or Texas toast
1 cup crispy rice cereal
½ cup unsweetened, finely shredded coconut
Oil in mister
Mixed berries, confectioners' sugar, and maple syrup, for serving (optional)

1. In a shallow 1½-quart baking dish, whisk eggs, coconut milk, brown sugar, pumpkin pie spice, and salt. Trim crusts off bread, if desired. Place rice cereal in a shallow bowl and crush with a flat-bottomed dry measuring cup or a glass. Stir in coconut. Soak bread in the egg, for about 10 seconds, then dip into the cereal-coconut mixture, again coating on both sides. Spray tops with oil. 2. Select the "AIR FRY" function of Ninja Foodi digital air fry oven, set the temperature to 375 degrees F/ 190 degrees C and set the time to 8 minutes. Press the Start/Pause button and begin preheating. Working in batches, place bread in air fryer basket, oil side down; spray top with oil. Air-fry for 8 minutes or until golden brown. Transfer to a parchment-lined cookie sheet and keep warm in a 300 degrees F/ 150 degrees C oven. 3. Serve with mixed berries, confectioners' sugar, and maple syrup, if desired.
Per Serving: Calories 685; Fat 40g; Sodium 509mg; Carbs 72g; Fiber 6g; Sugar 15g; Protein 509g

Air Fryer Pumpkin Fritters

Prep time: 5 minutes | Cook time: 9 minutes | Serves: 8

For The Fritters
1 (16.3-ounce, 8-count) package refrigerated biscuit dough
½ cup chopped pecans
¼ cup pumpkin purée
¼ cup sugar
1 teaspoon pumpkin pie spice
2 tablespoons unsalted butter, melted

For The Glaze
1 cup powdered sugar
1 teaspoon pumpkin pie spice
1 tablespoon pumpkin purée
2 tablespoons milk (plus more to thin the glaze, if necessary)

To Make the Fritters
1. Select the "AIR FRY" function of Ninja Foodi digital air fry oven, set the temperature to 330 degrees F/ 165 degrees C and set the time to 10 minutes. Press the Start/Pause button and begin preheating. Grease the air fryer basket or spray an air fryer–size baking sheet with olive oil or cooking spray. 2. Turn the biscuit dough out onto a cutting board. 3. Cut each biscuit into 8 pieces. 4. Once you cut all the pieces, place them in a medium mixing bowl. 5. Add the pecans, pumpkin, sugar, and pumpkin pie spice to the biscuit pieces and toss until well combined. 6. Shape the dough into 8 even mounds. 7. Drizzle butter over each of the fritters. 8. Place the fritters directly in the greased air fryer basket, or on the greased baking sheet set in the air fryer basket. 9. Bake for 7 minutes. 10. Check to see if the fritters are done. The dough should be cooked through and solid to the touch. If not, cook for 1 to 2 minutes more. 11. Using tongs, gently remove the fritters from the air fryer. Let cool for about 10 minutes before you apply the glaze.
To Make the Glaze
1. In a mixing bowl, mix the powdered sugar, pumpkin pie spice, pumpkin, and milk until smooth. If it seems more like icing, it is too thick. It should coat a spoon and be of a pourable consistency. 2. Drizzle the glaze over the fritters.
Per Serving: Calories 341; Fat 16g; Sodium 608mg; Carbs 47g; Fiber 2g; Sugar 26g; Protein 5g

Chocolate-Frosted Doughnuts

Prep time: 5 minutes | Cook time: 5 minutes | Serves: 4

1 (16.3-ounce / 8-count) package refrigerated biscuit dough
¾ cup powdered sugar
¼ cup unsweetened cocoa powder
¼ cup milk

1. Select the "AIR FRY" function of Ninja Foodi digital air fry oven, set the temperature to 330 degrees F/ 165 degrees C and set the time to 5 minutes. Press the Start/Pause button and begin preheating. Grease the air fryer basket. 2. Unroll the biscuit dough onto a cutting board and separate the biscuits. 3. Using a 1-inch biscuit cutter or cookie cutter, cut out the center of each biscuit. 4. Place the doughnuts into the air fryer. 5.Bake for 5 minutes. 6. Using tongs, remove the doughnuts from the air fryer and let them cool slightly before glazing. 7. Meanwhile, in a mixing bowl, Add the powdered sugar, unsweetened cocoa powder, and milk and mix until smooth. 8. Dip your doughnuts into the glaze and use a knife to smooth the frosting evenly over the doughnut. 9. Let the glaze set before serving.
Per Serving: Calories 233; Fat 8g; Sodium 590mg; Carbs 37g; Fiber 2g; Sugar 15g; Protein 5g

Chocolate Chip Cookies

Prep time: 5 minutes | Cook time: 5 minutes | Serves: 25

1 cup (2 sticks) unsalted butter, at room temperature
1 cup granulated sugar
1 cup brown sugar
2 large eggs
½ teaspoon vanilla extract
1 teaspoon baking soda
½ teaspoon salt
3 cups all-purpose flour
2 cups chocolate chips

1. Select the "BAKE" function of Ninja Foodi digital air fry oven, set the temperature to 340 degrees F/ 170 degrees C and set the time to 5 minutes. Press the Start/Pause button and begin preheating. Spray an air fryer–size baking sheet with cooking spray. 2. In a bowl, cream the butter along with sugars. 3. Mix in the eggs, vanilla, baking soda, salt, and flour until well combined. Fold in the chocolate chips. 4. Knead the dough so everything is mixed. 5. Drop heaping spoonfuls of dough onto the baking sheet about 1 inch apart. 6. Set the baking sheet into the air fryer. 7. Bake for 5 minutes. 8. When the cookies are golden brown and cooked through, use silicone oven mitts to remove the baking sheet from the air fryer and serve.
Per Serving: Calories 280; Fat 13g; Sodium 156mg; Carbs 38g; Fiber 0g; Sugar 24g; Protein 3g

Strawberry Cake

Prep time: 10 minutes | Cook time: 35 minutes | Serves: 6

1 pound strawberries, chopped
1 cup cream cheese, soft
¼ cup swerve
1 tablespoon lime juice
1 egg, whisked
1 teaspoon vanilla extract
3 tablespoons coconut oil, melted
1 cup almond flour
2 teaspoons baking powder

1. Select the "AIR FRY" function of Ninja Foodi digital air fry oven, set the temperature to 350 degrees F/ 175 degrees C and set the time to 35 minutes. Press the Start/Pause button and begin preheating. 2. In a bowl, mix all the ingredients, stir well and pour this into a cake pan lined with parchment paper. 3. Put the pan in the air fryer, cook for 35 minutes, cool down, slice and serve.
Per Serving: Calories 200; Fat 6g; Sodium 111mg; Carbs 4g; Fiber 2g; Sugar 2g; Protein 6g

Chocolate and Avocado Cream

Prep time: 5 minutes | Cook time: 20 minutes | Serves: 4

2 avocados, peeled, pitted and mashed
3 tablespoons chocolate, melted
4 tablespoons erythritol
3 tablespoons cream cheese, soft

1. Select the "AIR FRY" function of Ninja Foodi digital air fry oven, set the temperature to 340 degrees F/ 170 degrees C and set the time to 20 minutes. Press the Start/Pause button and begin preheating. 2. In a pan, combine all the ingredients, whisk, put the pan in the fryer and cook for 20 minutes. 3. Divide into bowls and serve cold.
Per Serving: Calories 200; Fat 6g; Sodium 147mg; Carbs 4g; Fiber 2g; Sugar 2g; Protein 5g

Blueberry Pie

Prep time: 5 minutes | Cook time: 18 minutes | Serves: 6

2 frozen pie crusts
2 (21-ounce) jars blueberry pie filling
1 teaspoon milk
1 teaspoon sugar

1. Select the "BAKE" function of Ninja Foodi digital air fry oven, set the temperature to 310 degrees F/ 155 degrees C and set the time to 15 minutes. Press the Start/Pause button and begin preheating. Thaw pie crust for 30 minutes on the countertop. 2. Place crust into the bottom of a 6-inch pie pan. 3. Pour the filling, then cover it with the other crust, being careful to press both crusts together around the edge to form a seal. 4. Trim off any excess pie dough. 5. Cut venting holes in the top crust with a knife or a small decoratively shaped cookie cutter. 6. Brush the crust with milk, then spread the sugar over it. 7. Place the pie in the air fryer basket, bake for 15 minutes. 8. Check the pie after 15 minutes. If it needs additional time, reset the timer and bake for an additional 3 minutes. 9. Using silicone oven mitts, remove the pie from the air fryer and let cool for 15 minutes before serving.
Per Serving: Calories 537; Fat 14g; Sodium 313mg; Carbs 101g; Fiber 3g; Sugar 58g; Protein 2g

Apple Hand Pies

Prep time: 5 minutes | Cook time: 7 minutes | Serves: 8

1 package prepared pie dough
½ cup apple pie filling
1 large egg white
1 tablespoon Wilton White Sparkling Sugar
Caramel sauce, for drizzling

1. Select the "AIR FRY" function of Ninja Foodi digital air fry oven, set the temperature to 350 degrees F/ 175 degrees C and set the time to 5 minutes. Press the Start/Pause button and begin preheating. Grease the air fryer basket with oil. 2. Lightly flour a clean work surface. Lay out the dough on the work surface. 3. with help of biscuit cutter, cut out 8 circles from the dough. 4. Gather up the dough, form it into a ball, and re-roll them. Using the biscuit cutter, cut out the remaining dough. 5. Add apple pie filling to the center of each circle. 6. With help of fork seal the edges. 7. Brush the egg wash over the top, then sprinkle with sparkling sugar. 8. Place the hand pies in the greased air fryer basket. They should be spaced so that they do not touch one another. 9. Bake for 5 minutes. When they are done, the crust should be golden brown. Drizzle with caramel sauce, if desired.
Per Serving: Calories 120; Fat 5g; Sodium 144mg; Carbs 17g; Fiber 0g; Sugar 3g; Protein 1g

Avocado Pudding

Prep time: 5 minutes | Cook time: 25 minutes | Serves: 6

4 small avocados, peeled, pitted and mashed
2 eggs, whisked
1 cup coconut milk
¾ cup swerve
1 teaspoon cinnamon powder
½ teaspoon ginger powder

1. Select the "AIR FRY" function of Ninja Foodi digital air fry oven, set the temperature to 350 degrees F/ 175 degrees C and set the time to 25 minutes. Press the Start/Pause button and begin preheating. 2. In a bowl, mix all the and whisk well. Pour into a pudding mold, put it in the air fryer and cook for 25 minutes. Serve warm.
Per Serving: Calories 192; Fat 8g; Sodium 121mg; Carbs 5g; Fiber 2g; Sugar 3g; Protein 4g

Stevia Avocado Cake

Prep time: 5 minutes | Cook time: 40 minutes | Serves: 6

2 tablespoons ghee, melted
1 cup coconut, shredded
1 cup mashed avocado
3 tablespoons stevia
3 teaspoons cinnamon powder

1. Select the "AIR FRY" function of Ninja Foodi digital air fry oven, set the temperature to 340 degrees F/ 170 degrees C and set the time to 40 minutes. Press the Start/Pause button and begin preheating. 2. In a bowl, mix all the ingredients and stir well. Pour this into a cake pan lined with parchment paper, place the pan in the fryer and cook for 40 minutes. 3. Cool the cake down, slice and serve.
Per Serving: Calories 192; Fat 4g; Sodium 322mg; Carbs 5g; Fiber 2g; Sugar 3g; Protein 7g

Cherry Cobbler

Prep time: 5 minutes | Cook time: 35 minutes | Serves: 4

1 cup all-purpose flour
1 cup sugar
2 tablespoons baking powder
¾ cup milk
8 tablespoons (1 stick) unsalted butter
1 (21-ounce) can cherry pie filling

1. In a mixing bowl, mix the flour with sugar, and baking powder. Add the milk and mix until well blended. 2. Melt the butter in microwave-safe bowl about 45 seconds. 3. Pour the butter into the bottom of an 8-by-8-inch pan, then pour in the batter and spread it in an even layer. Pour the pie filling over the batter. Do not mix; the batter will bubble up through the filling during cooking. 4. Select the "BAKE" function of Ninja Foodi digital air fry oven, set the temperature to 320 degrees F/ 160 degrees C and set the time to 20 minutes. Press the Start/Pause button and begin preheating. Bake for 20 minutes. 5. Check the cobbler. When the cobbler is done, the batter will be golden brown and cooked through. If not done, bake and recheck for doneness in 5-minute intervals. Overall cooking time will likely be between 30 and 35 minutes. 6. Remove from the air fryer and let cool slightly before serving.
Per Serving: Calories 706; Fat 24g; Sodium 219mg; Carbs 121g; Fiber 2g; Sugar 52g; Protein 6g

Banana Cake

Prep time: 5 minutes | Cook time: 30 minutes | Serves: 4

⅓ cup brown sugar
4 tablespoons (½ stick) unsalted butter, at room temperature
1 ripe banana, mashed
1 large egg
2 tablespoons granulated sugar
1 cup all-purpose flour
1 teaspoon ground cinnamon
1 teaspoon vanilla extract
½ teaspoon ground nutmeg

1. Spray a 6-inch Bundt pan with cooking spray. 2. In a medium mixing bowl, cream the brown sugar and butter until pale and fluffy. 3. Mix in the banana and egg. 4. Add the granulated sugar, flour, ground cinnamon, vanilla, and nutmeg and mix well. 5. Spoon the batter into the pan. 6. Place the pan in the air fryer basket. 7. Select the "AIR FRY" function of Ninja Foodi digital air fry oven, set the temperature to 320 degrees F/ 160 degrees C and set the time to 30 minutes. Press the Start/Pause button and begin preheating. Bake for 15 minutes. 8. It will likely take about 30 minutes total baking time to fully cook. 9. Using silicone oven mitts, remove the Bundt pan from the air fryer. 10. Let cool for about 10 minutes. Place a plate upside-down (like a lid) over the top of the Bundt pan. Carefully flip the plate and the pan over, and set the plate on the counter. Lift the Bundt pan off the cake. Frost as desired.
Per Serving: Calories 334; Fat 13g; Sodium 104mg; Carbs 49g; Fiber 2g; Sugar 22g; Protein 5g

Bundt Cake

Prep time: 5 minutes | Cook time: 30 minutes | Serves: 4

1¾ cups all-purpose flour
2 cups sugar
¾ cup unsweetened cocoa powder
1 teaspoon baking soda
1 teaspoon baking powder
½ cup vegetable oil
1 teaspoon salt
2 teaspoons vanilla extract
2 large eggs
1 cup milk
1 cup hot water

1. Spray a 6-inch Bundt pan with cooking spray. 2. In a large mixing bowl, combine the flour, sugar, cocoa powder, baking soda, baking powder, oil, salt, vanilla, eggs, milk, and hot water. 3. Pour the batter into the pan and set the pan in the air fryer basket. 4. Select the "AIR FRY" function of Ninja Foodi digital air fry oven, set the temperature to 330 degrees F/ 165 degrees C and set the time to 20 minutes. Press the Start/Pause button and begin preheating. Bake for 20 minutes. 5. It will likely take about 30 minutes total baking time to fully cook. 6. Using silicone oven mitts, remove the Bundt pan from the air fryer. 7. Let cool for about 10 minutes. Place a plate upside down (like a lid) over the top of the Bundt pan. Carefully flip the plate and the pan over, and set the plate on the counter. Lift the Bundt pan off the cake.
Per Serving: Calories 924; Fat 34g; Sodium 965mg; Carbs 155g; Fiber 6g; Sugar 104g; Protein 14g

Fudge Brownies

Prep time: 5 minutes | Cook time: 20 minutes | Serves: 6

8 tablespoons (1 stick) unsalted butter, melted
1 cup sugar
1 teaspoon vanilla extract
2 large eggs
½ cup all-purpose flour
½ cup cocoa powder
1 teaspoon baking powder

1. Spray a 6-inch air fryer–safe sheet pan with cooking spray or grease the pan with butter. 2. In a mixing bowl, mix the butter and sugar, then add the vanilla and eggs and beat until well combined. 3. Add the flour with cocoa powder, and baking powder and mix until smooth. 4. Pour the batter into the prepared pan. 5. Select the "AIR FRY" function of Ninja Foodi digital air fry oven, set the temperature to 350 degrees F/ 175 degrees C and set the time to 20 minutes. Press the Start/Pause button and begin preheating. Bake for 20 minutes. Once the center is set, use silicon oven mitts to remove the pan from the air fryer. 6. Let cool slightly before serving.
Per Serving: Calories 338; Fat 18g; Sodium 132mg; Carbs 46g; Fiber 2g; Sugar 34g; Protein 4g

Cream Cheese Muffins

Prep time: 15 minutes | Cook time: 11 minutes | Serves: 4

4 teaspoons cream cheese
1 egg, beaten
½ teaspoon baking powder
1 teaspoon vanilla extract
4 teaspoons almond flour
4 teaspoons coconut flour
2 tablespoons heavy cream
2 teaspoons Erythritol
Cooking spray

1. Make the muffin batter: mix up cream cheese, egg, baking powder, vanilla extract, almond flour, coconut flour, heavy cream, and Erythritol. 2. Then spray the air fryer muffin molds with cooking spray. Pour the batter in the muffin molds (fill ½ part of every mold). 3. Select the "AIR FRY" function of Ninja Foodi digital air fry oven, set the temperature to 365 degrees F/ 185 degrees C and set the time to 15 minutes. Press the Start/Pause button and begin preheating. Insert the muffin molds in the air fryer and cook the dessert for 11 minutes. 4. Cool the cooked muffins and remove them from the molds.
Per Serving: Calories 229; Fat 19.5g; Sodium 233mg; Carbs 8.3g; Fiber 4g; Sugar 6g; Protein 8.3g

Blackberries Cake

Prep time: 10 minutes | Cook time: 25 minutes | Serves: 4

2 eggs, whisked
4 tablespoons swerve
2 tablespoons ghee, melted
¼ cup almond milk
1 and ½ cups almond flour
1 cup blackberries, chopped
½ teaspoon baking powder
1 teaspoon lemon zest, grated
1 teaspoon lemon juice

1. Select the "AIR FRY" function of Ninja Foodi digital air fry oven, set the temperature to 340 degrees F/ 170 degrees C and set the time to 25 minutes. Press the Start/Pause button and begin preheating. 2. In a bowl, mix all of the ingredients and whisk well. 3. Pour this into a cake pan that fits the air fryer lined with parchment paper, put the pan in your air fryer and cook for 25 minutes. 4. Cool the cake down, slice and serve.
Per Serving: Calories 193; Fat 5g; Sodium 311mg; Carbs 4g; Fiber 1g; Sugar g; Protein 4g

Raspberry Avocado Cake

Prep time: 10 minutes | Cook time: 30 minutes | Serves: 4

4 ounces raspberries
2 avocados, peeled, pitted and mashed
1 cup almonds flour
3 teaspoons baking powder
1 cup swerve
4 tablespoons butter, melted
4 eggs, whisked

1. Select the "AIR FRY" function of Ninja Foodi digital air fry oven, set the temperature to 340 degrees F/ 170 degrees C and set the time to 30 minutes. Press the Start/Pause button and begin preheating. 2. In a bowl, mix the ingredients, toss, pour this into a cake pan that fits the air fryer after you've lined it with parchment paper, put the pan in the fryer and cook for 30 minutes. 3. Leave the cake to cool down, slice and serve.
Per Serving: Calories 193; Fat 4g; Sodium 178mg; Carbs 5g; Fiber 2g; Sugar 3g; Protein 5g

Cauliflower Rice and Plum Pudding

Prep time: 5 minutes | Cook time: 25 minutes | Serves: 4

1 and ½ cups cauliflower rice
2 cups coconut milk
3 tablespoons stevia
2 tablespoons ghee, melted
4 plums, pitted and roughly chopped

1. Select the "AIR FRY" function of Ninja Foodi digital air fry oven, set the temperature to 340 degrees F/ 170 degrees C and set the time to 25 minutes. Press the Start/Pause button and begin preheating. 2. In a bowl, mix all ingredients, toss, divide into ramekins, put them in the air fryer, and cook for 25 minutes. Cool down and serve.
Per Serving: Calories 221; Fat 4g; Sodium 159mg; Carbs 3g; Fiber 1g; Sugar 2g; Protein 3g

Coconut Cookies

Prep time: 15 minutes | Cook time: 10 minutes | Serves: 6

3 tablespoons coconut oil, softened
4 tablespoons coconut flour
2 tablespoons flax meal
2 tablespoons Monk fruit
1 teaspoon poppy seeds
½ teaspoon baking powder
½ teaspoon lemon juice
¼ teaspoon ground cardamom
Cooking spray

1. In the mixing bowl, put coconut oil, coconut flour, flax meal, and Monk fruit. 2. Then add poppy seeds, baking powder, lemon juice, and cardamom. 3. With the help of the fingertips, knead the soft but non-sticky dough. Then make the cookies from the dough. 4. Select the "BAKE" function of Ninja Foodi digital air fry oven, set the temperature to 375 degrees F/ 190 degrees C and set the time to 10 minutes. Press the Start/Pause button and begin preheating. Grease the air fryer basket with cooking spray. 5. Place the cookies in the air fryer and cook them for 10 minutes.
Per Serving: Calories 95; Fat 8.7g; Sodium 126mg; Carbs 4g; Fiber 2.8g; Sugar 2g; Protein 1.6g

Coconut Cake with Cheese

Prep time: 25 minutes | Cook time: 30 minutes | Serves: 4

2 teaspoons cream cheese
1 teaspoon Truvia
1 teaspoon vanilla extract
½ cup heavy cream
1 egg, beaten
1 teaspoon baking powder
1 teaspoon apple cider vinegar
1½ cups coconut flour
2 tablespoons butter, softened
Cooking spray

1. Pour heavy cream in the bowl. Add vanilla extract, egg, baking powder, apple cider vinegar, and butter. Stir the liquid until homogenous. 2. Then add coconut flour. Whisk the liquid until smooth. 3. Spray the pound cake mold with cooking spray. Pour the pound cake batter in the mold. Flatten its surface with the help of the spatula. 4. Select the "AIR FRY" function of Ninja Foodi digital air fry oven, set the temperature to 365 degrees F/ 185 degrees C and set the time to 30 minutes. Press the Start/Pause button and begin preheating. Put the mold with the pound cake in the air fryer and cook it for 30 minutes. 5. When the cake is cooked, cool it to room temperature. 6. Meanwhile, in the shallow bowl whisk together cream cheese and Truvia. 7. Then spread the surface of the pound cake with sweet cream cheese. 8. Slice the dessert on the servings.
Per Serving: Calories 339; Fat 20.5g; Sodium 144mg; Carbs 28.7g; Fiber 18g; Sugar 10g; Protein 10.9g

Delicious Berry Pudding

Prep time: 5 minutes | Cook time: 15 minutes | Serves: 6

2 cups coconut cream
⅓ cup blackberries
⅓ cup blueberries
3 tablespoons swerve
Zest of 1 lime, grated

1. Select the "AIR FRY" function of Ninja Foodi digital air fry oven, set the temperature to 340 degrees F/ 170 degrees C and set the time to 15 minutes. Press the Start/Pause button and begin preheating. 2. In a blender, combine all the ingredients and pulse well. Divide this into 6 small ramekins, put them in your air fryer and cook for 15 minutes. Serve cold.
Per Serving: Calories 173; Fat 3g; Sodium 144mg; Carbs 4g; Fiber 1g; Sugar 3g; Protein 4g

Chia Pudding

Prep time: 10 minutes | Cook time: 25 minutes | Serves: 6

2 cups coconut cream
6 egg yolks, whisked
2 tablespoons stevia
¼ cup chia seeds
2 teaspoons cinnamon powder
1 tablespoon ghee, melted

1. Select the "AIR FRY" function of Ninja Foodi digital air fry oven, set the temperature to 340 degrees F/ 170 degrees C and set the time to 25 minutes. Press the Start/Pause button and begin preheating. 2. In a bowl, mix all the ingredients, whisk, divide into 6 ramekins, place them all in your air fryer and cook for 25 minutes. 2. Cool the puddings down and serve.
Per Serving: Calories 180; Fat 4g; Sodium 321mg; Carbs 5g; Fiber 2g; Sugar 3g; Protein 7g

Nutty Cookies

Prep time: 15 minutes | Cook time: 10 minutes | Serves: 6

½ cup butter, softened
1 cup coconut flour
3 oz macadamia nuts, grinded
½ teaspoon baking powder
3 tablespoons Erythritol
Cooking spray

1. In the mixing bowl, mix up butter, coconut flour, grinded coconut nuts, baking powder, and Erythritol. Knead the non-sticky dough. 2. Divide the dough into small pieces and roll them into balls. 3. Press every cookie ball gently to get the shape of cookies. 4. Select the "AIR FRY" function of Ninja Foodi digital air fry oven, set the temperature to 365 degrees F/ 185 degrees C and set the time to 10 minutes. Press the Start/Pause button and begin preheating. the air fryer to 365 degrees F/ 185 degrees C. Grease the air fryer basket with cooking spray. 5. Put the uncooked cookies in the air fryer and cook them for 8 minutes. Then cook for extra 2 minutes at 390 degrees F/ 200 degrees C to get the light brown crust.
Per Serving: Calories 331; Fat 29.4g; Sodium 147mg; Carbs 14.2g; Fiber 2g; Sugar 6g; Protein 5.3g

Homemade Whipped Cream Cake

Prep time: 15 minutes | Cook time: 25 minutes | Serves: 12

1 cup almond flour
½ cup coconut flour
¼ cup coconut oil, melted
3 eggs, beaten
1 teaspoon baking powder
1 teaspoon vanilla extract
1 teaspoon cream cheese
2 tablespoons Splenda
½ cup whipped cream

1. In the mixing bowl mix up almond flour, coconut flour, coconut oil, eggs, baking powder, vanilla extract, and cream cheese. Whisk the mixture well with the help of the immersion blender. 2. Then line the air fryer sheet pan with baking paper. Pour the cake batter in the baking pan. Select the "AIR FRY" function of Ninja Foodi digital air fry oven, set the temperature to 355 degrees F/ 180 degrees C and set the time to 25 minutes. Press the Start/Pause button and begin preheating. Put the sheet pan in the air fryer and cook it for 25 minutes. 3. Then cool the cake well. 4. Meanwhile, mix up Splenda and whipped cream cheese. Spread the cake with whipped cream mixture.
Per Serving: Calories 119; Fat 9.3g; Sodium 322mg; Carbs g; Fiber 2.3g; Sugar 6g; Protein 3g

Butter Cheese Crumble

Prep time: 20 minutes | Cook time: 25 minutes | Serves: 4

½ cup coconut flour
2 tablespoons butter, softened
2 tablespoons Erythritol
3 oz peanuts, crushed
1 tablespoon cream cheese
1 teaspoon baking powder
½ teaspoon lemon juice

1. Select the "AIR FRY" function of Ninja Foodi digital air fry oven, set the temperature to 330 degrees F/ 165 degrees C and set the time to 25 minutes. Press the Start/Pause button and begin preheating. 2. In the mixing bowl mix up coconut flour, butter, Erythritol, baking powder, and lemon juice. Stir the mixture until homogenous. 3. Meanwhile, mix up peanuts and cream cheese. 4. Grate the frozen dough. 5. Line the air fryer mold with baking paper. Then put ½ of grated dough in the mold and flatten it. Top it with cream cheese mixture. 6. Then put remaining grated dough over the cream cheese mixture. Place the mold with the crumble in the air fryer and cook it for 25 minutes.
Per Serving: Calories 252; Fat 19.6g; Sodium 320mg; Carbs 13.1g; Fiber 7.8g; Sugar 6g; Protein 8.8g

Sweet Cheese Balls

Prep time: 2 hours | Cook time: 5 minutes | Serves: 4

1 tablespoon cream cheese
3 oz goat cheese
2 tablespoons almond flour
1 tablespoon coconut flour
1 egg, beaten
1 tablespoon Splenda
Cooking spray

1. Mash the goat cheese and mix it up with cream cheese. Then add egg, Splenda, and almond flour. Stir the mixture until homogenous. 2. Then make 4 balls and coat them in the coconut flour. Freeze the cheese balls for 2 hours. Select the "AIR FRY" function of Ninja Foodi digital air fry oven, set the temperature to 390 degrees F/ 200 degrees C and set the time to 5 minutes. Press the Start/Pause button and begin preheating. Then place the frozen balls in the air fryer, spray them with cooking spray and cook for 5 minutes or until the cheese balls are light brown.
Per Serving: Calories 224; Fat 16.8g; Sodium 211mg; Carbs 7.7g; Fiber 2.3g; Sugar 5g; Protein 11.4g

Chocolate Almond Candies

Prep time: 15 minutes | Cook time: 2 minutes | Serves: 4

1 oz almonds, crushed
1 oz dark chocolate
2 tablespoons peanut butter
2 tablespoons heavy cream

1. Select the "AIR FRY" function of Ninja Foodi digital air fry oven, set the temperature to 390 degrees F/ 200 degrees C and set the time to 2 minutes. Press the Start/Pause button and begin preheating. 2. Chop the chocolate and put it in the air fryer mold. 3. Add peanut butter and heavy cream. Stir the mixture and transfer in the air fryer. Cook it for 2 minutes or until it starts to melt. 4. Then line the air tray with parchment. Put the crushed almonds on the tray in one layer. 5. Then pour the cooked chocolate mixture over the almonds. Flatten gently if needed and let it cool. 6. Crack the cooked chocolate layer into the candies.
Per Serving: Calories 154; Fat 12.9g; Sodium 278mg; Carbs 7.4g; Fiber 1.9g; Sugar 6g; Protein 3.9g

Almond Flour Peanut Biscuits

Prep time: 20 minutes | Cook time: 35 minutes | Serves: 6

4 oz peanuts, chopped
2 tablespoons peanut butter
½ teaspoon apple cider vinegar
1 egg, beaten
6 oz almond flour
¼ cup of coconut milk
2 teaspoons Erythritol
1 teaspoon vanilla extract
Cooking spray

1. In the bowl mix up peanut butter, apple cider vinegar, egg, almond flour, coconut milk, Erythritol, and vanilla extract. 2. When the mixture is homogenous, add peanuts and knead the smooth dough. 3. Then spray the cooking mold with cooking spray and place the dough inside. Select the "AIR FRY" function of Ninja Foodi digital air fry oven, set the temperature to 350 degrees F/ 175 degrees C and set the time to 35 minutes. Press the Start/Pause button and begin preheating. Put the mold with biscuits in the air fryer and cook it for 25 minutes. 4. Then slice the cooked biscuits into pieces and return back in the air fryer. Cook them for 10 minutes more. 5. Cool the cooked biscuits completely.
Per Serving: Calories 334; Fat 29.1g; Sodium 177mg; Carbs 10.8g; Fiber 5.2g; Sugar 5g; Protein 13.4g

Cinnamon Squash Pie

Prep time: 15 minutes | Cook time: 35 minutes | Serves: 6

2 tablespoons Splenda
1 tablespoon Erythritol
5 eggs, beaten
4 tablespoons coconut flakes
¼ cup heavy cream
1 teaspoon vanilla extract
1 teaspoon butter
¼ teaspoon ground cinnamon
4 oz Kabocha squash, peeled

1. Grate the Kabocha squash. Then grease the baking mold with butter and put the grated Kabocha squash inside. 2. In the mixing bowl mix up Splenda, Erythritol, coconut flakes, heavy cream, vanilla extract, and ground cinnamon. 3. Then pour the liquid over the Kabocha squash. Stir the mixture gently with the help of the fork. 4. Select the "AIR FRY" function of Ninja Foodi digital air fry oven, set the temperature to 365 degrees F/ 185 degrees C and set the time to 35 minutes. Press the Start/Pause button and begin preheating. Put the mold with pie in the air fryer and cook it for 35 minutes. 5. Cool the cooked pie to the room temperature and cut into the servings.
Per Serving: Calories 116; Fat 7.2g; Sodium 120mg; Carbs 6.7g; Fiber 0.6g; Sugar 4g; Protein 5.1g

Healthy Seeds and Almond Cookies

Prep time: 15 minutes | Cook time: 9 minutes | Serves: 6

1 teaspoon chia seeds
1 teaspoon sesame seeds
1 tablespoon pumpkin seeds, crushed
1 egg, beaten
2 tablespoons Splenda
1 teaspoon vanilla extract
1 tablespoon butter
4 tablespoons almond flour
¼ teaspoon ground cloves
1 teaspoon avocado oil

1. Put the chia seeds, sesame seeds, and pumpkin seeds in the bowl. Add egg, Splenda, vanilla extract, butter, avocado oil, and ground cloves. 2. Then add almond flour and mix up the mixture until homogenous. 3. Select the "AIR FRY" function of Ninja Foodi digital air fry oven, set the temperature to 375 degrees F/ 190 degrees C and set the time to 9 minutes. Press the Start/Pause button and begin preheating. Line the basket with baking paper. With the help of the scooper, make the cookies and flatten them gently. 4. Place the cookies in the air fryer. Arrange them in one layer. Cook the seeds cookies for 9 minutes.
Per Serving: Calories 180; Fat 13.7g; Sodium 147mg; Carbs 9.6g; Fiber 3g; Sugar 6g; Protein 5.8g

Nutty Pear Biscotti Crumble

Prep time: 20 minutes | Cook time: 65 minutes | Serves: 6

7-inch cake pan or ceramic dish
3 pears, peeled, cored and sliced
½ cup brown sugar
¼ teaspoon ground ginger
1 teaspoon ground cinnamon
⅛ teaspoon ground nutmeg
2 tablespoons cornstarch
1¼ cups (4 to 5) almond biscotti, coarsely crushed
¼ cup all-purpose flour
¼ cup sliced almonds
¼ cup butter, melted

1. Combine the pears, brown sugar, ginger, cinnamon, nutmeg and cornstarch in a bowl. Toss to combine and then pour the pear mixture into a greased 7-inch cake pan or ceramic dish. 2. Combine the crushed biscotti, flour, almonds and melted butter in a medium bowl. Toss with a fork until crumbles. Sprinkle the biscotti crumble over the pears and cover the pan with aluminum foil. 3. Select the "AIR FRY" function of Ninja Foodi digital air fry oven, set the temperature to 350 degrees F/ 175 degrees C and set the time to 60 minutes. Press the Start/Pause button and begin preheating. 4. Air-fry for 60 minutes. Remove the aluminum foil and air-fry for an additional 5 minutes to brown the crumble layer. 5. Serve warm with cream.
Per Serving: Calories 330; Fat 15g; Sodium 155mg; Carbs 47g; Fiber 5g; Sugar 27g; Protein 5g

Coconut Cream Pie

Prep time: 15 minutes | Cook time: 25 minutes | Serves: 4

4 tablespoons coconut cream
1 teaspoon baking powder
1 teaspoon apple cider vinegar
1 egg, beaten
¼ cup coconut flakes
1 teaspoon vanilla extract
½ cup coconut flour
4 teaspoons Splenda
1 teaspoon xanthan gum
Cooking spray

1. Put all liquid in the bowl: coconut cream, apple cider vinegar, egg, and vanilla extract. 2. Stir the liquid until homogenous and add baking powder, coconut flakes, coconut flour, Splenda, and xanthan gum. Stir the until you get the smooth texture of the batter. 3. Spray the air fryer cake mold with cooking spray. Pour the batter in the cake mold. Select the "AIR FRY" function of Ninja Foodi digital air fry oven, set the temperature to 330 degrees F/ 165 degrees C and set the time to 25 minutes. Press the Start/Pause button and begin preheating. Put the cake mold in the air fryer basket and cook it for 25 minutes. 4. Then cool the cooked pie completely and remove it from the cake mold. Cut the cooked pie into servings.
Per Serving: Calories 110; Fat 6.6g; Sodium 238mg; Carbs 9.9g; Fiber 3.9g; Sugar 5g; Protein 2.1g

Conclusion

Ninja Foodi Digital Air Fryer Oven has everything you need in one convenient package. Although the air fryer oven technology isn't new, Ninja Foodi has managed to innovate by releasing an 8-in-1 multipurpose digital oven. There are various unique qualities of this oven that will astound you, with toasting and roasting at the top of the list.

In Ninja Foodi Digital Air Fryer, you can make a variety of easy recipes for perfectly cooked cuts of meat, tender fish, or freshly roasted veggies. The air fryer can even bake up a decadent dessert! Pick up a recipe and begin your wonderful exploring journey!

Appendix 1 Measurement Conversion Chart

VOLUME EQUIVALENTS (LIQUID)

US STANDARD	US STANDARD (OUNCES)	METRIC (APPROXIMATE)
2 tablespoons	1 fl.oz	30 mL
¼ cup	2 fl.oz	60 mL
½ cup	4 fl.oz	120 mL
1 cup	8 fl.oz	240 mL
1½ cup	12 fl.oz	355 mL
2 cups or 1 pint	16 fl.oz	475 mL
4 cups or 1 quart	32 fl.oz	1 L
1 gallon	128 fl.oz	4 L

VOLUME EQUIVALENTS (DRY)

US STANDARD	METRIC (APPROXIMATE)
⅛ teaspoon	0.5 mL
¼ teaspoon	1 mL
½ teaspoon	2 mL
¾ teaspoon	4 mL
1 teaspoon	5 mL
1 tablespoon	15 mL
¼ cup	59 mL
½ cup	118 mL
¾ cup	177 mL
1 cup	235 mL
2 cups	475 mL
3 cups	700 mL
4 cups	1 L

TEMPERATURES EQUIVALENTS

FAHRENHEIT(F)	CELSIUS (C) (APPROXIMATE)
225 °F	107 °C
250 °F	120 °C
275 °F	135 °C
300 °F	150 °C
325 °F	160 °C
350 °F	180 °C
375 °F	190 °C
400 °F	205 °C
425 °F	220 °C
450 °F	235 °C
475 °F	245 °C
500 °F	260 °C

WEIGHT EQUIVALENTS

US STANDARD	METRIC (APPROXINATE)
1 ounce	28 g
2 ounces	57 g
5 ounces	142 g
10 ounces	284 g
15 ounces	425 g
16 ounces (1 pound)	455 g
1.5pounds	680 g
2pounds	907 g

Appendix 2 Air Fryer Cooking Chart

Vegetables	Temp (°F)	Time (min)	Meat and Seafood	Temp (°F)	Time (min)
Asparagus	375	4 to 6	Bacon	400	5 to 10
Baked Potatoes	400	35 to 45	Beef Eye Round Roast (4 lbs.)	390	45 to 55
Broccoli	400	8 to 10	Bone to in Pork Chops	400	4 to 5 per side
Brussels Sprouts	350	15 to 18	Brats	400	8 to 10
Butternut Squash (cubed)	375	20 to 25	Burgers	350	8 to 10
Carrots	375	15 to 25	Chicken Breast	375	22 to 23
Cauliflower	400	10 to 12	Chicken Tender	400	14 to 16
Corn on the Cob	390	6	Chicken Thigh	400	25
Eggplant	400	15	Chicken Wings (2 lbs.)	400	10 to 12
Green Beans	375	16 to 20	Cod	370	8 to 10
Kale	250	12	Fillet Mignon (8 oz.)	400	14 to 18
Mushrooms	400	5	Fish Fillet (0.5 lb., 1-inch)	400	10
Peppers	375	8 to 10	Flank Steak(1.5 lbs.)	400	10 to 14
Sweet Potatoes (whole)	380	30 to 35	Lobster Tails (4 oz.)	380	5 to 7
Tomatoes (halved, sliced)	350	10	Meatballs	400	7 to 10
Zucchini (½-inch sticks)	400	12	Meat Loaf	325	35 to 45
			Pork Chops	375	12 to 15
			Salmon	400	5 to 7

Frozen Foods	Temp (°F)	Time (min)	Meat and Seafood	Temp (°F)	Time (min)
Breaded Shrimp	400	9	Salmon Fillet (6 oz.)	380	12
Chicken Burger	360	11	Sausage Patties	400	8 to 10
Chicken Nudgets	400	10	Shrimp	375	8
Corn Dogs	400	7	Steak	400	7 to 14
Curly Fries (1 to 2 lbs.)	400	11 to 14	Tilapia	400	8 to 12
Fish Sticks (10 oz.)	400	10	Turkey Breast (3 lbs.)	360	40 to 50
French Fries	380	15 to 20	Whole Chicken (6.5 lbs.)	360	75

Frozen Foods	Temp (°F)	Time (min)	Desserts	Temp (°F)	Time (min)
Hash Brown	360	15 to 18			
Meatballs	380	6 to 8	Apple Pie	320	30
Mozzarella Sticks	400	8	Brownies	350	17
Onion Rings (8 oz.)	400	8	Churros	360	13
Pizza	390	5 to 10	Cookies	350	5
Pot Pie	360	25	Cupcakes	330	11
Pot Sticks (10 oz.)	400	8	Doughnuts	360	5
Sausage Rolls	400	15	Roasted Bananas	375	8
Spring Rolls	400	15 to 20	Peaches	350	5

Appendix 3 Recipes Index

Made in the USA
Monee, IL
08 September 2024

65326027R00090